CCNA® Certification
ALL-IN-ONE
FOR DUMMIES®

by Silviu Angelescu

WILEY

Wiley Publishing, Inc.

CCNA® Certification All-in-One For Dummies®

Published by
Wiley Publishing, Inc.
111 River Street
Hoboken, NJ 07030-5774

www.wiley.com

Copyright © 2010 by Wiley Publishing, Inc., Indianapolis, Indiana

Published by Wiley Publishing, Inc., Indianapolis, Indiana

Published simultaneously in Canada

For general information on our other products and services, please contact our Customer Care Department within the U.S. at 877-762-2974, outside the U.S. at 317-572-3993, or fax 317-572-4002.

For technical support, please visit www.wiley.com/techsupport.

Wiley also publishes its books in a variety of electronic formats. Some content that appears in print may not be available in electronic books.

Library of Congress Control Number: 2010922557

ISBN: 978-0-470-48962-8

Manufactured in the United States of America

10 9 8 7 6 5 4 3

WILEY

About the Authors

Silviu Angelescu is a network and software engineer, consultant and technical trainer, specialized in data networks, storage networks and virtualization. He has worked as network and software engineer, consultant and corporate trainer for more than ten years at various high-tech companies and academic institutions, such as, Network Appliance (NetApp), Computer Associates (CA), CGI, Dawson College, and the University of Montreal. Silviu also ran a consulting business for training organizations, designing, developing, and deploying scheduling software and network services. He graduated in Computer Science at the University of Montreal and is currently an engineer and trainer in the Research Triangle Park, in North Carolina, USA.

Andrew Swerczek is a network engineer, computer lab instructor, and technical writer with over twenty years experience in the Information Technology field. He has worked for various governmental agencies and contractors including the US Department of Defense and Wang Laboratories. Andrew has achieved many IT industry certifications such as CCNA, CNE, CNA, CIW, DCSNP, NACA, FCA, IBA, i-Net+, Network+, Server+, and A+. He is a graduate from the London School of Journalism, owns a small business, and currently resides in the Harz Mountains region, in Germany.

Author's Acknowledgments

I would like to thank Katie Feltman, Pat O'Brien, John Edwards, and Bruce Tomlin: thanks for your hard work, support and patience. A lot of work goes into publishing and producing a book: I want to thank everyone at Wiley who worked behind the scenes to keep this project on track and make it happen.

I also want to thank Andrew Swerczek for his hard work and contribution to this book: Chapters one to five in Book II, Chapters one to four in Book VI, Chapters one to four in Book VII. Thanks also to Ed Tetz for his contribution: Chapters two to five in Book V.

Publisher's Acknowledgments

We're proud of this book; please send us your comments at http://dummies.custhelp.com. For other comments, please contact our Customer Care Department within the U.S. at 877-762-2974, outside the U.S. at 317-572-3993, or fax 317-572-4002.

Some of the people who helped bring this book to market include the following:

Acquisitions, Editorial, and Media Development

Project Editor: Pat O'Brien

Senior Acquisitions Editor: Katie Feltman

Copy Editor: John Edwards

Technical Editor: Bruce Tomlin

Editorial Manager: Kevin Kirschner

Media Development Project Manager: Laura Moss-Hollister

Media Development Assistant Project Manager: Jenny Swisher

Media Development Associate Producer: Shawn Patrick

Editorial Assistant: Amanda Graham

Sr. Editorial Assistant: Cherie Case

Cartoons: Rich Tennant (www.the5thwave.com)

Composition Services

Project Coordinator: Kristie Rees

Layout and Graphics: Christin Swinford, Christine Williams

Proofreaders: Melissa Cossell, Jessica Kramer, Toni Settle

Indexer: Broccoli Information Mgt.

Special Help: Anne Sullivan

Publishing and Editorial for Technology Dummies

    Richard Swadley, Vice President and Executive Group Publisher

    Andy Cummings, Vice President and Publisher

    Mary Bednarek, Executive Acquisitions Director

    Mary C. Corder, Editorial Director

Publishing for Consumer Dummies

    Diane Graves Steele, Vice President and Publisher

Composition Services

    Debbie Stailey, Director of Composition Services

Contents at a Glance

Table of Contents

Chapter 2: Wireless Local Area Network (WLAN) Security 693

Chapter 3: Wireless Local Area Network (WLAN) Operation Modes 703

Chapter 4: Managing Cisco Wireless Local Area Networks.......719

Introduction

The CCNA certification is a well-recognized certification, and having this certification will serve as a basic foundation for a number of other IT certifications that you may pursue. The exam tests your knowledge of Cisco hardware and software used in today's networking world, and the certification is one of the most popular certifications that IT professionals attain to prove their networking hardware and software knowledge.

Cisco Certified Network Associates (CCNA) are in high demand on the job market worldwide and the pay is not bad at all, believe me. By becoming a CCNA you increase your chances to obtain a better job, a promotion, or simply a better pay.

You bought this book because you need a complete, straight to the point, easy to understand study guide and reference book about Cisco networking technologies, products, best practices and certification. Whether you are a seasoned technology expert, or you are just starting in the high tech world, this book will help you improve your knowledge, skills, and hands-on experience with Cisco networking products.

About This Book

This book is designed to be a hands-on, practical guide to help you pass the CCNA exam. This book is written in a way that helps you understand complex technical content and prepares you to apply that knowledge to real-world scenarios.

I understand the value of a book that covers the points needed to pass the exams, but I also understand the value of ensuring that the information helps you perform IT-related tasks when you are on the job. That is what this book offers you — key points to pass the exams combined with practical information to help you in the real world, which means that this book can be used in more than one way:

+ **An exam preparation tool:** Because my goal is to help you pass the A+ exams, this book is packed with exam-specific information. You should understand everything that is in this book before taking the exams.

+ **A reference:** Rely on my extensive experience in the IT industry not only to study for (and pass) the exams but also to help you perform common computer-related tasks on the job. I hope you find this book a useful tool that you can refer to time and time again in your career.

Foolish Assumptions

I make a few assumptions about you as a reader and have written this book with these assumptions in mind:

✦ **You are interested in obtaining the CCNA.** After all, the focus of this book is helping you pass the exams.

✦ **You will study hard and do as much hands-on work as possible.** There is a lot of content on the exam, and you will most likely need to read over the information a few times to ensure that you understand the content. You should also experiment as much as possible after you read a particular topic

How This Book Is Organized

Like all *All-In-One For Dummies* books, chapters are organized into mini-books. The chapters in each minibook are related by a specific exam theme or topic:

✦ Book I: Networking Basics

✦ Book II: TCP/IP

✦ Book III: Switching with Cisco Switches

✦ Book IV: Routing With Cisco Routers

✦ Book V: Wireless Networks

✦ Book VI: Network Security

✦ Book VII: Wide Area Networks (WAN)

The Appendix gives you an overview of what you can find on the CD-ROM that accompanies the book.

Icons Used in This Book

I use a number of icons in this book to draw your attention to pieces of useful information.

Information that would be helpful to you in the real world is indicated with a Tip icon. Expect to find shortcuts and timesavers here.

This icon is used to flag information that may be useful to remember on the job.

 Information that could cause problems to you or to the computer is indicated with a Warning icon. If you see a Warning icon, make sure you read it. The computer you save may be your own.

 Detailed information that is not needed for the exams or that is a step above the knowledge you absolutely need to know for the exams is indicated with a Technical Stuff icon.

Feedback

If you would like to learn more about Cisco networking technologies, or if you would like to find out more about related technologies, such as virtualization, and storage networks, or if you would like to comment about this book, feel free to contact me at: sil@silange.com.

Where to Go from Here

Get started! You can just turn the page and go!

Book I

Networking Basics

The 5th Wave   By Rich Tennant

"Thanks to Sarbanes—Oxley, we've got more internal controls than a warehouse full of Imodium."

Contents at a Glance

Chapter 1: Introducing Computer Networks

Exam Objectives

- ✔ Describing the purpose and functions of computer networks
- ✔ Describing common network applications
- ✔ Describing common networking devices
- ✔ Describing the operation flow of computer networks and seeing how networking devices control the operation flow
- ✔ Describing the impact of applications (Voice over IP and Video over IP) on a network
- ✔ Describing the components required for network and Internet communications
- ✔ Describing the topologies of computer networks

CNA certification not only attests your knowledge about Cisco networking, but it also attests your knowledge about networking technologies in general. This is one of the reasons why CCNA certification is the gold-standard certification in the networking industry.

Purpose of Computer Networks

You link computers in a network for the same reason that people network. People networks are necessary to accomplish tasks that cannot be accomplished by a single individual. The same applies to computers. Computer networks were developed to aggregate the computing power of several individual computers into initially local networks, then campus networks, then metropolitan networks, then countrywide networks, and finally, global networks.

A computer network is a group of *computer host devices* that communicate with each other. To enable this communication, the computer host devices are connected using wired or wireless connections. The communication is controlled by network software running on the computer host devices and on *network devices.*

Computer host devices can be any other devices used to access the network, including servers, workstations, personal computers, smart phones, and laptops.

Network devices can be any devices that stand between computer host devices, including switches, routers, hubs, repeaters, and firewalls.

Network devices control and optimize communication between host devices.

Network applications

What's the purpose? Here are just a few network application examples:

✦ **World Wide Web:** Technically, this is a network application that allows the exchange of text pages coded in Hypertext Markup Language (HTML) using the Hypertext Transfer Protocol (HTTP). Initially, these HTML pages only supported hyperlinks to jump from one page to another. Now, HTTP and HTML have been augmented with dynamic extensions to allow a much more advanced, rich, multimedia Web experience than just jumping from one page to another.

✦ **Electronic mail:** I am sure that you have extensively used this one. This is a network application that allows the exchange of messages between two hosts. In fact, studies show that e-mail is by far the most commonly used network application.

✦ **File transfer and file sharing:** This network application allows the transfer of files from one computer host device to another. Several variations of this application exist, such as File Transfer Protocol (FTP), Secure FTP (SFTP), Network File System (NFS), and Server Message Block (SMB), but all versions serve the same purpose: to transfer files from one network host to another.

✦ **Remote control:** This network application allows you to control a computer host remotely from another host in the network. As with file transfer, several remote control applications exist, such as Windows Remote Desktop, Virtual Network Computing (VNC), and remote shell (rsh).

✦ **Voice over IP (VoIP) and Video over IP:** This network application allows the transfer of voice and video signals over the Internet Protocol. Many Web sites stream video over the Internet today. These sites use some VoIP network application to wrap their video content in IP packets and send them over the network to the computer host that requested the streamed video content. Another example of VoIP is Cisco IP phones, which are being adopted today by many organizations to save costs by concentrating their phone and data traffic over the same IP infrastructure.

✦ **Shared network storage:** This network application connects advanced specialized storage devices to a storage network, making them accessible to any computer host connected to that storage network. Storage networks can be either

  • Isolated, that is, connecting only to a few computer hosts locally

  • Connected to other data networks

✦ **High availability (HA) and parallel processing:** This network application enables computer hosts to act as a single logical host, sometimes also called a *computer cluster.* The hosts use clustering software that manages the logical "supercomputer." The clustering software needs to have those physical computers interconnected in a network.

Computer clusters are used for the following:

  • *High availability:* Several levels of high availability exist, but generally speaking, HA implies that whenever one of the physical computers in the cluster fails, the remaining computer(s) takes over the load of the failed computer.

  • *Parallel processing:* In parallel processing, all physical computers in the cluster can process data at the same time, thereby improving processing speed and reliability.

Both HA and parallel processing require a network connection between the physical computer hosts involved.

Operation Flow of Computer Networks

I now describe some examples of how computer hosts communicate in a network. Suppose that three computers are connected in a simple network using a hub, as shown in Figure 1-1.

Figure 1-1:
A simple network: Three hosts connected to a hub.

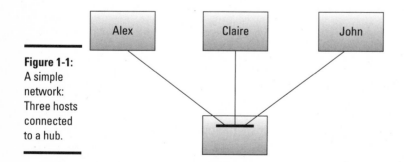

A *hub* works very much like a multiplexer, or a multiple socket power bar: Hosts Alex, John, and Claire connect to the hub, and they can "speak" and "hear" each other. The hub acts somewhat like a public meeting room where Alex, John, and Claire can meet and exchange ideas without seeing and without really knowing each other. They can all talk and hear each other in that room, but first, they need to get acquainted.

Suppose that host Alex wants to communicate with host John. To initiate the communication, Alex needs to know the address of John.

Alex needs to know John's logical address on the network, also called his IP address, and John's network interface card (NIC) physical address, also known as the MAC address:

✦ Alex needs John's logical (IP) address to establish a connection between his upper-layer network protocols and applications and John's upper-layer network protocols and applications.

✦ Alex needs John's NIC physical (MAC) address to establish a connection between his network interface card and John's to transmit electrical signals between the NICs, over the network.

So, how does Alex obtain John's logical (IP) address when he only knows his name? Alex needs to do a *name resolution,* to resolve the host name (John) to his IP address. Alex has several options:

✦ Alex can query a *name server,* also known as a *Domain Name System (DNS) server* to obtain the IP address of John. DNS servers keep tables of host names and their corresponding IP addresses. Whenever they are queried for the IP address of a host, they search the host name in their table, and if they find it, they return the IP address.

✦ Alex can use a *hosts* file that would list John and his corresponding IP address. All hosts can have a local hosts file that lists the hosts in the network with their corresponding IP address.

This is a simple method to resolve host names to IP addresses, but hosts files need to be maintained manually. Consequently, this method does not scale. DNS servers are typically used instead.

In this example, Alex and John are in the same network. In this case, Alex can simply broadcast a request to resolve John's host name to his IP address. The broadcast is sent to the IP broadcast address of the network. You read more about the IP broadcast address in Book II, Chapter 3. John, like everyone else in the network, can hear the broadcast and can respond with his IP address.

So now, Alex has John's logical IP address, but he still needs to obtain his physical (MAC) address to establish a connection between the NICs. Alex can simply broadcast a request to obtain John's MAC address.

The broadcast is sent to the data link layer broadcast address, which is FF:FF:FF:FF:FF:FF. This is the standard broadcast address to query for MAC addresses. John eventually responds with his MAC address.

Alex's broadcast queries are the equivalent of Alex (the person) asking out loud in the public meeting room: "I am Alex and I would like to communicate with John, but I don't have his address. If you are John, can you please send me your address?" Both John and Claire can hear Alex. John responds with his address. Claire, on the other hand, simply discards Alex's query. So, Alex's query is just noise for Claire. This noise is not good especially if the meeting room (the network) is large. Furthermore, if Claire also wants to talk to John, she would also have to shout out "I am Claire, and I would like to communicate with John, but I don't have his address. If you are John, can you please send me your address?"

Alex and Claire could be shouting at the same time, in which case John would not hear either one of them. They would likely have to repeat their requests. Worse yet, even after Alex and Claire have obtained John's address, they will still communicate out loud and potentially at the same time. Whenever they need to tell something to John, they will shout out, "John, I am sending you this message, blah, blah, blah." Both Claire and Alex could try to address John at the same time.

You can see that in larger meeting rooms (networks), this would become a major problem. Thus, it is best to limit the size of the meeting room, in other words, to limit the size of the network. But, what if you really need to have a lot of people meeting in that room? You can divide the group by some criteria, such as interests or geographical location, for example, and channel the intergroup communication using mediators to limit noise in the room. Basically, you are *segmenting* the group. You probably guessed that you do exactly the same thing in computer networks.

So, two basic issues are at hand:

+ **"Noise" generated by broadcast queries:** One computer sends a broadcast query to every other device in the network to obtain an IP address or a MAC address, and eventually the target computer responds. Meanwhile, all computers in the *broadcast domain* have "heard" the broadcast request. They were disturbed by a request that does not concern them. If lots of broadcast requests are being sent on the network by hosts that just joined the network, for example, a *broadcast storm* can occur: Everyone is disturbed by everyone's broadcast request, and the network performance is considerably impacted.

+ **Message collision:** After two computers know about each other and they start to communicate, they send data frames on the link that is shared by all other computers in that network segment. If two computers try to send frames at the same time, on the same wire, the frames collide.

In that case, both computers back off: They stop sending frames, they wait a little while, and they try to resend. You have no guarantee that the frames will not collide again when they are resent. Typically, there are few chances that they collide again, because the two computers wait random time periods that are likely different. However, collisions do happen, and they can slow a network considerably. Remember the meeting room example: The more people in the room, the more chances that everyone tries to speak at the same time. It's the same with computers: The more hosts you add to a network segment, the more chances of having frame collisions. It's best to keep network segments as small as possible.

You can *segment a network* using a data link layer *switch* instead of a hub. Data-link switches are also called Layer 2 switches, because the data link layer is the second layer in the TCP/IP protocol stack. In fact, every time I talk about a switch in this book, I refer to a Layer 2 switch. Switches segment networks into one *collision domain* per port. A collision domain is a logical space where messages can collide.

You need to understand the following networking concepts for the CCNA test:

✦ A *collision domain* is a logical network space where frames can collide, because several hosts are sharing the bandwidth of the network medium and they can potentially send frames on the wire at the same time.

   It is best to segment networks into several smaller collision domains to reduce the chances of having frame collisions.

✦ *Bandwidth* is the maximum amount of information (in bits/second) that can be transmitted on a transmission medium.

✦ A *hub* is basically a multiplexed connection device: All devices connected to a hub can send frames to all other devices connected to the hub. A hub sends frames it receives on all ports, except on the port where the frame is received. Thus, even if a frame is only addressed to one of the six hosts plugged in to the hub, in reality, all five hosts, other than the sending host, will receive the frame. Four hosts will have to discard the frame because it is not addressed to them. Some hubs also amplify the electrical signal before sending it on all ports other than the originating port. Those hubs are also *repeaters.*

✦ A *repeater* is a hub that not only sends the frames on all ports other the originating port, but it also amplifies the electrical signal. Amplifying the electrical signal allows the hub to send over longer distances. Most hubs on the market today also amplify the electrical signal. Thereby, most hubs are also repeaters. However, do not assume this during the CCNA test.

+ A *switch* is smarter (and more expensive) than a hub: It learns about devices that send frames into the switch. A switch builds a MAC address table that lists the MAC address of the host device that is sending on each port. Whenever a frame enters the switch, the switch looks at the destination MAC address of the frame. Then, the switch looks into its MAC address table and identifies the port that corresponds to the destination MAC address of the frame. It then sends the frame only on that port.

+ A *bridge* works very similarly to a switch, except that it uses software instead of hardware application-specific integrated circuit (ASIC) processors to process the MAC address filtering and forwarding. Consequently, a bridge is typically slower and less expensive than a switch. Switches have become very affordable lately, however, and it is very rare to find bridges on the market anymore.

Figure 1-2 shows the same simple network of Figure 1-1, but I exchanged the hub with a switch.

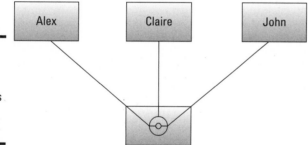

Figure 1-2:
A simple
network:
Three hosts
connected
to a switch.

This creates three collision domains, one for each port of the switch. Whenever host Alex needs to send a frame to host John, he will tag the frame with John's destination MAC address. Switches learn about MAC addresses connected to their ports, and they build an internal table that lists which MAC address is connected to each port. When the switch receives the frame from Alex, it looks at the destination MAC address in the frame and then it looks in its internal MAC address table. The switch identifies the port where the destination MAC address is connected and forwards the frame only on that port. In other words, in the example, Alex's frame sent to John does not disturb Claire. This dramatically reduces collision chances and thereby improves network performance.

Switches limit the collision domain, but they do not limit the broadcast domain. The switch broadcasts requests on all ports. Broadcast domains can be limited by either using virtual local-area networks (VLANs) on a switch or by segmenting the network and using routers to route between the different subnets.

Topologies of Computer Networks

Networks can be arranged in various topologies, or layouts. The most common topologies are as follows:

✦ **Point-to-point:** Two hosts connect directly to each other, as shown in Figure 1-3. The sending end of one host is connected to the receiving end of the other host. In its simplest form, the two hosts are connected with a crossover cable. This is usually the case in serial connections.

Figure 1-3:
Point-
to-point
topology.

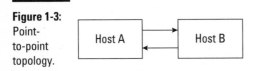

✦ **Star:** Hosts connect to a central device, as shown in Figure 1-4. All traffic flows through the central device. The star topology is also known as a hub-and-spoke topology. Ethernet networks using hubs or switches and twisted-pair cabling are star topologies.

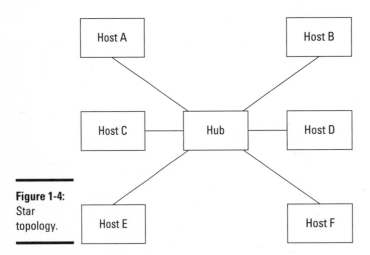

Figure 1-4:
Star
topology.

✦ **Ring:** Hosts are connected sequentially in a daisy-chain fashion, as shown in Figure 1-5. Traffic flows around the ring. The last host in the ring is connected to the first host, thereby closing the ring. Token Ring is the typical ring topology example. Fiber Distributed Data Interface (FDDI) is also a ring topology.

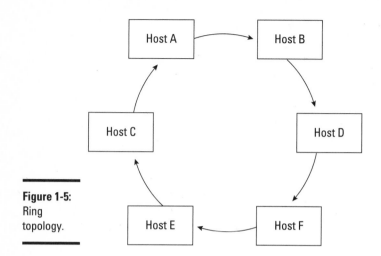

Figure 1-5:
Ring
topology.

✦ **Bus:** As shown in Figure 1-6, hosts are connected through a single cable, usually coaxial cable. Ethernet networks using coaxial cable are bus topologies.

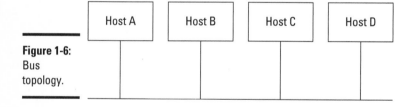

Figure 1-6:
Bus
topology.

✦ **Mesh:** Multiple hosts are connected point to point to each other in a mesh topology, as shown in Figure 1-7. These are multiple point-to-point connections that typically link every host in the network with every other host in the network. You find two types of mesh topologies:

• *Full-mesh topologies* provide several connections between hosts in the network, thereby improving reliability. The cost is high, though.

• *Partial-mesh topologies* are a good compromise because they can offer multiple connections for certain mission-critical hosts, yet they present cost savings over full-mesh configurations.

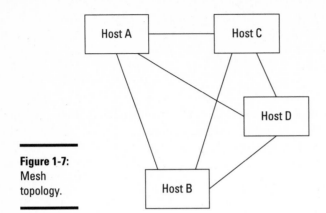

Figure 1-7:
Mesh
topology.

Prep Test

1 **Computer networks do which of the following?**

A ○ Allow computer hosts to communicate data between each other

B ○ Provide a user interface to control computer hosts

C ○ Provide a user interface to control networking devices

D ○ Operate solar power stations

2 **Networking devices do which of the following?**

A ○ Provide an operating system for the Internet

B ○ Allow users to use more than one computer at once

C ○ Control and optimize communication between host devices

D ○ Allow users to use more than one user interface at once

3 **A hub does which of the following?**

A ○ Modifies the MAC address of a data-link frame to allow transmission over longer distances

B ○ Sends frames it receives on all ports, except on the port where the frame is received

C ○ Amplifies the electrical signal to allow transmission over longer distances

D ○ Sends frames it receives only on the port that corresponds to the destination MAC address of the data-link frame

4 **A switch does which of the following?**

A ○ Modifies the MAC address of a data-link frame to allow transmission over longer distances

B ○ Sends frames it receives on all ports, except on the port where the frame is received

C ○ Amplifies the electrical signal to allow transmission over longer distances

D ○ Sends frames it receives only on the port that corresponds to the destination MAC address of the data-link frame

Answers

1 **A.** Allow computer hosts to communicate data between each other. Networks allow computers to communicate. See *"Purpose of Computer Networks."*

2 **C.** Control and optimize communication between host devices. Network devices manage the communication between host devices. Review *"Purpose of Computer Networks."*

3 **B.** Sends frames it receives out on all ports, except on the port where the frame is received. Hubs send out frames on all ports except on the incoming port. Read *"Operation Flow of Computer Networks."*

4 **D.** Sends frames it receives only on the port corresponding to the destination MAC address of the data-link frame. Switches send frames only on the destination port. Check out *"Operation Flow of Computer Networks."*

Chapter 2: The OSI Reference Model

Exam Objectives

- Describing the OSI reference model
- Describing the purpose and basic operation of each layer in the OSI reference model
- Describing the benefits of the OSI reference model
- Describing the purpose and basic operation of the protocols in the OSI and TCP/IP models
- Associating network devices to each layer in the OSI reference model

This chapter covers the Open Systems Interconnection (OSI) networking reference model. You discover the seven layers, their purpose, and how they relate to each other. The data encapsulation concept is also introduced.

Introduction to the OSI Reference Model

The International Organization for Standardization (ISO) defined the Open Systems Interconnection (OSI) reference model to standardize networking of devices from different vendors. The OSI reference model is mostly an architecture blueprint that networking and computer device manufacturers implement. The OSI model has never been implemented exactly as defined. The TCP/IP protocol stack is the closest implementation available today.

Seven Layers

The OSI reference model is designed in seven functional layers. Each layer has a precise mission, and each layer works fairly independently of the upper and lower layers. Upper layers use the services provided by lower layers, but the internal workings of each layer are not visible to other layers.

This independence is achieved through *encapsulation* and very clearly defined interfaces between layers. Here are the layers in a nutshell:

✦ Top layers build an application data payload that is divided by the lower *transport layer* into several small data chunks called *segments.* Each segment is numbered so that the receiving host can reassemble the application data.

✦ The transport segments are then forwarded down to the *network layer,* which tags each segment with logical source and destination addresses and some control information, and hands over the resulting shippable data packet to the lower *data link layer.*

✦ The *data link layer* adds the physical source address of the sender and the physical destination address of the receiver if the receiver is located in the same local network as the sender. If the receiver is not located in the same local network as the sender, the data link layer adds the physical destination address of the gateway in the local network. The *gateway* of a local network is usually a router that connects the local network to other networks.

Here are the basic ideas behind encapsulation:

✦ Each layer encapsulates the data and control data of upper layers within its own control data.

✦ The data chunk encapsulated within the control data of each layer travels from the sending host to the receiving host.

✦ The receiving host unwraps the successive control information layers that encapsulate the data.

✦ Top layers on the sending host hand off the data to the transport layer and trust the transport layer (and the layers beneath transport) to ship it to the receiving host.

✦ The data ends up being sliced into smaller chunks. The data is also augmented with control information at each layer. The control information added by each layer is wrapped around by the control data of the lower layers on the sending host.

✦ The data is unwrapped on the receiving host.

The seven layers as defined by the OSI reference model are shown in Figure 2-1.

Layer 7: Application

This layer represents the various network applications such as e-mail reader, Web browser, Hypertext Transfer Protocol (HTTP), File Transfer Protocol (FTP), and Network File System (NFS).

✦ The application layer provides a user interface and processes network data.

✦ The application layer on the sending host produces the network data to be transmitted from the sender host.

✦ The application layer on the receiving host consumes the network data produced and transmitted by the sender host.

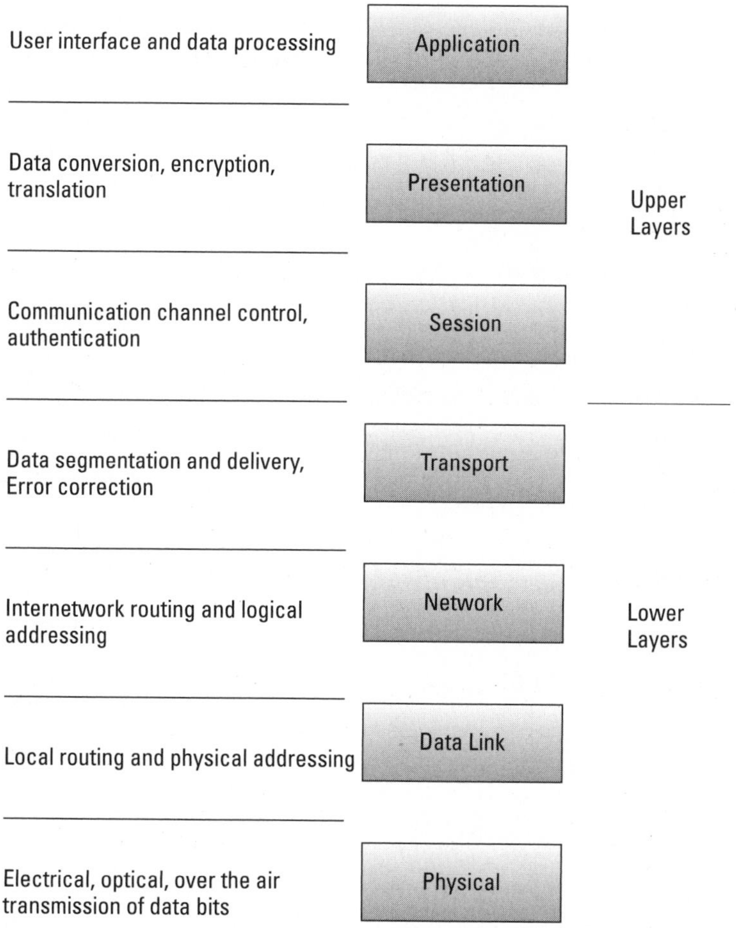

User interface and data processing	Application	
Data conversion, encryption, translation	Presentation	Upper Layers
Communication channel control, authentication	Session	
Data segmentation and delivery, Error correction	Transport	
Internetwork routing and logical addressing	Network	Lower Layers
Local routing and physical addressing	Data Link	
Electrical, optical, over the air transmission of data bits	Physical	

Figure 2-1:
The OSI
Reference
Model

Layer 6: Presentation

This layer is mostly concerned with data format. It converts the data between different formats so that both the sender and the receiver can use heterogeneous data. For example, mail messages contain various data formats: text, application attachments, video, audio, and graphical signature.

+ The presentation layer on the sending host receives the data payload from the application layer.

+ The presentation layer on the sending host converts the data into a format that is easily transportable over the network.

+ The presentation layer on the receiving host converts the data from the network format back to its native format that can be easily interpreted, used, and displayed by the application layer above.

Layer 5: Session

Some applications need to open logical communication channels between the computer hosts. Logical communication channels (sessions) maintain data about the communication established between the network application running on the sending host and the network application running on the receiving host. The session layer does the following:

+ Opens and maintains logical communication channels between network applications running on the sending host and network applications running on the receiving host.

+ Handles authentication: Some network applications use authentication mechanisms before they open a logical communication channel (session) with a remote host.

Layer 4: Transport

The transport layer manages the transport of data between two hosts over a network. In a nutshell, the transport layer does the following:

+ Slices the data to be transmitted into small chunks called *data segments* that can be easily sent over the network medium.

+ Reassembles the data in order on the receiving host.

  Data segments are not guaranteed to arrive in order at destination since they may use different routes to reach the destination host. The transport layer is responsible to reassemble the data in order on the receiving host.

Layer 3: Network

The network layer routes *data packets* across networks that link the sending and the receiving host. In a nutshell, the network layer does the following:

✦ Chooses the best route to send packets between hosts.

✦ Assigns logical addresses to all devices in the network to be able to identify each source host and each destination host, as well as each network through which packets need to be routed.

   Logical addresses are assigned at the network protocol level. Physical addresses are assigned on a physical device, such as a network card.

✦ Receives each data segment from the transport layer on the sending host and wraps it in a *data packet* along with routing data. The packet is sent down to the data link layer to send it over the network physical medium.

✦ On the receiving host, the network layer unwraps the packet received to extract the data segment and sends it up to the transport layer.

   Several protocols operate at the network layer, such as IP, IPX, AppleTalk, and SNA, but the CCNA test is only concerned with IP.

The Internet Protocol (IP) is the TCP/IP implementation of the network layer. IP addresses are logical addresses provided by the IP in TCP/IP.

Cisco routers are Layer 3 (network layer) devices. You read more about Cisco routers in Book IV.

Layer 2: Data link

The data link layer does the following:

✦ Transmits the data on the physical medium.

✦ Routes the data locally on the physical network medium. The data link layer uses physical addresses assigned to each physical network device in the local network to route data from one physical device to another.

✦ The data link layer receives each packet from the network layer on the sending host and wraps it in a *data frame* along with local routing data.

✦ The data link layer sends each data frame down to the physical layer to code an electrical or optical signal to transmit the data frame over a wire or over the air (wireless transmission).

✦ On the receiving host, the data link layer unwraps the data frame received to extract the packet and sends it to the network layer.

Switches are traditionally considered Layer 2 (data link layer) devices. However, many advanced switches operate at multiple layers of the OSI Reference Model. You read more about Cisco switches in Book III.

Layer 1: Physical

The physical layer provides the electrical, optical, or over-the-air connection between the sending host device and the receiving host device. This typically involves copper or fiber-optic cabling, or wireless radio connections, patch panels, signal repeaters, submarine cables, or satellites.

CCNA certification does not require you to be a space science expert. However, you do need to understand that data is always converted into bits that can be transmitted over a medium using electrical current or optical signals that simulate a 1 (signal) or a 0 (no signal).

In a nutshell, the physical layer defines mechanical, electrical, optical, radio, procedural, and functional standards to enable the transmission of data-link (Layer 2) frames over a certain transmission medium.

These standards define how a physical link is built, activated, maintained, and deactivated to enable transmissions between *DTE (data terminal equipment)* and *DCE (data communications equipment)*.

DTEs are host devices. DCEs are network devices, that is, any device that stands between two host devices.

Most hubs amplify the electrical signal; therefore, they are really repeaters with several ports. Hubs and repeaters are Layer 1 (physical layer) devices.

Benefits of the OSI Reference Model

A layered network model, such as the OSI reference model, has several advantages:

✦ Independently operating layers with clearly defined interlayer interfaces allow layers to evolve internally without impact on other layers. As long as a layer continues to interact the same way with upper and lower layers, it can change internally to adapt to new technologies and needs.

✦ The network communication problem is divided into smaller problems. By dividing the network communication process into several precise tasks and by assigning a specific layer to each task, it's easier to manage the whole process. It also allows each layer to specialize to specific network communication contexts. For example, the physical layer constantly changes to support new transmission media. However, other layers do not need to change because the physical layer interacts using the same interfaces with upper layers, even if a new transmission medium is added to the support list. Thus, the network model as a whole can adapt to support new media with localized change at the physical layer only.

✦ A network reference model provides a blueprint for all manufacturers, guaranteeing compatibility of varied devices from various manufacturers.

Prep Test

1 **What is the Open Systems Interconnection (OSI) reference model?**

A ○ A cabling standard that phone and networking companies implement

B ○ A computer host architecture blueprint that computer device manufacturers implement

C ○ A network architecture blueprint that network and computer device manufacturers implement

D ○ A network device architecture blueprint that network device manufacturers implement

2 **How does the OSI reference model guarantee independence of layer functionality?**

A ○ By encapsulating data at each layer and by defining clear interfaces between each layer

B ○ By allowing network and computer device manufacturers to implement proprietary layers

C ○ By allowing communication between computer hosts over a network

D ○ By optimizing the network route between computer hosts

3 **What is the function of the application layer of the OSI reference model?**

A ○ Segments and delivers data, correcting transmission errors

B ○ Opens and maintains communication channels, authenticating data communications

C ○ Converts data, encrypts data, and translates data

D ○ Manages the user interface and processes data before handing it off to the user

4 **What is the function of the presentation layer of the OSI reference model?**

A ○ Segments and delivers data, correcting transmission errors

B ○ Opens and maintains communication channels, authenticating data communications

C ○ Converts data, encrypts data, and translates data

D ○ Manages the user interface and processes data before handing it off to the user

5 **What is the function of the session layer of the OSI reference model?**

A ○ Segments and delivers data, correcting transmission errors

B ○ Opens and maintains communication channels, authenticating data communications

C ○ Converts data, encrypts data, and translates data

D ○ Manages the user interface and processes data before handing it off to the user

6 **What is the function of the transport layer of the OSI reference model?**

A ○ Segments and delivers data, correcting transmission errors

B ○ Opens and maintains communication channels, authenticating data communications

C ○ Converts data, encrypts data, and translates data

D ○ Manages the user interface and processes data before handing it off to the user

7 **What is the function of the network layer of the OSI reference model?**

A ○ Segments and delivers data, correcting transmission errors

B ○ Manages electrical, optical, and over-the-air transmission of data bits

C ○ Routes data frames locally and manages local physical addressing

D ○ Routes data packets between networks and manages global logical addressing

8 **What is the function of the data link layer of the OSI reference model?**

A ○ Segments and delivers data, correcting transmission errors

B ○ Manages electrical, optical, and over-the-air transmission of data bits

C ○ Routes data frames locally and manages local physical addressing

D ○ Routes data packets between networks and manages global logical addressing

9 **What is the function of the physical layer of the OSI reference model?**

A ○ Segments and delivers data, correcting transmission errors

B ○ Manages electrical, optical, and over-the-air transmission of data bits

C ○ Routes data frames locally and manages local physical addressing

D ○ Routes data packets between networks and manages global logical addressing

Answers

1 **C.** A network architecture blueprint that network and computer device manufac-turers implement. The Open Systems Interconnection (OSI) reference model is a network architecture blueprint that network and computer device manufacturers implement. Review *"Introduction to the OSI Reference Model."*

2 **A.** Encapsulating data at each layer and by defining clear interfaces between each layer. The OSI reference model guarantee independence of layer function-ality by encapsulating data at each layer and by defining clear interfaces between each layer. Check the *"Seven Layers"* section.

3 **D.** Managing the user interface, and processing data before handing it off to the user. The application layer of the OSI reference model manages the user inter-face, and processes the data before handing it off to the user. Review the *"Layer 7: Application"* section.

4 **C.** Converting data, encrypting data, and translating data. The presentation layer of the OSI reference model converts, encrypts and translates the data. Review the *"Layer 6: Presentation"* section.

5 **B.** Opening and maintaining communication channels, authenticating data com-munications. The session layer of the OSI reference model opens and maintains communication channels, and authenticates data communications. Check *"Layer 5: Session."*

6 **A.** Segmenting and delivering data, correcting transmission errors. The transport layer of the OSI reference model segments and delivers the data, and corrects any transmission errors. Review *"Layer 4: Transport."*

7 **D.** Routing data packets between networks and managing global logical address-ing. The network layer of the OSI reference model routes data packets between networks and manages global logical addressing. Review the *"Layer 3: Network"* section.

8 **C.** Routing data frames locally and managing local physical addressing. The data link layer of the OSI reference model routes data frames locally and manages local physical addressing. Check out the *"Layer 2: Data Link"* section.

9 **B.** Managing electrical, optical and over the air transmission of data bits. The physical layer of the OSI reference model manages electrical, optical and over the air transmission of data bits. Review the *"Layer 1: Physical"* section.

Chapter 3: Introducing the TCP/IP Protocol Suite

Exam Objectives

- Describing the TCP/IP network protocol family
- Describing the purpose and basic operation of each layer in the TCP/IP network protocol family
- Describing the benefits of the TCP/IP network protocol family
- Describing the purpose and basic operation of the protocols in the TCP/IP network protocol family
- Associating network devices to each layer in the TCP/IP network protocol family
- Describing how TCP/IP protocols relate to each layer in the OSI reference model
- Describing connection-oriented and connectionless data transport
- Demonstrating TCP flow control features, such as sequencing, acknowledgments, and the TCP sliding window
- Demonstrating the TCP three-way handshake process
- Describing the purpose and basic operation of TCP ports
- Describing the difference and the relationship between MAC addresses and IP addresses
- Demonstrating the Address Resolution Protocol (ARP)

*R*ead this chapter to find out about the Transmission Control Protocol/ Internet Protocol (TCP/IP) suite. TCP/IP is one of the most important topics on the CCNA test.

You first look at a diagram of the TCP/IP protocol suite that illustrates how TCP/IP relates to the OSI network reference model. Next, you review each TCP/IP layer and the most common protocols and applications that operate at each layer.

Introduction to the TCP/IP Protocol Suite

The Open Systems Interconnection (OSI) reference model is mostly an architecture blueprint for networking and computer device manufacturers. The OSI model has never been implemented exactly as defined. The TCP/IP protocol family is the closest implementation available today. Read the following sections to get acquainted with the TCP/IP protocol stack.

TCP/IP implements almost the same networking layers as the OSI reference model. However, some TCP/IP protocols work at more than one level, as shown in Figure 3-1.

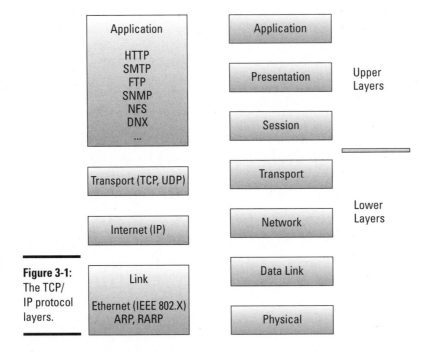

Figure 3-1: The TCP/IP protocol layers.

Layer 7: Application

The application layer represents the various network applications such as e-mail reader and Web browser.

It is important to distinguish between Layer 7 protocols and Layer 7 software applications. For example, you use Web-browsing software to view Web pages that are transferred to your computer using the Hypertext Transfer Protocol (HTTP). Web pages are coded in Hypertext Markup

Language (HTML) text format. The Web browser is a Layer 7 network application. The HTTP protocol is a Layer 7 protocol.

Some TCP/IP protocols at Layer 7

The following TCP/IP protocols are found at Layer 7:

+ **SMTP:** Simple Mail Transfer Protocol is used to transfer, edit, and display e-mail messages.

+ **HTTP:** Hypertext Transfer Protocol is used to transfer text in HTML
  format from one host to another. HTML is the Hypertext Markup
  Language that marks up text with hyperlinks to allow jumping from one
  text document to another. The Web is based on HTTP and HTML.

+ **FTP:** File Transfer Protocol is used to transfer files between hosts.

+ **NFS:** Network File System is used to share file systems over the network.

+ **SNMP:** Simple Network Management Protocol is used to provide a distributed network management framework to monitor and manage host
  and network devices over the network.

+ **DNS:** Domain Name System is a protocol that helps keep track of host
  names and logical (IP) addresses in a network.

+ **DHCP:** Dynamic Host Configuration Protocol is used to assign dynamic
  logical addresses (IP addresses) to hosts in a network.

Some TCP/IP software applications at Layer 7

The following TCP/IP software applications are found at Layer 7:

+ **E-mail application:** This application is used to read, edit, archive, and
  otherwise manage e-mail messages. E-mail applications typically use
  SMTP to send and receive e-mails to and from remote hosts. E-mail
  applications also work at Layer 6, the presentation layer. For example,
  e-mail applications use the Multipurpose Internet Mail Extensions
  (MIME) protocol to convert audio, video, picture, graphical, and even
  software application contents in e-mail messages into a format that can
  be displayed, rendered, or played on the receiving host. Whenever you
  send audio or video, your e-mail application also uses MIME to code
  the audio/video contents within the e-mail message in a format that is
  easily transferable over the network. Remember that Layer 6 is doing
  the data conversion.

+ **Web browser:** A browser is used to view Web pages. Web browsers use
  HTTP to transfer Web pages to and from your computer. Web browsers also work at the presentation layer because they need to convert
  and render non-HTML format that may be embedded in an HTML
  Web page. For instance, when you browse a Web page that contains a

video-streaming window, the Web page contains code embedded into the HTML text to instruct the Web browser on how to play that video stream. Remember that Layer 6 is doing the data conversion.

Layer 6: Presentation

The presentation layer is mostly concerned with data format. It converts the data between different formats so that both the sender and the receiver can use heterogeneous data. Layer 6 protocols and Layer 6 software applications exist. For example, MIME is a Layer 6 protocol that is used by e-mail software programs and Web browsers (Layer 6 applications) to convert e-mail contents that are not text into a data format that can be viewed, rendered, or otherwise processed on the computer host.

Some TCP/IP protocols at Layer 6

The following TCP/IP protocols are found at Layer 6:

✦ **MIME:** Multipurpose Internet Mail Extensions are used to allow e-mail applications to convert e-mail message contents other than text into a data format that is supported on the receiving host. MIME is also used to code nontext data into an outgoing mail message.

✦ **Unicode:** Modern e-mail applications and Web browsers use Unicode at the presentation layer to convert characters between the character set of the sender and the character set of the receiver. Unicode provides a standard way to code characters in different character sets, including multi byte characters for some languages.

Some TCP/IP software applications at Layer 6

The following TCP/IP software applications are found at Layer 6:

✦ **E-mail application:** E-mail applications use the MIME protocol to convert audio, video, picture, graphical, and even software application contents in e-mail messages.

✦ **Web browser:** Browsers also use the MIME protocol to convert non-HTML contents in Web pages.

Layer 5: Session

The session layer maintains a logical communication channel between a network application running on the sending host and a network application running on the receiving host. Sometimes the session layer also provides authentication services when sessions are established.

The following TCP/IP protocols are found at Layer 5:

✦ **Telnet:** A protocol used to open login sessions on a computer host.

✦ **RPC:** Remote-procedure call protocol is used to allow the execution of procedures (programs) on remote hosts.

✦ **iSCSI:** The Internet small computer system interface protocol allows you to send SCSI commands over a TCP/IP network. iSCSI is used to interconnect specialized storage devices and computer hosts using a TCP/IP network.

Layer 4: Transport

The transport layer slices up the data to be transmitted into small chunks called *data segments* that can be easily sent over the network medium. The segments may end up taking different routes to get to their destination. Consequently, they may arrive in different order. The transport layer on the receiving host reorders the data segments. The transport layer also provides some error-detection mechanisms. It also insulates the upper layers from network implementation details below, by providing a generic data transfer protocol to upper layers, no matter how the network is implemented underneath.

For example, the network layer can be implemented with the Internet Protocol (IP), the AppleTalk protocol, or the Novell Netware IPX protocol. In all cases, the transport layer presents the same interface up to the session layer while using the appropriate network layer protocol underneath.

Connectionless transport

Data can be sent between two hosts without establishing a logical connection between sending and receiving hosts. Connectionless transport protocols do not guarantee reliable delivery of data segments. However, they are a bit faster than connection-oriented transport protocols, because they do not need to spend time to establish and maintain connections. User Datagram Protocol (UDP) is a connectionless transport protocol.

Connection-oriented transport

A transport protocol that establishes a logical connection between the sending and the receiving hosts is called a *connection-oriented transport protocol*. Connection-oriented transport protocols usually guarantee *reliable delivery* of data segments. However, they are a bit slower than connectionless transport protocols, because they need to spend some time to establish and maintain the connection. Transmission Control Protocol (TCP) is a connection-oriented transport protocol.

Connection-oriented transport involves both creating a logical connection between the sending and the receiving hosts, and an exchange of *acknowledgments* between the hosts. Data segments are *sequenced,* allowing them to be sent in any order and reassembled on the receiving host.

Flow control is also part of connection-oriented reliable data transport. Flow control involves the sender and the receiver coordinating to sustain an optimal data transfer flow: As the receiver processes the data segments, it acknowledges reception to the sender. The sender then sends more segments.

The most common TCP/IP protocols at Layer 4

Common TCP/IP protocols at Layer 4 are as follows:

✦ **TCP:** Transport Control Protocol is a connection-oriented transport protocol. TCP guarantees reliable transmission.

✦ **UDP:** User Datagram Protocol is a connectionless transport protocol. UDP does not guarantee reliable transmission.

TCP flow control

The TCP transport protocol is a connection-oriented protocol that can control the flow of data transmission to guarantee reliable transmissions.

TCP on the sending host establishes a logical connection to TCP on the receiving host. This step is called *three-way handshake, call setup,* or *virtual circuit setup.* The sending host and the receiving host use this connection, or virtual circuit, to coordinate their data transfer. The connection is terminated when no more data needs to be transferred. Any host can initiate TCP connections. The host that initiates the TCP connection becomes the *sending* host. The other host is the *receiving* host. However, TCP connections allow both hosts to send and receive TCP segments. TCP controls the flow of segments in each direction of a connection independently using sender and receiver sequence numbers.

Three-way handshake

The first step to establish a TCP connection involves a *three-way handshake.* You may also hear the term *call setup* or *virtual circuit setup.* These are synonyms. Here is how the three-way handshake **process** works:

1. The host that initiates the network communication sends a TCP "Synchronize" (SYN) message to the receiving host to notify it that it wants to establish a TCP connection. This message contains, among other things, the sender starting sequence number for the TCP transmission.

2. The starting sequence number is the sequence number of the first TCP segment to transfer from sender to receiver. The sending and the receiving host then negotiate connection parameters.

3. The receiving host replies with a TCP "Synchronize" (SYN) message that contains the receiver starting sequence number. This message also sends an acknowledgment (ACK) to the sending host, indicating that the receiving host did receive the first TCP "Synchronize" message.

4. The sending host sends back an acknowledgment (ACK) to the receiving host to let it know that it did receive the receiver starting sequence number and that it is ready to send.

    At this point, the *bidirectional* TCP connection is established. TCP connections are bidirectional, because both hosts send SYN and ACK messages to each other to synchronize and guarantee a reliable data transfer.

Figure 3-2 illustrates the three-way handshake process.

Here's what's going on in Figure 3-2:

+ **Step 1:** The first step of the three-way handshake process involves sending a TCP "Synchronize" (SYN) request from host Alex to host Claire. Host Alex requests to open a TCP connection with host Claire. The SYN request contains the starting sequence number of the segments that host Alex sends to host Claire. This first segment sequence number is 1.

+ **Step 2:** Claire accomplishes two things with a single segment sent back to Alex. She first acknowledges that she received the segment with sequence 1 from Alex and that she is ready to receive his next segment with sequence 2. Second, she also informs Alex that her starting sequence number is 25.

+ **Step 3:** Alex acknowledges to Claire that he received her segment with sequence 25 and that he is ready to receive her next segment with sequence 26. Alex also tells Claire that this is his second segment, segment with sequence 2.

+ **Step 4:** Claire sends her segment 26 to inform Alex that she received his segment 2 and that she is ready to receive Alex's segment 3.

At this point, the TCP connection is established, and the actual data transfer can begin.

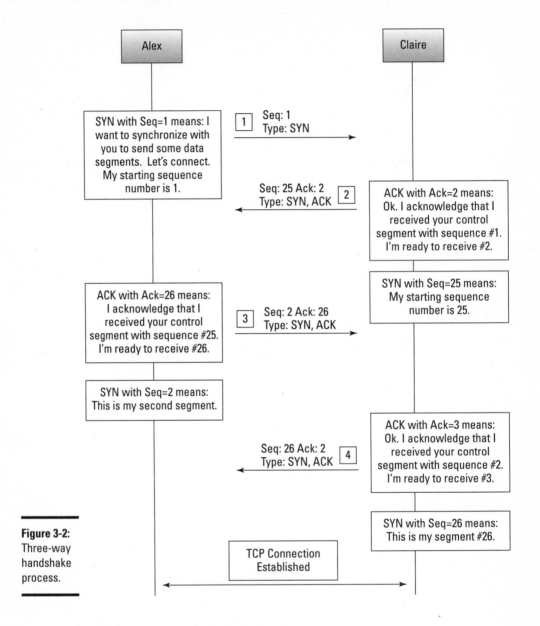

Figure 3-2: Three-way handshake process.

Alex

Claire

SYN with Seq=1 means: I want to synchronize with you to send some data segments. Let's connect. My starting sequence number is 1.

1 Seq: 1
Type: SYN

Seq: 25 Ack: 2
Type: SYN, ACK 2

ACK with Ack=2 means: Ok. I acknowledge that I received your control segment with sequence #1. I'm ready to receive #2.

SYN with Seq=25 means: My starting sequence number is 25.

ACK with Ack=26 means: I acknowledge that I received your control segment with sequence #25. I'm ready to receive #26.

3 Seq: 2 Ack: 26
Type: SYN, ACK

SYN with Seq=2 means: This is my second segment.

ACK with Ack=3 means: Ok. I acknowledge that I received your control segment with sequence #2. I'm ready to receive #3.

Seq: 26 Ack: 2
Type: SYN, ACK 4

SYN with Seq=26 means: This is my segment #26.

TCP Connection Established

Sequencing and acknowledgments

TCP connections are bidirectional: They allow both hosts to send and receive TCP segments. TCP controls the flow of segments in each direction of a connection independently using sender and receiver sequence numbers. Thus, TCP connections maintain two sets of sequence numbers: sender sequence numbers and receiver sequence numbers. The sender sequence numbers control the flow of segments sent by the sending host, host Alex in the previous example. The receiver sequence numbers control the flow of segments sent by the receiving host. Each segment that needs to be sent in either direction is sequenced (numbered) within the sender or receiver sequencing set, depending in which direction the segment travels.

Sequencing is also used to determine the order of the data segments. Data segments need to be reassembled in the correct order when they arrive at the destination on the receiving host, because they can get there in any order, depending on network conditions. TCP on the receiving host uses the sequence number of each data segment to determine its order during reassembly.

During transmission, errors can occur due to electrical interference, collisions, or link failure. TCP's use of sequencing and acknowledgments allows not only the control of the bidirectional transfer flow but also the correction of transmission errors by retransmitting segments that are lost or damaged. After a TCP connection is established using the three-way handshake process, TCP uses the *positive acknowledgment and retransmission (PAR)* process to ensure that all segments are received within a certain time period. Here's how PAR works:

1. Sending host starts a timer when it sends a segment. The sending host retransmits the segment if it does not receive a reception acknowledgment after a certain timeout period.

2. Sending host keeps track of the sequence number of each segment it transmits and expects reception acknowledgments for each one of them.

3. Receiving host sends acknowledgments back to the sending host for each segment it receives. The acknowledgment contains the sequence number of the next segment expected by the receiving host.

Figure 3-3 illustrates a simple data segment transfer between hosts Alex and Claire after they have established a TCP connection.

This figure continues the TCP connection established in Figure 3-2. Here, Alex starts sending data segments to Claire:

+ **Step 1:** Alex sends the first data segment in TCP segment 3. Segment 3 follows Alex's segments 1 and 2 sent during the three-way handshake process in Figure 3-2. Alex also acknowledges reception of Claire's segment 26, expecting 27.

+ **Step 2:** Claire acknowledges that she received Alex's segment 3 and that she is ready to receive Alex's segment 4. Claire's ACK is sent to Alex in Claire's segment 27.

◆ **Step 3:** Alex sends the second data segment in TCP segment 4. He also acknowledges to Claire that he received her segment 27 and that he is ready to receive 28.

◆ **Step 4:** Claire acknowledges that she received Alex's segment 4 and that she is ready to receive Alex's segment 5. Claire's ACK is sent to Alex in Claire's segment 28.

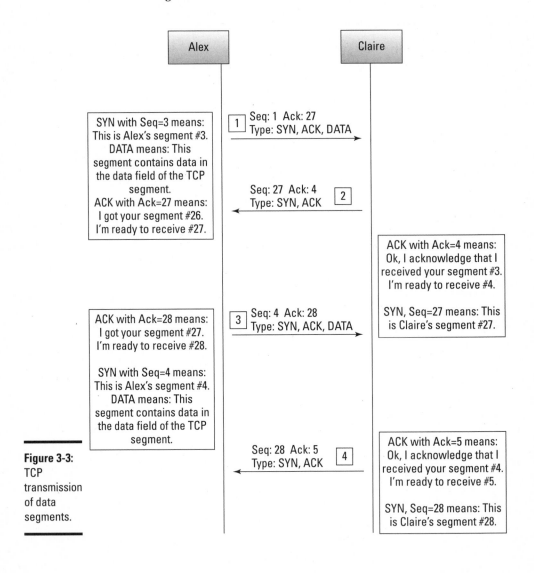

Figure 3-3:
TCP transmission of data segments.

TCP sliding window

Figure 3-3 illustrates how the TCP connection-oriented transport protocol uses sequencing and acknowledgments to guarantee a reliable transmission. However, you can see that in Figure 3-3, Alex waits to receive an acknowledgment from Claire before sending his next data segment. This is a waste of time. If Alex is ready to send, he should send instead of waiting for acknowledgments for each segment before sending the next one. The *TCP sliding window* enables Alex to do just that.

The TCP sliding window specifies how many segments Alex can send before it stops and waits for an acknowledgment from Claire. Consider that Alex and Claire agree on a TCP sliding window of 5:

+ Alex sends five segments and waits for at least one acknowledgment before sending segment 6.

+ The five segments are traveling through the network and eventually reach Claire, potentially in a different order.

+ Claire stashes these segments in a temporary area in memory called a *buffer* and processes them one by one.

+ As segments are processed, she sends an acknowledgment for each one of them.

+ As Alex receives acknowledgments, he sends more segments.

+ If Claire gets overloaded with too many segments to process, or if her memory is running low and she needs to shrink the buffer a little bit, she can decrease the TCP window size during the transfer.

+ Alex would then adjust by sending fewer segments.

So far, I've talked about TCP window size being measured in segments to keep things simple, but in reality, the TCP window size is measured in bytes.

Figure 3-4 illustrates a typical data-segment transfer between hosts Alex and Claire with a TCP window.

This figure continues the TCP connection established in Figure 3-2. Contrary to Figure 3-3, though, this figure also shows a typical TCP transmission with a TCP window of 3 that is decreased to 2 midway through the data transfer:

+ **Step 1:** The TCP window size is 3 segments. Alex sends the first three data chunks in segments 3, 4, and 5. Alex also acknowledges reception of Claire's segment 26, expecting 27.

+ **Step 2:** Claire acknowledges Alex's segments 3 and 4, but not 5. She's still expecting 5, although Alex has already sent it. Claire's ACKs for segments 3 and 4 are sent to Alex in Claire's segment 27 and 28, respectively.

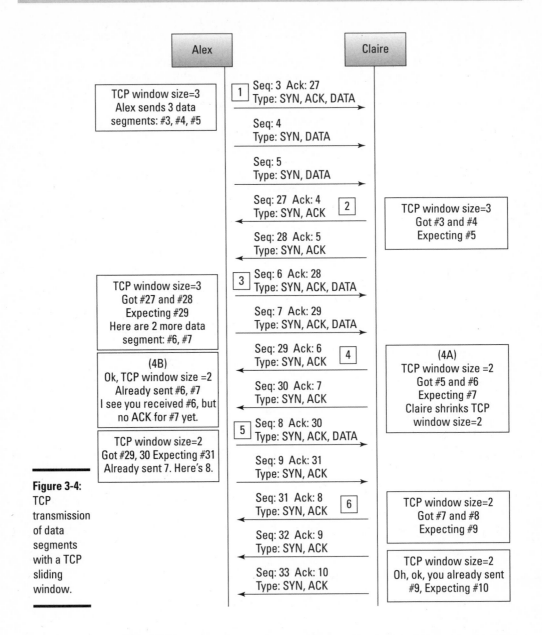

Figure 3-4:
TCP
transmission
of data
segments
with a TCP
sliding
window.

Alex

Claire

TCP window size=3
Alex sends 3 data
segments: #3, #4, #5

1 | Seq: 3 Ack: 27
Type: SYN, ACK, DATA

Seq: 4
Type: SYN, DATA

Seq: 5
Type: SYN, DATA

Seq: 27 Ack: 4
Type: SYN, ACK | 2

TCP window size=3
Got #3 and #4
Expecting #5

Seq: 28 Ack: 5
Type: SYN, ACK

TCP window size=3
Got #27 and #28
Expecting #29
Here are 2 more data
segment: #6, #7

3 | Seq: 6 Ack: 28
Type: SYN, ACK, DATA

Seq: 7 Ack: 29
Type: SYN, ACK, DATA

Seq: 29 Ack: 6
Type: SYN, ACK | 4

(4A)
TCP window size =2
Got #5 and #6
Expecting #7
Claire shrinks TCP
window size=2

(4B)
Ok, TCP window size =2
Already sent #6, #7
I see you received #6, but
no ACK for #7 yet.

Seq: 30 Ack: 7
Type: SYN, ACK

TCP window size=2
Got #29, 30 Expecting #31
Already sent 7. Here's 8.

5 | Seq: 8 Ack: 30
Type: SYN, ACK, DATA

Seq: 9 Ack: 31
Type: SYN, ACK

Seq: 31 Ack: 8
Type: SYN, ACK | 6

TCP window size=2
Got #7 and #8
Expecting #9

Seq: 32 Ack: 9
Type: SYN, ACK

Seq: 33 Ack: 10
Type: SYN, ACK

TCP window size=2
Oh, ok, you already sent
#9, Expecting #10

✦ **Step 3:** Alex sends two more data chunks in TCP segments 6 and 7. The TCP window size is 3 with just one segment in it (segment 5), which leaves two slots available. Hence, Alex can send two data segments at this point. He also acknowledges to Claire that he received her segments 27 and 28 and that he is ready to receive 29.

✦ **Step 4:** Claire acknowledges that she received Alex's segments 5 and 6 and that she is ready to receive Alex's segment 7. Keep in mind that Alex has actually already sent segment 7, but Claire is busy enough with segments 5 and 6 at this point. She shrinks the TCP window size to 2 segments, either because she needs to reduce the reception buffer size or maybe because she is overwhelmed by having three segments in the buffer, but two is good. Claire's ACKs for segments 5 and 6 are sent to Alex in Claire's segments 29 and 30, respectively. Alex readjusts his TCP window size to 2 segments.

✦ **Step 5:** Alex sends one more data chunk in TCP segment 8. He also acknowledges reception of Claire's segment 29 and 30, expecting 31 next.

✦ **Step 6:** Claire acknowledges that she received Alex's segments 7 and 8 and that she is ready to receive Alex's segment 9. Keep in mind that Alex has actually already sent segment 9 to acknowledge reception of Claire's segment 30. Thus, Claire acknowledges reception of Alex's segment 9, now expecting 10.

TCP connection-oriented data transfer involves the following:

✦ Performing a three-way handshake to set up the connection, also called a virtual circuit

✦ Using sequencing to identify each data segment and its order

✦ Using acknowledgments to guarantee data delivery

✦ Using bidirectional flow control to coordinate the sending and receiving of segments for optimal data transfer

UDP simplicity

The User Datagram Protocol (UDP) is a connectionless transport protocol that does not guarantee reliable transmission. UDP is not as chatty as TCP: Hosts that transfer data using TCP need to exchange many segments just to open a connection during the three-way handshake process. They need to exchange many more segments to acknowledge reception of every single data segment. These flow control data segments add some overhead to TCP transmissions.

UDP does not add flow control overhead because

✦ UDP is connectionless, so there's no need to send segments to do a three-way handshake to establish a connection.

✦ UDP makes no use of sequencing.

✦ UDP does not send acknowledgments.

✦ UDP does not guarantee reception of data segments.

Consequently, UDP is faster than TCP and can be good enough in some data-transfer scenarios such as DNS lookups and TFTP transfers. However, despite being chatty, TCP is by far the most widely used transport protocol in TCP/IP networks. It's nice to have warranty even if it costs a little more.

TCP/IP ports

Both TCP and UDP use ports to identify the source and destination network applications that are involved in data transmission.

Every host has a logical (IP) address and a physical (MAC) address. On the other hand, more than one network application may be running on each host. For example, you can have an e-mail program and a Web browser open at the same time on your host. So, how does your Web browser connect to a Web server, considering that the Web server host has only one IP address and may also be running an e-mail server application? Answer: By using standard TCP/IP ports. A standard TCP/IP port exists for HTTP (the protocol used by Web browsers), a standard TCP/IP port exists for SMTP (the protocol used by some e-mail readers), and so on. All network applications use a TCP/IP port to allow the sending application to connect to the receiving application. Hence, even if you run multiple network applications on the same host, as long as each network application has its own TCP/IP port, a TCP or UDP data transmission can be accomplished.

TCP/IP ports are defined by the IANA (Internet Assigned Numbers Authority). Here are the port number ranges currently defined:

✦ **0–1023:** Well-known TCP/IP ports. These ports are reserved for standard TCP/IP network applications and protocols.

✦ **1024–49151:** Registered TCP/IP ports. These ports are reserved for applications that are registered by various corporations. However, many companies today are using the private TCP/IP ports range instead.

✦ **49152–65535:** Private TCP/IP ports. These ports are available for anyone to use. Companies that write network applications typically allow the users to configure the TCP/IP ports manually in this port number range. This is a flexible and reliable solution for most network applications.

Table 3-1 lists some well-known reserved TCP/IP ports.

Table 3-1		Some Well-Known TCP/IP Ports	
TCP	*Port*	*UDP*	*Port*
HTTP	80, 8080	DHCP	67, 68
HTTPS	443	SNMP	161
SMTP	25	BOOTP	67,68

TCP	Port	UDP	Port
DNS	53	RIP	520, 521
POP	110	NTP	123
Telnet	23	IRC	194
SSH	22	SMB	445
FTP	20, 21	Syslog	514

Layer 3: Network

One of the most important functions of network layer devices and protocols is choosing the best route to send packets between hosts. This is called *routing*. The CCNA certification tests routing knowledge extensively because Cisco routers are the de facto standard today for routing packets at the network level. Consequently, you need to have a good understanding of routing. Routing and Cisco routers are covered in detail in Book IV.

The network layer also assigns logical addresses (IP addresses) to all devices in the network to be able to identify each source host, each destination host, and each network through which packets need to be routed. Logical addresses are assigned at the network protocol level as opposed to physical addresses, which are assigned on a physical device, such as network card.

Some TCP/IP protocols at Layer 3

The following TCP/IP protocols are found at Layer 3:

✦ **IP:** Internet Protocol is used to deliver data packets over a packet-switched network from a source host to a destination host based on their respective IP addresses. IP comes in two versions: IP version 4 (IPv4) and IP version 6 (IPv6). IPv4 is currently the most widely used version.

✦ **ICMP:** Internet Control Message Protocol is used to send error and status messages about network operations and available services, mostly by host and network devices. The most typical use of ICMP is the `ping` command, which allows you to verify whether a host or network device is reachable over the IP network from another host or network device.

✦ **IPsec:** Internet Protocol Security is used to secure IP data packet deliveries.

The Internet Protocol (IP) is the most important TCP/IP protocol that operates at the network layer. IP addresses are logical addresses provided by the IP in TCP/IP.

Hierarchy of IP addresses

Logical addressing at the network layer is *hierarchical:*

+ A limited range of IP addresses identifies a few global networks.

+ Global networks interconnect large and medium networks that use another specific range of IP addresses.

+ Large and medium networks interconnect smaller networks that use yet another specific range of IP addresses.

The *hierarchical IP addressing* scheme facilitates routing.

To understand this, think about a real street address, which is composed of the following:

+ Street number

+ Street name

+ Neighborhood name for larger cities

+ City name

+ State name

+ Country name

Routing at the network layer in computer networks works similarly to courier services:

+ A few extremely large global networks (think countries) interconnect other large networks.

+ Large-sized networks (think states or provinces) interconnect medium-sized networks (think cities).

+ Medium-sized networks interconnect smaller networks (think neighborhoods).

+ Small-size networks interconnect mini-networks (think streets).

+ Finally, computer hosts are found within each of the mini-networks (think street numbers).

Computer hosts embed the sender and receiver IP address in each data packet they send to another computer:

✦ If the receiving computer host is in the same network as the sender (living on the same street), the packet is simply routed locally at the data link layer using the physical address (the MAC address).

✦ If the receiving computer host is not in the same network as the sender, the packet is handed off to a *gateway* to be routed outside the network. A gateway is a router that links a network to another network.

✦ The gateway looks at the logical address (IP address) of the receiving computer host and determines in which network it is located (on which street).

✦ If the gateway knows about the network of the receiving computer host (it knows the street; it's in the same city), it sends the data packet to that network.

✦ If the gateway does not know the destination network, it hands the packet to the higher-up gateway.

I now take a closer look at how routing works at the network layer. Figure 3-5 shows the Alex, Claire, and John simple network connected to a remote network through the Internet. The remote network connects Marius, Monica, and Sophie.

Figure 3-5 shows the Alex, Claire, John network, network 192.168.25.0, interconnected over a wide-area network to the Marius, Monica, Sophie network, network 192.168.67.0. Remember that every network, every network device, and every host in a network have a logical address assigned by a protocol that operates at the network layer. The Internet Protocol assigns IP addresses in the case of TCP/IP. Recall also that IP addresses are hierarchical. They have a part that identifies the network and a part that identifies the host device. The size of network part and the size of the host part of a TCP/IP address vary according to the network it describes.

Observe that a switch interconnects hosts locally in networks 192.168.25.0 and 192.168.67.0. To keep things simpler, I will refer to these networks as network 25 and network 67. The first part of the IP address is the same for all devices in this example, so I will not refer to it in the following text. Each switch is connected to a router that serves as a gateway to exit that network. In other words, anytime a host in network 25 sends a data packet to a receiver in network 67, the packet is handed over by switch 25 to the gateway of the local network, the router 25<>51.

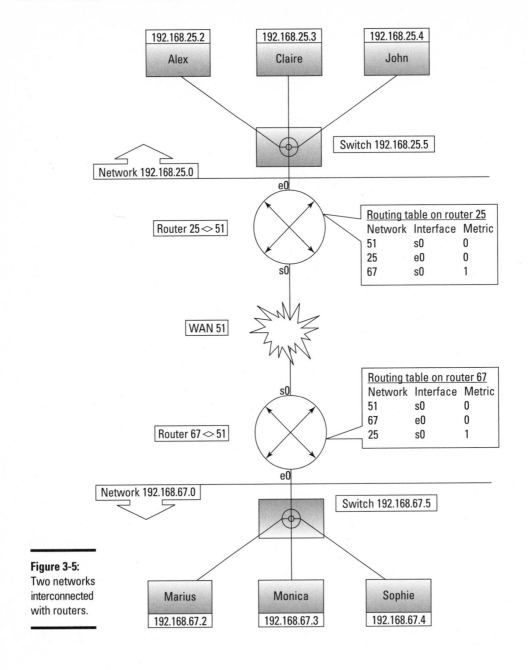

Figure 3-5:
Two networks interconnected with routers.

Routing tables

How does the router know where to send the data packet? Routers keep a *routing table* in memory. Routing tables keep track of the following:

+ Each network known

+ Router interface through which each network can be reached

+ Metrics associated with each route

Routers keep one routing table for each protocol, because each protocol has its own addressing scheme and metrics. If you run IP (IPv4), IPv6, and AppleTalk on the same router, that router will keep a routing table for IPv4, a routing table for IPv6, and a routing table for AppleTalk.

For example, assume that Claire needs to send a data packet to Marius:

+ The packet is tagged with Claire's IP address (192.168.25.3) as sender.

+ The packet is tagged with Marius's IP address (192.168.67.2) as receiver.

+ The packet leaves Claire on her network card and reaches router 25<>51 through switch 192.168.25.5.

+ Router 25<>51 searches for network 67 in its routing table:

  • It finds that network 67 is reachable through interface s0, which stands for serial 0.

  • Hence, router 25<>51 sends the packet on interface s0 into network 51 (the WAN).

+ The packet travels through the WAN and eventually enters router 67<>51 on interface s0.

+ Router 67<>51 examines the receiver address in the packet and finds 192.168.67.2:

  • Router 67<>51 searches for network 67 in its routing table.

  • It finds that network 67 is reachable through interface e0, which stands for Ethernet 0.

  • Router 67<>51 sends the packet on interface e0 into network 67 to the destination host Marius identified by 192.168.67.2.

How do routers 25<>51 and 67<>51 build their routing tables? By exchanging information about the networks they know about. In other words, router 25<>51 constantly communicates with router 67<>51 to exchange information about the networks and routes they each know about. Over time, as each router finds out about new networks, and new routes to those networks, the collective information about networks and routes gets more and more accurate.

Routing and routed protocols

Two types of protocols operate at the network layer: routed protocols and routing protocols:

✦ *Routed protocols* are used to route *data packets*. For example, IP (IPv4) is a routed protocol, and so are IPv6, AppleTalk, IPX, and SNA.

✦ *Routing protocols* are used to send *route update packets*. Route update packets carry information about new networks and new routes. Routers send each other route update packets whenever a new network is created or a new route is enabled. Some of the most common routing protocols are Routing Information Protocol (RIP), RIPv2, Enhanced Interior Gateway Routing Protocol (EIGRP), and Open Shortest Path First (OSPF). Different routing protocols use different metrics to decide which routes are better than others. To keep things simple, in the example, I just show one metric in the routing tables: the number of hop counts. The number of hop counts is the number of networks a data packet has to go through before reaching the destination network. In this case, to reach network 67 from network 25, a data packet needs to go through network 51, thus one hop.

Routing at the network layer involves

✦ *Hierarchical logical addressing*: Assign a network layer protocol level address to each network, network device and host device.

✦ *Routed protocols*: Use routed protocols to tag each packet with source and destination hierarchical addresses to allow routing of the data packet through networks as needed.

✦ Route packets on optimal routes.

✦ *Routing tables*: Maintain routing tables on routers listing networks, paths to networks and *metrics* for each path.

✦ *Routing protocols*: Use routing protocols to exchange network, routes, and metric information between routers to help find optimal routes as fast as possible.

Layer 2: Data Link

The data link layer transmits data on a physical medium. This layer also routes data locally to the next hop on the physical network medium. The data link layer uses physical addresses (MAC addresses) assigned to each physical network device in the local network to route data from one physical device to another. These addresses are called *Media Access Control (MAC)* addresses in TCP/IP. MAC addresses uniquely identify a specific network device, such as a switch or a router, or a network interface card (NIC) in a computer host device.

The data link layer is defined in TCP/IP by the IEEE 802.X (Ethernet) standard.

The data link layer receives each packet from the network layer on the sending host and wraps it up in a *data frame* along with local routing data. The data frame is sent down to the physical layer to code an electrical or optical signal to transmit it over a wire, or over the air (wireless transmission). On the receiving host, the data link layer unwraps the data frame received to extract the packet and sends it up to the network layer.

Some TCP/IP protocols at Layer 2

You find the following TCP/IP protocols at Layer 2:

✦ **ARP:** Address Resolution Protocol is used to resolve (find) the physical (MAC) address of a host or network device, when only its logical (IP) address is known.

✦ **RARP:** Reverse Address Resolution Protocol is used to resolve (find) the logical (IP) address of a host or network device, when only its physical (MAC) address is known.

✦ **CSMA/CD:** Carrier sense multiple access collision detect protocol is used to allow the host and network device to share the bandwidth of a given interconnection medium. You find out more about CSMA/CD in Book I Chapter 6.

Consider again the example shown in Figure 3-5. This time you'll look at it from a data link layer perspective. Assume again that Claire needs to send a data packet to Marius:

1. The packet is first tagged with Claire's IP address (192.168.25.3) (the sender)

2. The packet is also tagged with Marius's IP address (192.168.67.2) (the receiver)

3. The packet leaves Claire and reaches router 25<>51 through switch 192.168.25.5. So, does Claire send her packet to the 25<>51 router? Well, Claire needs to figure out the physical (MAC) address where this packet should be sent.

Address resolution

The *Address Resolution Protocol (ARP)* is used to resolve (find) a physical (MAC) address for a host or network device, when only its logical (IP) address is known. Claire uses ARP now:

1. Claire looks into her Address Resolution Protocol (ARP) table, searching for the IP address of the destination host and its corresponding MAC address. In other words, she searches the ARP table for IP address 192.168.67.2 (Marius's IP address) and hopes to find the corresponding MAC address. The ARP table stores responses to previous ARP requests.

2. If Claire does not find an entry for Marius in her ARP table, she broadcasts an ARP request.

3. All devices in network 25 see the ARP request, including router 25<>51.

4. Router 25<>51 examines the destination IP address. It is an address in network 67, a remote network.

5. Router 25<>51 responds with its own MAC address.

6. Claire saves the MAC address of router 25<>51 in her MAC address table.

7. Claire builds a data-link frame with her MAC address as source and the 25<>51 router MAC address as destination. She puts the IP packet inside the data-link frame and sends the frame to router 25<>51.

8. Router 25<>51 receives the data frame sent by Claire.

9. Router 25<>51 strips out the data-link frame and extracts the IP packet from it. It then searches its routing table for network 67. It finds that network 67 is reachable through interface s0.

10. Router 25<>51 builds a new data-link frame that fills the destination field with the MAC address of the next hop in network 51, assuming that the next hop in the WAN is also using Ethernet at the data link layer.

11. Router 25<>51 sends the data-link frame out on interface s0 to the next hop in network 51 (the WAN). Within network 51, each router repeats the same process.

12. The packet travels through the WAN and eventually enters router 67<>51 on interface s0.

13. Router 67<>51 strips out the data-link frame (which contains its own MAC address as destination) and extracts the IP packet from it.

14. Router 67<>51 examines the receiver IP address and finds 192.168.67.2.

15. Router 67<>51 searches for network 67 in its routing table. It finds that network 67 is reachable through interface e0, which stands for Ethernet 0.

16. Router 67<>51 builds a new data-link frame with Marius's MAC address (192.168.67.2) in the destination field. It encapsulates the IP packet within the new data-link frame. The 67<>51 router obtains Marius's MAC address the usual way: either by finding it in its ARP table or by broadcasting an ARP request on network 67 to look for the MAC address that corresponds to Marius's IP address.

17. Router 67<>51 sends the data-link frame out on interface e0. The data-link frame encapsulates the IP packet and is tagged with the MAC address of host Marius.

18. Marius receives the data-link frame and realizes that it is for him because it's tagged with his MAC address in the destination field.

Clare would jump over Steps 1 to 6 and send the data link frame directly to the 25<>51 router whenever she needs to send a packet to a host in a remote network if a default gateway (router 25<>51) is recorded on Claire.

Cisco switches are Layer 2 (data link layer) devices. You read more about Cisco switches in Book III, Chapter 2.

You find out more about the TCP/IP data link layer, including IEEE 802.X (Ethernet), in Book I, Chapter 6, and in Book II.

The data link layer is concerned with local area networks. Particularly, data link handles local routing of data frames in local area networks:

✦ *Media Access Control (MAC) address*: A unique physical address assigned to each network device, and to each host device NIC port. The IEEE 802.3 standard defines the structure of a MAC address.

✦ *Logical Link Control (LLC)*: Data link layer protocol that identifies the network layer protocol that generated the data packet. The LLC header in the data link layer frame is filled with the identifier of the originating network layer protocol, among other things. The data link layer on receiving host analyzes the LLC header to determine the target network protocol. Then, the LLC header is stripped off from the data link frame and the contents of the frame handed up to the network protocol identified by the LLC header.

✦ *Address Resolution Protocol (ARP)*: Data link layer protocol that is used to resolve (find) the physical (MAC) address of a host or network device, when only its logical (IP) address is known.

✦ *Carrier Sense Multiple Access and Collision Detection (CSMA/CD)*: Data link layer protocol allowing host and network devices to share the bandwidth of the same transmission medium. You learn more about CSMA/CD in the *Local Area Networks* chapter in this book.

Layer 1: Physical

The physical layer provides the electrical, optical, or over-the-air connection between the sending host device and the receiving host device. This typically involves copper or fiber-optic cabling, or wireless radio connections, patch panels, signal repeaters, submarine cables, or satellites. The physical layer defines the mechanical, electrical, optical, radio, procedural, and functional standards to enable the transmission of data-link (Layer 2) data frames over a certain transmission medium.

The physical layer is defined in TCP/IP by the IEEE 802.X (Ethernet) standard.

Prep Test

1 **Which of the following describes a Web browser?**

   A ○ Layer 7 (application) protocol

   B ○ Layer 7 software application

   C ○ Layer 6 (presentation) software application

   D ○ All of the above

2 **In connection-oriented transport, which of the following occurs?**

   A ○ Sending and receiving hosts exchange TCP acknowledgments.

   B ○ Sending and receiving hosts sequence their TCP segments.

   C ○ Sending and receiving hosts perform a three-way handshake.

   D ○ All of the above.

3 **What does the three-way handshake process allow two hosts to do?**

   A ○ Open a bidirectional TCP connection

   B ○ Open a bidirectional IP channel

   C ○ Open a bidirectional UDP session

   D ○ All of the above

4 **What happens whenever a TCP segment is missing at destination?**

   A ○ The receiving computer host aborts transmission.

   B ○ The sending computer host aborts transmission.

   C ○ The receiving computer host requests a retransmission.

   D ○ The sending computer host requests a retransmission.

5 **What does the positive acknowledgment and retransmission (PAR) TCP process ensure?**

   A ○ That all TCP segments are received within a certain time period

   B ○ That all UDP segments are received within a certain time period

   C ○ That all TCP/IP segments are received within a certain time period

   D ○ That all IP segments are received within a certain time period

6 **What do TCP and UDP ports allow multiple network applications to do?**

   A ○ Resolve the MAC address of the computer host they run on

   B ○ Connect to network interface card (NIC) drivers

   C ○ Connect their sending and receiving counterparts on the same sending and receiving computer hosts

   D ○ Resolve the IP address of the computer host they run on

7 **Name one of the main functions of Layer 3 (network layer) TCP/IP protocols.**

A ○ Manage the electrical aspect of network links

B ○ Choose the best route to send data packets between hosts, even when the hosts are separated by several networks

C ○ Choose the best route to send data frames between hosts, only when the hosts are located within the same local network

D ○ All of the above

8 **IP addresses are hierarchical to facilitate which of the following?**

A ○ Counting the number of hosts in a network

B ○ Counting the number of networks in a network

C ○ Routing of data packets in local and global networks

D ○ Routing of data frames in local networks

9 **A routed protocol is a Layer 2 (network layer) protocol that does which of the following?**

A ○ Route data packets

B ○ Send route update packets

C ○ Route data packets and send route update packets

D ○ All of the above

10 **A routing protocol is a Layer 2 (network layer) protocol that does which of the following?**

A ○ Route data packets

B ○ Send route update packets

C ○ Route data packets and send route update packets

D ○ All of the above

11 **What do Media Access Control (MAC) addresses uniquely identify?**

A ○ A specific wide-area network (WAN)

B ○ A specific local-area network (LAN)

C ○ A specific network device, such as a switch or a router, or a network interface card (NIC) in a computer host device

D ○ All of the above

Answers

1 **B.** Layer 7 software application. A Web browser is a Layer 7 software application. Review the *"Layer 7: Application"* section.

2 **D.** All of the above. In connection-oriented transport, sending and receiving hosts exchange TCP acknowledgments, sequence their TCP segments, and perform a three-way handshake to establish a connection before they start their communication. See *"TCP flow control."*

3 **A.** Open a bi-directional TCP connection. The three-way handshake process allows two hosts to open a bi-directional TCP connection. See *"Three-way handshake."*

4 **C.** The receiving computer host requests a re-transmission. Whenever a TCP segment is missing at destination, the receiving computer host requests a re-transmission. Review *"Sequencing and acknowledgments."*

5 **A.** All TCP segments are received within a certain time period. The positive acknowledgment and retransmission (PAR) TCP process ensures that all TCP segments are received within a certain time period. Review *"Sequencing and acknowledgments."*

6 **C.** Connect their sending and receiving counterparts on the same sending and receiving computer hosts. TCP and UDP ports allow multiple network applications to connect their sending and receiving counterparts on the same sending and receiving computer hosts. Review the *"Layer 4: Transport"* section.

7 **B.** Choose the best route to send data packets between hosts even when the hosts are separated by several networks. One of the main functions of Layer 3 (network layer) TCP/IP protocols is to choose the best route to send data packets between hosts even when the hosts are separated by several networks. Review the *"Layer 3: Network"* section.

8 **C.** Routing of data packets in local and global networks. The User Datagram Protocol (UDP) is a connectionless transport protocol that does not guarantee reliable transmission. Check out *"UDP Simplicity."*

9 **A.** Route data packets. A routed protocol is a Layer 3 (network layer) protocol that routes data packets. Review *"Routing and routed protocols."*

10 **B.** Send route update packets. A routing protocol is a Layer 3 (network layer) protocol that sends route update packets and manages the routes known by the router. Check *"Routing and routed protocols."*

11 **C.** Network device, such as a switch or a router, or a network interface card (NIC) in a computer host device. Media Access Control (MAC) addresses uniquely identify a network device, such as a switch or a router, or a network interface card (NIC) in a computer host device. Review the *"Layer 2: Data Link"* section.

Chapter 4: Data Encapsulation

Exam Objectives

↙ **Describing data encapsulation**

↙ **Describing how data encapsulation relates to the OSI network reference model**

↙ **Describing how data encapsulation enables the layers of the OSI network reference model to be independent of each other**

↙ **Describing protocol data units (PDUs) and showing how they relate to data encapsulation**

Read this chapter to find out about *data encapsulation:* what it is, how it works, and what its purpose is. You also read about *protocol data units (PDUs)* and see how they relate to data encapsulation. Diagrams illustrate data encapsulation and wrapping and unwrapping of PDUs at each OSI layer.

Introducing Data Encapsulation

Network models, including TCP/IP, use *encapsulation* and very clearly defined interfaces between layers to achieve independence of layer functionality.

Independence of layer functionality is crucial because it allows layers to evolve internally without impacting other layers. As long as a layer continues to interact the same way with upper and lower layers, it can change internally to adapt to new technologies and needs.

Independence of layer functionality also divides the network communication process into several precise specialized subprocesses. Each network model layer handles a specific subprocess. This eases management of the whole network communication process. It also allows each layer to specialize to specific network communication contexts, even to new unforeseen contexts. For example, the physical layer is constantly updated for new transmission media. However, this does not imply that the upper layers need to change as well. Thus, the network model as a whole can adapt to support new media with localized change at the physical layer.

Here's how encapsulation works:

✦ A computer host device needs to send some data across the network to a remote computer host.

✦ Data is modified by the upper-layer protocols as necessary and put in protocol data units.

Protocol data units (PDUs) are the basic data container used by each protocol to exchange data between hosts in a network. Each PDU contains data payload and control information that helps the protocol to figure out what to do with the data payload. The control information is usually stored in the header of the PDU, and sometimes in the trailer as well. Figure 4-1 illustrates each layer, its PDU, and how data is encapsulated in successive PDUs.

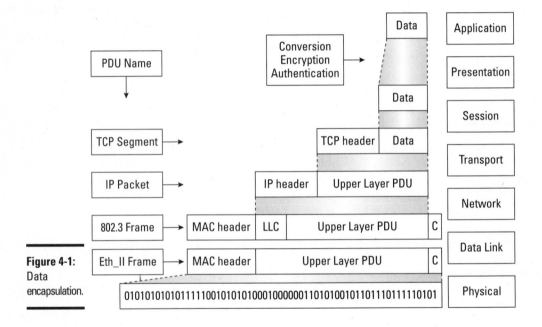

Figure 4-1: Data encapsulation.

✦ On the sending host, each layer does the following:

1. Receives a PDU from the upper layer.

2. Builds its own PDU containing the upper-layer PDU encapsulated within its own PDU built with a header and optionally a trailer around the upper-layer PDU.

   The original data payload ends up being encapsulated in several nested PDUs, one for each layer.

✦ On the receiving host, each layer does the following:

1. Receives a PDU from the lower layer

2. Strips out the lower-layer header and trailer because it doesn't need them

3. Extracts its own PDU, containing a control header, data payload, and optionally a control trailer

What a lower protocol considers data payload is in reality the original data payload nested within upper-layer PDUs. This is by design: Nesting PDUs guarantees layer independence. A lower-level PDU does not sneak into an upper-layer PDU. It considers the upper-layer PDU to be data payload and it doesn't touch it.

It is important to realize that each layer on the sending host communicates with its corresponding layer on the receiving host. Some layers, such as the TCP transport protocol in the transport layer, maintain a communication session between the sender and the receiver to guarantee reliable transmission and processing of PDUs.

Figure 4-2 shows the following:

✦ How each network layer interacts with its upper and lower layers to wrap and unwrap PDUs

✦ How equivalent layers on sender and receiver communicate with each other using control information in PDUs

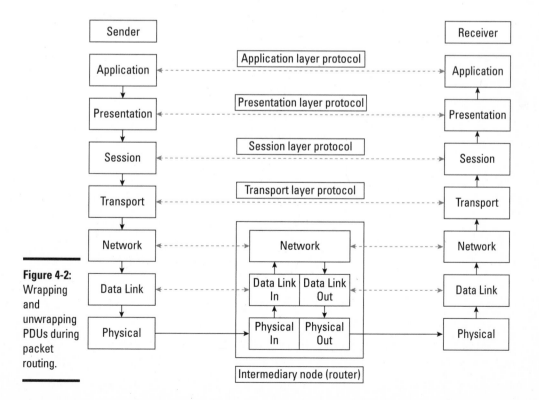

Figure 4-2: Wrapping and unwrapping PDUs during packet routing.

Observe that network and data link layers on intermediate nodes, which are typically routers, unwrap their PDUs, change the control information, and rebuild new PDUs to reach the next hop in the network.

Application, presentation, and session layers are typically called the top or *upper layers:*

1. The PDU is data at the *application layer,* such as the text of an e-mail message.

2. The application layer PDU is converted, encrypted, and translated at the *presentation layer* and encapsulated in control information headers to allow the receiving host to reconvert and unencrypt the data to its original format.

3. The presentation layer PDU that encapsulates the application layer PDU at this point may be further augmented with *session layer* control information.

   For example, an authenticated session may be opened between communicating hosts by the session layer. Control information about the authenticated session is added in a session layer header. The presentation layer PDU augmented with the session layer header becomes the session layer PDU. At this point, the session layer PDU encapsulates (contains) the presentation layer PDU, which in turn encapsulates the application layer PDU.

4. The session layer PDU is handed down to the *transport layer.*

   The transport layer first divides the session layer PDU into several small data chunks called *segments.* Each segment is numbered so that the receiving host can reassemble the application data.

5. The transport layer PDUs (the segments) are then forwarded down to the network layer, which tags each segment with logical source and destination addresses and some routing information and hands over the resulting shippable data *packet* to the lower data link layer.

6. The *data link layer* builds a data-link *frame* by adding the physical source address of the sender and the physical destination address of the receiver if the receiver is located in the same local network as the sender.

   If the receiver is not located in the same local network as the sender, the data link layer adds the physical destination address of the gateway in the local network to the data-link frame.

   The gateway of a local network is usually a router that connects the local network to other networks. The data link PDU (the data-link *frame*) is handed down to the physical layer.

At this point, the data link PDU (data link *frame*), encapsulates (contains) the network PDU (*packet*), which encapsulates the transport PDU (*segment*). The transport PDU in turn contains the session PDU, which encapsulates the presentation PDU, which in turn encapsulates the application layer PDU.

7. The *physical layer* converts each data-link *frame* into a series of binary signals. The binary signals are then transmitted over a wired or wireless connection to the next physical hop.

At the physical and data link layers, only the next hop is considered. The network layer keeps track of the final destination, even if the receiver is hundreds of miles away and several network hops away.

Prep Test

1 **What does independence of layer functionality allow?**

A ○ Layers to change internally without impacting other layers

B ○ Layers to interact with network hardware

C ○ Layers to interact with network software

D ○ Layers to migrate from one operating system to another

2 **Describe protocol data units (PDUs).**

A ○ Basic encryption method that allows a network interface card (NIC) to send encrypted data packets over the network

B ○ Basic encoding method that allows a network interface card (NIC) to send data packets over the network

C ○ Basic data container used by each protocol to exchange data between hosts in a network

D ○ Basic data container used by each protocol to set up a virtual circuit

3 **Each protocol data unit (PDU) contains which of the following?**

A ○ Data payload and control information about the local computer host

B ○ Data payload and control information that helps the protocol figure out what to do with the data payload

C ○ Data payload and control information about devices in the network

D ○ Data payload and control information about the remote computer host

4 **On the sending host, what is the function of each layer?**

A ○ Receives a PDU from the upper layer

B ○ Builds its own PDU containing the upper-layer PDU encapsulated within its own PDU

C ○ Encapsulates original data payload in several nested PDUs, one for each layer

D ○ All of the above

5 **On the receiving host, what is the function of each layer?**

A ○ Receives a PDU from the lower layer

B ○ Strips out the lower-layer header and trailer because it doesn't need them

C ○ Extracts its own PDU, containing a control header, data payload, and optionally a control trailer

D ○ All of the above

Answers

1 **A.** The independence of layer functionality allows each network layer to change without affecting the other layers. Review *"Introducing Data Encapsulation."*

2 **C.** Protocol data units (PDUs) are the basic data container used by each protocol to exchange data between hosts in a network. See *"Introducing Data Encapsulation."*

3 **B.** Each PDU contains data payload and control information that helps the protocol to figure out what to do with the data payload. The control information is usually stored in the header of the PDU, and sometimes in the trailer as well. Read *"Introducing Data Encapsulation."*

4 **D.** All of the above. Each layer on the sending host receives a PDU from the upper layer, builds its own PDU by adding control information in the header and/or trailer of the new PDU, and encapsulates the original PDU received from the upper layer within the new PDU. Check out *Figure 4-2: Wrapping and unwrapping PDUs during packet routing.*

5 **D.** All of the above. Each layer on the receiving host receives a PDU from the lower layer, strips out the lower-layer header and trailer because it doesn't need them, and extracts its own PDU, containing a control header, data payload, and optionally a control trailer. Review *Figure 4-2: Wrapping and unwrapping PDUs during packet routing.*

Chapter 5: Binary, Hexadecimal, and Decimal Numbering Systems

Exam Objectives

- ✔ Understanding decimal, hexadecimal, and binary numbering systems
- ✔ Converting numbers between the decimal, hexadecimal, and binary numbering systems
- ✔ Memorizing the major powers of 2 and understanding their relationship to corresponding binary numbers
- ✔ Differentiating between the bit, byte, and nibble

Read this chapter to find out about the *binary, hexadecimal,* and *decimal* numbering systems. The chapter covers the following topics:

+ How numbers are built based on a certain power base

+ How to convert numbers from one numbering system to another

+ Major powers of base 2 and their relationship to memory and disk size

+ Standard numbering systems notation

+ The first 15 numbers in the binary, hexadecimal, and decimal systems

+ The relationship between the hexadecimal and binary numbering systems and bits, bytes, and nibbles

It is important to read this chapter if you are not familiar with the binary, hexadecimal, and decimal numbering systems. You need to understand numbering systems and know how to convert numbers between the various systems. Don't worry if you are not familiar with these concepts yet. They sound much more complicated than they really are. Understanding numbering systems helps you not only when dealing with networks but also when dealing with other computer components and systems.

Several networking features and protocols rely on binary and hexadecimal numbers to code bit maps, subnet masks, and network addresses, among other things. It is important to understand numbering systems because they have implications on many features and protocols in networking.

Decimal Numbers

You have been using decimal numbers and learning how to count and calculate using decimal numbers since elementary school. So, you know that decimal numbers are built using digits 0 to 9. Ten digits can be used to build a number. That's why it's called the decimal system (*deci* means 10 in Latin). It is also called the base 10 numbering system, because all numbers in the decimal system are based on a power of 10.

The position of a digit in a decimal number determines its value. You learned in school that two-digit decimal numbers are worth 10 or more, three-digit numbers are 100 or more, four-digit numbers are 1,000 or more, and so on. For example, 11 and 36 are two-digit numbers, 120 and 250 are three-digit numbers, and 1,492 and 2,009 are four-digit numbers.

Have you ever wondered why when you place digit 2 in the third position from the right you mean 200, whereas if you place the digit 2 in the fourth position from the right you mean 2,000? There is a mathematical explanation.

All numbering systems are built on a certain base number. In the case of the decimal system, it is built on 10. That's why the decimal system is also called a 10-based numbering system, or simply base 10.

So here's how it works:

Position of digit from the right	4	3	2	1	0
Digit you place in that position	a	b	c	d	e
Value of number	$a*10^4 + b*10^3 + c*10^2 + d*10^1 + e*10^0$				

The value of each digit is built by multiplying the corresponding base 10 number by the digit placed in that position. For instance, the value of digit 3 is calculated by multiplying the base 10^3 by the digit placed in position 3. The nice thing about base 10 is that the power tells you how many trailing 0s you need to add after 1. So, 10^2 is two 0s after 1, which is 100; 10^3 is three 0s after 1, which 1,000; 10^4 is four 0s after 1, which is 10,000; and so on.

The value of the whole number is the sum of the values of each digit.

Consider the following example:

Position of digit from the right	4	3	2	1	0
Digit you place in that position	5	0	3	4	5
Value of number	$5*10^4 + 0*10^3 + 3*10^2 + 4*10^1 + 5*10^0 = 50,345$				

This is the magic of the decimal numbering system: What you see is what you get.

Binary Numbers

Binary numbers are quite simple. They only contain 0s and 1s. They are called binary numbers because they can only have two possible digits. You can see that 1 and 0 can easily be represented by "electrical signal," "no electrical signal." That's why all computer systems at their most basic level operate on binary numbers. Everything is converted to 1s and 0s, which are represented electrically by "signal," "no signal" in electronic circuits.

The binary system is similar to the decimal system:

✦ The position of a digit in a binary number determines the value.

✦ The binary system is built on 2, because you only have 2 digits to work with.

✦ The binary system is also called a 2-based numbering system, or simply base 2.

So here's how it works:

Position of digit from the right	4	3	2	1	0
Digit you place in that position	a	b	c	d	e
Value of number	$a*2^4 + b*2^3 + c*2^2 + d*2^1 + e*2^0$				

The value of each digit is built by multiplying the corresponding base 2 number by the digit placed in that position. Keep in mind though that whereas you can use digits 0 to 9 in the decimal system, you can only use digits 0 and 1 in the binary system.

For instance, the value of digit 3 is calculated by multiplying the base 2^3 with the digit placed in position 3.

The value of the whole number is the sum of the values of each digit.

Consider the following example:

Position of digit from the right	4	3	2	1	0
Digit you place in that position	0	0	1	0	1
Value of number	$0*2^4 + 0*2^3 + 1*2^2 + 0*2^1 + 1*2^0 = 5$				

The corresponding decimal value of the binary number 00101 is 5.

Consider another example:

Position of digit from the right	4	3	2	1	0
Digit you place in that position	1	0	1	0	1
Value of number	$1*2^4 + 0*2^3 + 1*2^2 + 0*2^1 + 1*2^0 = 21$				

The corresponding decimal value of the binary number 10101 is 21.

It is a good idea to become acquainted with a few base 2 numbers, because many measurements in the computer industry are based on base 2 numbers. For example, bandwidth, memory size, and hard drive space are usually expressed in base 2 numbers.

Table 5-1 lists the first 17 powers of 2. The table also illustrates the relationship between these numbers and common memory and disk multipliers used in the industry.

Table 5-1	Major Powers of 2		
Power of 2	*Kilo Multiplier*	*Mega Multiplier*	*Giga Multiplier*
$2^0 = 1$	—	—	—
$2^1 = 2$	—	—	—
$2^2 = 4$	—	—	—
$2^3 = 8$	—	—	—
$2^4 = 16$	—	—	—
$2^5 = 32$	—	—	—
$2^6 = 64$	—	—	—
$2^7 = 128$	—	—	—
$2^8 = 256$	¼ K	¼ M	¼ G
$2^9 = 512$	½ K	½ M	½ G
$2^{10} = 1,024$	1 K	1 M	1 G
$2^{11} = 2,048$	2 K	1 M	1 G
$2^{12} = 4,096$	4 K	4 M	4 G
$2^{13} = 8,192$	8 K	8 M	8 G
$2^{14} = 16,384$	16 K	16 M	16 G
$2^{15} = 32,768$	32 K	32 M	32 G
$2^{16} = 65,536$	64 K	64 M	64 G

The multiplier columns relate the value of the kilo, mega, and giga multipliers in the binary system — 1,024 (2^{10}) — to the K, M, and G designations. This is different from the value of the kilo, mega, and giga multiplier in the decimal system, which is 1,000 (10^3). In a nutshell:

✦ K means 1,024 in binary and 1,000 in decimal.

✦ M means 1,024*1,024 in binary and 1,000*1,000 in decimal.

✦ G means 1,024*1,024*1,024 in binary and 1,000*1,000*1,000 in decimal.

Some computer manufacturers use the decimal value of the kilo, mega, and giga multipliers instead of the binary value to market their products. For example, hard drive space is usually marketed using the decimal multipliers, not the binary multipliers. For example, a hard drive that is marketed as 30 gigabytes is usually 30*1,000*1,000*1,000 bytes, not 30*1,024*1,024*1,024 bytes. Hence, the drive is actually a bit smaller than 30 gigabytes.

Here are some examples of how these multipliers are used:

✦ 4 KB of cache memory means 4,096 bytes. 4,096 bytes * 8 bits/byte = 32,768 bits. Bytes are explained in the section "Bits, nibbles, and bytes," later in this chapter.

✦ 4 MB of RAM means 4,096 million bytes. 4,096,000 bytes * 8 bits/byte = 32,768,000 bits.

✦ 4 GB of RAM means 4,096 billion bytes. 4,096,000,000 bytes * 8 bits/byte = 32,768,000,000 bits.

Can you imagine working with a binary number that contains 32,768,000,000 digits (just 1s and 0s)? This is when the hexadecimal numbering system comes in handy.

Hexadecimal Numbers

Hexadecimal numbers are built using 16 digits, 0 to 9 and A to F. Digits 0 to 9 represent values up to 9. Digits A to F represent values 10 to 15. So, at the base, the hexadecimal system is 0,1,2,3,4,5,6,7,8,9,A,B,C,D,E,F, which corresponds to 0,1,2,3,4,5,6,7,8,9,10,11,12,13,14,15 in decimal. In other words, there is no change compared to the decimal system for 0 to 9. However, 10, 11, 12, 13, 14, and 15 become A, B, C, D, E, and F.

Sixteen possible digits exist in the hexadecimal numbering system. The nice thing about the hexadecimal system is that it is based on 16, which is 2^4. A single hexadecimal digit represents exactly 8 bits or 1 byte. Recall that 1 byte contains 8 bits. This means that you can represent a byte with a single hexadecimal value. This system is much easier to work with compared to dealing with 8 0s and 1s in the binary system.

The hexadecimal system is similar to the decimal system:

✦ The position in which a digit is placed in a hexadecimal number determines the value.

✦ The hexadecimal system is built on 16, because you have 16 digits to work with.

✦ The hexadecimal system is also called a 16-based numbering system, or simply base 16.

So here's how it works:

Position of digit from the right	4	3	2	1	0
Digit you place in that position	a	b	c	d	e
Value of number	$a*16^4 + b*16^3 + c*16^2 + d*16^1 + e*16^0$				

The value of each digit is built by multiplying the corresponding base 16 number by the digit placed in that position. Keep in mind though that whereas you can use digits 0 to 9 in the decimal system, you can now also use digits A to F for values above 9 in the hexadecimal system.

For instance, the value of digit 3 is calculated by multiplying the base 16^3 with the digit placed in position 3.

The value of the whole number is the sum of the values of each digit.

Consider an example:

Position of digit from the right	4	3	2	1	0
Digit you place in that position	0	0	1	1	0
Value of number	$0*16^4 + 0*16^3 + 1*16^2 + 1*16^1 + 0*16^0 = 272$				

The corresponding decimal value of the hexadecimal number 00110 is 272.

Consider another example:

Position of digit from the right	4	3	2	1	0
Digit you place in that position	0	7	3	9	5
Value of number	$0*16^4 + 7*16^3 + 3*16^2 + 9*16^1 + 5*16^0 = 29,599$				

The corresponding decimal value of the hexadecimal number 07395 is 29,599.

Consider another example:

Position of digit from the right	4	3	2	1	0
Digit you place in that position	D	5	C	9	A
Value of number	$13*16^4 + 5*16^3 + 12*16^2 + 9*16^1 + 10*16^0 = 875,824$				

The corresponding decimal value of the hexadecimal number D5C9A is 875,824.

As you see, one of the advantages of hexadecimal numbers is their ability to represent large numbers with relatively few digits compared to the decimal system, and especially compared to the binary system. The later section "Bits, nibbles, and bytes" shows you another interesting characteristic of hexadecimal numbers: They can easily represent binary values grouped by 8 bits.

Table 5-2 lists the first 15 numbers in the decimal, hexadecimal, and binary numbering systems. You should memorize these numbers because they will help you understand subnet masks, bit masks, memory, and disk sizing.

Table 5-2	Hexadecimal, Binary, and Decimal Values	
Hexadecimal	*Binary*	*Decimal*
0	0000	0
1	0001	1
2	0010	2
3	0011	3
4	0100	4
5	0101	5
6	0110	6
7	0111	7
8	1000	8
9	1100	9
A	1010	10
B	1011	11
C	1100	12
D	1101	13
E	1110	14
F	1111	15

Numbering systems notation

So how do you know whether 100 is being expressed in decimal or in hexadecimal notation? The industry uses a standard "0x" prefix to indicate hexadecimal numbers.

Another equivalent notation is 100_{16}. In fact, any number in any base can be written like this. For example, 251 in decimal can be written as 251_{10}, and 4 in binary can be written as 100_2. However, it is rare to see this type of notation for decimal and binary numbers. Binary numbers are easy to spot because they only contain 0s and 1s, and decimal numbers are assumed to be decimal unless indicated otherwise.

Bits, nibbles, and bytes

So now you understand how the numbering systems work and how they relate to each other. One last thing that I want to show you in this chapter is how numbers can be organized in bits, nibbles, and bytes.

A *bit* is one single binary value. So, it is a single-digit binary number that is either 0 or 1.

A *nibble* is a group of 4 bits. A nibble is also a single hexadecimal digit. That is one of the reasons why it is so easy to represent a binary number in hexadecimal: Every group of 4 bits is a hexadecimal digit.

A *byte* is a group of 8 bits. A byte is also 2 nibbles. In many ways, a byte is the basic unit of measure in the computer industry. Most western characters are represented by a byte. Memory size and hard drive space are measured in megabytes (million bytes), gigabytes (billion bytes), and terabytes (trillion bytes).

Assume that you want to represent the letter A in binary. The *American Standard Code for Information Interchange* table, also known as the *ASCII* table, defines each standard alphabet letter as 1 byte. Letter A is coded as 0100 0001. Table 5-3 shows the breakdown of letter A.

Table 5-3	Letter A Notations	
Binary	*Hexadecimal*	*Decimal*
0100 0001	41	65
Nibble 1 Nibble 2	—	—

Notice how each binary nibble — each group of 4 bits — maps exactly to each hexadecimal digit. This is nice because it makes conversions between hexadecimal and binary numbering systems easy. The next section describes this conversion.

Converting binary to hexadecimal

You saw in the previous section that

✦ 4 bits comprise

- 1 nibble

- 1 hexadecimal digit

- ½ byte

✦ 8 bits comprise

- 2 nibbles

- 2 hexadecimal digits

- 1 byte

Hence, when converting numbers from binary to hexadecimal, you can

✦ Separate the binary number in groups of 4 bits (nibbles).

✦ Convert each nibble to hexadecimal.

✦ Concatenate the hexadecimal number you obtain: The result is the converted hexadecimal number.

Some examples follow.

Convert 10101_2 to hexadecimal:

1. Separate the binary number into nibbles starting from the right. Pad with leading 0s if necessary: $0001\ 0101_2$.

2. Convert each nibble to its corresponding hexadecimal number:

- $0001_2 = 1_{16}$

- $0101_2 = 5_{16}$

3. Concatenate the hexadecimal digits in the order of the original binary number:

- Original number is $0001\ 0101_2$

- Concatenated hex number is 15_{16}

  Answer: $10101_2 = 15_{16}$

Convert 110101_2 to hexadecimal:

1. Separate the binary number into nibbles starting from the right. Pad with leading 0s if necessary: $0011\ 0101_2$.

2. Convert each nibble to its corresponding hexadecimal number:

   - $0011_2 = 3_{16}$
   - $0101_2 = 5_{16}$

3. Concatenate the hexadecimal digits in the order of the original binary number:

   - Original number is $0011\ 0101_2$
   - Concatenated hex number is 35_{16}

     Answer: $110101_2 = 35_{16}$

Convert 10011110101_2 to hexadecimal:

1. Separate the binary number into nibbles starting from the right. Pad with leading 0s if necessary: $0100\ 1111\ 0101_2$.

2. Convert each nibble to its corresponding hexadecimal number:

   - $0100_2 = 4_{16}$
   - $1111_2 = F_{16}$
   - $0101_2 = 5_{16}$

3. Concatenate the hexadecimal digits in the order of the original binary number:

   - Original number is $0100\ 1111\ 0101_2$
   - Concatenated hex number is $4F5_{16}$

   Answer: $10011110101_2 = 4F5_{16}$

Converting hexadecimal to binary

The same method can be used to convert hexadecimal numbers to binary notation:

1. Convert each digit of the hexadecimal to a binary nibble, padding the nibble with leading 0s if necessary.

2. Concatenate the binary nibbles you obtain: The result is the converted hexadecimal number.

Here are some examples.

Convert 16_{16} to binary:

1. Convert each hexadecimal digit to its corresponding binary nibble:

- $1_{16} = 0001_2$ (observe how you pad 1_2 with three leading 0s)
- $6_{16} = 0110_2$

2. Concatenate the nibbles in the order of the original hexadecimal number:

- Original number is 16_{16}
- Concatenated hex number is $0001\ 0110_2$

Answer: $16_{16} = 10110_2$

Convert $16FA_{16}$ to binary:

1. Convert each hexadecimal digit to its corresponding binary nibble:

- $1_{16} = 0001_2$
- $6_{16} = 0110_2$
- $F_{16} = 1111_2$
- $A_{16} = 1010_2$

2. Concatenate the nibbles in the order of the original hexadecimal number:

- Original number is $16FA_{16}$
- Concatenated hex number is $0001\ 0110\ 1111\ 1010_2$

Answer: $16FA_{16} = 1\ 0110\ 1111\ 1010_2$

Convert $DC14FA_{16}$ to binary:

1. Convert each hexadecimal digit to its corresponding binary nibble:

- $D_{16} = 1101_2$
- $C_{16} = 1100_2$
- $1_{16} = 0001_2$
- $4_{16} = 0100_2$
- $F_{16} = 1111_2$
- $A_{16} = 1010_2$

2. Concatenate the nibbles in the order of the original hexadecimal number:

- Original number is $DC14FA_{16}$
- Concatenated hex number is $1101\ 1100\ 0001\ 0100\ 1111\ 1010_2$

Answer: $DC14FA_{16} = 1101\ 1100\ 0001\ 0100\ 1111\ 1010_2$

Prep Test

1 Which of the following computer and network features rely on the properties of the hexadecimal and binary numbering systems?

A ○ Bit maps

B ○ Subnet masks

C ○ Network addresses

D ○ All of the above

2 Convert 10101_2 to decimal notation.

A ○ 21

B ○ 1

C ○ 4D

D ○ F

3 Convert 16_{10} to binary notation.

A ○ 10010

B ○ 01001

C ○ 10000

D ○ 10110

4 Convert 64_{10} to binary notation.

A ○ 1000000

B ○ 1101010

C ○ 1111010

D ○ 0010101

5 Convert 10101_2 to hexadecimal notation.

A ○ F

B ○ D

C ○ 15

D ○ 14

6 What does a nibble correspond to?

A ○ 4 bits

B ○ 1 hexadecimal digit

C ○ ½ byte

D ○ All of the above

7 What does a byte correspond to?

A ○ 4 bits

B ○ 1 hexadecimal digit

C ○ 8 bits

D ○ All of the above

8 Convert 110101_2 to hexadecimal notation.

A ○ F

B ○ 35

C ○ 25

D ○ D1

9 Convert 10011110101_2 to hexadecimal notation.

A ○ 4F5

B ○ 4D5

C ○ 5E1

D ○ D32

10 Convert 16_{16} to binary notation.

A ○ 111

B ○ 10110

C ○ 15

D ○ 0101

11 Convert $16FA_{16}$ to binary notation.

A ○ 1110111011000

B ○ 1011001101001

C ○ 1011011111010

D ○ 0101001100101

12 Convert $DC14FA_{16}$ to binary notation.

A ○ 001011110101011010101111

B ○ 111010100101111110100101

C ○ 010111010011101001010101

D ○ 110111000001010011111010

Answers

1 **D.** All of the above. Review the chapter introduction.

2 **A.** 21. Read *"Binary Numbers."*

3 **C.** 10000. See *"Binary Numbers."*

4 **A.** 1000000. Look over *"Binary Numbers."*

5 **C.** 15. Review *"Converting binary to hexadecimal."*

6 **D.** All of the above. Refer to *"Bits, nibbles, and bytes."*

7 **C.** 8 bits. See *"Bits, nibbles, and bytes."*

8 **B.** 35. Look over *"Converting binary to hexadecimal."*

9 **A.** 4F5. Read *"Converting binary to hexadecimal."*

10 **B.** 10110. Review *"Converting hexadecimal to binary."*

11 **C.** 1011011111010. Refer to *"Converting hexadecimal to binary."*

12 **D.** 110111000001010011111010. Look over *"Converting hexadecimal to binary."*

Chapter 6: Local-Area Networks (LANs)

Exam Objectives

✓ Identifying and choosing Ethernet LAN type, duplex mode, and speed

✓ Identifying and choosing Ethernet cabling and connectors

✓ Describing collision domains and their impact on network performance

✓ Describing how collision domains relate to CSMA/CD

✓ Identifying and choosing methods to minimize collision domains

✓ Identifying Ethernet operations at the data link layer

✓ Identifying Ethernet operations at the physical layer

*O*n the CCNA exam, local-area networks are related to Ethernet, Layer 2 switches, and cabling. Read this chapter to find out about Ethernet and related standards and technologies, including cabling and an introduction to Layer 2 switching. The exam asks about the CSMA/CD protocol, and about the distinction between half-duplex and full-duplex transmission modes in Ethernet. It also expects you to know about the IEEE 802.X Ethernet standards. In this chapter, you discover CSMA/CD and half- and full-duplex transmission modes. This chapter shows how Ethernet operates at both the data link and physical layers.

Introduction to Local-Area Networks

Local-area networks, known as LANs, interconnect host devices over short distances. LANs can support high speed and a fairly large bandwidth. LAN traffic can be controlled with bridges and switches. Hubs are also used to interconnect hosts in a LAN.

Switches are preferred over hubs, because switches limit the collision domain.

Ethernet Networking

Ethernet networking is a standard LAN implementation that specifies characteristics of LAN operation at the physical and data link layers. Ethernet is defined by the IEEE 802.3 standard specification. It now spans both wired and wireless connections.

At its inception, Ethernet was designed as a contention media access control mechanism to control access to bandwidth on a common link shared by several connected host devices. Ethernet, by design, broadcasts data frames on a shared medium, so it's collision prone. Layer 2 switches and full-duplex transmission mode reduce and even eliminate the risk of collisions.

CSMA/CD protocol

Ethernet uses the *carrier sense multiple access collision detect (CSMA/CD)* protocol. Whenever several computer hosts share the bandwidth on a common network medium, there's a risk of frame collisions. CSMA/CD was developed to mitigate this risk.

1. Whenever a host device needs to send a frame over the network medium, it first listens to the wire (carrier sense) to see whether another host is transmitting over the shared network medium:

  • If the wire is clear, the host sends its frame over the shared network medium.

  • If the wire is already busy carrying frames, the host waits until no activity exists on the wire and then it sends the frame.

2. The host continues to monitor the network medium to ensure that no other host starts sending frames.

3. If after listening to the wire and determining that it is clear, two sending hosts simultaneously attempt to transmit, they will detect each other's signal and send a jam signal to notify all hosts that a frame collision has occurred and that they need to stop sending.

4. If collisions occur after 15 retries, the hosts time out.

An Ethernet network that sustains lots of frame collisions is subject to

  ✦ Low throughput

  ✦ Low transmission reliability

  ✦ Congestion

  ✦ Delay in transmissions

Although CSMA/CD mitigates the risk of frame congestion, if a host needs to constantly back off from transmitting because collisions are occurring, it will decrease the performance of network applications on that host. CSMA/CD provides a mechanism to detect and work around frame collision, but it does not prevent collisions from happening.

Connecting more hosts in the same network segment (in other words, in the same collision domain) means that you have more chances to have frame collisions. You can limit the size of the collision domain using bridges and switches to segment the network into one *collision domain* per port. (Book III, Chapter 1 shows how to use Layer 2 switches to minimize collision domains.)

Keep the following points in mind for the exam:

✦ CSMA/CD provides a mechanism to **s**ense (listen to) the **c**arrier (CS) used for **m**ultiple **a**ccess (MA) and to **d**etect frame **c**ollisions (CD) when they occur.

✦ Whenever collisions occur, CSMA/CD cleans up the transmission medium and handles staggered retransmissions.

✦ Retransmissions decrease network performance.

Duplex communication

Duplex communication works in both directions between two devices. The most important difference is whether devices can send and receive at the same time.

Half-duplex

By default Ethernet is *half-duplex:* Devices can't send and receive at the same time. A single pair of wires is used for both sending and receiving frames.

Ethernet coaxial cabling supports only half-duplex transmission.

Because frame collisions occur and need to be mitigated with CSMA/CD, the theoretical throughput of half-duplex Ethernet is rarely achieved. Half-duplex throughput is usually 30–40 percent of theoretical throughput. For example, a 100BASE-T half-duplex connection is supposed to deliver up to 100 Mbps. However, you will more likely get 40 Mbps in half-duplex mode due to frame collisions.

Full-duplex

Full-duplex Ethernet can send and receive at the same time. It uses at least two pairs of wires to send and receive frames at the same time (one connection path per pair). This is usually the case when you use Ethernet twisted-pair cabling. Full-duplex twisted-pair connections provide point-to-point connections between the transmitter on the sending host and the receiver on the receiving host. This eliminates frame collisions and speeds data transfer.

Category 3, 5, 5e, and 6 twisted-pair cabling support both half-duplex and full-duplex transmission. Full-duplex is typically used with twisted-pair.

Using full-duplex twisted-pair connections, you can theoretically achieve full throughput in both directions. Considering the 100BASE-T example, with full-duplex twisted-pair, you should be able to get 100 Mbps sending and 100 Mbps receiving, for a total bandwidth of 200 Mbps. However, you will likely get less than 100 Mbps because of factors that distort the signal, such as electrical noise and crosstalk.

Full-duplex twisted-pair is the recommended cabling solution for Ethernet, because it allows full-duplex connections and it improves network throughput and reliability by eliminating frame collisions. Particularly, use full-duplex twisted-pair to connect hosts to switches, interconnect switches, or interconnect hosts using a crossover cable.

Ethernet Standards

You find various Ethernet implementations. Ethernet standards specify the following technical implementation details:

+ Topology

+ Bandwidth

+ Transmission mode

+ Cabling

+ Maximum range

Ethernet is defined by a collection of IEEE 802.3 standards. Four main families of Ethernet are grouped according to bandwidth supported and cabling used. See Table 6-1. Standards in bold are the most common.

Table 6-1		Ethernet Standards		
Commercial Name	*Standard Name*	*IEEE*	*Cabling*	*Max. Bandwidth*
Ethernet	10BASE2	802.3	Thin coaxial	10 Mbps
	10BASE5		Thick coaxial	
	10BASE-T		UTP Cat3, Cat5	
Fast Ethernet	100BASE-T4	802.3u	UTP Cat3	100 Mbps
	100BASE-TX		**UTP Cat5**	
	100BASE-FX		MM fiber	
Gigabit Ethernet	**1000BASE-T**	802.3ab	**UTP Cat5, 5e**	1000 Mbps
	1000BASE-SX		SM/MM fiber	
	1000BASE-LX		SM/MM fiber	
10 Gigabit Ethernet	**10GBASE-T**	802.3an	**UTP Cat6, 6a**	10000 Mbps

10-Mbps Ethernet (IEEE 802.3)

You find three versions of early 10-Mbps Ethernet implementations:

✦ 10BASE5 (Thicknet)

✦ 10BASE2 (Thinnet)

✦ 10BASE-T

Two of them use coaxial cabling. One of them uses twisted-pair cabling.

All 10-Mbps Ethernet implementations use half-duplex communication.

10BASE5 (Thicknet)

This is the original Ethernet standard. A 10BASE5 single thick coaxial cable has to be tapped (using a vampire tap or clamp) to connect a host device to the core and to the screen of the cable. This standard (specifically the type of cable and connection) is obsolete.

10BASE5 offers the following features:

✦ Cabling: 10BASE5 (thick coaxial cable, also called Thicknet)

✦ Topology: Bus

✦ Bandwidth: 10 Mbps

✦ Transmission mode: Half-duplex

✦ Range: 500 meters

10BASE2 (Thinnet)

This is a cabling variation of the original Ethernet standard. It is easier to connect the 10BASE2 thin coaxial cable than the 10BASE5 thick coaxial cable, because 10BASE2 host device network interface cards (NICs) use a BNC connector. Thus, the coaxial cable does not need to be tapped to connect to it. 10BASE2 coaxial cables must have terminators at each end.

10BASE2 has the following features:

✦ Cabling: 10BASE2 (thin coaxial cable, also called Thinnet)

✦ Topology: Bus

✦ Bandwidth: 10 Mbps

✦ Transmission mode: Half-duplex

✦ Range: 185 meters

10BASE-T

This is a cabling and topology variation of the original Ethernet standard.

Twisted-pair cables are much easier to connect than coaxial cables because they use RJ-45 connectors that are similar to RJ-11 telephone connectors. 10BASE-T networks can be connected using Category 3, Category 5, or Category 5e cables. Cat3 and Cat5/5e cables have four pairs of conductors; however, 10BASE-T only uses two of the four pairs.

This is the most common standard in 10-Mbps Ethernet implementations, with the following features:

✦ Cabling: 10BASE-T (twisted-pair: Cat3 or Cat5)

✦ Topology: Star

✦ Bandwidth: 10 Mbps

✦ Transmission mode: Half-duplex

✦ Range: 100 meters

Fast Ethernet (100-Mbps)

You find the following versions of 100-Mbps Fast Ethernet implementations:

✦ Fast Ethernet over twisted-pair

✦ Fast Ethernet over fiber-optic

Some versions support only half-duplex transmission mode, but most are full-duplex.

Fast Ethernet over twisted-pair

The most common versions of Fast Ethernet over twisted-pair cabling are described in the following sections.

100BASE-T4 (IEEE 802.3u)

This is a faster version of 10BASE-T over Cat3 cabling. In this case, all four pairs of conductors in the Cat3 twisted-pair are used. This is half-duplex transmission with the following features:

✦ Cabling: 100BASE-T4 (twisted-pair: Cat3)

✦ Topology: Star

✦ Bandwidth: 100 Mbps

✦ Transmission mode: Half-duplex

✦ Range: 100 meters

100BASE-T2 (IEEE 802.3y)

This is a variation of 100BASE-T4 that uses just two of the four pairs in a Cat3 twisted-pair. 100BASE-T4 supports full-duplex transmissions, because two pairs can be used to transmit and two pairs to receive simultaneously. 100BASE-T2 is equivalent to 100BASE-TX, but it uses Cat3 instead of Cat5 cabling. However, 100BASE-T2 implementations are almost nonexistent. 100BASE-TX is the norm today for Fast Ethernet.

100BASE-T2 has the following features:

✦ Cabling: 100BASE-T2 (twisted-pair: Cat3)

✦ Topology: Star

✦ Bandwidth: 100 Mbps

✦ Transmission mode: Full-duplex

✦ Range: 100 meters

100BASE-TX (IEEE 802.3u)

Like 100BASE-T2, 100BASE-TX uses just two of the four pairs in a twisted-pair. Unlike 100BASE-T2, though, 100BASE-TX uses Cat5 (or Cat5e), not Cat3, twisted-pair cabling. Cat5 and Cat5e are superior to Cat3 cabling. Because two pairs can be used to transmit and two pairs to receive simultaneously, 100BASE-TX supports full-duplex transmissions.

100BASE-TX, described as follows, is the norm today for Fast Ethernet:

✦ Cabling: 100BASE-TX (twisted-pair: Cat5 or better UTP)

✦ Topology: Star

✦ Bandwidth: 100 Mbps

✦ Transmission mode: Full-duplex

✦ Range: 100 meters

Fast Ethernet over fiber-optic

The following sections describe the most common versions of Fast Ethernet over fiber-optic cabling.

Fiber-optic cabling is more expensive than twisted-pair, but it can connect networks over longer distances and is not susceptible to EMI (electromagnetic interference), RFI (radio frequency interference), channel attenuation, or crosstalk.

100BASE-FX (IEEE 802.3u)

This is a cabling variation of the Fast Ethernet standard. Multimode fiber-optic cabling is used in this case, instead of copper-based twisted-pair cabling. 100BASE-FX uses long-wavelength laser transmission (1300 nm) that is typically more expensive than short-wavelength laser or LED optic transmission. 100BASE-FX supports full-duplex transmission with a range of up to 2 km. It also supports half-duplex transmission with a range of only 400 meters to allow collision detection. Even longer distances can be reached with single-mode fiber-optic cabling.

100BASE-FX cabling has the following features:

✦ Cabling: 100BASE-FX (1300-nm multimode fiber-optic)

✦ Topology: Star

✦ Bandwidth: 100 Mbps

✦ Transmission mode: Half-duplex and full-duplex

✦ Range: 400 meters (half-duplex) or 2 km (full-duplex)

100BASE-SX (IEEE 802.3u)

This is a cabling variation of the 100BASE-FX standard. Short-wavelength (850-nm) multimode fiber-optic cabling is used in this case, instead of long-wavelength (1300-nm) multimode fiber-optic cabling. 100BASE-SX, described as follows, is typically more affordable than 100BASE-FX, but its range is shorter:

✦ Cabling: 100BASE-SX (850-nm multimode fiber-optic)

✦ Topology: Star

✦ Bandwidth: 100 Mbps

✦ Transmission mode: Half-duplex and full-duplex

✦ Range: 300 meters

Gigabit Ethernet (1000-Mbps)

Gigabit Ethernet, also known as GigE, can be implemented with twisted-pair or fiber-optic cables.

Gigabit Ethernet over twisted-pair

The 1000BASE-T and 1000BASE-TX standards are the most common versions of Gigabit Ethernet over twisted-pair cables. The choice between 1000BASE-T and 1000BASE-TX depends on the type of cabling available and on network application requirements.

Category 5 and 5e twisted-pair cabling can link 1000BASE-T networks. Category 6 and 7 twisted-pair can link both 1000BASE-T and 1000BASE-TX networks. However, Cat6 and Cat7 cables are more expensive and less common than Cat5 and Cat5e. Hence, 1000BASE-T is currently the norm in Gigabit Ethernet over twisted-pair.

Some network applications specifically require two simultaneous 1000-Mbps links over the same cable. For these applications, Cat 6 or Cat 7 (1000BASE-TX) is required.

1000BASE-T (IEEE 802.3ab)

This is a bandwidth variation of the 100BASE-TX standard. Unlike 100BASE-TX, 1000BASE-T uses the four pairs in a Cat5, Cat5e, Cat6, or Cat7 cable. 1000BASE-T supports full-duplex transmission with a range of up to 100 meters.

The main advantage of 1000BASE-T over 100BASE-TX is obviously the increased bandwidth. Note that although Cat5 supports 1000BASE-T, Cat5e is recommended because the enhanced Cat5e adds specifications for far-end crosstalk. With the following features, this is the most common standard in Gigabit Ethernet implementations:

✦ Cabling: 1000BASE-T (twisted-pair Cat5 or Cat5e)

✦ Topology: Star

✦ Bandwidth: 1000 Mbps

✦ Transmission mode: Full-duplex

✦ Range: 100 meters

1000BASE-TX (IEEE 802.3ab)

This is a variation of the 1000BASE-T standard. Unlike 1000BASE-T, 1000BASE-TX uses just two of the four pairs in a Cat6 or Cat7 cable. 1000BASE-TX supports full-duplex transmission with a range of up to 100 meters. Because only two of the four pairs are used, Cat6 and Cat7 can support two 1000BASE-TX links on the same cable.

1000BASE-TX networks connected with Cat6 cabling are used in GigE applications that require larger bandwidth than 1000Mbps, such as multimedia content development and streaming, videoconferencing, highly available data centers, and distribution layer cabling. The 1000BASE-TX standard provides a total bandwidth of 2000Mbps using two 1000BASE-TX links on the same Cat6 or Cat7 cable.

If you use network equipment that supports 10 Gigabit Ethernet (10GigE) you could use 10GigE instead of GigE over Cat6. Using 10GigE instead of GigE provides higher bandwidth (10000Mbps instead of just 2000Mbps) over Cat6 cabling.

1000BASE-TX has the following features:

✦ Cabling: 1000BASE-TX (twisted-pair Cat6 or better)

✦ Topology: Star

✦ Bandwidth: 2000 Mbps (two 1000BASE-TX links over Cat6 or Cat7)

✦ Transmission mode: Full-duplex

✦ Range: 100 meters

Gigabit Ethernet over fiber-optic

The following sections describe the most common versions of Gigabit Ethernet over fiber-optic cables. The choice among these versions depends on the type of fiber-optic cable available and on the required range.

1000BASE-LX (IEEE 802.3z)

1000BASE-LX uses long-wavelength laser transmission (1270-nm or 1355-nm) that is typically more expensive than short-wavelength laser or LED optic transmission. 1000BASE-LX supports full-duplex transmission at 1000 Mbps with a range of up to 5 km using single-mode fiber cables, and up to 550 meters using multimode fiber cables.

1000BASE-LX offers the following features:

✦ Cabling: 1000BASE-LX (1270-nm or 1355-nm single-mode or multimode fiber-optic)

✦ Topology: Star

✦ Bandwidth: 1000 Mbps

✦ Transmission mode: Full-duplex

✦ Range: 550 meters (multimode fiber) or 5 km (single-mode fiber)

1000BASE-SX (IEEE 802.3z)

1000BASE-SX uses short-wavelength laser transmission (770-nm or 860-nm) that is typically more affordable than long-wavelength laser transmission. 1000BASE-SX supports full-duplex transmission at 1000 Mbps with a range of up to 550 meters using 62.5/125 microns with low-modal-bandwidth fiber cables, and up to 220 meters using 50/100 microns with high-modal-bandwidth fiber cables.

1000BASE-SX has the following features:

✦ Cabling: 1000BASE-SX (770- to 860-nm single-mode or multimode fiber-optic)

✦ Topology: Star

✦ Bandwidth: 1000 Mbps

✦ Transmission mode: Full-duplex

✦ Range: 220 or 550 meters

1000BASE-LH (IEEE 802.3z)

This is a variation of 1000BASE-LX that uses higher-quality laser optics. 1000BASE-LH has a longer range than 1000BASE-LX.

1000BASE-LH is not a standard term, but it is commonly accepted in the industry to designate 1000BASE-LX with 1300- or 1310-nm fiber cabling.

1000BASE-LH offers the following features:

✦ Cabling: 1000BASE-LH (1300-nm or 1310-nm single-mode or multimode fiber-optic)

✦ Topology: Star

✦ Bandwidth: 1000 Mbps

✦ Transmission mode: Full-duplex

✦ Range: Up to 10 km (single-mode fiber)

1000BASE-ZX (IEEE 802.3z)

This is a variation of 1000BASE-LX that uses 1550-nm-wavelength fiber transmission. 1000BASE-ZX has better range than both 1000BASE-LX and 1000BASE-LH. Keep in mind that 1000BASE-ZX, like 1000BASE-LH, is not a standard term, but it is commonly accepted in the industry. 1000BASE-ZX designates Ethernet transmission over 1550-nm-wavelength fiber cabling.

1000 BASE-ZX has the following features:

✦ Cabling: 1000BASE-ZX (1550-nm single-mode or multimode fiber-optic)

✦ Topology: Star

✦ Bandwidth: 1000 Mbps

✦ Transmission mode: Full-duplex

✦ Range: 70 km (single-mode fiber)

10 Gigabit Ethernet (10000-Mbps)

10 Gigabit Ethernet, also known as 10GigE, can be implemented with twisted-pair or with fiber-optic cables. 10 Gigabit Ethernet only supports full-duplex transmissions.

10 Gigabit Ethernet over twisted-pair

The 10GBASE-T standard is the most common version of 10 Gigabit Ethernet over twisted-pair cables. 10GBASE-T uses Category 6 UTP cabling.

The IEEE 802.3an-2006 standard was introduced in 2006 to connect devices at 10000 Mbps using Cat6 cabling. It is currently the fastest Ethernet standard. 10GBASE-T only supports full-duplex transmission with a range of up to 100 meters.

The 10GBASE-T standard, with the following features, is the most common version of 10 Gigabit Ethernet over twisted-pair cables:

✦ Cabling: 10GBASE-T (twisted-pair Cat6 or Cat6a)

✦ Topology: Star

✦ Bandwidth: 10000 Mbps

✦ Transmission mode: Full-duplex

✦ Range: 55 meters with Cat6 or 100 meters with Cat6a

10 Gigabit Ethernet over fiber-optic

The 10GBASE-SR, 10GBASE-LR, and 10GBASE-ER standards are the most common versions of 10 Gigabit Ethernet over fiber-optic cabling. The choice among these versions depends on the type of fiber-optic cable available and on the required range. Other standards can reach longer ranges than the ones listed here, but they are beyond the scope of CCNA certification.

10GBASE-SR (IEEE 802.3 C49 64B/66B)

10GBASE-SR is a standard for short-range (SR) 10GigE connections using MMF (multimode fiber) optic cabling. 10GBASE-SR uses short-wavelength laser transmission (850-nm) that is typically less expensive than long-wavelength laser or LED optic transmission.

10GBASE-SR offers the following features:

+ Cabling: 10GBASE-SR (850-nm multimode fiber-optic)
+ Topology: Star
+ Bandwidth: 10000 Mbps
+ Transmission mode: Full-duplex
+ Range: 82 meters (standard MMF) and up to 300 meters (latest OM3 MMF)

10GBASE-LR (IEEE 802.3 C49 64B/66B)

10GBASE-LR is a standard for long-range (LR) 10GigE connections using SMF (single-mode fiber) optic cabling. 10GBASE-LR uses long-wavelength laser transmission (1310-nm) that is typically more expensive than short-wavelength laser transmission.

10GBASE-LR has the following features:

+ Cabling: 10GBASE-LR (1310-nm multimode fiber-optic)
+ Topology: Star
+ Bandwidth: 10000 Mbps
+ Transmission mode: Full-duplex
+ Range: 10 km (standard) and up to 25 km (using certain optical modules)

10GBASE-ER (IEEE 802.3 C49 64B/66B)

10GBASE-ER is a standard for extended-range (ER) 10GigE connections using SMF (single-mode fiber) optic cabling. 10GBASE-ER uses long-wavelength laser transmission (1550-nm) that is typically more expensive than short-wavelength laser transmission.

10GBASE-ER offers the following features:

+ Cabling: 10GBASE-ER (1550-nm multimode fiber-optic)
+ Topology: Star
+ Bandwidth: 10000 Mbps
+ Transmission mode: Full-duplex
+ Range: 40 km

Ethernet in the OSI Model

Ethernet specifications and hardware fulfill two of the roles of the OSI layer model.

Data link layer

Ethernet implements some of the features and functions of the data link layer. The mission of the data link layer is to

+ Manage access to the transmission media

+ Control transmission flow

+ Route data link frames *locally* between NICs connected to the local network

Ethernet implements some of these functions.

Physical addressing: MAC address

Ethernet uses the Media Access Control (MAC) address to route data-link frames locally in a LAN. Host NICs and network devices built to comply with the Ethernet IEEE 802.3 standard have a MAC address assigned by their manufacturer. MAC addresses are unique and theoretically unchangeable. They are also sometimes called hardware or physical addresses because they are physically linked to a specific host NIC or network device.

A MAC address is a unique 48-bit number, or 6 bytes, or 12 hexadecimal values, for example, 00-00-0F-F0-EF-AC or 00-AC-03-2B-1F-03.

Figure 6-1 illustrates the structure of a MAC address.

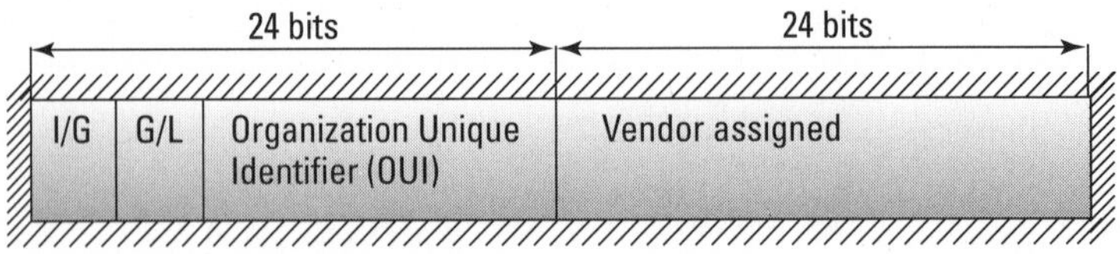

Figure 6-1: MAC address.

Ethernet uses the MAC address to uniquely identify each host and network device connected to a LAN:

+ **The *Organizational Unique Identifier (OUI):*** Identifies the manufacturer (assigned by the IEEE)

✦ **The vendor-assigned part:** A unique value that manufacturers assign to each of the devices they produce

✦ **The *Individual/Group (I/G)* bit:**

- 1 if this is a broadcast or multicast MAC address

- 0 if this is an individual MAC address, the MAC address of a specific device

✦ **The *Global/Local (G/L)* bit:**

- 0 if this is a globally assigned MAC address (a MAC address assigned by the IEEE)

- 1 if this is a locally assigned MAC address (a MAC address assigned by the manufacturer)

Data-link frame as implemented by Ethernet

The data-link frames encapsulate the data payload received from the network layer into a data unit that contains information about the sender, information about the receiver, and some control data. The sender and receiver information is represented by their respective MAC addresses. These are

✦ Destination MAC address field (D-M)

✦ Source MAC address field (S-M)

Figure 6-2 shows the structure of an Ethernet_II data-link frame.

Figure 6-2:
Ethernet_II frame (standard MAC encapsulation).

Pre 8 bytes	D-M 6 bytes	S-M 6 bytes	Type 2 bytes	Data 46 tp 1500 bytes	FCS

Figure 6-3 shows the structure of an Ethernet 802.3 data-link frame.

Figure 6-3:
Ethernet 802.3 frame (LLC and MAC encapsulation).

Pre 8 bytes	D-M 6 bytes	S-M 6 bytes	Length 2 bytes	LLC 8 bytes	Data 38 to 1492 bytes	C 4 bytes

Ethernet frames contain the following fields:

◆ The *Pre* field contains the preamble synchronization bits that help the receiving host device lock on the bit stream.

◆ The *D-M (Destination MAC Address)* field is the MAC address of the receiving host device. The D-M can be an individual MAC address or a broadcast or multicast MAC address.

◆ The *S-M (Source MAC Address)* field is the MAC address of the sending host device. The S-M can only be an individual MAC address.

◆ The *T (Type)* field in the Ethernet_II frame specifies the network layer protocol that created the data payload that is encapsulated in the data field. The Ethernet_II frame format is the most common.

◆ The *L (Length)* field in the 802.3 Ethernet frame indicates the length of the data stream in the data part of the frame.

The *Logical Link Control (LLC)* header in the 802.3 Ethernet frame is 7, 8, or 9 bytes long depending on implementation and contains the following fields:

◆ 1 byte identifying a Source Service Access Point (SSAP)

◆ 1 byte identifying a Destination Service Access Point (DSAP)

◆ 3, 4, or 5 bytes for control, depending on implementation

◆ 2 bytes identifying the type of the network layer protocol that created the data payload

The 802.3 Ethernet frame uses a Source Service Access Point (SSAP) and a Destination Service Access Point (DSAP) that identify a subnetwork layer protocol service access point that uses the link layer service. The 802.3 Ethernet frame does contain a type field, the last 2 bytes of the LLC header. However, because the maximum size of the data payload is fixed at 1500 bytes, by adding an LLC header, the data-link frame space available for data is decreased.

Ethernet_II is the most common implementation. Thus, you see a Type field instead of the Length and LLC fields in most data-link frames today.

The *Data* field is the network layer packet that contains, for example, an IP packet that encapsulates either a Transmission Control Protocol (TCP) or a User Datagram Protocol (UDP) segment. The Data field is between 46 and 1500 bytes long in Ethernet_II, depending on the size of the IP packet. You can set the *maximum transmission unit (MTU)* from 68 to 1500 bytes to configure the IP packet size. The Internet Protocol version 4 (IPv4) standard requires routers and switches to support a minimum MTU size of 576 bytes. It is not recommended to set the MTU size below 576 bytes because transmission performance will decrease. If you set the MTU size higher than 576 bytes, make sure that all routers and switches in the transmission path support an MTU higher than 576.

It is best practice to keep the MTU size set to the same value on all devices in a network to avoid unnecessary frame fragmentation and reassembly.

The *FCS (Frame Check Sequence)* field, stores a cyclic redundancy check (CRC) value:

1. The sending host calculates this field based on the contents of the frame it sends.

2. The receiving host recalculates the CRC based on the frame received and checks the CRC field against the calculated CRC.

3. If the two correspond, the frame is deemed valid. Otherwise, the frame is dropped, and the sending host will need to retransmit the frame.

Physical layer

Ethernet standards specify physical topology, bandwidth, transmission mode, cabling, and maximum range. Thus, Ethernet also operates at the physical layer: Cables, electrical transmission parameters, and topology are physical devices.

Many cabling options are available with Ethernet. Some cables offer higher bandwidth, or longer range, but they are more expensive than cables offering lower bandwidth and shorter range.

When designing a network, the trick is to realize that the number of hosts that you need to connect in a LAN determines the potential size of the collision domain. If you have only about three to five hosts, you may be able to go with a hub and Cat3 LAN; you can forget about coaxial cable altogether. However, because Layer 2 switches and Cat5 have been very affordable for several years, it is best to replace the hub and Cat3 solution with a layer 2 switch and Cat5 or Cat5e. For a reasonable price, you get full-duplex transmission and one collision domain per switch port, using layer 2 switches and Cat5 or better. A LAN connected with layer 2 switches and Cat5 or better is faster, more reliable, and more scalable than a LAN implemented with hubs and Cat3. On the other hand, if you need to connect hundreds or thousands of hosts into a single LAN, you definitely need to limit the collision domain with layer 2 switches and Cat5, Cat5e, Cat6, or Cat6a. The choice between Cat5, Cat5e, Cat6, or Cat6a cabling depends on bandwidth, range and budget requirements.

Considering bandwidth, it may be nice to have 10 Gigabit Ethernet (10GigE) brought to every host in the LAN, but is it really necessary? In most cases, the current cost of 10GigE is too high to implement it up to every host on the LAN. A hybrid approach may be best: Use 10GigE with Cat6 or Cat6a to interconnect switches and routers at the core of the LAN, and use Gigabit Ethernet (GigE) with Cat5e — or even Fast Ethernet with Cat5 — for local host access to the access layer switches.

The Electronic Industries Alliance and the Telecommunications Industry Association (EIA/TIA) define Ethernet physical specifications. This particularly involves standard cabling and connectors to be used in Ethernet networks.

EIA/TIA-568-B cabling standard

The *EIA/TIA-568-B cabling standard* was developed to define a blueprint for data-communication cabling for commercial buildings as well as for data-communication cabling between buildings. The standard defines cable system architecture, cable installation requirements, cable termination, cable types, distances, and connectors.

EIA/TIA-568-B defines a hierarchical cabling architecture: A main cross-connect (MCC) links to intermediate cross-connects (ICCs) using backbone cabling in a star topology. The ICCs link to horizontal cross-connects (HCCs).

The Cisco hierarchical networking model fits nicely in the hierarchical cabling architecture standard defined by EIA/TIA-568-B. You find out about the Cisco Hierarchical Networking Model in Book I, Chapter 9.

T568B and T568A termination standards

The *T568A* and *T568B* termination standards define the pin and conductor pair assignments for 4- or 8-conductor Cat3, Cat5, Cat5e, Cat6, Cat6a, and Cat7 cables. Particularly, T568A and T568B define the pin-out, or wire layout, of the *8 Position 8 Contact (8P8C)* connector, also known as *RJ45*. This connector looks very similar to an RJ11 telephone connector; it's just a bit larger.

Ethernet cabling

All copper cables are exposed to *channel attenuation,* also known as inherent attenuation. Channel attenuation is the loss of signal strength as the electrical signal travels through the transmission medium. Cables are also exposed to *crosstalk.* Crosstalk is signal interference that occurs when two cables run next to each other. Twisting the cables together in pairs almost completely eliminates the crosstalk effect. This is the whole idea behind twisted-pair cables. In fact, as you have already seen, various categories of unshielded twisted-pair cable exist: Cat3, Cat5, Cat5e, Cat6, and Cat7.

The main difference between twisted-pair categories is the number of wire twists per foot in each pair of wires. The more twists, the more chances to cancel out crosstalk and the higher the category. To further protect the cable against electrical interference, shielded twisted-pair (STP) cable can be used. Unshielded twisted-pair (UTP) cabling is by far the most common type of twisted-pair cabling due to its lower cost and greater flexibility, however, STP is recommended for environments that have high electromagnetic fields, such as industrial environments."

Straight-through cables

A cable that is wired as T568A at both ends is a straight-through cable. Straight-through cables are used to

Book I
Chapter 6

**Local-Area
Networks (LANs)**

✦ Connect host devices to network devices

✦ Connect routers to switches or hubs

Only pins 1, 2, 3, and 6 are used for Ethernet and FastEthernet because Ethernet and FastEthernet (except 100BASE-T4) use only two of the four pairs of wires in a cable. Gigabit Ethernet (GigE) and 10 Gigabit Ethernet (10GigE) use all eight pins because GigE and 10GigE standards utilize all four pairs of wires in a cable.

A standard Ethernet and FastEthernet straight-through connection is shown in Figure 6-4.

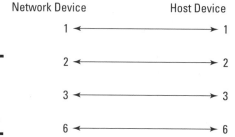

Figure 6-4:
Straight-
through
connection.

Crossover cables

A twisted-pair cable that is wired as T568A at one end and as T568B at the other end is a crossover cable.

Crossover cables are used to interconnect switches to switches, hubs to hubs, hosts to hosts, hubs to switches, and routers directly to hosts. A crossover connection is shown in Figure 6-5.

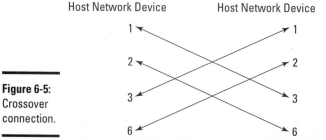

Figure 6-5:
Crossover
connection.

Rollover cables

A rollover cable flips all connections: Pin 1 on one end is pin 8 at the far end, pin 2 is pin 7, pin 3 is pin 6, and so on.

Rollover cables are not used for Ethernet connections, but they are very important in the Cisco world. Rollover cables are used to connect to the console serial port of a router from a PC. You can use HyperTerminal or any other terminal emulation application on your PC, using a rollover cable and a RJ45-to-USB or a RS232-to-USB adapter. A rollover connection is shown in Figure 6-6.

Host   Router Console

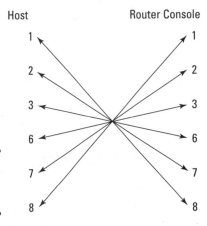

Figure 6-6:
Rollover
connection.

The following list summarizes the different types of Ethernet cables:

+ Straight-through cables are used to connect a sending device to a receiving device: host sends to switch, switch sends to router, router sends back to switch, switch sends back to host.

+ Crossover cables are used to interconnect similar devices: switches to switches, hubs to hubs, and hosts to hosts. Two exceptions exist: hubs to switches and hosts to routers directly.

Think of it this way: Crossover cables are used to connect sending devices to sending devices. You need to cross over the cable to connect the send wire to the receive pin at the other end.

+ Rollover cables are used to connect a host directly to a switch or router console.

Prep Test

1 Which of the following describes Ethernet?

A ○ A standard twisted-pair implementation that specifies characteristics of twisted-pair cabling operation at the physical and data link layers

B ○ A standard WAN implementation that specifies characteristics of WAN operation at the physical and data link layers

C ○ A standard fiber-optic implementation that specifies characteristics of fiber-optic cabling operation at the physical and data link layers

D ○ A standard LAN implementation that specifies characteristics of LAN operation at the physical and data link layers

2 What is the main purpose of the CSMA/CD protocol?

A ○ To monitor a shared carrier medium used by several computer hosts to transmit data and to detect frame collisions when they occur

B ○ To monitor a shared network interface card (NIC) used by several computer hosts to transmit data and to detect frame collisions when they occur

C ○ To monitor MAC addresses of incoming traffic on a network interface card (NIC) on a computer host and to detect frame collisions when they occur

D ○ To monitor MAC addresses of full-duplex traffic on a network interface card (NIC) on a computer host and to detect frame collisions when they occur

3 What does the CSMA/CD back-off algorithm control?

A ○ The jam signal emitted by a sending host when a frame collision occurs

B ○ How much time computer hosts wait before they start sending again when a frame collision occurs

C ○ The timeout for sending data-link frames when a frame collision occurs

D ○ The boot time of the network interface card (NIC)

4 Which of the following describes full-duplex transmissions?

A ○ Data frames are transmitted in one direction only over a single pair of wires

B ○ Data frames are transmitted in both directions, simultaneously, over a single pair of wires

C ○ Data frames are transmitted in both directions, simultaneously, over two pairs of wires

D ○ Data frames are transmitted in both directions, simultaneously, over two wires

5 **What is the maximum bandwidth of Fast Ethernet?**

A ○ 10000 Mbps
B ○ 10 Mbps
C ○ 1000 Mbps
D ○ 100 Mbps

6 **What is the maximum bandwidth of Ethernet?**

A ○ 10000 Mbps
B ○ 10 Mbps
C ○ 1000 Mbps
D ○ 100 Mbps

7 **What is the maximum bandwidth of Gigabit Ethernet (GigE)?**

A ○ 10000 Mbps
B ○ 10 Mbps
C ○ 1000 Mbps
D ○ 100 Mbps

8 **What is the maximum bandwidth of 10 Gigabit Ethernet (10GigE)?**

A ○ 10000 Mbps
B ○ 10 Mbps
C ○ 1000 Mbps
D ○ 100 Mbps

9 **What is the most common Fast Ethernet standard?**

A ○ 10BASE-T
B ○ 100BASE-TX
C ○ 1000BASE-T
D ○ 10GBASE-T

10 **What is the most common Ethernet standard?**

A ○ 10BASE-T
B ○ 100BASE-TX
C ○ 1000BASE-T
D ○ 10GBASE-T

Answers

1 **D.** A standard LAN implementation that specifies characteristics of LAN operation at the Physical and Datalink Layers. Ethernet is a standard LAN implementation that specifies characteristics of LAN operation at the Physical and Datalink Layers. Review *"Ethernet Networking."*

2 **A.** Monitor a shared carrier medium used by several computer hosts to transmit data, and detect frame collisions when they occur. The CSMA/CD protocol monitors a shared carrier medium used by several computer hosts to transmit data, and detect frame collisions when they occur. See *"CSMA/CD protocol."*

3 **B.** How much time computer hosts wait before they start sending again when a frame collision occurs. The CSMA/CD back-off algorithm controls how much time computer hosts wait before they start sending again when a frame collision occurs. Check *"CSMA/CD protocol."*

4 **C.** Data frames are transmitted in both directions, simultaneously, over two pairs of wires. In full-duplex transmissions, data frames are sent in both directions, simultaneously, over two pairs of wires. Review *"Duplex communication."*

5 **D.** 100 Mbps. The maximum bandwidth of Fast Ethernet is 100 mega bits per second. See *"Fast Ethernet (100 Mbps)."*

6 **B.** 10 Mbps. The maximum bandwidth of the base Ethernet standard (IEEE 802.3) is 10 mega bits per second. Check *"10-Mbps Ethernet (IEEE 802.3)."*

7 **C.** 1000 Mbps. The maximum bandwidth of Gigabit Ethernet (GigE) is 1000 mega bits per second, which is equivalent to 1 gigabit per second (1000 megs = 1 gig). Review *"Gigabit Ethernet (1000-Mbps)."*

8 **A.** 10000 Mbps. The maximum bandwidth of 10 Gigabit Ethernet (10GigE) is 10000 mega bits per second, which is equivalent to 10 gigabits per second (10000 megs = 10 gig). See *"10 Gigabit Ethernet (10000-Mbps)."*

9 **B.** 100BASE-TX. The most common Fast Ethernet standard is 100BASE-TX. Check *"Table 6-1 Ethernet standards."*

10 **A.** 10BASE-T. The most common 10Mbps Ethernet standard over copper wire is 10BASE-T. See *"Table 6-1 Ethernet standards."*

Chapter 7: Introducing Wide-Area Networks (WANs)

Exam Objectives

✔ Describing wide-area networks (WANs)

✔ Describing the purpose of data communication service providers

✔ Differentiating between LAN and WAN operations and features

✔ Identifying different methods for connecting to a WAN

*Y*ou get acquainted with WANs (wide-area networks) in this chapter. You find out about the various types of WAN connections. The pros and cons of each type of connection are reviewed. You discover more about WANs in Book VII.

Introducing Wide-Area Networks

Wide-area networks span long distances. They interconnect the following:

+ MANs (metropolitan-area networks)
+ CANs (campus-area networks)
+ LANs (local-area networks)

Telecommunication companies build and maintain WANs. Telecom companies lease bandwidth, or dedicated connections, to other companies that need to interconnect their LANs over long distances. The telecom companies that provide shared bandwidth or dedicated connections over their WANs are also called *service providers*.

Data communication service providers invest in telecommunication infrastructure such as terrestrial and submarine cabling, satellites and earth base stations, microwave base stations, and other wireless links to be able to provide a fast, reliable worldwide data communication infrastructure.

You find four types of WAN connections:

+ Dedicated leased line
+ Circuit-switched

+ Packet-switched
+ Cell-switched

Dedicated Leased Line Connections

A *dedicated leased line* is a data communication connection that is used exclusively by one customer. The customer leases the data communication line from a service provider.

The service provider installs a data communication link between the customer's sites. Only that customer uses the data communication link. Sometimes, the communication line may already exist, and the service provider simply reserves it for the customer.

Advantages of leased lines

The main advantages of dedicated lease connections are as follows:

+ **Highly available bandwidth:** The customer can use all the bandwidth of the connection because no one else shares the same line. Depending on the type of link, maximum bandwidth can reach approximately 45 Mbps:
  - T1 link: 1.544 Mbps
  - T2 link: 6.312 Mbps
  - T3 link: 44.736 Mbps
+ **Privacy:** No other users share the leased line. Hence, no other user can disturb the traffic of the customer leasing the line.
+ **Reliability:** Fewer chances exist to have traffic spikes, conflicting setups, and conflicting network applications, because only one customer is using the line.
+ **Customization:** The connection line can be configured and customized to the particular needs of that customer, including quality of service (QoS), traffic management, and encryption.

Disadvantage of leased lines

The main disadvantages of dedicated leased lines are as follows:

+ **Cost:** Dedicated leased lines are expensive, and they get more expensive as the distance increases between connected sites.
+ **Multiple PPP links:** Whenever more than two sites are connected, a dedicated leased line needs to be configured for each site in a point-to-point topology. This increases costs.

Dedicated leased line protocols

Dedicated leased lines use point-to-point protocols such as the following:

✦ High-Level Data Link Control (HDLC) Protocol

✦ Point-to-Point Protocol (PPP)

✦ Serial Line Internet Protocol (SLIP)

Read Book VII, Chapters 1, 2, and 3 to find out about these protocols.

Circuit-Switched Connections

Circuit-switched connections use the telephone communication infrastructure to send and receive data over telephone lines.

Telephone lines are either analog or digital:

✦ **Analog:** These are standard telephone lines. Digital data needs to be converted to analog signals using a *modem* before sending the data over analog telephone lines. Analog signals received from a telephone line are converted back to digital signals by a modem.

✦ **Digital:** These are the newer telephone lines. Two digital circuit-switched connection technologies exist:

  • *ISDN (Integrated Services Digital Network):* Introduced before ADSL. ISDN was a popular alternative to dialup modems. However, it has been superseded by ADSL today.

  • *ADSL (asymmetric digital subscriber line):* Introduced in the mid-1990s. ADSL was initially much more expensive than ISDN, hence ISDN's initial popularity. As ADSL costs went down, it became the standard for circuit-switched connections.

Advantage of circuit-switched connections

The main advantage of this solution is availability: All major telecommunication companies offer ADSL connectivity in areas where they operate.

Disadvantages of circuit-switched connections

The main disadvantages of this solution are as follows:

✦ **Low speeds (especially with ISDN):**

  • 19.2–128 Kbps (ISDN)

  • 1.5–3 Mbps (ADSL)

✦ **High cost:** Costs are typically pay-per-use, so they tend to add up.

Circuit-switched connection protocols

Similar to dedicated leased lines, circuit-switched connections use point-to-point protocols such as the following:

✦ High-Level Data Link Control (HDLC) Protocol

✦ Point-to-Point Protocol (PPP)

✦ Serial Line Internet Protocol (SLIP)

Packet-Switched Connections

Packet-switched connections are a shared bandwidth technology: Users connect to a service provider network and share the bandwidth of that service provider and the bandwidth of its external link to other networks.

Advantages of packet-switched connections

The main advantages of packet-switched connections are as follows:

✦ **Inexpensive:** Packet-switched connections are less expensive than dedicated leased lines and circuit-switched connections. Customers connecting through packet-switched links share the infrastructure deployed by the service provider to support their collective connectivity needs. Hence, they also share the costs of that infrastructure.

✦ **High speed:** Depending on the type of link, maximum bandwidth can reach approximately 45 Mbps. However, several users share the bandwidth. Available speeds are as follows:

- T1: 1.544 Mbps
- T2: 6.312 Mbps
- T3: 44.736 Mbps

✦ **QoS:** Although several users share the bandwidth, service providers now offer QoS (quality of service) guarantees. This increases reliability and brings the service level of packet-switched connections almost on par with dedicated leased lines.

✦ **Easy setup:** The customer can connect one of the serial interfaces on his router to his service provider's network in one location. The customer can also connect serial interfaces from routers at remote locations to the service provider network. This interconnects the customer's sites through the service provider network, while sharing the bandwidth of the service provider with other users. Consequently, this is a fairly straightforward and cost-effective solution to interconnect remote sites over long distances.

Disadvantage of packet-switched connections

The main disadvantage of packet-switched connections is shared bandwidth. Several users share the bandwidth of the service provider with packet-switched connections. This represents some challenges:

✦ **Reliability:** More chances exist to have traffic spikes, conflicting setups, and conflicting network applications because several customers are sharing the bandwidth of the service provider.

✦ **Limited customization:** Customer-specific configurations such as QoS, traffic management, and encryption need to be done without affecting other users' configurations.

✦ **Security:** Data exchanged between remote sites goes through the service provider network that also carries other customers' data.

Packet-switched connection protocols

Packet-switched connections use the following packet-switching protocols:

✦ **X.25:** The initial packet-switching WAN protocol. X.25 is considered to be the grandfather of Frame Relay.

✦ **Frame Relay:** Newer, improved version of X.25. Frame Relay is the most commonly used packet-switching protocol today.

Read Book VII, Chapters 1 and 4 to find out about these protocols.

Cell-Switched Connections

Cell-switched connections are very similar to packet-switched connections with the exception that cell-switched frames have a fixed size whereas packet-switched frames vary in size. For this reason, cell-switched connections tend to be faster than packet-switched connections, especially under heavy traffic.

Advantages of cell-switched connections

The main advantages of cell-switched connections over packet-switched connections are as follows:

✦ **Speed:** Cell-switched connections are faster than packet-switched connections. Cell-switched connections use fixed-size frames as opposed to the variable-size frames in packet-switched connections. Hence, there is no delay in finding the length of each data frame in cell-switched connections. Maximum bandwidth can reach 155 Mbps.

✦ **Best suited for simultaneous data, voice, and video connections:** Voice and video traffic needs to be converted back and forth between analog and digital signals.

Coders/decoders (codecs) perform these conversions in real time. Recall that cell-switched connections are faster than packet-switched connections because there is no need to resolve the length of each frame in cell-switched connections. Codecs operate better with fixed-length data frames because these data frames can be processed faster; codecs operate better with cell-switched connections.

Disadvantages of cell-switched connections

The main disadvantages of cell-switched connections over packet-switched connections are as follows:

✦ **Overhead:** Cell-switched connections — the *Asynchronous Transfer Mode (ATM)* protocol — segment variable-length data frames into fixed-length cells of 48 bytes for data plus 5 bytes for the control header: 53 byte cells. The sending router or switch needs to spend some processing power (*overhead*) to segment the variable-length data frames into fixed-length cells. Similarly, the receiving router or switch needs to spend some processing power (overhead) to reassemble the fixed-length cells into variable-length data frames.

✦ **Bandwidth wasted:** Some cells are not filled with data. All cells have 48 bytes available for data, but an incoming variable-length frame can be smaller than 48 bytes. In that case, some of the 48 bytes of the ATM cell are empty. Those empty bytes in the ATM cell are wasting bandwidth because they are still transferred over the WAN.

Cell-switched connection protocols

Cell-switched connections use the Asynchronous Transfer Mode (ATM) protocol.

Read Book VII, Chapter 1 to find out about the ATM protocol.

Prep Test

1 **Describe wide-area networks (WANs).**

A ○ They span long distances.

B ○ They interconnect local-area networks (LANs).

C ○ They interconnect all the networks that make up the Internet.

D ○ All of the above.

2 **A dedicated leased line is which of the following?**

A ○ A data communication line that is built by a customer

B ○ A data communication line that is used exclusively by one customer

C ○ A data communication line that is shared by a few customers

D ○ All of the above

3 **Advantages of dedicated leased lines include which of the following?**

A ○ Privacy

B ○ Reliability

C ○ Highly available bandwidth

D ○ All of the above

4 **What is the main disadvantage of circuit-switched connections?**

A ○ Low speed

B ○ Lack of privacy

C ○ High cost

D ○ Low reliability

5 **Circuit-switched connections use which of the following protocols?**

A ○ Point-to-Point Protocol (PPP)

B ○ Serial Line Internet Protocol (SLIP)

C ○ High-Level Data Link Control (HDLC) Protocol

D ○ All of the above

6 **What is the main disadvantage of packet-switched connections?**

A ○ Low speed

B ○ Shared bandwidth

C ○ High cost

D ○ Low reliability

Answers

1 **D.** All of the above. Wide-area networks (WANs) span long distances. They interconnect local-area networks (LANs). They interconnect all the networks that make up the Internet. Review *"Introducing Wide-Area Networks."*

2 **B.** A dedicated leased line is a data communication connection that is used exclusively by one customer. See *"Dedicated Leased Line Connections."*

3 **D.** All of the above. Dedicated leased lines are best suited for environments that need privacy, reliability, and highly available bandwidth. Look over *"Dedicated Leased Line Connections."*

4 **C.** The main disadvantage of circuit-switched connections is their high cost. See *"Circuit-Switched Connections."*

5 **D.** All of the above. Circuit-switched connections use point-to-point WAN protocols such as PPP, SLIP, and HDLC. Review *"Circuit-Switched Connections."*

6 **B.** Shared bandwidth. The main disadvantage of packet-switched connections is sharing the bandwidth of the medium. Check out *"Packet-Switched Connections."*

Chapter 8: Introducing Wireless Networks

Exam Objectives

- Describing the purpose and functions of wireless networks
- Describing the standards associated with wireless media
- Identifying and describing the purpose of the components in wireless networks
- Comparing and contrasting wireless security features and capabilities

*W*ireless networks are short- or medium-range networks that connect host devices using airwaves (radio) instead of cables. Wireless connections exist in a large variety of applications both for LAN and WAN connections.

Wireless LAN (WLAN)

Probably the most familiar and common wireless networking standard is the IEEE 802.11 wireless fidelity standard for LAN wireless connection. The IEEE 802.11 standard, also known as *Wi-Fi,* defines a blueprint and implementation specification to implement short-range, high-speed wireless connections. The CCNA exam focuses on LAN wireless connections, so it's important to understand wireless LANs.

Wireless WAN

In terms of WAN applications, wireless connections are used for moderate ranges of up to 20 miles. Several technologies exist, some of which can concentrate the airwave signals into a directional beam, thereby increasing range. Microwave transmission is a form of wireless connection that can span very long distances, either on earth or through telecommunication satellites. Wireless WANs are beyond the scope of the CCNA exam.

Benefits and Costs of Wireless Networks

The main advantage of wireless LANs is the elimination of wired connections:

✦ No need to run cables across the building

✦ No need to buy and install connectors

✦ No need to buy and install local distribution patch panels

In short, wireless connections allow tremendous flexibility. The disadvantages are as follows:

✦ Lack of reliability

✦ Limited range

✦ Piggybacking

✦ Potential security issues

Security Risks

One of the biggest issues in wireless networks is security. Because data transmission is done through airwaves, and because TCP/IP does not encrypt data by default, the potential exists for eavesdropping.

If TCP/IP security protocols are used, even if data packets are *sniffed,* the contents cannot be read, unless sniffers can break the encryption. However, most TCP/IP transmissions are unencrypted. So, a security risk clearly exists when transmitting data over airwaves in wireless networks.

A *packet sniffer* is a network application that "listens" to IP packets traveling through a network. Packet sniffers usually trap all IP packets and display or log their contents. Packet-sniffing tools were originally designed for network troubleshooting, but they are now used for a variety of purposes, including hacking and eavesdropping.

Another issue is *piggybacking.* If your wireless network is open, anyone can connect to it. Your neighbor, or someone passing by on the street, can use a wireless device to connect to your network. They may not necessarily have bad intentions (for example, sniffing your data), but they are still using your bandwidth.

The IEEE 802.11 standard defines several mechanisms to mitigate piggybacking and security risks: SSID (service set identifier), Wired Equivalent Privacy (WEP), Wi-Fi Protected Access (WPA), and MAC Address Filtering.

Service set identifier (SSID)

A service set identifier (SSID) identifies each wireless network. By default, the SSID is broadcast over the airwaves so that any wireless device and any host operating system can know about the existence of the wireless network. You can turn off the broadcasting of the SSID over the air. This basically hides the name (the SSID) of the wireless network. Wireless devices cannot detect the wireless network unless its SSID is broadcast.

However, you can connect a wireless device to a "hidden" wireless network by typing its SSID in the network SSID options box in the device wireless configuration tool. The idea is this: You know the SSID of your wireless network because you configured it. Hence, you can type that SSID in the network SSID options box in the device wireless configuration tool. Your neighbor, or someone walking by on the street, does not know the SSID of your wireless network, and even if she scans the air for wireless networks, she cannot find your network SSID because it's not broadcast. Unless she knows the SSID of your network, she cannot connect to your wireless network.

Tools are available that can find wireless networks even if their SSID is hidden (that is, not broadcast). Hiding the SSID makes it more difficult for piggybackers to find the wireless network.

Hiding the SSID is a bit like an automobile alarm system: It does not prevent pros from stealing the car, but it limits the number of potential attacks.

Wired Equivalent Privacy (WEP)

WEP is the first wireless security protocol that was introduced to secure the over-the-air communication between *wireless access point (WAP)* devices and wireless *network interface card (NIC)* devices. It's very easy to configure but not very secure.

WEP uses a 64-bit or 128-bit encryption key generated on the WAP device. The key must be provided to all wireless devices that need to connect to the secured wireless network. The 128-bit encryption key is a bit more secure (harder to crack, or "guess") than the 64-bit encryption key. No additional performance penalty is incurred to generate a 128-bit encryption, but there's more data to transfer over the wireless network. Hence, if network performance is most important, do not use encryption or use 64-bit encryption. If security is most important, use 128-bit encryption, or better yet, use WPA-2.

Wi-Fi Protected Access (WPA)

WPA is a security certification program that was created by the *Wi-Fi Alliance* to secure wireless networks. The Wi-Fi Alliance is a group of wireless device manufacturers. The group includes Cisco. One the goals of the WPA program is to provide a more secure alternative to the Wired Equivalent Privacy (WEP) security protocol previously used in wireless networks.

Two versions of WPA wireless security exist today: WPA-1 and WPA-2.

WPA-1

WPA-1 is an improvement over WEP. WPA-1 uses *Temporal Key Integrity Protocol (TKIP)*. The *basic input-output system (BIOS)* of most wireless network interface cards, even as old as 1999, can be upgraded to support WPA-1. However, wireless access point (WAP) devices require modification to support WPA-1. Hence, most WAP devices built before 2003 do not support WPA-1. To summarize, most wireless devices, both NICs and WAPs, and host operating systems built after 2003, support WPA-1.

The Wi-Fi Alliance tests and certifies wireless NIC and WAP devices to determine whether they comply with the WPA-1 standard. If they do, a WPA-1 logo is visible on the packaging and on the device.

WPA-2

WPA-2 is defined by the IEEE 802.11i standard. This fixes WEP shortcomings as well as some flaws discovered in TKIP used in WPA-1. WPA-2 does not use TKIP. Instead, it uses the *Counter Mode with Cipher Block Chaining Message Authentication Code Protocol (CCMP)* encryption algorithm, which is considered fully secure. WPA-2 is currently the most secure wireless security protocol.

Not all wireless NIC and WAP devices support WPA-2. Particularly, devices manufactured before 2004 do not typically comply with the WPA-2 Wi-Fi certification. The Wi-Fi Alliance tests and certifies wireless NIC and WAP devices to determine whether they comply with the WPA-2 standard. If they do, a WPA-2 logo is visible on the packaging and on the device.

MAC address filtering

Another way to control devices that are allowed to connect to a wireless network is filtering by MAC address. Most WAP devices allow creating a list of MAC addresses that can connect to the wireless network. The MAC address of each device that needs to connect to the wireless network is added to the list. The WAP then refuses connection to any wireless device that is not in the "allowed MAC address" list.

This may be a good solution for small- to medium-size wireless networks. However, it becomes difficult to manage in larger wireless networks when many wireless devices need to connect.

Prep Test

1 **What is the main advantage of wireless LANs?**

  A ○ Elimination of wired connections

  B ○ Elimination of crosstalk

  C ○ Elimination of signal attenuation

  D ○ All of the above

2 **What is a disadvantage of wireless LANs?**

  A ○ Limited range

  B ○ Piggybacking

  C ○ Potential security risks

  D ○ All of the above

3 **Describe wireless networks.**

  A ○ Short- or medium-range networks that connect host devices using satellites

  B ○ Short- or medium-range networks that connect host devices using airwaves

  C ○ Short- or medium-range networks that connect host devices using optical fiber

  D ○ All of the above

4 **Wireless local-area networks (WLANs) are standardized by which of the following standards?**

  A ○ IEEE 802.3w

  B ○ IEEE 802.11w

  C ○ IEEE 802.11

  D ○ All of the above

5 **WLAN security issues can be mitigated using which of the following?**

  A ○ Wi-Fi Protected Access (WPA)

  B ○ MAC address filtering

  C ○ Wired Equivalent Privacy (WEP)

  D ○ All of the above

Answers

1 **A.** The main advantage of wireless connections is the elimination of wired connections. Review *"Benefits and Costs of Wireless Networks."*

2 **D.** All of the above. Wireless networks are typically unreliable, provide a limited range, and are exposed to piggybacking and packet sniffing. Check out *"Benefits and Costs of Wireless Networks."*

3 **B.** Wireless networks connect host devices over short or medium distances using airwaves. Read *"Benefits and Costs of Wireless Networks."*

4 **C.** The IEEE 802.11 standard defines the characteristics and specifications of wireless networks. See *"Introducing Wireless Networks."*

5 **D.** All of the above. Several methods are available to mitigate the inherent security risks of wireless networks, including WPA, MAC address filtering, and WEP. Review *"Security Risks."*

Chapter 9: Network Design

Exam Objectives

✓ Describing the Cisco hierarchical network model

✓ Describing the characteristics and purpose of each layer in the Cisco hierarchical network model

✓ Describing the benefits associated with designing networks based on the Cisco hierarchical network model

✓ Identifying the Cisco devices suited for each layer in the Cisco hierarchical network model

You find out about the Cisco hierarchical network design model in this chapter. You see how Cisco conceptually divides networks into three layers:

✦ Core layer

✦ Distribution layer

✦ Access layer

Cisco Hierarchical Network Model

Cisco defines a network design model that is hierarchical: Three layers define the type of connectivity needed between devices in the network. The Cisco hierarchical model also defines where specific services should best be offered in a network. For example, you may want to create access control lists at the distribution layer, not at the access layer. On the other hand, you may want to handle segmentation at the access layer.

Core Layer

The *core layer* is the layer that sits at the center of the network. This layer is also called the *backbone*. Ultimately, traffic from all devices in the network may end up being routed to the core of the network. The core layer is "where networks meet." Large routers typically interconnect at the core layer. Major global networks are organized around several main backbones to which thousands of core layer routers connect. Backbone links are typically highly available and extremely fast links that provide very high bandwidth.

The core layer specializes in providing very high-speed, very highly available connectivity between large global networks. No host devices are typically connected at the core level. Only very fast, multiple-port, highly available routers connect at this layer. A failure at the core layer affects all host devices that need to send traffic through that backbone.

To handle the huge volume of network traffic bubbling up from the distribution and access layers, the core layer must maintain the following:

✦ High speed

✦ Low latency

✦ High availability

✦ High reliability

The following sections describe some best practices when designing core layer connectivity.

Highly available core

When designing core layer connectivity, you need to ensure that the core of the network is highly available — in other words, ensure that the core continues to work even if a component of the core fails. For example, even if a router connecting at the core layer fails, the core of the network should continue to handle traffic on redundant routers and redundant links.

The keyword here is *redundancy:* You need to have redundancy built in to the core layer. You can achieve redundancy in two ways:

✦ Use one or a few *service provider class* devices that are highly redundant, such as a Cisco Carrier Routing System (CRS-1) blade router.

✦ Use multiple, interconnected *enterprise-class routers and switches,* such as the Cisco 7600 series (router) or the Cisco 6500 series (switch).

In both cases, you also need to configure the *service provider–class* or the *enterprise-class* routers with the following:

✦ Redundant links to each distribution layer router

✦ Redundant links to the network backbone

✦ Redundant power supplies

✦ Redundant cooling systems

Redundancy allows you to guarantee traffic operation at the core layer.

Most core routers on the market today, such as the Cisco CRS-1, have resiliency and top performance built in. The Cisco CRS-1 is composed of several routers within the same box.

The CRS-1 uses blade hardware architecture:

✦ *Blade hardware* architecture involves one cabinet, or *chassis,* with several processing *blades.* Blade architecture provides top-speed processing and resiliency using parallel processing on the blades while using minimal footprint, power, and cooling.

✦ Each processing blade is a router built on circuit boards that slide inside the chassis.

✦ All blades interconnect to a *backplane.*

Avoid changing the core layer setup as much as possible. If expansion is needed, it is best to expand an existing core router by adding processing blades instead of exchanging the whole core router with another one. Also, it is best to test upgrades in a testing and development environment before upgrading the production core router.

Fast core

When designing core layer connectivity, you need to ensure that the core of the network is working at the top speeds supported for the backbone links. Core routers available today support top backbone speeds of 10 gigabits per second (Gbps) to 40 Gbps.

Backbone speeds have been steadily increasing over the past decade, and everything seems to point to further increases in speed in the future. Hence, today's top-notch core router will not be a top-notch core router in three to five years. Backbone bandwidth requirements will likely increase, and a core router that supports 40 Gbps today may be too slow in the future. For example, in the 1990s, backbone bandwidth was typically 155 Mbps. By 2000, it had increased to 2.5 Gbps. Today, backbone speeds are usually 10 Gbps, with some links blazing at 40 Gbps.

To offer adequate core layer speed, it is best to use the fastest core routers on the market. However, you can do the following things to improve speed, no matter which core router you choose:

✦ Avoid enabling any services that would slow the core router. It is best to enable these services on routers operating at the distribution or access layer. For example, on core routers:

• Avoid routing between virtual local-area networks (VLANs)

- Avoid controlling access using access control lists
- Avoid filtering packets
- Avoid interconnecting LANs

✦ Avoid connecting end devices, such as host devices, at the core layer. The core layer specializes in providing very high-speed, very highly available connectivity between large global networks. This is no place for connecting end devices. The core layer is solely reserved for internetwork connectivity.

✦ Avoid enabling slower routing protocols, such as Routing Information Protocol (RIP), on core routers.

✦ Avoid connecting access layer switches directly at the core layer. Access layer traffic needs to be concentrated in a few distribution layer routers that connect to the core layer. This ensures that core bandwidth is not wasted dealing with traffic that shouldn't go to the core in the first place.

Routing protocols use different metrics and methods to determine the best route for a packet. Some methods are faster than others. It is best practice to use only the fastest routing protocols on core routers, such as the following:

✦ OSPF (Open Shortest Path First)

✦ EIGRP (Enhanced Interior Gateway Routing Protocol)

✦ IS-IS (Intermediate System–to–Intermediate System)

You read more about routing protocols, metrics, and methods they use to determine routes in Book IV.

For example, in Figure 9-1, a host connected to switch A1 may need to send a packet to a host connected to switch A2. The packet should be properly routed at the distribution layer by router A without ever disturbing the core router. The packet does not need to reach network B, so you don't need to route it to the core layer. If you plugged switch A1 and A2 directly into the core router, instead of using the distribution layer router A, the packet would have to go through the core router, which wastes precious core network bandwidth.

Figure 9-1 illustrates how the core layer, the distribution layer, and the access layer interconnect to provide an optimal hierarchical network.

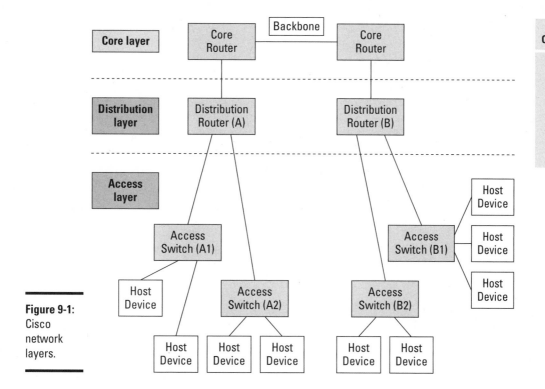

Figure 9-1:
Cisco
network
layers.

Distribution Layer

The *distribution layer* links the core layer to the access layer. The distribution
layer is also called the *workgroup layer*.

The distribution layer is involved in routing packets between nodes connected
at the access layer. Packets may need to be routed to a different network,
which may be located within the same distribution layer network, or
through the core layer in a different distribution layer network. Routers
typically interconnect at the distribution layer.

The main functions performed by switches and routers at the distribution
layer are as follows:

✦ Finding the best network route for packets

✦ Filtering packets

✦ Interconnecting LANs

✦ Connecting LANs to WANs

✦ Relaying packets to the core layer as needed

✦ Securing networks

Distribution layer switches and routers are best suited for the following:

✦ **Routing packets between access and core layer routers:** Similar to core routers, you should enable only faster routing protocols (OSPF, EIGRP, IS-IS) on distribution routers. However, if access layer routers have slower routing protocols enabled (such as RIP), you should also enable those protocols on distribution routers.

✦ **Managing access lists:** You should configure access lists at the distribution layer because this is the entry point into local-area networks (LANs). Use Layer 2 switches to manage access lists because Layer 2 switches are faster than routers.

✦ **Filtering packets:** Similar to access lists, you should configure packet filtering at the distribution layer because this is the entry point into LANs.

✦ **Translating network addresses (NAT — Network Address Translation):** Some LANs at the access layer may have their own private addressing scheme.

The distribution layer is the entry point into LANs. Hence, you should configure NAT at the distribution layer to translate public WAN IP addresses into private LAN IP addresses.

✦ **Managing firewalls:** *Firewalls* isolate the internal private network from the outside public networks (the Internet) to filter IP packets and control access to internal network resources.

You should enable and manage firewalls at the distribution layer because most internal networks operate at the access layer and sometimes at the distribution layer. The distribution layer is the entry point in internal networks.

✦ **Routing packets between VLANs:** Virtual local-area networks (VLANs) are bound to internal networks. As mentioned previously, internal networks operate at the access layer and sometimes at the distribution layer.

The distribution layer is the entry point in internal networks. So, distribution layer switches and routers are best suited to manage inter-VLAN routing.

Access Layer

The *access layer* is the layer that interconnects host devices to LANs. The access layer is where workgroup LANs are defined.

This layer is also called the *desktop layer,* because it usually involves interconnecting desktop computers and concentrating their traffic into a distribution layer switch or router.

Switches, small routers, and computer host devices typically interconnect at the access layer.

Most services that are bound to a particular LAN are typically enabled at the access layer. For example, traffic segmentation is typically configured at the access layer, because traffic is usually segmented on a per-LAN basis, or on a per-VLAN basis.

The main functions performed by switches and routers at the access layer are as follows:

✦ Connecting host devices to a LAN

✦ Segmenting network traffic using switched LANs and VLANs

✦ Relaying traffic to switches and routers at the distribution layer

Benefits

There are several benefits of designing and implementing networks in such a hierarchical way. You realize the following benefits when you implement the Cisco hierarchical network model:

✦ Specialization

✦ Scalability

✦ Limitation of problem domain

Specialization

Each layer offers a specific set of services and interconnectivity type:

✦ **Access layer:** Host devices and other end-node devices connect only at the access layer, which is optimized for endpoint connections and local network traffic handling.

✦ **Distribution and core layers:** Routers, on the other hand, specialize in efficient and optimal routing of data packets between networks. Hence, they typically operate at the distribution and core layer, which are optimized for bulk and backbone traffic handling. No end-device connections are done at the distribution and core layers.

Scalability

It is easy to scale up a hierarchical network. Each layer can expand both laterally and vertically.

Considering Figure 9-1, you can easily add additional host devices to the network by expanding at the *access layer*. It is important, however, to calculate the bandwidth required for additional nodes and expand the links at the distribution and core layer if necessary. Each layer can be designed with some future capacity growth in mind. For example, you can plan for a certain number of ports and links at the access layer. Not all ports are connected on day 1. However, over time, as you add host devices, these links are used.

To support higher bandwidth, you can expand at the *distribution and core layers*. You can also plan for additional bandwidth capacity at the distribution and core layers without necessarily enabling and using all this potential bandwidth capacity on day 1. For example, you can deploy routers with two or four ports at the distribution layer, even if you only use one port on day 1. This leaves room to increase bandwidth capacity at the distribution layer by using the additional router ports in the future.

A fine balance exists between planning for future capacity growth and wasting money. In the example, a two-port router at the distribution layer, with one uplink port being used on day 1, may be a better solution than a four-port router with one uplink port being used on day 1, from a financial perspective. On the other hand, if the network grows fairly fast, and it gets to the point where you need three uplink ports to the core layer, you would wish you had a four-port router instead of a two-port router at the distribution layer, because it is more economical to connect and enable port 3 on a four-port router than to add and connect a new two-port router. It all depends on the future growth forecast, in other words, how quickly the additional bandwidth will be needed. It also depends on high-availability requirements. For example, even if you consider that four uplink ports will be needed fairly soon, you may still decide to implement two two-port routers instead of a single four-port router to be able to continue to provide connectivity to the core layer in case one of the routers fails.

Cisco offers products that allow you to fine-tune the balance between planning for future capacity growth and wasting money up front. Higher-end Cisco switches and routers typically have expansion module slots. This lets you start with a router/switch with a lower number of ports and add ports as your needs increase. Upper limits still exist (as well as models in the same product line with more expansion slots than others), but for a slightly higher initial cost, you can add more interfaces without buying new equipment. The higher initial cost of a modular switch or router is in some cases lower than the cost of a switch/router that provides all the ports you'll need for future growth over the upcoming months/years. You can also replace an expansion module depending on network changes such as a different type of WAN. Cisco modular products allow considerable flexibility in the way you design and implement your network.

Limitation of problem domain

Troubleshooting network problems is simplified in a Cisco hierarchical network, because each layer offers a specific set of services and interconnectivity. Hence, you need to investigate only problems related to that specific set of services and interconnectivity at any particular network layer. For example, if a host device cannot connect to the network, you typically investigate its connectivity at the access layer only. You don't need to look at the distribution layer if other hosts in the same network can connect to the distribution and core layers.

Prep Test

1 What is one of the layers defined by the Cisco hierarchical network model?

A ○ Data link layer

B ○ Session layer

C ○ Access layer

D ○ Presentation layer

2 The core layer in the Cisco hierarchical network model is the layer that provides which of the following?

A ○ Very high-speed, very highly available connectivity between large local networks

B ○ Very high-speed, very highly available connectivity between large global networks

C ○ Very high-speed, very highly available connectivity for hosts

D ○ Very high-speed, very highly available connectivity for IP phones

3 To ensure that the core layer in the Cisco hierarchical network model is highly available, you need to do which of the following?

A ○ Design redundancy into the network: redundant routing, redundant links to distribution layer, redundant power supplies, redundant cooling systems

B ○ Design the network using blade hardware only: use only blade-based routers when designing core layer connectivity

C ○ Design the core layer using Layer 2 switches only

D ○ All of the above

4 What should you do to ensure that the core layer in the Cisco hierarchical network model is fast?

A ○ Avoid enabling any services that would slow the core router

B ○ Avoid connecting end devices such as host devices at the core layer

C ○ Avoid enabling slower routing protocols on core routers

D ○ All of the above

5 The distribution layer in the Cisco hierarchical network model is the layer that does which of the following?

A ○ Links the session layer to the access layer

B ○ Links the data link layer to the access layer

C ○ Links the core layer to the access layer

D ○ Links the presentation layer to the access layer

6 **What are distribution layer switches and routers best suited to do?**

A ○ Find the best network route for packets into and out of LANs and WANs

B ○ Filter packets

C ○ Interconnect LANs and connect LANs to WANs

D ○ All of the above

7 **What do distribution layer switches and routers manage?**

A ○ NAT (Network Address Translation), ACLs (access control lists), firewalls, inter-LAN and inter-VLAN routing

B ○ NAT (Network Address Translation), ACLs (access control lists), firewalls, routing within LANs and routing within VLANs

C ○ NAT (Network Address Translation), ACLs (access control lists), firewalls

D ○ All of the above

8 **What is the function of the access layer in the Cisco hierarchical network model?**

A ○ Interconnects core routers to LANs

B ○ Interconnects end devices such as hosts to LANs

C ○ Interconnects distribution routers to LANs

D ○ Interconnects end devices such as hosts to core routers

9 **Name some of the benefits of designing networks according to the Cisco hierarchical network model.**

A ○ Specialization

B ○ Scalability

C ○ Limitation of problem domain

D ○ All of the above

Answers

1 **C.** Access layer. The Cisco hierarchical network model defines three layers: access, distribution, and core. Review *"Cisco Hierarchical Network Model."*

2 **B.** The core layer in the Cisco hierarchical network model is the layer that provides very high-speed, very highly available connectivity between large global networks. Check out *"Core Layer."*

3 **A.** To ensure that the core layer in the Cisco hierarchical network model is highly available, you need to design redundancy into the network: redundant routing, redundant links to the distribution layer, redundant power supplies, and redundant cooling systems. Read *"Core Layer."*

4 **D.** All of the above. To ensure that the core layer in the Cisco hierarchical network model is fast, you should avoid enabling any services that would slow the core router, avoid connecting end devices such as host devices at the core layer, and avoid enabling slower routing protocols on core routers. See *"Core Layer."*

5 **C.** The distribution layer in the Cisco hierarchical network model is the layer that links the core layer to the access layer. Look over *"Distribution Layer."*

6 **D.** All of the above. Distribution layer switches and routers are best suited to find the best network route for packets into and out of LANs and WANs, to filter packets, and to interconnect LANs and to connect LANs to WANs. Review *"Distribution Layer."*

7 **D.** Distribution layer switches and routers typically manage NAT (Network Address Translation), ACLs (access control lists), firewalls, and inter-LAN and inter-VLAN routing. See *"Distribution Layer."*

8 **B.** The access layer in the Cisco hierarchical network model interconnects end devices such as hosts into LANs. *Check out "Access Layer."*

9 **D.** All of the above. The main benefits of designing networks according to the Cisco hierarchical network model are specialization, scalability, and limitation of problem domain. Look over *"Benefits."*

Chapter 10: Introducing Cisco Hardware and Software

Exam Objectives

✓ Identifying software components in Cisco devices

✓ Describing the characteristics and purpose of the Cisco Internetwork Operating System (IOS)

✓ Identifying Cisco network management software products and their purpose

✓ Identifying hardware components in Cisco devices

✓ Reviewing best practices for selecting Cisco hardware and software products for a specific network design

✓ Describing system memory organization on Cisco devices

✓ Describing device configurations on Cisco switches and routers

✓ Using the Cisco IOS command-line interface (CLI)

✓ Using Cisco graphical user interfaces (GUIs)

Read this chapter to get acquainted with Cisco hardware and software products. You find out about the main hardware components of Cisco devices. You discover software that runs on Cisco devices, including the Cisco Internetwork Operating System, shortly known as IOS. You read about the characteristics and purpose of Cisco IOS. You see that the same IOS can be used to manage both Layer 2 Cisco switches and Layer 3 Cisco routers. You also see how to use the IOS command-line interface (CLI) as well as the graphical user interface (GUI) to manage Cisco devices. Context-sensitive help is discussed as well.

Introducing Cisco Products

You probably know the difference between hardware and software:

✦ **Hardware:** Physical devices that you install, connect to a power supply, and interconnect with network cables. In the Cisco world and in the context of this book, *hardware* means a Cisco switch, a Cisco router, cables, computer hosts, or Cisco IP phones.

✦ **Software:** Computer programs that are installed on a physical device to configure and manage the device, to provide a user interface, to operate the device, and to troubleshoot the device. In the Cisco world and in the context of this book, *software* means the Cisco Internetwork Operating System (IOS), the Cisco Network Assistant (CNA), the Cisco Security Device Manager (SDM), or the Cisco Device Manager (DM).

The following sections describe the Cisco hardware and software products that you need to know for the CCNA test.

Cisco software

Cisco provides various software products. You do not need to know about all of them for the CCNA test. However, you will be tested on your knowledge of the Cisco IOS, Cisco CNA, and Cisco SDM. Each of these three software products is described in the following sections.

Cisco IOS

The Cisco IOS (Internetwork Operating System) is Cisco's proprietary switch and router operating system. The Cisco IOS is stored in flash memory on the Cisco device.

Cisco IOS operates all major Cisco switch and router series, from the entry-level Cisco Catalyst 2960 switch series to the top-of-the-line Cisco Catalyst 6500 switch series, and from the entry-level Cisco 1800/2600/2800 router series to the top-of-the-line Cisco 12000 router series. This is good. You can learn the Cisco IOS working with an entry-level Cisco Catalyst 2960 switch series and with an entry-level Cisco 1800/2600/2800 router series and use that knowledge with any Cisco switch or router, even with top-of-the-line Cisco Catalyst 6500 series switches and with top-of-the-line Cisco 12000 router series.

Cisco Device Manager

The Cisco Device Manager is a Web-based tool that is installed on all Cisco switches and routers at the factory. To access this tool, you need to browse to the management IP address of the Cisco switch or router from a computer host connected to the network. The Cisco Device Manager Web application is part of the Cisco IOS software package, and it's stored in the Cisco device flash memory.

Cisco CNA

The Cisco Network Assistant (CNA) is a Java-based application used to monitor and manage Cisco switches and routers from a central management console. Cisco CNA is available for Windows, Mac OS X, and Linux. It provides a graphical user interface (GUI) that allows the network administrator to have both global and detailed views of the Cisco networking environment. Cisco CNA is stored on the hard drive of the computer host where it's installed.

Cisco SDM

The Cisco Security Device Manager (SDM) is a computer application used to monitor and manage Cisco routers from a central management console. Cisco SDM is available for Windows. It provides a graphical user interface (GUI) that allows the network administrator to have both global and detailed views of the Cisco routing environment.

Cisco software in read-only memory (ROM)

Four software programs are stored in ROM on Cisco devices. These programs are the first programs that the Cisco device runs upon powering up. They are used to verify and bootstrap the Cisco device, during startup, prior to loading the Cisco IOS and transitioning into normal operation mode.

These software programs are as follows:

+ **Power-on self test (POST):** This program is used to verify the Cisco device hardware. It is the first program the Cisco device runs when you power it up.

+ **Bootstrap program:** This program brings up the Cisco device by loading the Cisco IOS stored in flash memory. The bootstrap program is run right after the POST.

+ **Boot Image (Rx-boot):** The Boot Image (Rx-boot) is a subset of the Cisco IOS. The Rx-boot image is used to download the Cisco IOS to the Cisco device from a Trivial File Transfer Protocol (TFTP) server whenever the IOS needs to be upgraded, or whenever the IOS needs to be replaced. The Rx-boot image is accessed from the (boot)> prompt on a Cisco device.

+ **ROM Monitor (ROMMON):** The ROM Monitor is used to maintain, test, and troubleshoot the configuration stored in ROM and in the flash memory of the Cisco device. ROMMON is also used to troubleshoot hardware problems. Most management features provided by ROMMON can also be done with Rx-boot. It is best practice to use Rx-boot whenever possible. ROMMON is typically used to change the value stored in the *configuration register* or as a last resort when booting problems cannot be fixed with Rx-boot. ROMMON is accessed from the rommon> prompt on a Cisco device. To get to the rommon> prompt, you need to break out of the bootstrap process by pressing Ctrl+Break while the Cisco device is booting up. The configuration register is explained in the section "Cisco device memory," later in this chapter.

Cisco hardware

Cisco provides various hardware products. You do not need to know about all of them for the CCNA test. However, you will be tested on a few things. You need to be able to differentiate Cisco hardware product types. You also need to know best practices for using Cisco hardware products.

Differentiate Cisco hardware products

You need to know the difference between various networking devices. You need to know how a switch is different from a hub or a bridge. You also need to know how switches, hubs, and bridges are different from routers.

Best practices for using Cisco hardware products

You need to understand best practices for using entry-level and top-of-the-line products. For example, you need to know that top-of-the-line switches and routers are best suited for the core layer or for the distribution layer of the network. Entry-level and midrange switches and routers are best suited for the access layer or for the distribution layer.

Top-of-the-line switches and routers manage specialized services in a network, such as the Spanning Tree Protocol (STP) root bridge role, inter-VLAN routing, and gateway connectivity. These services are used throughout the network. Hence, they need to run on a highly efficient and highly available switch or router.

Cisco device memory

Five areas comprise the memory of Cisco devices. These memory areas are used to store static and dynamic device configuration data. These memory areas are as follows:

✦ **Read-only memory (ROM):** The ROM stores programs and data necessary to start up the Cisco device. This memory keeps its contents even when the Cisco device is powered down. ROM is kept on EPROM (erasable programmable read-only memory) chips.

✦ **Flash memory:** The flash memory stores the Cisco IOS. Flash memory keeps its contents even when the Cisco device is powered down. Flash memory is kept on EEPROM chips, on PCMCIA cards, or on CompactFlash cards. The PCMCIA and CompactFlash cards can be accessed either internally on the Cisco device motherboard or externally through a PCMCIA or CompactFlash external slot.

✦ **Nonvolatile random-access memory (NVRAM):** The NVRAM stores the *startup configuration*. This is the configuration that Cisco IOS loads when it boots up. NVRAM keeps its contents even when the Cisco device is powered down.

✦ **Random-access memory (RAM):** The RAM stores the *running configuration.* This is the dynamic data that changes while the Cisco device is in normal operation mode. This includes the Address Resolution Protocol (ARP) cache (MAC address tables), routing tables, STP data, VLAN data, EtherChannel configuration data, and temporary buffers. RAM does not keep its contents when the Cisco device is powered down. Upon startup, RAM is initialized with contents from NVRAM.

✦ **Configuration register:** The configuration register is a 2-byte (16-bit) area of NVRAM that holds a numeric value that defines how the Cisco device starts up. By default, the value stored in the configuration register instructs the bootstrap program to load the Cisco IOS from flash memory and to load the startup configuration from NVRAM. You can change the value of the configuration register from the ROMMON prompt. To get to the `rommon>` prompt, you need to break out of the bootstrap process by pressing Ctrl+Break while the Cisco device is booting up.

Introducing Cisco Device Configurations

You find two configurations on Cisco switches and routers: the startup configuration and the running configuration.

Startup configuration

The startup configuration is the configuration that the Cisco IOS loads when it boots up. The startup configuration is stored in NVRAM, which keeps its contents even when the Cisco device is powered down.

Cisco switches and routers start in setup mode to allow you to create a startup configuration whenever no startup configuration exists in NVRAM. After you complete the setup mode, you are prompted to save the configuration to NVRAM. If you answer yes, the configuration you created is saved to NVRAM: It becomes the startup configuration. You can also manually save the current configuration to NVRAM by using the `copy running-config startup-config` Cisco IOS command.

Cisco devices use the startup configuration data to configure the device before normal operation starts. The Cisco IOS loads the startup configuration from NVRAM into RAM. At that point, the startup configuration becomes the running configuration. The switch is up and ready in normal operation mode.

Running configuration

The running configuration is the dynamic data that changes while the Cisco device is in normal operation mode. This includes the ARP cache (MAC address tables), routing tables, STP data, VLAN data, EtherChannel configuration data, and temporary buffers. The Cisco IOS loads the startup configuration from NVRAM into RAM during the boot process. After it's in RAM, the startup configuration becomes the running configuration and can change dynamically.

You can save the running configuration to NVRAM to replace the startup configuration with updated data. To do this, use the `copy running-config startup-config` Cisco IOS command. You can also save the running configuration to a file on a computer host.

Meet the Cisco IOS User Interface

Read the following sections to find out about the Cisco IOS user interface, including the command-line interface (CLI) and the graphical user interfaces (GUIs) available.

It's important to get familiar with the IOS CLI and GUI interfaces because you will be tested on them in the CCNA exam.

Cisco IOS command-line interface (CLI)

The Cisco IOS command-line interface (CLI) is a text-based interface that is integrated into the IOS. When a switch or router boots up, the IOS loads the startup configuration from NVRAM and displays the IOS prompt, waiting for commands.

The Cisco device is in *user EXEC* mode at this point: You, the device administrator, can enter IOS commands at the IOS prompt. The Cisco IOS processes your commands and displays results. Next, the IOS displays the prompt again, waiting for more commands.

Command-line operation modes

Before you explore the details of the IOS command-line interface, it's a good idea to understand the various command-line modes of the Cisco IOS. The Cisco IOS CLI operates in one of the following modes:

✦ **Setup mode:** Initial setup mode

✦ **User EXEC mode:** Normal operation mode

✦ **Privileged EXEC mode:** Privileged operation mode

✦ **Global configuration mode:** Commands that affect the configuration of the whole device

✦ **Specific configuration mode:** Commands that affect only a specific part of the device

The following sections describe each of these operation modes.

Setup mode

Setup mode is the initial configuration mode. Cisco switches and routers start in setup mode whenever no startup configuration exists in NVRAM. The IOS setup mode guides you through the steps to initially configure your switch or router by asking a few questions. You can either complete the setup mode questionnaire or exit out of it before completion. Either way, after you exit from setup mode, the Cisco IOS transitions from setup mode to user EXEC mode.

User EXEC mode

The *user EXEC* mode is the normal operation mode on Cisco switches and routers. The Cisco IOS displays the user EXEC prompt and waits for commands.

User EXEC prompt

The Cisco IOS user EXEC prompt is composed of the switch or router host name followed by the character >. Switches are all named "Switch" by default. Routers are all named "Router" by default.

You should give a meaningful host name to your switches and routers. You don't want to use the same name for all your switches, and you don't want to use the same name for all your routers, right?

✦ This is the user EXEC prompt for a switch with the default host name of "Switch":

```
Switch>
```

✦ This is the user EXEC prompt for a switch with the host name of "SW1":

```
SW1>
```

✦ This is the user EXEC prompt for a router with the default host name of "Router":

```
Router>
```

✦ This is the user EXEC prompt for a switch with the host name of "RT1":

```
RT1>
```

Privileged EXEC mode

The *privileged EXEC* mode is the advanced operation mode of Cisco switches and routers. Cisco designed the privileged mode to filter access to IOS commands that can have adverse effects on the Cisco device and its configuration. The idea is to allow only experienced administrators to run commands in privileged mode. You can set different passwords for user EXEC mode and for privileged EXEC mode.

You should have different passwords for user EXEC mode and for privileged EXEC mode, and provide the privileged EXEC mode password only to experienced administrators.

To enter privileged mode, execute the `enable` Cisco IOS command (or just en in its short form). You execute `enable` or en at the user EXEC prompt. Next, the IOS prompts you for the privileged EXEC mode password if you have configured a different password for privileged EXEC mode. After you enter the privileged EXEC mode password, the Cisco IOS displays the privileged EXEC mode prompt and waits for commands.

To exit from privileged EXEC mode back to user EXEC mode, execute the `disable` Cisco IOS command.

Privileged EXEC prompt

The Cisco IOS privileged EXEC prompt is comprised of the switch or router host name followed by the # character. Switches are all named "Switch" by default. Routers are all named "Router" by default. You should give a meaningful host name to your switches and routers.

The following example shows how to enable privileged EXEC mode. You are not prompted for a privileged EXEC mode password in this case. Why? No specific password has yet been set for privileged EXEC mode, so the user EXEC mode password is accepted.

```
Switch>enable (or en)
Switch#
```

The following is the same example on a switch named "SW1." Here you also use the `disable` command to exit to the user EXEC prompt:

```
SW1>enable (or en)
SW1#disable
SW1>
```

The same commands work on a router named "RT1":

```
RT1>enable (or en)
RT1#disable
RT1>
```

Global configuration mode

The *global configuration* mode is used for commands that affect the configuration of the whole Cisco device. In other words, if you need to execute some commands that modify the behavior of either the whole switch or the whole router you need to set the IOS in global configuration mode. You can only enable global configuration mode from privileged EXEC mode.

To set the Cisco IOS in global configuration mode, execute the `configure`
`terminal` IOS command (or just `config t`, in its short form). You execute
`configure terminal` or `config t` at the privileged EXEC prompt.

Global configuration prompt

The Cisco IOS global configuration prompt is comprised of the switch or
router host name followed by `(config)#`.

You need to enable privileged mode first by executing `enable` at the user
EXEC prompt and then executing `configure terminal`.

Here is an example where you enter global configuration mode from user
EXEC mode:

```
SW1>enable (or en)
SW1#configure terminal (or config t)
SW1(config)#
```

The same commands work on a router named "RT1":

```
RT1>enable (or en)
RT1#configure terminal (or config t)
RT1(config)#
```

If you need to run a command that is not available in global configuration
mode, you can prefix the command with `do` to execute it in privileged EXEC
mode. The `do` prefix allows you to temporarily exit the configuration mode
to run just that command.

For example:

```
SW1(config)#do show running-config
```

The `show running-config` command is not available in configuration
mode, only in privileged mode. So, theoretically, you cannot run this command
at the `(config)` prompt. You would have to exit to privileged mode, run
`show running-config`, and come back to configuration mode. Cisco
provides the `do` prefix to allow you to run nonconfiguration commands from
the configuration prompt.

Specific configuration mode

The *specific configuration* mode is used for commands that affect the
configuration of either just one part or one range of components of the Cisco
device. Typically, you need to set the IOS in specific configuration mode
when you need to work on a few interfaces (or ports) on your switch or on
your router.

To set the Cisco IOS in specific configuration mode, you need to select the components you want to work with. You select components from the global configuration prompt. In other words, to transition to the specific configuration mode, you first need to set the IOS in global configuration mode by executing the `configure terminal` IOS command (or just `config t` or `conf t` in its short forms). You execute `configure terminal` or `config t` at the privileged EXEC prompt. After you are in global configuration mode, you can select the components you want to work with and thereby transition the IOS to specific configuration mode.

For example, if you need to configure interface fastethernet0/1, you need to set the IOS in global configuration mode and then select the fa0/1 interface using the `interface` IOS command:

```
SW1>enable (or en)
SW1#configure terminal (or config t)
SW1(config)#interface fastethernet0/1 (or int fa0/1)
SW1(config-if)#
```

Specific configuration prompt

The Cisco IOS specific configuration prompt is comprised of the switch or router host name followed by `(config-<component>)#`.

You need to enable privileged mode first by executing `enable` at the user EXEC prompt and then execute `configure terminal`.

The previous example showed how to enter interface configuration mode from user EXEC mode. Note that the prompt is `SW1(config-if)#` in interface configuration mode. The term `if` is an abbreviation for interface.

Here is another example where you select the console access line component:

```
SW1>enable (or en)
SW1#configure terminal (or config t)
SW1(config)#line console 0 (or line con 0)
SW1(config-line)#
```

Observe that the specific configuration prompt is different: `SW1(config-line)#`. The `<component>` part of the specific configuration prompt changes according to which component you select.

If you need to run a command that is not available in specific configuration mode, you can prefix the command with `do` to execute it in privileged EXEC mode. The `do` prefix allows you to temporarily exit the specific configuration mode to run just that command.

For example:

```
SW1(config-if)#do show running-config
```

The `show running-config` command is not available in interface configuration mode, only in privileged mode. So, theoretically, you cannot run this command at the `(config-if)` prompt. You would have to exit to privileged mode, run `show running-config`, and come back to interface configuration mode. Cisco provides the `do` prefix to allow you to run nonconfiguration commands from the specific configuration prompt.

Selecting a component to work with

In the previous section, you read that you must select switch or router components to work with before you execute commands that affect only some parts of the switch.

Typically this involves selecting switch or router interfaces, or ports, and setting the switch or router in interface configuration mode before configuring the ports. You use the `interface` Cisco IOS command to select interfaces to work with and to transition the switch or router into interface configuration mode.

You can also select other components to configure, such as access lines using the `line` Cisco IOS command.

For example, the following IOS CLI segment selects the console access line to set a console password for that line:

```
SW1>enable (or en)
SW1#configure terminal (or config t)
SW1(config)#line console 0 (or line con 0)
SW1(config-line)#password my_password
SW1(config-line)#login
SW1(config-line)#exit
SW1(config)#exit
SW1#disable
SW1>
```

Observe the `configure terminal` command that transitions the switch into global configuration mode. Note the `line` command, which enables the line configuration mode. Observe also the IOS prompt changing from the default `SW1>` to global configuration `SW1(config)#` to line configuration `SW1(config-line)#`.

Here is the same example, using the same commands, on router RT1:

```
RT1>enable (or en)
RT1#configure terminal (or config t)
RT1(config)#line console 0 (or line con 0)
RT1(config-line)#password my_password
RT1(config-line)#login
RT1(config-line)#exit
RT1(config)#exit
RT1#disable
RT1>
```

Selecting a component range to work with

You can select a range of components to work with, instead of selecting just one component. This is very useful when you need to configure several similar components with the same settings. For example, the following IOS CLI segment selects the whole range of VTY (Virtual Terminal Line) access lines to set the same Telnet password for all VTY lines on the switch:

```
SW1>enable (or en)
SW1#configure terminal (or config t)
SW1(config)#line vty 0?
   <0-15> last line number
SW1(config-line)#line vty 0-15
SW1(config-line)#password my__telnet_password
SW1(config-line)#login
SW1(config-line)#exit
SW1(config)#exit
SW1#disable
SW1>
```

Observe the `configure terminal` command, which transitions the switch into global configuration mode. Note the `line vty 0-15` command, which selects lines 0 to 15 and enables line-range configuration mode. Observe also the IOS privileged mode prompt changing from the default `SW1#` to global configuration `SW1(config)#` to line configuration `SW1(config-line)>`.

Here is the same example, using the same commands, on router RT1:

```
RT1>enable (or en)
RT1#configure terminal (or config t)
RT1(config)#line vty 0?
   <0-15> last line number
RT1(config-line)#line vty 0-15
RT1(config-line)#password my__telnet_password
RT1(config-line)#login
RT1(config-line)#exit
RT1(config)#exit
RT1#disable
RT1>
```

Command shortcuts

You may have already noticed that many IOS commands can be used in their short form. Both forms are accepted by the Cisco IOS. Both forms are also accepted on the CCNA test. Table 10-1 shows some examples.

Table 10-1	Common Cisco IOS Commands — Short Forms
Command	*Short Forms*
show	sho, sh
interface	interf, inter, int

Command	Short Forms
`fastethernet`	`fasteth`, `fast`, `fa`
`copy running-config startup-config`	`copy run start`, `copy ru st`
`no shutdown`	`no shut`, `no sh`
`configure terminal`	`config t`, `conf t`

 You can type just a few characters of any command and press Enter. The short form you type may be accepted. If it isn't, the Cisco IOS will display an error. However, use the full-length command during the CCNA test, if you are unsure about a short form.

Command-line errors

The Cisco IOS parses the commands you type, including the abbreviated commands, after you press Enter. If you mistype a command or if the command is invalid, the IOS displays one of these errors: invalid input, ambiguous command, or incomplete command.

Invalid input

 The IOS displays the `%Invalid input` error message whenever a command is misspelled or cannot be run at the current prompt.

Double-check spelling and the command-line operation mode.

Ambiguous command

The IOS typically displays the `%Ambiguous command` error message when the command you typed is too short to determine which command you really mean.

 Double-check the short form of the command, or enter the command in its full-length form.

Incomplete command

The IOS displays the `%Incomplete command` error message when command arguments are missing from the command line.

Double-check the required arguments for the command you entered.

Default answers

The Cisco IOS is designed to suggest answers whenever possible. Suggested answers, also called default answers or default options, are shown between brackets next to the question. To keep a suggested answer, simply press Enter.

For example, the following IOS CLI segment copies the current running configuration from RAM to the startup configuration file in NVRAM:

```
SW1#copy running-config startup-config (or copy run start)
Destination filename [startup-config]? <press Enter>
Building configuration...
[OK]
SW1#
```

The second line asks where you want to copy the running configuration to. The default destination is the `startup-config` file in NVRAM. Observe how the Cisco IOS suggests the default destination between brackets — [startup-config] — before the question mark. To keep the default answer, just press Enter.

Enabling and disabling components and services

Sometimes you need to enable or disable certain components or services on a Cisco switch or router. You do this by prefixing an IOS command with the no qualifier.

For example, the following IOS CLI segment enables authentication prompting on the console access line using the `login` IOS command:

```
SW1>enable (or en)
SW1#configure terminal (or config t)
SW1(config)#line console 0 (or line con 0)
SW1(config-line)#password my_password
SW1(config-line)#login
SW1(config-line)#exit
SW1(config)#exit
SW1#exit
SW1>
```

To disable authentication prompting on the console access line, you would run the `login` command prefixed with no:

```
SW1>enable (or en)
SW1#configure terminal (or config t)
SW1(config)#line console 0 (or line con 0)
SW1(config-line)#no login
SW1(config-line)#exit
SW1(config)#exit
SW1#exit
SW1>
```

Context-sensitive help

The Cisco IOS CLI is designed to provide contextual help. You can list available commands along with a brief summary for each command. You can also get help about a particular command by typing the command verb followed by the ? character. This is useful when you are unsure about the arguments of a specific command. Many IOS commands have more than one argument. You may want to find out more about a specific argument. You can do this by typing the command along with the arguments you know and a ? character instead of the argument that you want to find out more about.

Listing commands

You can list available commands by typing ? at the IOS prompt. It is important to understand that commands you see in the help list are contextual: The list contains only commands that can be executed in the current IOS command-line operation mode. For example, the password command you used previously can only be executed in privileged EXEC line configuration operation mode. Hence, the Cisco IOS help command (the ? command) only lists the password command if you already executed enable (to transition the IOS to privileged EXEC mode), followed by configure terminal (to transition the IOS to global configuration mode), followed by line console 0 (to transition the IOS to line configuration mode). Here is an example:

First you list commands available in user EXEC mode:

```
RT1>?
Exec commands:
  access-enable    Create a temporary Access-List entry
  access-profile   Apply user-profile to interface
  clear            Reset functions
  connect          Open a terminal connection
  crypto           Crypto
  disable          Turn off privileged commands
  disconnect       Disconnect an existing network connection
  enable           Turn on privileged commands
  exit             Exit from the EXEC
  help             Description of the interactive help system
  lock             Lock the terminal
  login            Log in as a particular user
  logout           Exit from the EXEC
  modemui          Start a modem-like user interface
  mrinfo           Request neighbor and version information from a multicast
                   router
  mstat            Show statistics after multiple multicast traceroutes
  mtrace           Trace reverse multicast path from destination to source
  name-connection  Name an existing network connection
  pad              Open a X.29 PAD connection
  ping             Send echo messages
  ppp              Start IETF Point-to-Point Protocol (PPP)
  resume           Resume an active network connection
  rlogin           Open an rlogin connection
  show             Show running system information
  slip             Start Serial-line IP (SLIP)
  ssh              Open a secure shell client connection
  systat           Display information about terminal lines
  tclquit          Quit Tool Comand Language  shell
  telnet           Open a telnet connection
  terminal         Set terminal line parameters
  traceroute       Trace route to destination
  tunnel           Open a tunnel connection
  udptn            Open an udptn connection
  voice            Voice Commands
  where            List active connections
```

```
x28                 Become an X.28 PAD
x3                  Set X.3 parameters on PAD
```

Observe that the `password` command is not listed, because you cannot execute the `password` command in user EXEC mode.

Next, enable the privileged EXEC mode using the `enable` command and list the commands available using the `?` help command again:

```
RT1>enable                         (or en)
RT1#?
Exec commands:
  access-enable     Create a temporary Access-List entry
  access-profile    Apply user-profile to interface
  access-template   Create a temporary Access-List entry
  alps              ALPS exec commands
  archive           manage archive files
  audio-prompt      load ivr prompt
  auto              Exec level Automation
  bfe               For manual emergency modes setting
  call              Reload IVR call application, accounting template
  ccm-manager       Call Manager Application exec commands
  cd                Change current directory
  clear             Reset functions
  clock             Manage the system clock
  cns               CNS agents
  configure         Enter configuration mode
  connect           Open a terminal connection
  copy              Copy from one file to another
  crypto            Crypto
  debug             Debugging functions (see also 'undebug')
  delete            Delete a file
  dir               List files on a filesystem
  disable           Turn off privileged commands
  disconnect        Disconnect an existing network connection
  enable            Turn on privileged commands
  erase             Erase a filesystem
  exit              Exit from the EXEC
  help              Description of the interactive help system
  isdn              Run an ISDN EXEC command on an ISDN interface
  lock              Lock the terminal
  login             Log in as a particular user
  logout            Exit from the EXEC
  microcode         microcode commands
  modemui           Start a modem-like user interface
  monitor           Monitoring different system events
  more              Display the contents of a file
  mrinfo            Request neighbor and version information from a multicast
                    router
  mrm               IP Multicast Routing Monitor Test
  mstat             Show statistics after multiple multicast traceroutes
  mtrace            Trace reverse multicast path from destination to source
  name-connection   Name an existing network connection
  ncia              Start/Stop NCIA Server
  no                Disable debugging functions
  pad               Open a X.29 PAD connection
  ping              Send echo messages
  ppp               Start IETF Point-to-Point Protocol (PPP)
  pwd               Display current working directory
  reload            Halt and perform a cold restart
```

```
rename          Rename a file
restart         Restart Connection
resume          Resume an active network connection
rlogin          Open an rlogin connection
rsh             Execute a remote command
sdlc            Send SDLC test frames
send            Send a message to other tty lines
setup           Run the SETUP command facility
show            Show running system information
slip            Start Serial-line IP (SLIP)
squeeze         Squeeze a filesystem
ssh             Open a secure shell client connection
start-chat      Start a chat-script on a line
systat          Display information about terminal lines
tclquit         Quit Tool Comand Language  shell
tclsh           Tool Comand Language a shell
telnet          Open a telnet connection
terminal        Set terminal line parameters
test            Test subsystems, memory, and interfaces
traceroute      Trace route to destination
tunnel          Open a tunnel connection
udptn           Open an udptn connection
undebug         Disable debugging functions (see also 'debug')
upgrade         Upgrade firmware
verify          Verify a file
voice           Voice Commands
where           List active connections
write           Write running configuration to memory, network, or terminal
x28             Become an X.28 PAD
x3              Set X.3 parameters on PAD
```

Observe that many more commands are available in privileged EXEC mode than in user EXEC mode. However, the `password` command is still not listed because the IOS is not yet in line configuration mode. So, next you need to execute the `configure terminal` command to transition the IOS into global configuration mode, run `line console 0` to transition the IOS into line configuration mode, and run the `?` help command again:

```
RT1#? configure terminal (or config t)
Enter configuration commands, one per line.  End with CNTL/Z.
RT1(config)#line console 0
RT1(config-line)#?
Line configuration commands:
  absolute-timeout        Set absolute timeout for line disconnection
  access-class            Filter connections based on an IP access list
  activation-character    Define the activation character
  autocommand             Automatically execute an EXEC command
  autocommand-options     Autocommand options
  autohangup              Automatically hangup when last connection closes
  autoselect              Set line to autoselect
  buffer-length           Set DMA buffer length
  data-character-bits     Size of characters being handled
  databits                Set number of data bits per character
  default                 Set a command to its defaults
  disconnect-character    Define the disconnect character
  dispatch-character      Define the dispatch character
  dispatch-machine        Reference a TCP dispatch state machine
  dispatch-timeout        Set the dispatch timer
  domain-lookup           Enable domain lookups in show commands
  editing                 Enable command line editing
```

```
escape-character         Change the current line's escape character
exec                     Configure EXEC
exec-banner              Enable the display of the EXEC banner
exec-character-bits      Size of characters to the command exec
exec-timeout             Set the EXEC timeout
exit                     Exit from line configuration mode
flowcontrol              Set the flow control
flush-at-activation      Clear input stream at activation
full-help                Provide help to unprivileged user
help                     Description of the interactive help system
history                  Enable and control the command history function
hold-character           Define the hold character
insecure                 Mark line as 'insecure' for LAT
international            Enable international 8-bit character support
ip                       IP options
ipv6                     IPv6 options
length                   Set number of lines on a screen
location                 Enter terminal location description
lockable                 Allow users to lock a line
logging                  Modify message logging facilities
login                    Enable password checking
logout-warning           Set Warning countdown for absolute timeout of
                         line
modem                    Configure the Modem Control Lines
monitor                  Copy debug output to the current terminal line
motd-banner              Enable the display of the MOTD banner
no                       Negate a command or set its defaults
notify                   Inform users of output from concurrent sessions
ntp                      Configure NTP
padding                  Set padding for a specified output character
parity                   Set terminal parity
password                 Set a password
private                  Configuration options that user can set will
                         remain in effect between terminal sessions
privilege                Change privilege level for line
refuse-message           Define a refuse banner
rotary                   Add line to a rotary group
rxspeed                  Set the receive speed
script                   specify event related chat scripts to run on the
                         line
session-disconnect-warning  Set warning countdown for session-timeout
session-limit            Set maximum number of sessions
session-timeout          Set interval for closing connection when there is
                         no input traffic
special-character-bits   Size of the escape (and other special) characters
speed                    Set the transmit and receive speeds
start-character          Define the start character
stop-character           Define the stop character
stopbits                 Set async line stop bits
telnet                   Telnet protocol-specific configuration
terminal-type            Set the terminal type
timeout                  Timeouts for the line
transport                Define transport protocols for line
txspeed                  Set the transmit speeds
vacant-message           Define a vacant banner
width                    Set width of the display terminal
x25                      X25 protocol-specific configuration
```

Now the `password` command shows up in the command listing.

Anytime you are unsure about which IOS command-line mode is required to execute a specific command, you can use the Cisco IOS contextual help system to find out. Follow these steps:

1. **Run the ? help command in user EXEC mode.**

You can run the command in user EXEC mode if it shows up in the list returned by the ? help command at the user EXEC prompt.

2. **If the command does not show up in the list, set the IOS in privileged EXEC mode by executing `enable` at the user EXEC prompt and run the ? help command again.**

You can run the command in privileged EXEC mode if it shows up in the list returned by the ? help command at the privileged EXEC prompt.

3. **If the command still does not show up in the list, set the IOS in privileged EXEC, global configuration mode by running `configure terminal` at the privileged EXEC prompt and run the ? help command again.**

You can run the command in privileged EXEC, global configuration mode if it shows up in the list returned by the ? help command at the privileged EXEC, global configuration mode prompt.

4. **If the command still does not show up in the list, it may be a command that requires selecting a particular component to work with, such as interfaces or access lines, as in previous examples:**

a. Set the IOS in privileged EXEC, specific configuration mode by selecting the component or the range of components to work with (using, for example, the `interface` or the `line` command).

b. Run the ? help command again. The command should show up in the help list.

If the command doesn't appear, double-check the component selection command: Make sure that you use the `interface` command if you're working with interfaces; make sure that you use the `line` command if you're working with access lines.

Listing command arguments

You can list available command arguments by typing ? after the command verb at the IOS prompt. It's important to understand that arguments you see in the help list are contextual. Here's an example:

```
RT1>enable (or en)
RT1#? configure terminal (or config t)
Enter configuration commands, one per line.  End with CNTL/Z.
RT1(config)#line ?
  <0-70>   First Line number
```

```
aux       Auxiliary line
console   Primary terminal line
tty       Terminal controller
vty       Virtual terminal
x/y       Slot/Port for Modems

RT1(config)#line aux ?
  <0-0>   First Line number

RT1(config)#line console ?
  <0-0>   First Line number

RT1(config)#line tty ?
  <1-64> First Line number

RT1(config)#line vty ?
  <1-15> First Line number
```

Observe that `line` ? lists available keywords for the first argument of the `line` command. Next, you list available keywords for the second argument of the `line` command using the `line` *<first_arg>* ? help command. The available keywords for the second argument of the `line` command depend on the first argument:

✦ `aux`: Only one auxiliary port exists on this Cisco device, so you can only enter 0 for the second argument when the first argument is `aux`. Hence, `line aux` ? reports <0-0>.

✦ `console`: Only one console port exists on this Cisco device, so you can only enter 0 for the second argument when the first argument is `console`. Hence, `line console` ? reports <0-0>.

✦ `tty`: This Cisco device has 65 TTY access lines, so you can enter a number between 0 and 64 for the second argument when the first argument is `tty`. Hence, `line tty` ? reports <0-64>.

✦ `vty`: This Cisco device has 16 VTY access lines, so you can enter a number between 0 and 15 for the second argument when the first argument is `vty`. Hence, `line vty` ? reports <0-15>.

You can also find out the characteristics of the Cisco device you're working on using the contextual help command. In the previous example, you found out how many TTY and VTY access lines are available on the Cisco device. If the Cisco device had more VTY access lines, help would report that. For example, if your Cisco device had 128 VTY access lines, the `line vty` ? help command would report <0-127>.

Cisco IOS graphical user interface (GUI)

The following sections describe the Cisco IOS GUIs. You find out about the Cisco Device Manager, the Cisco Network Assistant, and about the Cisco Security Device Manager.

Cisco Device Manager

The Cisco Device Manager is a Web-based tool that is installed on all Cisco switches and routers at the factory. To access this tool, you need to browse to the management IP address of the Cisco switch or router from a computer host connected to the network. The Cisco Device Manager Web application is part of the Cisco IOS software package and is stored in the Cisco device's flash memory.

To load the Cisco Device Manager, open a Web browser on a computer that has network access to your switch or router and browse to the management IP address of the switch or router, as shown in Figure 10-1.

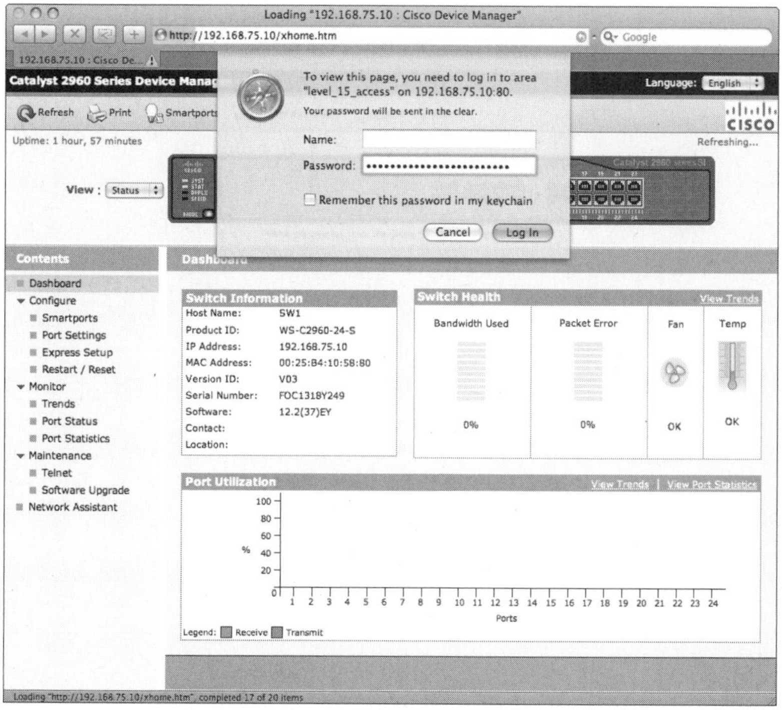

Figure 10-1:
Cisco Device Manager login.

Observe that you may need to log in to your switch or router with level_15_ access (privileged access) to monitor and configure the device, if you already set a privileged mode password. If you did not yet set a privileged mode password on your switch or router, you do not see this login prompt: The device is not yet secure; you can log in without a password.

After you are logged in, you are looking at the dashboard. Figure 10-2 illustrates the dashboard view of a Cisco Catalyst 2960 switch.

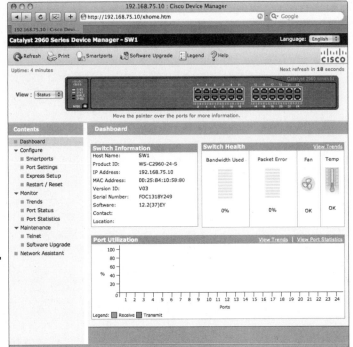

Figure 10-2:
Cisco
Device
Manager
dashboard.

You see a view of your switch. Ports that are up and connected show up in green, as does port FastEthernet0/1, shortly known as fa0/1 (port 1 in Figure 10-2). The dashboard shows information about the switch, switch health, and port utilization data. The left side of the screen is reserved for the Contents menu.

The Smartports and Port Settings items allow you to configure the ports of the switch. Figure 10-3 illustrates the Port Settings form. All ports are enabled by default. All ports autonegotiate speed and transmission duplex mode.

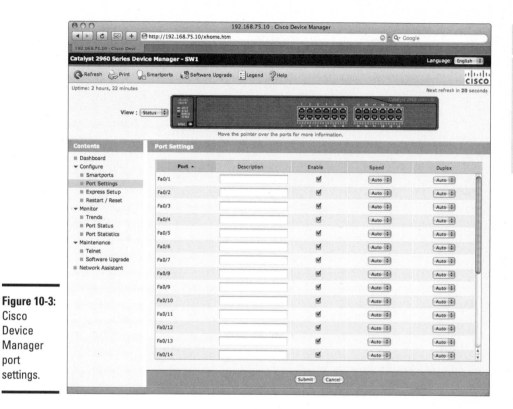

Figure 10-3:
Cisco
Device
Manager
port
settings.

The Port Settings Web form allows you to configure the ports on your
switch. For each port you can do the following:

✦ **Enter a description:** This is a short comment that describes the purpose of
the port. For example, "Connects to computer host Claire" or "Connects
to switch SW2."

✦ **Enable the port:** All ports are enabled by default.

✦ **Configure the speed:** The speed is automatically negotiated by default.
You would only need to configure it to a specific value if you connect the
port to a device that cannot automatically negotiate the transmission
speed.

✦ **Configure the duplex mode:** The transmission duplex mode is
automatically negotiated by default. You would only need to configure
it to a specific value if you connect the port to a device that cannot
automatically negotiate the transmission duplex mode.

Figure 10-4 illustrates the Express Setup menu and the corresponding
Express Setup Web form.

Figure 10-4: Cisco Device Manager Express Setup menu.

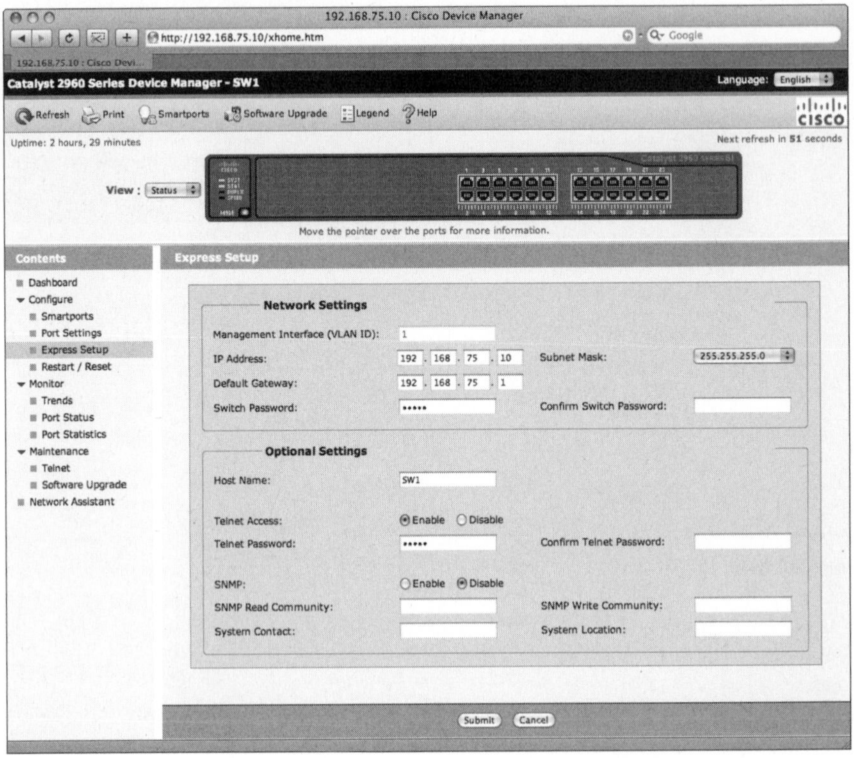

The Express Setup Web form allows you to initially configure your switch. Observe that the form already displays values in Figure 10-4. This switch has already been set up. You can use the Express Setup Web form to change the basic setup of the switch. Keep in mind that changing the network settings can affect your ability to connect to the Cisco Device Manager on the switch. You read more about Express Setup in Book III, Chapter 2.

Figure 10-5 illustrates the Restart/Reset menu and the corresponding Restart/Reset Web form.

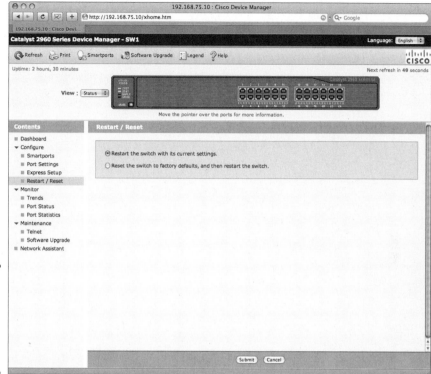

Figure 10-5:
Cisco
Device
Manager
Restart/
Reset menu.

The Restart/Reset Web form allows you to

✦ **Restart the switch:** This is restarting the switch with the current
configuration.

✦ **Reset the switch:** This is resetting the switch to the default factory
configuration and restarting the switch with the default settings.

Figure 10-6 illustrates the Port Status menu and the corresponding Port
Status Web form.

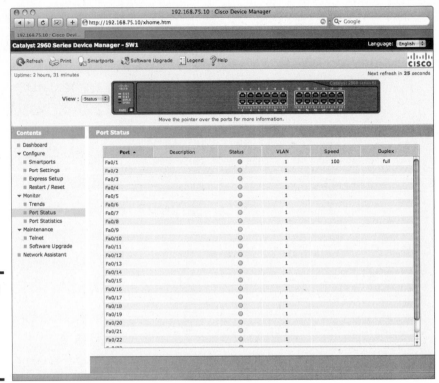

Figure 10-6:
Cisco
Device
Manager
Port Status
menu.

The Port Status Web form allows you to monitor the current state of the switch ports. You can monitor the following:

+ **Port description:** This is a short comment that describes the purpose of the port.

+ **Ports status:** This is solid green if the port is up; it is solid grey otherwise.

+ **Port VLAN:** The VLAN to which the port belongs. Access ports belong to a single given VLAN (virtual local-area network): They carry traffic only for that VLAN. Trunk ports do not belong to any VLAN: They carry traffic for all VLANs. You find out more about VLANs in Book III, Chapter 5.

+ **Port speed:** The maximum bandwidth supported by the port.

+ **Port duplex mode:** The current transmission duplex mode of the port.

Figure 10-7 illustrates the Telnet menu and the corresponding Telnet Web form.

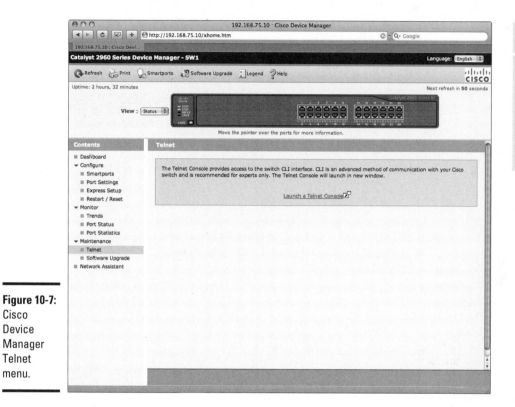

Figure 10-7:
Cisco
Device
Manager
Telnet
menu.

The Telnet Web form allows you to open a Telnet session to log in at the command-line prompt of your switch using one of the virtual type terminal (VTY) access lines. Clicking the Launch a Telnet Console link launches the default Telnet client application on your computer, opening a Telnet session to the IP address of your switch.

Figure 10-8 illustrates the Software Upgrade menu and the corresponding Software Upgrade Web form.

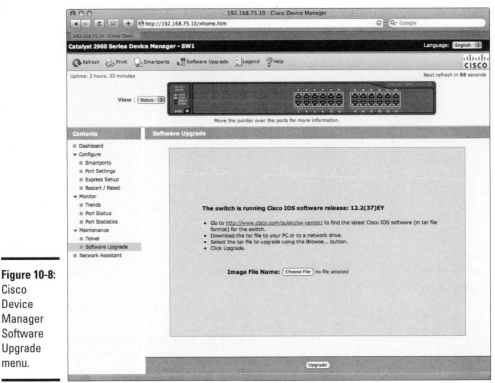

Figure 10-8:
Cisco
Device
Manager
Software
Upgrade
menu.

The Software Upgrade Web form allows you to upgrade the Cisco Internetwork Operating System (IOS) installed on your switch. Here is the procedure you need to follow to upgrade the IOS on your switch:

1. **Click the** `http://www.cisco.com/public/sw-center/` **link to access the latest version of the Cisco IOS on Cisco's Web site.**

2. **Download the Cisco IOS image (tar file) to your computer hard drive.**

3. **Click the Choose File button and browse to the location where you saved the Cisco IOS image (tar file) on your computer hard drive.**

4. **Select the Cisco IOS image (tar file).**

5. **Click the Upgrade button to upgrade the Cisco IOS on your switch with the Cisco IOS image file you just downloaded to your computer.**

Cisco Network Assistant (CNA)

The Cisco Network Assistant, shortly known as CNA, is a Java-based software application used to monitor and manage Cisco switches and routers from a central management console. CNA is available for Windows, Mac OS X, and Linux. It provides a graphical user interface (GUI), allowing the network administrator to have both global and detailed views of the Cisco networking environment. CNA is stored on the hard drive of the computer host where it is installed.

Although CNA monitors and manages both Cisco switches and Cisco routers, it is intended more for switches than for routers. Routers are typically monitored and managed using either the Cisco SDM (Security Device Manager) tool or the Cisco SDM Express tool.

You download the CNA software package from the Cisco Web site (www. cisco.com). CNA is provided for free by Cisco. The Cisco Device Manager Web application provides a direct link to the CNA software package download site at Cisco.com, as illustrated in Figure 10-9.

Figure 10-9:
CNA
download
link in Cisco
Device
Manager.

Figure 10-10 illustrates the CNA Connect Web form.

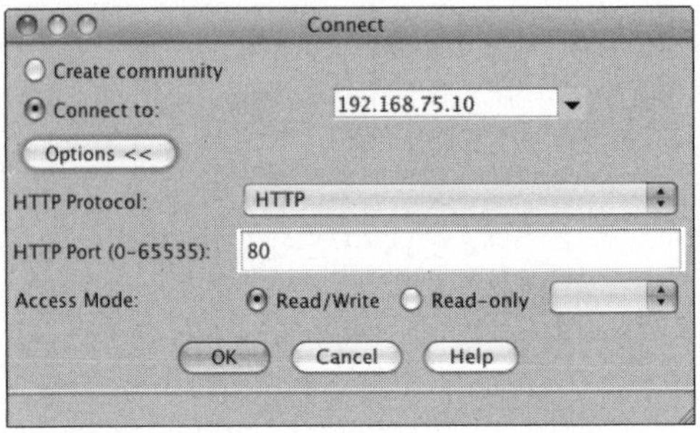

Figure 10-10:
CNA
Connect
form.

You need to enter the host name or IP address of the switch or router you want to connect to. Observe that you can specify the HTTP port used for this connection. The HTTP port is configurable on Cisco switches and routers. You can connect only to monitor the configuration of the device (*read-only* connection) or to monitor and change the configuration of the device (*read/write* connection).

Figure 10-11 illustrates the CNA login Web form.

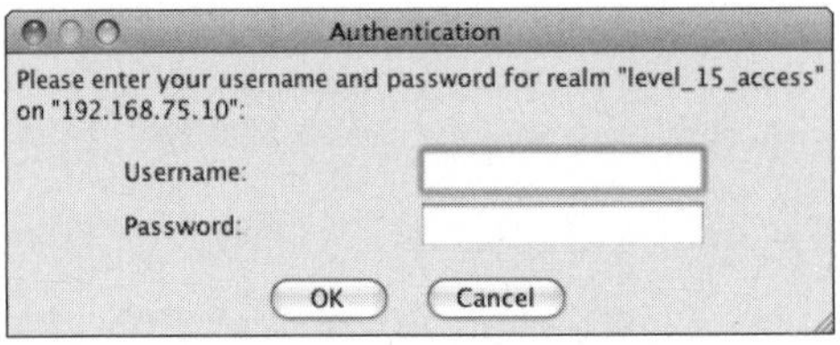

Figure 10-11:
CNA login
form.

You need to enter a username and password that give you level_15_access to the switch or router configuration. Permission level_15_access allows you to run commands in privileged EXEC mode. You can leave the username blank and enter the privileged EXEC password that you set on your switch or router. If you did not set a privileged EXEC password yet on your switch or router, leave both the username and the password blank and click the OK button.

Figure 10-12 illustrates the CNA Topology View.

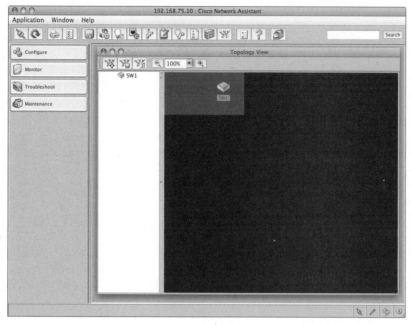

Figure 10-12:
CNA
Topology
View.

You see a view of switch SW1 in this example. If the switch were interconnected to other switches, routers, or computer hosts, you would see them as well in the topology view. The topology view is very useful because it provides a global view of your Cisco network.

Figure 10-13 illustrates the CNA Configure menu.

You use the CNA Configure menu and Web forms to configure any device in your Cisco network. The items on the CNA Configure menu vary according to the device you select in the topology view.

Figure 10-14 illustrates the CNA Monitor menu.

You use the CNA Monitor menu and Web forms to monitor various items in your Cisco network. The items on the CNA Monitor menu vary according to the device you select in the topology view. You can monitor devices using the Inventory menu. You can view port statistics using the Port Statistics menu. Bandwidth graphs provide a graphical representation of the bandwidth usage on Cisco devices in your network. You can also monitor access control lists (ACL Reports) and the Address Resolution Protocol (ARP).

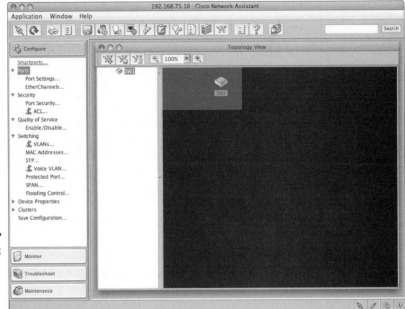

Figure 10-13:
CNA
Configure
menu.

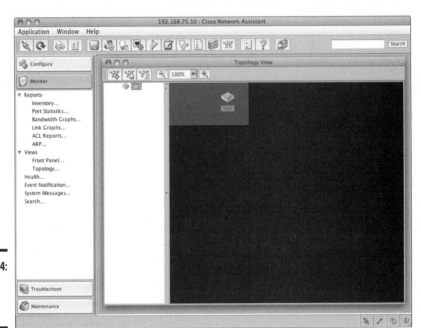

Figure 10-14:
CNA
Monitor
menu.

Figure 10-15 illustrates the CNA Troubleshoot menu.

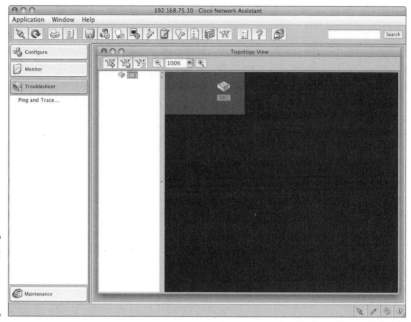

Figure 10-15:
CNA
Troubleshoot
menu.

You use the CNA Troubleshoot menu and Web forms to troubleshoot various items in your Cisco network. The items on the CNA Troubleshoot menu vary according to the device you select in the topology view. The most widely used troubleshooting tool in this menu is by far the Ping and Trace tool.

Figure 10-16 illustrates the CNA Maintenance menu.

You use the CNA Maintenance menu and Web forms to maintain your Cisco network. The items on the CNA Maintenance menu vary according to the device you select in the topology view.

Here is a summary of the options available for Cisco switches and routers:

✦ **Software Upgrade:** Upgrade the Cisco IOS software on Cisco switches and routers in your network.

✦ **File Management:** Manage the Cisco IOS software image files on Cisco switches and routers in your network.

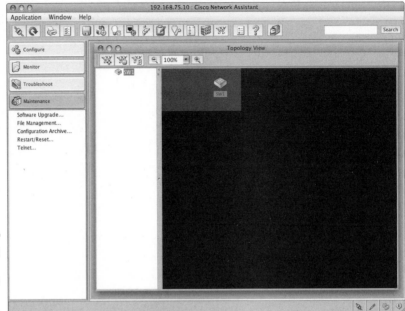

Figure 10-16:
CNA
Maintenance
menu.

+ **Configuration Archive:** Back up the Cisco IOS software image files of your Cisco switches and routers to a configuration archive. Manage the Cisco configuration archive.

+ **Restart/Reset:** Reboot the Cisco device currently selected in the topology view. Restart reboots the Cisco device, keeping the current startup configuration. Reset resets the Cisco device to factory-default configuration and reboots it.

+ **Telnet:** Open a Telnet session to the Cisco device currently selected in the topology view.

Cisco Router and Security Device Manager (SDM)

The Cisco Router and Security Device Manager (SDM) is a computer application used to monitor and manage Cisco routers from a central management computer host. Cisco SDM is available for Windows. It provides a graphical user interface (GUI) that allows network administrators to have both global and detailed views of the Cisco routing environment.

The Cisco Router and Security Device Manager (SDM) is comprised of the following:

- ✦ **Cisco SDM server:** The Cisco SDM server is a microapplication stored in flash memory on recent Cisco routers. It provides information about the router to the Cisco SDM client. It also executes commands on the router as requested by the Cisco SDM client.

- ✦ **Cisco SDM client:** The Cisco SDM client connects and authenticates to the Cisco SDM server on a router from a remote computer host to gather information about the router and to run commands on the router. The Cisco SDM client is a Windows software application. You install the Cisco SDM client on a PC. After it is installed, the Cisco SDM client is stored and loaded from the hard drive of that PC.

Installing the Cisco SDM client on a PC

The Cisco SDM client Windows installation package is available in the following ways:

- ✦ **Cisco Router and Security Device Manager CD:** This CD is shipped with all recent Cisco routers.

- ✦ **Cisco Web site:** You can download the Cisco SDM client software package from Cisco's Web site (www.cisco.com).

To install the Cisco SDM client on your PC, double-click the Cisco SDM client Windows installation package.

The Cisco SDM Installation Wizard prompts you whether you want to install Cisco SDM on your computer, on the router, or both on the computer and on the router, as shown in Figure 10-17.

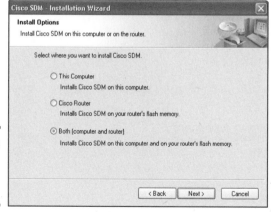

Figure 10-17: SDM installation destination.

If your router has the Cisco SDM (server) package already installed in flash memory, you do not need to install SDM on the router; you install it only on your computer.

Next, if you chose to install the Cisco SDM (server) package on your router, the Installation Wizard prompts you to authenticate to the router. The installation wizard needs to authenticate with a level_15_access (privileged) access level to the router to be able to install the SDM server microapplication in the flash memory of the destination router. You need to enter the router's IP address, and the username and password of a user that has a level_15_ access (privileged) permission level to the router, as shown in Figure 10-18.

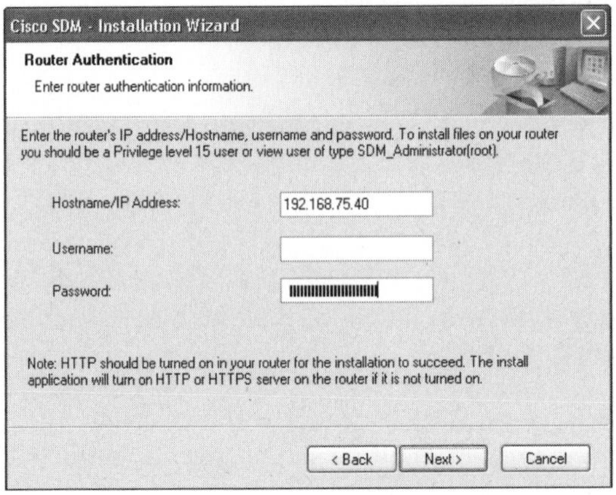

Figure 10-18:
SDM server
destination
router login.

Now, the Cisco SDM Installation Wizard prompts you to specify a default router to which it connects. The SDM client connects and authenticates to the default router to gather information about the router and the network and to run commands on the router. The default target router runs the SDM server microapplication.

Figure 10-19 shows the default target router selection.

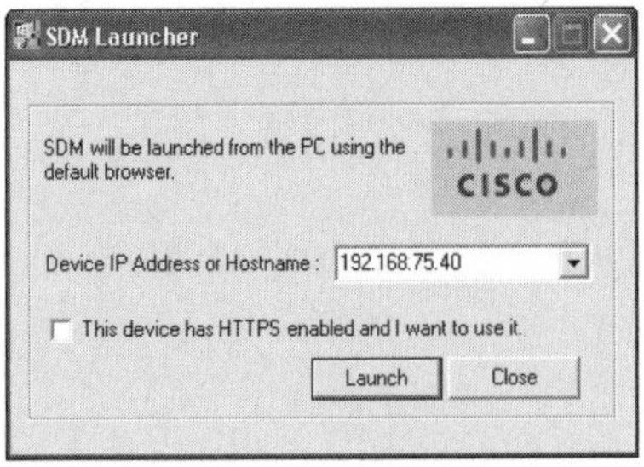

Figure 10-19:
SDM target
router
selection.

Next, the Installation Wizard prompts you to authenticate to the target router. You need to specify a user that has a level_15_access (privileged) permission level on the target router. The SDM client authenticates to the target router using the level_15_access (privileged) access level to gather information about the router and the network and to run commands on the router.

Figure 10-20 shows the default target router login.

Figure 10-20:
SDM target
router login.

The Cisco SDM Installation Wizard now displays a progress screen, as shown in Figure 10-21. This screen informs you that SDM is loading and shows the version of SDM (V 2.5 in this case) and the IP address of the default target router (192.168.75.40 in this case).

In some cases, Cisco SDM may prompt you to authenticate again to the target router, as shown in Figure 10-22. Similar to Figure 10-20, you need to specify a user that has a level_15_access (privileged) permission level on the default target router.

Cisco SDM is supported by most Cisco routers, except older models, such as the Cisco 2600 series. If SDM does not support your router, you see an "Unsupported Router" message, as shown in Figure 10-23.

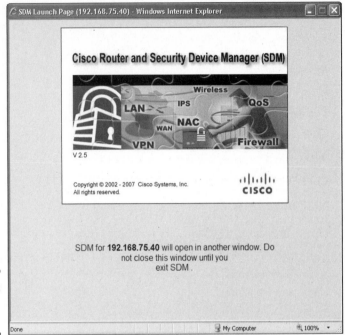

Figure 10-21:
SDM
loading.

Figure 10-22:
SDM target
router
second
login.

Figure 10-23:
SDM
unsupported
router.

Launching the Cisco SDM client on a PC

To launch the Cisco Router and Security Device Manager (SDM) on a Windows computer host, follow these steps:

1. **Choose Start.**

2. **Select All Programs.**

3. **Choose Cisco Systems⇨Cisco SDM⇨Cisco SDM.**

   SDM prompts you to select the target router. Refer to Figure 10-19.

4. **Enter the IP address of the target router.**

5. **Click the Launch button.**

   SDM prompts you twice to authenticate to the target router. You need to specify a user that has a level_15_access (privileged) permission level on the default target router. Refer to Figures 10-20 and 10-22.

6. **Enter the username and password of a user that has a level_15_access (privileged) access to your target router.**

7. **Click the OK button.**

   SDM displays its welcome (Home) screen, as shown in Figure 10-24.

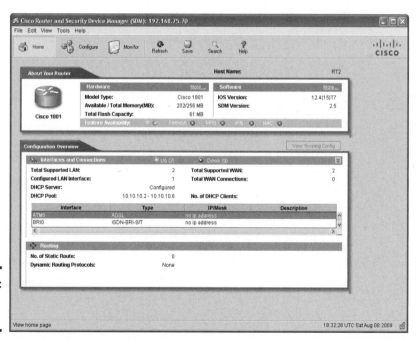

Figure 10-24:
SDM Home
screen.

The SDM Home screen displays basic information about your target router. SDM offers two modes of operation:

✦ **Configure:** Observe the Configure button on the SDM toolbar. You can configure your target router using the configure operation mode.

✦ **Monitor:** Observe the *Monitor* button on the SDM toolbar. You can monitor your target router using the monitor operation mode.

Using SDM, you can configure the following features on your target router:

✦ Interfaces and connections

✦ Firewall and ACLs (access control lists)

✦ VPN (Virtual Private Network)

✦ Security audit

✦ Routing

✦ NAT (Network Address Translation)

✦ Intrusion prevention

✦ QoS (quality of service)

✦ NAC (Network Admission Control)

You configure these features by clicking the corresponding button in the vertical toolbar shown in Figure 10-25. This opens the corresponding configuration forms and wizards in the right pane of the screen. Figure 10-25 shows the SDM Interfaces and Connections configuration form.

Using SDM, you can monitor the following features on your target router:

✦ Overview status of your router

✦ Interface status

✦ Firewall status

✦ VPN status

✦ Traffic status

✦ QoS (quality of service) status

✦ NAC (Network Admission Control) status

✦ Logging status

✦ IPS (intrusion prevention system) status

✦ 802.1x authentication status

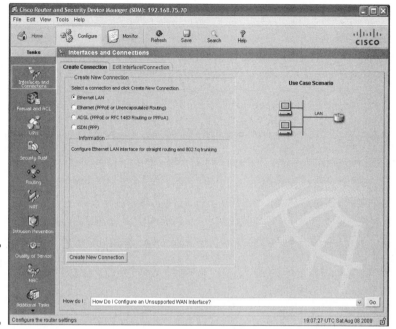

Figure 10-25:
SDM
Configure
screen.

You monitor these features by clicking the corresponding button in the vertical toolbar shown in Figure 10-26. This opens the corresponding monitoring form in the right pane of the screen. Figure 10-26 shows the SDM Interface Status monitoring form.

Cisco Router and Security Device Manager Express (SDM Express)

Cisco replaced the Cisco Device Manager with an *Express* version of the Cisco Router and Security Device Manager (SDM) on more recent routers. When you browse to the management IP address of more recent routers, you launch the Cisco SDM Express software application. The Cisco SDM Express software application is comprised of the following:

✦ **Cisco SDM server:** The Cisco SDM server is a microapplication stored in flash memory on recent Cisco routers. It provides information about the router to the Cisco SDM client. It also executes commands on the router as requested by the Cisco SDM client.

✦ **Cisco SDM Express Web-based client:** The Cisco SDM Express Web-based client connects and authenticates to the Cisco SDM server on a router from a Web browser on a remote computer host to gather information about the router and to run commands on the router. The Cisco SDM Express client is a Java-based, Web-based software application. You do not need to install the Cisco SDM Express client on your PC. The Web browser on your PC loads the Cisco SDM Express client automatically when you browse to the IP address of a router that supports the Cisco SDM Express client.

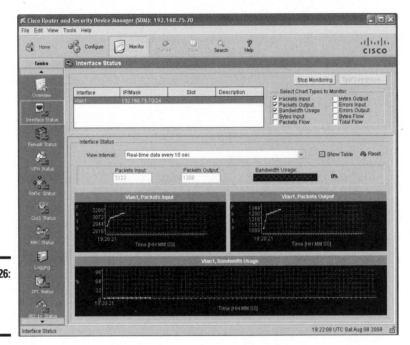

Figure 10-26:
SDM
Monitor
screen.

To launch the Cisco Router and Security Device Manager (SDM) Express edition on a Windows computer host, browse to the management IP address of the target router and follow these steps:

1. **Log in to your router by entering the username and password of a user that has level_15_access (privileged) access to your target router.**

SDM Express prompts you to authenticate to the target router. You need to specify a user that has a level_15_access (privileged) permission level on the default target router. Cisco provides a level_15_access (privileged) user named cisco, identified by password cisco. You can use this user to log in to your router. This user is intended to be a temporary user: Cisco allows you to log in only once using cisco/cisco. You need to create your own level_15_access (privileged) user for ongoing router management. Refer to Figure 10-27.

2. **Click the OK button.**

Figure 10-27:
SDM
Express
login.

The Cisco SDM Express client displays a progress screen, as shown in
Figure 10-28. This screen informs you that SDM Express is loading and shows
the version of SDM (V 2.5 in this case) and the IP address of the default
target router (192.168.75.70 in this case).

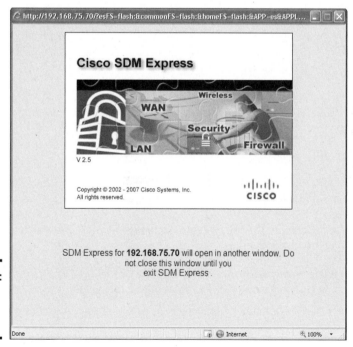

Figure 10-28:
SDM
Express
loading.

SDM Express displays its welcome (Overview) screen, as shown in Figure 10-29.

Figure 10-29: SDM Express Overview screen.

The SDM Express Overview screen displays basic information about the following:

+ Your target router

+ The router's LAN (local-area network)

+ The router's WAN (wide-area network)

You can perform the following tasks using the SDM Express router management application:

+ **Basic configuration:** Observe the Basic Configuration item on the Tasks menu, as shown in Figure 10-30. The Basic Configuration form is used to

 • Create a management user (in this example, Admin007)

 • Set a privileged encrypted password (secret password)

 • Set the host name of your router

 • Set the domain name of your router

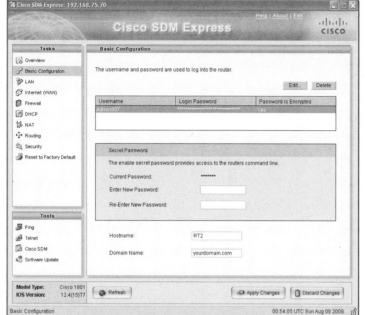

Figure 10-30:
SDM
Express
Basic
Configuration
form.

✦ **LAN configuration:** Observe the LAN item on the Tasks menu. The LAN form, shown in Figure 10-31, is used to configure the following:

- The IP address of Ethernet interfaces on your router (in this example, interface Vlan1 is configured with IP 102.168.75.70)

- The subnet mask of Ethernet interfaces on your router (in this example, interface Vlan1 is configured with subnet mask 255.255.255.0)

✦ **WAN configuration:** Observe the Internet (WAN) item on the Tasks menu. The Internet (WAN) form, shown in Figure 10-32, is used to configure interfaces to WANs (wide-area networks). Routers typically serve as gateways from a LAN into WANs. You configure your WAN links on this form. In this example, you can configure ATM and ADSL WAN links.

✦ **Firewall configuration:** Observe the Firewall item on the Tasks menu. The Firewall form is used to configure firewall rules to filter incoming and outgoing IP packets.

✦ **DHCP (Dynamic Host Configuration Protocol) configuration:** Observe the DHCP item on the Tasks menu. The DHCP form, shown in Figure 10-33, is used to configure the starting and ending IP addresses that can be assigned by your router to DHCP clients. A *DHCP client* is a computer host device or a network device that does not have an assigned IP address; the device requests an IP address from your router.

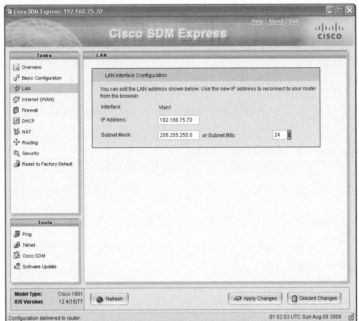

Figure 10-31:
SDM
Express LAN
configuration.

Figure 10-32:
SDM
Express
WAN
configuration.

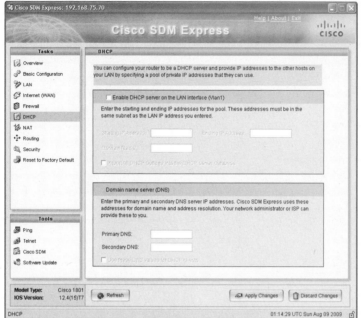

Figure 10-33:
SDM
Express
DHCP
configuration.

✦ **NAT configuration:** Observe the NAT item on the Tasks menu. The NAT form is used to configure Network Address Translation to translate public WAN IP addresses into local private LAN IP addresses.

✦ **Static routing configuration:** Observe the Routing item on the Tasks menu. The Routing form, shown in Figure 10-34, is used to configure default static routes to other networks. Routers exchange information about networks they know; this is *dynamic routing.* However, you can specify a default route that your router can use to get to other networks. Default routes can be specified over any interface on your router. In other words, you connect that interface to another network, and then you enter the *static route* information in the Routing form in SDM Express.

✦ **Security configuration:** Observe the Security item on the Tasks menu, as shown in Figure 10-35. The Security form is used to

• Disable services that can pose security risks

• Enable services that enhance security on your router

• Encrypt passwords

• Synchronize your router's clock to an external reference clock

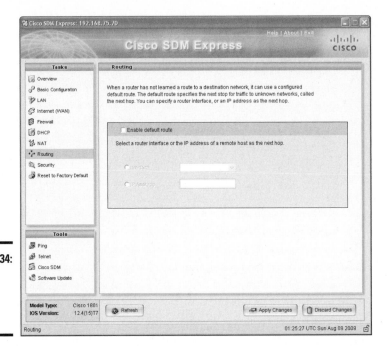

Figure 10-34:
SDM
Express
static
routing.

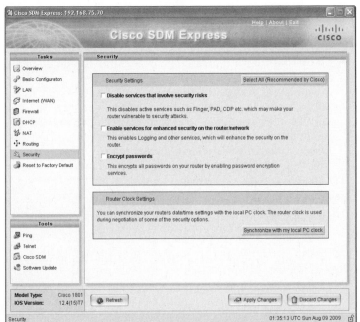

Figure 10-35:
SDM
Express
security
configuration.

✦ **Reset to factory default:** The Reset to Factory Default form allows you to do the following:

- Save the current running configuration of your router to a file on your computer host. Before you reset your router to factory default settings, you may want to save the current configuration to a file. You can reload this configuration from the file, later on, if you need to. Think of this as a safety net: It's risky to reset a router. You may lose valuable configuration data. You should save the current configuration in a file, just in case.

- Reset the router to factory default settings. Click the Reset Router button to reset the router.

The SDM Express router management application offers the following tools (refer to the lower-left corner of Figure 10-36):

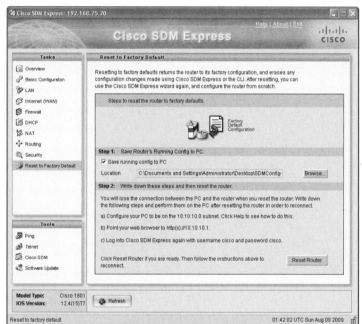

Figure 10-36:
SDM
Express
Reset to
Factory
Default
form.

✦ **Verify connectivity to another device in the network (Ping):** Observe the Ping item on the Tools menu. The Ping form is used to verify connectivity to other computer host devices and network devices in the network.

✦ **Open a Telnet session to your router from the computer host (Telnet):**
Observe the Telnet item on the Tools menu.

✦ **Launch the Cisco SDM management application (Cisco SDM):** Observe
the Cisco SDM item on the Tools menu. You can launch the full version of
Cisco SDM from SDM Express using the Cisco SDM tool in SDM Express.

✦ **Update the software on your Cisco router (Software Update):** You can
use this tool to update the software on your router. You can update the
software by applying updates to the router memory

- From Cisco's Web site (www.cisco.com)

- From your computer host (local PC)

- From a CD

Prep Test

1 What is the Cisco IOS?

   A ○ Cisco's proprietary switch and router operating system

   B ○ Cisco's proprietary Web-based switch and router network management system

   C ○ Cisco's proprietary switch and router memory routing protocol

   D ○ Cisco's proprietary Web-based switch and router device management software application

2 What is the Cisco Device Manager?

   A ○ Cisco's proprietary switch and router operating system

   B ○ Cisco's proprietary Web-based switch and router network management system

   C ○ Cisco's proprietary switch and router memory routing protocol

   D ○ Cisco's proprietary Web-based switch and router device management software application

3 When does the power-on self test (POST) run?

   A ○ Immediately after the Cisco IOS loads on a switch or router

   B ○ Immediately after the startup configuration loads on a switch or router

   C ○ Immediately after the flash memory is initialized on a switch or router

   D ○ Immediately after a Cisco switch or router is powered up

4 What is the main purpose of the bootstrap program, also known as the boot loader?

   A ○ To bring up a Cisco switch or router by loading the startup configuration from flash memory to RAM

   B ○ To bring up a Cisco switch or router by loading the Cisco IOS from flash memory to RAM

   C ○ To bring up a Cisco switch or router by loading the running configuration from flash memory to RAM

   D ○ To bring up a Cisco switch or router by loading the Cisco Device Manager from flash memory to RAM

5 **What is the main purpose of the ROM Monitor microprogram, also known as ROMMON?**

A ○ To maintain, test, and troubleshoot the power consumption of a Cisco device

B ○ To maintain, test, and troubleshoot the console port of a Cisco device

C ○ To maintain, test, and troubleshoot the configuration stored in ROM and in the flash memory of a Cisco device

D ○ To maintain, test, and troubleshoot the ROM port of a Cisco device

6 **It is best practice to use entry-level switches, such as the Cisco Catalyst 3560, at which of the following layers?**

A ○ Access and distribution layer

B ○ Distribution and core layer

C ○ Core layer

D ○ Access and core layer

7 **What does the flash memory on a Cisco switch or router store?**

A ○ The startup configuration of a Cisco switch or router

B ○ The image file of the Cisco IOS

C ○ The Cisco Device Manager software application program

D ○ All of the above

8 **Where is the Cisco switch and router running configuration loaded from?**

A ○ The running configuration file during startup

B ○ Cisco's Web site during startup

C ○ The startup configuration file during startup

D ○ All of the above

9 **The Cisco IOS command-line interface operates in setup mode to do which of the following?**

A ○ Initially configure the ROM Monitor (ROMMON) microprogram

B ○ Initially configure the Cisco Device Manager software application

C ○ Initially configure the IOS

D ○ Initially configure the switch or router

10 **The Cisco IOS command-line interface operates in privileged configuration mode to do which of the following?**

A ○ Configure the ROM Monitor (ROMMON) microprogram

B ○ Configure the Cisco Device Manager software application

C ○ Configure the IOS

D ○ Configure the switch or router

Answers

1 **A.** Cisco's proprietary switch and router operating system. The Cisco IOS is Cisco's proprietary switch and router operating system. Review *"Cisco IOS."*

2 **D.** Cisco's proprietary Web-based switch and router device management software application. The Cisco Device Manager is Cisco's proprietary web-based switch and router device management software application. Check *"Cisco Device Manager."*

3 **D.** Immediately after a Cisco switch or router is powered up. The power-on self test (POST) runs immediately after a Cisco switch or router is powered up. See *"Cisco software in read-only memory (ROM)."*

4 **B.** Bring up a Cisco switch or router by loading the Cisco IOS from Flash memory to RAM. The main purpose of the bootstrap program is bringing up a Cisco switch or router by loading the Cisco IOS from Flash memory to RAM. Review *"Cisco software in read-only memory (ROM)."*

5 **C.** Maintain, test and troubleshoot the configuration stored in ROM and in the Flash memory of a Cisco device. The main purpose of the ROM Monitor micro program is to maintain, test and troubleshoot the configuration stored in ROM and in the Flash memory of a Cisco device. See *"Cisco software in read-only memory (ROM)."*

6 **A.** Access and distribution layer. It is best practice to use entry-level switches at the access and distribution layers. Review *"Best practices for using Cisco hardware products."*

7 **D.** All of the above. The flash memory on a Cisco switch or router stores the startup configuration, the image file of the Cisco IOS, and the Cisco Device Manager software application program. See *"Cisco device memory."*

8 **C.** Is loaded from the startup configuration file during startup. The Cisco switch and router running configuration is loaded from the startup configuration file during startup. Review *"Introducing Cisco Device Configurations."*

9 **D.** Initially configure the switch or router. The Cisco IOS command-line interface operates in setup mode to initially configure the switch or router. Check *"Startup configuration."*

10 **D.** Configure the switch or router. The Cisco IOS command-line interface operates in privileged configuration mode to configure the switch or router. Review *"Meet the Cisco IOS User Interface."*

Book II

TCP/IP

The 5th Wave   By Rich Tennant

TECH SOLUTIONS

Try unplugging it and then plugging it back in.

What kind of money did you use?

We should see the can right down here.

Bobby! What do you know about a Buthel VP 500 vending machine?!

Cola

OPEN

Contents at a Glance

Chapter 1: Introducing TCP/IP

Exam Objectives

✔ Understanding the purpose of TCP/IP

✔ Revealing the components of TCP/IP

✔ Exposing the OSI reference model

✔ Understanding the function of each layer in the OSI model

✔ Examining data encapsulation

✔ Comparing differences in the DoD and OSI models

*I*n almost every aspect of our daily computing lives, we are communicating, researching, and relying on the Internet, a culmination of some of the finest inventions ever conceived. From the humble beginnings of the telephone and telegraph to radio broadcasts and computers, the Internet has allowed us to "get connected." From online banking to online dating, more than 1.5 billion users use this great tool for education and entertainment, conducting business, and connecting globally with others. Just as we use speech and more than 6,800 different languages to transmit thoughts and ideas, this interconnected web of networks also needed its own language for communication. This language is TCP/IP.

Transmission Control Protocol (TCP) and Internet Protocol (IP) are a set of protocols — a standard set of rules that control and enable communication among computers — developed to allow data exchange and sharing of resources across a network. All hosts that speak this same language on the network can understand one another and communicate together. This language, or protocol, defines how messages are formatted and how errors are handled. A networking world without these rules and protocols in place would probably resemble the ancient Tower of Babel.

You must have a strong understanding of TCP/IP protocols, the OSI reference model and its seven layers, and TCP/IP encapsulation methods to do well on the exam. You will see many questions on the test regarding TCP/IP and its suite of protocols. I briefly examine the Open Systems Interconnection (OSI) and DoD (Department of Defense) conceptual models that provide a framework for TCP/IP and other protocols. I also cover the different components of TCP/IP and data encapsulation. For an in-depth review of the TCP/IP layers and protocols, see Book II, Chapter 2.

TCP/IP communication

TCP/IP allows many different operating systems and computer platforms to interoperate with one another seamlessly over a computer network. A computer network is a collection of computers or devices that communicate together over a shared transmission medium. This transmission medium is the physical cabling and network interfaces that direct and support network traffic. And whether you are running Microsoft Windows, Sun Solaris, Ubuntu Linux, Novell Netware, or MAC OS X, TCP/IP will function regardless of operating system or hardware manufacturer type. This allows all of these different entities to interact and understand one another using one language, a great advantage of TCP/IP.

TCP/IP is designed with one major goal in mind; to *decentralize* network communications. If a single node on the network fails, other devices continue to function independently and are uninfluenced by the failed system. Unlike centralized management, this gives nodes an equal share and priority on the network. This is a key feature of TCP/IP. A decentralized network using TCP/IP is enhanced further by using decentralized features of dynamic routing, which you find out more about in Chapters 2 and 3 of Book II.

TCP/IP is based on a defined set of rules for how data communication protocols operate; these rules are defined in the Open Systems Interconnection (OSI) model. This model examines each function of the protocol stack within TCP/IP and computer networking. Actually, TCP/IP may be better defined using the four-layer Department of Defense (DoD) model approach I discuss in the section "TCP/IP in the DoD model," later in this chapter.

We pioneered this

In the late 1960s, the Advanced Research Projects Agency (ARPA) was tasked with finding an efficient means of connecting various computer sites for the purpose of sharing research data. It has been rumored that ARPA began investigating ways of creating this reliable interconnection of remote networks with the sole purpose that these networks would continue to function during, and even withstand, a nuclear attack in wartime scenarios. This is, in fact, a myth. Although network survivability during major losses of the network was highly desired, especially by the U.S. government, ARPA's need for a robust network was more due to unreliable equipment and its connecting links than, say, a nuclear threat.

Combined with valuable experimental research on data transfer technology from laboratories in the United States, France, and the United Kingdom, ARPA successfully created a topology-independent, *packet-switching* network that allowed communication among all types of operating systems and hardware platforms. This open-architectural design of ARPANET would grow over the years to eventually form what we now know as the Internet, an internetworking of networks.

The goal of this new packet-switching network was to optimize traffic load and ensure delivery of data, increasing robustness of communication. The sending computer would assign each packet with a destination address and sequence number, and each block of data could then be routed independently yet still be reassembled in proper order by the receiving node, allowing multiple packets to travel different paths to the desired destination. Reassembly of these packets in the correct sequence would then be processed by the receiving computer.

Splitting data into packets would prove to be much more desirable than *circuit-switching* technology, which transmitted data from source to destination using a dedicated, reserved connection. The inflexible nature of circuit switching would make the line unavailable for other connections until the call was terminated. Messages could be transferred all at once using the entire available bandwidth of the circuit, but the main disadvantage was that no other connection could use the bandwidth until the connection was terminated and a new one established. ARPA would later adopt packet-switching technology as the foundation for ARPANET, with packet-switching proving to be the core method of internetwork communications.

Components of TCP/IP

The following list describes the components that make up the TCP/IP suite:

✦ **Internet Protocol (IP):** The most important, underlying protocol of the TCP/IP suite, *IP* handles data exchange between computers using small data packets called *datagrams,* determining the best route for delivery. Any available path chosen by the datagram may be taken to reach the destination. IP does not handle delivery verification like TCP does and is only concerned with sending and receiving data. Check out Figure 1-1 for an example of IP and TCP packet headers.

✦ **Transmission Control Protocol (TCP):** *TCP* is a connection-oriented protocol responsible for reliable delivery of data between applications, ensuring that data sent by the source machine is received properly by the destination machine. TCP enables the sending of messages from both source and destination machines to communicate connection status and inserts header information into each packet, allowing error-free delivery and checking for unauthorized modification of packet data.

✦ **User Datagram Protocol (UDP):** A *connectionless,* best-effort protocol useful for sending datagrams in any order and without delivery guarantee, assuming that other applications or protocols can handle the required error checking and handshaking. Having less data to transmit, UDP datagrams are smaller and delivered faster than TCP packets, but lack the reliable nature that TCP provides. As you can see in Figure 1-2, UDP does not provide error checking and handshaking as does the more reliable TCP.

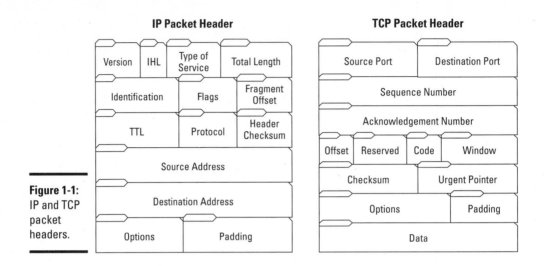

Figure 1-1: IP and TCP packet headers.

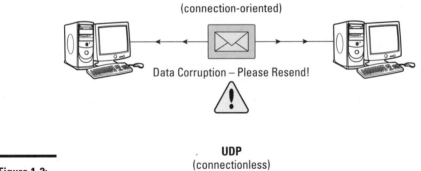

Figure 1-2: TCP versus UDP communications.

✦ **Hypertext Transfer Protocol (HTTP):** The request and response protocol used for Web browsers to transfer files, text, and graphics over the Internet between clients and servers. The client, possibly a home or business user using a Web browser, would initiate a communication request and receive a response from a remote server machine hosting the Internet Web site, establishing a connection through TCP port 80. An HTTP or Web site address starts with the prefix `http://`.

✦ **File Transfer Protocol (FTP):** An application protocol in the TCP/IP stack for transmitting files between network nodes using port 21 for control and port 20 for data. The most common use of FTP is downloading files from the Internet. Thousands of public and private FTP sites exist, allowing restricted or anonymous access to unlimited amounts of data. FTP address syntax is similar to HTTP, using `ftp://` as its convention.

✦ **Telnet:** A client/server protocol using the reliable connection-oriented transport mechanisms of TCP. Telnet sets up nonencrypted data communication between client and server on TCP port 23 and allows local client machines to access remote hosts as if the user were physically sitting at the remote node. In Figure 1-3, you can see an example of Telnet communications. This method of access is vulnerable to data interception by malicious users and lacks secure authentication. *Secure Shell (SSH)* protocol has replaced Telnet in most remote-access environments and provides stronger security and authentication features.

✦ **Domain Name System (DNS):** An Internet naming protocol used for addressing and naming remote computer systems. The DNS lookup process translates commonly used, simple names into long, difficult-to-remember numeric IP addresses (which are stored on DNS servers). This feature eliminates the need for a Web user to remember a Web site's IP address, such as *192.168.176.56.* Instead, DNS allows a user to enter a DNS Web site address (such as *www.sitename.com*) and retrieves the IP address transparently. Check out Figure 1-4 for an explanation of the DNS lookup process.

✦ **Dynamic Host Configuration Protocol (DHCP):** A protocol used for dynamic IP addressing and network configuration of clients issued from a central server. This dramatically reduces administration overhead and allows automatic network configuration to DHCP clients by sending a broadcast message to the DHCP server, requesting issue of a network IP address, subnet mask, DNS server address, default gateway, and other needed data. In Figure 1-5, you can see an example of a DHCP client requesting an IP lease from a DHCP server.

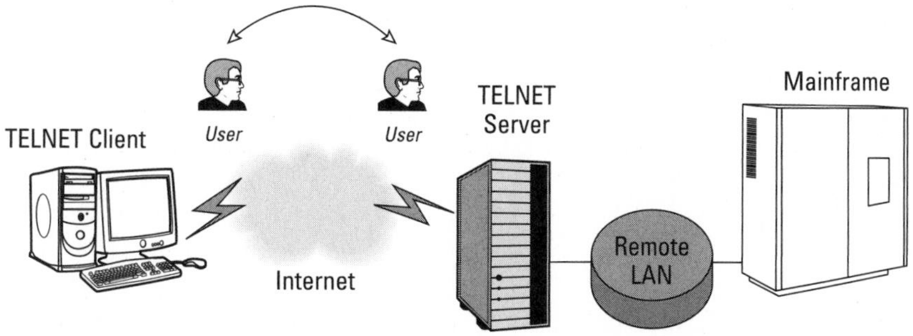

**Book II
Chapter 1**

Introducing TCP/IP

Figure 1-3:
Telnet communi-
cations.

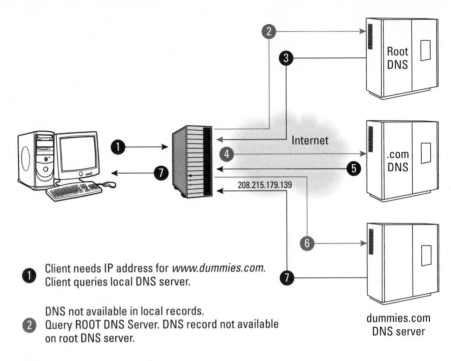

① Client needs IP address for *www.dummies.com*.
Client queries local DNS server.

② DNS not available in local records.
Query ROOT DNS Server. DNS record not available
on root DNS server.

③ Returns DNS address of .com DNS server

④ Local DNS now queries .com DNS Server.
DNS record not available.

Figure 1-4:
Domain
Name
System
lookup.

⑤ Returns DNS address of dummies.com DNS server

⑥ Local DNS contacts dummies.com DNS server,

⑦ Returns IP address for www.dummies.com.

Figure 1-5:
Dynamic
Host
Configuration
Protocol.

DHCP Client

DHCP Server

① DHCP Discover – IP address Request ⟶

② DHCP Offer – IP Address Offer

③ DHCP Request – IP Address Selection ⟶

④ DHCP ACK – IP Address Acknowledgement

✦ **Internet Protocol Security (IPsec):** A security method that uses packet encryption and authentication techniques to secure IP communications. Internet Key Exchange (IKE), Authentication Headers (AHs), and Encapsulating Security Payload (ESP) handle negotiation, authentication, protection, and security duties and are some of the protocols used in this suite.

✦ **Address Resolution Protocol (ARP):** ARP is used to map a host machine's hardware Ethernet MAC address from the host's known IP address. The client sends a request to a remote host asking for resolution of a certain address, and the remote host identifies the required address and returns the query to the client. This is useful for identifying and communicating with Ethernet hosts on a local-area network (LAN).

✦ **Reverse Address Resolution Protocol (RARP):** A protocol that provides the reverse method of finding the IP address from a host's known hardware address.

✦ **Network Time Protocol (NTP):** A protocol that's used by computer systems over IP networks to time-synchronize with each other using a reference time source.

✦ **Open Shortest Path First (OSPF):** A dynamic routing protocol used by routers and network devices to exchange routing information. OSPF exchanges routing information between network devices, with the goal of building a routing map of the entire network. OSPF detects changes in data routes automatically, recognizes link failures, and reroutes traffic to build a loop-free environment.

✦ **Network File System (NFS):** A file-sharing system that allows access to remote data as if it were located on the local host.

✦ **Internet Control Message Protocol (ICMP):** A protocol that provides error and statistic handling for connectivity verification, sending out messages when a datagram is unable to reach its destination. When a gateway or router is unable to forward a datagram, or when a gateway can deliver a datagram on a shorter route, an ICMP message is delivered to the client. This protocol is often used by system administrators who want to verify that routers are sending packets correctly and to the proper destination address. The ICMP `ping` command is used to test whether another host is available over an IP network. This is accomplished by sending an ICMP "echo request" packet to a target interface and waiting for a reply.

✦ **Post Office Protocol 3 (POP3):** A standard protocol for e-mail retrieval from a remote server working on TCP port 110. An e-mail server stores electronic mail messages that can be retrieved all at once by remote systems using e-mail client software. A typical connection lasts long enough to download a user's e-mail and then disconnects while the retrieved e-mail is deleted from the server.

Book II
Chapter 1

Introducing TCP/IP

✦ **Internet Message Access Protocol (IMAP):** Another protocol used for e-mail retrieval on port 143 by remote clients that support both offline and online modes of operation. Unlike POP3, IMAP provides both connected and disconnect modes of operation and allows simultaneous, multiple user access to the same mailbox.

✦ **Simple Mail Transfer Protocol (SMTP):** A protocol for sending messages reliably and efficiently. (POP3 and IMAP are usually considered e-mail *receiving* protocols, while SMTP provides e-mail services typically used for *sending* messages.) Small text commands are used for negotiation and transmission control over a TCP data stream connection.

Introducing the major TCP/IP layers and protocols

Computers and networks also follow a structured model that describes how data flows from one source to another. The Open Systems Interconnection (OSI) reference model describes a set of rules for digital communication between hardware and software.

The OSI reference model

The OSI reference model, shown in Figure 1-6, was designed by the International Organization for Standardization (ISO) and defines how data is moved between a source and destination computer's software applications over a network. Delivering the data using seven conceptual layers defined by the ISO, these layers divide network communications architecture in a top-to-bottom approach. Moving up the OSI model from the bottommost layer to the top, services are *provided* to the next-uppermost layer (by the layer just below it), while services are *received* from the topmost layer to each next-lower layer. Each layer is responsible for a specific, exclusive set of functions not handled at any other layer.

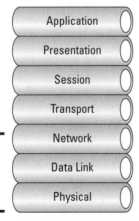

Figure 1-6:
The OSI
reference
model.

The main purposes of this model are to allow compatibility among various computer manufacturers' network hardware and to provide a structured method for designing network protocols. Equipment from different vendors on the same network would communicate seamlessly together using the OSI model as a reference. Network protocols designed to follow this layered architecture offer a real advantage to networking equipment manufacturers. Each manufacturer can design its equipment using this model as a blueprint, guaranteeing compatibility and functionality.

Digital information sent from one machine to another using this model flows from the top of the OSI model (where the user interacts with the computer using software), starting at the application layer of the sending computer and traveling down this theoretical stack into the presentation, session, transport, network, data link, and physical layers.

Data arrives at the physical layer and is transported by a physical means (such as the LAN cabling and network adapter) to the receiver's computer. Then the data travels back up the invisible stack to arrive at the destination computer's application program (possibly a Web browser making an HTTP request). See Figure 1-7.

You may be wondering how the OSI layers communicate with each other. Each layer has a defined set of responsibilities and is independent of the layers above and below it. Communication is possible with layers above and below a given layer on the same system and its peer layer on the other side of the connection. The network layer may prepare and hand data off to either the transport or data link layer, depending on the direction of network traffic. If data is being received, it flows up the stack. Data that is being sent travels down the stack. The network layer on the sending computer also communicates with the network layer on the receiving computer, its peer layer. See Figure 1-8.

These layers are not actually moving data through the network and should not be confused with protocols used for communication. Network protocols are tasked with moving the data through a network and follow the rules put in place by the OSI model. Some protocols operate at different layers in the stack than other protocols, depending on function, and implement the layers' functionality.

The seven layers consist of upper and lower layers and are shown from the highest layer to the lowest (refer back to Figure 1-6):

✦ Layer 7: Application layer

✦ Layer 6: Presentation layer

✦ Layer 5: Session layer

- ✦ Layer 4: Transport layer
- ✦ Layer 3: Network layer
- ✦ Layer 2: Data link layer
- ✦ Layer 1: Physical layer

Commit the OSI model to memory. A good way to remember the names of each layer is to use the mnemonic device "**A**ll **P**eople **S**eem **T**o **N**eed **D**ata **P**rocessing" (from the top down), or in reverse order, "**P**lease **D**o **N**ot **T**hrow **S**ausage **P**izza **A**way."

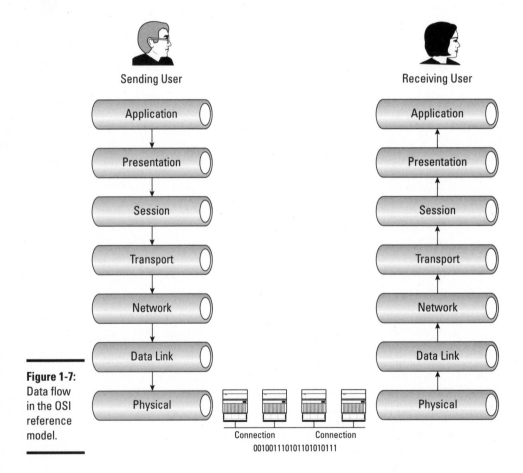

Figure 1-7: Data flow in the OSI reference model.

Sending User

Receiving User

Application

Presentation

Session

Transport

Network

Data Link

Physical

Connection   Connection
001001110101101010111

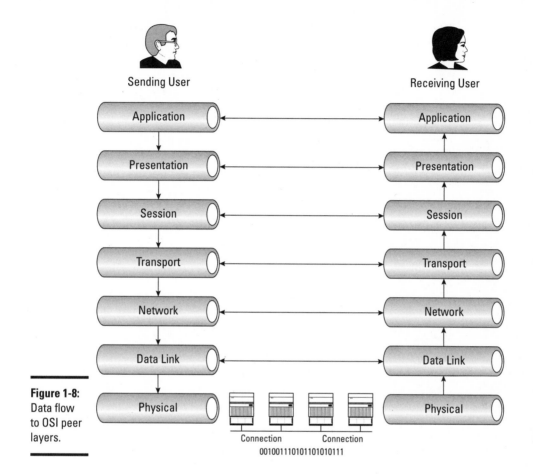

**Book II
Chapter 1**

Introducing TCP/IP

Figure 1-8:
Data flow
to OSI peer
layers.

The seven OSI layers

The upper and lower layers have different responsibilities and are split accordingly. The *upper* layers, shown in Figure 1-9, include the *application, presentation,* and *session* layers and are tasked with software application communications:

Figure 1-9:
The OSI
model upper
layers.

✦ **Application layer:** The application layer is responsible for application-specific end-user processes and is the closest layer to the actual end user. Typical functions of the application layer include communication synchronization, resource availability determination, and identification of partners for communication. Some examples of application layer protocols include Hypertext Transfer Protocol (HTTP), File Transfer Protocol (FTP), Simple Mail Transfer Protocol (SMTP), and Telnet.

✦ **Presentation layer:** The presentation layer, also referred to as the *syntax layer,* formats and encrypts data over the network. It also provides data to the application layer in a format it can understand. Translation is performed between application and network formats, ensuring that no compatibility issues exist.

✦ **Session layer:** The last of the upper layers is the session layer. It is responsible for controlling computer connections between local and remote applications. It initiates, controls, and terminates sessions using full-duplex, half-duplex, or simplex operations.

The *lower* layers, shown in Figure 1-10, provide data transportation services using both hardware and software methods for flow control, addressing, and routing over the network and make up the *transport, network, data link,* and *physical* layers:

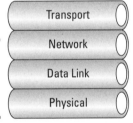

Figure 1-10:
The OSI model lower layers.

✦ **Transport layer:** The transport layer provides seamless data transfer between computer systems using flow control and end-to-end error recovery, keeping track of datagram delivery and retransmitting lost packets. TCP and the connectionless UDP operate at this level.

✦ **Network layer:** The network layer is responsible for transporting data between networks and is also called the *routing* layer. All routed networks connected to the Internet function at this level using the Internet Protocol, and data is transferred in a series of hops. Internetworking, switching, routing, addressing, error handling, congestion control, and packet sequencing are handled here.

✦ **Data link layer:** The data link layer resides above and manages errors from the physical layer and is divided into two sublayers:

- The *Media Access Control (MAC) layer,* useful for controlling network access

- The *Logical Link Control (LLC) layer,* responsible for frame synchronization, flow control, and error checking

The data link layer also encodes and decodes data packets into bits and manages errors from the physical layer, promoting reliable delivery on the physical medium.

✦ **Physical layer:** The physical layer resides at the bottom of the stack and defines the physical hardware used on the network, such as network interface cards, host bus adapters, repeaters, hubs, and cabling.

For the test: WAN technology uses telephone companies (and other carriers) to transmit data over long geographic distances and functions at the two lowest OSI layers. Although also considered to be a network layer function, WAN operation is generally considered to function at the physical and data link layers.

Book II
Chapter 1

Introducing TCP/IP

TCP/IP in the DoD model

Although the protocol architecture of TCP/IP follows the guidelines of the seven-layer OSI approach, TCP/IP more closely resembles a four-layer approach of the *DoD model* architecture. The DoD model conceptually referred to here is shown using fewer layers, but basic theory remains the same. Instead of data traveling through the seven-layer OSI model, data passes down through *four basic layers,* with each layer responsible for handing off control to the next adjoining layer. In this and the following sections, I give you a closer look at each layer and describe how this process works.

The four layers are listed here from the highest layer to the lowest:

✦ Layer 4: Application layer

✦ Layer 3: Transport layer

✦ Layer 2: Internet layer

✦ Layer 1: Network access layer

Data in the DoD model is sent from the host machine and travels down the stack, starting at the application layer and passing through the transport, Internet, and network access layers. The data is then transmitted over the network medium and returned up the four layers to the receiving host.

The four DoD layers

As shown in Figure 1-11, the four major components of the DoD model are the application, transport, Internet, and network access layers. Each layer has a specific responsibility and is listed here from the highest layer to the lowest:

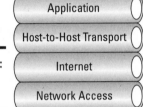

Figure 1-11:
The DoD
model.

+ **Application layer:** The top layer in the DoD model roughly combines the functionality of the three upper layers described in the OSI model, namely, the application, presentation, and session layers. This is where user information is handled and packaged for delivery to the transport layer.

+ **Transport layer:** The Transmission Control Protocol and User Datagram Protocol reside at the transport, or host-to-host, layer and provide valuable services in data delivery and error correction. TCP is the traffic cop and makes sure that the data gets to its intended destination, while UDP is unconcerned with verifying reliable delivery of packets.

+ **Internet layer:** The Internet layer resides between the transport and network access layers and is the foundation of IP networking. The Internet Protocol is associated at this layer and is responsible for delivering packets across interconnected networks.

+ **Network access layer:** Like the physical layer in the OSI model, the network access layer is responsible for delivering data across the physical network hardware.

Demystifying data encapsulation

Encapsulation in telecommunications is defined as the inclusion of one data structure inside another so that the first data structure is temporarily hidden from view. Data is encapsulated and decapsulated in this way as it travels through the different layers of the OSI and DoD models.

Starting from the application layer and moving downward, user information is formed into data and handed to the presentation layer for encapsulation. The presentation layer encapsulates the data provided by the application layer and passes it on to the session layer. The session layer synchronizes with the corresponding session layer on the destination host and passes the data to the transport layer, which converts the data into *segments* and delivers these segments from source to destination. The network layer encapsulates the segments from the transport layer into packets, or datagrams, and gives a network *header* defining the source and destination IP addresses. These packets of data are given to the data link layer and converted into *frames.* Frames are then converted into *binary data,* ready for network transfer. This process is shown in Figure 1-12.

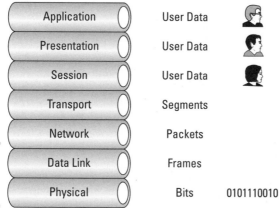

Figure 1-12:
Data encapsulation.

Data encapsulation by OSI layer is described in the following table:

Layer	Encapsulation
Application	User data
Presentation	User data
Session	User data
Transport	Segments
Network	Packets or datagrams
Data link	Frames
Physical	Bits

User information goes through a five-step process during encapsulation to arrive at the physical wire:

1. User information is processed by the application, presentation, and session layers and prepares the data for transmission.

    For example, Robert opens his Web browser application on his laptop and types in the URL `http://www.cisco.com`.

2. The upper layers present the data to the transport layer, which converts the user data into segments.

    Continuing with the example, Robert's data request passes down from the upper layers to the transport layer and a header is added, acknowledging the HTTP request.

3. The network layer receives the segments and converts them into packets.

    The transport layer passes the data down to the network layer, where source and destination information is added, providing the address to the destination.

4. The data link layer converts the packets into frames.

    The data link layer frames the packets and adds the Ethernet hardware address of the source computer and the MAC address of the nearest connected device on the remote network.

5. The physical layer receives the data frames and converts them into binary format.

    Data frames are converted into bits and transmitted over the network, returning Robert's requested Web page.

Prep Test

1 Which layer of the OSI model is responsible for reliable delivery of data across the physical network?

A ○ Network layer

B ○ Data link layer

C ○ Transport layer

D ○ Physical layer

2 Transmission Control Protocol operates at which OSI layer?

A ○ Transport layer

B ○ Network layer

C ○ Session layer

D ○ Data link layer

3 Which layer of the OSI model is responsible for managing sessions between applications?

A ○ Presentation layer

B ○ Application layer

C ○ Transport layer

D ○ Session layer

4 Which of the following are *not* steps in the data-encapsulation process? (Choose two.)

A ○ Segments are converted into frames

B ○ User information is converted into data

C ○ Frames are converted into bits

D ○ Packets are converted into frames

E ○ Data is converted into packets

5 What does SMTP stand for?

A ○ Sending Mail Transfer Protocol

B ○ Simple Mail Transfer Protocol

C ○ Simple Method Timing Protocol

D ○ Simple Management Transfer Protocol

6 **The User Datagram Protocol operates at which OSI layer?**

A ○ Transport layer
B ○ Network layer
C ○ Session layer
D ○ Data link layer

7 **TCP/IP is based on which type of technology?**

A ○ Circuit-switching
B ○ Packet-switching
C ○ Frame-switching
D ○ Header-switching

8 **Which layer of the OSI model theoretically resides closest to the end user?**

A ○ Presentation layer
B ○ Data link layer
C ○ Application layer
D ○ Physical layer

9 **TCP is considered to be what type of protocol?**

A ○ Connectionless
B ○ Proprietary
C ○ Session-oriented
D ○ Connection-oriented

10 **Which layer in the DoD model is responsible for routing IP packets?**

A ○ Physical layer
B ○ Session layer
C ○ Network layer
D ○ Internet layer

Answers

1 **B.** Data link layer. The reliable delivery of data across the physical medium is the task of the data link layer. See *"The seven OSI layers."*

2 **A.** Transport layer. TCP guarantees reliable delivery of data at the transport layer. Take a look at *"The seven OSI layers."*

3 **D.** Session layer. The session layer is responsible for managing sessions between applications. Review *"The seven OSI layers."*

4 **A, E.** Segments are converted into packets and data is converted into segments. Read *"Demystifying data encapsulation."*

5 **B.** Simple Mail Transfer Protocol. Review *"Components of TCP/IP."*

6 **A.** UDP operates at the transport layer. See *"The seven OSI layers."*

7 **B.** Packet-switching. The TCP/IP protocol is based on packet-switching technology. Refer to *" TCP/IP communication."*

8 **C.** Application layer. The user sends data that is first received by the application layer. Review *"The seven OSI layers."*

9 **D.** TCP is connection-oriented and provides reliable data communication. Check out *"Components of TCP/IP."*

10 **D.** Internet layer. The other three listed layers are OSI layers, not DoD layers. Review *"TCP/IP in the DoD model."*

Chapter 2: TCP/IP Layers and Protocols

Exam Objectives

✓ Describing the purpose and function of each TCP/IP layer

✓ Understanding data encapsulation

✓ Identifying and explaining data flow through the OSI layers

✓ Describing the purpose and basic operation of the protocols in the TCP/IP family

✓ Describing common Ethernet wiring and cabling standards

✓ Examining hardware addressing and bridge segmentation at the data link layer

✓ Interpreting differences between routing and routed protocols

✓ Identifying distance vector and link-state protocols

✓ Determining TCP transport mechanisms

✓ Describing the protocols used at the application layer for network and Internet communications

✓ Differentiating between the OSI and TCP layered models

*1*t is time to dig a little deeper into the TCP/IP family of protocols and reveal a little more of the OSI and DoD models. I break down each layer inside the OSI model and magnify its inner workings. Protocols that reside at each of these layers are discussed along with the rules and standards for transmitting, sending, and verifying data. Then, the TCP/IP model is compared to the OSI framework, providing required knowledge to pass the CCNA examination. While the CCNA exam will test your knowledge in both areas of the OSI model and the TCP/IP model, you should memorize each layer in each of the models and know all their functionalities. By the time you are done studying and are ready to take the exam, you should be dreaming in layers!

Information Exchange through the OSI Layer

As you can see from Figure 2-1, the OSI model is comprised of seven conceptual layers that deal with application and data transfer functions. The upper and lower layers have different responsibilities and are split accordingly. The upper layers include the application, presentation, and session layers and are tasked with software application communications. The lower layers provide data transportation services using both hardware and software methods for flow control, addressing, and routing over the network and make up the transport, network, data link, and physical layers. Each layer typically communicates with three other layers: the layer above, layer below, and *peer* to its own layer:

✦ The *service provider* is the layer offering its services to the adjoining layer, the *service user*.

✦ The *service access point* (SAP) is a meeting point where these source and destination requests take place.

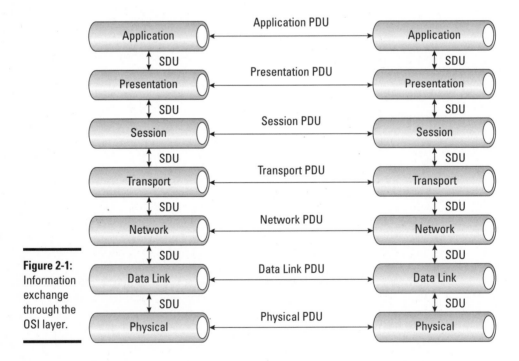

Figure 2-1:
Information
exchange
through the
OSI layer.

Examples of SAPs are port identifiers in UDP and TCP transmissions.

Individual layers communicate by adding control information called *headers* and *trailers* to data using *protocol data units (PDUs)* and *service data units (SDUs)*. Messages that traverse up or down the stack on the local machine are SDUs. Messages sent across peer-to-peer layers from source to destination machines are PDUs. The specific name of each data structure changes depending on the current location of that PDU or SDU in the model. Traveling down the stack, the SDU is known as

✦ A *segment* at the transport layer

✦ A *packet* at the network layer

✦ A *frame* at the data link layer

✦ Raw *bits* at the physical layer

Each layer adds its own header and trailer information inside the PDU/SDU. This is termed *encapsulation* and is revealed in Figure 2-2. As information descends down the stack, header and trailer information is added to it. The information is passed across the physical medium of the network and returns up the conceptual layers of the receiving machine, with each layer reversing the process, stripping off the header of its peer layer, and passing the information up the stack until it reaches the user's application. This is known as *deencapsulation*.

Book II Chapter 2

TCP/IP Layers and Protocols

Data Encapsulation

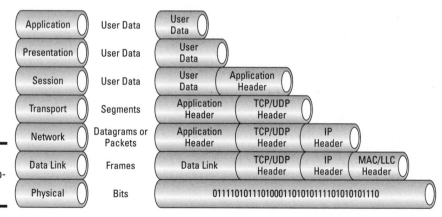

Figure 2-2: Data encapsulation.

Memorize the encapsulation method and order:

1. User data

2. Segments

3. Packets

4. Frames

5. Bits

OSI Layers and Protocols

Now I take a deeper look at the seven layers of the OSI model, the protocols, and how data flows through each layer of the stack.

The physical layer: Layer 1

The physical layer is the first layer located at the bottom of the OSI model and carries bits of data — digital 0s and 1s — over the network medium. This layer resides furthest away from the end user and closest to the network hardware.

Some examples of network hardware at this layer include fiber-optic and Ethernet cabling, repeaters, hubs, modems, and network adapters.

The physical layer takes logical data from the data link layer and converts it into a signal over physical, electrical, or mechanical interfaces. The physical layer specifies the following:

✦ The types of media, connectors, and signals used

✦ Their voltage requirements, distance limitations, and wire transmission speed

All upper layers must hand off their communications to the residing layer below them, with all information eventually passing through the physical layer. No network communication would be possible without this layer. All LAN protocols operate at the physical and data link layers of the OSI model.

Layer 1 characteristics are as follows:

✦ Physical media and connectors

✦ Signaling and voltage levels

✦ Data rates and transmission distances

Ethernet cabling standards

Since its conception in 1972, a variety of standards have been set by the Institute of Electrical and Electronics Engineers (IEEE) for LAN technology. The IEEE 802.3 standardizes Ethernet LAN technology at the physical and data link layers and defines collision detection using *carrier sense multiple access collision detect (CSMA/CD)*. The IEEE 802.3 specification also defines *half-duplex* and *full-duplex* transmissions:

✦ Half-duplex allows two-way communications but in only one direction at a time, much like the functionality of a "walkie-talkie" system.

✦ Full-duplex allows bidirectional communication simultaneously using two physical twisted pairs of wire, proving a significant performance boost over half duplex mode.

Book II
Chapter 2

TCP/IP Layers and
Protocols

Ethernet 802.3 uses both full- and half-duplex modes of communication, with full-duplex using one set of twisted-pair wiring for transmission and one for reception of data.

IEEE specifications and guidelines exist for fiber-optic, twisted-pair, and coaxial cabling. A few of the most popular Ethernet standards you need to know are as follows:

✦ **10BASE-T:** Transmits a 10-Mbps signal over a bus network topology in a star network using twisted-pair Ethernet cable with a maximum distance of 100 meters to the local-area network's hub or switch.

   A major advantage of twisted-pair cabling is the relatively low cost.

✦ **100BASE-T:** The Fast Ethernet family based on an extension of the 802.3 specification and having the same maximum distance as 10BASE-T. The major difference is that 100BASE-T transmits signals at 100 Mbps using Category 5 cabling.

✦ **1000BASE-T:** Sets the standard transmission rate at 1 Gbps (GbE or GigE) over Category 5e twisted-pair cabling.

✦ **10GBASE-T:** The new emerging standard for Gigabit Ethernet, 10GBASE-T sets the transmission rate at 10 times that of 1000BASE-T, at up to 100 meters using Category 6/6a cabling.

The first number in the naming convention refers to transmission speed. *BASE* is short for *baseband,* meaning that each signal completely controls the wire, and *T* denotes twisted-pair wiring. All three of these standards support half- and full-duplex operation and use RJ-45 connectors.

Ethernet wiring standards

The Electronic Industries Alliance (EIA) and Telecommunications Industry Association (TIA) set the standard for U.S. telecommunications networks and LAN cables and have separated them into the following categories:

✦ **Category 1:** Cat1 (actually Anixter level 1) is untwisted wire used in older telephone wiring installations and is not recognized under the EIA/TIA-586 standard. A cable must be rated as Category 3 or higher to belong in the EIA/TIA grouping.

✦ **Category 2:** Cat2 (actually Anixter level 2) uses solid wire in twisted pairs formerly used in Apple LocalTalk and Token Ring networks, transmitting data at a maximum of 4 Mbps. Cat2 is also not recognized under the EIA/TIA-586 standard.

✦ **Category 3:** Cat3 is 24 AWG twisted-pair copper cable used in older 10BASE-T networks and provides 16 MHz of bandwidth. Cat3 supports communications up to 10 Mbps and has been superseded by the more popular Category 5 cable.

Cat3 is still found in installations that require telephone and VoIP services.

✦ **Category 4:** Cat4 supports data speeds up to 16 Mbps and provides 20 MHz of bandwidth. Cat4 is generally found in Token Ring networks and is no longer popular. Like Category 3, it has also been superseded by Category 5 cable.

✦ **Category 5:** Cat5 consists of four twisted pairs of copper wires insulated from each other in a single cable using 8P8C (RJ-45) connectors. By twisting cable pairs, crosstalk and line noise are minimized. Cat5 cables are either shielded or unshielded. EIA/TIA-568-A specifications state that this cable can transmit data up to 150 Mbps, with a maximum distance of 100 meters (328 feet). Cat5 has been the most popular type of cable over the last several years.

Cat5 can be found in many 100BASE-TX and 1000BASE-T networks today.

✦ **Category 5e:** First published in 2000, Cat5e is an updated version of Cat5 cable and uses bidirectional and full four-pair transmission for improved performance over Gigabit Ethernet. Cat5 and Cat5e are very similar and maintain the same cable speed and distance limitations.

Cat5e is preferred over Cat5 for 1000BASE-T networks because of its improved performance characteristics defined in EIA/TIA-568-B.

✦ **Category 6/6a:** Like Cat5, Category 6 cable consists of four twisted pairs of copper wires and is typically referred to as the standard for Gigabit Ethernet. Supporting 10 Gigabit Ethernet, or 10GBASE-T, this 22 to 24 AWG cable is also backward compatible with 10/100/1000BASE-T networks and has a maximum distance of 100 meters. When used in 10GBASE-T environments, that distance drops to approximately 50 meters. Category 6 also has higher specification requirements than previous categories. Category 6a doubles the specifications of Cat6 and is used in 10GBASE-T networks.

✦ **Category 7/7a:** Cat7 consists of four twisted pairs of copper wires with shielding added to each wire pair and uses either 8P8C standard connectors or TERA connectors at each end. Cat7 cable raises the requirements for noise levels and signal-leaking crosstalk over Category 6 and is used for 10GBASE-T networks. Cat7 cable is rated at 600 MHz and Cat7a at 1000 MHz.

Cabling below Category 5 specifications should never be used in new local-area network installations!

The data link layer: Layer 2

The function of data link layer is to receive messages from the network layer and transmit them as *frames* to the physical layer, providing the physical source and delivery addresses of host network machines for node-to-node frame delivery. As you can see in Figure 2-3, this is the nearest logical layer to the physical layer in the OSI model and detects errors occurring on Layer 1.

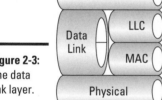

Figure 2-3:
The data
link layer.

The data link layer verifies that messages are transmitted to the proper devices on the network.

Common Layer 2 protocols are as follows:

✦ Frame Relay

✦ Ethernet

✦ ATM

✦ Token Ring

✦ Cisco Discovery Protocol

✦ FDDI

**Book II
Chapter 2**

**TCP/IP Layers and
Protocols**

+ HDLC

+ PPP

Layer 2 characteristics are as follows:

+ Physical hardware addressing

+ Data transportation using frames over the physical layer

  Hardware MAC addresses are used to transmit data frames!

The data link layer consists of two sublayers, called the Media Access Control (MAC) sublayer and the Logical Link Control (LLC) sublayer:

+ **Media Access Control (MAC) sublayer:** This is the "traffic cop" of the data link layer and is responsible for controlling communication with the physical layer and transporting data frames across the physical network.

  One example of this control over an electrical bus is the *carrier sense multiple access collision detect (CSMA/CD)* protocol, which helps avoid data collisions on an Ethernet network. As you can see in Figure 2-4, data collisions occur when two or more devices on the same network transmit data simultaneously. CSMA/CD provides the rules of communication for Ethernet networks, allowing each device in the broadcast domain its "turn" sending data.

  The MAC sublayer is also tasked with data framing — taking or encapsulating packets from the network layer and adding *header* and *trailer* information. These frames contain the hardware addresses, or 48-bit MAC addresses, of both source and destination machines. The MAC sublayer is the addresser and deliverer of frames — the error detector — and the interface between the LLC and the physical layer.

  Substantial collisions on an Ethernet network result in data congestion, delayed response, and low throughput!

+ **Logical Link Control (LLC) sublayer:** This is the interface between the MAC sublayer and the network layer, providing the means for connectionless or connection-oriented services over a data link between two hosts. The LLC sublayer manages data transmission speeds across the physical medium using flow control mechanisms and allows multiple, dissimilar protocol streams to coexist on the same link, such as IP or IPX.

  Service access points (SAPs) consisting of the *source service access point (SSAP)* and the *destination service access point (DSAP)* are logical markers that assist in locating upper-layer services on remote hosts.

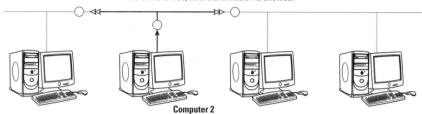

Computer 2 listens for network traffic.
If the line is free, data transmission is allowed.

Computer 2

If computer 1 and computer 3 both listen and transmit data at the same time, a collision occurs. Each computer stops
transmission and waits a predetermined amount of time before retransmission occurs.

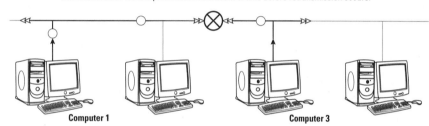

Figure 2-4:
CSMA/CD.

Computer 1   Computer 3

Data framing

Data framing at the data link layer consists of control information such as
source and destination address, preamble, length, and user data sent using
Layer 2 frames.

As shown in Figure 2-5, each frame begins with a *preamble,* or synchronization
bit, for handshaking with receiving machines. The *Start of Frame Delimiter*
marks the end of the preamble and precedes the 48-bit source and
destination MAC addresses. The source address is always a single unicast
network hardware address, although the destination address may contain
unicast, multicast, or broadcast addresses. The *Length or Type* field specifies
which protocol is used in data encapsulation. Following the type field are the
User Data and *CRC Checksum* fields.

Typical Ethernet Frame

Figure 2-5:
Data
framing.

Preamble	Start of Frame Delimiter	Destination Ethernet Address	Source Ethernet Address	Length or type	Data	Frame Check Sequence
Used for bit synchronization					Varies from	
62 bits	2 bits	48 bits	48 bits	16 bits	46–1500 bytes	32 bits

Cyclic redundancy check

The cyclic redundancy check (CRC) is designed to verify data in a network using a CRC code hash function by comparing the source and destination data values. CRC is responsible for data integrity by detecting errors and discarding corrupted data. This check is performed without CRC repairing the data. If retransmission of bad data is necessary, it is handled by other protocols. The sending source calculates the CRC value and sends the information to the destination machine. The receiving host also performs the calculation, and if they match, the data is deemed error-free by both hosts. If they do not match, the data is discarded.

ARP and RARP

Address Resolution Protocol (ARP) determines the unknown data-link (Layer 2) address (the MAC address) of a network device using the known Layer 3 IP address. An ARP command-line example is shown in Figure 2-6 and may include the following command-line parameters:

Command	*Function*
ARP -a	Displays entries in ARP table
ARP -s 192.168.1.101 00-0f-1f-9c-2d-ad	Adds static entry to table

Figure 2-6: ARP command-line screen shot.

Reverse Address Resolution Protocol (RARP) performs the opposite of ARP and determines the network address using the known hardware address.

Segmenting with bridges

Bridges work at the data link layer and connect multiple network segments into a single, logical network, increasing scalability. If the physical limitations of a network have been reached, bridges allow extending the network further. Bridges filter and forward frames based on MAC address and can assist in filtering and reducing congested network traffic.

A *forwarding table* with these hardware addresses is stored on the bridge, which communicates using the *Spanning Tree Protocol (STP)*. Spanning Tree Protocol was originally developed by the Digital Equipment Corporation (DEC) and ensures that data reaches its target only once, creating a loop-free environment and preventing network flooding and broadcast storms. The bridge blocks any redundant ports so as not to create new loops.

Important facts to keep in mind regarding bridges, hubs, and switches are as follows:

+ Bridges and switches operate at the data link layer.

+ Bridges can segment networks but do not isolate multicast or broadcast traffic.

+ Layer 2 switches forward and filter traffic and use loop avoidance and hardware address discovery features.

+ Replacing a hub with a switch reduces network congestion.

+ Bridges use the MAC address to forward frames, and routers use logical IP addresses to forward packets.

A Layer 2 hardware address looks like this: *00:aa:00:64:c6:08*

A Layer 2 broadcast address looks like this: *FF:FF:FF:FF:FF:FF*

The network layer: Layer 3

The main goal of the network layer is the addressing and routing of connectionless or connection-oriented communications between source and destination networks. The network layer is responsible for determining the best method of transferring traffic — a data packet — between nodes. By gathering network topology information, routing protocols at the network layer attempt to determine the optimal delivery path of packets. Each router in an internetwork shares its routing information with other connected routers, forming a networking map of interconnected devices. These routers can also be used to split networks into logical subnetworks, or subnets.

When a sending computer wants to send data to another machine, a broadcast message is sent, requesting the MAC address of the recipient's computer (see the section "The data link layer: Layer 2," earlier in this chapter). This is done to determine whether the target resides on the local or remote network:

✦ If the MAC address is found on the local network, data is transferred to the target node without traversing the router.

✦ If the packet is addressed to a target node on a remote network, the router uses this network map to deliver the packet to the proper subnet, or next available *hop,* to the destination.

A hop, or *metric,* refers to the best-path distance determination in forwarding packets over a router's *interface* using IP addressing.

I take a closer look at IP addressing and subnetting in Chapters 3 and 4 of Book II.

Layer 3 characteristics are as follows:

✦ Connectionless and connection-oriented data transport to logical addresses (IP) in separate broadcast domains

✦ Host addressing and message forwarding between networks

Routing versus routed protocols

Routing protocols are network layer protocols that allow networking equipment called routers to statically establish or dynamically advertise and learn routes to other networks:

✦ *Static routes* must be manually configured by a system administrator.

When a network undergoes configuration or topology changes, these networks have to be manually updated by the network administrator.

✦ *Dynamic routes* are discovered automatically by the routing protocol in use and do not require manual intervention by a system administrator.

These routing protocols are then able to determine addressing require-ments, newly formed routing paths, and the best and quickest ways to these destinations.

Dynamic and static routes are the two ways to determine the best-path route on Cisco routers!

A *routed* protocol is assigned to an interface on the router and determines the method of packet delivery. A *routing* protocol determines the path of packets through the network.

Distance vector and link-state routing protocols

Routing protocols are categorized into two main classes, distance vector and link-state, as follows:

✦ **Distance vector:** The dynamic distance vector protocols make a destination calculation based on vector, or traffic interface, direction and measure distance by metric hop count. This is based on the number of hosts the data must pass through to reach its destination. Common distance vector protocols are Enhanced Interior Gateway Routing Protocol (EIGRP) and Routing Information Protocol (RIP).

✦ **Link-state:** These are routing protocols that track the connections of each link, constructing a network map of the internetwork and sharing it with all its neighboring nodes, or routers. Algorithms are employed to determine the shortest path to a particular destination, and individual routers share the routing tables of their own links. Open Shortest Path First (OSPF) is a link-state routing protocol.

As you can see in Figure 2-7, some routing protocols at the network layer include RIP, OSPF, IGRP, EIGRP, and BGP. I now examine some of these protocols:

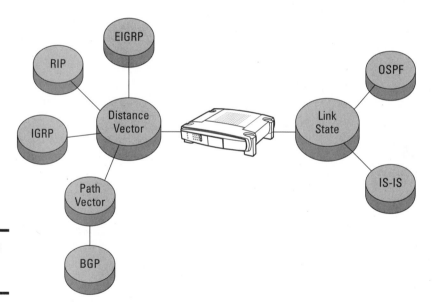

Figure 2-7:
Routing
protocols.

✦ **Routing Information Protocol (RIP):** A distance vector routing protocol that uses hop counts to measure the distance between networks. Each hop (typically a router) between the source and destination is given a value, and entries are added and updated in the routing table. RIP also minimizes loops by limiting route hops. RIP — an *Interior Gateway Protocol (IGP)* — sends routing updates to other routers if the network topology changes. RIP has a maximum hop count of 15.

✦ **Interior Gateway Routing Protocol (IGRP):** A proprietary protocol developed by Cisco Systems that allows network devices to exchange important data regarding the advertisements of routes. Routers using IGRP send routing updates to each other every 90 seconds and are not burdened by the hop-count limitations set by RIP. IGRP provides the following features:

- Provides scalability

- Updates the network during topology changes

- Supports multiple paths between source and destination

- Shows calculations based on bandwidth, delay, loading, reliability, and MTU factors

- Provides poison reverse, split horizon, holddowns, and flash updates

✦ **Enhanced Interior Gateway Routing Protocol (EIGRP):** Uses the same distance vector algorithms and metrics as the obsolete IGRP but supersedes IGRP with improvements on convergence times and scalability.

EIGRP supports variable-length subnet mask (VLSM) and arbitrary route summarization, combining the advantages of link-state and distance vector protocols. Data collected by EIGRP is stored in routing, topology, and neighbor tables and discovered by using simple hello messages sent to neighboring routers. After discovery is complete, routing tables are exchanged, and EIGRP calculates least-cost, nonloop, best-method paths.

✦ **Open Shortest Path First (OSPF):** A nonproprietary, dynamic, link-state Interior Gateway Protocol (IGP) used in routing packets based on IP addresses throughout a single routing domain. OSPF detects routing changes and link failures and dynamically corrects itself very quickly. OSPF uses a shortest path first method of route determination and supports VLSM, tagging, and route source authentication.

✦ **Border Gateway Protocol (BGP):** An interdomain path vector routing protocol that maintains and exchanges reachability information with other BGP-available networks by maintaining an IP routing table. BGP is a path vector protocol that uses defined rules and network policies to determine the best path to a particular destination.

✦ **Intermediate System–to–Intermediate System (IS-IS):** An Interior Gateway, link-state routing protocol that uses complex algorithms to determine the best path to a network. IS-IS is employed in medium- to large-scale networks; it offers very fast convergence and is widely scalable. It provides network topology information by rapidly flooding the network with new routing information.

As you can see from Figure 2-8, network segmentation (splitting a network into two parts) using a router separates broadcast traffic!

Network before router segmentation

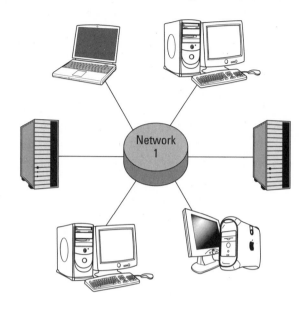

Network after router segmentation

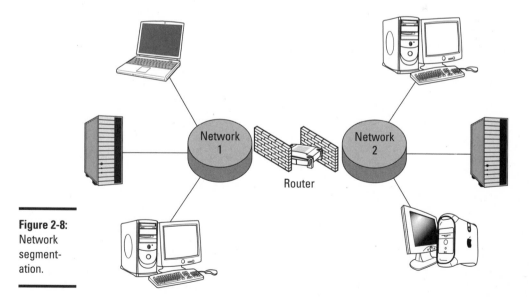

Figure 2-8:
Network
segment-
ation.

A routed protocol example is shown in Figure 2-9. Here is a list of the routed protocols:

✦ **Internet Protocol (IP):** The most popular routed protocol over LAN or WAN links and is included in the TCP/IP family of protocols. IP uses routable data called *packets* that contain address and control information to transfer information via connectionless, best-effort delivery services. IP addresses contain network and host addresses and are four octets in length. I look at this 32-bit IP addressing scheme in detail in Book II, Chapter 3.

✦ **Internetwork Packet Exchange (IPX):** Another network layer protocol (used by Novell NetWare operating systems) that is similar in function to, but less popular than, IP-based networks. IPX is a proprietary, connectionless, datagram protocol that uses a 32-bit network address (network number) and a 48-bit host addressing scheme (MAC address).

✦ **Internet Control Message Protocol (ICMP):** A TCP/IP family protocol that works at the network layer. ICMP is used to report errors and deliver messages with valuable user data, such as *destination host unreachable, time exceeded,* and *echo requests.* ICMP is used in determining route availability and can return a destination unreachable message if the end route is unavailable. A form of ICMP echo request is using the `ping` command to test connectivity across routes or hops. ICMP uses Time-To-Live (TTL) calculations (that reach 0) to prevent routing loops.

ICMP generates an echo reply to ping requests and sends destination unreachable messages to hosts. ICMP is implemented with *all* TCP/IP hosts!

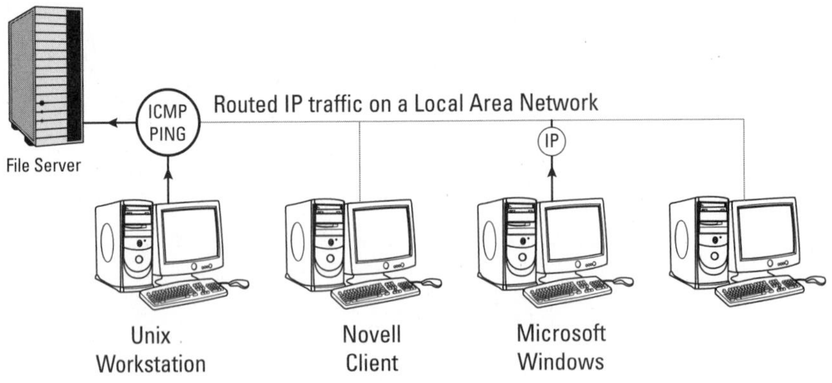

Figure 2-9:
Routed
protocols.

File Server

ICMP PING

Routed IP traffic on a Local Area Network

IP

Unix Workstation

Novell Client

Microsoft Windows

The transport layer: Layer 4

This fourth layer of the OSI model governs the logical session between two host machines and their transport layers, providing a seamless connection between nodes, which are invisible to the end user. This offers reliable and stable source-to-target data transfers for the upper-layer protocols.

Protocols functioning at this layer typically are concerned with data integrity, data sequencing, and flow control and are considered to be either

✦ Connection-oriented

  Connection-oriented protocols use handshaking to verify proper data delivery.

✦ Connectionless

  Connectionless protocols use less overhead than connection-oriented protocols but do not check for delivery of data and are considered unreliable.

Layer 4 characteristics are as follows:

✦ End-to-end virtual node establishment

✦ Multiplexing

✦ Reliable data transmission

✦ Flow control

Some examples of Layer 4 protocols include the following:

✦ **Transmission Control Protocol (TCP):** A connection-oriented protocol responsible for IP packet delivery using a virtual full-duplex, reliable transmission of data from source to destination nodes. TCP ensures that data arrives intact and in the same order it was sent. It is a *sliding window protocol* that can handle timeouts and retransmissions of data. Sliding window is used for transmission flow control and uses a series of acknowledgments (ACKs) and records frame sequences. TCP also provides *multiplexing,* meaning that multiple upper-layer data streams can be combined and transported over a single connection.

  TCP establishes connection, transmits data, and then terminates the connection. TCP uses acknowledgments to provide reliable transport.

✦ **User Datagram Protocol (UDP):** The other major transport protocol at this layer. UDP differs from TCP in that UDP has no reliability checking or handshaking between hosts, and receipt of datagrams is never acknowledged by the receiving machine. LAN broadcast messages are an example of UDP datagrams.

The advantage of UDP over TCP is that overhead traffic is reduced due to UDP's connectionless nature! Refer to Figure 2-10 for a complete listing of differences between TCP and UDP.

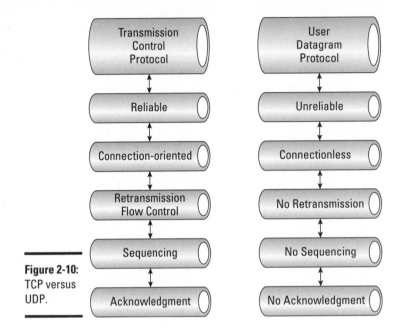

Figure 2-10:
TCP versus
UDP.

The session layer: Layer 5

The session layer provides synchronization and data-exchange features between two applications in the upper-layer stack and manages the link between the nodes. It provides data-checking procedures during communication sessions and can retransmit lost data in the event of a connection failure. The session layer can operate in either half- or full-duplex mode, and known protocols include PPTP, RPC, SSH, and NETBIOS. Application program interfaces (APIs) are known as session layer tools and allow upper-layer communications using a standard set of services. Viewing Figure 2-11, you see an example of session layer communications.

Layer 5 characteristics are as follows:

✦ Provides communication sessions between end-user processes

✦ Manages data exchange from peer presentation layers

✦ Provides Transmission Control Protocol (TCP) sockets

TCP sockets are the combination of IP addresses and port numbers and are considered bidirectional endpoints that allow the communication process to occur. TCP sockets are paired between a client and server machine. The server is tasked with listening for client requests and then creates a connection on a specific port.

HTTP Client requests Web page from
Web Server

Internet
Web Server

HTTP Client

**Book II
Chapter 2**

**TCP/IP Layers and
Protocols**

Figure 2-11:
Session
layer
communi-
cations.

Network user accesses home directory files

File Server

Network User

The presentation layer: Layer 6

The second layer nearest to the end user is the presentation layer; it deals with *data syntax* between communicating application layers.

Layer 6 is the translator of the OSI model and converts application layer data back to the application layer on the peer node. It also handles data encryption and data compression duties but is the only layer that performs *data conversion.* Presentation layer data standards include ASCII, EBCDIC, HTML, JPEG, MIDI, MPEG, QuickTime, and Rich Text Format (RTF). *Multipurpose Internet Mail Extension (MIME)* encoding is also done at the presentation level.

Layer 6 characteristics are as follows:

✦ Delivers and formats data for the application layer

✦ Provides data encryption and data compression

The application layer: Layer 7

The application layer provides the services needed for applications to access protocols and has message-handling, file transfer, and error control features. The end user synchronizes data and transfers files through application programs and network operating systems.

The application layer synchronizes data and file transfers between host-to-host communications. An end user saving data to a network share or querying a remote database would be an example of an application layer process. During data access, the application layer process relies on the underlying lower session layer to establish the connection.

Layer 7 characteristics are as follows:

+ Is the layer closest to the end user
+ Provides network services to end-user applications

The following are application layer protocols:

+ **Hypertext Transfer Protocol (HTTP):** A client/server request/response protocol designed to share resources between a client's Web browser and a Web server. When a Web user types `http://` in the URL address of the Web browser, an HTTP protocol request is made to the Web server. The Web server responds by returning text, graphics, or video to the user. The exchange of information is made possible by using a specific port or socket to transfer the data. The standard port used for HTTP communications is port 80.

+ **File Transfer Protocol (FTP):** Allows sharing of files between remote computers in a reliable manner. The TCP/IP protocol provides a command-line FTP utility that enables file- and directory-sharing services between remote systems. FTP operations are processed through TCP port 21.

+ **Simple Mail Transfer Protocol (SMTP):** Transfers e-mail between IP-based systems on TCP port 25 using a series of text commands to exchange instructions between hosts. A host is either an end user, Mail User Agent (MUA), or Mail Transfer Agent (MTA). A typical computer user receives e-mail from a mail server using POP3 or IMAP and delivers e-mail via SMTP.

+ **Terminal Emulation Protocol, or Telnet:** A client-server protocol that allows users to type and execute commands on a remote host as if the user were physically sitting in front of the machine. Telnet provides a mechanism that allows a remote logon to a remote workstation, over a remote network. Telnet is considered a security risk and does not encrypt data or provide authentication services. Telnet operates on TCP port 23.

+ **Network File System (NFS):** Offers transparent access to remote resources over the network. Users may access files remotely as if the files were locally stored data. This allows the network administrator to store files in a central location, with users relying on NFS for access. This service is provided to the end user by mounting the available share.

+ **Simple Network Management Protocol (SNMP):** The TCP/IP network management protocol that delivers the state and condition of monitored networking devices. Health status reports of network-attached devices may be delivered to any polling network management consoles. Administrative alerts can be set by the system administrator to issue warnings on critical system failures. SNMP agents monitor the network and return information to requesting SNMP management systems. SNMP uses UDP port 161 for general messages and port 162 for trap messages.

✦ **Post Office Protocol 3 (POP3):** Downloads and stores e-mail from SMTP mail servers using TCP port 110. POP3 downloads all messages addressed to the user at one time and does not allow selective downloading of mail. After all messages have been received by the POP3 client, the POP3 client disconnects, and the stored e-mail is deleted from the database on the mail server.

✦ **X Windows:** A graphical user interface (GUI) used for communicating between X terminals and UNIX workstations.

✦ **Internet Small Computer Systems Interface (iSCSI):** Transfers SCSI commands over IP networks. iSCSI is used for remote storage data access across local- and wide-area networks. Clients, or initiators, send SCSI data requests to target SCSI storage devices that are usually storage-area networks (SANs). iSCSI communications allow long-distance file access over the existing network topology.

Book II Chapter 2

TCP/IP Layers and Protocols

✦ **Domain Name System (DNS):** A network service that associates alphanumeric host names to a particular IP address of a network host commonly found on the Internet. DNS names consist of a *host name* followed by a *domain name,* which combined create a *fully qualified domain name.* For example, www.cisco.com (cisco is the host name, and .com is the domain) is much easier for users to remember than IP addresses like 192.168.172.147. This functionality of finding IP addresses from the domain name is called *name resolution* and is performed by DNS servers.

✦ **Dynamic Host Configuration Protocol (DHCP):** The protocol used to assign authorized network clients with an IP address, subnet mask, default gateway, and DNS server configuration information. This automates system administration tasks and prevents network administrators from having to perform redundant configuration tasks on every network device. Adding new clients to the network using DHCP is extremely easy and minimizes user intervention.

The DHCP client initially sends a broadcast message asking for information from the DHCP server usually found on the local-area network. This request is processed by the DHCP server, and IP information and lease times are returned to the client. After the IP addressing information is received, the client may begin to communicate with other IP-based machines.

TCP/IP Layers and Protocols

I now examine how the TCP/IP, or Department of Defense (DoD) data communications, model is structured and define its layers.

In Figure 2-12, you can see the key differences between the OSI and DoD models.

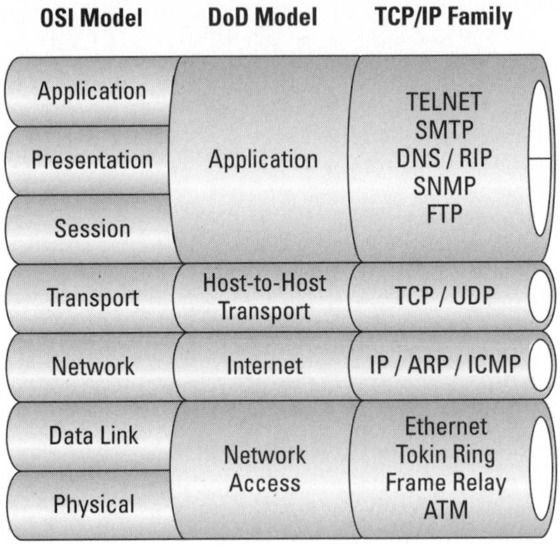

OSI Model	DoD Model	TCP/IP Family
Application		TELNET
Presentation	Application	SMTP DNS / RIP
Session		SNMP FTP
Transport	Host-to-Host Transport	TCP / UDP
Network	Internet	IP / ARP / ICMP
Data Link	Network Access	Ethernet Tokin Ring
Physical		Frame Relay ATM

Figure 2-12: The OSI versus the DoD model.

The network access layer: Layer 1

The network access layer is the lowest layer in the DoD model and functions like the OSI physical layer by specifying the physical hardware requirements for data transmission. This layer uses hardware MAC addresses to deliver data on the same local network and uses a frame check sequence (FCS) to verify data integrity.

The Internet layer: Layer 2

The Internet layer functions similarly to the network layer in the OSI model. All IP-routed traffic goes through the Internet layer to reach the proper destination. Each IP packet contains routing and addressing information and is explained in the next chapter. Internet layer protocols include IP, ICMP, ARP, and RARP.

The host-to-host transport layer: Layer 3

The transport layer, or host-to-host layer, matches the form and function of its OSI layer of the same name. Each application uses a port or socket number to establish a remote connection using TCP.

The application layer: Layer 4

The application layer is the combination of the functions of all three uppermost layers in the OSI model: the application, presentation, and session layers. Protocols include SMTP, DNS, NFS, FTP, and RIP.

Prep Test

1 Which protocol prevents bridging loops?

- **A** ○ Spanning Tree Protocol
- **B** ○ Border Gateway Protocol
- **C** ○ Open Shortest Path First Protocol
- **D** ○ Transmission Control Protocol

2 Which function of Ethernet networks prevents data collisions?

- **A** ○ TCP/IP
- **B** ○ CSMA/CD
- **C** ○ IGRP
- **D** ○ 802.3

3 Which layer of the OSI model contains the MAC and LLC sublayers?

- **A** ○ Physical layer
- **B** ○ Network layer
- **C** ○ Transport layer
- **D** ○ Data link layer

4 Which protocol does not acknowledge receipt of data?

- **A** ○ User Datagram Protocol
- **B** ○ User Datagram Packet
- **C** ○ Transmission Control Protocol
- **D** ○ Internet Control Message Protocol

5 Which of the following is a valid MAC address?

- **A** ○ 192.168.101.1
- **B** ○ 0100111011100100
- **C** ○ 00-0f-1f-9c-2d-ad
- **D** ○ 255.255.255.0

6 Data framing occurs at which OSI layer?

- **A** ○ Transport layer
- **B** ○ Network layer
- **C** ○ Data link layer
- **D** ○ Session layer

7 **What is the correct order of data encapsulation starting from the application layer to the physical layer?**

A ○ Bits, Frames, Packets, Segments, User Data

B ○ User data, Frames, Packets, Segments, Bits

C ○ User data, Packets, Segments, Frames, Bits

D ○ User data, Segments, Packets, Frames, Bits

8 **Which layer of the OSI model most closely resembles the network access layer in the DoD model?**

A ○ Physical layer

B ○ Network layer

C ○ Data link layer

D ○ Transport layer

9 **Which OSI layer is responsible for multiplexing?**

A ○ Data link

B ○ Transport

C ○ Session

D ○ Network

10 **ARP determines the _____ address by using the known _____ address.**

A ○ Hardware, IP

B ○ MAC, HEX

C ○ IP, MAC

D ○ Ethernet, RARP

11 **Which of the following are routing protocols? (Choose all that apply.)**

A ○ IP

B ○ BGP

C ○ EIGRP

D ○ UDP

E ○ OSPF

12 **TCP sockets consist of the _____ and _____.**

A ○ MAC address, ICMP packets

B ○ frames, segments

C ○ IP address, MAC address

D ○ IP address, port number

Answers

1 **A.** Spanning Tree Protocol. Spanning Tree Protocol prevents bridging loops at the data link layer. Review *"Segmenting with bridges."*

2 **B.** CSMA/CD. CSMA/CD stands for carrier sense multiple access collision detect and prevents collisions on an Ethernet network. Check out *"The data link layer: Layer 2."*

3 **D.** Data link layer. The MAC and LLC sublayers both reside in the data link layer. Read *"The data link layer: Layer 2."*

4 **A.** User Datagram Protocol. UDP is connectionless and does not acknowledge receipt of delivery. See *"The transport layer: Layer 4."*

5 **C.** Ethernet MAC addresses consist of 48-bit hardware addresses such as 00-0f-1f-9c-2d-ad. Refer to *"The data link layer: Layer 2."*

6 **C.** Data link layer. The data link layer is responsible for framing data. Review *"The data link layer: Layer 2."*

7 **D.** The correct order is User data, Segments, Packets, Frames, Bits. Read *"Information Exchange through the OSI Layer."*

8 **A.** Physical layer. The network access layer of the DoD Model is comparable to the OSI's physical layer. Review *"TCP/IP Layers and Protocols."*

9 **B.** Transport layer. Multiplexing is a function at the transport layer. Check out *"The transport layer: Layer 4."*

10 **A.** ARP determines the Ethernet (MAC) hardware address using the known IP (network) address. Review *"ARP and RARP."*

11 **B, C, E.** BGP, EIGRP, and OSPF are all considered routing protocols. Read *"Routing versus routed protocols."*

12 **D.** IP address, port number. TCP sockets consist of IP addresses and port numbers. See *"The session layer: Layer 5."*

Chapter 3: IP Addressing

Exam Objectives

✓ Describing the purpose of IP addressing

✓ Identifying responsible IP address issuing authorities and their methods

✓ Separating IP addresses using network and host ID bits

✓ Understanding the differences between public and private addressing

✓ Identifying reserved addresses

✓ Describing the three major classes of network addressing

✓ Interpreting subnet masking techniques

✓ Explaining broadcasting

✓ Describing Address Resolution Protocol and its purpose

This chapter explores the purpose and hierarchy of IP addressing in detail. I examine the process of logical network and host addressing, subnet masks, and the classes of logical IP addressing. Private and broadcast addresses are clarified, and real-world addressing examples are given so that you will have a clear understanding of how IP addressing works. This is essential information needed to pass the exam. But never fear! Understanding IP addressing is not as difficult as you may think!

The Purpose of IP Addresses — It's All about the Delivery

The major purpose of IP addressing is to exchange data across the network between two hosts using *datagrams,* or *packets.* Packets are broken-up independent pieces of data that consist of header and trailer information, and they contain source and delivery addresses, along with various control information. These source and destination addresses allow packets to reach the proper destination; the packets can then be reassembled in the proper sequence by the receiving machine.

Three important components are involved in the delivery of IP packets:

✦ The individual *IP address* is used to identify each host on the network.

✦ The *gateway address* is used to get these packets to the correct network.

✦ The *subnet mask* separates the IP address into a network portion and a host portion.

I examine subnet masking later in this chapter.

This addressing technique is similar to how the post office uses your home address to deliver your mail. Without the proper address, delivery would be impossible. The IP address, gateway address, and subnet mask are three essential items in the IP addressing scheme. Internet Protocol version 4 (IPv4) allows a grand total of 4,294,967,296 available IP addresses. This may sound like a lot, but more than 30 million addresses are reserved for special purposes. Also, thousands of new networks from around the world are being created daily, and available IP addresses are disappearing quickly. Eventually, the IP address pool will be depleted. I cover one solution to this problem (IPv6) in Book II, Chapter 5. For now, I focus on how and where you get these IPv4 addresses.

The show IP interface brief command on the router displays a summary of its configured IP address, default gateway, and subnet mask.

The Hierarchy of IP Addresses — Who's in Charge?

Assigning unique IP addresses for each network around the globe is no easy task:

✦ The *Internet Assigned Numbers Authority (IANA)* is responsible for worldwide IP address assignment and DNS root zone management.

The IANA is operated by the *Internet Corporation for Assigned Names and Numbers (ICANN),* which delegates large blocks of IP addresses to a *Regional Internet Registry (RIR).*

✦ RIRs are assigned IP allocation responsibilities based on geographic location and hand down further assignment to a *Local Internet Registry (LIR).* There are five RIRs including the American Registry for Internet Numbers (ARIN), RIPE Network Coordination Centre (Europe, Middle East, Central Asia), Asia-Pacific Network Information Centre (APNIC), Latin American and Caribbean Internet Addresses Registry (LACNIC), and African Network Information Centre (AfriNIC).

✦ LIRs work with local *Internet service providers (ISP)* to assign IP addresses to individual organizations.

Network and host addressing

Each device on a TCP/IP (IPv4) network uses a unique 4-byte, or 32-bit, decimal IP address for communication and is composed of two distinct parts: a *network address* and a *host address.* This addressing scheme is known as *dotted-decimal notation,* where each byte (8 bits) in the IP address is called an *octet.* IP addresses are four octets long and house the address of the host machine and the network to which it belongs. Each octet is then separated by a dot.

Figure 3-1 shows a typical IP address:

172.16.10.100

8 bits/ 1 byte	8 bits/ 1 byte	8 bits/ 1 byte	8 bits/ 1 byte

Figure 3-1:
IP address
example.

172	16	10	100
Octet	Octet	Octet	Octet

Network   32-bit IP Address   Host

In this IP address example, the first octet is 172. This value on the IP address class list lands between 128 and 191 and is designated as a Class B network. In a Class B network with a default subnet mask (16 bits), 172.16 is the network portion of the address, and 10.100 is the host portion of the address on the 172.16 network. See the following section for further information on IP address classes.

IP ignores the host portion of the IP address and only uses the network portion to route packets between networks. Then the complete four-octet IP address is used to make final delivery decisions to the exact node on the destination network.

Each of these four octets contains a decimal value from 0 to 255 that is translated into binary format by the computer. Each bit in the 8-bit octet has an assigned value of 128, 64, 32, 16, 8, 4, 2, or 1. An octet (decimal) value of 0 would look like 00000000 in binary. An octet (decimal) value of 255 would be represented in binary as all 1s, or 11111111. I explain the significance of the binary numbering scheme as I examine the distinct classes of IP addresses in the next section.

Classes of IP addresses

IPv4 addressing is divided into five structured classes of addresses (A, B, C, D, and E), which help in identification and ease of administration:

✦ The first three classes — A, B, and C — are the main, publicly available classes and are the most well known.

✦ Classes D and E are reserved for multicast and experimental purposes.

Classes are determined by investigating the first few binary bits of an IP address. These starting bits are called *high-order bits* and start with either a 0 or a 1. These bits are read by IP software to determine the logical network and host addresses of devices. Figure 3-2 takes a closer look at the rules that define each address class.

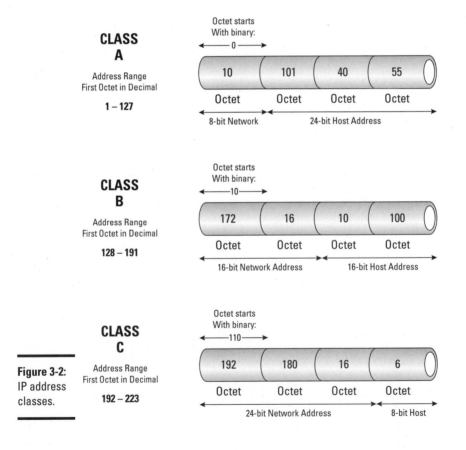

Figure 3-2: IP address classes.

✦ **Class A (0–127):** Only 128 Class A networks are available in the IPv4 addressing scheme, and these are reserved for large organizations:

- The first bit in the IP address is 0 and identifies it as Class A.

- The remaining 7 bits of the first octet are network-identifying bits.

- The last 24 bits are reserved for host-bit addresses and are available for use by more than 16 million Class A network hosts.

In Figure 3-3, you can see the upper and lower network possibilities for a Class A network in binary notation.

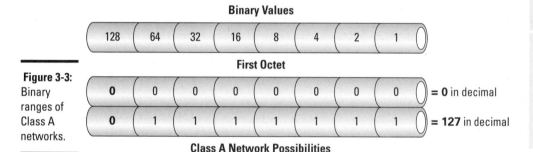

Figure 3-3:
Binary ranges of Class A networks.

✦ **Class B (128–191):** Comprised of medium-sized organizations and identified by the first 2 bits of the IP address:

- The first 2 bits are represented by 1 0 in binary format (the first bit is a 1, and the second is a 0).

- The following 14 bits in the first two octets are used for network addresses.

- The remaining 16 bits are used for host addressing.

Class B allows 16,384 networks, with each network containing up to 65,536 hosts. Figure 3-4 lists the upper and lower network possibilities for Class B networks in binary notation.

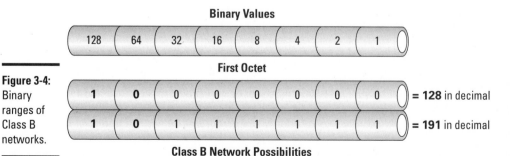

Figure 3-4:
Binary ranges of Class B networks.

✦ **Class C (192–223):** The most commonly found networks on the Internet are Class C networks and use 1 1 0 as the first 3 bits of the address. The next 21 bits are used for network addressing, and the last 8 bits specify the host addresses. There are more than 2 million possible addresses for Class C networks, with each of these networks containing up to 254 hosts. The upper and lower network possibilities for Class C networks in binary notation are listed in Figure 3-5.

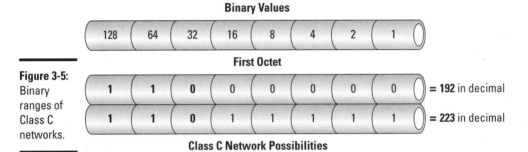

Figure 3-5:
Binary ranges of Class C networks.

✦ **Class D (224–239):** Used for *multicasting* purposes and not for general network addressing. For this reason, Class D addresses are not issued to the public or available for commercial use. These addresses start with 1 1 1 0 as the first 4 network bits in the first octet, which are used to address groups of IP devices all at the same time. In Figure 3-6, you can see the reserved binary structure of Class D networks. Also, refer to RFC 1112 for more information.

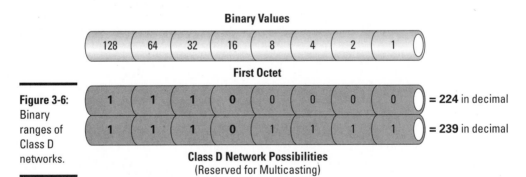

Figure 3-6:
Binary ranges of Class D networks.

✦ **Class E (240–254):** Addresses reserved for research and experimental purposes. Class E addresses are not issued for commercial use. Class E addressing uses 1 1 1 1 as the first 4 bits in the address, as shown in Figure 3-7.

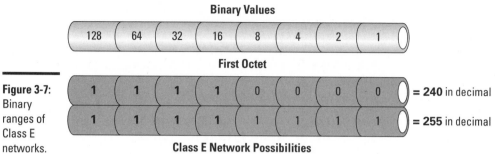

Figure 3-7:
Binary
ranges of
Class E
networks.

By referring to Figure 3-8, you can now get a complete overall picture of address classes, IP address ranges, and number of hosts available per network depicted in decimal notation.

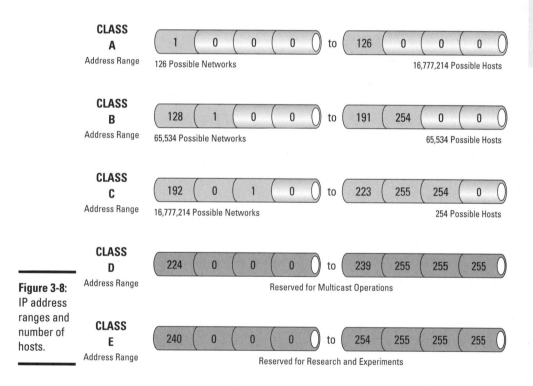

Figure 3-8:
IP address
ranges and
number of
hosts.

Other reserved addresses

You have just seen how Class D and E networks (starting at 224) are reserved for special purposes and not available for host addressing. There are other reserved addresses as well. Two of the main ones are designated for the *default route* and *loopback address*. The default route address is represented as 0.0.0.0 and is used to simplify the routing information that IP uses. Any route lookup failure defaults back to this route. The loopback address space is 127.0.0.0 and is used for testing and treating a local host as if it were remote to the network. This virtual network interface can be used to send data between client and server applications on the same machine. I examine other reserved address space allocations for private networking in the section "Private IP Addresses — We Reserve the Right . . .," later in this chapter.

Host numbers 0 and 255 are reserved for network identification and broadcasting, respectively. You find out more about these a little later in the chapter.

Understanding network ID, host ID, and subnet masks

To understand IP address resolution, you need to understand how to decode the IP address and extract the two main identifiers:

✦ A network ID (the network bits)

✦ A host ID (the bits the system administrator controls locally when assigning IP addresses)

The network ID identifies the network, and the host ID identifies the host on the local-area network.

You can decipher the network ID, the *subnets*, and the host IDs available from each IP address by analyzing its binary equivalent. Using Figure 3-9, I compare an IP address using the decimal system and its binary equivalent.

Figure 3-9:
IP address represented in decimal and binary.

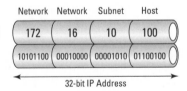

IP addresses with all decimal 0s in the host address octets represent the network segment and are reserved (not issued to network clients).

I now take a look at network and host addressing using the IP address example of 172.16.10.100. You already know that 172.16 is the network portion and 10.100 is the host portion of this Class B network address. The entire 172.16 network is specified using 0s, or written as 172.16.**0.0**, and is not assignable to any network client. This IP represents the entire 172.16 network "wire" and is reserved. The 172.16 network can be subdivided or split into subnetworks, or subnets, using, or "borrowing," from the host portion of the IP address as follows:

172.16.**1**.0	Subnet 1 on network 172.16.0.0
172.16.**2**.0	Subnet 2 on network 172.16.0.0
172.16.**3**.0	Subnet 3 on network 172.16.0.0
172.16.**16**.0	Subnet 16 on network 172.16.0.0

**Book II
Chapter 3**

IP Addressing

These subnetworks are divided logically into smaller groups but still remain a part of the 172.16.0.0 network. Subnets are logical divisions of IP-based networks split into smaller groups for increased flexibility and traffic management. More efficient addressing schemes may be implemented, and broadcast traffic can be reduced. These divided subnets remain under the same single (local) administration and use *subnet masking* techniques, which "borrow" bits from the host portion of the IP address. I examine subnetting in detail throughout Book II, Chapter 4.

For now, just keep in mind a few subnetting basics:

✦ A subnet mask — or subnet address — is used by routers to assist in determining the network portion of an IP address from the host portion.

✦ The subnet mask is a 32-bit value just like the IP address. The binary 1 bits correspond to the network and subnet portions of the address. The 0 bits are host representatives. In Figure 3-10, you can see a standard subnet mask and its equivalent value in binary. Underneath the standard mask is a subnetted example and its network ID value in binary.

✦ Three standard masks exist for Class A, B, and C networks:

• Standard Class A subnet mask: 255.0.0.0

• Standard Class B subnet mask: 255.255.0.0

• Standard Class C subnet mask: 255.255.255.0

In each case, the decimal value of 255 represents all 1s (11111111) in binary format.

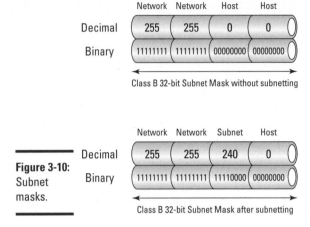

Class B 32-bit Subnet Mask without subnetting

Figure 3-10:
Subnet
masks.

Class B 32-bit Subnet Mask after subnetting

Private IP Addresses — We Reserve the Right . . .

The global shortage of IPv4 addresses is a real problem. One "Band-Aid" fix for this shortage is a *private IP addressing* solution. Private IP addressing was originally conceived to address this problem by using IP addresses that are not globally allocated by the RIR. That means that anyone can assign and use this block of reserved IP addresses on his or her network without the need to register them with the IANA. These private IP addresses are not routable on the public Internet (private IPs are routable inside the private organization's network) and are unable to access the Internet without assistance.

Network Address Translation (NAT) or a *proxy server* is required to allow hosts with private IP addresses access to the Internet.

The address ranges for these private networks are as follows:

Class	From	To
A	10.0.0.0	10.255.255.255
B	172.16.0.0	172.31.255.255
C	192.168.0.0	192.168.255.255

One common use of NAT and private IP addressing is found in home networks. Each home user is typically assigned one IP address for Internet access. If the home user needs Internet access for five PCs, this creates a problem. Network Address Translation (enabled on the home user's router) allows Internet access for each machine assigned a private IP address. A

NAT-enabled router receives packets from the local network and analyzes and modifies each packet header, replacing the internal IP address with the public address of the router. This appears to the outside world as if all internal private traffic is occurring from one public IP address assigned to the router. This example is actually called *NAT overload* or *Port Address Translation (PAT)*. I examine NAT and PAT in detail in Book VI, Chapter 3.

The benefits of private IP addressing are as follows:

✦ Allows entire private network to use a small number of public IP addresses, or even a single public IP address

✦ Provides increased security for local hosts by obscuring the actual network addressing scheme

✦ Preserves IPv4 address space

Broadcasting — Shouting to the World!

A broadcast address is a reserved address used to send data to all nodes in the same collision domain.

This differs from *unicasting,* which addresses only one specific host, and *multicasting,* which is used to specify a group of systems (not all) on the same subnet.

Broadcast information reaches every machine on the same network segment (not separated by a gateway router) and is useful for exchanging service announcements and state availability of nodes on the local network. Gateway routers do not pass broadcast traffic and can be used to segment networks to minimize collisions and unwanted traffic.

Broadcast IP addresses are determined from the IP address and subnet mask of the individual subnet. Before I get into Layer 3 broadcasts, I first need to revisit how broadcasting works at Layer 2.

Replacing Layer 2 hubs with either Layer 2 or Layer 3 switches also creates *segmentation* and decreases collision domains.

Although a router can pass broadcast messages between subnetworks, routers are usually configured to block broadcasts from traversing their interfaces. This reduces and separates traffic between subnets, improving individual network performance.

Data-link Layer 2 broadcasts

A hardware broadcast, or MAC broadcast, is a data frame that is transmitted on an Ethernet network simultaneously to all devices on the local subnet. These broadcast frames do not traverse the Layer 3 gateway (router). A Layer 2 frame broadcast is recognizable by the reserved destination MAC address of FF:FF:FF:FF:FF:FF.

Broadcast addresses are always the highest IP address in an individual network or subnet. Addresses that identify the network are always the lowest.

Network Layer 3 broadcasts

A network Layer 3 broadcast is a message sent to all devices or interfaces located in an IP network, or subnet. These data packets are usually defined as either *limited (flooded)* or *direct* broadcasts. A limited or flooded broadcast is sent from one network interface to all other network interfaces on the same network segment. This type of broadcast is not forwarded by routers and stays local on the same segmented network. It is represented by the IP address 255.255.255.255. A direct broadcast may traverse the router to reach its destination and has the form of x.x.255.255.

This datagram is viewed by the router as a regular packet and is not considered a broadcast message until it reaches the intended subnet. Figure 3-11 shows an example of a Layer 3 flooded broadcast:

✦ Network IP = 172.16.0.0

✦ Subnet = 255.255.0.0

✦ IP broadcast = 172.16.255.255

Figure 3-12 shows another type of broadcast. This is an example of a Layer 3–directed broadcast and traverses the router into the remote network:

✦ Network IP = 172.16.16.0

✦ Subnet = 255.255.255.0

✦ IP broadcast = 172.16.16.255

Some examples of IP broadcasts are:

✦ DHCP packets

✦ RIP routing table updates

✦ ARP requests

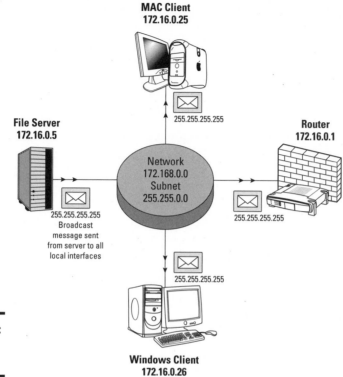

MAC Client
172.16.0.25

File Server
172.16.0.5

255.255.255.255

Router
172.16.0.1

Network
172.168.0.0
Subnet
255.255.0.0

255.255.255.255

255.255.255.255
Broadcast
message sent
from server to all
local interfaces

255.255.255.255

Figure 3-11:
Broadcast
example A.

Windows Client
172.16.0.26

Book II
Chapter 3

IP Addressing

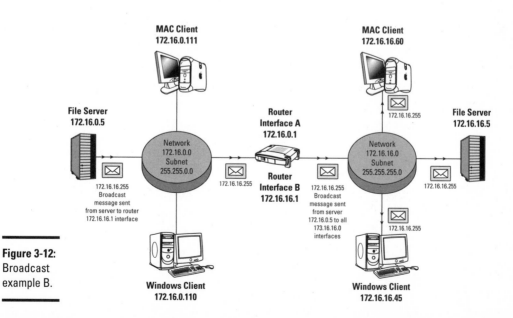

MAC Client
172.16.0.111

MAC Client
172.16.16.60

File Server
172.16.0.5

Router
Interface A
172.16.0.1

File Server
172.16.16.5

172.16.16.255

Network
172.16.0.0
Subnet
255.255.0.0

172.16.16.255

Router
Interface B
172.16.16.1

172.16.16.255

Network
172.16.16.0
Subnet
255.255.255.0

172.16.16.255

172.16.16.255
Broadcast
message sent
from server to router
172.16.16.1 interface

172.16.16.255
Broadcast
message sent
from server
172.16.0.5 to all
173.16.16.0
interfaces

172.16.16.255

Figure 3-12:
Broadcast
example B.

Windows Client
172.16.0.110

Windows Client
172.16.16.45

Address Resolution Protocol — ARP's on the Case, Sherlock!

Communication between nodes on the same network is made possible by Layer 2 MAC addressing. To share information, each host is assigned a physical address (usually burned into the ROM of the network adapter) and must know the MAC address of the recipient's interface. When these physical addresses are unknown, they must be discovered to allow communications between hosts. That's where Address Resolution Protocol (ARP) begins its investigative duties.

The purpose of ARP

ARP requests allow network clients to dynamically discover these unknown hardware addresses by "ARPing" for them using the known IP address. After sending an ARP request for a known IP to all workstations on the LAN, the answering (target) interface returns its MAC address to the ARP requester, and an ARP cache entry is made. This ARP cache contains a map of the IP-to-MAC address resolutions and saves the address to the table, avoiding further broadcast traffic on the network until the ARP cache is flushed. This ARP table is dynamic and is checked before broadcasting the next ARP request, which helps minimize broadcast traffic.

Proxy ARP

Devices that intercept ARP requests destined for other hosts use a technique called *proxy ARP*. This service is usually handled by routers and intercepts and answers the ARP requests intended for other nodes.

This is used on nodes not configured with a default gateway.

And what about RARP?

Reverse Address Resolution Protocol (RARP) provides the inverse operations of ARP and requests IP addresses from known hardware addresses. An example of RARP would be a diskless workstation connecting to the network on bootup and "RARPing" for an IP address using its known (burned-in) MAC address.

Physical (MAC) addresses are used in delivery of data packets between nodes on the same local network. Logical (IP) addresses are used to determine packet delivery to nodes on the destination internetwork.

Prep Test

1 Which part of an IP address identifies specific devices on the network?

- A ○ Network ID
- B ○ Third octet
- C ○ First 2 bits
- D ○ Host ID

2 Which of the following are routable Class A IP host addresses? (Choose two.)

- A ○ 10.0.0.54
- B ○ 126.0.0.1
- C ○ 82.82.82.82
- D ○ 127.22.34.100
- E ○ 0.54.9.7

3 Which command can be used to verify internal TCP/IP stack functionality?

- A ○ ping 192.168.1.1
- B ○ ping 127.0.0.1
- C ○ ping 10.0.0.1
- D ○ ping 172.168.0.1

4 What is the binary number 01111101 in decimal?

- A ○ 6
- B ○ 140
- C ○ 125
- D ○ 126

5 Which of the following is the broadcast address for network 172.168.0.0 with a 255.255.0.0 subnet mask?

- A ○ 172.168.16.254
- B ○ 172.168.0.1
- C ○ 172.168.255.255
- D ○ 255.255.255.254

6 Which of the following are reserved IP addresses and cannot be issued to public hosts? (Choose three.)

A ○ 127.0.0.100

B ○ 172.31.1.1

C ○ 0.5.77.21

D ○ 126.4.16.36

E ○ 111.62.54.4

F ○ 191.6.7.8

7 Which part of a Class A IP address using a standard 8-bit subnet mask identifies the host ID?

A ○ First octet

B ○ First, second, and third octet

C ○ First and second octet

D ○ Second, third, and fourth octet

8 Which settings must be configured on a host to pass IP traffic across an inter-network? (Choose three.)

A ○ ICMP

B ○ Default gateway

C ○ Loopback address

D ○ IP address

E ○ MAC address

　F　Subnet mask

9 Which protocol investigates the network for an IP address from the known hardware address?

A ○ RARP

B ○ ICMP

C ○ ARP

D ○ ARP proxy

10 Select some of the benefits of private IP addressing? (Choose all that apply.)

A ○ Does not require NAT

B ○ Increased security

C ○ Saves IPv4 address space

D ○ Allows entire private network to use one public IP address

Answers

1 **D.** Host ID. The host portion of the IP address specifies the individual nodes on the network. Review *"Network and host addressing."*

2 **B, C.** 126.0.0.1 and 82.82.82.82. Both IPs 82.82.82.82 and 126.0.0.1 are valid Class A network addresses. See *"Classes of IP addresses."*

3 **B.** `ping 127.0.0.1`. Loopback testing is done using the 127.0.0.0 reserved address space. Refer to *"Other reserved addresses."*

4 **C.** 125. The decimal value of 125 is 01111101 in binary form. Review *"Classes of IP addresses."*

5 **C.** 172.168.255.255. The broadcast address for the 172.168.0.0 network is 172.168.255.255. Read *"Network Layer 3 broadcasts."*

6 **A, B, C.** 127.0.0.100, 172.31.1.1, 0.5.77.21. The 127 range is reserved for loopback testing. The 172 address range is used for private IP addressing and is not routable over the Internet. The 0 address range is reserved for the default path. See *"Other reserved addresses."*

7 **D.** The second, third, and fourth octet. The first octet in a Class A network using the 255.0.0.0 subnet mask represents the network ID. The second, third, and fourth octets represent the host IDs. Check out *"Understanding network ID, host ID, and subnet masks."*

8 **B, D, F.** Default gateway, IP address, subnet mask. The IP address, default gateway, and subnet mask are all required by the client to transfer IP packets across the WAN. Read *"The Purpose of IP Addresses — It's All about the Delivery."*

9 **A.** RARP. RARP provides the inverse functionality of ARP and retrieves IP addresses from known MAC addresses. Review *"And what about RARP?"*

10 **B, C, D.** Increased security, saves IPv4 address space, allows entire private network to use one public IP address. Three important reasons to use private IPs are to maximize local network security, minimize depletion of global IP availability, and use one public IP (NAT). Read *"Private IP Addresses — We Reserve the Right . . ."*

Chapter 4: Subnetting

Exam Objectives

✔ Describing the purpose and function of subnetting

✔ Dividing networks into smaller pieces called subnets

✔ Understanding proper subnetwork planning

✔ Describing classless interdomain routing

✔ Identifying CIDR slash notation

✔ Subnetting Class A, B, and C networks

✔ Using hexadecimal and binary conversion

✔ Understanding subnet zero

✔ Identifying and using variable-length subnet masks (VLSMs)

✔ Explaining summarization

✔ Understanding the ANDing process

This chapter examines and provides detailed examples of how subnetting works and why it is used in so many organizations around the world. A proper understanding of subnetting is essential for passing the CCNA exam. I discuss how to create subnets and how to determine the subnet and number of hosts from the IP address. I take a look at classless interdomain routing (CIDR) and its uses and provide you with examples of subnetting from the three major classes, A, B, and C. Variable-length subnet masks (VLSMs) and summarization are also discussed.

Before even scheduling your CCNA test, you should know this chapter forward, backward, inside out, and upside down! So now I get right to it . . . Subnetting 101!

Subnetting Basics

The IP address is comprised of the network ID and host ID fields, with a logically invisible separating line dividing the two. This dividing line can be shifted, or "moved to the right," by the network administrator to add configuration flexibility to the local-area network. Logical networks may be added to the configuration of the local infrastructure by reducing the amount of allowed hosts on the network. By subtracting available hosts, the amount of available networks or subnets is increased.

Subnets are logically defined groups of smaller networks represented by the same network and subnet ID in the IP address. This can represent individual departments in a corporate environment, all separated by unique network IDs. Using subnetting, the Accounting, Human Resources, and Legal Affairs offices may be split into logical groupings of smaller networks that still reside in the overall corporate network. In Figure 4-1, you can see a typical organization split into departmental subnets. But why do this?

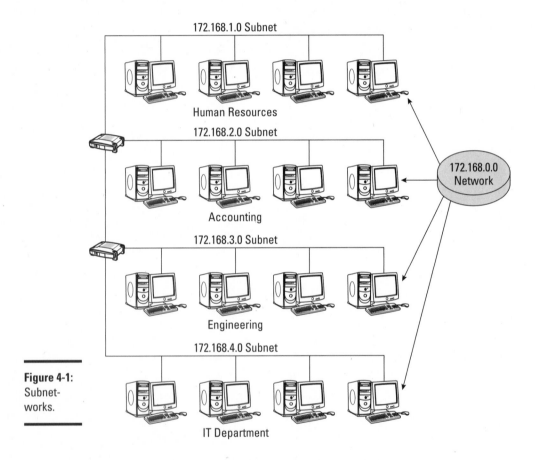

172.168.1.0 Subnet

Human Resources

172.168.2.0 Subnet

Accounting

172.168.3.0 Subnet

Engineering

172.168.4.0 Subnet

IT Department

172.168.0.0 Network

Figure 4-1:
Subnet-
works.

Purpose of subnetting

One of the main reasons for subnetting is to split one large network into smaller, logical chunks of space. This makes things easier to manage and also keeps problems restricted to their own subnets. Broadcast traffic is minimized throughout the network and is contained in each group's network structure. This helps significantly with troubleshooting issues and isolating problems on the network.

Another good reason for subnetting is having two portions of the network that are geographically separated from one another. Each remote site connects using a router's WAN link and uses separate network IDs in the IP address to split them logically. They still belong to the same overall corporate network but are divided into subnets for management and location-related reasons. As shown in Figure 4-2, if you move your logical dividing line to the right and increase your network ID bits, you increase the amount of networks. This decreases the amount of allowed hosts on the network, and address usage as a whole becomes more efficient. The outside world still sees the network as one complete network, but inside the organization, the structure has been modified and grouped into smaller pieces. There are some additional benefits to using this approach.

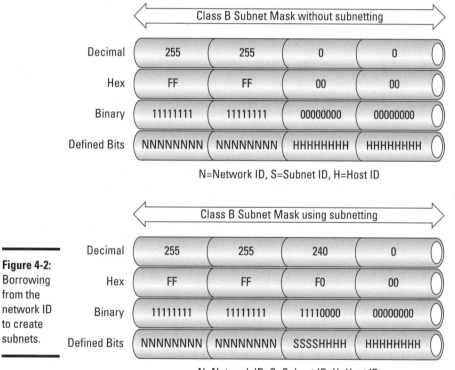

Figure 4-2: Borrowing from the network ID to create subnets.

Individual departments may have very different volumes of network traffic. One department may have a high volume of daily network traffic and another department, a significantly lower amount. If these departments coexist on the same logical network, they will be competing for network bandwidth and can cause major delays in data access times. By separating or segmenting the two departments, each department is allocated its own bandwidth, and data collisions are minimized. Data traffic from one subnet will not interfere with the other subnet. This separation of subnetworks is also beneficial for subnets using different LAN protocols on the same network. A very good reason to subnet is to separate a Token Ring network from an Ethernet network.

Subnet masks

Subnet masking is used to recognize or reveal the subnet contained in the IP address. Every node on the same subnet must have the same subnet mask. The subnet mask helps you to decode the IP address and decipher the individual network bits, subnet bits, and host — or interface — bits. Network devices use the subnet mask to determine which part of the IP is a network address and which part is the interface. By using the IP address and subnet mask, networking devices can calculate which devices are located on the same subnet, on a different subnet on the same organizational network, or on a completely different network.

Like the IP address, the subnet mask consists of a 32-bit binary numbering system that is represented in decimal notation. The first decimal value in the first octet of a subnet mask is always 255.*x.x.x.* This means that all first 8 bits are "on," or written as 11111111 in binary.

Using subnetting, the 1 bits always represent the network and subnet portion of the IP address, and the 0 bits represent the hosts on the network. As you read in the previous chapter, standard masks exist for Class A (255.0.0.0), B (255.255.0.0), and C (255.255.255.0) networks. These default masks are used when no subnetting is required. Things get a little more interesting when you need to take one network and split it into several subdivisions of networks. In Figure 4-2, you saw how a default mask is represented in binary compared to a network using subnetting. Figure 4-3 shows possible bit positions as related to subnet masking for individual subnets.

The portion of the subnet mask that defines the individual subnets is not fixed and is not required to fit exactly into each octet. Bits that define the subnetwork occupy binary space that formerly belonged to the host ID exclusively, splitting the host octet into a subnet and host portion.

Although byte-sized (1 octet/8 bits) subnet masking is used and easier to read, subnet addressing relies on bits as the determining boundary factor, not the individual octets! Also, subnet masks are only used on the local network, and all subnetworks appear as one large network to the outside world.

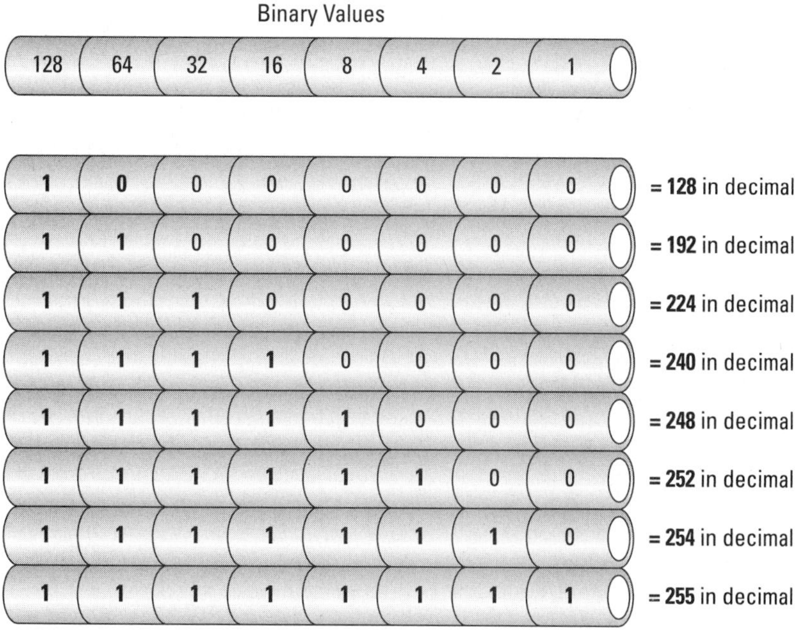

Binary Values

128	64	32	16	8	4	2	1

1	0	0	0	0	0	0	0	= **128** in decimal
1	1	0	0	0	0	0	0	= **192** in decimal
1	1	1	0	0	0	0	0	= **224** in decimal
1	1	1	1	0	0	0	0	= **240** in decimal
1	1	1	1	1	0	0	0	= **248** in decimal
1	1	1	1	1	1	0	0	= **252** in decimal
1	1	1	1	1	1	1	0	= **254** in decimal
1	1	1	1	1	1	1	1	= **255** in decimal

Figure 4-3:
Subnet
mask bit
positions.

Creating subnets

A good measure of proper planning is required before deciding to break up a large organizational network into logical subnets:

✦ You must first determine how many individual subnets you need today, also considering future growth requirements.

✦ Another tricky factor to consider is deciding how many host addresses and network interfaces will be needed on each of these subnets.

By determining the amount of networks and the number of hosts on each network, you can choose an appropriate subnet mask.

When creating subnets, the host octet value of 0 in dotted-decimal is reserved for the network segment address and is not used for host addressing. Also, the host octet decimal value of 255 is reserved for messaging to all hosts and is represented as a broadcast message.

I have already discussed how subnetting improves network performance and divides a network into smaller pieces. A downside to subnetting is that routing complexity is increased as subnets are added. Solid planning and good network documentation are essential. I now take a deeper look into the planning process and subnet creation throughout the remainder of this chapter.

Subnet mask, network ID, host ID, and broadcast IP

I first review the relationship among subnet masks, network and host IDs, and the broadcast IP address for a given subnet by examining the following example.

Assume that you have a network address of 172.16.0.0 with the default subnet mask of 255.255.0.0. You then "borrow" from the host portion (host portions are the third and fourth octet) or shift over 1 complete byte of the subnet mask, extending the network portion of the subnet mask to cover the entire third octet. The subnet mask would then look like this: 255.255.255.0. Your change looks like this in binary:

11111111.11111111.00000000.00000000

to

11111111.11111111.**11111111**.00000000

The first 16 bits in both examples define the original network ID. The change comes in the third octet, which has now morphed from a host ID octet to a subnetted one. The fourth octet is now used for hosts using the new mask compared to the third and fourth octets from the standard mask.

You have just created an 8-bit subnet by changing the default mask from 255.255.0.0 to 255.255.255.0. What does this give you for choices when planning your organizational subnet structure? Discounting the reserved network segment — or "wire" — dotted-decimal address of 0 and the reserved broadcast decimal address of 255, you can now assign 254 unique host addresses on 256 unique subnets, instead of the 65,534 host addresses on a single network provided by the default mask.

So for instance, subnet 172.16.1.0 has the host range possibilities of 172.16.1.1–172.16.1.254, with 172.16.1.255 reserved as the broadcast address for that subnet. I examine typical examples of Class A, B, and C subnetting in an upcoming section, but for now, I turn my attention to classless interdomain routing.

Classless interdomain routing (CIDR)

Classless interdomain routing — pronounced *cider* for short — was created to solve the problems introduced by the *classful* (A–E) addressing scheme and to prevent address space depletion. CIDR uses a masking technique (instead of a classful addressing one) to determine the target network, eliminating the classful configuration limitations and preventing the waste of classful system addressing. In classful addressing, the amount of assignable host and network addresses available to the system administrator can be excessive and prove to be very inefficient.

An organization given a Class A network address may have only a few thousand hosts connected to the network, but this class allocates the addressing capability for over 16 million hosts. The shortage of Class B IP addresses led ISPs to issue ranges of Class C network addresses that can accommodate an organization's need while saving Class B address space.

These classes (especially class C networks) also proved to be a serious burden on networking equipment due to the rapid size growth and inefficiency of the routing tables. Just think of all the Class A, B, and C network possibilities that would have to be stored in each router's Internet routing table!

By eliminating this classful system for a classless one, a more efficient use of address space is introduced, which allocates only the addressing space currently needed for that particular network. As shown in Figure 4-4, classless interdomain routing uses masking techniques to create subnetworks other than what a default mask allows. The subnetwork mask is then built using the bits borrowed from the host ID and recognized as network ID bits. Using CIDR and route aggregation, which I discuss later in this chapter, a flexible system of addressing and routing is realized, beneficial for the router's processor and memory performance and reducing the size of routing tables. Classful addressing is then discarded and replaced with *CIDR notation.*

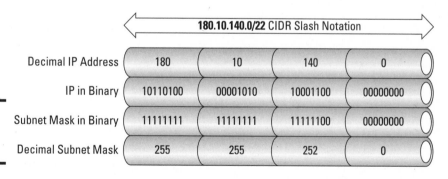

Figure 4-4: CIDR notation.

In the previous IP address examples, you can determine which class an IP address belongs to by categorizing it in one particular class list (A, B, or C). With CIDR notation, this is no longer the case. You cannot identify a particular class by examining the octets alone. You must use a modified method of examining the subnet mask. In CIDR notation, you follow the IP address with the amount of bits assigned as the network ID, often called the *prefix length.* This CIDR, or *slash notation,* is written as follows:

180.10.140.0/22

As shown in Figure 4-4, the value 22 after the slash represents 22 "on" or 1 bits of the network ID in binary. The remaining 10 bits are "off" or 0 and represent host bits. Writing 180.10.140.0/22 is just a shortened form of writing out the entire IP and subnet mask together:

180.10.140.0 255.255.252.0

Using CIDR slash notation, there is no need to know or fit the IP address in a certain class. The network ID and host IDs are easily identified from the bit values assigned by the prefix length. Take a look at the CIDR addressing table listed in Figure 4-5.

Net. bits	Host bits	Subnet Mask	CIDR Notation	Number of Hosts	# of Equivalent "Classful" Networks		
					Class A	Class B	Class C
1	31	128.0.0.0	/1	2,147,483,646	128	-	-
2	30	192.0.0.0	/2	1,073,741,822	64	-	-
3	29	224.0.0.0	/3	536,870,910	32	-	-
4	28	240.0.0.0	/4	268,435,454	16	-	-
5	27	248.0.0.0	/5	134,217,726	8	-	-
6	26	252.0.0.0	/6	67,108,862	4	-	-
7	25	254.0.0.0	/7	33,554,430	2	-	-
8	24	255.0.0.0	/8	16,777,214	1	256	-
9	23	255.128.0.0	/9	8,388,606	1/2	128	-
10	22	255.192.0.0	/10	4,194,302	1/4	64	-
11	21	255.224.0.0	/11	2,097,150	1/8	32	-
12	20	255.240.0.0	/12	1,048,574	1/16	16	-
13	19	255.248.0.0	/13	524,286	1/32	8	-
14	18	255.252.0.0	/14	262,142	1/64	4	-
15	17	255.254.0.0	/15	131,070	1/128	2	-
16	16	255.255.0.0	/16	65,534	1/256	1	256
17	15	255.255.128.0	/17	32,766	-	1/2	128
18	14	255.255.192.0	/18	16,382	-	1/4	64
19	13	255.255.224.0	/19	8,190	-	1/8	32
20	12	255.255.240.0	/20	4,094	-	1/16	16
21	11	255.255.248.0	/21	2,046	-	1/32	8
22	10	255.255.252.0	/22	1,022	-	1/64	4
23	9	255.255.254.0	/23	510	-	1/128	2
24	8	255.255.255.0	/24	254	-	1/256	1
25	7	255.255.255.128	/25	126	-	-	1/2
26	6	255.255.255.192	/26	62	-	-	1/4
27	5	255.255.255.224	/27	30	-	-	1/8
28	4	255.255.255.240	/28	14	-	-	1/16
29	3	255.255.255.248	/29	6	-	-	1/32
30	2	255.255.255.252	/30	2	-	-	1/64

Figure 4-5: CIDR addressing table.

IP Address Class and Subnet Mask

Here are a few important considerations regarding subnet planning and addressing:

+ How many subnets are currently needed today?

+ How many subnets will be needed in the future?

+ How many assignable host addresses will be needed on each individual subnet?

+ How many interfaces or hosts must the largest subnet support?

+ How many hosts will exist on future subnets?

Things can prove to be quite complicated when planning for future growth in a network:

+ Analyze the organization's current needs.

  If 6 subnets are required today, use the binary *powers of two* ($2n$) numbering system to calculate the subnet requirements. Understanding this binary numbering system is essential for proper subnet deployment planning. 2^3 ($2*2*2$) gives you a total of 8 usable subnets, which meets the minimum requirement of 6. This equation is calculated by multiplying $2 \times 2 = 4$ and then $4 \times 2 = 8$. This is represented in binary as 11100000 as you move from left to right, taking host ID bits and changing them to network, or subnet ID, bits.

+ Take future growth into consideration.

  Maybe you are expecting your 6 subnets to possibly double to 12 over the next few years and decide on an addressing plan of 12 maximum subnets. 2^3 gives you 8 subnets but no longer meets your requirements of 12. 2^4 ($2*2*2*2$) is your next $2n$ possibility and gives you 16 maximum address spaces for the 12 planned subnets, with 4 remaining subnets for future expandability. This does limit your expansion possibilities in the future if you have miscalculated. These 16 subnets also must have large enough address spaces to support the maximum number of required hosts on each subnet.

As you move up the ladder and start increasing the amount of subnetworking possibilities, your available host addresses decline.

Class C IP address subnets

You use this binary "powers of two" numbering system to define Class C subnets. You have been assigned an IP address of 204.1.1.0 with a /24 prefix length (255.255.255.0) and require a maximum of 10 host interfaces on 12 subnets. 2^4 provides you with 16 subnets (2*2*2*2=16) and designates 4 additional network bits (**24**) for subnetting, moving from a /24 bit mask to a /28 bit mask. This leaves 28 bits for the network ID and 4 bits for host IDs. You can see the new subnet mask:

Before: 204.1.1.0/24 (255.255.255.0)

After: 204.1.1.0/28 (255.255.255.240)

Four bits remain for assigning (up to 14 maximum) host addresses on each subnet and meet your requirements of 10 interfaces per subnet.

Two host addresses are lost (2^4=16–2=14 host IDs) for network and broadcast addresses. The host addresses of all 0s and all 1s are reserved!

By creating many subnets, you have reduced your host addressing space considerably and would quickly run out of assignable addresses when additional workstations are added to each subnet. I am just using this as an example to better explain subnetting. Make sure to always find the proper balance between subnet and host allocation.

In Figure 4-6, 16 subnets and 4 additional network bits (starting from 0 to 15) are specified. All subnets are multiples of 16. You can quickly verify each subnet value by continually adding the subnet value to itself (incrementing subnets by 16 in this case).

IP subnet zero

Referring to Figure 4-6, subnet zero is the first address created in the subnetting scheme and matches the original network IP address. In the past, it had been strongly recommended to avoid using this address for subnets because this is identical to the original network address before subnetting. RFC 1878 currently designates this address as a valid subnet and can be used in the subnet addressing scheme. So how can you verify the difference between the address for the entire network and the first subnet? It's all in the CIDR slash notation:

✦ The 204.1.1.0/24 prefix length (255.255.255.0) represents the entire network.

✦ 204.1.1.0/28 notation (255.255.255.240) represents the first subnet 0.

They both use the same IP address but are handled differently by classless routing protocols due to the four-position bit jump and subnet mask assignment change (/24 vs. /28).

	Binary					Decimal			Prefix Length
Original IP	11001100	00000001	00000001	00000000	=	204	1	1	0	/24
Subnet 0	11001100	00000001	00000001	**0000**0000	=	204	1	1	0	/28
Subnet 1	11001100	00000001	00000001	**0001**0000	=	204	1	1	16	/28
Subnet 2	11001100	00000001	00000001	**0010**0000	=	204	1	1	32	/28
Subnet 3	11001100	00000001	00000001	**0011**0000	=	204	1	1	48	/28
Subnet 4	11001100	00000001	00000001	**0100**0000	=	204	1	1	64	/28
Subnet 5	11001100	00000001	00000001	**0101**0000	=	204	1	1	80	/28
Subnet 6	11001100	00000001	00000001	**0110**0000	=	204	1	1	96	/28
Subnet 7	11001100	00000001	00000001	**0111**0000	=	204	1	1	112	/28
Subnet 8	11001100	00000001	00000001	**1000**0000	=	204	1	1	128	/28
Subnet 9	11001100	00000001	00000001	**1001**0000	=	204	1	1	144	/28
Subnet 10	11001100	00000001	00000001	**1010**0000	=	204	1	1	160	/28
Subnet 11	11001100	00000001	00000001	**1011**0000	=	204	1	1	176	/28
Subnet 12	11001100	00000001	00000001	**1100**0000	=	204	1	1	192	/28
Subnet 13	11001100	00000001	00000001	**1101**0000	=	204	1	1	208	/28
Subnet 14	11001100	00000001	00000001	**1110**0000	=	204	1	1	224	/28
Subnet 15	11001100	00000001	00000001	**1111**0000	=	204	1	1	240	/28

Figure 4-6: Defining Class C subnet addresses.

Defining the Subnet Addresses
204.1.1.0/28

Book II Chapter 4

Subnetting

If you are unable to use subnet zero on your network, always remember to subtract 2 from the subnets column, exactly as done with host addressing. See Figures 4-6 and 4-7 for details.

Subnet zero is enabled by default on all routers using Cisco IOS Release 12 and higher. CLI syntax usage is `ip subnet-zero` to enable and `no ip subnet-zero` to disable this feature.

Host addressing assignments

Now that you have defined and created your 16 individual subnets, you must determine the number of host addresses allowed on each subnet and the broadcast address belonging to each subnet.

In the running example, you borrowed 4 bits from the host field and changed them to network bits, which changed your mask and left you with 4 bits for host addressing. These 4 bits provide 16 host addresses minus 2 ($2^4=16-2=14$ host IDs) for network and broadcasting, as shown in Figure 4-7. By viewing this figure, you can see that host address ranges always fall between the subnet address and the broadcast address.

Subnet #	Subnet Address	Start Host Address		End Host Address	Broadcast Address
0	0	204.1.1.1	TO	204.1.1.14	15
1	16	204.1.1.17	TO	204.1.1.30	31
2	32	204.1.1.33	TO	204.1.1.46	47
3	48	204.1.1.49	TO	204.1.1.62	63
4	64	204.1.1.65	TO	204.1.1.78	79
5	80	204.1.1.81	TO	204.1.1.94	95
6	96	204.1.1.97	TO	204.1.1.110	111
7	112	204.1.1.113	TO	204.1.1.126	127
8	128	204.1.1.129	TO	204.1.1.142	143
9	144	204.1.1.145	TO	204.1.1.158	159
10	160	204.1.1.161	TO	204.1.1.174	175
11	176	204.1.1.177	TO	204.1.1.190	191
12	192	204.1.1.193	TO	204.1.1.206	207
13	208	204.1.1.209	TO	204.1.1.222	223
14	224	204.1.1.225	TO	204.1.1.238	239
15	240	204.1.1.241	TO	204.1.1.254	255

Figure 4-7: Defining Class C host addresses.

Defining the Host Addresses
204.1.1.0/28

Referring to Figure 4-8, a complete listing of possibilities for Class C subnetting is given, including the following:

✦ Number of subnet bits used

✦ Number of host and network possibilities per subnet mask

✦ Broadcast addressing assignments

Subnet bits	Subnet Mask	Number of Subnets	Number of Hosts	Broadcast Address
0	255.255.255.0	0	254	N.N.N.255
1	255.255.255.128	2	126	N.N.N.S+129
2	255.255.255.192	4	62	N.N.N.S+63
3	255.255.255.224	8	30	N.N.N.S+31
4	255.255.255.240	16	14	N.N.N.S+15
5	255.255.255.248	32	6	N.N.N.S+7
6	255.255.255.252	64	2	N.N.N.S+3

Figure 4-8: Subnet table — Class C.

Table of Class C Subnet Structure

N=Network, S=Subnet

Class B IP address subnets

Now that you have seen exactly how subnets and hosts are determined using a Class C IP address, I take a look at another example using a Class B network. You have been issued a network IP address of 180.10.0.0 with the default mask of 255.255.0.0. This is written as 180.10.0.0/16 in CIDR notation. A total of 100 hosts per network segment on 50 subnets is required, using the $2n$ binary numbering system to determine the amount of hosts and subnets. How many bits must you borrow from the host field and change into network bits to support 100 hosts on 50 subnets?

2^6 provides you with an address range of 64 (2*2*2*2*2*2=64) and designates 6 additional network bits for subnetting, moving from a /16 bit mask (255.255.0.0) to a /22 bit mask (255.255.252.0). You now have 22 bits for the network ID and 10 bits left over for host ID addressing, giving you 64 possible networks and 1,022 hosts.

This would accommodate your requirements for 100 workstations on 50 subnets but leaves very few options for adding additional future network segments. Because you only require 100 hosts, you can steal 1 more bit from those hosts and add it to the network side of the mask. 180.10.0.0/16 has now changed from 180.10.0.0/22 to 180.10.0.0/23 (255.255.254.0) with 9 bits reserved for hosts, as shown in Figure 4-9. This 1-bit jump has just doubled your possible subnets to 128 and cut your possible hosts in half (from 1,022 to 510). You still can support 100 interfaces per subnet, but you have planned for future network growth by adding additional subnets.

	Binary					Decimal				Prefix Length
Original IP	10110100	00001010	00000000	00000000	=	180	10	0	0	/16
Subnet 0	10110100	00001010	**00000000**	00000000	=	180	10	0	0	/23
Subnet 1	10110100	00001010	**00000010**	00000000	=	180	10	2	0	/23
Subnet 2	10110100	00001010	**00000100**	00000000	=	180	10	4	0	/23
Subnet 3	10110100	00001010	**00000110**	00000000	=	180	10	6	0	/23
Subnet 4	10110100	00001010	**00001000**	00000000	=	180	10	8	0	/23
Subnet 5	10110100	00001010	**00001010**	00000000	=	180	10	10	0	/23
Subnet 6	10110100	00001010	**00001100**	00000000	=	180	10	12	0	/23
Subnet 7	10110100	00001010	**00001110**	00000000	=	180	10	14	0	/23
Subnet 8	10110100	00001010	**00010000**	00000000	=	180	10	16	0	/23
Subnet 9	10110100	00001010	**00010010**	00000000	=	180	10	18	0	/23
Subnet 10	10110100	00001010	**00010100**	00000000	=	180	10	20	0	/23
Subnet 11	10110100	00001010	**00010110**	00000000	=	180	10	22	0	/23
Subnet 12	10110100	00001010	**00011000**	00000000	=	180	10	24	0	/23

Figure 4-9:
Defining
Class B
subnet
addresses.

Ending With ...

	Binary					Decimal				Prefix Length
Subnet 127	10110100	00001010	**11111110**	00000000		180	10	254	0	/23

Defining the Subnet Addresses
180.10.0.0/23

In Figure 4-9, each of the 128 newly created subnets is listed in order from 0 to 127. Each subnet uses the 7 bits of the third octet borrowed from the host ID and converts them to network bits. Then you determine your host IP address ranges by examining how many bits remain in the host ID field. These 9 bits provide 512 host addresses minus 2 (2^9 =512–2=510 host IDs) for network and broadcasting, as shown in Figure 4-10. Again, host address ranges always fall between the subnet address and the broadcast address. Broadcast addresses are easily determined by subtracting 1 from the next subnet address.

Figure 4-11 shows a complete listing of possibilities for Class B subnetting, including the number of subnet bits used, the number of host and network possibilities per subnet mask, and the broadcast addressing assignments.

A Class B network using a 255.255.255 subnet mask allows 254 hosts on 256 separate subnets!

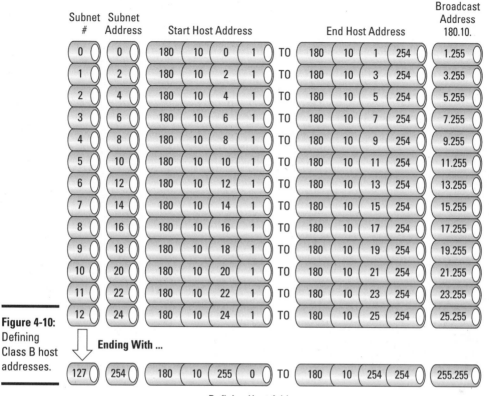

Figure 4-10:
Defining
Class B host
addresses.

Defining Host Addresses
180.10.0.0/23

Class A IP address subnets

A Class A network provides only 254 subnets but allows more than 16 million hosts on those subnets. For the last subnetting example, you split a Class A network address using the following details:

Network address: 15.0.0.0

Subnet mask: 255.0.0.0

CIDR notation: 15.0.0.0/8

Number of subnets/hosts required now: 4 subnets / 1500 hosts per subnet

Number of estimated subnets/hosts for future use: 25 subnets / 5000 hosts

Total subnets/hosts required: 29 subnets / 6500 hosts per subnet

Subnet bits	Subnet Mask	Number of Subnets	Number of Hosts	Broadcast Address
0	255.255.0.0	0	65,534	N.N.255.255
1	255.255.128.0	2	32,766	N.N.S+124.255
2	255.255.192.0	4	16,382	N.N.S+63.255
3	255.255.224.0	8	8,190	N.N.S+31.255
4	255.255.240.0	16	4,094	N.N.S+15.255
5	255.255.248.0	32	2,046	N.N.S+7.255
6	255.255.252.0	64	1,022	N.N.S+3.255
7	255.255.254.0	128	510	N.N.S+1.255
8	255.255.255.0	256	254	N.N.S.255
9	255.255.255.128	512	126	N.N.S+127
10	255.255.255.192	1,024	62	N.N.S+63
11	255.255.255.224	2,048	30	N.N.S+31
12	255.255.255.240	4,096	14	N.N.S+15
13	255.255.255.248	8,192	6	N.N.S+7
14	255.255.255.252	16,384	2	N.S.S+3

Figure 4-11:
Subnet
table —
Class B.

Table of Class B Subnet Structure
N=Network, S=Subnet

You can start by stealing some bits! Because you are using the $2n$ numbering system again to perform calculations, you cannot create exactly 29 subnets. By only borrowing 1, 2, 3, or 4 host bits, this would not give you enough subnets to fulfill your requirements. You get your required 29 subnets (you must create 32 subnets) by taking 5 host bits and morphing them into network bits. 2^5 (2*2*2*2*2) provides you with an address range of 32 subnets and gives you a new CIDR notation/prefix length of 15.0.0.0/13 (255.248.0.0). Using Figure 4-12, you can now review your Class A bit assignments.

Here's a helpful technique to use: Take 256 and subtract 248 (taken from the new subnet mask of 255.248.0.0), leaving a value of 8. Eight is the first subnet value and also the block size of your address range. As shown in Figure 4-13, by continuously adding the first subnet value to itself, you can define your additional subnets down to the last one.

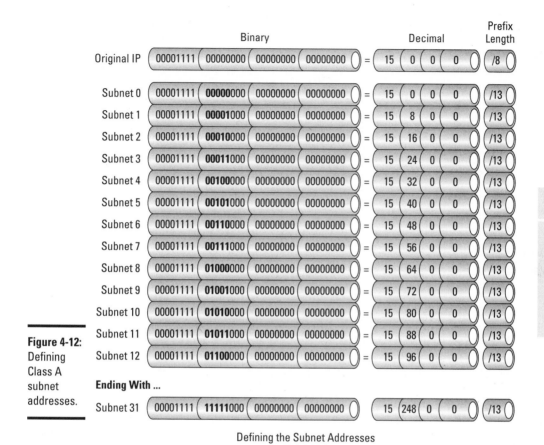

Figure 4-12:
Defining
Class A
subnet
addresses.

Defining the Subnet Addresses
15.0.0.0/13

In Figure 4-14, you can see the subnet table for Class A networks.

Remember these important factors during the planning and design phase of your organization's subnet deployment:

✦ How many subnets will your chosen subnet mask provide?

You determine this by using the powers of two. 2^3 denotes three 1 bits borrowed from the host ID (which equals 11100000 in binary) and provides 8 subnets (2*2*2=8).

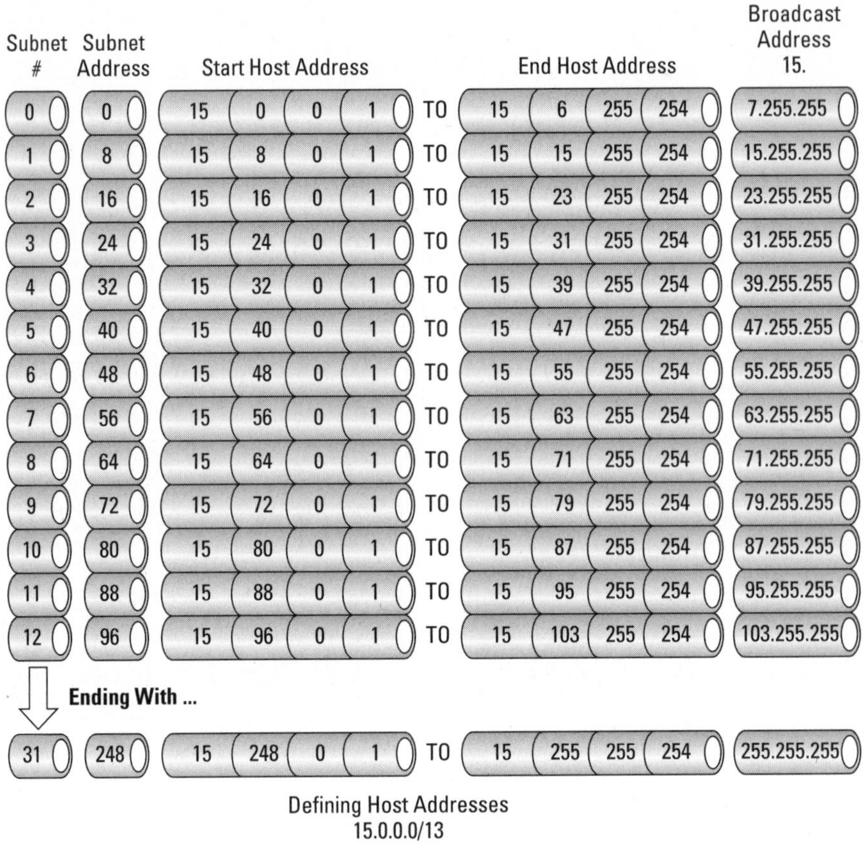

Subnet #	Subnet Address	Start Host Address					End Host Address				Broadcast Address 15.
0	0	15	0	0	1	TO	15	6	255	254	7.255.255
1	8	15	8	0	1	TO	15	15	255	254	15.255.255
2	16	15	16	0	1	TO	15	23	255	254	23.255.255
3	24	15	24	0	1	TO	15	31	255	254	31.255.255
4	32	15	32	0	1	TO	15	39	255	254	39.255.255
5	40	15	40	0	1	TO	15	47	255	254	47.255.255
6	48	15	48	0	1	TO	15	55	255	254	55.255.255
7	56	15	56	0	1	TO	15	63	255	254	63.255.255
8	64	15	64	0	1	TO	15	71	255	254	71.255.255
9	72	15	72	0	1	TO	15	79	255	254	79.255.255
10	80	15	80	0	1	TO	15	87	255	254	87.255.255
11	88	15	88	0	1	TO	15	95	255	254	95.255.255
12	96	15	96	0	1	TO	15	103	255	254	103.255.255

Ending With ...

31	248	15	248	0	1	TO	15	255	255	254	255.255.255

Figure 4-13: Defining Class A host addresses.

Defining Host Addresses
15.0.0.0/13

✦ How many hosts are available on these subnets?

You can calculate this by counting all remaining host bits in binary in the same fashion as you determined your number of subnets. The difference is that you count up the host bits, or 0 bits, that are not used by the network or subnet address. 11100000 would represent 3 "on" network bits and the remaining five 0 bits ($2^5=2*2*2*2*2=32-2$) would allow 30 hosts.

✦ What are the subnet and broadcast addresses?

You can determine subnet addresses by taking 256 and subtracting the subnet mask 255.255.255.248. This gives your block size range of 8 (256–248=8). To define all subnets, continue doubling this block size in increments of 8 until you reach your subnet mask (248).

✦ What are the valid host ranges?

The hosts are always located between the subnet and broadcast addresses. With your example block size of 8, valid host ranges would be .1–.6, with a network address of .0 and a broadcast of .7.

Subnet bits	Subnet Mask	Number of Subnets	Number of Hosts	Broadcast Address
0	255.0.0.0	0	16,777,214	N.255.255.255
1	255.128.0.0	2	8,388,606	N.S+127.255.255
2	255.192.0.0	4	4,194,302	N.S+63.255.255
3	255.224.0.0	8	2,097,150	N.S+31.255.255
4	255.240.0.0	16	1,048,574	N.S+15.255.255
5	255.248.0.0	32	524,286	N.S+7.255.255
6	255.252.0.0	64	262,142	N.S+3.255.255
7	255.254.0.0	128	131,070	N.S+1.255.255
8	255.255.0.0	256	65,534	N.S.255.255
9	255.255.128.0	512	32,766	N.S+127.255
10	255.255.192.0	1,024	16,382	N.S+63.255
11	255.255.224.0	2,048	8,190	N.S+31.255
12	255.255.240.0	4,096	4,094	N.S+15.255
13	255.255.248.0	8,192	2,046	N.S+7.255
14	255.255.252.0	16,384	1,022	N.S+3.255
15	255.255.254.0	32,768	510	N.S+1.255
16	255.255.255.0	65,536	254	N.S.255
17	255.255.255.128	131,072	126	N.S+127
18	255.255.255.192	262,144	62	N.S+63
19	255.255.255.224	524,288	30	N.S+31
20	255.255.255.240	1,048,576	14	N.S+15
21	255.255.255.248	2,097,152	6	N.S+7
22	255.255.255.252	4,194,304	2	N.S+3

Figure 4-14: Subnet table — Class A.

Table of Class A Subnet Structure
N=Network, S=Subnet

Hexadecimal-to-binary conversion

Hexadecimal (base 16) numbering uses 16 values starting with 0–9 through A–F and increases in value in increments of 1. Two hexadecimal numbers together equal 1 byte (one 8-bit octet) and is easier to read than its binary counterpart.

The following steps allow you to determine hex-to-binary equivalents:

1. Convert each hexadecimal value to decimal.

2. Convert each decimal number into 4-bit binary and write them out, from left to right, as one, long 32-bit address.

To convert from binary to hexadecimal, just reverse the process.

Here are the hex values as they equate in decimal:

Hex	0 1 2 3 4 5 6 7 8 9 A B C D E F
Decimal	0 1 2 3 4 5 6 7 8 9 10 11 12 13 14 15

Now take a closer look at how this works using the hexadecimal value of **10db**:

Hexadecimal	**1**	**0**	**D**	**B**
Decimal	1	0	13	11
Binary	0001	0000	1101	1011
32-bit address		0001000011011011		

Hex-to-binary conversion is very simple if you remember each hex value (0–9, A–F) and its decimal equivalent (0–15). Practice binary, hex, and decimal conversions until you can do them in your sleep.

Variable-Length Subnet Masks (VLSMs)

So far, you have seen the advantages of how subnetting increases your network configuration possibilities and saves address space. One major downside to subnetting is that the subnet ID is the same bit length throughout the entire network for all subnets. This creates a problem when one subnet must accommodate many more hosts than the other subnets. You can plan for this by setting up each subnet to accommodate the largest amount of hosts required, but it is not very efficient and it wastes address space.

Purpose of VLSM

A variable-length subnet mask (VLSM) is an advanced form of subnetting that allows subnets of variable lengths to all coexist under one network. The purpose of VLSM is to adjust your simple, same-size subnets to better accommodate the size requirements of your physical networks. Subnets of various lengths can be defined to better match the number of interfaces required per subnet.

To understand VLSM, view it as an address space–saving subnetting tool that subnets your subnets! Figure 4-15 provides an example of a network before and after VLSM subnetting is applied.

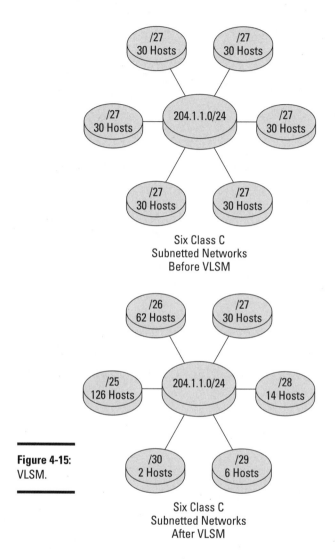

Six Class C
Subnetted Networks
Before VLSM

Book II
Chapter 4

Subnetting

Figure 4-15:
VLSM.

Six Class C
Subnetted Networks
After VLSM

Assigning subnets of variable lengths to separate interfaces on the router is possible with VLSM. This allows classless routing protocols such as Enhanced Interior Gateway Routing Protocol (EIGRP), Open Shortest Path First (OSPF), and Routing Information Protocol version 2 (RIPv2) to function with VLSM, while classful protocols such as RIP and IGRP do not. These classful protocols do not carry separate information for each subnet and assume that all subnets are using the same mask. This limitation is overcome using classless routing and VLSM.

VLSM design guidelines

Although more complex than standard subnetting, VLSM is designed and very similar to CIDR. VLSM enables subnetworking of your internal organizational subnets and can be applied as much as needed throughout the network, as long as enough host bits are available to steal from your network address block. Figure 4-16 shows the process of subnetting a network using VLSM.

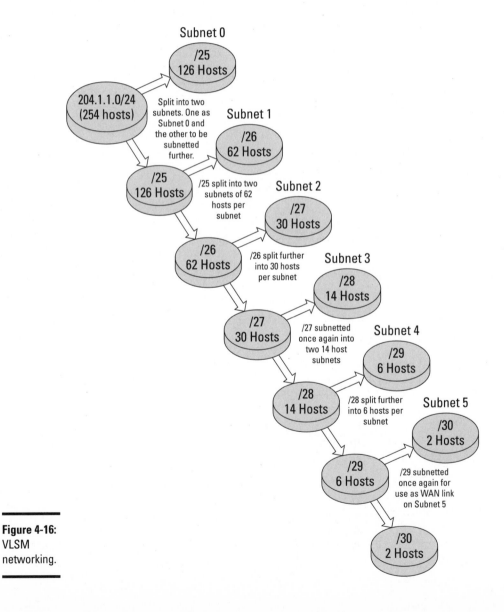

Figure 4-16:
VLSM
networking.

Optimizing IP addressing with VLSM

You can review the example of a subnetted VLSM network in Figure 4-16 by using the Class C network address of 204.1.1.0/24. You divide this network into two /25 subnetworks by stealing 1 bit from the first available host ID bit field. This gives you two subnets, 204.1.1.0/25 and 204.1.1.128/25. The 204.1.1.0/25 network is used for subnet 0 and the other will continue to be manipulated and divided again into two new /26 subnets, 204.1.1.128/26 and 204.1.1.192/26. This is done by stealing the next available host ID bit and gives you a total of 62 hosts per subnet. You then dedicate 204.1.1.128/26 for subnet 1, and the other subnet is used to create two new /27 subnets. The process continues in this fashion until you run out of host ID bits to steal and have defined all your subnets.

The VLSM subnet table is shown in Figure 4-17.

Subnet number	Address / Mask	Subnet Mask	Number of Hosts	Assignable Range
0	204.1.1.0/25	255.255.255.128	126	204.1.1.1 - 204.1.1.126
1	204.1.1.128/26	255.255.255.192	62	204.1.1.129 - 204.1.1.190
2	204.1.1.192/27	255.255.255.224	30	204.1.1.193 - 204.1.1.222
3	204.1.1.224/28	255.255.255.240	14	204.1.1.225 - 204.1.1.238
4	204.1.1.240/29	255.255.255.248	6	204.1.1.241 - 204.1.1.246
5	204.1.1.248/30	255.255.255.252	2	204.1.1.249 - 204.1.1.250

Figure 4-17: VLSM subnet table — Class C.

Summarization

VLSM breaks apart network addresses into smaller subnets. *Summarization,* often called *route aggregation* or *supernetting,* is the consolidation of many individual routes into a single route advertisement. This is the *reverse process of subnetting,* with the network and host ID dividing line moved to the left instead of the right. This supernet is a block of subnets addressed as one complete network and allows multiple network IDs to be combined under one distinct network address. This proves less taxing for bandwidth and hardware requirements and slows the growth of internetworking routing tables. The summarization process allows minimum impact to routing tables by consolidating a group of subnets into one routing table entry. By summarizing routes and having less routing table entries, less of a burden is placed on routing hardware; CPU and memory resource requirements are therefore reduced.

The main advantages of route summarization are as follows:

+ Bandwidth requirements reduced
+ Router CPU and memory requirements reduced
+ Routing table size reduced

Summarization investigated

I now focus my attention on how a router views individual routes compared to route summarization. In Figure 4-18, four individual routes are listed:

+ 204.1.4.0/24
+ 204.1.5.0/24
+ 204.1.6.0/24
+ 204.1.7.0/24

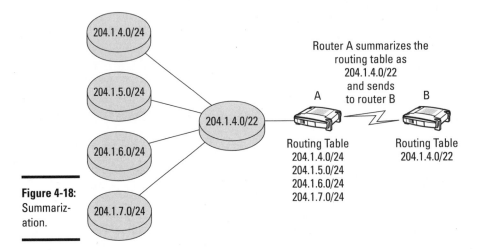

Figure 4-18: Summarization.

These four addresses are then combined, or summarized, into the address 204.1.4.0/22 by using the following procedure:

1. Convert all addresses into binary format.

2. Identify only the common bits from the four addresses, ignoring all other bits.

3. Convert these common bits back into decimal.

You have your summarization routing address.

By totaling all of those common bits, it is easy to figure out your prefix length (subnet mask).

The process is expounded using Figure 4-19.

Summarization and VLSM

Summarization works best when using contiguous blocks of subnets, as is the case in Figures 4-18 and 4-19, and requires a classless routing protocol that supports VLSM. EIGRP, BGP, RIPv2, OSPF, and IS-IS all support summarization. For review, the main steps of route aggregation are as follows:

1. Convert the decimal address to binary.

2. Identify the common bits only.

3. Convert the common bits back to decimal for summary routing address.

4. Count the common bits to determine the prefix length.

Routers dynamically learn routes to subnetworks by their routing protocols.

Book II
Chapter 4

Subnetting

	Binary					Decimal				Prefix Length
Subnet 3	**11001100**	**00000001**	00000011	00000000	=	204	1	3	0	/24
Subnet 4	**11001100**	**00000001**	**00000100**	00000000	=	204	1	4	0	/24
Subnet 5	**11001100**	**00000001**	**00000101**	00000000	=	204	1	5	0	/24
Subnet 6	**11001100**	**00000001**	**00000110**	00000000	=	204	1	6	0	/24
Subnet 7	**11001100**	**00000001**	**00000111**	00000000	=	204	1	7	0	/24
Subnet 8	**11001100**	**00000001**	00001000	00000000	=	204	1	8	0	/24

Figure 4-19: Summarization revealed.

Defining Summarization
204.1.4.0/22

Common bits are listed in **bold print**.
Subnet 3 & 8 do not have the same common bits
as do subnets 4-7 and are not included in the
summarization address.

The ANDing process

When devices on separate subnets or networks want to communicate with one another, calculations are performed to determine whether the target device is local or remote to the sending machine. This binary AND operation is performed on the sending machine to determine whether to send packets directly to a host locally on the same subnet or to the default gateway, or router.

The rules are simple when ANDing binary numbers. In binary ANDing, 1 + 1 = 1. Any other combination equals 0! The ANDing process contains these steps:

1. The sending host ANDs its own IP address with its own subnet mask.

2. The sending host then takes its own IP and ANDs it with the destination host's subnet mask.

3. The results are compared to determine the location of the destination host. If both ANDing processes produce the same result, the target host is local. If the AND process produces unequal results, the host is remote.

This process ignores host IDs and is only concerned with determining the network location. Here is an example of the AND process in binary using sending host 204.1.1.120/25 and target host 204.1.1.195:

Source IP
11001100.00000001.00000001.01111000 = 204.1.1.120

Source mask
11111111.11111111.11111111.10000000 = 255.255.255.128

ANDing result
11001100.00000001.00000001.00000000 = 204.1.1.0

Destination IP
11001100.00000001.00000001.11000011 = 204.1.1.195

Destination mask
11111111.11111111.11111111.10000000 = 255.255.255.128

ANDing result
11001100.00000001.00000001.10000000 = 204.1.1.128

As you can see from the results, source and destination devices are on separate subnets and would require a router to exchange packets.

Prep Test

1 How many hosts are available on the 200.100.15.0/24 network?

- **A** ○ 126
- **B** ○ 62
- **C** ○ 254
- **D** ○ 32

2 What is the purpose of VLSM?

- **A** ○ Splits a network into equal parts
- **B** ○ Creates sub-subnets of various lengths
- **C** ○ Optimizes and load-balances routing traffic
- **D** ○ Automatically updates routing tables

3 Which command disables (default-enabled) IP subnet zero on the router?

- **A** ○ `0 ip subnet-zero`
- **B** ○ `off ip subnet zero`
- **C** ○ `disable ip subnet-zero`
- **D** ○ `no ip subnet-zero`

4 How many bits must you borrow from a Class B host ID to get the subnet mask of 255.255.224.0?

- **A** ○ 2
- **B** ○ 3
- **C** ○ 5
- **D** ○ 4

5 Which of the following represents the reverse process of subnetting? (Choose three.)

- **A** ○ Supernetting
- **B** ○ Route aggregation
- **C** ○ VLSM
- **D** ○ Summarization
- **E** ○ Subnet masking
- **F** ○ Converting binary to dotted-decimal

6 What are important reasons for subnetting a network? (Choose three.)

A ○ Routing table size reduction

B ○ Troubleshooting and problem isolation

C ○ Separating broadcast traffic

D ○ Ease of management

E ○ Requires less planning

7 Which routing protocols support VLSM? (Choose all that apply.)

A ○ IGRP

B ○ EIGRP

C ○ RIP

D ○ IS-IS

E ○ OSPF

F ○ BGP

8 Your Class C network requires 10 subnets with 10 hosts per subnet. Which subnet mask is correct?

A ○ 255.255.255.0

B ○ 255.255.255.240

C ○ 255.255.240

D ○ 255.255.255.248

9 Which of the following networks would use the subnet mask of 255.0.0.0 by default? (Choose all that apply.)

A ○ 180.1.5.0

B ○ 129.0.0.1

C ○ 105.0.0.0

D ○ 0.6.0.5

10 What type of IP address is 204.201.210.4?

A ○ Host IP

B ○ Broadcast IP

C ○ Network IP

D ○ Multicast IP

Answers

1 **C.** 254. There are 254 (256–2) hosts addresses available on this network. Review *"Subnetting Basics."*

2 **B.** Creates sub-subnets of various lengths. VLSM allows creation of subnets of various lengths to better accommodate the number of interfaces required per subnet. Read *"Variable-Length Subnet Masks (VLSMs)."*

3 **D.** `no ip subnet-zero`. The `no ip subnet-zero` command is used to disable this feature on the router. Check out *"IP subnet zero."*

4 **B.** 3 bits. You steal the first 3 host ID bits (from left to right) and convert them to decimal (224), giving you the mask 255.255.224.0, or /19 in CIDR notation. Review *"IP Address Class and Subnet Mask."*

5 **A, B, D.** Route aggregation, supernetting, and summarization are all terms used to denote the consolidation of many individual routes into a single route advertisement. Read *"Summarization."*

6 **B, C, D.** Separating broadcast traffic, problem isolation, and simplified management are all benefits of subnetting. Review *"Purpose of subnetting."*

7 **B, D, E, F.** Classless routing protocols such as EIGRP, BGP, RIPv2, OSPF, and IS-IS all support VLSM. Check out *"Summarization and VLSM."*

8 **B.** 255.255.255.240. Borrowing 4 host bits from the fourth octet allows 14 hosts on 16 subnetted networks. Refer to *"Classless interdomain routing (CIDR)."*

9 **C.** 105.0.0.0. 105.0.0.0/8 is the only valid Class A address. See *"Subnetting Basics."*

10 **A.** Host IP. 204.201.210.4 is a Class C host address. Review *"IP Address Class and Subnet Mask."*

Chapter 5: Internet Protocol Version 6 (IPv6)

Exam Objectives

- ✓ Understanding IPv6
- ✓ Identifying IPv4 and IPv6 differences
- ✓ Examining IPv6 addressing
- ✓ Reviewing IPv6 configuration
- ✓ Routing with IPv6
- ✓ Migrating IPv4 to IPv6
- ✓ Implementing dual-stack IPv4/IPv6 protocols
- ✓ Tunneling through both IP versions

Arriving at the final chapter on the TCP/IP family, you have surely amassed a wealth of knowledge on the subject by now. I have gone over 32-bit IPv4 addressing, classifying, and subnetting fundamentals and introduced you to the popular protocols and layering methods. Now I turn your attention to a new and improved Internet protocol version, namely IPv6. On the CCNA examination, you will find various test questions regarding the technical requirements and addressing scheme of IPv6. I provide all the knowledge required to answer any IPv6 questions on the test.

Internet Protocol Version 6 (IPv6)

IPv4's 32-bit addressing scheme currently specifies roughly 4 billion hosts on 16 million networks. Considering Network Address Translation (NAT) and private addressing, this sounds like an overwhelmingly large enough number to provide ample address space for the entire networked world. You should not forget that many of these addresses are reserved and not available for host assignment. Also, the A, B, and C address classes have remarkably inflated the internetwork's routing tables and proven to be a very wasteful method of IP assignment. A new and improved version of the Internet protocol and addressing solution was announced in the mid 1990s (RFC 2460) and was tasked with solving IPv4's many shortcomings. Enter IPv6!

By examining IPv4's pitfalls, you can recognize the need for a more flexible Internet addressing method. The realization that the entire IPv4 address pool would eventually be depleted forced Internet designers and engineers to rethink address space allocation. In the early 1990s, the Internet Engineering Task Force (IETF) created a series of groups with the mission of designing the successor to IPv4. Development began on a "Next Generation Internet Protocol" (IPng), and standardization of IP version 6 followed in 1998.

Version 5 was already assigned to another developing protocol — the Internet Stream Protocol — and this is the reason for the jump from version 4 to 6.

Although both versions function similarly, IPv4 and IPv6 use different types of packet header formatting and addressing lengths. As you can see in Figure 5-1, IPv6 packet headers are more efficient and greatly simplified compared to IPv4 header information. This helps to reduce processing overhead during transmission. The majority of IPv4 protocols can function with IPv6, despite these packet header incompatibilities, and require very little modification other than the larger 128-bit address support. IPv6 has been designed to transition easily to IPv4 with minimum disruption to current network configuration, while improving on IPv4's features.

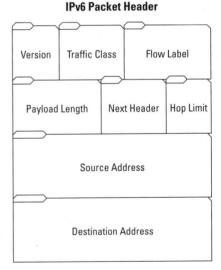

Figure 5-1:
IPv4 versus
IPv6 packet
headers.

IPv6 is supported in Cisco IOS Release 12.2 and later.

The Benefits of IPv6

The major benefits and features of IPv6 include the following:

✦ **Larger address space:** The main limitations with IPv4 are the imposed address space limitations and eventual complete loss of addressing capability. IPv6 was designed to overcome IPv4's 32-bit limitations by introducing much larger 128-bit addresses and providing an address pool that is virtually inexhaustible.

✦ **Stateless autoconfiguration:** A feature used to issue and generate an IP address without the need for a Dynamic Host Configuration Protocol (DHCP) server:

  • Routers send router advertisements (RAs) to network hosts containing the first half, or first 64 bits, of the 128-bit network address.

  • The second half of the address is generated exclusively by the host and is known as the *interface identifier.* The interface identifier uses its own MAC address, or it may use a randomly generated number. This allows the host to keep hardware addresses hidden for security reasons and helps an administrator mitigate security risks.

✦ **More efficient packet headers:** IPv6 uses a simpler header design than IPv4. The enhanced design allows routers to analyze and forward packets faster. Fewer header fields must be read, and header checksums are completely discarded in IPv6. More efficient packet headers improve network performance and save valuable router resources.

✦ **Changes in multicast operation:** Support for multicasting in IPv6 is now mandatory instead of optional, as with IPv4. The multicasting capabilities in IPv6 completely replace the broadcasting functionality found in IPv4. IPv6 replaces broadcasting with an "all-host" multicasting group.

✦ **Increased security:** Another optional feature found in IPv4, IP Security (IPsec) measures are now considered mandatory and implemented natively in IPv6.

✦ **Additional mobility features:** Mobile IPv6 allows a mobile IPv6 node to change links or locations and still maintain one permanent address.

✦ **Integrated quality of service (QoS):** Integrated QoS in IPv6 packet headers provides improved packet management. Routers are now able to organize, prioritize, and forward packets more efficiently than with previous implementations.

Almost all operating systems available today provide support for IPv6. Some operating systems provide "out of the box" support, while others depend on additional installation packages. Host operating systems that support IPv6 include

+ BSD

+ Linux

+ Solaris, AIX, HP-UX, Tru64, OpenVMS

+ Microsoft Windows (XP or higher)

+ MAC OS X (10.2 or higher)

Introducing IPv6 Addressing

IPv6 is an Internet protocol that uses a 128-bit hexadecimal addressing method called *colon hexadecimal notation.* This method supports a much wider address space than IPv4. More than *340,282,366,920,938,463,463,37 4,607,431,768,211,456,* or *3.4×1038,* addresses are available! This is enough address space to issue each person on the planet approximately $5×10^{28}$ addresses, or trillions of addresses. It's fairly safe to say that the topic of address exhaustion is now completely exhausted!

What do all of these astronomical numbers really translate to? Flexibility! You can assign different functions on your networks to specific bit ranges in the IP address without facing address exhaustion, allowing improved network design and troubleshooting efficiency. Subnet masks are no longer used in IPv6, although subnets are still determined by prefix length notation.

IPv6 hexadecimal addresses are *eight sets of 16-bit groups separated by colons,* as shown in Figure 5-2. The hexadecimal address would look this in decimal:

47.238.18.18.66.15.0.0.0.0.6.44.245.126.212.31

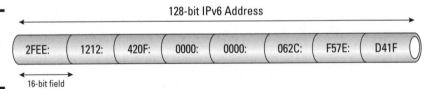

Figure 5-2: IPv6 128-bit address example.

128-bit IPv6 Address

| 2FEE: | 1212: | 420F: | 0000: | 0000: | 062C: | F57E: | D41F |

16-bit field

You can transform your hexadecimal IP address into decimal notation by splitting the address into 8-bit sections and counting the 1s, or "on" bits, in binary. Take the first 16-bit group and split the 2F from the EE. 2F in binary is represented as 00101111, which equals 47 in decimal.

Hexadecimal is not case sensitive, so both "2FEE" and "2fee" have the same value.

Address space is divided and allocated into sections based on IPv6 prefix notation, as shown in Figure 5-3.

IPv6 Prefix Notation	Allocation	Reference
0000::/8	Reserved by IETF	RFC4291
0100::/8	Reserved by IETF	RFC4291
0200::/7	Reserved by IETF	RFC4048
0400::/6	Reserved by IETF	RFC4291
0800::/5	Reserved by IETF	RFC4291
1000::/4	Global Unicast	RFC4291
2000::/3	Reserved by IETF	RFC4291
4000::/3	Reserved by IETF	RFC4291
6000::/3	Reserved by IETF	RFC4291
8000::/3	Reserved by IETF	RFC4291
A000::/3	Reserved by IETF	RFC4291
C000::/3	Reserved by IETF	RFC4291
E000::/4	Reserved by IETF	RFC4291
F000::/5	Reserved by IETF	RFC4291
F800::/6	Reserved by IETF	RFC4291
FC00::/7	Unique Local Unicast	RFC4193
FE00::/9	Reserved by IETF	RFC4291
FE80::/10	Link Local Unicast	RFC4291
FEC0::/10	Reserved by IETF	RFC3879
FF00::/8	Multicast	RFC4291

Figure 5-3:
IPv6
address
space.

Who's the assigning authority?

IPv6 address assignment is handled similarly to IPv4 address allocation. Management of IPv6 addresses has been delegated from the *Internet Corporation Assigned Names and Numbers (ICANN)* to the *Internet Assigned Numbers Authority (IANA),* which in turn has been handed over to five *regional Internet registries (RIRs):*

✦ **The American Registry for Internet Numbers (ARIN):** Serving North America

✦ **The Réseaux IP Européens Network Coordination Centre (RIPE NCC):** Supporting Europe, the Middle East, and the former Soviet Union

✦ **The Asian Pacific Network Information Centre (APNIC):** Supporting Asia and Australia

✦ **The African Network Information Centre (AfriNIC):** Responsible for Africa and the Indian Ocean

✦ **The Latin American and Caribbean Internet Addresses Registry (LACNIC):** Serving Latin America and the Caribbean

These five RIRs delegate addressing responsibilities further to

✦ Local Internet registries (LIRs)

✦ Internet service providers (ISPs)

IPv6 address notation

IPv6 128-bit addresses consist of two logical parts:

✦ The top 64 bits represent the global routing prefix (plus the subnet ID).

✦ The remaining 64 bits contain the host interface identifier.

The ultimate deciding factor of where the network portion ends and the host portion starts remains the responsibility of the prefix length value (much like IPv4 CIDR notation). This network/host split is not hard-coded into the address and can be configured according to network requirements.

The host address functions the same way as the 48-bit hexadecimal MAC address in IPv4, but has now added 16 additional bits. The host address in IPv6 is created using the hardware MAC address from the host interface and is termed a *64-bit Extended Unique Identifier (EUI-64).* If privacy is a concern, the host can use a randomly generated number instead of the MAC address to identify itself on the network.

These long addresses probably appear more confusing and complicated than the 32-bit addressing that you are used to with IPv4. Instead of representing IP addresses in dotted-decimal notation, you now use a hexadecimal approach. A method is available to shorten 128-bit hex addresses that have leading 0s in each 16-bit group. These unnecessary leading 0s may be omitted, as shown in Figure 5-4; this is called *zero compression.* The rules for zero compression are simple: Only *one* consecutive series of 0s (separated by colons) may be removed per address. Double colons (::) are inserted into the address as a placeholder to represent the discarded 0s.

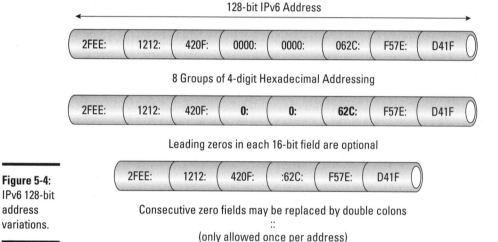

128-bit IPv6 Address

| 2FEE: | 1212: | 420F: | 0000: | 0000: | 062C: | F57E: | D41F |

8 Groups of 4-digit Hexadecimal Addressing

| 2FEE: | 1212: | 420F: | 0: | 0: | 62C: | F57E: | D41F |

Leading zeros in each 16-bit field are optional

| 2FEE: | 1212: | 420F: | :62C: | F57E: | D41F |

Consecutive zero fields may be replaced by double colons
::
(only allowed once per address)

Figure 5-4:
IPv6 128-bit address variations.

Additional legal zero compression examples are as follows:

BA02:**0:0:0:0:0:0**:1 = BA02**::**1 — Six consecutive 0s are denoted by using the double colon.

FC55:**0:0:0**:3030:2340:0210:0010 = FC55**::**3030:2340:0210:0010 — A string of three consecutive 0s are again replaced by the double colon.

CA12:0:0:75BA:0:0:62DC:CA01 = CA12**::**75BA:0:0:62DC:CA01 *or* CA12:0:0:75BA**::**62DC:CA01 may be used, but not both.

0:0:0:0:0:0:0:0 = :: — All 0s represented by the double colon.

0:0:0:0:0:0:0:1 = ::1 — Internal loopback address.

It's easy to find out how many 16-bit words the double colons replace by subtracting the amount of visible groups from 8. So, in the first previous example, BA02::1 has two visible groups with a set of double colons. By subtracting 2 from 8, you find out that six 16-bit groups are represented by the double colon.

The following is an example of *illegal* zero compression:

FC55::3030:2340::0010 — More than one set of double colons is not allowed. You also cannot determine how many 16-bit groups each double colon set replaces.

Another method to shorten these long addresses is to remove leading 0s from each 16-bit group:

0C55:0030:0001:0210:F010:0708:0050:00DF may be shortened and written as C55:30:1:210:F010:708:50:DF.

The network portion of the address is determined by the prefix length value following the address. IPv6 addresses are followed by a slash and decimal number indicating the bit count, much like IPv4 CIDR notation. The following value

0C55:0030:0001:0210:F010:0708:0050:00DF/64

indicates that the first 64 bits are prefix (or network) bits.

Refer to the hexadecimal conversion chart in Table 5-1 to help understand and decode IPv6 addresses.

Table 5-1				Values for Each 16-bit Group			
Hex	0	1	2	3	4	5	6	7
Hex	0	1	2	3	4	5	6	7
Decimal	0	1	2	3	4	5	6	7
Binary	0000	0001	0010	0011	0100	0101	0110	0111
Hex	8	9	A	B	C	D	E	F
Decimal	8	9	10	11	12	13	14	15
Binary	1000	1001	1010	1011	1100	1101	1110	1111

IPv6 address types

You find three types of IPv6 addresses:

✦ **Unicast:** Packet delivery that is designed for host-to-host communications. Unicast packets are directed and delivered to a single interface. One unicast address is assigned per interface.

✦ **Multicast:** Addresses that are assigned to a specific "multicast group" of interfaces. IPv6 multicasting functions similarly to IPv4 broadcasting and is described as "one-to-many" IP communications. Because no broadcast address exists in IPv6, the "all-nodes" multicast address is used to designate a group of interfaces.

Compared to IPv4 broadcasting, IPv6 multicasting provides a much more efficient means of group communications. It is no longer necessary for all interfaces on the subnet to receive the same broadcast message, saving valuable CPU processes and reducing network traffic.

✦ **Anycast:** Packets that are sent and received by only one member (interface) per anycast group. This is described as "one-to-one-of-many" communications and delivers packets to the closest interface (in routing distance) in the anycast group. Anycast addresses use the same syntax as unicast addressing, and hosts are unable to recognize the difference between unicast and anycast packets.

There is an important difference to remember regarding anycast and multicast delivery. Anycast packets are only sent to one host in an anycast group, compared to packets reaching "all hosts" in the multicast group.

IPv6 reserves — The "special"ists

IPv6 dedicates a large amount of address space for testing and other special purposes. As shown in Figure 5-5, the *special addressing* group types are as follows:

:: — The unspecified address: Consists of all 0s and is sent by hosts that do not know its own address. A network device sending a DHCP request would be an example of using the unspecified address. The unspecified address is 0:0:0:0:0:0:0:0, or written as a set of double colons.

::1 — The loopback address: As in IPv4, the loopback address is used for testing stack operability on a single interface, and packets are looped back, or returned, to the same sending device. Packets are not transmitted to remote machines. The loopback address is 0:0:0:0:0:0:0:1, or written as a set of double colons followed by the number 1.

FE80::/10 — Link-local addresses: The first group of bits starting with FE in hex represent private addresses. These addresses are used much like the private addresses in IPv4 and cannot be routed. Packets that are sent to these private addresses stay on the local network and do not traverse routers to outside organizations. This is analogous to the IPv4 autoconfiguration addresses 169.254.0.0/16.

FF00::/8 — Multicast addresses: The first group of bits (1111 1111) starting with FF in hex represent dedicated multicast addressing. IPv6 multicasting is used similarly and can be compared to IPv4 broadcasting.

IPv6 Prefix Notation	Type	Description
: : /128 (0:0:0:0:0:0:0:0)	Unspecified Address	Used in software when no known IP address is available.
: : 1/128 (0:0:0:0:0:0:0:1)	Loopback Address	The IP stack loops packets destined for this address back to itself.
2001 : db8 : : / 32	Reserved Global Unicast Addresses	Used as an example address in documentation. See RFC 3849.
FE80 : : / 10	Link-Local Unicast Addresses	Only valid on the local physical network
FF00 : : / 8	Multicast Address	Used in Multicasting addressing

Figure 5-5: Special IPv6 addresses.

Configuring IPv6

To configure IPv6 on Cisco devices, you must enable IPv6 on the interface you intend to use for traffic forwarding. Because IPv6 is disabled by default in the Cisco router's IOS, you must first allow forwarding of IPv6 traffic on the network. The steps are as follows:

1. **Enable IPv6 routing:** Enable the router to pass IPv6 traffic using the `ipv6 unicast-routing` command in IOS global configuration mode.

2. **Configure IPv6 addressing:** Each interface expected to forward IPv6 traffic must be configured with an IPv6 address. A link-local address is assigned automatically by configuring a global or site-local address to the interface, which activates that particular interface for IPv6. The interface also joins the following multicast groups automatically:

   - *Solicited-node multicast group:* FF02:0:0:0:0:1:FF00::/104 used for all unicast/anycast addresses assigned to that interface. Used in the Neighbor Discovery Protocol (NDP).

   - *All-nodes multicast group:* FF02:0:0:0:0:0:0:1 used for all link-local nodes.

   - *All-routers multicast group:* FF02:0:0:0:0:0:0:2 used for all link-local routers.

3. **Verify IPv6 addressing and address configuration:** IPv6 packet processing verification and proper interface configuration can be viewed by examining the running configuration and interface information.

To configure a Cisco interface for IPv6 in the IOS, enter privileged EXEC/ global configuration mode and specify the interface type and number:

```
Router>enable
Router#configure terminal
Router(config)#interface type number
```

Then designate the IPv6 network or address assigned to the interface and enable IPv6 processing on the interface. The ipv6-prefix/address arguments with the prefix length must be in standard colon hexadecimal notation, such as *2001:0CC8:0:1::/64.*

```
Router(config-if)#ipv6 address ipv6-prefix/prefix-length eui-64
```

**Book II
Chapter 5**

Configuring site-local and global addresses is done without the eui-64 or link-local prefixes. Using eui-64 configures an interface identifier in the low-order 64 bits of the address. Or, use the following:

```
Router(config-if)#ipv6 address ipv6-address/prefix-length link-local
```

**Internet Protocol
Version 6 (IPv6)**

The link-local identifier allows configuration of a link-local address other than the one automatically configured by default. Link-local addresses only communicate with nodes on the same network. Another alternative is as follows:

```
Router(config-if)#ipv6 address ipv6-prefix/prefix-length anycast
```

This method specifies an IPv6 anycast address. You may also use the following:

```
Router(config-if)#ipv6 enable
```

Using the `ipv6 enable` command automatically configures a link-local address on the interface and enables the interface for IPv6 processing. Now, exit interface configuration mode and enable the interface to forward unicast datagrams:

```
Router(config-if)#exit
Router(config)#ipv6 unicast-routing
```

You can now verify that IPv6 is enabled and properly configured to a particular interface by viewing the running configuration:

```
Router#show running-config
Building configuration...
Current configuration : 22324 bytes
! Last configuration change at 13:34:21 EST Tue Jun 4 2009
! NVRAM config last updated at 04:14:16 EST Tue Jun 4 2009 by drew
hostname dummies
ipv6 unicast-routing
interface Ethernet0
no ip route-cache
```

```
no ip mroute-cache
no keepalive
media-type 10BaseT
ipv6 address 3FFE:C00:0:1::/64 eui-64
```

The running configuration shows that IPv6 unicast-routing is enabled and that you are assigned an IPv6 address. Now you can view the configured Ethernet interface:

```
Router#show ipv6 interface ethernet 0
Ethernet0 is up, line protocol is up
IPv6 is enabled, link-local address is FE80::260:3EFF:FE11:6770
Global unicast address(es):
3FFE:C00:0:1:260:3EFF:FE11:6770, subnet is 3FFE:C00:0:1::/64
Joined group address(es):
FF02::1
FF02::2
FF02::1:FF11:6770
MTU is 1500 bytes
ICMP error messages limited to one every 500 milliseconds
ND reachable time is 30000 milliseconds
ND advertised reachable time is 0 milliseconds
ND advertised retransmit interval is 0 milliseconds
ND router advertisements are sent every 200 seconds
ND router advertisements live for 1800 seconds
Hosts use stateless autoconfig for addresses
```

The show command tells you that IPv6 is enabled, gives you the link-local address, informs you of stateless autoconfiguration, and lists the three assigned group addresses.

Address autoconfiguration — DHCP who?

Address autoconfiguration allows IPv6 hosts to self-configure themselves with IP addressing and other information without the need for a server. In IPv4, you either specify a static IP address or enable DHCP addressing to provide required *stateful* information to hosts. Stateful addressing is delivered to clients using a centrally managed server. With *stateless* IPv6 autoconfiguration, neither a DHCP server nor static IP is necessary. Stateless configuration allows devices to generate their own addresses and adjust according to the state of the network.

The steps involved in address autoconfiguration are as follows:

1. **Generate a link-local address:** The device creates a 64-bit host identifier using its own 48-bit hardware address and adds a trailing 16-bit hex value of *0xFFFE*. The 48-bit hardware address and the added 16-bit value of 0xFFFE combine to form the host identifier. The universal/local bit of the MAC address is always the seventh bit and gets "flipped" from 0 to 1. This process is called *MAC-to-EUI64 conversion* and determines the interface ID of the device.

Another method can be used to generate the link-local address without using a MAC address. Instead of using the hardware address of an interface, a random "token" value is generated by the device. This can cause problems if two devices on the network randomly generate the same token. The chances are minimal, but testing must be done to eliminate the possibility that this token value is identically generated and used somewhere else on the same local network.

2. **Test the uniqueness of the link-local address:** The host sends a *neighbor solicitation message* by employing the *Neighbor Discovery Protocol (NDP)*. NDP verifies the uniqueness of the link-local address. Because two nodes may not share the same interface ID, the node listens on the network for a neighbor advertisement. If duplicate addresses exist (most likely from using a "token" value instead of the MAC address), a new interface ID must be generated.

3. **Assign the link-local address to the interface:** The device assigns the newly generated link-local address to its interface. Assigning the link-local address depends on the previous step and will execute only when the address uniqueness test passes.

4. **Host contacts the router on the local network:** The host contacts the router in one of two ways. The host may either listen to *router advertisements (RAs)* or send its own router solicitation message. In either case, the requesting node contacts the router, requesting additional information needed for network address configuration. The router responds and informs the host how to determine its globally unique network address. For networks employing stateful configurations, DHCPv6 contact information is provided to the host.

5. **Globally unique network address is formed:** The host combines the interface ID with the router-issued network prefix to create the globally unique network address.

A dynamic approach

While stateless address autoconfiguration has removed the major reasons for deploying DHCP services in IPv4, DHCPv6 may still be used in IPv6 networks to provide stateful addressing assignment.

Why would you use DHCPv6 instead of stateless address autoconfiguration?

✦ A network administrator may want to have complete control over which addresses are assigned to which clients.

✦ Additional information needs to be distributed via DHCPv6 that would not ordinarily be possible otherwise.

An example would be updating reverse DNS information for IPv6 addresses.

Regardless, passing network addresses and configuration information to nodes via User Datagram Protocol (UDP) remains the main goal of DHCPv6.

I examine the differences of DHCP in IPv4 and IPv6:

✦ DHCPv6 is no longer based on the inefficient BOOTP protocol and has been completely redesigned.

✦ Single DHCPv6 requests may issue addresses to all node interfaces in one exchange.

✦ DHCPv6 uses multicast solicit messaging.

Here is the DHCP client/server request/response process in a nutshell:

✦ The client uses its link-local address to send a multicast *solicit* message requesting a DHCP lease.

✦ The DHCP server receives the client message using a reserved, link-scoped multicast address and responds with an *advertise* message.

Implementing and configuring a DHCPv6 server on a Cisco router are done as follows:

```
Router>enable
Router#configure terminal
Router(config)#ipv6 dhcp pool poolname
Router(config)#domain-name domain
Router(config-dhcp)#dns-server ipv6-address
Router(config-dhcp)#prefix-delegation ipv6-prefix/prefix length client-DUID [iaid
    iaid] [lifetime]
Router(config-dhcp)#prefix-delegation pool poolname [lifetime {valid-lifetime |
    preferred-lifetime}]
Router(config-dhcp)#exit
Router(config)#interface type number
Router(config-if)#ipv6 dhcp server poolname [rapid-commit] [preference value]
    [allow-hint]
```

The dhcp pool command specifies the address pool name and creates the pool. The domain-name and dns-server commands specify the domain name in use and the IP address of the DNS server. *Prefix delegation* assigns the IPv6 prefix length address and registered lifetime. Finally, the DHCP server pool is assigned to a specific interface.

ICMPv6

Internet Control Message Protocol version 6 (ICMPv6) is an integral part of IPv6 and functions just as it does in IPv4. ICMPv6 is used by nodes for reliability testing (using the ping command) and for reporting errors during packet handling. ICMPv6 messages are divided into two categories: *error messages* and *informational messages*. These are defined by their high-order bits in the message type field of each packet:

✦ 0–127 is the range for error messages.

✦ 128–255 are used for informational messages.

ICMPv6 packets are used for *path MTU discovery, Neighbor Discovery Protocol (NDP),* and the *Multicast Listener Discovery (MLD) Protocol.*

MLD is tasked with discovering nodes that want to send/receive multicast packets to specific multicast addresses using IPv6 routers. Neighbor Discovery uses ICMP messages to determine link-layer addresses of hosts that reside on the same network using solicitation messages. Router advertisement (RA) messages are also handled by ICMPv6.

Routing with IPv6

The Internet is a collection of IP-based packet-switching networks known individually as *autonomous systems (ASs)*. Each of these subnets may use one or more system administrators to deploy routing protocols inside the organization, known as Interior Gateway Protocols (IGPs). To connect individual networks and to pass routing information between them, an Exterior Gateway Protocol (EGP) is enabled.

System administrators may either

✦ Manually update routing tables, which is called *static routing*

✦ Use an automatically configured *dynamic routing* approach

The purpose and goal of routing IPv4 and IPv6 packets remain the same: to forward packets efficiently from sender to receiver interfaces.

Static routing — Gimme some static!

Static routing is implemented essentially the same way as in IPv4. Static routes are configured and stored in static routing tables and maintained on the router itself. This may improve routing performance but also increases network management and administrative tasks.

Routers using an IPv6 static configuration have the following benefits over dynamically configured networks:

✦ Less bandwidth requirements

✦ Security and resource efficiency

✦ No CPU usage during route calculations

The drawbacks are that static routes must be manually reconfigured by the network administrator if the network topology undergoes any changes. Static routes can provide increased security for certain links on large networks or are optimally used for small networks with only one connection to the outside world.

The following code configures an IPv6 static route using the Cisco IOS `ipv6 route` command:

```
Router>enable
Router#configure terminal
Router(config)#ipv6 route ipv6-prefix/prefix-length {ipv6-address | interface-
    type interface-number [ipv6-address]} [administrative-distance]
    [administrative-multicast-distance | unicast | multicast][tag tag]
```

Introducing IPv6 routing protocols

IPv6 relies on the same routing protocols as does IPv4, although some modifications and upgrades were made to provide the additional requirements of IPv6. I examine three of the most popular Interior Gateway Protocols modified for IP version 6:

✦ RIPng (RIP next generation)

✦ EIGRPv6

✦ OSPFv3

RIPng into the next generation

Routing Information Protocol next generation (RIPng) is a distance vector protocol based on RIPv2, designed for deployment in medium-sized networks and functioning similarly to RIP in IPv4. RIPng is designed for use with routers only and carries a maximum 15-hop radius, which limits its use in large networking environments.

The major purpose of RIPng is to provide route computation between routers every 30 seconds. IPv4 split horizon and poison reverse functionality are still ingrained within RIPng, along with slow convergence after the network topology changes.

Updated RIPng features include the following:

✦ Uses IPv6 as the method of transport.

✦ Uses IPv6 prefix/next-hop addressing.

✦ RIP updates via multicast group FF02::9.

✦ Request and response updates are received on UDP port 521.

The following code configures or enables RIPng from the IOS interface configuration mode:

1. Enter privileged EXEC/global configuration mode:

```
Router>enable
Router#configure terminal
```

2. Select the interface to configure:

```
Router(config)#interface type number
```

3. Enable RIPng on the interface:

```
Router(config-if)#ipv6 rip name enable
```

EIGRPv6

Enhanced Interior Gateway Routing Protocol version 6 (EIGRPv6) is another advanced distance vector protocol that also works similarly to the EIGRP protocol used in IPv4. EIGRPv6 is still easy to configure and uses the Diffusing Update Algorithm (DUAL) for loop-free, fast convergence times. Some highlights of EIGRPv6 are as follows:

✦ Configures EIGRPv6 on an interface without requiring an assigned global IPv6 address.

✦ Uses the `router-id` configuration command to enable the protocol.

✦ Requires the `no shutdown` command to be issued before routing is started.

✦ Enabling EIGRPv6 on passive interfaces is not required.

✦ Route filtering is performed using the `distribute-list prefix-list` command.

The network and interface to be used must be enabled from interface configuration mode. To turn on the routing process and enable EIGRPv6, enter router configuration mode. Then follow these steps:

To turn on the routing process and enable the EIGRPv6 routing protocol, configure as follows:

1. Enter privileged EXEC/global configuration mode:

```
Router>enable
Router#configure terminal
```

2. Enable routing of IPv6 packets:

```
Router(config)#ipv6 unicast-routing
```

3. **Create an EIGRP IPv6 routing process and enter router configuration mode (occurs automatically when you issue the** `Router` **command):**

   ```
   Router(config-if)#ipv6 router eigrp as-number
   ```

4. **Assign the unique fixed router ID:**

   ```
   Router(config-router)#router-id {ip-address | ipv6-
       address}
   ```

5. **Issue the** `no shutdown` **command:**

   ```
   Router(config-router)#no shutdown
   ```

6. **Specify the interface to be configured:**

   ```
   Router(config)#interface fastethernet 0/0
   ```

7. **Enable IPv6 processing on the interface:**

   ```
   Router(config-if)#ipv6 enable
   Router(config-if)#ipv6 eigrp as-number
   ```

8. **Issue the** `no shutdown` **command to bring up the interface:**

   ```
   Router(config-if)#no shutdown
   ```

9. **Type** exit **to return to global configuration mode:**

   ```
   Router(config-if)#exit
   ```

10. **Type** exit **again to return to privileged EXEC mode:**

    ```
    Router(config)#exit
    ```

11. **Copy the running configuration to the startup configuration:**

    ```
    Router#copy run start
    ```

The `autonomous system number` and `no shutdown` commands are required to designate and enable EIGRPv6 on the router. You then select the proper interface for configuration and enable EIGRP on that interface.

OSPFv3

Open Shortest Path First version 3 (OSPFv3) is a link-state routing protocol based on OSPFv2 using a hierarchical method of dividing large autonomous systems. OSPF makes routing decisions based on the state of the attached links that connect source to destination. Network link-state information is collected and stored in a database and propagated using a series of *link-state advertisements (LSAs)*. This database is used to create the routing tables used by OSPF. IP addressing information has been removed from OSPF packet headers.

OSPFv3 uses multicast addresses FF02::5 and FF02::6 to send updates and acknowledgments. Enhanced features include the following:

✦ Transmits IPv6 prefixes and supports multiple 128-bit addresses per interface.

✦ IPsec authentication replaces OSPF protocol authentication.

✦ Runs over a link instead of a subnet.

✦ Uses "ships in the night" integrated parallel routing. "Ships in the night" provides simultaneous OSPFv3 and OSPFv2 operation, allowing both IPv4 and IPv6 packets to be forwarded.

To configure or enable OSPFv3, you must first enable unicast routing and IPv6 on the interface.

1. **Enter privileged EXEC/global configuration mode and select the particular interface:**

```
Router>enable
Router#configure terminal
Router(config)#interface type number
```

2. **Enable and assign OSPF to the interface on the router:**

```
Router(config-if)#ipv6 ospf process-id area area-id
    [instance instance-id]
```

Migrating to IPv6

Many organizations realize the eventual necessity of migrating to IPv6, even if they are anticipating a daunting process ahead. They may be comfortable and fully satisfied with IPv4's functionality and current network configuration. However, the IPv4 comfort level will not last forever. The clock is ticking, and time is running short. But the problem may lie with agencies that don't realize the budget, planning, and technical expertise requirements needed for migration. In actuality, the migration process is less painful than some may think.

Here are a few points to remember when planning a migration to IPv6:

✦ **Develop a plan.** Start working on a plan now before it is time to migrate. A complete transition to IPv6 can take years, so start planning thoroughly now. Address assignment, routing, DNS, and application support are areas that must be considered for deployment.

✦ **Analyze the organization's network management system.** The majority of network management systems currently support IPv4 only. Additional funds may be required to upgrade the existing IPv4 network management system to IPv6, or an entirely new system may be needed to support IPv6.

✦ **Evaluate network security.** Unauthorized network access is still a major concern with IPv6. Both firewalls and intrusion detection systems are invaluable.

✦ **Enable IPv6 on the network.** Start activating IPv6 on the network core, or backbone, to the desktop. Applications may then follow suit and be migrated individually, depending on greatest organizational priority.

Migration methods

To successfully migrate to IPv6, you must maintain backward compatibility with current IPv4 hosts and networks. The IETF has recommended migration methods to follow that can ease the Internet conversion process to IPv6. A few methods I focus on are as follows:

✦ Dual-stack — IPv4 and IPv6 protocol stacks

✦ Tunneling — IPv6 through IPv4 and vice versa

✦ Translating addresses using NAT-PT

Dual-stack — IPv4 and IPv6 protocol stacks

Dual-stack environments allow functionally of both IPv4/IPv6 protocols and applications to coexist on the same network. This approach splits the traffic into two separate networks, so separate security strategies are also required:

✦ Using IPv4 addresses in the dual-stack approach, the IPv4 protocol stack is used. Likewise for IPv6 address, the IPv6 stack is used.

✦ If the destination address is an IPv6 address with an embedded IPv4 address, IPv6-to-IPv4 encapsulation is performed.

In Figure 5-6, I examine another scenario that depicts dual-stack technology. The sending host machine is transmitting both IPv4 and IPv6 protocol stacks, each destined for a separate network. The host's IPv6 packets travel to the IPv6 network, while the IPv4 traffic is routed to the IPv4 network.

Tunneling IPv6 through IPv4

Encapsulation of IPv6 packets within IPv4 packets is made possible by tunneling. As you can see in Figure 5-7, IPv6 tunneling allows IPv6-enabled host interfaces to connect to other IPv6 devices using the existing IPv4network. IPv6 transmissions across IPv4 internetworks are made transparent and ease IPv6 deployment. Without tunneling, there would be no means for IPv6 hosts to communicate with each other over an IPv4 network. Each tunnel is considered a single point-to-point link, and every packet forwarded through a tunnel constitutes one hop. Tunneling endpoints require support for both the IPv4 and IPv6 protocol stacks.

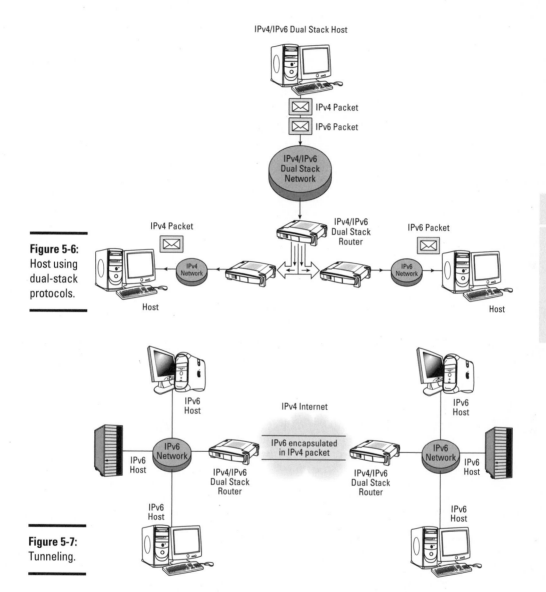

Figure 5-6:
Host using
dual-stack
protocols.

Figure 5-7:
Tunneling.

Some Cisco IPv6-supported tunneling methods are as follows:

✦ **Manual:** A point-to-point connection between two IPv6 domains. The
   link is established using an IPv4 backbone and assigning an IPv6 address
   to the tunneling interface. One IPv4 source and destination address are
   assigned, one on each end of the tunnel. The tunnel routers are required
   to provide dual-stack IPv4/IPv6 support. Establishing a manual tunnel
   may be done between routers or between a host and a router.

✦ **Generic routing encapsulation (GRE)/IPv4 compatible:** This is similar to manual tunneling, except GRE tunneling may use many different protocols to deliver data. Tunnels may carry IPv6 data using GRE as the "carrier" protocol and IPv4 or IPv6 as the "transport" protocol. The network administrator may determine the "passenger" protocol by examining the information stored in the IP header.

✦ **6to4:** Automatic 6to4 tunneling also operates similarly to manual tunneling, with one major exception. 6to4 tunnels are point-to-multipoint instead of point-to-point. The end-to-end connection used in manual tunneling does not exist in 6to4 tunneling. Instead, the IPv4 address embedded in the IPv6 address is used to locate the tunnel's endpoints. Each site's tunnel endpoint must use a globally unique IPv4 address, and the border router must support dual-stack operation. The tunnel destination is extracted from the IPv6 address and is determined by the IPv4 address of the border router. Tunneling IPv6 addresses start with the prefix 2002::/16, formatted as follows:

> 2002:*border-router-IPv4-address*::/48

Following the embedded IPv4 address are 16 bits used to number local networks.

✦ **Intra-Site Automatic Tunnel Addressing Protocol (ISATAP):** ISATAP is used to create a virtual IPv6 link within a local IPv4 network. ISATAP is used when no IPv6 infrastructure is available on the local network and system administrators would like to test IPv6 hosts on their current IPv4 infrastructure.

The following commands implement manual tunneling on Cisco routers:

1. **Enter privileged EXEC/global configuration mode:**

```
Router>enable
Router#configure terminal
```

2. **Specify the interface to be configured for tunneling and the tunneling number, and enter interface configuration mode:**

```
Router(config)#interface tunnel tunnel-number
```

3. **Specify the IPv6 network assigned to the interface, and enable IPv6 processing on the interface:**

```
Router(config-if)#ipv6 address ipv6-prefix/prefix-
    length [eui-64]
```

4. **Specify the source and destination IPv4 addresses:**

```
Router(config-if)#tunnel source {ip-address |
    interface-type interface-number}
Router(config-if)#tunnel destination ip-address
```

5. **Specify the tunnel mode:**

```
Router(config-if)#tunnel mode ipv6ip
```

The `tunnel mode ipv6ip` command assigns IPv6 as the passenger protocol and specifies IPv4 as both the encapsulation and transport protocol for the manual IPv6 tunnel.

 Hosts and routers that use tunneling of IPv6 packets over IPv4 networks utilize a special IPv6 unicast address called an *IPv4-compatible IPv6 address.* This address carries a 32-bit IPv4 address in the last low-order bits and looks like *x:x:x:x:x:x:d.d.d.d,* where *x* is an IPv6 hexadecimal address and *d* represents the standard IPv4 address. Another type of address, called an *IPv4-mapped IPv6 address,* is also used to embed IPv4 addresses inside an IPv6 address. This type of address is dedicated to represent IPv4-only hosts that do not support IPv6.

Translating addresses using NAT–Protocol Translation

Network Address Translation–Protocol Translation (NAT-PT) provides bidirectional address translation between IPv4/IPv6 hosts or domains, and is designed to alleviate migration burdens for organizations transitioning from IPv4 to IPv6. This translation service acts as a buffer and allows IPv4 hosts to communicate directly with IPv6 hosts, and vice versa. Dual-stack networks with minimal IPv6 hosts may enable NAT-PT on routers to communicate with IPv4-only networks and hosts.

One main advantage of NAT-PT is that all configuration is done at the router level, with no changes needed at the host. This allows IPv6 implementation with no disruption to current network infrastructure. NAT-PT should not be used when connectivity is needed between a dual-stack IPv4/IPv6 host and an IPv4-only or IPv6-only hosts. Cisco recommends tunneling over NAT-PT in certain cases to eliminate the possibility of double translation.

NAT-PT uses *Stateless IP/ICMP Translation (SIIT) Algorithm* and acts as a dedicated device to translate between IPv6 and IPv4. NAT-PT activates a pool of IPv4 addresses and assigns them dynamically to IPv6 nodes. IPv4-to-IPv6 address bindings provide transparent routing of datagrams by binding addresses in an IPv6 network with addresses in IPv4 networks, and vice versa. In Figure 5-8, you can see how NAT–Protocol Translation operates.

Use the following steps to implement NAT-PT on Cisco routers:

1. **Enter privileged EXEC/global configuration mode:**

```
Router>enable
Router#configure terminal
```

2. **Assign an IPv6 prefix as a global NAT-PT prefix:**

```
Router(config)#ipv6 nat prefix ipv6-prefix/prefix-length
```

3. **Specify an interface type and number, and place the router in interface configuration mode:**

```
Router(config)#interface type number
```

4. **Assign an IPv6 address to the interface and enable IPv6 processing:**

```
Router(config-if)#ipv6 address ipv6-prefix {/prefix-
    length | link-local}
```

5. **Enable NAT-PT on the interface and exit interface configuration mode:**

```
Router(config-if)#ipv6 nat
Router(config-if)#exit
```

6. **Select an interface and place the router in interface configuration mode:**

```
Router(config)#interface type number
```

7. **Specify an IP address and mask assigned to the interface, and enable IP processing on the interface:**

```
Router(config-if)#ip address ip-address mask
    [secondary]
```

8. **Enable NAT-PT on the interface:**

```
Router(config-if)#ipv6 nat
```

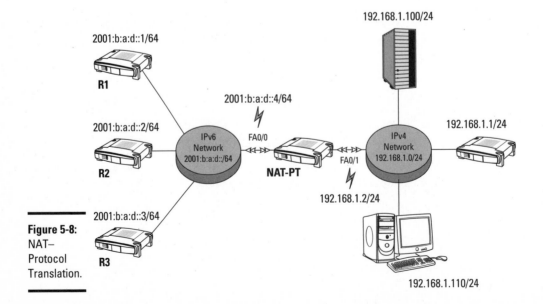

Figure 5-8:
NAT–
Protocol
Translation.

Prep Test

1 Which addresses represent the 128-bit loopback address in IPv6? (Choose two.)

A ○ ::1

B ○ 00:00:00:00::127

C ○ 127.0.0.1

D ○ 0:0:0:0:0:0:0:1

2 Which of the following are valid IPv6 addresses? (Choose three.)

A ○ FC55::3030:2340::0010

B ○ BA02::1

C ○ 182.80.10.1

D ○ CD01:245F:0000:15CE:0000:589A:FABC:0001

E ○ CA12::75BA:0:0:62DC:CA01

3 Which address types are used in IPv6? (Choose three.)

A ○ Multicast

B ○ Anycast

C ○ Broadcast

D ○ Unicast

E ○ Localcast

4 Which feature of IPv6 allows a client to receive an IP address without the use of a DHCP server?

A ○ IPsec

B ○ QoS

C ○ Stateless autoconfiguration

D ○ Mobile IP

5 Which addresses are used by the unspecified address? (Choose two.)

A ○ FE80::/10

B ○ ::

C ○ 0:0:0:0:0:0:0:0

D ○ FF00::/8

6 Which answer best describes hexadecimal colon notation?

A ○ 64-bit addressing

B ○ Eight octets separated by colons

C ○ Four 8-bit octets

D ○ Eight sets of 16-bit groups separated by colons

7 Which command is used to enable IPv6 routing in the Cisco IOS?

A ○ ipv6 unicast-routing

B ○ ipv6 route add

C ○ ipv6 anycast routing

D ○ ipv6 enable on

8 Which decimal and binary values equal "AB" in hexadecimal? (Choose two.)

A ○ 142

B ○ 171

C ○ 11100110

D ○ 10101010

E ○ 10101011

F ○ 37

9 Which addresses are valid IPv6 addresses? (Choose two.)

A ○ 0C:55:00:30:00:01:02:10:F0:10:07:08:00:50:00:DF

B ○ 0C55::1541:CDF8:0708:0050::00DF

C ○ 0C55::F010:0708:0050:00DF

D ○ 0C55:0030:0001:F010:0708:0050::00DF

10 Which packet delivery method uses a one-to-one-of-many approach?

A ○ Multicast

B ○ Anycast

C ○ Unicast

D ○ Broadcast

11 What are the main benefits of IPv6? (Choose three.)

A ○ Larger address space

B ○ Stateless autoconfiguration

C ○ Optional IPsec

D ○ Mobile IPv4

E ○ Increased packet header efficiency

Answers

1 **A, D.** The loopback address in IPv6 is 0:0:0:0:0:0:0:1 and is represented as ::1 in shortened form. 127.0.0.1 is the loopback address in IPv4. Review *"IPv6 reserves — The "special"ists."*

2 **B, D, E.** BA02::1, CD01:245F:0000:15CE:0000:589A:FABC:0001, and CA12::75BA:0:0:62DC:CA01 are all valid addresses. FC55::3030:2340::0010 uses two sets of double colons and is not a valid address. 182.80.10.1 is an IPv4 address. See *"IPv6 address notation."*

3 **A, B, D.** IPv6 uses unicast, multicast, and anycast addresses. Broadcast addressing is no longer used in IPv6. Take a look at *"IPv6 address types."*

4 **C.** Stateless autoconfiguration enables hosts to generate IPv6 addresses. Check out *"The Benefits of IPv6."*

5 **B, C.** ::, 0:0:0:0:0:0:0:0. Both 0:0:0:0:0:0:0:0 and the shortened form :: represent the unspecified address. FE80::/10 is the link-local address, and FF00::/8 is the multicast address. Review *"IPv6 reserves — The "special"ists."*

6 **D.** Eight sets of 16-bit groups separated by colons. IPv6 uses 128-bit addressing. Refer to *"Introducing IPv6 Addressing."*

7 **A.** The `ipv6 unicast-routing` CLI command is used to enable IPv6 traffic. Read *"Configuring IPv6."*

8 **B, E.** 171, 10101011. The binary value 10101011 and decimal value 171 are equal to the hexadecimal value of AB. See *"Introducing IPv6 Addressing"* and *"IPv6 address notation."*

9 **C, D.** 0C55::F010:0708:0050:00DF and 0C55:0030:0001:F010:0708:0050::00DF are valid IPv6 addresses. Review *"IPv6 address notation."*

10 **B.** Anycasting delivers packets to only the closest interface in routing distance in the anycast group. Check out *"IPv6 address types."*

11 **A, B, E.** Larger address space, increased packet header efficiency, and stateless autoconfiguration are all IPv6 benefits. IPsec is mandatory in IPv6. Mobile IPv4 is not a feature of IPv6. See *"The Benefits of IPv6."*

Book III

Switching with Cisco Switches

The 5th Wave   By Rich Tennant

"My spam filter checks the recipient address,
http links, and any writing that panders to
postmodern English romanticism with conceits
to 20th-century graphic narrative."

Contents at a Glance

Chapter 1: Introducing Layer 2 Switches

Exam Objectives

✔ Describing data link OSI Layer 2 and how it relates to Layer 2 switches

✔ Describing the purpose of a Layer 2 switch

✔ Differentiating a Layer 2 switch from a hub or a bridge

✔ Describing the basic Layer 2 switch functions

✔ Managing Layer 2 switch port security

✔ Describing how a Layer 2 switch handles unicast, multicast, and broadcast transmissions

✔ Describing MAC address table thrashing and broadcast storms

*R*ead this chapter to find out about Layer 2 switches.

Layer 2 — Data Link Layer Review

Layer 2 in the Open Systems Interconnection (OSI) is the data link layer. The data link layer transmits data on the physical medium. The data link layer uses physical addresses assigned to each physical network device in the local network to route data from one physical device to another. These addresses are called Media Access Control (MAC) addresses in TCP/IP. MAC addresses uniquely identify a specific network device, such as a switch or a router, or a network interface card (NIC), in a host device.

The data link layer has the following features:

✦ Receives each packet from the network layer on the sending host

✦ Wraps up the packet in a *data frame* along with local routing data (the physical MAC address)

✦ Sends the data frame to the physical layer to code an electrical or optical signal

The physical layer transmits the data frame over a wire or over the air (wireless transmission).

On the receiving host, the data link layer does the following:

✦ Unwraps the data frame received

✦ Extracts the packet out of the data frame

✦ Sends the packet up to the network layer

The TCP/IP protocol is used at Layer 2 for data link operations. Ethernet, defined by the IEEE 802.X standards, operates at Layer 2 to handle data link functions. Hence, whenever you consider Layer 2 in TCP/IP, you really need to think about Ethernet and physical MAC addresses. Layer 2, the data link layer, is only concerned with local-area networks (LANs). The mission of the data link layer is to handle data frame transmission locally between two devices connected on a LAN. The data link layer is concerned with LANs, implemented with Ethernet, and addressed using physical MAC addresses.

Layer 2 switches use the MAC address of each device that transmits data-link frames through the switch to decide whether to forward that frame on an outbound port. Layer 2 switches also remember MAC addresses of connected devices to decide on which outbound port to send data-link frames.

Purpose of a Layer 2 Switch

To understand the purpose of a Layer 2 switch, you need to know a little bit about older computer networks. First-generation LANs were connected using a single coaxial cable. Host devices in the LAN shared the bandwidth of that cable. Figure 1-1 illustrates such a network. Observe that hosts Alex, Claire, and John are connected to the same coaxial cable. The bandwidth is shared. Worse yet, everyone sees all frames sent on the cable: Alex sends a frame to John, but Claire also sees the frame and needs to discard it because it is not addressed to her. You can imagine that Claire needs to spend some time discarding frames, and so do Alex and John whenever they see a frame that is not addressed to them. This is not efficient.

Hubs

Later, hubs were introduced to interconnect several host devices using one cable for each device. This greatly simplified connections because each host was connected individually to the hub. It is very easy to connect or disconnect a host to a hub by simply plugging or unplugging the network cable linking the host to the hub. Hub networks were typically deployed using twisted-pair cable instead of coaxial cable. RJ-45 connectors were used, which greatly simplified connections.

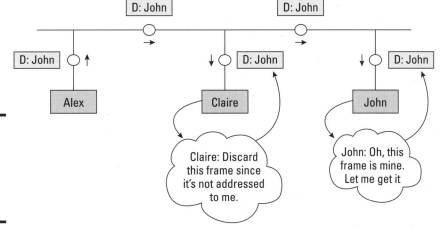

Figure 1-1:
Flat bus
network
with single
collision
domain.

A hub works very much like a multiple socket power bar: Data sent into a hub is sent out to all host devices connected to that hub except to the host that sent the data in. In other words, a hub forwards a data frame on all outbound ports, except on the port through which the frame came in.

Host devices share the bandwidth of the medium both when connected using coaxial cables and when connected using hubs. Because hosts share the same cable or the same hub, hosts can potentially send data frames at the same time on the medium. Hence, data frames can collide.

Ethernet uses carrier sense multiple access collision detect (CSMA/CD) to control data frame collisions. This works well to work around collisions, but it does consume bandwidth. The CSMA/CD collision-detection and back-off algorithms can consume a lot of bandwidth. This is why in older networks, only 50–60 percent of the bandwidth was really usable for data frame transmission. The rest was wasted dealing with data frame collisions. The solution to this problem is to limit the collision domain, to make it as small as possible. This decreases or eliminates the risk of collision. That's where Layer 2 bridges and Layer 2 switches come into play.

Figure 1-2 shows a hub-based network. This solution provides an easier way to connect the hosts, but the hosts share the hub and the bandwidth. The hub does not filter the frames.

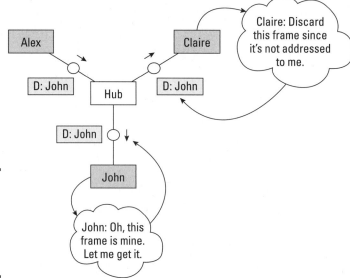

Figure 1-2:
Hub-based network with single collision domain.

Bridges

Bridges, like hubs, are used to interconnect devices in a LAN using a point-to-point connection for each device. Unlike hubs, bridges were the first network device that was able to limit the collision domain.

Bridges, like switches, create one collision domain per port and can forward data frames only on the outbound port that reaches the destination of the frame, as opposed to hubs, which send the frame out on all ports.

Think about it this way:

✦ A hub is like phone conferencing. Everyone on the phone call hears what you say.

✦ A bridge or a switch is like a normal telephone call: Only the person you call hears what you say.

A bridge is slower than a switch because it uses software instead of hardware application-specific integrated circuits (ASICs) to learn about MAC addresses and to decide whether to forward a data frame. Otherwise, a bridge works like a switch.

Switches

A Layer 2 switch is a network device that creates one collision domain per port and forwards data frames only on the outbound port that reaches the destination of the frame. Switch characteristics are as follows:

✦ Switches are faster than bridges because they use hardware ASICs instead of software to perform their operations.

✦ Switches are typically faster than routers because they do not need to look at the network layer (Layer 3) IP packet header. They only inspect the data-link (Layer 2) frame to look at the source and destination MAC address of the frame. This is why they are called Layer 2 switches: They only operate on the data-link (Layer 2) frame.

Figure 1-3 shows a switched network. This solution has several advantages:

✦ It provides an easier way to connect the hosts.

✦ The hosts work in their own isolated collision domain (one per port). Hence, frames do not collide.

✦ The switch filters the frames and forwards them only to the outbound port connected to the destination host. This is much more efficient than flooding the frame out on all ports, as hubs do.

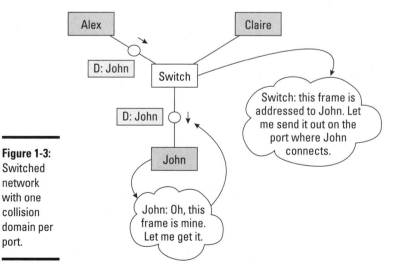

Figure 1-3:
Switched network with one collision domain per port.

The features of hubs, bridges, and switches are outlined in Table 1-1.

Table 1-1	Hubs, Bridges, and Switches		
Feature	*Hubs*	*Bridges*	*Switches*
Technology	Broadcasting	Software switching	ASIC switching
Duplex	Half	Half	Half/Full
Speed	Turtle	Bear	Leopard
VLAN support	No	No	Yes
Collision domain	Whole hub	1 per port	1 per port
Broadcast domain	Whole hub	Whole bridge	1 per VLAN

Basic Switch Functions

A Layer 2 switch must accomplish three tasks:

✦ Learn about the MAC addresses of devices connected to the switch

✦ Decide whether to forward frames it receives from host devices or other switches

✦ Avoid creating any Layer 2 loops

The following sections explain each of these functions in detail.

Address learning

Layer 2 switches learn the MAC addresses of devices connected to the switch as follows:

✦ The switch inspects each data frame that enters the switch. It saves the port number where the frame entered along with the source MAC address of that frame. The MAC address and the corresponding port number are saved in a MAC address table.

✦ As devices send frames into the switch, the switch slowly builds a complete MAC address table that contains

• The MAC address of each device connected

• The port number through which that device is sending frames into the switch

Figure 1-4 illustrates hosts Alex, Claire, and John interconnected in a Layer 2 switch. The MAC address table is empty at this point because none of the hosts have sent frames into the switch.

Figure 1-5 illustrates hosts Alex, Claire, and John interconnected in a Layer 2 switch. Here, Alex sends a frame to Claire. The switch inspects the data-link (Ethernet) frame and registers the source MAC address in the MAC address table along with the switch port through which the frame came in. Hence, the switch knows about Alex at this point.

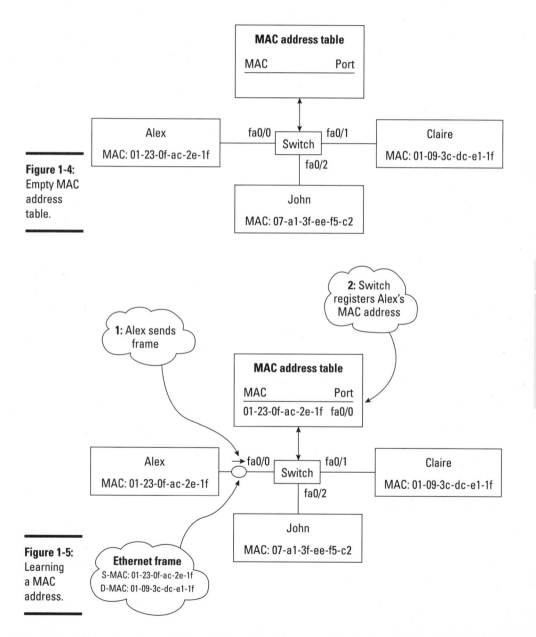

Figure 1-4: Empty MAC address table.

Figure 1-5: Learning a MAC address.

Next, suppose that Claire responds to Alex: Claire sends a frame back to Alex. The switch inspects the data-link (Ethernet) frame and registers the source MAC address in the MAC address table along with the switch port through which the frame came in. Hence, the switch also learns about Claire at this point. Figure 1-6 illustrates the state of the MAC address table when the switch knows about Alex and Claire.

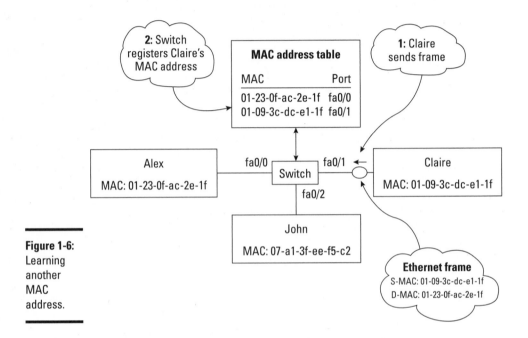

Figure 1-6:
Learning another MAC address.

Eventually, John will also send a frame into the switch. At that point, the switch would register John's MAC address along with the switch port where John sent the frame in.

Figure 1-7 shows the complete MAC address table that stores the MAC address of each host and the switch port where they connect. This is the state of the MAC address table after each host has sent at least one frame through the switch. The switch keeps the MAC address table in its flash memory as long as the switch is powered on. However, if a host sends no frames for a certain amount of time, its MAC address is removed from the MAC address table to keep the table clean and current.

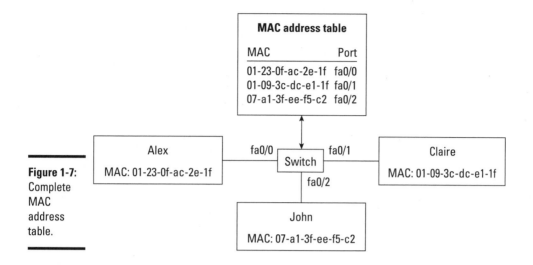

Figure 1-7: Complete MAC address table.

Flooding, forwarding, and filtering frames

Layer 2 switches need to decide whether to forward frames they receive. They also need to figure out over which outbound port they forward the frame. To do this, switches use the MAC address table:

1. The switch inspects each frame that enters on an inbound port: It looks at the source and destination MAC address of the frame.

2. The switch searches for the destination MAC address of the frame in the MAC address table:

   - If the switch finds the destination, the switch forwards the frame on the outbound port saved in the MAC address table for that destination MAC address.

   - If the switch does not find the destination MAC address in its MAC address table, it forwards the frame out on all outbound ports except on the one through which that frame came in.

Flooding a frame

Recall from an earlier section that initially, the MAC address table is empty, as shown in Figure 1-4. When Alex sends a frame to Claire, the switch learns about Alex, but it still does not know about Claire at this point. How does the switch know where to send Alex's frame? It doesn't. So the switch *floods* the frame out on all ports except the port through which it came in, that is, the port where Alex connects. Figure 1-8 illustrates this.

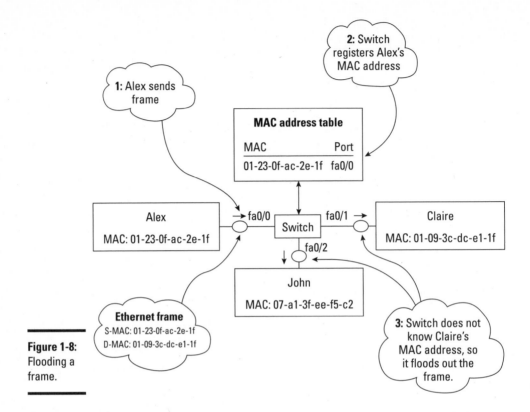

Figure 1-8:
Flooding a
frame.

Forwarding a frame

Claire responds to Alex: Claire sends a frame back to Alex. In this case, the
switch knows about Alex because it has just registered his MAC address
in the MAC address table when Alex sent the initial frame. So, the switch
forwards the frame *only* out on the port where Alex connects. Figure 1-9 illustrates this.

Filtering a frame

Assume that the network has been changed, as shown in Figure 1-10. Host
Monica was added to the network. Observe that John and Monica are interconnected with a hub, and the hub connects to the switch. Assume that
John sends a frame to Monica. First, John's frame enters the hub. The hub
floods the frame out on all ports except the sending port, that is, except
the port where John connects. So, the frame goes out to Monica and to the
switch. At this point, Monica receives the frame.

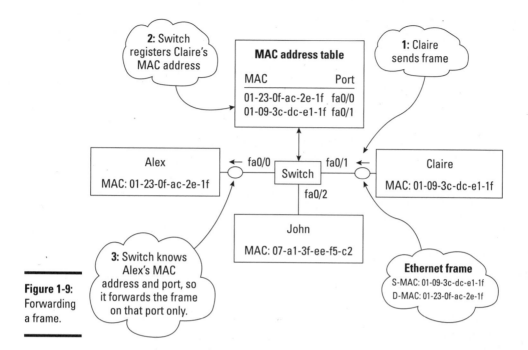

Figure 1-9:
Forwarding
a frame.

Now, the switch looks at the destination MAC address and searches it in the MAC address table. It does not find it. Hence, the switch would normally flood the frame out on all ports except on the incoming port, that is, except on e0/2. However, the switch does have MAC addresses registered for ports e0/0 and e0/1 that are different from the destination MAC address (D-MAC) of John's frame. So, the switch *filters* the frame because it is not for any of the hosts plugged in to its outgoing ports. Filtering a frame basically means discarding it without sending it out on any ports.

Next, assume that Monica sends a frame back to John. First, Monica's frame enters the hub. The hub floods it out on all ports except on the sending port, that is, except on Monica's port. So, the frame goes out to John and to the switch. At this point, John receives the frame. Figure 1-11 illustrates this situation.

The switch uses the frame to learn about Monica's MAC address, and filters the frame. So here it goes.

The switch first registers Monica's MAC address in the MAC address table. Observe that it registers it to the same outgoing switch port as John's MAC address. This is normal, because from the switch's perspective, both John and Monica come in on the same port: e0/2. That's the port where the hub connects.

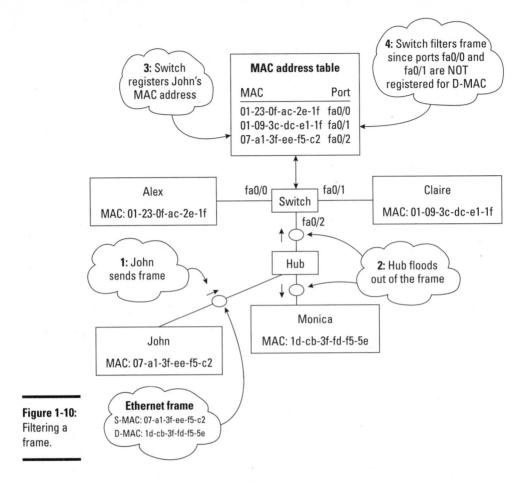

Figure 1-10:
Filtering a
frame.

Next, the switch looks at the source MAC address and at the destination MAC address: They are both connected to the same switch port. Hence, the switch simply discards the frame because there is no point in sending it back to where it came from. In this case, the switch also filters the frame: It does not forward it out on any ports.

Basically, the switch assumes that if the sender and the receiver are connected to the same switch port, this is either

✦ A host sending a frame to itself

✦ A host sending a frame to another host connected locally into a hub

In both cases, the destination host should have already received the frame, so there is no need to forward it back to the same port.

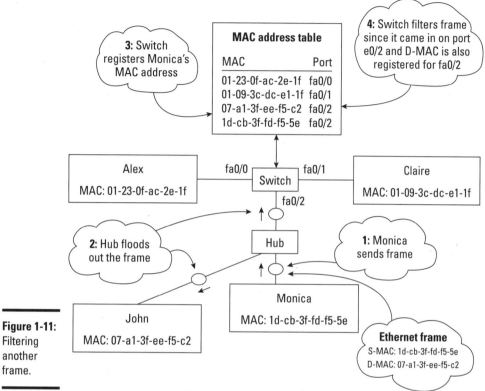

Figure 1-11:
Filtering
another
frame.

Avoiding loops

Data-link (Ethernet) frames do not expire. An Ethernet frame sent to an unknown MAC address can bounce forever in the network. This is not good because it wastes bandwidth. This problem is exacerbated when several switches are interconnected with redundant links. It is best practice to use redundant links to interconnect Layer 2 switches to mitigate interswitch link failure risks. However, this amplifies the risk to have frames bouncing back and forth between switches.

Figure 1-12 shows two switches interconnecting hosts Alex, Claire, John, and Monica. Suppose that the MAC address tables are empty on both switches because none of the hosts has sent any frames yet. Here's an example:

1. Assume that Alex sends a frame to Claire. Recall from Figure 1-8 that the first time Alex sends a frame to Claire, the switch learns about Alex, but it still does not know about Claire. So, switch SW1 needs to flood the frame out on all ports except the port through which it came in, that is, the port where Alex connects to SW1.

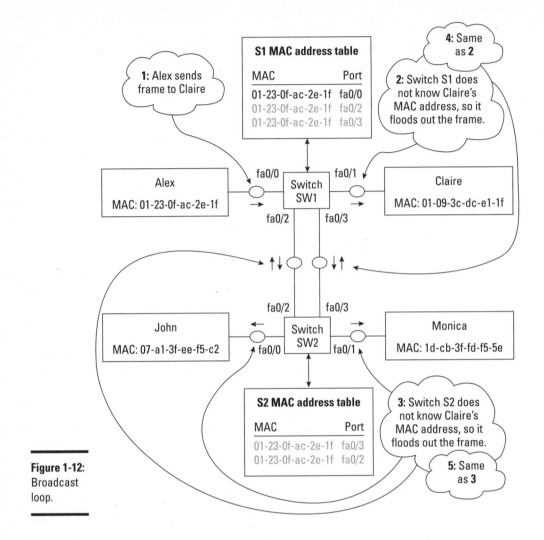

Figure 1-12: Broadcast loop.

2. Switch SW1 floods the frame out on all ports except the port through which it came in. The frame reaches switch SW2. Switch SW2 does not know about Claire either, so it also needs to flood the frame out on all ports except the port through which it came in.

3. Switch SW2 floods the frame out on all ports except the port through which it came in.

Because two links are connecting the SW1 and SW2 switches, the frame that came in through fa0/2 on SW2 is flooded out on fa0/3, and the frame that came in through fa0/3 on SW2 is flooded out on fa0/2. Hence, switch SW1 gets the frame back, twice: on fa0/2 and on fa0/3.

4. Because SW1 still does not know Claire's MAC address, it floods the frame again on both fa0/2 and fa0/3. SW2 receives the frame again, twice: on fa0/2 and on fa0/3.

5. Because SW2 still does not know Claire's MAC address, it floods the frame out again on all ports, including fa0/2 and fa0/3, and so on.

This is a typical example of a *broadcast storm:* a broadcast frame that bounces forever among switches interconnected with redundant links.

Observe another problem in Figure 1-12. Because switches SW1 and SW2 receive the same frame on two different ports, they register the source MAC address (S-MAC) of host Alex for both ports. This is a problem because the switch does not know over which port it needs to send frames out to Alex whenever D-MAC is set to Alex's MAC address in a frame. This is a typical example of *MAC address table thrashing.*

Broadcast storms and MAC address table thrashing are both caused by loops between Layer 2 switches interconnected with redundant links. To avoid loops and bouncing frames, the *Spanning Tree Protocol (STP)* is used on Layer 2 switches. STP is explained in detail in Book III, Chapter 4.

Address learning: The process by which a Layer 2 switch learns which MAC address is connected to each switch port. The process involves the switch saving the port number where each frame enters along with the source MAC address of that frame. The incoming port number and the MAC address are saved in a MAC address table.

Flooding: The process by which a Layer 2 switch forwards a frame out on all outbound ports except on the port through which that frame came in. A switch floods a frame whenever it does not find the frame's destination MAC address in the MAC address table. It also floods broadcast frames.

Forwarding: The process by which a Layer 2 switch forwards a frame on the outbound port saved in the MAC address table for that destination MAC address.

Filtering: The process by which a Layer 2 switch discards a frame without sending it out on any ports. A switch filters a frame whenever the frame's source MAC address and frame's destination MAC address are registered to the same switch port, according to the MAC address table.

Avoiding loops: The process by which Layer 2 switches eliminate transmission loops created by redundant interswitch links. The Spanning Tree Protocol (STP) handles this process. Spanning Tree Protocol (STP) is discussed in detail in Book III, Chapter 4.

**Book III
Chapter 1**

Introducing Layer 2
Switches

Broadcast storm: A broadcast frame that bounces forever among switches interconnected with redundant links. Broadcast storms waste bandwidth and may thrash the MAC address table.

MAC address table thrashing: Multiple ports attached to the same MAC address. The switch does not know on which outgoing port it can reach that MAC address.

Managing Port Security

Figure 1-11 shows a situation that can trigger some security risks and performance issues: You added host Monica to a network by simply plugging both Monica and John into a hub-connected to the switch. Now, both Monica and John are using the switch port that was originally reserved only for John.

While this is a quick-and-easy way to expand the network, it may not be the best way to do it, especially in very large LANs. For example, assume that you have an Ethernet jack in each cubicle in a large company office. As you can see, you can plug a hub or another switch into any Ethernet jack and add as many hosts as you want in that cubicle. This can turn into a major security and performance issue.

It is not secure to add uncontrolled host devices to a company network. It can also be a performance issue because the access and distribution network layers are probably designed to handle only one host, or maybe two hosts per cubicle. If a user adds a hub or a switch and plugs several hosts into the same Ethernet jack through the hub or the switch, the network load originating from that cubicle could increase above planned levels.

So, how can you configure the port to limit it to just John or to a certain maximum number of hosts? You can set filters and limits on each switch port using the `switchport port-security` Cisco command.

Filter based on MAC address

You can set the port to only support a specific MAC address using the `switchport port-security mac-address <MAC>` command. For example, you can run `switchport port-security mac-address 07-a1-3f-ee-f5-c2` to set the port to only allow John to connect.

Setting a static filter on a specific MAC address may not be a flexible solution. If you need to change the network interface card (NIC) in the John host, for example, you would have to change the filter on your switch to allow the MAC address of the new NIC. The sticky option is probably a better option. The sticky option is explained shortly.

Filter based on number of devices connected

You can set the port to only support a certain maximum number of devices connected using the `switchport port-security maximum <max#>` command.

Filter based on sticky MAC address

The most interesting port security option is the *sticky* option. The sticky option basically allows you to specify that the MAC address of the first device to send through that port will stick to the port. You can even specify how many devices stick to the port. The command is `switchport port-security mac-address sticky`. Next, you specify how many MAC addresses you allow to stick to the port using the `switchport port-security maximum <max#>` command.

In other words, if you replace `<max#>` with 2 in this command, you have the first two MAC addresses stick to that port. This is a more flexible alternative to filtering on actual MAC addresses.

Action triggered by filter

You can choose what action the switch needs to take should the filter or the limit be broken. You can use the `switchport port-security violation <action>` command to do this. For example, to have the port shut down upon a policy violation, you can run the `switchport port-security violation shutdown` command.

**Book III
Chapter 1**

Introducing Layer 2
Switches

Before you run any of the `switchport` commands, you first need to enter the Cisco switch configuration terminal using the `configure terminal` command. You can also use the short form of this command: `config t`. Next, you need to select a port to work with using the `interface <interface#>` command. Again you can use the short form: `int <interface#>`. For example, to work with the first Fast Ethernet interface on your switch, you can run `int fastethernet 0/0` or the even shorter form `int fa 0/0`. Then, you can execute the previous commands.

Read more about Cisco commands in Book III, Chapter 2.

Transmitting Unicast, Multicast, and Broadcast

So far in this chapter, you've seen how Layer 2 switches behave during unicast transmissions. A *unicast* transmission involves one device sending frames to a single target device. Only two devices are involved in unicast transmissions: the sending device and the target device. The device can be a host or a network device, such as a switch or a router.

A *multicast* transmission involves a device sending frames to multiple target devices. Note that a single device can send multiple frames to multiple devices, but *multicast* really means the device sending the *same* frame to multiple target devices. Normally, a multicast group is created, and target devices are added to the group. By default, a Layer 2 switch that receives a frame addressed to a multicast MAC address floods that frame out on all ports except on the port through which the frame came in.

You can configure the switch to send the frame only to the ports of the devices in the multicast group. However, those configuration options are beyond the scope of the CCNA test.

Multicast transmissions are typically used to stream data out to a group of hosts, for example, in IP-based video or audioconferencing.

A *broadcast* transmission involves a device sending frames to all devices in its local network. Whereas multicast transmissions involve the sending device and a specific subset of target devices in the local network, broadcast transmissions involve the sending device and *all* devices in the local network. Whenever a frame contains a destination MAC address (D-MAC) of FF-FF-FF-FF-FF-FF, it is considered to be a broadcast frame. A Layer 2 switch always floods out broadcast frames on all ports except on the port in which the frame came in.

Broadcast transmissions are typically used whenever a host tries to find a target device. For instance, you saw previously in Figure 1-5 that Alex sends a frame to Claire. The figure shows that Alex fills the Ethernet frame with his MAC address in S-MAC and Claire's MAC address in D-MAC. Here's the question: How does Alex know Claire's MAC address? Well, before Alex can send that frame, it needs to find Claire's MAC address.

To determine Claire's MAC address, Alex first looks into his Address Resolution Protocol (ARP) table, searching for the MAC address corresponding to the IP address of Claire. The ARP table is a table where responses to previous ARP requests are cached. If Alex does not find an entry in its ARP table that corresponds to Claire's IP address, it broadcasts an ARP request. In other words, it sends an ARP request packaged in a frame with the destination MAC address (D-MAC) set to FF-FF-FF-FF-FF-FF. The switch automatically floods the frame out on all ports when D-MAC is set to the FF-FF-FF-FF-FF-FF broadcast MAC address. All devices in the local network see the ARP request. Claire eventually responds with her MAC address. Alex saves Claire's MAC address in his ARP table. The next time, Alex will find Claire's MAC address in his ARP table. He will fill the D-MAC field with Claire's MAC address without having to broadcast another ARP request. So, you just saw a typical use for broadcast transmissions. Each host builds its ARP table the same way: using ARP request broadcasts.

Unicast transmission: Involves a device sending a frame to a single target device.

Multicast transmission: Involves a device sending a frame to multiple target devices.

Broadcast transmission: Involves a device sending a frame to all devices in its local network.

Prep Test

1 The data link layer, Layer 2 in the OSI network reference model, is represented in TCP/IP by which of the following?

A ○ IP addresses

B ○ Ethernet

C ○ EtherChannel

D ○ All of the above

2 What is the main function of the data link layer?

A ○ To handle data frame transmission locally between two devices connected on a local-area network (LAN)

B ○ To handle data frame transmission between two devices connected on a wide-area network (WAN)

C ○ To handle IP packet routing locally between two nodes connected on a local-area network (LAN)

D ○ To handle IP packet routing between two nodes connected on a wide-area network (WAN)

3 Layer 2 switches rely on the _____ to determine whether they forward data-link frames on an outgoing port.

A ○ Firmware version

B ○ IP address

C ○ MAC address

D ○ All of the above

4 How does a hub forward a data frame?

A ○ Only on the outbound port where the target firmware connects

B ○ Only on the outbound port where the target IP address connects

C ○ Only on the outbound port where the target MAC address connects

D ○ On all outbound ports, except on the port through which the frame came in

5 **Describe how a Layer 2 switch learns addresses.**

A ○ The switch saves the port number where each data frame enters the switch along with the source IP address of that frame in the IP address table.

B ○ The switch saves the port number where each data frame enters the switch along with the source MAC address of that frame in the MAC address table.

C ○ The switch saves the port number where each data frame enters the switch along with the source firmware version of that frame in the MAC address table.

D ○ The switch saves the port number where each data frame enters the switch along with the source firmware version of that frame in the IP address table.

6 **Describe how a Layer 2 switch floods a frame.**

A ○ The switch eliminates redundant interswitch links.

B ○ The switch sends a data frame only on the outgoing port where the destination device can be reached.

C ○ The switch sends a data frame on all outgoing ports except on the port where it entered the switch.

D ○ The switch discards a data frame.

7 **Describe how a Layer 2 switch forwards a frame.**

A ○ The switch eliminates redundant interswitch links.

B ○ The switch sends a data frame only on the outgoing port where the destination device can be reached.

C ○ The switch sends a data frame on all outgoing ports except on the port where it entered the switch.

D ○ The switch discards a data frame.

8 **Describe how a Layer 2 switch avoids loops.**

A ○ The switch blocks redundant interswitch links using STP.

B ○ The switch sends a data frame only on the outgoing port where the destination device can be reached.

C ○ The switch sends a data frame on all outgoing ports except on the port where it entered the switch.

D ○ The switch discards a data frame.

9 **Unicast transmission involves which of the following?**

A ○ A device sending a frame to multiple target devices

B ○ A device sending a frame to all devices in its local network

C ○ A device sending a frame to a single target device

D ○ All of the above

Answers

1 **B.** Ethernet. The data link layer, Layer 2 in the OSI network reference model, is represented in TCP/IP by Ethernet. Refer to *"Layer 2 — Data Link Layer Review."*

2 **A.** The main function of the data link layer is to handle data frame transmission locally between two devices connected on a local-area network (LAN). Check out *"Layer 2 — Data Link Layer Review."*

3 **C.** MAC address. Layer 2 switches inspect the destination MAC address of each frame entering the switch to determine whether to forward the frame on an outgoing port. Review *"Basic Switch Functions."*

4 **D.** Hubs always forward frames on all outbound ports, except on the port through which the frame entered the hub. Hubs multiplex the data frames from one ingoing port to multiple outgoing ports. Peruse *"Purpose of a Layer 2 Switch."*

5 **B.** To learn addresses, a Layer 2 switch saves the port number where each data frame enters the switch along with the source MAC address of that frame in the MAC address table. Check out *"Address learning."*

6 **C.** A Layer 2 switch floods a frame by sending the frame on all outgoing ports except on the port where it entered the switch. Read *"Flooding, forwarding, and filtering frames."*

7 **B.** A Layer 2 switch floods a frame by sending the frame only on the outgoing port where the destination device can be reached. Review *"Flooding, forwarding and filtering frames."*

8 **A.** Eliminates redundant interswitch links. A Layer 2 switch avoids switching loops by eliminating redundant interswitch links. Check out *"Avoiding loops."*

9 **C.** A device sending a frame to a single target device is a unicast transmission. Read *"Transmitting Unicast, Multicast, and Broadcast."*

Chapter 2: Managing a Switch Using Cisco IOS

Exam Objectives

✔ **Connecting to a Cisco switch**

✔ **Understanding the startup process of a Cisco switch**

✔ **Configuring a Cisco switch**

✔ **Managing Cisco switch configurations**

✔ **Managing Cisco switch authentication**

Managing a Cisco switch is very similar to managing a Cisco router. Most IOS commands are the same for switches and routers, but the output differs in some cases. Most IOS commands and GUI tools are available for both switches and routers. Some GUI tools are only available for routers, such as the Cisco Router and Security Device Manager (SDM) and SDM Express. Other GUI tools are only available for switches, such as the Cisco Device Manager. You find out about switch management IOS commands and GUI tools in this chapter.

Best Practice for Using Cisco Switches

When designing networks, the key point to remember is that top-of-the-line switches are best suited for either the *core layer* or the *distribution layer* of the network. Entry-level and midrange switches are best suited for either the *access layer* or the *distribution layer*. Cisco defines three layers in a network: the core layer, distribution layer, and access layer.

Top-of-the-line switches manage specialized services in a network, such as STP root bridge role, VLAN Membership Policy Server (VMPS), VLAN Trunking Protocol (VTP) domain control, Inter-VLAN routing, and LAN gateway connectivity.

These services are used throughout the network. Hence, they need to run on a highly efficient and highly available switch.

Figures 2-1 and 2-2 show the front and rear panels, respectively, of a Cisco Catalyst 2960, 24-port entry-level switch.

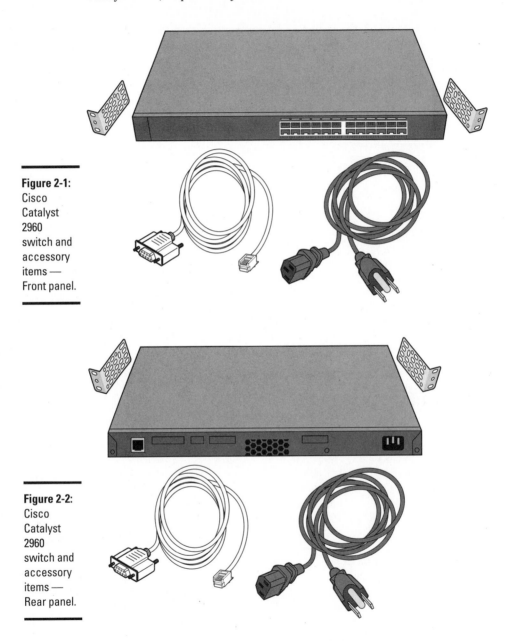

Figure 2-1:
Cisco
Catalyst
2960
switch and
accessory
items —
Front panel.

Figure 2-2:
Cisco
Catalyst
2960
switch and
accessory
items —
Rear panel.

Connecting to a Cisco Switch

Unlike a computer host, Cisco switches do not have a keyboard, monitor, or mouse device to allow direct user interaction. Cisco switches can be managed by connecting either locally or remotely to the switch from a computer host. You basically leverage the computer host user interface to interact with the Cisco switch.

Connecting locally

Cisco switches have several ports. Think of switch ports as plugs where you connect either computer hosts or other network devices.

Some switch ports are reserved for other purposes than network connectivity. These are the console port and the auxiliary port on a Cisco switch.

Console port

The *console port* is used to connect a management computer host to the switch using a rollover cable. You use this port whenever you want to connect locally to the console of your switch. The console is the default monitoring and configuration input and output facility of the switch. All Cisco devices have a *console facility,* where the Cisco operating system (IOS) displays status messages, error messages, diagnostic messages, and user prompts.

Think of the console facility as a virtual computer monitor and keyboard:

✦ Switch output messages are going to the virtual computer monitor.

✦ Switch user input is gathered using the virtual keyboard.

To access the console facility, you need to connect to the console port on your switch. You use a rollover cable connected at one end to the console port of your switch and connected at the other end to the management computer host.

Figure 2-3 illustrates a Cisco Catalyst switch with a management computer host connected to the switch's console port using a rollover cable. This figure illustrates the rear panel of the switch.

After you physically connect the switch to your computer using a rollover cable, you need to use a terminal emulation application on your management computer to open a serial terminal connection to your switch. The following applications support terminal emulation:

◆ HyperTerminal

◆ TeraTerm

◆ SecureCRT

You need to configure a connection profile for your Cisco switch using specific RS232 serial communication parameters:

◆ Baud rate: 9600

◆ Data bits: 8

◆ Parity: none

◆ Stop bits: 1

◆ Flow control: none

Serial communications (RS232) are governed by these parameters. Older computer hosts used to have serial communications ports (RS232) named COM1, COM2, COM3, and so on. Since the invention of USB, serial ports are being phased out. Your laptop probably has several USB ports but no serial port.

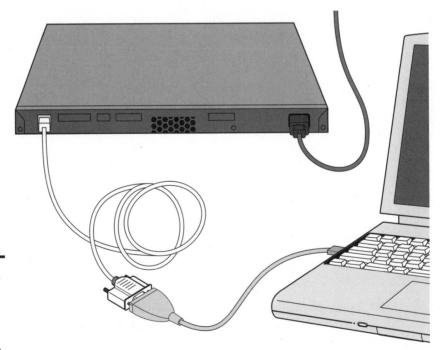

Figure 2-3:
Cisco
Catalyst
switch
console
connection.

Serial/USB port adapters are on the market. If you do not have a serial port on your computer, you need one of these adapters. Serial/USB port adapters create a virtual serial port on your computer by emulating an RS232 serial port using the USB physical port. Both RS232 and USB are standards that define serial communication frameworks.

Figure 2-4 illustrates a DB9 serial-to-USB converter (on the right in the picture). The switch rollover cable (on the left in the picture) plugs in to the converter. The converter plugs in to one of the USB ports on the laptop.

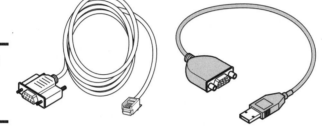

Figure 2-4:
Serial-to-USB port adapter.

Auxiliary port

The *auxiliary* port is used to connect a management computer host to the switch using a rollover cable, similarly to the *console* port. However, you use this port whenever you want to connect a modem locally to the auxiliary port. Next, you configure the modem to receive calls from a management computer host over a telephone line. After the management computer host establishes a modem connection to the switch, you are connected to the *console facility* of the switch. This port is really used for remote connections to your switch, but you still need to connect an answering modem locally to the auxiliary port of the switch. Note that some switches do not have an auxiliary port.

Having a modem answering calls and allowing console connections to the switch from remote computer hosts are security risks. It is important to configure passwords to challenge console port and auxiliary port connections. You will see how to configure console, auxiliary, and VTY (virtual terminal) passwords in the "Managing Cisco IOS Authentication" section later in this chapter.

Figure 2-5 illustrates a Cisco Catalyst switch with a management computer host connected to the switch's auxiliary port using two modems.

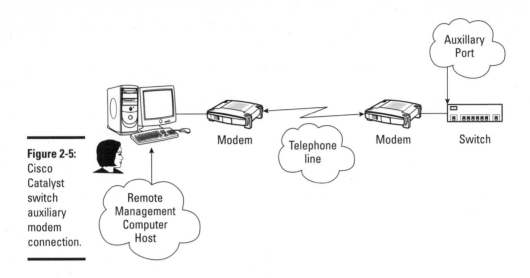

Figure 2-5:
Cisco
Catalyst
switch
auxiliary
modem
connection.

Connecting remotely

It's nice to be able to connect locally to a switch, but in a typical networking environment, you would have several switches. Some switches may not be located on the same floor or even in the same building as where you are located. So you can connect remotely to a Cisco switch. You can connect to both the switch console and its terminal window from a remote management computer host.

You can connect remotely to Cisco switches in several ways:

✦ Connect to the auxiliary port of the switch using a modem connection. This connects you to the console of the switch from a remote location.

✦ Connect to the network IP address of the switch using Telnet or other terminal emulation software. Each switch has a network IP address that identifies the switch as an IP node in the network. You can connect to this IP address using any Telnet or secure Telnet application, just as you connect to a computer host using Telnet or secure Telnet.

✦ Connect to the console IP address of the switch using a Console Terminal Server. You can configure a Console Terminal Server that makes the switch console facility available at a specific IP address and at a specific TCP/IP port number in the network. You can connect to this `IP:port` address using any Telnet application.

It is important to configure passwords to challenge console port, auxiliary port, and VTYconnections. You see how to configure console, auxiliary, and VTYpasswords in the "Configuring a Cisco Switch" and the "Managing Cisco Switch Authentication" sections, later in this chapter.

Figure 2-6 illustrates a Cisco Catalyst switch with a management computer host connected to the switch IP address using Telnet.

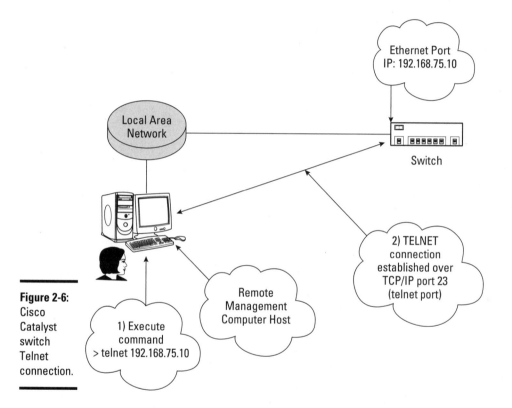

Figure 2-6: Cisco Catalyst switch Telnet connection.

Book III
Chapter 2

Managing a Switch
Using Cisco IOS

Figure 2-7 illustrates a Cisco Catalyst switch with a management computer host connected to the switch console via a Terminal Server.

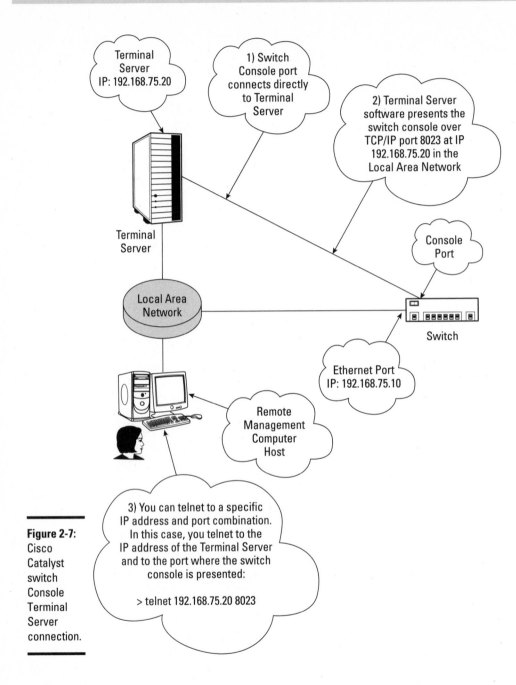

Terminal
Server
IP: 192.168.75.20

1) Switch
Console port
connects directly
to Terminal
Server

2) Terminal Server
software presents the
switch console over
TCP/IP port 8023 at IP
192.168.75.20 in the
Local Area Network

Terminal
Server

Console
Port

Local Area
Network

Switch

Ethernet Port
IP: 192.168.75.10

Remote
Management
Computer
Host

3) You can telnet to a specific
IP address and port combination.
In this case, you telnet to the
IP address of the Terminal Server
and to the port where the switch
console is presented:

> telnet 192.168.75.20 8023

Figure 2-7:
Cisco
Catalyst
switch
Console
Terminal
Server
connection.

Cisco Switch Startup Process

A Cisco switch always follows the same process when it is powered up:

1. **Run the POST: The Cisco switch runs the power-on self test.**

The POST is a microprogram, stored in ROM, that is used to verify basic functionality of the Cisco switch hardware.

2. **Boot up: The Cisco switch runs the *bootstrap program,* also known as the *boot loader software.***

The boot loader is a microprogram, stored in ROM, that is used to bring up the switch and transition it to normal operation mode by loading the Cisco IOS from flash memory. If the boot loader does not find a valid Cisco IOS in flash memory, it tries to load the IOS from either

- A TFTP server
- ROM

On switches, the bootstrap program also initializes the central processing unit (CPU) registers. CPU registers control where physical memory is mapped, how much memory is mapped, memory speed, and a few parameters that are beyond the scope of CCNA.

3. **Load the IOS: The Cisco IOS loads into RAM.**

By default, the Cisco IOS is loaded from flash memory. However, if the bootstrap program does not find a valid IOS in flash memory, it tries to load it from a TFTP server, if one is configured.

If no TFTP server is configured, or if no valid IOS is on the TFTP server, the bootstrap program loads the Rx-boot image from ROM. (The Rx-boot image is a subset of the Cisco IOS operating system.) The Rx-boot image is used to manage the boot process. The Rx-boot image comes up with the (boot)> prompt, where you can run various commands to manage the boot process. For instance, you can manually specify a location from which to load the IOS image.

4. **Load the startup configuration.**

After the Cisco switch loads the IOS in RAM, the IOS loads the device *startup configuration* from NVRAM. The startup configuration is loaded into RAM and becomes the *running configuration,* the configuration that changes dynamically while the Cisco device is running.

At this point, the Cisco device is in normal operation mode, ready for business.

**Book III
Chapter 2**

**Managing a Switch
Using Cisco IOS**

The following IOS CLI segment shows a Cisco Catalyst 2960 switch starting up for the first time.

```
Using driver version 1 for media type 1
Base ethernet MAC Address: [ ... output cut ... ]
Xmodem file system is available.
The password-recovery mechanism is enabled.
Initializing Flash...
mifs[2]: 0 files, 1 directories
mifs[2]: Total bytes      :    3870720
mifs[2]: Bytes used       :       1024
mifs[2]: Bytes available  :    3869696
mifs[2]: mifs fsck took 0 seconds.
mifs[3]: 516 files, 19 directories
mifs[3]: Total bytes      :   27998208
mifs[3]: Bytes used       :    8684544
mifs[3]: Bytes available  :   19313664
mifs[3]: mifs fsck took 6 seconds.
...done Initializing Flash.
done.
```

The first part of the preceding example shows output from the bootstrap program. It shows the media driver version being used on the switch and the MAC address of the switch. It also shows that Xmodem connectivity is enabled. The password recovery mechanism is enabled. Finally, the CPU registers are initialized to map flash memory structures.

The output of the preceding example starts at the second step in the process (bootup). You do not see the output from the first step of the process (POST) here. The first part of the POST only displays messages upon test failures.

```
Loading "flash:c2960-lanlite-mz.122-37.EY/c2960-lanlite-mz.122-37.EY.bin"...@@@@@
    @@@@@@@@@@@@@@@@@@@@@@@@@@@@@@@@@@@@@@@@@@@@@@@@@@@@@@@@@@@@@@@@@@@@@@@@@@@@@@
    @@@@@@@@@@@@@@@@@@@@@@@@@@@@@@@@@@@@@@@@@@@@@@@@@@@@@@@@@@@@@@@@@@@@@@@@@@@@
File "flash:c2960-lanlite-mz.122-37.EY/c2960-lanlite-mz.122-37.EY.bin"
    uncompressed and installed, entry point: 0x3000
executing...
```

This part loads the Cisco IOS from flash memory and executes it in RAM. The bootstrap program loads the `c2960-lanlite-mz.122-37.EY/c2960-lanlite-mz.122-37.EY.bin` IOS image located in the `flash:` memory structure.

```
        Restricted Rights Legend
Use, duplication, or disclosure by the Government is
subject to restrictions as set forth in subparagraph
(c) of the Commercial Computer Software - Restricted
Rights clause at FAR sec. 52.227-19 and subparagraph
(c) (1) (ii) of the Rights in Technical Data and Computer
Software clause at DFARS sec. 252.227-7013.

        Cisco Systems, Inc.
        170 West Tasman Drive
        San Jose, California 95134-1706
```

```
Cisco IOS Software, C2960 Software (C2960-LANLITE-M), Version 12.2(37)EY, RELEASE
    SOFTWARE (fc2)
Copyright (c) 1986-2007 by Cisco Systems, Inc.
Compiled Thu 28-Jun-07 18:07 by antonino
Image text-base: 0x00003000, data-base: 0x00D00000

Initializing flashfs...
Using driver version 1 for media type 1
mifs[3]: 0 files, 1 directories
mifs[3]: Total bytes     : 3870720
mifs[3]: Bytes used      : 1024
mifs[3]: Bytes available : 3869696
mifs[3]: mifs fsck took 0 seconds.
mifs[3]: Initialization complete.

mifs[4]: 516 files, 19 directories
mifs[4]: Total bytes     : 27998208
mifs[4]: Bytes used      : 8684544
mifs[4]: Bytes available : 19313664
mifs[4]: mifs fsck took 1 seconds.
mifs[4]: Initialization complete.

...done Initializing flashfs.
```

This part shows the name and version of the Cisco IOS. The flash memory file system is initialized.

```
POST: CPU MIC register Tests : Begin
POST: CPU MIC register Tests : End, Status Passed

POST: PortASIC Memory Tests : Begin
POST: PortASIC Memory Tests : End, Status Passed

POST: CPU MIC interface Loopback Tests : Begin
POST: CPU MIC interface Loopback Tests : End, Status Passed

POST: PortASIC RingLoopback Tests : Begin
POST: PortASIC RingLoopback Tests : End, Status Passed

POST: PortASIC CAM Subsystem Tests : Begin
POST: PortASIC CAM Subsystem Tests : End, Status Passed

POST: PortASIC Port Loopback Tests : Begin
POST: PortASIC Port Loopback Tests : End, Status Passed

Waiting for Port download...Complete

cisco WS-C2960-24-S (PowerPC405) processor (revision C0) with 61440K/4088K bytes
    of memory.

Last reset from power-on
1 Virtual Ethernet interface
24 FastEthernet interfaces
The password-recovery mechanism is enabled.

64K bytes of flash-simulated non-volatile configuration memory.

[ ... Some Serial, Assembly, Revision numbers cut ... ]
```

```
Model number: WS-C2960-24-S

[ ... More Serial, Assembly, and Revision numbers cut ... ]

Switch   Ports  Model       SW Version   SW Image
------   -----  -----       ----------   ----------
*   1    24     WS-C2960-24-S 12.2(37)EY   C2960-LANLITE-M

Press RETURN to get started!
```

This part shows the results of the second part of the POST and lists information about hardware components of this switch. This is a 24-port switch. All ports are compliant to the Fast Ethernet standard. The maximum bandwidth supported by Fast Ethernet is 100 Mbps. This switch has 64K in nonvolatile RAM (NVRAM).

```
[ ... Some status messages cut ... ]

Cisco IOS Software, C2960 Software (C2960-LANLITE-M), Version 12.2(37)EY, RELEASE
   SOFTWARE (fc2)
Copyright (c) 1986-2007 by Cisco Systems, Inc.
Compiled Thu 28-Jun-07 18:07 by antonino

Would you like to terminate autoinstall? [yes]: yes

        --- System Configuration Dialog ---

Would you like to enter the initial configuration dialog? [yes/no]: no
Switch>
```

This part shows the final stage of the boot process (load startup configuration). Because this is a new switch, no startup configuration exists.

The IOS asks whether you would like to enter the initial configuration dialog. This dialog allows you to quickly configure the switch as follows:

✦ IP address

✦ Default gateway (router)

✦ Subnet mask

✦ Console password

✦ Host name

✦ Telnet password

Configuring a Cisco Switch

Cisco switches ship with several items:

✦ Console rollover cable: This is the cable you need to connect to the console port on the switch.

✦ AC power cord.

✦ 19-inch rack mounting brackets.

✦ Getting Started documentation CD.

These items are needed to initially power up and configure the switch. First, use the mounting brackets to mount the switch in a standard EIA-310-D data center rack. Next, connect the power cord to the power feed of the EIA-310-D data center rack. Before you power up the switch, you may want to review the Getting Started documentation on the CD provided with the switch.

Initial switch configuration

Cisco switches are not configured when they are new. They do not have a startup configuration. Cisco switches (like the example in Figure 2-8) can interconnect computer hosts locally in an isolated network comprised of the switch itself and the computer hosts, even without a startup configuration. However, if you need to interconnect the switch to another switch or if you need to connect the switch to a gateway to reach remote networks, you need to create a startup configuration.

Book III
Chapter 2

Managing a Switch
Using Cisco IOS

Figure 2-8:
Cisco
Catalyst
2960
switch and
accessory
items.

Cisco switches revert to setup mode anytime no startup configuration is saved in NVRAM. This happens in two situations:

✦ The device is new: No startup configuration exists on new devices.

✦ The startup configuration has been deleted: You can delete the startup configuration using IOS commands or using the Mode button to reset the switch.

You should verify the switch and create a startup configuration before you start using the switch, even if you use the switch only to interconnect computer hosts locally in an isolated network comprised of the switch itself and some computer hosts. If you ever decide to expand this small network by adding another switch and more computer hosts, or if you decide to connect this small network to a gateway to reach the Internet, you definitely need a startup configuration in NVRAM.

You can create a startup configuration using one of the following methods:

✦ Filling in the Express Setup Web form

✦ Using the switch Autoinstall feature

✦ Using the initial configuration dialog

✦ Using the Cisco IOS setup mode commands

Express Setup mode

Cisco provides a utility, named *Express Setup,* that allows you to initially configure the switch. You run Express Setup when you power on the switch the first time to configure the following settings on the switch:

✦ IP address

✦ Default gateway (router)

✦ Subnet mask

✦ Console password

✦ Host name

✦ Telnet password

To set the switch in Express Setup mode, press and hold the Mode button for 3 seconds. Release the button when all LEDs are green.

Next, browse to the IP address of the switch. This loads the Express Setup form, as illustrated in Figure 2-9.

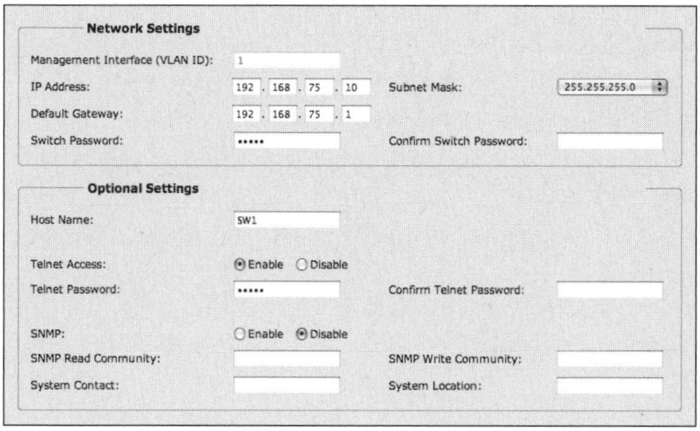

Figure 2-9:
Cisco
Catalyst
2960
Express
Setup Web
form.

Initializing the switch using the initial configuration dialog

The CCNA test expects you to know how to initialize the switch using the
Cisco IOS setup mode.

The first time you power on a Cisco switch, it has no startup configuration
in NVRAM. You can connect to the console of the switch to get access to the
IOS prompt. The switch will be in setup mode, because no startup configuration exists. In setup mode, the IOS asks you to configure the following:

✦ IP address

✦ Default gateway (router)

✦ Subnet mask

✦ Enable and Enable secret password

✦ Host name

✦ Telnet password

If choose not to configure the switch and use it without a startup configuration, you can avoid or abort setup mode using one the following methods:

✦ Exit setup mode by pressing Ctrl+C.

✦ Answer no when setup mode asks whether you want to configure
the switch.

✦ Answer no when setup mode asks whether you want to save the configuration at the end of the series of setup questions.

You should verify the switch and create a startup configuration before you start using the switch, even if you use the switch only to interconnect computer hosts locally in an isolated network comprised of the switch itself and some computer hosts.

Here is an example of the initial setup mode dialog:

```
Using driver version 1 for media type 1
Base ethernet MAC Address: 00:25:b4:10:58:80
Xmodem file system is available.
The password-recovery mechanism is enabled.

[ ... some boot messages cut ... ]

Loading "flash:c2960-lanlite-mz.122-37.EY/c2960-lanlite-mz.122-37.EY.bin"...@
    @@@@@@@@@@@@@@@@@@@@@@@@@@@@@@@@@@@@@@@@@@@@@@@@@@@@@@@@@@@@@@@@@@@@@@@@@@@@@
    @@@@@@@@@@@@@@@@@@@@@@@@@@File "flash:c2960-lanlite-mz.122-37.EY/c2960-
    lanlite-mz.122-37.EY.bin" uncompressed and installed, entry point: 0x3000
executing...

        Restricted Rights Legend

Use, duplication, or disclosure by the Government is
subject to restrictions as set forth in subparagraph
(c) of the Commercial Computer Software - Restricted
Rights clause at FAR sec. 52.227-19 and subparagraph
(c) (1) (ii) of the Rights in Technical Data and Computer
Software clause at DFARS sec. 252.227-7013.

        Cisco Systems, Inc.
        170 West Tasman Drive
        San Jose, California 95134-1706

Cisco IOS Software, C2960 Software (C2960-LANLITE-M), Version 12.2(37)EY, RELEASE
    SOFTWARE (fc2)
Copyright (c) 1986-2007 by Cisco Systems, Inc.
Compiled Thu 28-Jun-07 18:07 by antonino
Image text-base: 0x00003000, data-base: 0x00D00000

[ ... some boot messages cut ... ]

Press RETURN to get started!

[ ... some boot messages cut ... ]
```

The first part of the output, shown in the preceding example, displays various boot messages. The switch is now up and running.

Because no startup configuration exists in NVRAM, the IOS first asks whether you would like to let the switch run the Autoinstall feature to automatically configure the switch with a baseline configuration:

✦ If you answer yes to this question, or if you just press Enter to keep the default answer, the switch automatically configures itself with a baseline configuration to allow minimum functionality. After the autoinstall process completes, your switch is operational.

✦ If you answer no to the autoinstall question, the IOS next asks whether you want to run the initial configuration dialog. You type **yes** as follows to run the initial configuration dialog.

```
Would you like to terminate autoinstall? [yes]: <no>

        --- System Configuration Dialog ---

Would you like to enter the initial configuration dialog? [yes/no]: yes

At any point you may enter a question mark '?' for help.
Use ctrl-c to abort configuration dialog at any prompt.
Default settings are in square brackets '[]'.

Basic management setup configures only enough connectivity
for management of the system, extended setup will ask you
to configure each interface on the system

Would you like to enter basic management setup? [yes/no]: yes
Configuring global parameters:

  Enter host name [Switch]: SW1

  The enable secret is a password used to protect access to
  privileged EXEC and configuration modes. This password, after entered, becomes
    encrypted in the configuration.
  Enter enable secret: my_priv_encrypt_password

  The enable password is used when you do not specify an
  enable secret password, with some older software versions, and some boot
    images.
  Enter enable password: my_priv_password

  The virtual terminal password is used to protect
  access to the router over a network interface.
  Enter virtual terminal password: my_telnet_password
  Configure SNMP Network Management? [no]:
```

The second part of the output, shown in the preceding example, prompts you to set a host name and passwords on your switch. In this example

✦ Name the switch SW1.

✦ Set the encrypted privileged mode password to my_priv_encrypt_ password.

✦ Set the unencrypted privileged mode password to my_priv_password.

✦ Set the VTY access line password to my_telnet_password.

The next section of the initial configuration dialog, shown in the following example, displays a summary of the Ethernet interfaces (ports) available on your switch.

```
Current interface summary

Any interface listed with OK? value "NO" does not have a valid configuration
```

Book III
Chapter 2

Managing a Switch
Using Cisco IOS

```
Interface        IP-Address  OK? Method Status    Protocol
Vlan1            unassigned  YES unset  down      down
FastEthernet0/1  unassigned  YES unset  down      down
FastEthernet0/2  unassigned  YES unset  down      down

 [... some output cut ...]

FastEthernet0/23 unassigned  YES unset  down      down
FastEthernet0/24 unassigned  YES unset  down      down

Enter interface name used to connect to the
management network from the above interface summary: vlan1

Configuring interface Vlan1:
Configure IP on this interface? [no]: yes
 IP address for this interface: 192.168.75.10
 Subnet mask for this interface [255.255.255.0] :
 Class C network is 192.168.75.0, 24 subnet bits; mask is /24
Would you like to enable as a cluster command switch? [yes/no]: no
```

The third part of the output, shown in the preceding example, prompts you to set up a management interface for the switch. You choose the first VLAN interface: VLAN ID 1. You set an IP address and subnet mask on the management interface.

VLAN 1, the first VLAN, is reserved for management purposes. It is sometimes called the administrative VLAN.

The next section of the initial configuration dialog, shown in the following example, displays a summary of the configuration that will be created on your switch.

Only the secret password is encrypted by default: the encrypted privileged mode password.

You can also encrypt the other passwords for increased security using the `service password-encryption` command.

```
The following configuration command script was created:

hostname SW1
enable secret 5 $1$3GJW$pVC5U4qVd1bzy5x8kDkwa.
enable password my_priv_password
line vty 0 15
password my_telnet_password
no snmp-server
!
!
interface Vlan1
no shutdown
```

```
ip address 192.168.75.10 255.255.255.0
!
interface FastEthernet0/1
!
interface FastEthernet0/2
!
interface FastEthernet0/3
!
interface FastEthernet0/4
!

[... some output cut ...]

interface FastEthernet0/22
!
interface FastEthernet0/23
!
interface FastEthernet0/24
!
end
```

The last section of the initial configuration dialog, shown in the following example, prompts you to do one of the following:

✦ Save the configuration you just created to NVRAM.

✦ Return to the setup without saving the configuration you just created.

✦ Go straight to the IOS prompt without saving the configuration you just created.

You choose "2" to save the configuration you just created to NVRAM. This configuration becomes the startup configuration.

```
[0] Go to the IOS command prompt without saving this config.
[1] Return back to the setup without saving this config.
[2] Save this configuration to nvram and exit.

Enter your selection [2]:

Building configuration...
[OK]
Use the enabled mode 'configure' command to modify this configuration.

SW1>
```

Initializing the switch using Cisco IOS setup mode commands

You can configure the switch settings manually using Cisco IOS setup mode commands at any time.

The following sections show you a few basic Cisco IOS configuration commands that you can use at any time to configure your Cisco device.

Naming the switch

You can name your switch using the `hostname` Cisco IOS command. You should name all your switches using meaningful names to ease identification and management of each switch.

To configure the host name of the switch, run the following commands:

```
Switch>enable (or en)
Switch#configure terminal (or config t)
Switch(config)#hostname SW1
SW1(config)#exit
SW1#disable
SW1>
```

Configuring management IP address for the switch

You can configure an IP address and an IP gateway for your switch using the `ip address` and `ip default-gateway` Cisco IOS commands. This allows you to connect to the switch from remote locations using either Telnet or HTTP.

To configure the management IP address and default gateway on your switch, run the following commands:

```
SW1>enable (or en)
SW1#configure terminal (or config t)
SW1(config)#interface vlan1 (or int vlan1)
SW1(config-if)#ip address 192.168.75.10 255.255.255.0
SW1(config-if)#no shutdown
SW1(config-if)#exit
SW1(config)#ip default-gateway 192.168.75.1
SW1(config)#exit
SW1#disable
SW1>
```

The first two commands (`enable` and `configure terminal`) set the IOS in privileged global configuration mode. You can now run commands that configure global switch settings, that is, settings that apply to the whole switch.

The `interface vlan1` command selects an interface to work with. In this example, you select vlan1. Cisco switches support several virtual LANs (VLANs). They are numbered from 1 to 4094. The first VLAN, VLAN 1, is reserved for switch management. It is called the management (or administrative) VLAN. This is the VLAN on which you want to set the management IP address and the management default IP gateway.

The `ip address 192.168.75.10 255.255.255.0` command sets the IP address and the subnet mask on the interface that you selected previously. Observe that the IOS prompt now shows `SW1(config-if)#`. Config-if means that you are configuring an interface (`if`) right now.

The `no shutdown` command starts up the VLAN 1 interface. Recall that you enable components and services on a Cisco switch using the component or service name. You disable components and services on a Cisco switch using the component or service name prefixed with the `no` keyword. Here, shutdown is actually a state, not a component or service. An interface is either shut down or not shut down (started up). To summarize:

✦ To shut down an interface, select it and execute `shutdown`.

✦ To start an interface, select it and execute `no shutdown`.

The `ip default-gateway 192.168.75.1` command sets the default gateway for the switch. Observe that you first exit from the interface configuration mode (`SW1(config-if)# exit`) because the default gateway applies to the whole switch, not just to an interface. Now, you are back in global configuration mode (`SW1(config)#`).

The Cisco IOS prompt is designed to show you the configuration mode that you're in:

✦ `(config)`: You are in global configuration mode.

In this mode, you can execute commands that configure global switch settings, that is, settings that apply to the whole switch.

✦ `(config-if)`: You are in interface configuration mode.

In this mode, you can execute commands that configure switch interface settings, that is, settings that apply to just one interface of the switch. You select the interface to work with using the `interface` command.

✦ `(config-if-range)`: You are in interface range configuration mode.

In this mode, you can execute commands that configure a range of switch interfaces, that is, settings that apply to a range of interfaces on the switch. You select the range of interfaces to work with using the `interface range` command.

Configuring passwords

You can configure authentication passwords for your switch using the `password` and `login` Cisco IOS commands. By default, new Cisco devices do not have a password configured.

You can configure several passwords for different types of access:

✦ **Console password:** Used for console access through the console port or through a Console Terminal Server.

✦ **Auxiliary password:** Used for console access through the auxiliary port using a modem.

+ **VTY lines password:** Virtual type terminal (VTY) lines are used for Telnet and Secure Shell (SSH) access. They are called virtual type terminal (VTY) lines because no physical terminal is connected to the switch. You connect a computer host to the network and access the switch remotely using the switch management IP address. A terminal emulation program on the computer host emulates a physical terminal (TTY).

+ **Privileged password:** Used for privileged mode access. Privileged mode is an "expert" management operation mode used to run some Cisco IOS commands.

The console port and the auxiliary port are enabled by default, even if no password is specified for them. This is a security risk. It is best practice to specify at least a console password on new Cisco devices.

The VTY lines (Telnet and Secure Shell) are disabled by default. You need to specify a password for the VTY lines to enable them.

To configure passwords, you need to instruct the Cisco device to prompt for authentication. You use the `login` Cisco IOS command to do this.

Best practice

At a minimum, you should set passwords for console and VTY access to secure access through the console port and to enable and secure remote access through Telnet or SSH.

The following sections describe how to configure passwords for console and VTY access using Cisco IOS commands.

Console password

To configure the console password, run the following commands:

```
SW1>enable (or en)
SW1#configure terminal (or config t)
SW1(config)#line console 0 (or line con 0)
SW1(config-line)#password my_password
SW1(config-line)#login
SW1(config-line)#exit
SW1(config)#exit
SW1#disable
SW1>
```

The first two commands (`enable` and `configure terminal`) set the IOS in privileged global configuration mode. You can now run commands that configure global switch settings, that is, settings that apply to the whole switch.

The `line console 0` command selects the console line. Cisco devices have only one console line: console 0.

The `password my_password` command sets the `my_password` password on the console access line.

Finally, you instruct the Cisco device to prompt for authentication by entering the `login` Cisco IOS command. From now on, anytime you connect to the console line, you will be prompted to provide a password. The password you provide must be `my_password`. To disable the authentication prompt, issue `line console 0` again and enter the `no login` command.

You use the `exit` commands to exit the `config-line` mode and to exit the `(config)` global configuration mode.

Telnet password

To configure a password for the VTY lines, run the following commands:

```
SW1>enable (or en)
SW1#configure terminal (or config t)
SW1(config)#line vty 0 ?
   <0-15> last line number
SW1(config-line)#line vty 0-15
SW1(config-line)#password my_telnet_password
SW1(config-line)#login
SW1(config-line)#exit
SW1(config)#exit
SW1#disable
SW1>
```

The first two commands (`enable` and `configure terminal`) set the IOS in privileged global configuration mode. You can now run commands that configure global switch settings, that is, settings that apply to the whole switch.

The `line vty 0 ?` command asks the Cisco IOS how many VTY lines are available. The response (`<0-15> last line number`) shows that 16 VTY lines are available on this particular switch (you can have 16 simultaneous Telnet sessions opened to this switch). Now, you can configure a password either on one of the VTY lines (by selecting that particular line) or on all VTY lines (by selecting the whole 0–15 line range).

The `line vty 0-15` command selects the whole 0–15 VTY line range. Cisco devices have several VTY *access lines.* Older switches used to have only four VTY lines. Newer switches have as many as 1,180 VTY lines. It is best practice to query the Cisco IOS about how many VTY lines are available.

You have two main reasons to have several VTY access lines on a Cisco device:

✦ **Allowing you to connect to the switch and connect to another device from the switch:** Two VTY lines are needed in this case: one line to connect into the switch and another line to connect out of the switch to another device.

◆ **Allowing several administrators to work on the switch:** In large networks, more than one administrator may manage the network. More than one administrator may need to connect from a remote location to the same switch using Telnet or SSH. This is typical with large core switches.

The `password my_telnet_password` command sets the `my_telnet_password` password on the VTY access lines. You can set a different password on each line. However, this is not recommended. You don't know which VTY line you are on when you log in, so you wouldn't know which password to enter. Best practice is to select the whole range of VTY lines and set the same password on all of them.

Finally, you instruct the Cisco device to prompt for authentication by entering the `login` Cisco IOS command. From now on, anytime you connect to any of the VTY lines, you will be prompted to provide a password. The password you provide must be `my_telnet_password`. To disable the authentication prompt, issue `line vty 0-15` again and enter the `no login` command.

After you run the initial setup IOS commands, the switch has a startup configuration saved in NVRAM. The switch is reachable on the IP network. You can now connect to the switch either locally to its console or auxiliary port, or remotely to its IP address, as explained previously in the "Connecting to a Cisco Switch" section.

Configuring banners

You can configure a banner for your switch using the `banner` Cisco IOS command. The purpose of a banner is to display a brief message about the switch when you log in. This is useful when you have many switches spread out across multiple sites. It helps identifying the switch you log in to and its configuration and usage guidelines.

Banners are also useful for legal reasons: You can add a security warning in the banner message to warn users against unauthorized logins to the switch.

Although this does not prevent the user from logging in to the switch, it does provide grounds for legal action in the case of unauthorized logins. Always use passwords to secure your switches.

Four types of banners are available:

◆ **Message of the day (MOTD) banner:** This is the first banner to display when a user connects to a switch, regardless of the type of connection. This banner is used to display a message for all users connecting to the switch, *before* they log in. This is typically used for an unauthorized access warning.

✦ **Login banner:** This banner is displayed on TTY or VTY terminals after the MOTD banner.

This banner is typically used to display information about the switch and to provide guidelines on how to log in and use the switch.

✦ **Incoming terminal connection banner:** This banner is displayed on reverse TTY or VTY terminals after the MOTD banner.

This banner is used for the same reasons as the login banner. The only difference is the type of terminal connection: You can specify additional information in this banner for users connecting with reverse TTY or VTY terminals.

✦ **EXEC process creation banner:** This banner is displayed whenever an EXEC process is created, after the user is logged in. An EXEC process is created for each user EXEC prompt.

User EXEC prompts are established for each user connected to the switch, after they log in successfully. Hence, the EXEC process creation banner is displayed after the login/incoming banners, and after the MOTD banner.

To configure an MOTD banner on your switch, run the following commands:

```
SW1>enable (or en)
SW1#configure terminal (config t)
SW1(config)#banner motd -
Enter TEXT message. End with character '-'.
$This switch is property of silange.com networks. Unauthorized access is
    prohibited. Please disconnect if you are not a silange.com employee,
    customer, or business partner.
-
SW1(config)#
```

The `banner motd -` command starts the banner text editor using `'-'` as the delimiting character. The delimiting character is used by the IOS to determine when you are done typing the banner text. You enter the banner text of your choice and end by typing the delimiting character (`'-'` in this case) and pressing Enter. The delimiting character can be any character, but it is important to understand that you cannot use that character within the text of the banner. Cisco IOS would interpret that as the end of the banner text.

Resetting a Cisco switch

Express Setup and IOS setup mode run whenever no startup configuration exists in NVRAM. In other words, the switch reverts to setup mode anytime no startup configuration exists in NVRAM. Normally, this only happens when the switch is new and not yet configured.

However, you may want to clear the current configuration in NVRAM and start a new configuration from scratch. This is typically a last-resort trouble-shooting method: When problems affect the switch and no troubleshooting method fixes the problems, your last resort is to reset the switch and recon-figure it.

If you need to run Express Setup or the IOS setup again, you need to reset the switch. Resetting the switch clears the configuration of the switch.

After it is reset, the switch is in the state it was when you purchased it:

+ No IP address

+ No host name

+ No default gateway (router)

+ No subnet mask

+ No console password

+ No Telnet password

+ No startup configuration

You should back up the startup configuration of a switch to a backup com-puter host before resetting the switch. You learn how to backup the startup configuration file to a backup computer host in the "Managing Cisco Switch Configuration" section in this chapter.

To reset the switch and clear its startup configuration from NVRAM using the Mode button, follow these steps:

1. **Press and hold the Mode button.**

   The switch LEDs begin blinking after a few seconds.

2. **Continue to hold the Mode button.**

   The LEDs stop blinking after about 7 seconds. The switch reboots.

3. **Release the Mode button after the LEDs stop blinking and the switch starts rebooting.**

   The switch comes back up in setup mode without a startup configura-tion in NVRAM.

Managing Cisco switch configuration

Ongoing, you can manage your switch using the following:

✦ Cisco IOS commands

✦ The Cisco Device Manager Web tool

✦ The Cisco Network Assistant (CNA) tool

The Cisco Device Manager and the Cisco Network Assistant are two graphical user interface (GUI)–based tools that allow you to manage your switch and its startup and running configurations from a remote location using a computer host. Their GUI is much easier to use and more intuitive than Cisco IOS commands.

You find out about Cisco IOS switch configuration management commands in the following sections.

Managing the switch boot process

Cisco switches always follow the same boot process when they are powered up. This process involves four stages:

1. **Run the POST:** The Cisco switch runs the power-on self test to verify basic functionality of the Cisco switch hardware.

2. **Boot up:** The Cisco switch runs the *bootstrap program* to bring up the switch and transition it to normal operation mode by loading up the first Cisco IOS image from flash memory.

3. **Load the IOS:** The Cisco IOS loads into RAM from flash memory.

4. **Load the startup configuration:** After the Cisco switch loads the IOS in RAM, the IOS loads the device *startup configuration* from NVRAM. The startup configuration is loaded into RAM and becomes the *running configuration,* the configuration that changes dynamically while the Cisco device is running. At this point, the Cisco device is in normal operation mode, ready for business.

This process is also called the *automatic boot process.* The switch automatically boots up with current options and loads the startup configuration.

Boot command

By default, the Cisco *bootstrap program* loads the first Cisco IOS image file from flash memory when the switch is powered up. In some cases, you may need to boot a specific IOS image file from flash memory. For example, suppose that you download a new Cisco IOS image file that contains additional features, but you would like to test it on your switch before you remove the original IOS image file. You can configure the switch to boot with the new IOS image file using the `boot` command.

The `boot` command allows you to configure the boot process of a Cisco switch. You can do the following:

✦ Control which Cisco IOS image file is loaded

✦ Control which startup configuration file is loaded

✦ Enable Ctrl+Break during booting

✦ Enable manual booting

✦ Change the size of the NVRAM area that is formatted in Cisco IFS format

You can use the Cisco IOS contextual help to see the options available with the `boot` command:

```
SW1>
SW1>enable (or en)
Password: my_priv_encrypt_password
SW1#configure terminal (or config t, or conf t)
SW1(config)#
SW1(config)#boot ?
  boothlpr    Boot Helper System Image
  buffersize  Specify the size for filesystem-simulated NVRAM
  config-file           Configuration File
  enable-break          Enable Break while booting
  helper                Helper Image(s)
  helper-config-file    Helper Configuration File
  manual                Manual Boot
  private-config-file   Private Configuration File
  system                System Image
SW1(config)#exit
SW1#disable
SW1>
```

Observe that you need to be in privileged global configuration mode to execute the `boot` command.

The `boothlpr` option is beyond the scope of the CCNA test.

The `buffersize` option allows you to specify the size of the NVRAM buffer (memory area) that is formatted in Cisco IOS File System (IFS). You may need to increase the size of the IFS buffer if you need to store additional Cisco IOS images in flash memory.

The `config-file` option allows you to specify which configuration file is loaded during the boot process. This is useful when you need to test alternate configurations stored in different startup configuration files.

The `enable-break` option enables the Ctrl+Break key-combination option during the boot process. This allows you to interrupt the startup of the switch by pressing Ctrl+Break.

The `helper` and `helper-config-file` options are beyond the scope of the CCNA test.

The `manual` option enables manual booting. This allows you to boot the switch manually: The automatic boot process interrupts and displays the `switch:` manual boot prompt. You can manually boot the switch from the `switch:` manual boot prompt, controlling which IOS image is loaded and which configuration file is loaded. You can also use the `switch:` manual boot prompt to troubleshoot startup problems on your switch.

The `private-config-file` option allows you to specify which private configuration file is loaded during the boot process. This is useful when you need to test alternate private configurations stored in different startup configuration files. Private configuration files are used to store secured configuration data such as cryptographic encryption keys used for SSH.

The `system` option allows you to boot a specific Cisco IOS image file. This is useful in cases when, for example, you download a new Cisco IOS image file, containing additional features, and you would like to test it on your switch.

Here is an example in which you set your switch to boot with a specific Cisco IOS image file stored in flash memory:

```
SW1>
SW1>enable (or en)
Password:my_priv_encrypt_password
SW1#configure terminal (or config t, or conf t)
SW1(config)#
SW1(config)#boot system flash:/c2960-lanlite-mz.122-37.EY
SW1(config)#exit
SW1#disable
SW1>
```

Observe that you need to be in privileged global configuration mode to execute the `boot` command.

You can use the `show boot` command to verify the current boot options on a switch:

```
SW1>
SW1>enable (or en)
Password: my_priv_encrypt_password
SW1#show boot
BOOT path-list        : flash:/c2960-lanlite-mz.122-37.EY
Config file           : flash:/config.text
Private Config file   : flash:/private-config.text
Enable Break          : no
Manual Boot           : no
HELPER path-list      :
Auto upgrade          : yes
```

```
Auto upgrade path   :
NVRAM/Config file
        buffer size:    65536
SW1#disable
SW1>
```

Observe that you need to be in privileged EXEC mode to execute the `show boot` command. This command shows the current boot options. All options can be changed with the corresponding `boot` command, as explained earlier. After you change a boot option, you need to reboot your switch using the `reload` command in privileged EXEC mode.

Interrupting the boot process

In some cases, you may need to interrupt the automatic boot process to control some of the boot options. For example, you may have lost or forgotten the passwords on your switch. In this case, you do not want to boot the switch automatically, because you will be locked out of the switch by a password you do not have or do not remember. You need to break out of the boot process to reset the password.

You have three methods of interrupting the boot process on a Cisco switch:

+ Press the Mode button during the boot process. This is the simplest and default method to interrupt the boot process of a Cisco switch.

+ Change the boot process from automatic to manual and reboot the switch.

+ Enable the boot break option, reboot the switch, and press Ctrl+Break from a console connection during the boot process.

Interrupting the boot process with the Mode button

Follow these steps to interrupt the boot process of a Cisco switch using the Mode button on the front panel of the switch:

1. **Reboot the switch using the** `reload` **command in privileged EXEC mode.**

2. **Press the Mode button while the System LED (SYST) is flashing green within the first 15 seconds of the switch boot process.**

3. **Continue to press the Mode button until the System LED (SYST) flashes briefly amber and then turns solid green.**

4. **Release the Mode button when the System LED (SYST) becomes solid green.**

Interrupting the boot process by enabling the manual boot option

Follow these steps to interrupt the boot process of a Cisco switch using the manual boot option:

1. Enable the manual boot option.

2. Reboot the switch using the `reload` **command in privileged EXEC mode.**

You have the following options to control the manual boot option on a Cisco switch:

✦ To enable the manual boot option, run `boot manual` at the privileged global configuration prompt.

✦ To disable the manual boot option, run `no boot manual` at the privileged global configuration prompt.

The manual boot option is off by default. The switch boots up automatically without showing the `switch:` manual boot prompt.

Here is an example of how you enable manual boot:

```
SW1>enable (or en)
SW1#configure terminal (or config t)
Enter configuration commands, one per line.  End with CNTL/Z.
SW1(config)#boot manual
SW1(config)#
SW1(config)#do show boot (or do sh boot)
BOOT path-list       : flash:c2960-lanlite-mz.122-37.EY/c2960-lanlite-mz.122-37.
    EY.bin
Config file          : flash:/config.text
Private Config file  : flash:/private-config.text
Enable Break         : no
Manual Boot          : yes
HELPER path-list     :
Auto upgrade         : yes
Auto upgrade path    :
NVRAM/Config file
    buffer size:     65536

SW1(config)#exit
SW1#reload
    System configuration has been modified. Save? [yes/no]: n
    Proceed with reload? [confirm] <press Enter>

00:20:51: %SYS-5-RELOAD: Reload requested by console. Reload Reason: Reload
    command.

[... reboot output cut ...]

The system is not configured to boot automatically.  The
following command will finish loading the operating system
software:

    boot

switch:
```

The first two commands (`enable` and `configure terminal`) set the IOS in privileged global configuration mode. You can now run commands that configure global switch settings, that is, settings that apply to the whole switch.

Next, enable the manual boot process using the `boot manual` IOS command. Then, look at the current boot options using the `show boot` command. Observe that you use the `do` prefix because the `show` command does not run in configuration mode; you need to run it at the privileged EXEC prompt. Recall that the `do` Cisco IOS prefix allows you to run non-configuration commands in configuration mode.

Think of the `do` Cisco IOS prefix as an override option that allows you to momentarily exit configuration mode, run the command that follows the `do` prefix and come back into configuration mode. Note that the manual boot option is enabled now **(Manual Boot: yes)**.

The next few commands reboot the switch.

After the switch comes back up again, the bootstrap program interrupts the boot process and waits for commands at the `switch:` manual boot prompt.

Interrupting the boot process with Ctrl+Break

Follow these steps to interrupt the boot process of a Cisco switch using the Ctrl+Break key combination:

1. **Enable the boot process break option.**

2. **Reboot the switch using the** `reload` **command in privileged EXEC mode.**

3. **From a console connection, press Ctrl and Break simultaneously while the System LED (SYST) is flashing green within the first 15 seconds of the switch boot process.**

The following options allow you to control the boot process break option on a Cisco switch:

✦ To enable the boot process break option, run `boot enable-break` at the privileged global configuration prompt.

✦ To disable the boot process break option, run `no boot enable-break` at the privileged global configuration prompt.

The boot process break option is disabled by default.

Here is an example of how you enable the boot process break option:

```
SW1>enable (or en)
SW1#configure terminal (or config t)
Enter configuration commands, one per line.  End with CNTL/Z.
SW1(config)#boot enable-break
SW1(config)#
SW1(config)#do show boot (or do sh boot)
BOOT path-list        : flash:c2960-lanlite-mz.122-37.EY/c2960-lanlite-mz.122-37.
    EY.bin
Config file            : flash:/config.text
Private Config file : flash:/private-config.text
Enable Break           : yes
Manual Boot            : no
HELPER path-list       :
Auto upgrade           : yes
Auto upgrade path      :
NVRAM/Config file
    buffer size:    65536

SW1(config)#exit
SW1#reload
    System configuration has been modified. Save? [yes/no]: n
    Proceed with reload? [confirm] <press Enter>

00:20:51: %SYS-5-RELOAD: Reload requested by console. Reload Reason: Reload
    command.

[... reboot output cut ...]

[... Press CTRL-BREAK simultaneously ...]

The system boot process was interrupted.  The
following command will finish loading the operating system
software:

    boot

switch:
```

The first two commands (enable and configure terminal) set the IOS in privileged global configuration mode. You can now run commands that configure global switch settings, that is, settings that apply to the whole switch.

Next, enable the boot process break option using the boot enable-break IOS command. Then, look at the current boot options using the show boot command. Note that the enable break option is on now.

The next few commands reboot the switch.

After the switch comes back up again, from a console connection press Ctrl and Break simultaneously to interrupt the boot process. After it is interrupted, the bootstrap program waits for commands at the switch: manual boot prompt.

Introducing the switch manual boot prompt

No matter how you interrupt the boot process, you end up at the `switch:` manual boot prompt. The manual boot prompt allows you to control the boot process of the switch.

The bootstrap program displays a message informing you that you can enter the `boot` command to continue booting up the switch. You can use the help command (?) at the `switch:` boot prompt to see the manual boot commands and options available.

The IOS has not yet loaded the startup configuration at this point. In fact, the bootstrap program has not even loaded the IOS at this point.

Managing configurations

Two configurations are available on any Cisco switch: the startup configuration and the running configuration. The following sections review the characteristics of startup and running configurations and describe how to manage them on a Cisco switch.

Startup configuration

The startup configuration is the configuration that the Cisco IOS loads when it boots up. The startup configuration is stored in NVRAM, which keeps its contents even when the Cisco device is powered down.

Whenever no startup configuration exists in NVRAM, the switch starts in setup mode to allow you to create a startup configuration. After you complete the setup mode, you are prompted to save the configuration to NVRAM. If you answer yes, the configuration you created is saved to NVRAM; it becomes the startup configuration. You can also manually save the current configuration to NVRAM by using the `copy running-config startup-config` Cisco IOS command.

Cisco devices use the startup configuration data to configure the device before normal operation starts. The Cisco IOS loads the startup configuration from NVRAM into RAM. At that point, the startup configuration becomes the running configuration. The switch is up and ready in normal operation mode.

Running configuration

The running configuration is the dynamic data that changes while the Cisco device is in normal operation mode. This includes the following:

+ ARP cache (MAC address tables)
+ Routing tables
+ STP data

✦ VLAN data

✦ EtherChannel configuration data

✦ Temporary buffers

The Cisco IOS loads the startup configuration from NVRAM into RAM during the boot process. After it is in RAM, the startup configuration becomes the running configuration and can change dynamically.

You can save the running configuration to NVRAM to replace the startup configuration with updated data. To do this, use the `copy running-config startup-config` Cisco IOS command. You can also save the running configuration to a file on a computer host.

Saving the running configuration to NVRAM

To save the running configuration to NVRAM, run the following commands:

```
SW1>enable (or en)
SW1#copy running-config startup-config (or copy run start)
Destination filename [startup-config]? <press Enter>
Building configuration…
[OK]
SW1#
```

The first line shows the `copy` command. You can also use the short form of this command (`copy run start`).

The second line asks where you want to copy the running configuration to. You have several possible destinations:

✦ `startup-config`: Use this keyword to copy the current running configuration over the startup configuration in NVRAM.

✦ `flash`: Use this keyword to copy the current running configuration to a file in flash memory, alongside the Cisco IOS.

✦ `ftp`: Use this keyword to copy the current running configuration to an FTP server. This option is useful for backing up the switch configuration to a remote computer host.

✦ `archive`: This is similar to the `ftp` option, except that you archive to a tape- or disk-based backup system directly, instead of passing through a computer host.

Many more possible copy destinations exist. You can use the Cisco IOS contextual help system to find out more about the other possible copy destinations by running the following command:

```
SW1#copy running-config ? (or copy run ?)
```

The ? sign instructs the Cisco IOS to show you all the possible values that you can provide for the second argument of the `copy` command.

The default destination is the `startup-config` file in NVRAM. To keep the default answer, just press Enter. Sometimes the Cisco IOS prompts you to enter a value, and it shows the default answer in between brackets [ ]. To keep the default answer, just press Enter.

Monitoring the running configuration

To monitor the running configuration, run the following command:

```
SW1#show running-config (or sh run)
```

Monitoring the startup configuration

To monitor the startup configuration, run the following command:

```
SW1#show startup-config (or sh start)
```

Deleting the startup configuration

Resetting the switch erases the startup configuration from NVRAM and reboots the switch. Upon reboot, the switch starts in setup mode because no startup configuration exists in NVRAM. This allows you to clear the current configuration in NVRAM and build a new configuration from scratch.

This is typically a last-resort troubleshooting method: When problems affect the switch and no troubleshooting method fixes the problems, your last resort is to reset the switch and reconfigure it.

You can also reset the switch using the `erase startup-config` Cisco IOS command.

You should back up the startup configuration to a backup computer host before deleting it. You find out how to back up the configuration to a backup computer host later in this chapter.

To delete the startup configuration, run the following commands:

```
SW1>enable (or en)
SW1#erase startup-config
Erasing the nvram filesystem removes all configuration files!
Continue? [confirm] <press Enter to confirm>
[OK]
Erase of nvram: complete
SW1#
```

Observe that the `erase` command warns you that the NVRAM contents will be reinitialized and prompts you to confirm. The default answer is `confirm`. To confirm, just press Enter.

Switch configuration backup and recovery best practice

It is best practice to save the running configuration to both

+ The startup configuration file in NVRAM on the switch itself
+ A computer host

This protects you against a total failure of the switch. If the switch fails and you need to replace it with a new one, you don't want to have to re-create the startup configuration from scratch. If you have that configuration saved on a computer host, you can load the startup configuration from the computer host onto the new switch; you're now ready to go in production with the new switch.

Back up the switch running configuration to a computer host

To back up the running configuration to a computer host, run the following commands:

```
SW1>enable (or en)
SW1#copy running-config tftp (or copy run tftp)
Address or name of remote host []? 192.168.75.5
Destination filename [SW1-config]? <press Enter>
812 bytes copied in 0.910 secs (892 bytes/sec)
SW1#
```

The `copy running-config tftp` Cisco IOS command on the second line initiates copying the switch running configuration to a TFTP server.

The third line prompts you for the IP address or host name of the remote host destination. Observe that, in this example, the IOS does not suggest any destination IP address or hostname "[]". You can configure a default TFTP server on your switch. The IP address or hostname of that default TFTP server will then show up suggested between the square brackets.

The fourth line prompts you for the filename of the configuration file to be saved on the remote host. The switch name followed by `-config` is suggested by default. Simply press Enter to accept the suggested filename.

Now your running configuration is saved in a file named `SW1-config` on the remote computer host with IP address 192.168.75.5.

Book III
Chapter 2

Managing a Switch
Using Cisco IOS

Recover a switch configuration from a computer host

Suppose that you need to load a configuration from a remote host to your switch. The same `copy` Cisco IOS command allows you to recover a configuration from a remote host:

```
SW1>enable (or en)
SW1#copy tftp running-config (or copy tftp run)
Address or name of remote host []? 192.168.75.5
Source filename []? SW1-config
Destination filename [running-config]? <press Enter>
Accessing tftp://192.168.75.5/SW1-config...
Loading SW1-config from 192.168.75.5
[OK - 812 bytes]
812 bytes copied in 10.120 secs (80 bytes/sec)
SW1#
```

The `copy tftp running-config` Cisco IOS command on the second line copies the switch running configuration from a TFTP server.

The third line prompts you for the IP address or host name of the remote host destination. Observe that, in this example, the IOS does not suggest any source IP address or hostname "[]". You can configure a default TFTP server on your switch. The IP address or hostname of that default TFTP server will then show up suggested between the square brackets.

The fourth line prompts you for the source filename of the configuration file that you want to load from the remote host. Enter the name of a configuration file that you saved previously on the TFTP server. In this example, you enter the name of the configuration that you just copied to the TFTP server in the previous example ("SW1-config").

The fifth line prompts you for the destination filename. The `running-config` filename is suggested. This means that the configuration you load from the TFTP server will replace the current running configuration. Press Enter to accept the suggested choice.

Next, the `copy` command displays a few status messages.

At this point, your running configuration has been loaded from a file named `SW1-config` from a remote TFTP server host with IP address 192.168.75.5.

Managing switch configurations using Cisco IOS File System (IFS)

You saw in the previous two sections how to back up a switch configuration to a file on a computer host and how to restore a switch configuration from a backup file on a computer host. You used the `copy` Cisco IOS command to do this. This section shows you a new trick: how to manage the memory of a Cisco switch using Cisco IOS File System (IFS) commands.

You can manage the memory of a Cisco switch like a file system on a computer host. The Cisco IFS presents the memory of a Cisco switch as directories (or folders) and files within those directories, just like Microsoft Windows, Apple Mac OS X, Linux, or any other computer operating system presents the hard drive of a computer host as directories (or folders) and files.

The Cisco IFS commands are only available in privileged mode. So, you need to run the `enable` command first (or `en` in its short form).

First, verify the current directory:

```
SW1>enable (or en)
SW1#pwd
flash:
```

You are currently in the flash memory main directory, as shown by the `pwd` command. Next, run the Cisco IFS command `dir` to see the contents of flash memory on your switch:

```
SW1#dir
Directory of flash:/
    1  -rw-  15572992  <no date>  c2960-ik9o3s3-mz.123-1a.bin
16777216 bytes total (1204160 bytes free)
```

This shows that the flash memory on your switch contains a single Cisco IOS image named `c2960-ik9o3s3-mz.123-1a.bin`.

So, what other directories and files exist on your switch? You can easily find that using the `dir all-filesystems` Cisco IFS command:

```
SW1#dir all-filesystems
Directory of nvram:/

   27  -rw-    0         <no date>  startup-config
   28  ----    0         <no date>  private-config

29688 bytes total (29636 bytes free)
Directory of system:/

   10  drwx    0                   <no date>  its
    2  dr-x    0                   <no date>  memory
    1  -rw-    582                 <no date>  running-config
    9  dr-x    0                   <no date>  vfiles

No space information available
Directory of flash:/

    1  -rw-  15572992  <no date>  c2600-ik9o3s3-mz.123-1a.bin

16777216 bytes total (1204160 bytes free)
```

Observe that you have three main directories (file systems) on your Cisco switch:

✦ nvram: Stores the startup-config and private-config files.

✦ system: This is the RAM, which contains the running-config file.

✦ flash: This is the flash memory, which contains the Cisco IOS operating system image. This is the Cisco IOS image that the bootstrap program loads in RAM when the switch boots up.

You can list the contents of any of these main directories (file systems) individually using the dir and cd Cisco IFS commands. You can change your working directory from flash: to any of the main directories using the cd Cisco IFS command.

For example, issue the following command to list the contents of NVRAM:

```
SW1#dir nvram:/
Directory of nvram:/
   27  -rw-  0    <no date>  startup-config
   28  ----  0    <no date>  private-config
29688 bytes total (29636 bytes free)
```

Now, change the directory to the RAM directory (system) and look at the files and directories available there:

```
SW1#cd system:
SW1#dir
Directory of system:/
   10  drwx  0    <no date>            its
    2  dr-x  0    <no date>         memory
    1  -rw-  582  <no date>  running-config
    9  dr-x  0    <no date>         vfiles
```

Observe the running-config file. This is the current running configuration. You can copy a configuration file from a computer host to system:/running-config to load a configuration on the switch from a configuration backup file on a computer host.

To load a configuration on the switch from a configuration backup file on a computer host, run the following Cisco IFS commands:

```
SW1#copy tftp://192.168.75.5/SW1-confg system:/running-config
Destination filename [running-config]? <press Enter>
Accessing tftp://192.168.75.5/SW1-confg...
Loading SW1-confg from 192.168.75.5
[OK - 812 bytes]
812 bytes copied in 10.120 secs (80 bytes/sec)
SW1#
```

The `copy tftp://192.168.75.5/SW1-confg system:/running-config` command you use here is very similar to the `copy tftp running-config` command that you used in the previous section. The only difference is that you specify the path to the source and the path to the destination when you use the Cisco IFS version of the `copy` command.

You can also use this command to copy a configuration from a configuration backup file on a computer host to the `startup-config` file in NVRAM. Here is an example:

```
SW1#copy tftp://192.168.75.5/SW1-confg nvram:/startup-config
Destination filename [startup-config]? <press Enter>
Accessing tftp://192.168.75.5/SW1-confg...
Loading SW1-confg from 192.168.75.5
[OK - 812 bytes]
812 bytes copied in 10.120 secs (80 bytes/sec)
```

Managing Cisco Switch Authentication

You can configure several passwords for different types of access to your switch:

✦ **Console password:** Used for console access through the console port or through a Console Terminal Server.

✦ **Auxiliary password:** Used for console access through the auxiliary port using a modem.

✦ **VTY lines password:** Virtual type terminal (VTY) lines are used for Telnet and Secure Shell (SSH) access. They are called virtual type terminal lines because no physical terminal is connected to the switch. Instead, you connect a computer host to the network and access the switch remotely using the switch management IP address. A terminal emulation program on the computer host emulates a physical terminal (TTY).

✦ **Privileged password:** Used for privileged mode access. Privileged mode is an "expert" management operation mode used to run some Cisco IOS commands.

The console port and the auxiliary port are enabled by default, even if no password is specified for them. This is a security risk. It is best practice to specify at least a console password on new Cisco devices.

Privileged EXEC mode is *not* secured with a password by default on Cisco switches. By default, you can access privileged mode by executing the `enable` IOS command at the user EXEC prompt. It is best practice to configure a privileged mode password to secure access to advanced IOS commands that can adversely affect the functionality of the switch if misused.

The VTY lines (Telnet and Secure Shell) are disabled by default. You need to specify a password for the VTY lines to enable them.

To configure passwords, you need to instruct the Cisco device to prompt for authentication. You use the `login` Cisco IOS command to do this.

Console password

This section reviews how to configure a console password. To configure the console password, run the following commands:

```
SW1>enable (or en)
SW1#configure terminal (or config t)
SW1(config)#line console 0 (or line con 0)
SW1(config-line)#password my_password
SW1(config-line)#login
SW1(config-line)#exit
SW1(config)#exit
SW1#disable
SW1>
```

The first two commands (`enable` and `configure terminal`) set the IOS in privileged global configuration mode. You can now run commands that configure global switch settings, that is, settings that apply to the whole switch.

The `line console 0` command selects the console line. Cisco devices have only one console line: console 0.

The `password my_password` command sets the `my_password` password on the console access line.

Finally, you instruct the Cisco device to prompt for authentication by entering the `login` Cisco IOS command. From now on, anytime you connect to the console line, you will be prompted to provide a password. The password you provide must be `my_password`. To disable the authentication prompt, issue `line console 0` again and enter the `no login` command.

You use the `exit` commands to exit the `config-line` mode and to exit the (config) global configuration mode.

Telnet password

This section reviews how to configure a password for the VTY access lines. To configure a password for the VTY lines, run the following commands:

```
SW1>enable (or en)
SW1#configure terminal (or config t)
SW1(config)# line vty 0 ?
  <0-15> last line number
```

```
SW1(config-line)# line vty 0-15
SW1(config-line)# password my_telnet_password
SW1(config-line)# login
SW1(config-line)# exit
SW1(config)# exit
SW1#disable
SW1>
```

The first two commands (enable and configure terminal) set the IOS in privileged global configuration mode. You can now run commands that configure global switch settings, that is, settings that apply to the whole switch.

The line vty 0 ? command asks the Cisco IOS how many VTY lines are available. The response (<0-15> last line number) shows that 16 VTY lines exist on this particular switch. Now, you can configure a password either on one of the VTY lines (by selecting that particular line) or on all VTY lines (by selecting the whole 0–15 line range).

The line vty 0-15 command selects the whole 0–15 VTY line range. Cisco switches have several VTY *access lines*. Older switches used to have only four VTY lines. Newer switches have as many as 1,180 VTY lines. It is best practice to query the Cisco IOS about how many VTY lines are available.

Two main reasons exist to have several VTY access lines on a Cisco switch:

✦ **Allowing you to connect to the switch and connect to another device from the switch:** Two VTY lines are needed in this case: one to connect into the switch and another one to connect out of the switch to another device.

✦ **Allowing several administrators to work on the switch:** In large networks, more than one administrator may manage the network. More than one administrator may need to connect from a remote location to the same switch using Telnet or SSH. This is typical with large core switches.

The password my_telnet_password command sets the my_telnet_password password on the VTY access lines. You can set a different password on each line. However, this is not recommended because you don't know which VTY line you are on when you log in, so you wouldn't know which password to enter. Best practice is to select the whole range of VTY lines and to set the same password on all of them.

Finally, instruct the Cisco switch to prompt for authentication by entering the login Cisco IOS command. From now on, anytime you connect to any of the VTY lines, you will be prompted to provide a password. The password you provide must be my_telnet_password. To disable the authentication prompt, issue line vty 0-15 again and enter the no login command.

Auxiliary password

If your switch has an auxiliary port, it is best practice to secure access to the auxiliary port using a password. To configure the auxiliary password, run the following commands:

```
SW1>enable (or en)
SW1#configure terminal (or config t)
SW1(config)#line auxiliary 0 (or line aux 0)
SW1(config-line)#password my_aux_password
SW1(config-line)#login
SW1(config-line)#exit
SW1(config)#exit
SW1#disable
SW1>
```

The first two commands (`enable` and `configure terminal`) set the IOS in privileged global configuration mode. You can now run commands that configure global switch settings, that is, settings that apply to the whole switch.

The `line auxiliary 0` command selects the auxiliary line. Cisco switches have only one auxiliary line: auxiliary 0.

The `password my_password` command sets the `my_password` password on the auxiliary line.

Finally, you instruct the Cisco switch to prompt for authentication by entering the `login` Cisco IOS command. From now on, anytime you connect to the auxiliary line, you will be prompted to provide a password. The password you provide must be `my_password`. To disable the authentication prompt, issue `line auxiliary 0` again and enter the `no login` command.

You use the `exit` commands to exit the `config-line` mode and to exit the `(config)` global configuration mode.

Privileged password

It is best practice to set up a privileged password to secure access to advanced IOS commands that can adversely affect the functionality of the switch if misused. You can use two different commands to configure a privileged password:

✦ `enable password my_priv_password`: This command sets `my_priv_password` as the privileged password. This password is not encrypted by default. This command is supported in all IOS versions.

✦ `enable secret my_priv_encrypt_password`: This command sets `my_priv_ encrypt_password` as the privileged password. This password is encrypted. This command is supported in newer IOS versions.

Using the enable secret or the enable password commands, you configure a privileged password that is stored locally on your switch. The only difference between the two commands is that enable secret stores the password on the switch in encrypted form. This is more secure than enable password, which stores the password on the switch in unencrypted form.

Always use the Cisco IOS help to determine whether the enable secret command is available. If it is, use it to set the privileged password. It is best practice to encrypt the privileged password using the enable secret command whenever this command is available. Otherwise, encrypt passwords using the service password-encryption command in global configuration mode."

You can also configure your privileged password to be stored on a *Terminal Access Controller Access Control System (TACACS)* server. This is a good option in larger networks with many switches when it is better to configure the privileged password once, centrally, on a TACACS server, instead of configuring passwords on each of your switches.

To configure an encrypted privileged mode password, run the following commands:

```
SW1>enable (or en)
SW1#configure terminal (or config t)
SW1(config)#enable secret my_priv_encrypt_password
SW1(config)#exit
SW1#disable
SW1>
```

**Book III
Chapter 2**

Managing a Switch
Using Cisco IOS

Encrypting passwords

By default, passwords are stored in plain text in the running configuration in RAM and in the startup configuration file in NVRAM. You can view the passwords on your switch in plain text, using either the show running-config or the show startup-config command. This is a security risk. It is best practice to encrypt all passwords on your switch.

The privileged password is encrypted if you use the enable secret command. It is best practice to set a privileged password using the enable secret command to make sure that it is encrypted. So, if you use enable secret instead of enable password to set a privileged password, your privileged password is encrypted.

How about other passwords? Console, auxiliary, and Telnet (VTY) passwords are *not* encrypted, even if you use the enable secret command for the privileged password. You need to encrypt them using the service password-encryption command.

To encrypt passwords on your switch, run the following commands:

```
SW1>enable (or en)
SW1#configure terminal (or config t)
SW1(config)#service password-encryption
SW1(config)#exit
SW1#disable
SW1>
```

The first two commands (`enable` and `configure terminal`) set the IOS in privileged global configuration mode. You can now run commands that configure global switch settings, that is, settings that apply to the whole switch.

The `service password-encryption` command asks the Cisco IOS to encrypt all passwords except the privileged password that is already encrypted if the `enable secret` command was used.

Enabling Secure Shell (SSH)

Secure Shell (SSH) is similar to Telnet: It allows remote users to connect to the switch by using the switch IP address. SSH is more secure than Telnet, because it encrypts data exchanged between the remote management computer and the switch.

You should encrypt data exchanged between the remote management computer and the switch.

Consider this example: You need to change the passwords on a switch located in a remote data center. The data center is too far to walk to, so you need to connect to the switch remotely from your computer. While changing the passwords, you enter the passwords on the keyboard of your computer. If you are connected to the switch using Telnet, the data exchanged between your computer and the switch is in clear text. That data includes the new passwords that you type at your computer keyboard. Hence, passwords are sent over the Internet in clear text. This is a security risk. SSH avoids this security risk by encrypting data exchanged between your computer and the switch.

SSH uses encryption keys to encrypt the data exchanged in an SSH session. Cisco supports both SSH version 1.0 (also known as SSH v1 or SSH.1) and SSH version 2.0 (also known as SSH v2 or SSH.2). Cisco started to support SSH v2 beginning with IOS Release 12.1(19)E on some switch and router models.

If you get a `%Invalid input` error when you execute the `crypto key generate rsa` command, the Cisco IOS version on your switch does not support SSH. You may need to download the cryptographic software image from Cisco. To download the cryptographic IOS software image for your switch, log in to `www.cisco.com/public/sw-center/index.shtml`.

(You need to register at Cisco.com before downloading. Some software export limitations may apply.)

Figure 2-10 shows the Cisco Catalyst 2960 software download section at Cisco.com.

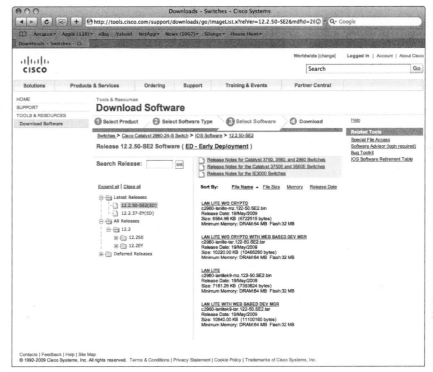

Figure 2-10:
Downloading Cisco Catalyst switch IOS images.

Four packages are available for each release:

✦ **LAN LITE w/o crypto:** This is the Cisco IOS image without cryptographic services. This IOS image does not support SSH.

✦ **LAN LITE w/o crypto with web-based DEV MGR:** This is the Cisco IOS image without cryptographic services, but it includes the Cisco Device Manager GUI. This IOS image does not support SSH.

✦ **LAN LITE:** This is the Cisco IOS image with cryptographic services. This IOS image supports SSH.

✦ **LAN LITE with web-based DEV MGR:** This is the Cisco IOS image with cryptographic services and with the Cisco Device Manager GUI. This IOS image supports SSH.

To enable SSH, you need to do the following:

✦ Ensure that the Cisco IOS image on your switch supports SSH.

✦ Ensure that you assigned a host name to your switch: SSH needs the host name to generate the encryption keys.

✦ Ensure that you assigned an IP domain name to your switch: SSH needs the IP domain name to generate the encryption keys.

✦ Create a local or TACACS administrator user and assign it a password: SSH cannot use the Telnet password that you assigned to the VTY access lines. You need to create a specific user that will be used to authenticate SSH sessions.

✦ Create the encryption keys.

✦ Configure SSH options such as session timeout and number of login retries.

✦ Enable SSH on the VTY lines of your switch.

Consider the following example:

```
SW1>enable (or en)
SW1#configure terminal (or config t)
```

The `enable` and `configure terminal` commands set the IOS in privileged global configuration mode. You can now run commands that configure global switch settings, that is, settings that apply to the whole switch.

```
SW1(config)#ip domain-name silange.com
```

The `ip domain-name silange.com` command sets the IP domain name for this switch. SSH needs the host name and the IP domain name to generate the encryption keys. Observe that you did not use the `hostname SW1` command here because the switch already has a host name that is different from the default Cisco "Switch" host name. If your switch was still named "Switch" and you try to run the `crypto` command, the IOS would prompt you to assign a host name to your switch.

```
SW1(config)#username Admin007 password Admin007Passwrd
SW1(config)#line vty 0 15
SW1(config-line)#login local
SW1(config-line)#exit
```

The `line vty 0 15` and `login local` commands enable local authentication on VTY lines 0 to 15.

You can also use TACACS authentication by executing `login tacacs` instead of `login local`. However, you would need to have a TACACS server configured, which is beyond the scope of CCNA.

Next, you exit the line configuration mode by executing `exit` at the `(config-line)` prompt.

Now, you create the SSH encryption keys for your switch. You execute the `crypto key generate rsa` command. This command generates public and private encryption keys based on the RSA encryption algorithm. It uses the `hostname.domain-name` combination of the switch to generate the keys. The `crypto` command also uses a modulus number to generate the keys. You can choose the number of bits used for the modulus number: between 360 and 2048. The higher the number of bits in the modulus number, the harder it is for a hacker to break the keys. So, it is better to have more bits in the modulus number. However, the more bits in the modulus number, the longer it takes to generate it. Modulo 1024 is used in this example, a good compromise between security and performance:

```
SW1(config)#crypto key generate rsa
  The name for the keys will be: SW1.silange.com
  Choose the size of the key modulus in the range of 360 to 2048 for your General
    Purpose Keys. Choosing a key modulus greater than 512 may take a few minutes.

  How many bits in the modulus [512]: 1024
  % Generating 1024 bit RSA keys ...[OK]
  *Mar  1 00:14:40.071: %SSH-5-ENABLED: SSH 1.5 has been enabled
```

Next, you look at the current SSH configuration on the switch using the `show ip ssh` command. Observe that you prefix this command with the `do` keyword because you cannot run `show ip ssh` in configuration mode. Recall that the `do` prefix allows you to run a privileged EXEC command from the privileged EXEC configuration prompt:

```
SW1(config)#do show ip ssh
  SSH Enabled - version 2.0
  Authentication timeout: 120 secs; Authentication retries: 3

SW1(config)#ip ssh time-out 60
SW1(config)#ip ssh authentication-retries 2
```

The `ip ssh time-out 60` and `ip ssh authentication-retries 2` commands configure a 60-second SSH session timeout and configure SSH to allow two login retries. Observe that the default timeout is 120 seconds and the default number of retries is 2, as shown by the `show ip ssh` command in the previous step.

Finally, you need to enable SSH as an input transport protocol on the VTY access lines. The `line vty 0 15` and `transport input ssh telnet` commands accomplish this.

Note that you enabled both SSH and Telnet as input transport protocols on the VTY access lines. If you removed the `telnet` keyword from the `transport input` command, only SSH would be enabled:

Book III
Chapter 2

Managing a Switch
Using Cisco IOS

```
SW1(config)#line vty 0 15
SW1(config-line)#transport input ssh telnet
SW1(config-line)#exit
```

The next two commands show the current SSH configuration on the switch
(show ip ssh) and the status of current SSH connections if any (show ssh):

```
SW1(config)#do show ip ssh
  SSH Enabled - version 2.0
  Authentication timeout: 60 secs; Authentication retries: 2
SW1(config)#do show ssh
  %No SSH server connections running.
SW1(config)#exit
SW1#disable
SW1>
```

Recovering switch passwords

What happens if you forget your passwords? Suppose, for example, that you
start a new job working at a company as the network administrator. The network consultant who set up the network infrastructure left without leaving
the passwords for some switches you have in your network. This happens
quite often, unfortunately. Theoretically, you would have to wipe out the
configuration of the switches and start from scratch. This is not productive.

The Cisco IOS provides a mechanism to recover passwords in case you lose
them or you do not remember them.

You need to have physical access to the switch to connect to its console
port. This is a good thing, because you don't want anyone else connecting
from a remote location through Telnet to be able to reset the passwords on
your switches.

The key point of the password recovery process is to boot up the Cisco
switch ignoring its current startup configuration, which contains the current
passwords. To do this, you need to interrupt the boot process of the switch
before the startup configuration is loaded from NVRAM to RAM.

Reviewing the switch manual boot process

You have three ways to interrupt the boot process on a Cisco switch.

Interrupting the boot process with the Mode button

Follow these steps to interrupt the boot process of a Cisco switch using the
Mode button on the front panel of the switch:

1. **Reboot the switch using the** reload **command in privileged EXEC
   mode.**

2. **Press the Mode button while the System LED (SYST) is flashing green
   within the first 15 seconds of the switch boot process.**

3. **Continue to press the Mode button until the System LED (SYST) flashes briefly amber and then turns solid green.**

4. **Release the Mode button when the System LED (SYST) becomes solid green.**

Enabling the manual boot option

Follow these steps to interrupt the boot process of a Cisco switch using the manual boot option:

1. **Enable the manual boot option.**

2. **Reboot the switch using the** `reload` **command in privileged EXEC mode.**

The following options allow you to control the manual boot option on a Cisco switch:

✦ To enable the manual boot option, run `boot manual` at the privileged global configuration prompt.

✦ To disable the manual boot option, run `no boot manual` at the privileged global configuration prompt.

The manual boot option is off by default: The switch boots up automatically without showing the `switch:` manual boot prompt.

Interrupting the boot process with Ctrl+Break

Follow these steps to interrupt the boot process of a Cisco switch using the Ctrl+Break key combination:

1. **Enable the boot process break option.**

2. **Reboot the switch using the** `reload` **command in privileged EXEC mode.**

3. **From a console connection, press Ctrl and Break simultaneously while the System LED (SYST) is flashing green within the first 15 seconds of the switch boot process.**

You have the following boot process break options on a Cisco switch:

✦ To enable the boot process break option, run `boot enable-break` at the privileged global configuration prompt.

✦ To disable the boot process break option, run `no boot enable-break` at the privileged global configuration prompt.

The boot process break option is disabled by default.

Reviewing the switch manual boot prompt

Regardless of how you interrupt the boot process, you end up at the `switch:` manual boot prompt. The manual boot prompt allows you to control the boot process of the switch.

The bootstrap program displays a message informing you that you can enter the `boot` command to continue booting up the switch.

You can use the help (?) command at the `switch:` boot prompt to see the manual boot commands and options available.

The IOS has not yet loaded the startup configuration at this point. In fact, the bootstrap program has not even loaded the IOS at this point.

You are now ready to start the password recovery process. This process varies depending on whether the password recovery feature is enabled on the switch.

Introducing the password recovery option

A switch administrator can disable the password recovery feature for security reasons. If the password recovery feature is disabled, the password can still be reset, but the switch configuration is reset as well. This prevents an unauthorized user from resetting the password and gaining access to a configured switch.

You control the password recovery feature availability using the `service password-recovery` IOS command. The `service password-recovery` IOS command needs to be run in privileged global configuration mode. You have the following options to control the password recovery feature on a Cisco switch:

✦ To enable password recovery, run `service password-recovery` at the privileged global configuration prompt.

✦ To disable password recovery, run `no service password-recovery` at the privileged global configuration prompt.

Password recovery process with password recovery enabled

The password recovery feature is enabled if you see the message `The password-recovery mechanism is enabled` during the boot process. Follow these steps to recover the password on a switch with the password recovery option enabled:

1. **Interrupt the normal boot process using one of the methods previously described.**

2. **Manually initialize the flash file system.**

3. **Hide the startup configuration file to prevent the IOS from loading it.**

4. **Boot the switch manually and wait for the IOS to finish loading in RAM.**

5. **Unhide the startup configuration file.**

6. **Manually load the startup configuration file from NVRAM to RAM.**

7. **Reset the password.**

8. **Save the running configuration over the startup configuration.**

9. **Revert the boot process to its default options.**

10. **Reboot the switch.**

Here is an example:

```
!Lines starting with "!" in this example are comments that
!explain certain commands within the example. Cisco IOS
!does not interpret lines starting with the "!" character.
!The IOS interprets these lines as comments, not as commands.

!The first few lines below restart the switch using the
!reload IOS command after the manual boot option was enabled.

SW1>en
SW1#reload
Proceed with reload? [confirm]

00:01:35: %SYS-5-RELOAD: Reload requested by console. Reload Reason: Reload
      command.

!The switch is now starting up. Observe the message in bold
!below, showing that password recovery is enabled.

Using driver version 1 for media type 1
Base ethernet MAC Address: 00:25:b4:10:58:80
Xmodem file system is available.
The password-recovery mechanism is disabled.

The system has been interrupted prior to initializing the
flash filesystem.  The following commands will initialize
the flash filesystem, and finish loading the operating
system software:

    flash_init
    boot

!next line manually initializes the flash file system
switch: flash_init

Initializing Flash...
mifs[2]: 0 files, 1 directories
mifs[2]: Total bytes    :   3870720
mifs[2]: Bytes used     :      1024
```

```
mifs[2]: Bytes available :    3869696
mifs[2]: mifs fsck took 0 seconds.
mifs[3]: 518 files, 19 directories
mifs[3]: Total bytes    :   27998208
mifs[3]: Bytes used     :    8687616
mifs[3]: Bytes available :   19310592
mifs[3]: mifs fsck took 5 seconds.
...done Initializing Flash.

switch:

!next line hides the startup-config by copying it under a
!  different name, thereby preventing the IOS from
!  loading the startup-config (config.text)
switch: rename flash:config.text flash:config.text.old
switch:

!next line manually boots the switch
switch: boot

Loading "flash:c2960-lanlite-mz.122-37.EY/c2960-lanlite-mz.122-37.EY.bin"...@@@@@
     @@@@@@@@@@@@@@@@@@@@@

[... boot output cut ...]

SW1>en

!next line un-hides the startup-config by putting config.text
!  back to its place in flash memory
SW1#rename flash:config.text.old flash:config-text

!next lines load config.text from flash (NVRAM) to RAM
SW1# copy flash:config.text system:running-config
Source filename [config-text]? <press Enter>
Destination filename [running-config]? <press Enter>

!at this point the startup-config (flash:config.text)
!  was loaded (manually) into RAM (system:running-config)

SW1# configure terminal      (or config t)

!next line sets the new password
SW1(config)# enable secret my_priv_encrypt_password

SW1(config)# exit

!next line replaces the startup-config file
!   in NVRAM (flash:config.text) with the current
!   running-config file in RAM (system:running-config)

SW1# copy running-config startup-config

!next line reboots the switch
SW1# reload

System configuration has been modified. Save? [yes/no]: yes
Proceed with reload? [confirm] <press Enter>

00:15:05: %SYS-5-RELOAD: Reload requested by console. Reload Reason: Reload command.

[... reboot output cut ...]
```

Observe that the password recovery feature is enabled on this switch.

Once you get to the `switch:` manual boot prompt, you need to manually initialize the flash file system using the `flash_init` boot command.

Next, you hide the startup configuration file in flash memory by copying it under a different name. This prevents the IOS from finding the startup configuration file in flash memory (`flash:config.text`) and loading it in RAM (`system:running-config`). Recall that you don't want the IOS to load the startup-config since it stores the current passwords that you want to reset.

Now, you manually boot the switch and wait for IOS to finish loading in RAM. You know the IOS finished loading when it displays the `SW1>` User EXEC Prompt.

Next, you unhide the startup configuration file in flash memory by copying it back under its original file name (`flash:config.text`).

You manually load the startup configuration in RAM overwriting the current running configuration of the switch. You do this by copying the startup configuration file from NVRAM (`flash:config.text`) to RAM (`system:running-config`).

At this point the startup-config (`flash:config.text`) has been loaded (manually) into RAM (`system:running-config`) and it became the current running-config.

Now, it's time to set the new password. This basically resets the password to a new one.

Finally, you replace the startup-config file in NVRAM (`flash:config.text`) with the current running-config file in RAM (`system:running-config`) and you reboot the switch.

Upon reboot the switch password is reset.

Password recovery process with password recovery disabled

The password recovery feature is disabled if you see the message The `password-recovery mechanism is disabled` during the boot process. In this case, you need to reset the whole configuration of the switch to be able to reset the password. This basically resets the switch to its default out-of-factory configuration. You need to ensure that you do not lose any valuable information about your network configuration when you do this. It is best practice to save the configuration of the switch before resetting it.

Follow these steps to recover the password on a switch with the password recovery option disabled:

1. **Interrupt the normal boot process using one of the methods described previously.**
2. **Accept to reset the switch to its default configuration.**
3. **Boot the switch manually and wait for the IOS to finish loading in RAM.**
4. **Reset the password.**
5. **Save the running configuration over the startup configuration.**
6. **Revert the boot process to its default options.**
7. **Reboot the switch.**

Here is an example:

```
!Lines starting with "!" in this example are comments that
!explain certain commands within the example. Cisco IOS
!does not interpret lines starting with the "!" character.
!The IOS interprets these lines as comments, not as commands.
!The first few lines below restart the switch using the
!reload IOS command after the manual boot option was enabled.
SW1>en
SW1#reload
Proceed with reload? [confirm]

00:01:35: %SYS-5-RELOAD: Reload requested by console. Reload Reason: Reload
    command.
!The switch is now starting up. Observe the message in bold
!below, showing that password recovery is disabled.
Using driver version 1 for media type 1
Base ethernet MAC Address: 00:25:b4:10:58:80
Xmodem file system is available.
The password-recovery mechanism is disabled.

The password-recovery mechanism has been triggered, but
is currently disabled.  Access to the boot loader prompt
through the password-recovery mechanism is disallowed at
this point.  However, if you agree to let the system be
reset back to the default system configuration, access
to the boot loader prompt can still be allowed.

!here the IOS prompts you to reset the configuration of the
!switch to be able to reset its password.
Would you like to reset the system back to the default configuration (y/n)? y

!next line manually boots the switch
switch:boot

Loading "flash:c2960-lanlite-mz.122-37.EY/c2960-lanlite-mz.122-37.EY.bin"...@@@@@
    @@@@@@@@@@@@@@@@@@@@@

[... boot output cut ...]
```

```
SW1>en
SW1#configure terminal (or config t)

!next line sets the new password
SW1(config)#enable secret my_priv_encrypt_password

SW1(config)#exit

!next line replaces the startup-config file
!   in NVRAM (flash:config.text) with the current
!   running-config file in RAM (system:running-config)

SW1#copy running-config startup-config

!next line reboots the switch
SW1#reload

System configuration has been modified. Save? [yes/no]: yes
Proceed with reload? [confirm] <press Enter>

00:15:05: %SYS-5-RELOAD: Reload requested by console. Reload Reason: Reload
    command.

[... reboot output cut ...]
```

Observe that the password recovery feature is disabled on this switch. You are prompted to reset the switch to its default out-of-factory configuration to reset the password. You answer y to the prompt.

Next, manually boot the switch and wait for the IOS to finish loading in RAM. You know that the IOS is finished loading when it displays the SW1> user EXEC prompt.

Now it's time to set the new password. This basically resets the password to a new one.

Finally, replace the startup-config file in NVRAM (flash:config. text) with the current running-config file in RAM (system:running-config) and reboot the switch.

Upon reboot, the switch is reset to its default out-of-factory configuration. The password of the switch is set to my_priv_encrypt_password. This is the password that you just set with the enable secret command during the password recovery procedure.

Prep Test

1 **Describe the Cisco IOS (Internetwork Operating System).**

A ○ Cisco's proprietary switch and router graphical user interface

B ○ Cisco's proprietary switch and router operating system

C ○ Cisco's proprietary switch and router console facility

D ○ All of the above

2 **What are some of the graphical user interfaces that you can use to manage a Cisco switch?**

A ○ Cisco Network Assistant (CNA) and Cisco Device Manager

B ○ Cisco Switch Windows Control Panel

C ○ Cisco Router and Security Device Manager (SDM)

D ○ All of the above

3 **What is the purpose of the boot image (Rx-boot) microprogram, accessible using the** `switch:` **manual boot prompt?**

A ○ Control the log level during the boot process

B ○ Control the power supply level during the boot process

C ○ Control the boot process

D ○ All of the above

4 **When does the POST (power-on self test) run?**

A ○ Immediately after the Cisco IOS loads on a switch or router

B ○ Immediately after the startup configuration loads on a switch or router

C ○ Immediately after the startup configuration loads on a switch or router

D ○ Immediately after a Cisco switch or router is powered up

5 **What is the main purpose of the bootstrap program, also known as the boot loader?**

A ○ To bring up a Cisco switch or router by loading the startup configuration from flash memory to RAM

B ○ To bring up a Cisco switch or router by loading the Cisco IOS from flash memory to RAM

C ○ To bring up a Cisco switch or router by loading the running configuration from flash memory to RAM

D ○ To bring up a Cisco switch or router by loading the Cisco Device Manager from flash memory to RAM

6 At what layer is it best practice to use entry-level switches, such as the Cisco Catalyst 2960 or the Cisco Catalyst 3560?

A ○ Access and distribution layer
B ○ Distribution and core layer
C ○ Core layer
D ○ Access and core layer

7 What does the flash memory on a Cisco switch store?

A ○ The startup configuration of a Cisco switch or router
B ○ The image file of the Cisco IOS operating system
C ○ The Cisco Device Manager software application program
D ○ All of the above

8 Where does a Cisco switch load its running configuration?

A ○ From the running configuration file during startup
B ○ From Cisco's Web site during startup
C ○ From the startup configuration file during startup
D ○ All of the above

9 When does the Cisco IOS command-line interface operate in setup mode?

A ○ To initially configure the ROM Monitor (ROMMON) microprogram
B ○ To initially configure the Device Manager software application
C ○ To initially configure the IOS
D ○ To initially configure the switch or router

10 When does the Cisco IOS command-line interface operate in privileged configuration mode?

A ○ To configure the ROM Monitor (ROMMON) microprogram
B ○ To configure the Device Manager software application
C ○ To configure the IOS
D ○ To configure the switch or router

Answers

1 **B.** Cisco's proprietary switch and router operating system. The Cisco IOS (Internetworking Operating System) is Cisco's proprietary switch and router operating system. Review the chapter introduction.

2 **A.** Cisco Network Assistant (CNA) and Cisco Device Manager. Some of the Graphical User Interfaces that you can use to manage a Cisco switch are the Cisco Network Assistant (CNA) and the Cisco Device Manager. Review the chapter introduction.

3 **C.** Maintain, test and troubleshoot the configuration stored in ROM and in the flash memory of a Cisco device. The purpose of the Boot image (Rx-boot) microprogram, accessible using the switch: manual boot prompt, is to maintain, test and troubleshoot the configuration stored in ROM and in the Flash memory of a Cisco device. Check *"Cisco switch startup process"* and *"Managing Cisco Switch Configuration."*

4 **D.** Immediately after a Cisco switch or router is powered up. The Power-On-Self-Test runs immediately after a Cisco switch is powered up. Check *"Cisco switch startup process."*

5 **B.** Bring up a Cisco switch or router by loading the Cisco IOS from flash memory to RAM. The main purpose of the bootstrap program, also known as the boot loader, is to bring up a Cisco switch by loading the Cisco IOS from Flash memory to RAM. See *"Cisco switch startup process."*

6 **A.** Access and distribution layer. It is best practice to use entry-level switches, such as the Cisco Catalyst 2960 or the Cisco Catalyst 3560, at the access and distribution layers. Review *"Best Practice For Using Cisco Switches."*

7 **D.** All of the above. The flash memory on a Cisco switch stores the startup configuration of a Cisco switch or router, the image file of the Cisco IOS operating system, and the Cisco Device Manager software application program. See *"Cisco switch startup process."*

8 **C.** Is loaded from the startup configuration file during startup. The running configuration of a Cisco switch is loaded from the startup configuration file during startup. Review *"Cisco switch startup process."*

9 **D.** Initially configure the switch or router. The Cisco IOS command line interface operates in setup mode to initially configure the switch or router. Review *"Initial switch configuration."*

10 **D.** Configure the switch or router. The Cisco IOS command line interface operates in privileged configuration mode to configure the switch. Review *"Managing Cisco Switch Authentication."*

Chapter 3: Controlling Network Traffic with Cisco Switches

Exam Objectives

✔ Describing how MAC addresses are handled in local and remote transmissions

✔ Describing Layer 2 switch modes

✔ Setting the duplex mode of a Layer 2 switch

✔ Reviewing MAC address table thrashing and broadcast storms and seeing how STP fixes these two issues

Read this chapter to find out how Cisco Layer 2 switches control and optimize traffic in a local-area network (LAN).

Sending to MAC Addresses in Remote Networks

In the following sections, you discover how a sending host device interacts with a Layer 2 switch and with a gateway (a router) to send frames to a target device located in a remote network. Most data transfers involve sending and receiving devices that are not located in the same LAN. Data frames need to be sent to the LAN gateway first. Next, the LAN gateway routes the data frames wrapped in packets through a wide-area network (WAN) to the destination LAN.

Sending frames within the LAN

A host determines the MAC address of a target device in the local network by first looking into its Address Resolution Protocol (ARP) table, searching for the MAC address that corresponds to the IP address of the target device:

✦ If the sending host finds an entry in its ARP table corresponding to the IP address of the target device, it simply writes that MAC address in the destination MAC address field in the Ethernet frame.

✦ If the sending host does not find an entry in its ARP table corresponding to the IP address of the target device, it broadcasts an ARP request. In other words, it sends an ARP request packaged in a frame with the destination MAC address set to the broadcast address: FF-FF-FF-FF-FF-FF. All devices in the LAN see the ARP request.

The target device eventually responds with its MAC address. The sending host saves the target's MAC address in its ARP table. The next time the sending host will find the target's MAC address in its ARP table.

Figure 3-1 illustrates how Alex, the sending host, interacts with the Layer 2 switch and with Claire, the target host, to find Claire's MAC address and to send her frames:

1. Alex looks up his ARP table to see whether he already has Claire's MAC address. He doesn't, so he needs to broadcast an ARP request.

2. Alex broadcasts an ARP request.

   The Ethernet frame contains Alex's MAC address in the S-MAC (source) field and the standard broadcast MAC address (FF-FF-FF-FF-FF-FF) in the D-MAC (destination) field.

3. The switch receives this frame, and upon inspection of the D-MAC field, it floods the frame out on all ports except the one through which it came in.

4. The frame reaches both John and Claire. John discards it, because it's not for him. Claire recognizes her own IP address in the ARP request, so she responds with her MAC address.

   The Ethernet frame contains Claire's MAC address in the S-MAC field and Alex's MAC address in the D-MAC field.

5. Alex receives Claire's frame that basically answers his ARP request.

   Alex now has Claire's IP address and her MAC address. He saves them both in his ARP table. So, the next time he needs to send something to Claire, he doesn't need to broadcast an ARP request again.

6. Now, Alex can send frames directly to Claire because he knows her MAC address. He reads Claire's MAC address from his ARP table and builds the Ethernet frame, putting his own MAC address in the S-MAC field and Claire's MAC address in the D-MAC field.

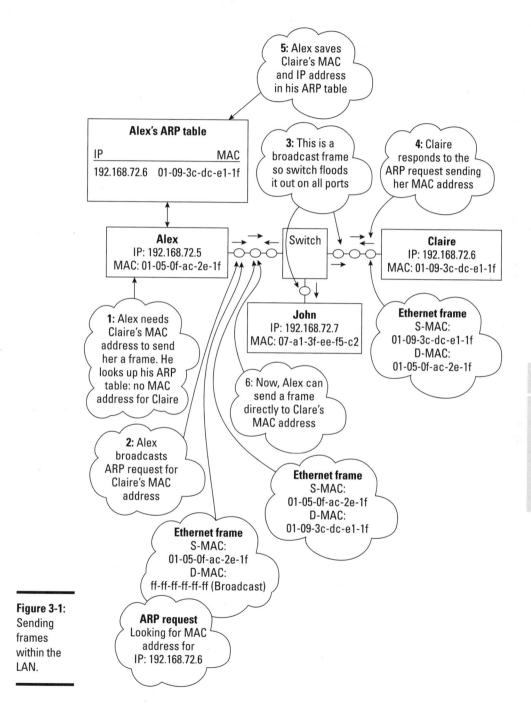

Book III
Chapter 3

Controlling Network
Traffic with Cisco
Switches

Figure 3-1:
Sending
frames
within the
LAN.

Sending frames to a remote network

What happens when the target device is *not* in the local network? It starts the same way as when the device is in the local network. The sending host first looks up its Address Resolution Protocol (ARP) table, searching for the MAC address that corresponds to the IP address of the target device:

✦ If the sending host finds an entry in its ARP table corresponding to the IP address of the target device, it simply writes that MAC address in the destination MAC address field in the Ethernet frame.

✦ If the destination device is located in a remote network, the host will never find the MAC address of the target host in its ARP table, but rather, it will find the MAC address of the LAN gateway.

The LAN gateway is the router device that routes data frames wrapped in IP packets from the LAN to a WAN and from the WAN back into the LAN. The sending host will never find the MAC address of the target host in its ARP table, but rather, it will eventually find the MAC address of the LAN gateway.

If the sending host does not find an entry in its ARP table corresponding to the IP address of the target device, it broadcasts an ARP request. In other words, it sends an ARP request packaged in a frame with the destination MAC address set to the broadcast address: FF-FF-FF-FF-FF-FF. All devices in the LAN see the ARP request, but the target device is not in the local network. So, it does not see the ARP request. However, the LAN gateway (that is, the router), like all devices in the LAN, does see the ARP request. It recognizes that the ARP request is for an IP address that is located in a remote network.

The router responds to the sending host with its own MAC address. In other words, the router tells the sending host: Anytime you need to send frames to this target device, send the frames to me, and I'll route the frames to the remote LAN where this target device is located. The sending host saves the gateway's MAC address in its ARP table. The next time the sending host needs to send to this same target device in a remote network, it will find the MAC address of the gateway in its ARP table. Hence, the sending host will send the frame to the router, directly, without broadcasting an ARP request.

Figure 3-2 illustrates how Alex, the sending host, interacts with the Layer 2 switch and with the gateway router, to find the gateway's MAC address and to send frames to Monica, the target host, in a remote network:

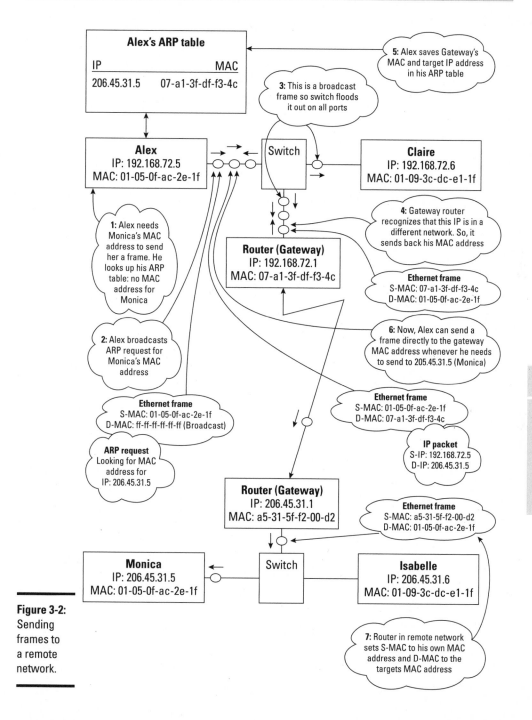

Figure 3-2:
Sending
frames to
a remote
network.

1. Alex looks up his ARP table to see whether he already has Monica's MAC address. He doesn't, so he needs to broadcast an ARP request.

2. Alex broadcasts an ARP request.

   The Ethernet frame contains Alex's MAC address in the S-MAC (source) field and the standard broadcast MAC address (FF-FF-FF-FF-FF-FF) in the D-MAC (destination) field.

3. The switch receives this frame, and upon inspection of the D-MAC field, it floods the frame out on all ports except the one through which it came in.

4. The frame reaches both Claire and the router that links this LAN to a WAN:

   - Claire discards the frame, because it's not for her.

   - The router recognizes that the IP address requested in the ARP is in a different network, so it sends back its MAC address. This enables Alex to send the frame to the router, and the router handles it from there.

   The Ethernet frame contains the router's MAC address in the S-MAC field and Alex's MAC address in the D-MAC field.

5. Alex receives the router's frame that basically answers his ARP request. Alex now saves Monica's IP address and the router's MAC address in his ARP table.

   The next time he needs to send something to Monica, he doesn't need to broadcast an ARP request again. He simply sends the frame to the router, and the router handles it from there.

6. Now, Alex can send frames to Monica without broadcasting an ARP request. He looks up Monica's IP address in his ARP table and builds the Ethernet frame, putting his own MAC address in the S-MAC field and the router's MAC address in the D-MAC field. Thus, the frame bound for Monica goes directly to the router now. The router sends the frame over the WAN to the gateway of the remote network where Monica is located.

7. The remote router encapsulates the IP packet in a new Ethernet frame that contains its MAC address in the S-MAC field and Monica's MAC address in the D-MAC field.

   Ethernet frames are always bound to a given LAN. The Ethernet frame in Alex's network involved Alex and his local gateway. The Ethernet frame in Monica's network involved Monica and the remote router (Monica's gateway). Ethernet frames always identify the next hop in a LAN: The source and destination MAC addresses change at each hop. In contrast, IP packets identify the sender and the receiver of the data payload. The source and destination IP addresses remain the same throughout the journey of a packet through networks linking the sender and the receiver.

Sending frames within a LAN: The destination MAC address of the frame is set to the MAC address of the target host device.

Sending frames to a remote network: The destination MAC address of the frame is set to the MAC address of the LAN gateway. The LAN gateway is a router that links the LAN to a WAN.

The destination MAC address of a Layer 2 data-link (Ethernet) frame is never set to the MAC address of a Layer 2 switch. A Layer 2 switch is merely a conduit that provides an optimized point-to-point link between the sending device and the target device.

The sending device is usually a host in the LAN. Hence, the source MAC address in the Ethernet frame is the MAC address of the sending host device.

The target device is either another host in the LAN or the LAN gateway. Hence, the destination MAC address in the Ethernet frame is either the MAC address of a target host device within the LAN or the MAC address of the LAN gateway.

Deciding the Fate of Frames

In the following sections, you find out about switching modes and how they control the fate of each frame: filtering, forwarding, or flooding the frame. One of the most important functions of a Layer 2 switch is to decide what to do with a frame it receives. The switch either

+ Filters (that is, discards) the frame

+ Forwards the frame out on a specific port

+ Sends the frame out on all ports except the port through which it came in

The following sections describe how the switch decides the fate of a frame.

Switching modes

Layer 2 switches support three switching modes: Store-and-forward, Cut-through, and Fragment-free

Store-and-forward

The *store-and-forward* switching mode follows this process:

1. The switch stores the entire frame in the switch buffer (temporary) memory.

2. FCS (frame check sequence) is run to ensure that the frame is valid.

3. The switch inspects the source MAC address and destination MAC address of the frame.

4. The switch saves the source MAC address along with the incoming port in the MAC address table.

5. The switch looks up the MAC address table for the destination MAC address:

   - If it finds the destination MAC address in the MAC address table, it *forwards* the frame only on the outgoing port registered in the MAC address table.

   - If it does not find the destination MAC address in the MAC address table, it *floods* the frame on all ports, except the port where the frame came in.

Cut-through

The *cut-through* switching mode is faster than the store-and-forward mode. In cut-through mode, the switch does not store the whole frame in its buffer memory. Instead, it processes the frame as soon as it receives the first 6 bytes of the frame:

1. The switch inspects the first 6 bytes of the Ethernet frame, looking at the destination MAC address.

2. The switch searches for an entry for the destination MAC address in its MAC address table.

3. Assuming that the destination MAC address has already been catalogued in the MAC address table, the switch *forwards* the bytes of the frame right away on the corresponding outgoing port, even before the rest of the frame has been completely received. If the destination MAC address is not in the MAC address table, the switch *floods* the frame on all ports, except the port where the frame came in.

The switch does *not* calculate the FCS before it forwards the frame. The cut-through mode speeds frame forwarding considerably, but at a price: Because the FCS is not calculated, both valid and invalid frames are forwarded. Normally, the receiving device can handle this. However, in networks with high traffic volume, by forwarding both valid and invalid frames, the switch unnecessarily overloads the network segment between the switch and the receiving device, which is not good. This is why some switch models still calculate the FCS and keep track of invalid frames. When the number of invalid frames passes a certain threshold, the switch reverts to store-and-forward mode.

Fragment-free

The *fragment-free* switching mode combines the advantages of both the store-and-forward mode and the cut-through mode. Valid Ethernet frames are normally at least 64 bytes in length. Fragment-free considers any frame that is at least 64 bytes to be valid.

A switch in fragment-free mode acts as follows:

1. The switch stores the first 64 bytes of a frame in the switch buffer.

2. It inspects the source MAC address and destination MAC address of the frame.

3. It saves the source MAC address along with the incoming port in the MAC address table.

4. The switch looks up the MAC address table for the destination MAC address:

   - If it finds the destination MAC address in the MAC address table, it *forwards* the frame only on the outgoing port registered in the MAC address table.

   - If it does not find the destination MAC address in the MAC address table, it *floods* the frame on all ports, except the port where the frame came in.

Fragment-free starts forwarding the frame as soon as its first 64 bytes have been received, as opposed to store-and-forward, which stores the whole frame before forwarding it. Hence, fragment-free is faster than store-and-forward. However, fragment-free is slower than cut-through, because cut-through forwards the frame as soon as the first 6 bytes have been received.

A switch in fragment-free mode discards any frame that is shorter than 64 bytes. Because frames shorter than 64 bytes are typically invalid frames, this lowers the risk of forwarding invalid frames. This is similar to the store-and-forward mode, which does not forward invalid frames.

Fragment-free mode does not calculate the FCS. This is similar to the cut-through mode. As in cut-through mode, some switches calculate the FCS anyway and revert to store-and-forward when the number of invalid frames passes a certain threshold.

Fragment-free is a good compromise between store-and-forward and cut-through switching modes:

✦ Store-and-forward is reliable, forwarding only valid frames, but slower because it always calculates the FCS.

✦ Cut-through is faster because it doesn't store the whole Ethernet frame before forwarding it, but is potentially unreliable because it may forward invalid frames.

✦ Fragment-free relies on the minimum valid Ethernet frame size to determine whether a frame is valid without calculating the FCS:

- Because most invalid frames are smaller than 64 bytes, fragment-free is quite reliable.

- Because fragment-free does not store more than 64 bytes of the frame in the switch buffer, it is quite efficient as well.

Switching in Half-Duplex and Full-Duplex Modes

The first few iterations of the Ethernet standard supported only half-duplex transmissions. Current Ethernet standards support both half-duplex and full-duplex transmission modes.

Reviewing half-duplex Ethernet

Half-duplex Ethernet uses a single pair of wires for both sending and receiving frames. Frame collisions occur and need to be mitigated with carrier sense multiple access collision detect (CSMA/CD), so half-duplex throughput is usually 30–40 percent of theoretical throughput. This means that in a typical 100BASE-T Ethernet network, although theoretical throughput is 100 Mbps, half-duplex only provides 30 to 40 Mbps. All hubs, bridges, and switches support half-duplex transmission mode. However, half-duplex Ethernet should only be used with older devices that do not support full-duplex Ethernet. In all other cases, it is best to use full-duplex Ethernet.

Reviewing full-duplex Ethernet

Full-duplex Ethernet uses two pairs of wires, or even four pairs of wires, to send and receive frames at the same time on several connection paths using one connection path per pair. Full-duplex twisted-pair connections provide a point-to-point connection between the transmitter on the sending host and the receiver on the receiving host. This eliminates frame collisions and speeds data transfer. Using full-duplex twisted-pair connections, you can theoretically achieve full throughput in both directions. Considering the 100BASE-T example, using full-duplex twisted-pair, you should be able to get 100 Mbps sending and 100 Mbps receiving, for a total bandwidth of 200 Mbps. However, in reality, you will likely get less than 100 Mbps due to potential electrical noise, crosstalk, and other factors that may distort the signal. Most Layer 2 switches support full-duplex transmission mode.

Duplex mode best practice

It is best practice to use full-duplex transmission mode because it improves network throughput and reliability by eliminating frame collisions. Particularly, always use full-duplex transmission mode to connect hosts to switches, and interconnect switches using full-duplex twisted-pair.

Configuring port duplex mode on a Cisco switch

You configure the transmission mode on a Cisco switch using the `duplex` IOS command. For example, to set the transmission mode of a switch interface in full-duplex mode, execute the following command:

```
SW1(config-if)#duplex full
```

To set the transmission mode of a switch interface in half-duplex mode, execute the following command:

```
SW1(config-if)#duplex half
```

By default, all switch ports are set to autonegotiate the duplex mode with the device that connects to the port. To manually set the duplex mode to autonegotiate, execute the following command:

```
SW1(config-if)#duplex auto
```

Configuring port speed on a Cisco switch

You can follow the `duplex` IOS command with the `speed` IOS command to set the speed of the interface. The `speed` command can configure the interface to run at various speeds: 10, 100, 1000, and auto.

Some interfaces are limited in the speeds they support. For example, a Fast Ethernet switch interface supports speeds only up to 100 Mbps. In this case, you can only set the Fast Ethernet interface speed to 10, 100, or auto.

Selecting a switch port

Before you run any of the `duplex` and `speed` commands, you need to select the port you want to configure:

1. Transition the IOS to privileged EXEC mode:

```
SW1>enable (or en)
```

2. Enable the Cisco switch configuration terminal:

```
SW1#configure terminal (or config t or conf t)
```

Book III
Chapter 3

Controlling Network
Traffic with Cisco
Switches

3. Select a port to work with using the interface <interface#> command.

Again, you can use the short form: int <interface#>. For example, to work with the first Fast Ethernet interface on your switch (0/0), you can run the following:

```
SW1(config)#int fastethernet 0/0 (or int fa 0/0)
SW1(config-if)#
```

Avoiding Loops with Spanning Tree Protocol (STP)

This section introduces the Spanning Tree Protocol (STP) that is used by Layer 2 switches to avoid loops in topologies with redundant interswitch links. The next chapter is devoted to a more detailed discussion of STP.

Whenever two Layer 2 switches are interconnected with redundant links, transmission loops may occur. Frames are continuously retransmitted on alternate links between switches, effectively causing frames to loop, or bounce, between switches. This can cause broadcast storms and MAC address table thrashing.

A broadcast frame that bounces forever between switches interconnected with redundant links causes a broadcast storm. Because each switch floods broadcast frames out on all ports, they continuously send the frame to each other on alternate links. Data-link (Ethernet) frames do not expire, so they can bounce forever between Layer 2 switches. The Spanning Tree Protocol helps avoid these broadcast storms.

MAC address tables can be thrashed when a MAC address is registered for more than one switch port. This may happen when the same Ethernet frame is received through more than one port on a given switch. It is common to get thrashed MAC address tables when loops exist in a network because frames are sent between switches on alternate ports. Hence, the same source MAC address in the frame is registered for each alternate port.

So, how exactly does STP eliminate loops in LANs? STP basically monitors the network and catalogs each link, particularly redundant links. Next, STP disables redundant links, setting up preferred, optimized links between switches. The preferred, optimized links are used under normal circumstances. Should any of the preferred links fail, one of the nonpreferred redundant links is enabled and used instead.

STP assigns a root bridge that acts sort of like the decision maker in the network. The term *root bridge* typically refers to a Layer 2 switch. It can also really be a bridge, but more commonly it is a switch. The root bridge decides which routes are preferred and which routes are nonpreferred.

The root bridge interacts with *nonroot bridges:* other switches in the LAN. STP is enabled on all switches in the LAN. The root bridge and the nonroot bridges have specific roles within STP.

Switch ports are categorized by whether they forward frames and whether they are the endpoints of a preferred, optimized link within the LAN.

STP operation, management, and optimization are covered in Book III, Chapter 4.

Prep Test

1 When sending data frames to a host in a remote network, the destination MAC address in the data frame is set to what?

A ○ The IP address of the destination host

B ○ The IP address of the LAN gateway

C ○ The MAC address of the destination host

D ○ The MAC address of the LAN gateway

2 When sending data frames to a host within the LAN, the destination MAC address in the data frame is set to what?

A ○ The IP address of the destination host

B ○ The IP address of the LAN gateway

C ○ The MAC address of the destination host

D ○ The MAC address of the LAN gateway

3 Hosts use the _____ to determine the MAC address of a target device.

A ○ UDP (User Datagram Protocol)

B ○ ARP (Address Resolution Protocol)

C ○ DHCP (Dynamic Host Configuration Protocol)

D ○ TCP (Transport Control Protocol)

4 Hosts need to broadcast _____ whenever their _____ does not contain the MAC address of a target device.

A ○ an ARP request, ARP table

B ○ a UDP request, UDP table

C ○ a DHCP request, DHCP table

D ○ a TCP request, TCP table

5 Which of the following describes the store-and-forward switching mode?

A ○ Stores only the first 64 bytes of the data frame before processing it

B ○ Does not store any bytes in the switch buffer before processing the data frame

C ○ Stores only the first 6 bytes of the data frame before processing it

D ○ Stores the entire data frame in the switch buffer before processing it

6 Which of the following describes the cut-through switching mode?

A ○ Stores only the first 64 bytes of the data frame before processing it

B ○ Does not store any bytes in the switch buffer before processing the data frame

C ○ Stores only the first 6 bytes of the data frame before processing it

D ○ Stores the entire data frame in the switch buffer before processing it

7 Which of the following describes the fragment-free switching mode?

A ○ Stores only the first 64 bytes of the data frame before processing it

B ○ Does not store any bytes in the switch buffer before processing the data frame

C ○ Stores only the first 6 bytes of the data frame before processing it

D ○ Stores the entire data frame in the switch buffer before processing it

8 How does the store-and-forward switching mode ensure that the data frame is valid?

A ○ By reading the FCS from the frame

B ○ By calculating the FCS and verifying it against the FCS stored in the frame

C ○ By discarding any data frame that is smaller than 64 bytes

D ○ By discarding any data frame that is larger than 64 bytes

9 How does the fragment-free switching mode ensure that the data frame is valid?

A ○ By reading the FCS from the frame

B ○ By calculating the FCS and verifying it against the FCS stored in the frame

C ○ By discarding any data frame that is smaller than 64 bytes

D ○ By discarding any data frame that is larger than 64 bytes

10 Although you can manually set the duplex mode and the speed of switch ports on a Cisco switch, by default, how are both the duplex mode and the speed set?

A ○ To the lowest value

B ○ To the highest value

C ○ Autonegotiated based on MAC address table entries

D ○ Autonegotiated with the device connecting in the switch port

Answers

1 **D.** When sending data frames to a host in a remote network, the destination MAC address in the data frame is set to the MAC address of the LAN gateway. Refer to *"Sending frames to a remote network."*

2 **C.** When sending data frames to a host in a remote network, the destination MAC address in the data frame is set to the MAC address of the destination host. Review *"Sending frames within the LAN."*

3 **B.** ARP (Address Resolution Protocol). Hosts use ARP to determine the MAC address of a target device. Check out *"Sending frames within the LAN."*

4 **A.** Hosts need to broadcast an ARP request whenever their ARP table does not contain the MAC address of a target device. If the ARP table does not contain the MAC address of the destination device, the sending host needs to broadcast an ARP request to find out the MAC address of the target device. Read *"Sending frames within the LAN."*

5 **D.** The store-and-forward switching mode stores the entire data frame in the switch buffer before processing it. Peruse *"Switching modes."*

6 **C.** The cut-through switching mode stores only the first 6 bytes of the data frame before processing it. Review *"Switching modes."*

7 **A.** The fragment-free switching mode stores only the first 64 bytes of the data frame before processing it. Check out *"Switching modes."*

8 **B.** The store-and-forward switching mode ensures that the data frame is valid by calculating the FCS and verifying against the FCS stored in the frame. Read *"Switching modes."*

9 **C.** The fragment-free switching mode ensures that the data frame is valid by discarding any data frame that is smaller than 64 bytes. See *"Switching modes."*

10 **D.** The duplex mode and the speed of switch ports on a Cisco switch are by default set to autonegotiate with the device connecting in the switch port. Review *"Switching in Half-Duplex and Full-Duplex Modes."*

Chapter 4: Spanning Tree Protocol (STP)

Exam Objectives

✔ Describing problems related to switching loops and seeing how STP fixes them

✔ Describing STP operation flow, root bridge, and nonroot bridge functions

✔ Managing STP root bridge selection

✔ Managing STP port type assignment

✔ Describing the STP convergence process

✔ Describing the STP port states

✔ Understanding best practices to decrease STP convergence duration

✔ Managing Cisco switch and port configuration options for STP

✔ Describing Rapid Spanning Tree Protocol (RSTP) improvements over STP

✔ Describing and managing EtherChannel

*Y*ou found out in previous chapters that switches are very often interconnected using redundant links to improve reliability of interswitch links. You also discovered that redundant links can create transmission loops, causing broadcast storms and MAC address table thrashing. Switches need to avoid transmissions loops when they are interconnected using redundant links.

Read this chapter to see how the Spanning Tree Protocol (STP) (IEEE 802.1d) can be used to help Layer 2 switches avoid loops. You see how to configure and manage STP. You are also introduced to STP port types. The convergence process flow is explained, along with some parameters you can set to control STP convergence. Finally, you see how the Rapid Spanning Tree Protocol (RSTP) (IEEE 802.1w) improves STP convergence speed.

Introducing the Spanning Tree Protocol (STP)

Layer 2 switches need to avoid switching loops. Here you see how switches can avoid switching loops using STP. The STP protocol is defined in the IEEE 802.1d standard.

Before I look at STP, I review the problem that STP resolves: data-link frames being continuously sent back and forth between Layer 2 switches interconnected with redundant links.

Data-link (Ethernet) frames do not expire. An Ethernet frame sent to an unknown MAC address can bounce around forever in the network. This is not good because it wastes bandwidth. This problem is exacerbated when several switches are interconnected with redundant links. It is best practice to use redundant links to interconnect Layer 2 switches to mitigate inter-switch link failure risks. However, this amplifies the risk of having frames bouncing back and forth between switches.

Figure 4-1 shows a typical dual-switch LAN with two interswitch links. Hosts Alex, Claire, John, and Monica are interconnected in a LAN using two switches connected with redundant interswitch links. Suppose that the MAC address tables are empty on both switches because none of the hosts have sent any frames yet.

Assume that Alex sends a frame to Claire:

1. The first time Alex sends a frame to Claire, the switch learns about Alex, but it still does not know about Claire. So, switch SW1 needs to flood the frame out on all ports except the port through which it came in, that is, the port where Alex connects to SW1.

2. Switch SW1 floods the frame out on all ports except the port through which it came in.

   The frame reaches switch SW2. Switch SW2 does not know about Claire either, so it also needs to flood the frame out on all ports except the port through which it came in.

3. Switch SW2 floods the frame out on all ports except the port through which it came in.

   Because you have two links connecting the SW1 and SW2 switches, the frame that came in through fa0/2 on SW2 is flooded out on fa0/3, and the frame that came in through fa0/3 on SW2 is flooded out on fa0/2. Hence, switch SW1 gets the frame back, twice: on fa0/2 and on fa0/3.

4. Because SW1 still does not know Claire's MAC address, it floods the frame again on both fa0/2 and fa0/3. SW2 receives the frame again, twice, on fa0/2 and on fa0/3.

5. Because SW2 still does not know Claire's MAC address, it floods the frame out again on all ports, including fa0/2 and fa0/3, and so on.

This is a typical example of a *broadcast storm:* a broadcast frame that bounces forever between switches interconnected with redundant links.

Observe another problem in Figure 4-1. Because switches SW1 and SW2 receive the same frame on two different ports, they register the source MAC address (S-MAC) of host Alex for both ports. This is a problem because the switch will not know over which port it needs to send frames out to Alex whenever D-MAC is set to Alex's MAC address in a frame. This is a typical example of *MAC address table thrashing.*

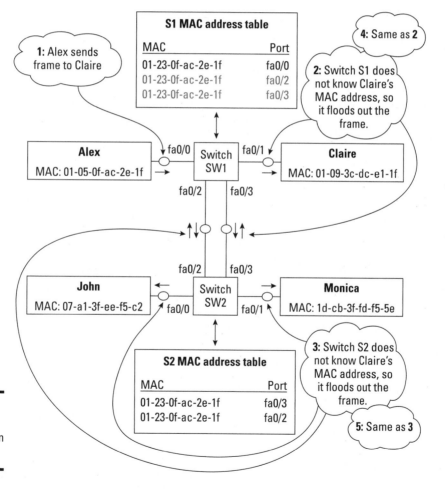

Figure 4-1:
Layer 2
transmission
loop.

Layer 2 transmission loops cause the following:

✦ **Broadcast storms:** A broadcast frame that bounces forever between switches interconnected with redundant links is called a broadcast storm. Broadcast storms waste bandwidth and may thrash the MAC address table.

✦ **MAC address table thrashing:** The MAC address table gets thrashed when multiple ports are attached to the same MAC address. The switch does not know on which outgoing port it can reach that MAC address.

To avoid loops and bouncing frames, enable the *Spanning Tree Protocol (STP)* on Layer 2 switches.

So, how exactly does STP eliminate Layer 2 loops in LANs? STP basically monitors the network and catalogs every link, particularly redundant links. Next, STP disables redundant links, setting up preferred, optimized links between switches:

✦ The preferred, optimized links are used under normal circumstances.

✦ Should any of the preferred links fail, one of the nonpreferred redundant links is enabled and used instead.

STP assigns a root bridge that acts sort of like the decision maker in the network. The term *root bridge* refers typically to a Layer 2 switch. It can also really be a bridge, but more commonly it is a switch. The root bridge decides which routes are preferred and which routes are nonpreferred.

The root bridge interacts with *nonroot bridges:* other switches in the LAN. STP is enabled on all switches in the LAN. The root bridge and the nonroot bridges have specific roles within STP.

Switch ports are categorized depending on whether they forward frames and depending on whether they are the endpoints of a preferred, optimized link within the LAN.

Root bridge: A Layer 2 switch (or bridge) that decides which routes are preferred and which routes are nonpreferred.

Nonroot bridge: A Layer 2 switch (or bridge) that is not a root bridge. Nonroot bridges coordinate with the root bridge to assist in the determination of preferred and nonpreferred routes from each nonroot bridge to the root bridge in the LAN.

STP Operation Flow

The Spanning Tree Protocol executes three operations to achieve a stable, loop-free LAN:

✦ **Electing STP root bridge:** The switch with the lowest *bridge ID* is elected the root bridge.

✦ **Assigning STP port types:** Each port on every switch in the LAN is assigned a type that defines its behavior. Switches communicate using STP to assign a type to their ports. This determines the ports' behavior to be either *forwarding* (that is, the port forwards data-link frames) or *blocking* (that is, the port sends no data-link frames).

✦ **Achieving STP convergence:** Convergence is the result of assigning port types. After switches have assigned a forwarding type or a blocking type to all ports that interconnect them, STP achieves a stable, loop-free LAN.

I now look at each of these steps in detail.

Electing a root bridge

STP's first step is to choose a root bridge. STP relies on the bridge ID to decide which switch should become the root bridge. STP chooses the switch with the lowest bridge ID to be the root bridge.

Bridge ID

The bridge ID is a number composed of the switch's MAC address and its STP priority. The STP priority on any given Layer 2 switch is by default 32768. So, because the priority of all switches is by default the same (32768), STP really chooses the switch with the lowest MAC address to be the root bridge.

Figure 4-2 shows an example with four switches having the same STP priority.

The switch with the lowest MAC address is chosen as the root bridge.

STP priority

What if the switch with the lowest MAC address is actually an old, slow switch? You wouldn't want the slowest switch in your LAN to become the root bridge because it will slow every other switch in your network. You can use the STP priority setting to control which switch will have the lowest bridge ID.

Best practice is to set the STP priority to a low value (smaller than the default 32768 STP priority) on the fastest switch in your LAN. This causes STP to choose the fastest switch in your LAN as the root bridge.

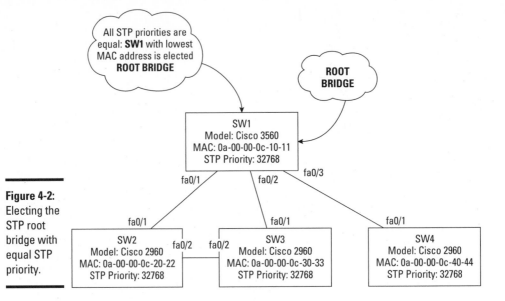

Figure 4-2:
Electing the STP root bridge with equal STP priority.

You can set the STP priority to any number between 0 and 61440. However, the STP priority value has to be a multiple of 4096. So, the STP priority values you can choose are 0, 4096, 8192, 12288, . . . 61440. If you set the STP priority to 0, that switch will be the root bridge.

It is not best practice to set the STP priority to 0 on more than one switch. Setting the STP priority to 0 on more than one switch would basically tell STP to use those switches as the root bridge. However, you can only have one root bridge in any given Layer 2 spanning tree, so STP will simply choose the switch with the lowest MAC address among the switches with STP priority set to 0.

Figure 4-3 shows the four switches example again, this time with a lower STP priority value set on the faster Cisco Catalyst 3560 SW2 switch.

Observe that the faster Cisco Catalyst 3560 switch with the lower STP priority value is chosen as the root bridge.

STP priority is VLAN-bound. In other words, each virtual LAN can have a different root bridge. However, this is not a common setup. Usually, all VLANs have the same root bridge. You can subdivide a LAN into several logical (virtual) LANs (VLANs) using the same physical equipment. In other words, you can have some devices communicate within one virtual LAN and other devices communicate within another virtual LAN on the same cables, switches, and routers. This allows you to identify and separate network traffic for different purposes on any given network.

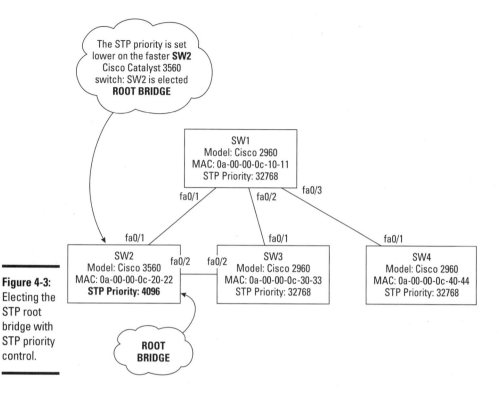

The STP priority is set lower on the faster **SW2** Cisco Catalyst 3560 switch: SW2 is elected **ROOT BRIDGE**

SW1
Model: Cisco 2960
MAC: 0a-00-00-0c-10-11
STP Priority: 32768

fa0/1   fa0/2   fa0/3

fa0/1   fa0/1   fa0/1

SW2
Model: Cisco 3560
MAC: 0a-00-00-0c-20-22
STP Priority: 4096

fa0/2   fa0/2

SW3
Model: Cisco 2960
MAC: 0a-00-00-0c-30-33
STP Priority: 32768

SW4
Model: Cisco 2960
MAC: 0a-00-00-0c-40-44
STP Priority: 32768

ROOT BRIDGE

Figure 4-3: Electing the STP root bridge with STP priority control.

STP priority related to the Cisco hierarchical network architecture

Cisco networks are designed using a hierarchical architecture. Three layers make up the Cisco hierarchical network architecture:

✦ Core layer

✦ Distribution layer

✦ Access layer

The *core layer* is the layer that sits at the center of the network. This layer is also called the *backbone.*

Ultimately, traffic from all devices in the network may end up being routed to the core of the network. The core layer is "where networks meet."

The *distribution layer* links the core layer to the access layer. This layer is also called the *workgroup layer.* The distribution layer is involved in routing packets between nodes connected at the access layer. Packets may need to be routed to a different network, which may be located within the same distribution layer network or up through the core layer in a different distribution layer network.

Book III
Chapter 4

Spanning Tree
Protocol (STP)

The *access layer* is the layer that interconnects host devices to LANs. The access layer is where workgroup LANs are defined. This layer is also called the *desktop layer,* because it usually involves interconnecting desktop computers and concentrating their traffic into a distribution layer switch or router. Switches, small routers, and computer host devices typically interconnect at the access layer.

Layer 2 switches are typically used at the access layer and at the distribution layer. It is important to understand that the larger the LAN, the more choices are available for a root bridge. As mentioned earlier, it is best practice to assign STP priorities to ensure that the fastest switch in the LAN becomes the root bridge.

Figure 4-4 shows a very large Cisco LAN that spans both the distribution and the access layers.

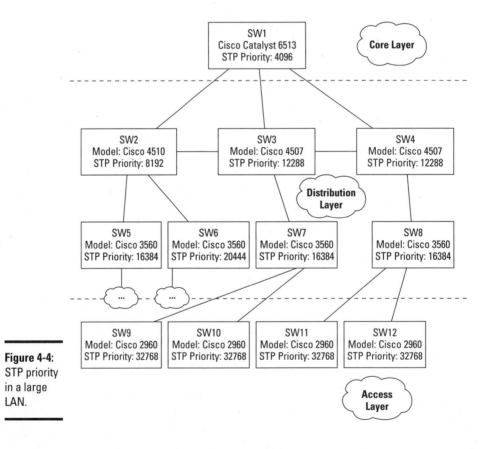

Figure 4-4:
STP priority
in a large
LAN.

Observe that you set the STP priority values in a hierarchical way to ensure that the fastest Cisco Catalyst 6500 series switch is elected the root bridge. One of the Cisco Catalyst 4500 series would be next in line for becoming the root bridge, should the 6500 series ever fail. You set the STP priority in a hierarchical way to ensure that one of the next-fastest switches is elected, if the root bridge ever fails or is unavailable. If you set the STP priorities all equal below the 6500 series, any of those switches could become the root bridge. Do you remember which one would, in that case? If you answered the one with the lowest MAC address because all STP priorities would be equal, you are right. Note also that within the same level, faster switches have lower STP priorities to ensure that they would be the first ones to become the root bridge, if necessary.

Assigning STP port types

The second step in the STP operation flow is assigning port types to every port in the network. STP assigns port types according to the cost of each path between the root switch and a nonroot switch.

STP path cost

Switches are typically interconnected using redundant links to increase resilience, should one of the links fail. Each of these links provides a connection path. Each path has a certain cost associated with it. The cost is defined according to the bandwidth of the link. Table 4-1 lists the costs associated with each Ethernet bandwidth.

Table 4-1	STP Path Cost for Each Ethernet Bandwidth
Bandwidth	*STP Cost*
10 Mbps	100
100 Mbps	19
1 Gbps	4
10 Gbps	2

STP prefers paths with lower costs. Looking at Table 4-1, you can see that STP prefers faster bandwidths. Consider a switch that has a 100-Mbps link and a 1-Gbps link connecting it to the root bridge. STP will designate the port that connects to the 1-Gbps link to be *root port,* the port that connects to the root bridge. The port connecting to the slower 100-Mbps link will be either a *designated port* or a *blocking port.* A designated port is a port that forwards data-link frames. A blocking port is a port that does not forward data-link frames. You read more about designated and blocking ports a bit later in this chapter.

**Book III
Chapter 4**

**Spanning Tree
Protocol (STP)**

Setting root ports

After switches have elected a root bridge, nonroot switches assign one of their ports to be their root port. The STP root port is the port that connects a switch to the STP root bridge. The port that is elected to be the root port is either

✦ A port that connects the nonroot switch directly to the root bridge

✦ A port that connects to the least expensive path (STP cost) to the root bridge

Switches communicate between themselves using STP to calculate the cost of each path to the root bridge. Each switch adds the cost of its own path to the cost received from the neighboring switches to determine the total cost of a given path to the root. After the costs of all paths to the root have been calculated, each switch assigns the root port to the port connecting to the path with the lowest cost.

Figure 4-5 illustrates a simple LAN with a root bridge switch and three non-root switches. Each nonroot switch sets one of its ports to be the root port.

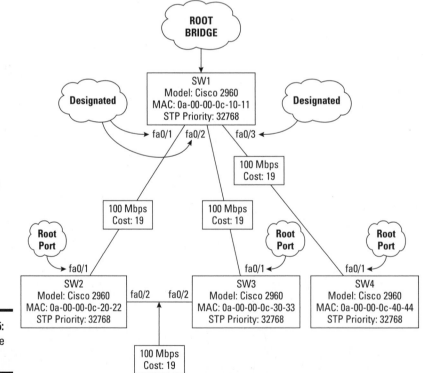

Figure 4-5:
Setting the root port.

Observe that each of the three nonroot switches chooses a root port that connects directly to the root bridge.

Note also that switch SW4 only has one link connecting it to the SW1 root bridge. In this case, there isn't a choice for the root port: It is the one port that connects SW4 to SW1, the root bridge.

The SW2 switch chooses the direct path to the root bridge because it is less costly than the path going through the SW3 switch. Similarly, the same is true for the SW3 switch.

The SW1 switch, the root bridge, has no root ports because it is the root bridge itself. SW1 only has designated ports.

Setting designated ports

After each switch assigned one of its ports to be the root port, connecting to the root bridge, the remaining ports are either *designated* or *blocking:*

✦ An STP designated port is a port that forwards data-link frames.

Each LAN segment needs to have a designated port, a port that forwards traffic in and out of that LAN segment.

✦ An STP blocking port is a port that does not forward data-link frames.

Figure 4-6 shows the same four switches, this time with root ports, with designated ports, and with blocking ports.

Observe the link between switch SW2 and SW3. Switches SW2 and SW3 need to decide which port is designated and which port is blocking on the link that interconnects them. Because both SW2 and SW3 connect to SW1, the root bridge, through a path with an STP cost of 19 (100 Mbps), the total STP cost to the root is the same in both directions on the SW2/SW3 link: The SW2 to SW3 to SW1 STP cost is 19 + 19, and SW3 to SW2 to SW1 is also 19 + 19. So, SW2 and SW3 cannot set their designated and blocking ports relying solely on the STP path cost. SW2 and SW3 need to look at other criteria to decide which port is designated and which port is blocking on the link that interconnects them. In this case, SW2 and SW3 look at their bridge ID: The switch with the lower bridge ID sets its port to be designated, while the switch with the higher bridge ID sets its port to be blocking. Recall that the bridge ID is a number composed of the switch's MAC address and its STP priority. Both SW2 and SW3 have the same STP priority, so SW2 wins because its MAC address is lower than SW3's MAC address.

Switches look at other criteria anytime a tie exists in the STP path cost. The following sections describe the criteria that switches analyze to decide which of their ports is the root port, which of their ports are designated ports, and which of their ports are blocking ports.

**Book III
Chapter 4**

**Spanning Tree
Protocol (STP)**

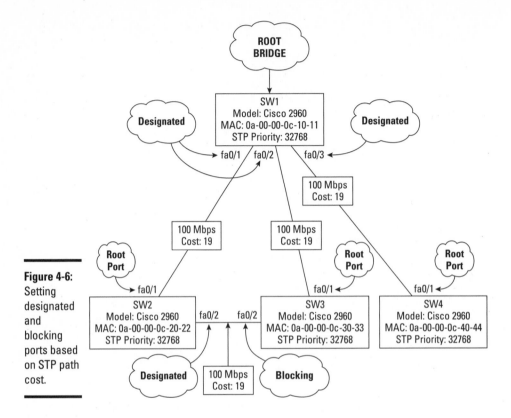

Figure 4-6:
Setting
designated
and
blocking
ports based
on STP path
cost.

Choosing ports according to STP path cost

The port that connects to the path reaching the root bridge with the lowest cumulative STP cost becomes either the root port or a designated port.

For example, SW2 connects to SW1, the root bridge, through port fa0/1. The STP cost of that path is 19. SW2 also connects to SW1, the root bridge, through port fa0/2, via SW3. The total STP cost of that path is 19 + 19 = 38. Because the fa0/2 STP cost of 38 is greater than the fa0/1 STP cost of 19, SW2 will set fa0/1 to be its root port.

Choosing ports according to bridge ID

If the switch has multiple ports and the STP path cost is the same for all ports, the port that connects to the path reaching the switch with the lowest bridge ID becomes either the root port or a designated port.

For example, Figure 4-7 adds a new switch, SW5 to the network. SW5 is connected to both SW2 and SW3, but it is not directly connected to SW1, the root bridge. Several routes exist from SW5 to SW1. One route is SW5 to SW2 to SW1. Similarly, another route is SW5 to SW3 to SW1. You can see that the STP cost is equal for these two routes: 19 + 19 = 38. In this case, SW5 will choose port fa0/1 that connects to SW2 to be its root port because SW2 has a lower bridge ID than SW3.

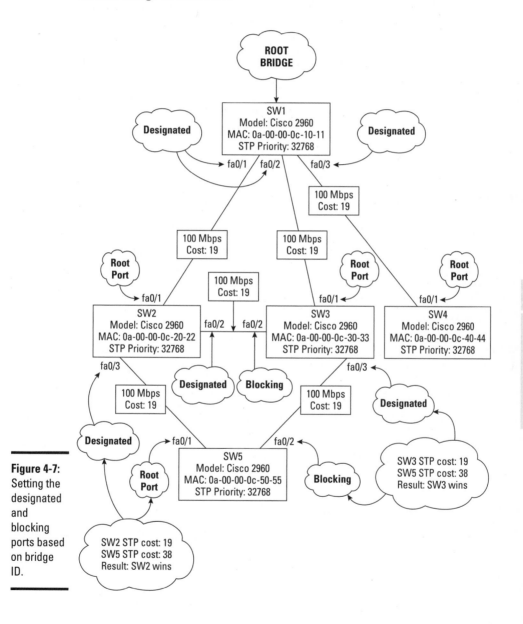

Book III Chapter 4

Spanning Tree Protocol (STP)

Figure 4-7: Setting the designated and blocking ports based on bridge ID.

Observe that the second port on SW5 connecting to SW3 ends up blocking. Here is why: After SW5 has chosen its root port, SW5 and SW3 communicate to decide how they assign the ports that interconnect them. Which port will be designated on that segment, and which port will be blocking? As usual, the STP path cost is analyzed first: The STP path cost from SW3 to the root bridge is 19. The STP path cost from SW5 to the root bridge is 19 + 19 = 38, because the root port on SW5 connects to SW2 and then SW2 connects to SW1. The STP path cost is greater on SW5 than on SW3, so SW3 wins. The port on SW3 becomes designated for the SW5-to-SW3 link. The port on SW5 becomes blocking for the SW5-to-SW3 link.

Choosing ports according to port number

If the switch has multiple ports, the STP path cost is the same for all ports, and the bridge ID is the same (that is, two links interconnecting the same two switches), the port with the lowest port number becomes either the root port or a designated port.

Setting blocking ports

Earlier you read that each LAN segment needs to have a designated port, a port that forwards traffic in and out of that LAN segment. The port at the other end of the link becomes a blocking port. An STP blocking port is a port that does not forward data-link frames, thereby closing the loop. A blocking port still receives data frames, but it sends no data frames out on the link. In other words, the link becomes one-way, from the designated port to the blocking port.

Achieving STP convergence

After switches have assigned a forwarding type or a blocking type to all ports that interconnect them, STP achieves a stable, loop-free LAN. This is a *converged network.* Convergence is the result of assigning port types to eliminate loops in the LAN.

Introducing bridge protocol data units (BPDUs)

Switches communicate by sending each other bridge protocol data units (BPDUs).

A BPDU is a special-purpose data-link frame that is multicast every 2 seconds. BPDUs contain information about STP path costs, bridge IDs, port IDs, and some other parameters that help switches to elect the root bridge and to decide how to assign port types to their respective ports.

Figure 4-8 illustrates the structure of IEEE 802.1d BPDU data-link frames.

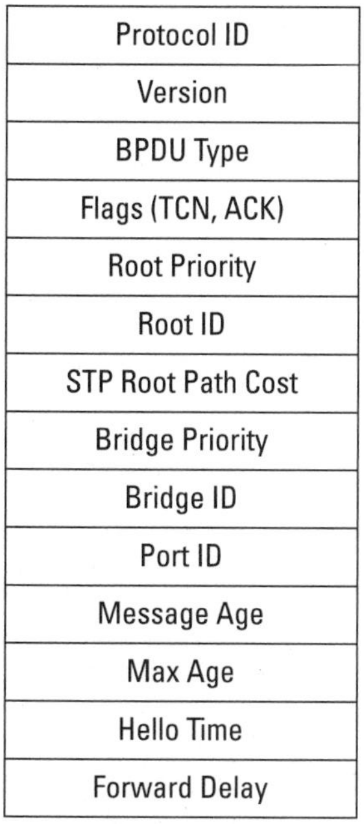

Protocol ID
Version
BPDU Type
Flags (TCN, ACK)
Root Priority
Root ID
STP Root Path Cost
Bridge Priority
Bridge ID
Port ID
Message Age
Max Age
Hello Time
Forward Delay

Figure 4-8:
Bridge
protocol
data unit
(BPDU)
structure.

Topology change notification (TCN) BPDUs

What if the topology of the LAN changes? What if you add or remove a link between two switches, or if you add or remove a switch? In that case, the switches involved send a topology change notification (TCN) BPDU.

A TCN is a specialized BPDU that informs every switch in the LAN that the topology has changed. At that point, switches need to go through the convergence process again: They need to reelect a root if the root bridge was affected by the topology change. Next, they need to decide how they set up their ports. Finally, they achieve a converged state.

STP port states

Ports on switches running STP are in one of the following states:

✦ **Blocking:** Ports start in the blocking state. A blocking port forwards no data-link frames. It listens to what's happening in the LAN: It receives and analyzes BPDUs. Having all ports blocking when a switch is powered up prevents the switch from creating and using transmission loops while STP is converging. A port that is an endpoint to an interswitch link stays in the blocking state unless it becomes a root port or a designated port during the STP convergence process.

A port can also transition to the blocking state if the switch receives a topology change notification (TCN) BPDU. Whenever the network topology changes, STP blocks all ports until the STP convergence process is restarted. A delay occurs before the STP convergence is restarted. Whenever a switch or a link fails or becomes unavailable, switches connected to the failing switch or link wait for 20 seconds before they start the STP convergence process. This 20-second wait is called the *max age timer*. You can view and change the max age timer using Cisco IOS commands.

Blocking state duration: 20 seconds (*max age timer*)

✦ **Listening:** Next, ports transition to the listening state. A listening port listens to BPDUs to prepare to transmit frames. A port in the listening state would only send and receive BPDUs without populating the MAC address table of the switch. This is the state in which switches communicate using BPDUs to assign a port type to the listening port. A port stays in the listening state for 15 seconds by default. The listening time and the learning time make up the *forward delay timer*. You can view and change the forward delay timer using Cisco IOS commands.

Listening state duration: 15 seconds (*forward delay timer — part 1*)

✦ **Learning:** Ports transition to the learning state. A learning port listens to BPDUs and populates its MAC address table. The purpose of the learning state is to allow the switch to gather information about the MAC address reachable on each port. A port in learning mode sends no data frames. A port stays in the learning state for 15 seconds by default. The listening time and the learning time make up the *forward delay timer*. You can view and change the forward delay timer using Cisco IOS commands.

Learning state duration: 15 seconds (*forward delay timer — part 2*)

✦ **Forwarding:** At this point, the port has become a root port, a designated port, or a blocking port. If the port is either root or designated, it transitions to the forwarding state. A port in the forwarding state can send and receive data frames.

✦ **Disabled:** A disabled port is basically a port that has been shut down manually by the switch administrator. Disabled ports do not participate in the network: They do not go through the convergence process, and they do not send or receive frames. They are basically turned off.

STP convergence duration

The STP convergence process takes some time to complete. During this time, no data communication passes through the switches involved. In other words, while switches go through the STP convergence process, host devices connected to the LAN do not have access to the network.

How long must the hosts wait before they get network access? Look at port-state default durations listed previously:

+ 20 seconds in the blocking state (max age timer)
+ 15 seconds in listening state (forward delay — part 1)
+ 15 seconds in the learning state (forward delay — part 2)

The total time is 50 seconds. Hence, hosts need to wait up to 50 seconds before they get network access anytime a switch is rebooted, or a link becomes unavailable. In other words, the network becomes unavailable for up to 50 seconds every time a change in topology occurs. This is not good. This is why Cisco and the IEEE improved STP to decrease STP convergence delays. These improvements are explained in the following sections.

Best practices to decrease STP convergence duration

It is best practice to set the STP priority to a low value (smaller than the default 32768 STP priority) on the fastest switch in your LAN. This causes STP to choose the fastest switch in your LAN as the root bridge.

Also, in larger LANs, when using several switches with various performance levels, it is best practice to set STP priority values in a hierarchical way according to the performance level of each group of switches to ensure that one of the next-fastest switches is elected the root bridge, if the root bridge ever fails or becomes unavailable.

Introducing Cisco Options for STP

Even when best practices are followed, the STP convergence delays may still be too long. You can use the following Cisco configuration options for STP to decrease STP convergence delays.

PortFast

The Cisco PortFast port option is used on ports that do not need to participate in STP. These are typically ports that do not interconnect switches, bridges, or hubs. For example, a switch port that connects directly to a host device using a single link does not need to participate in STP because there are no chances that that port will ever create a switching loop.

Enabling PortFast on a switch port basically turns off STP for that particular port. The advantage is that the port does not need to wait for the STP convergence to complete (up to 50 seconds) before it is active.

To configure PortFast on interface fa0/1, run the following commands:

```
SW1>en
SW1#configure terminal (or config t)
SW1(config)#interface fastethernet 0/1 (or int fa0/1)
SW1(config-if)#spanning-tree portfast
```

To configure PortFast on interfaces fa0/1 to fa0/4, run the following commands:

```
SW1>en
SW1#configure terminal (or config t)
SW1(config)#interface range fastethernet 0/1 - 4
SW1(config-if-range)#spanning-tree portfast
```

BPDUGuard

The BPDUGuard Cisco option is used in conjunction with the PortFast option on access layer switches. The PortFast option is dangerous if it is enabled by mistake on a port that interconnects switches: Enabling PortFast turns off STP on that port. This can potentially create a switching loop. The BPDUGuard option monitors the frames received on the PortFast-enabled port.

If the port ever receives a BPDU, it means that it is connected to a switch. In this case, BPDUGuard sets the port into an error-disabled state. This generates an error message on the switch console to inform the switch administrator that the port should not be PortFast-enabled. This situation can happen, for example, when an administrator mistakenly connects a switch to a port that was previously connected to a host. The port was PortFast-enabled because a host cannot create a switching loop. But now a switch connects to the port, so PortFast needs to be disabled. The BPDUGuard option ensures that an error is raised and that the port is disabled whenever this happens.

To configure BPDUGuard on interface fa0/1, run the following commands:

```
SW1>en
SW1#configure terminal (or config t)
SW1(config)#interface fastethernet 0/1 (or int fa0/1)
SW1(config-if)#spanning-tree bpduguard enable
```

To configure BPDUGuard on interfaces fa0/1 to fa0/4, run the following commands:

```
SW1>en
SW1#configure terminal (or config t)
SW1(config)#interface range fastethernet 0/1 - 4
SW1(config-if-range)#spanning-tree bpduguard enable
```

BPDUFilter

The BPDUFilter option prevents BPDU frames from entering or exiting a PortFast-enabled port. Without BPDUFilter enabled, a port that is PortFast enabled still receives BPDU frames. BPDUs are only useful in the context of STP. So, it makes sense to enable BPDUFilter to fence off the BPDUs on a port that is PortFast enabled because that port does not participate in STP.

If a BPDU reaches the PortFast-enabled port with the BPDUFilter option set, the PortFast option is disabled and the port starts to participate in STP. This is different from BPDUGuard: When a PortFast-enabled port with the BPDUGuard option set receives a BPDU, the port is turned off and an error is logged. BPDUFilter leaves the port on but turns off the PortFast option, thereby enabling STP on the port. You can use either the BPDUGuard option, the BPDUFilter option, or both on a PortFast-enabled port. Best practice is to use at least one of these options along with PortFast for ports that do not need to participate in STP.

To configure BPDUFilter on interface fa0/1, run the following commands:

```
SW1>en
SW1#configure terminal (or config t)
SW1(config)#interface fastethernet 0/1 (or int fa0/1)
SW1(config-if)#spanning-tree bpdufilter enable
```

To configure BPDUFilter on interfaces fa0/1 to fa0/4, run the following commands:

```
SW1>en
SW1#configure terminal (or config t)
SW1(config)#interface range fastethernet 0/1 - 4
SW1(config-if-range)#spanning-tree bpdufilter enable
```

UplinkFast

The UplinkFast Cisco option speeds STP convergence when at least one alternate or backup root port exists on the switch.

This option should only be enabled if an alternate root port exists. The alternate root port would be blocked in normal operation. If the root port fails or the link starting at the root port fails, UplinkFast switches right away to use the alternate root port without waiting for the STP convergence process to complete. This results in quicker failover time whenever the root port/link fails. This option is typically enabled on access layer switches that have redundant links to distribution layer switches.

Figure 4-9 illustrates the network shown in Figure 4-7 with an additional link between SW2 and SW5.

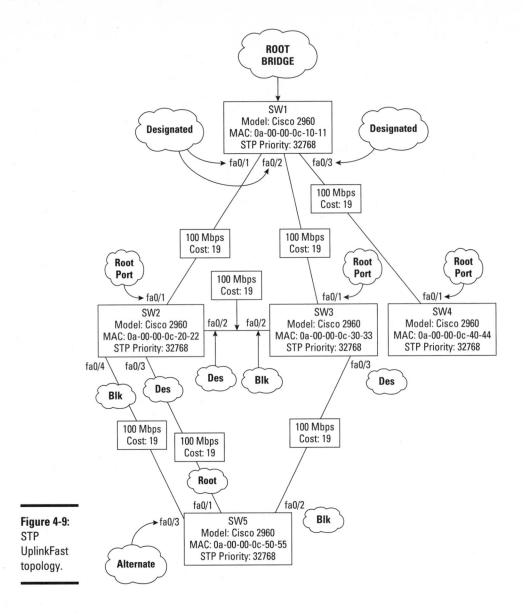

Figure 4-9:
STP
UplinkFast
topology.

In this setup, you can enable STP UplinkFast on switch SW5 because it has an alternate root port connecting it to switch SW2. Port fa0/3 on SW5 is now blocked. By enabling STP UplinkFast on SW5, port fa0/3, the alternate root port on SW5, would become root if the current root port, fa0/1, ever becomes unavailable, or if the link starting at fa0/1 on SW5 ever becomes unavailable.

To configure UplinkFast on switch SW5, run the following commands:

```
SW1>en
SW1#configure terminal (or config t)
SW1(config)#spanning-tree uplinkfast
```

BackboneFast

The BackboneFast Cisco option allows a switch to detect failures on links that are not connected directly to the switch. This option can be set on any switch including the root switch to allow all switches in the LAN to detect indirect link failures before TCN BPDUs are sent. This speeds STP convergence.

To configure BackboneFast on switch SW1, run the following commands:

```
SW1>en
SW1#configure terminal (or config t)
SW1(config)#spanning-tree backbonefast
```

Introducing Rapid Spanning Tree Protocol (RSTP)

Layer 2 switches need to avoid switching loops. However, STP convergence delays are a problem. Following STP best practices increases the chances to have a quick STP convergence after a topology change, but you have no guarantee that it will be any quicker than 50 seconds. Cisco-specific STP options also increase the chances to have a quick STP convergence after a topology change, but still, there is no guarantee that it will be any quicker than 50 seconds.

The Rapid Spanning Tree Protocol (RSTP) resolves this problem. The RSTP protocol is defined in the IEEE 802.1w standard. RSTP integrates the STP Cisco options described previously and adds more port types to decrease the time required to achieve STP convergence.

Shorter delay before STP recalculation (max age timer)

Remember that ports start in the blocking state whenever a switch is powered up. Switch ports also transition to the blocking state whenever a change in topology occurs (that is, whenever they receive a TCN BPDU). Switches wait for 20 seconds before they start the STP recalculation process. This 20-second wait time is called the *max age timer*.

Considering that BPDUs are sent every 2 seconds, STP switches wait for 10 BPDUs before they start the STP recalculation process.

RSTP reduces this 20-second delay. RSTP waits for just three BPDUs before it starts the STP convergence process. This considerably speeds the STP convergence process: a 6 max age timer delay in RSTP instead of the 20-second max age timer delay in STP.

Alternate port and backup port

RSTP adds two port types to the mix: *alternate ports* and *backup ports*. The purpose of these additional ports is to reduce STP convergence time by allowing switches in the LAN to have failover plans in the event that their root port or designated port fails.

The BPDUs in RSTP are extended to contain details not just about root, designated, and blocking ports, but also information about alternate and backup ports.

Alternate port

An *alternate port* is a port that becomes the root port in the event that the root port or the link starting at the root port fails or becomes unavailable.

The idea is to allow the switch to quickly use the alternate port as a root failover port without the need to go through the lengthy STP convergence process to find an alternate root port. The switch basically keeps in mind a "plan B" (alternate port) for the root port in the event that the current root port fails.

Backup port

A *backup port* is a port that becomes the designated port in the event that the designated port or the link starting at the designated port fails or becomes unavailable.

The idea is to allow the switch to quickly use the backup port as a designated failover port without the need to go through the lengthy STP convergence process to find an alternate designated port. The switch basically keeps in mind a "plan B" (backup port) for the designated port in the event that the current designated port fails.

Rapid Transitioning to Forwarding (RTF)

The IEEE 802.1w standard that defines RSTP adopted the Cisco PortFast port configuration option and named it Rapid Transitioning to Forwarding (RTF).

The same as the Cisco PortFast port configuration option, RTF speeds the STP convergence by transitioning *edge ports* very quickly to a forwarding state. A switch edge port is a port that connects to the edge of the network: a port that connects to an end device, such as a computer host, instead of connecting to another switch. These ports do not need to participate in STP, so they can transition to forwarding mode before STP convergence is achieved.

Enabling RSTP on a Cisco switch

RTF (PortFast) and other Cisco switch and port options for STP need to be enabled manually for RSTP as for STP. After Cisco switch and port options for STP have been set, you can turn on RSTP.

To enable RSTP on switch SW1, run the following commands:

```
SW1>en
SW1#configure terminal (or config t)
SW1(config)#spanning-tree mode rapid-pvst
```

EtherChannel

The STP convergence process assigns STP port types to all switches in the LAN, setting the ports in either the forwarding mode or blocking mode. On any given LAN segment, you only have one forwarding port. All other ports are blocking. The blocking ports would only be used if the current forwarding port fails.

Why would you have redundant links between switches if STP effectively shuts them down? Why would you spend extra money to have redundant links if you cannot use them? The additional links are only used for failover. Wouldn't it be nice if you could use these extra links to send data, thereby increasing the throughput of your LAN? That's exactly what EtherChannel does.

EtherChannel allows you to group several physical links into a single logical link. This is also called *port trunking* because you put several ports in a logical trunk. Cisco calls it *link aggregation* because you group several physical links together to create a single logical (aggregated) link. Both terms are valid because you group several ports in a trunk, thereby grouping several physical links in a single logical link.

You can group up to eight ports in a single trunk using EtherChannel.

EtherChannel and STP are friends

It is best practice to enable EtherChannel on redundant interswitch links when using STP. This groups redundant physical ports into a single logical port trunk. STP considers the whole port trunk to be a single link, so it will configure it to be forwarding (either a root port or designated port).

Although STP sees the port trunk as a single port, you still have several physical links between your switches. So, STP is happy because only one (logical trunk) port exists between the switches: You have no danger of creating a switching loop, so you don't need to block any ports. On the other hand, you still have several physical links between your switches to provide the desired redundancy.

Enabling EtherChannel on your redundant links provides three main advantages:

+ By grouping up to eight physical ports into a single logical port trunk, you add the bandwidth of each port to provide an *increased bandwidth* in the port trunk. For example, if you group eight Fast Ethernet ports into a port trunk, your total bandwidth in the port trunk would be 8 × 100 Mbps = 800 Mbps.

+ EtherChannel uses *load-balancing* algorithms to spread the network traffic across all ports in the port trunk. If one of the ports becomes overloaded, traffic is distributed across the remaining ports.

+ EtherChannel has built-in *fault tolerance:* If one port or link fails, EtherChannel sends traffic across the remaining ports in the trunk.

   Network applications consider the whole EtherChannel port trunk as a single network link, so they are not affected by a single port failure within the EtherChannel trunk. Better yet, STP also considers the whole EtherChannel port trunk as a single link, so STP recalculation is not necessary when a port fails within the EtherChannel trunk. STP recalculation would only be necessary if the whole EtherChannel port trunk fails. The EtherChannel port trunk would only fail when all the ports in the EtherChannel trunk fail.

EtherChannel versions

EtherChannel was initially developed by Cisco — actually, a company that Cisco acquired. Later, IEEE released the 802.3ad standard, which defines an open-standard version of EtherChannel. You can use either version on Cisco switches.

Port Aggregation Protocol (PAgP)

The Port Aggregation Protocol (PAgP) is the Cisco-proprietary protocol that can only be used on Cisco switches to manage EtherChannel.

Link Aggregation Control Protocol (LACP)

The Link Aggregation Control Protocol (LACP) is a protocol defined by the IEEE 802.3ad standard to manage EtherChannel. LACP can be used on any switch brands.

Enabling EtherChannel on SW2 and SW5

To use link aggregation on a redundant link between two switches, you need to enable EtherChannel on both switches. You can enable EtherChannel using the `interface port-channel` Cisco IOS command.

To configure EtherChannel on switch SW2 and assign interfaces fa0/3 to fa0/4 to the EtherChannel, run the following commands:

```
SW2>en
SW2#configure terminal (or config t)
SW2(config)#interface port-channel 1 (or int port-channel 1)
SW2(config-if)#exit
SW2(config)#interface range fastethernet 0/3 - 4
SW2(config-if-range)#channel-group 1 mode on
SW2(config-if-range)#exit
SW2(config)#
```

You need to run the previous commands on SW5 as well.

The `interface port-channel 1` command creates the port channel no. 1, also known as EtherChannel 1.

The `interface range fastethernet 0/3 - 4` command selects a range of physical interfaces to work with.

The `channel-group 1 mode on` command assigns the selected interface, or the selected interface range, to port channel group (EtherChannel) no. 1.

The `channel-group mode` command has a few options that control which port aggregation protocol is used to aggregate the physical ports in the EtherChannel you create. Recall that you can choose between two port (or link) aggregation protocols: Cisco's proprietary Port Aggregation Protocol (PAgP) and IEEE's 802.3ad standard named Link Aggregation Control Protocol (LACP). Table 4-2 summarizes the options available with the `channel-group mode` Cisco IOS command.

**Book III
Chapter 4**

**Spanning Tree
Protocol (STP)**

Table 4-2	Choosing a Port (Link) Aggregation Protocol	
Channel-group command	*Protocol*	*Behavior*
channel-group <channel #> mode on	LACP	Sends LACP frames to neighbor switch
channel-group <channel #> mode off	None	Port aggregation is off
channel-group <channel #> mode auto	PAgP passive	Waits for neighbor switch to send PAgP frames
channel-group <channel #> mode passive	LACP passive	Waits for neighbor switch to send LACP frame
channel-group <channel #> mode desirable	PAgP active	Sends PAgP frames to neighbor switch
channel-group <channel #> mode active	LACP active	Sends LACP frames to neighbor switch

Monitoring STP

By default, STP is enabled on Cisco switches. However, you need to set port options and switch-wide STP options manually. Also, RSTP needs to be enabled manually. The following sections show how to look at the current STP configuration on a switch.

To monitor STP configuration on a switch, run the ubiquitous Cisco IOS show command with the spanning-tree option.

Monitoring switch STP configuration

You need to be in the privileged EXEC mode (using the enable IOS command) for spanning-tree configuration monitoring:

+ Displaying general STP configuration:

    ```
    SW1#show spanning-tree
    ```

+ Displaying UplinkFast configuration:

    ```
    SW1#show spanning-tree uplinkfast
    ```

+ Displaying BackboneFast configuration:

    ```
    SW1#show spanning-tree backbonefast
    ```

✦ To display PortFast on interface fa0/1, run the following command:

```
SW1#show spanning-tree interface fastethernet 0/1
   portfast
```

✦ To display BPDUGuard on interface fa0/1, run the following command:

```
SW1#show spanning-tree interface fastethernet 0/1
   bpduguard
```

✦ To display BPDUFilter on interface fa0/1, run the following command:

```
SW1#show spanning-tree interface fastethernet 0/1
   bpdufilter
```

**Book III
Chapter 4**

**Spanning Tree
Protocol (STP)**

Prep Test

1 **What is the main purpose of STP?**

A ○ Routing IP packets

B ○ Avoiding switching loops

C ○ Managing network segmentation in LANs using UplinkFast Cisco technology

D ○ All of the above

2 **What is the main purpose of a root bridge?**

A ○ Routing IP packets

B ○ Managing port security in LANs using PortFast Cisco technology

C ○ Helping decide which ports and links are preferred and which ports and links are nonpreferred

D ○ None of the above

3 **What criteria are analyzed to select the root bridge?**

A ○ STP priority and MAC address of the switch

B ○ Port type and port state of the root port

C ○ MAC address table and port access credentials on the switch

D ○ All of the above

4 **What is best practice when setting STP priority?**

A ○ Set it equal on all switches

B ○ Set it in a hierarchical way based the number of licensed switch ports

C ○ Set it in a hierarchical way based on switch capabilities

D ○ Set it to the default value of 32768

5 **What determines the STP path cost?**

A ○ The number of ports (hops) of a link to the root bridge

B ○ The sum of the bandwidth of each segment of a link to the root bridge

C ○ The number of segments of a link to the root bridge

D ○ The duplex mode of ports (hops) of a link to the root bridge

6 **How does STP assign port types?**

A ○ According to port MAC address, bridge ID, and port number

B ○ According to port bootup order, port MAC address, and bridge ID

C ○ According to STP path cost, bridge ID, and port number

D ○ According to STP path cost, port number, and MAC address

7 **What are the STP port types?**

A ○ Root port, or designated port or blocking port

B ○ Root port, or alternate or backup port

C ○ Root port, fabric port, failover port

D ○ All of the above

8 **The main advantage of RSTP over STP is that it allows switches to do which of the following?**

A ○ Avoid loops

B ○ Wake up on LAN activity

C ○ Log STP status messages

D ○ Converge faster

9 **Describe the Cisco options for STP.**

A ○ They are useless when more than three switches are in the LAN.

B ○ They are enabled manually.

C ○ They are enabled by default when STP is started.

D ○ They are not available if RSTP is used.

10 **What are the main advantages of using EtherChannel to logically group redundant interswitch links?**

A ○ Fewer cables to run between switches, faster switch bootup time, cost

B ○ Load balancing, fewer link failures, increased bandwidth per physical link

C ○ Load balancing, fault tolerance, link aggregation

D ○ Load balancing, fewer link failures, link aggregation

11 **What is the Cisco IOS command used to monitor most STP?**

A ○ `show statistics`

B ○ `show spanning-tree`

C ○ `show STP`

D ○ `monitor STP`

Answers

1 **B.** Avoiding switching loops. The main purpose of STP is to help switches communicate to set their ports in root, designated, or blocking state to avoid switching loops. Refer to *"Introducing the Spanning Tree Protocol (STP)."*

2 **C.** Helping decide which ports and links are preferred and which ports and links are nonpreferred. STP calculates optimal routes to the root bridge to determine which ports are forwarding and which ports are blocking on each switch. See *"Electing a root bridge."*

3 **A.** STP priority and MAC address of the switch. Switches elect a root bridge according to the bridge ID of each switch. The bridge ID of each switch is a combination of the MAC address of the switch and its STP priority. Check out *"Electing a root bridge."*

4 **C.** Set STP priority in a hierarchical way based on switch capabilities to ensure that most powerful switches are always first in line to be elected root bridge. Review *"STP priority related to the Cisco hierarchical network architecture."*

5 **B.** The sum of the bandwidth of each segment of a link to the root bridge. Switches add the bandwidth of each link to the root bridge to determine the STP path cost. See *"Setting designated ports."*

6 **C.** According to STP path cost, bridge ID, and port number. These three criteria are analyzed to determine the STP type of each port. Refer to *"Setting designated ports."*

7 **A.** Root port, or designated port or blocking port. RSTP adds the alternate port and backup port. Check out *"Assigning STP port types."*

8 **D.** RSTP helps switches converge faster. Read *"Introducing Rapid Spanning Tree Protocol (RSTP)."*

9 **B.** They are enabled manually. Cisco options for STP are enabled manually either on the whole switch or on a particular port. See *"Introducing Cisco Options for STP."*

10 **C.** Load balancing, fault tolerance, link aggregation. EtherChannel groups several physical links into a single logical link, thereby balancing the load across all physical links in the trunk, tolerating one or a few link failures in the trunk and adding up the bandwidth of the physical links to use for the logical link. Refer to *"EtherChannel."*

11 **B.** The `show spanning-tree` command is the Cisco IOS command used to monitor most STP. Check out *"Monitoring STP."*

Chapter 5: Virtual Local Area Networks (VLANs)

Exam Objectives

✔ Describing the purpose and implications of VLANs

✔ Describing the benefits of using VLANs

✔ Creating and managing VLANs

✔ Identifying VLANs using Cisco ISL and IEEE 802.1q frame tagging

✔ Creating and managing VLAN port trunks

✔ Creating and managing EtherChannel logical ports

✔ Understanding the difference between Port Aggregation Protocol (PAgP) and Link Aggregation Control Protocol (LACP)

✔ Understanding the difference between a VLAN port trunk and an EtherChannel logical port

✔ Creating and managing VLAN port trunk over EtherChannel logical port

✔ Managing switch port types: access ports and trunk ports

✔ Managing VLAN port trunks using the Dynamic Trunking Protocol (DTP)

✔ Managing the VLAN Trunking Protocol (VTP)

✔ Managing inter-VLAN routing

*V*LANs are an important feature that allows you to subdivide a LAN into several logical (virtual) LANs (VLANs) using the same physical equipment. In other words, you could have some devices communicate within one virtual LAN and other devices communicate within another virtual LAN on the same cables, switches, and routers. You can identify and separate network traffic for different purposes on any given network using VLANs. The nice thing about VLANs is that you don't need to have separate physical networks to separate traffic within the LAN.

VLANs also limit the broadcast domain. Switches do not limit broadcast domains. A broadcast frame sent on a Layer 2 switch will reach every host and network device within that LAN. This may be a problem in a large LAN. VLANs fix this problem: Each VLAN is a broadcast domain. In other words, broadcast frames only reach host and network devices within the VLAN where the broadcast frame is sent. This dramatically improves the performance and reliability of LANs.

Introducing Virtual Local Area Networks (VLANs)

A VLAN is a logical grouping of network resources and host devices based on the ports where those hosts connect to the switch, or based on the MAC address of those hosts. A VLAN is basically a logical grouping of switch ports or MAC addresses. A VLAN can span more than one physical switch. This is interesting because you could have a VLAN that groups network and host devices across many switches in a network. Data-link frames can be tagged with a VLAN identifier to indicate that they are part of a certain VLAN.

Figure 5-1 illustrates three VLANs that group the computer hosts by business department.

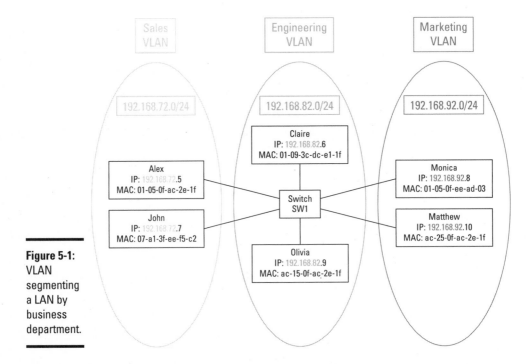

Figure 5-1:
VLAN segmenting a LAN by business department.

VLANs keep things tidy

The most apparent benefit of using VLANs is keeping things well organized by logically grouping your network along business departments and functions. You can even group network and host devices in VLANs by project. For example, if Engineering starts a new project and it needs to experiment with network connectivity, new hardware, and new software, it is a good idea to group the resources needed for that project into a specific VLAN.

This avoids running into a situation where the engineers run a test that would bring down the whole network.

VLANs subdivide the broadcast domain

Another benefit is not as apparent as keeping traffic separate along business functions. VLANs break up the broadcast domain:

✦ A *collision domain* is a logical network space where frames can collide because several hosts are sharing the bandwidth of the network medium and they can potentially send frames on the wire at the same time. It is best to *segment networks* into several smaller collision domains to lower the chances of having frame collisions. Layer 2 switches break up the collision domain by providing point-to-point links between devices connected to the switch.

✦ A *broadcast domain* is a logical network space where broadcast frames are sent. A broadcast frame is a data-link frame that is sent to all devices in the network. Broadcast frames are typically used to locate a device in the network. Layer 2 switches forward a broadcast frame out on all their ports except on the port where the broadcast frame entered the switch. This may become a problem in large networks. That's where VLANs enter the scene. VLANs basically subdivide the LAN into several virtual LANs. Broadcast frames are sent within a LAN. So, if you subdivide the LAN into several smaller VLANs, broadcast frames are only sent within each VLAN. That's the beauty of VLANs: They break up the broadcast domain.

This works quite nicely because most of the time, hosts need to communicate within their own VLAN. They need to communicate with hosts outside of their own VLAN more rarely. That's why it is best practice to organize VLANs along business departments and functions and/or along projects.

Referring to Figure 5-1, a computer in the Marketing group VLAN needs to access Marketing servers and computers most of the time. Only rarely does it need to communicate with a computer in the Engineering or Sales department.

Subdividing the network in the Marketing, Engineering, and Sales VLANs breaks up the broadcast domain into three subdomains: Marketing, Engineering, and Sales. So, a computer in Marketing broadcasts a frame that only reaches computers in Marketing whenever it needs to find the IP and MAC address of a server in Marketing to connect to it.

What if a computer in Marketing needs to find the IP and MAC address of a server in Sales or Engineering? In that case, routing needs to be enabled among those three VLANs. By default, data-link frames do not cross over from one VLAN to another. You need to specifically configure routing between VLANs to allow that. You see how to enable inter-VLAN routing later in this chapter.

There are many more reasons to use VLANs in a network. The following section reviews some of these benefits of VLANs and explains why you should use VLANs in your networks.

Benefits of VLANs

Here are the main benefits of using VLANs in your network:

✦ **Limit the size of each broadcast domain:** This is probably the most important benefit of VLANs. VLANs increase the number of broadcast domains and reduce the size of each broadcast domain. VLANs subdivide a LAN into several logical LANs. Broadcast frames are sent within a LAN. So, if you subdivide the LAN into several smaller VLANs, broadcast frames are only sent within each VLAN.

✦ **Improve security:** VLANs allow network administrators to logically group switch ports for specific purposes. They can assign users (computer hosts) to those VLANs by controlling the port where the computer host connects to the switch. Ports are assigned to the port group (VLAN) where that computer host needs to be. Those ports can be located on any switch in the network: A VLAN can span more than just one switch. This is a very efficient way to control access to network resources.

✦ **Improve network management and flexibility:** Previously you read that VLAN membership allows network administrators to control access to network resources. The nice thing is that they can manage this membership from a single location for all switches in the network. Better yet, by using dynamic VLAN membership, VLAN Trunking Protocol (VTP), and inter-VLAN routing, they can control access to network resources in a very large network with minimum effort.

✦ **Improve network usage and efficiency:** Network administrators assign network resources to a certain VLAN. Only computer hosts and network devices in that VLAN have access to those resources. Referring to Figure 5-1, a Marketing server should not be disturbed by requests from Engineering computers. By subdividing the network in three VLANs, you ensure that Engineering computers will not disturb Marketing servers and vice versa.

You can configure inter-VLAN routing to allow certain requests to cross over from one VLAN to another, but using VLANs, you have control; it is not all open access.

Managing VLANs

I now discuss how to create and manage VLANs. You discover VLAN 1, a special-purpose VLAN. You also find out about the difference between static and dynamic VLAN membership.

Create VLANs

To create a VLAN on a Cisco switch, you first use the `vlan` Cisco IOS command with the number that you want to assign to the new VLAN. You can assign a VLAN number between 2 and 4094. Then, you can name that VLAN using a name that identifies the purpose of the VLAN.

Create VLAN example

To create the Sales VLAN on switch SW1, run the following commands:

```
SW1>en
SW1#configure terminal (or config t)
SW1(config)#vlan 2
SW1(config-vlan)#name Sales
SW1(config-vlan)#exit
SW1(config)#
```

To create the other two VLANs shown in Figure 5-1, run the following commands:

```
SW1(config)>vlan 3
SW1(config-vlan)#name Engineering
SW1(config)#vlan 4
SW1(config-vlan)#name Marketing
SW1(config-vlan)#exit
SW1(config)#
```

Special-purpose VLANs

Looking at the previous example, you can see that you chose numbers 2, 3, and 4, respectively, for the Sales, Engineering, and Marketing VLANs.

Why did you not choose VLAN 1 for the Sales VLAN? VLAN 1 is a special-purpose VLAN. VLAN 1 is the administrative VLAN. Although you can assign ports to VLAN 1, Cisco recommends reserving that VLAN for switch and network management purposes only. VLAN 1 is the only VLAN that is precreated on a Cisco switch, and you cannot delete it.

By default, all ports on the switch are members of VLAN 1. Whenever you assign a port to a VLAN, you basically move the port out of VLAN 1 and into a new VLAN that you created.

Static and dynamic VLAN membership

How you assign ports to a VLAN depends on whether you're using static or dynamic VLAN membership.

A switch can have some ports configured with static VLAN membership and some ports configured with dynamic VLAN membership. Static and dynamic VLAN membership modes can coexist on the same switch. However, you should ensure that ports configured with dynamic VLAN membership connect to end devices, not to another switch.

Static VLAN membership

With *static VLAN membership,* you assign a specific port to a specific VLAN using the `switchport access vlan` Cisco IOS command.

Static VLAN membership is also called port-based VLAN membership because you control VLAN membership based on the port where the computer host connects to the switch.

This works quite well in small networks. However, if you need to move the computer host to a different port, you need to make sure that the new port is also configured in the correct VLAN. You may also need to change the VLAN membership of the port where the computer host used to connect, to disable access to the VLAN from that port, if that port remains unoccupied, for instance.

Port management and port-based (static) VLAN membership can become a daunting management task in larger networks. In that case, you may want to use dynamic VLAN membership instead.

Static VLAN membership port assignment example

To assign port 2 on switch SW1 to VLAN 2 (Sales), run the following commands:

```
SW1>en
SW1#configure terminal (or config t)
SW1(config)#interface fa0/2 (int fa0/2)
SW1(config-if)#switchport access vlan 2
SW1(config-if)#exit
SW1(config)#
```

Dynamic VLAN membership

With *dynamic VLAN membership,* you enable a service called VLAN Membership Policy Server (VMPS) on your switches. The VMPS keeps a table of the MAC addresses of all devices connected to your switch. You can assign each MAC address to a specific VLAN. This is great because, no matter where that device connects to your network, it will always be assigned to the correct VLAN. The MAC address of the device does not change, even if you connect the device to a different port on the switch, or even to a different switch. That MAC address is assigned to a specific VLAN on the VMPS. So, the device will always operate in the correct VLAN, no matter where it connects from.

Certain Cisco switch models, such as the Cisco Catalyst 2960 series, can only be configured as VMPS clients. You would have to configure VMPS on a Cisco Catalyst 3560 series or better.

Identifying VLANs

You can identify VLANs by their number and by their name. You found out previously that you assign a number between 2 and 4094 to VLANs that you create. VLAN 1 is reserved for administrative purposes only; it is best practice to assign your ports to other VLANs than VLAN 1. The number of a VLAN is also called the *VLAN ID*.

The following sections describe how a switch identifies a VLAN.

Tagging data-link frames with a VLAN ID

Data-link frames can be tagged with the VLAN ID. This allows any switch in the network to identify the VLAN that the frame belongs to. The VLAN ID tag changes the data-link frame: It adds a header and a trailer, in some cases. There are two methods for VLAN frame tagging:

✦ The Cisco Inter-Switch Link (ISL) proprietary method

✦ The IEEE 802.1q standard

Cisco ISL frame tagging

The Cisco ISL frame-tagging method encapsulates data-link frames in Cisco ISL frames by adding a 26-byte header and a 4-byte trailer to the original data-link frame. The header contains the VLAN ID, identifying the VLAN to which the encapsulated data-link frame belongs. The trailer includes a cyclic redundancy check (CRC) to ensure the validity of the ISL frame.

The Cisco ISL frame-tagging method is Cisco proprietary: It works only between Cisco switches. So, if the network contains switches from other vendors, using Cisco ISL may not be the best choice. In fact, Cisco is moving away from its proprietary Cisco ISL frame-tagging method to use the IEEE 802.1q standard instead.

The Cisco ISL frame-tagging method changes the size of the data-link (Ethernet) frame. This can be a problem if a switch or a computer host that does not support Cisco ISL ever receives the frame. Basically, this is a problem if anything else but a Cisco switch receives the frame. The modified data-link frame, encapsulated in a Cisco ISL tagged frame, is potentially larger than the maximum size of an Ethernet frame. Devices that do not support Cisco ISL would drop a Cisco ISL frame.

**Book III
Chapter 5**

Virtual Local Area
Networks (VLANs)

Some Cisco switch models do not support the Cisco ISL frame-tagging method anymore. For example, the Cisco Catalyst 2960 series switches support only the IEEE 802.1q frame-tagging standard. The Cisco Catalyst 3560 series switches, on the other hand, support both the Cisco ISL frame-tagging method and the IEEE 802.1q frame-tagging standard.

IEEE 802.1q frame tagging (a.k.a. dot1q)

The IEEE 802.1q frame-tagging standard changes the data-link frame header: It adds an "802.1q tag" that identifies the VLAN to which the modified data-link frame belongs. The 802.1q tag is 4 bytes long. Hence, the data-link frame size may be a bit larger than a normal Ethernet frame. However, this is not a problem, because all network devices, even computer host network interface cards (NICs), understand the IEEE 802.1q standard. Whenever they see an 802.1q tag in the Ethernet frame, they can simply extract it and process the rest of the data-link (Ethernet) frame.

The IEEE 802.1q standard is also known as the *dot1q* encapsulation method. In fact, you use the `switchport trunk encap dot1q` Cisco IOS command to set a trunk port to use the IEEE 802.1q VLAN ID frame-tagging standard.

VLAN Trunking

Connecting hosts and network resources by using a single switch may be an efficient setup in a small network, but it does not scale very well.

What happens if you need to add more computer hosts into that network but no more ports are available on the SW1 switch? What if one of the computer hosts needs to be moved to a different location? In both cases, you would need to add a second switch, SW2, to the network. But then, how do you interconnect the two switches, SW1 and SW2, and more importantly, how do you manage the three VLANs across two switches? This is when you need VLAN trunking.

VLAN trunking allows switches to send VLAN information across interswitch links that are configured as a trunk port. By using trunk ports, VLANs can span more than one switch. You can now add new computer hosts to the second switch, SW2, and have them operate in their corresponding VLAN that now spans SW1 and SW2.

Figure 5-2 illustrates an expanded network: You now have two switches, SW1 and SW2, that are interconnected by a trunk port. The three VLANs, Sales, Engineering, and Marketing, now span both switches SW1 and SW2. You can add computer hosts to either SW1 or SW2 and assign them to one of the three VLANs that span the whole network.

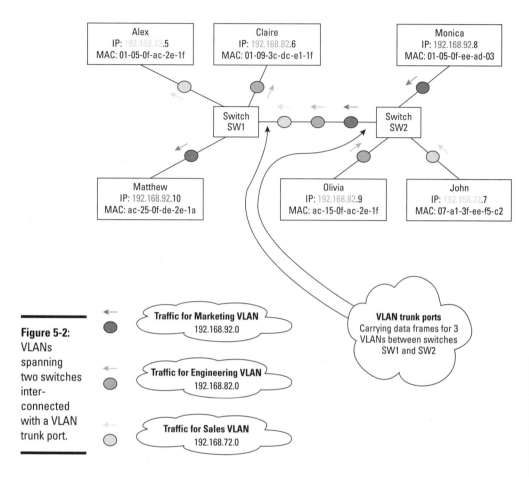

Figure 5-2: VLANs spanning two switches interconnected with a VLAN trunk port.

If you also use dynamic VLAN membership, you can move a computer host from SW1 to SW2, because that computer VLAN membership depends on the MAC address of the computer host, not on the SW1 switch port where it used to connect.

EtherChannel and VLANs are friends

It is best practice to enable EtherChannel on redundant interswitch links when using STP. It is also best practice to enable EtherChannel on redundant interswitch links when using VLANs. This groups redundant physical ports into a single logical port trunk. This is also called *port trunking* because you put several ports in a logical trunk. Cisco calls it *link aggregation* because you group several physical links together to create a single logical (aggregated) link. Both terms are valid because you group several ports in a trunk, thereby grouping several physical links in a single logical link.

You can group up to eight ports in a single trunk using EtherChannel.

Although switches see the EtherChannel port trunk as a single port, you still have several physical links between your switches. So, only one logical EtherChannel trunk port exists between the switches backed by several physical interswitch links to provide the desired redundancy. Using EtherChannel with VLANs provides the same advantages as using EtherChannel with STP: increased bandwidth, load balancing, and fault tolerance.

Increasing bandwidth with EtherChannel

By grouping up to eight physical ports into a single logical port trunk, you add the bandwidth of each port to provide an *increased bandwidth* in the port trunk. For example, if you group eight Fast Ethernet ports into a port trunk, your total bandwidth in the port trunk would be 8×100 Mbps = 800 Mbps.

Balancing the load with EtherChannel

EtherChannel uses *load-balancing* algorithms to spread the network traffic across all ports in the port trunk. If one of the ports becomes overloaded, traffic is distributed across the remaining ports.

Tolerating faults with EtherChannel

EtherChannel has built-in *fault-tolerance:* If one port or link fails, EtherChannel sends traffic across the remaining ports in the trunk. Network applications consider the whole port trunk as a single network link, so they are not affected by a single port failure within the trunk.

EtherChannel versions

EtherChannel was initially developed by Cisco — actually, a company that Cisco acquired. Later, IEEE released the 802.3ad standard, which defines an open version of EtherChannel. You can use either version on Cisco switches.

Port Aggregation Protocol (PAgP)

The Port Aggregation Protocol (PAgP) is the Cisco-proprietary protocol that can only be used on Cisco switches to manage EtherChannel.

Link Aggregation Control Protocol (LACP)

The Link Aggregation Control Protocol (LACP) is a protocol defined by the IEEE 802.3ad standard to manage EtherChannel. LACP can be used on any switch brands.

VLAN or EtherChannel trunking? Both?

VLAN port trunks and EtherChannel port trunks are different. However, switch ports can be configured to be both an EtherChannel port trunk and a VLAN port trunk.

It is best practice to configure VLAN port trunks over EtherChannel port trunks whenever redundant interswitch links are available.

VLAN port trunk

You create a VLAN port trunk by configuring a switch port to be a trunk port interconnecting two switches.

The key point here is that this port may be just a single physical connection, a single link, interconnecting the switches. It is still called a VLAN port trunk because that port carries data for all VLANs in the network. So, it is a port trunk in the sense that it carries data for more than one VLAN. It is not a port trunk in the sense that you group several physical links in a single logical link. So, by default, if you set a *single* physical or logical port to be a port trunk interconnecting two switches, that port is a VLAN port trunk.

The main purpose of a VLAN port trunk is to carry data for several VLANs over a *single* physical or logical link interconnecting two switches.

EtherChannel port trunk

You create an EtherChannel port trunk by grouping together *several* physical ports interconnecting two switches in a single logical port.

The key point here is that you group several physical links into a single logical link. So, an EtherChannel port trunk is a port trunk in the sense that you group several physical links into a single logical link.

The main purpose of an EtherChannel port trunk is to provide a single logical interswitch link backed by *several* physical interswitch links to provide increased bandwidth, load balancing, and fault tolerance on that interswitch link.

Configuring EtherChannel and VLAN trunking

You can configure ports to be both an EtherChannel port trunk and a VLAN port trunk. Follow these steps:

✦ Create an EtherChannel port trunk:

  1. Use the `interface port-channel` Cisco IOS command to create the EtherChannel port trunk.

2. Use the `interface range` Cisco IOS command to select the physical interfaces to assign to the EtherChannel port trunk.

3. Use the `channel-group <#> mode` command to assign the selected interfaces to the EtherChannel port trunk.

✦ Configure a VLAN trunk over an EtherChannel logical port trunk:

1. Use the `interface port-channel` Cisco IOS command to select the EtherChannel port.

2. Use the `switchport mode trunk` Cisco IOS command to set the EtherChannel port as a trunk port.

It is best practice to configure VLAN port trunks over EtherChannel port trunks whenever redundant interswitch links are available.

Figure 5-3 illustrates two switches that are interconnected with four physical links. Those links are grouped into an EtherChannel. The EtherChannel is configured as a VLAN trunk. The VLAN trunk carries frames for all VLANs in the network.

A VLAN trunk over EtherChannel is a bit like a freeway overpass:

✦ The physical Ethernet connections are like the support beams of the overpass.

✦ The EtherChannel logical port supported by the physical Ethernet connections is like the overpass flatbed held up by the support beams.

✦ The VLAN trunk carrying VLAN data frames is like the smooth asphalt surface that carries vehicles on top of the overpass flatbed.

The section "Managing VLAN trunk ports," later in this chapter, shows an example of how to configure a few physical ports in an EtherChannel port trunk. The example then shows how to configure a VLAN port trunk over the EtherChannel port trunk.

Introducing switch port types

Switch ports can be used either as access ports or as trunk ports:

✦ You can configure a switch port to be an access port or to be a trunk port manually, using the `switchport mode` Cisco IOS command.

✦ You can also use the *Dynamic Trunking Protocol (DTP)* to set the switch port operation mode automatically:

• DTP sets a switch port to be a trunk port if the port connects to another switch.

• DTP sets the port to be an access port if the port connects to an end device, such as a computer host or an IP telephone.

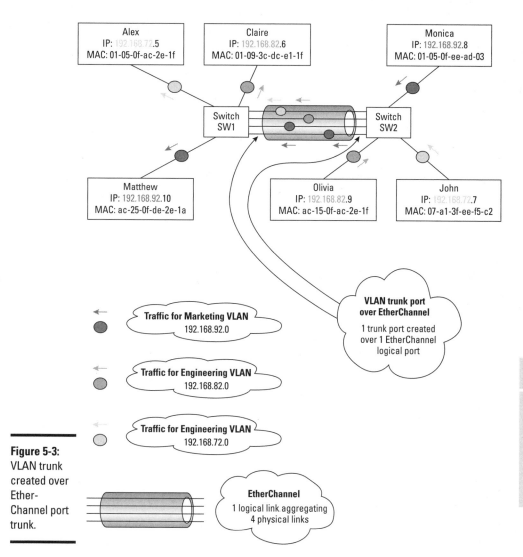

Figure 5-3:
VLAN trunk
created over
Ether-
Channel port
trunk.

Access ports

Access ports are ports that connect a switch to end devices, such as computer hosts. By default, switch ports are configured as access ports and they are all part of VLAN 1, the default administrative VLAN. It is best practice to create new VLANs and assign access ports to those new VLANs, avoiding using VLAN 1 for access ports.

Access ports can only be members of one VLAN, and they only carry traffic for that VLAN. Access ports always carry traffic in native Ethernet format. The switch removes the VLAN ID tag from the Ethernet frame before it hands off the frame out on an access port. Similarly, the switch adds the VLAN ID tag to Ethernet frames it receives through an access port from an end device. If the switch receives an Ethernet frame tagged with a VLAN ID from an access port, it drops the frame because it considers it invalid. This is a "free" security feature: It prevents connecting a switch to a port that should be used by a single end device. It is "free" because the switch does not have to do anything special to provide this security feature: Switches simply do not look at the source field of an Ethernet frame when that frame comes in on an access port. Recall that tagging an Ethernet frame with a VLAN ID increases the size of the frame over the normal Ethernet frame size. So, the switch sees an oversized frame coming in on an access port: It drops it as invalid because it is oversized. The VLAN assigned to an access port is also called the *configured VLAN*.

There is an exception to the rule that an access port can only be a member of one VLAN and that it can only carry traffic for that VLAN. Access ports can be part of a single *data* VLAN and carry *data* frames only for that VLAN. However, access ports can simultaneously be part of a VLAN reserved for Voice over IP (VoIP) and carry VoIP frames for that VLAN. In other words, access ports on newer switches can be configured with two VLANs: one VLAN for data and one VLAN for VoIP. This allows you to connect both a computer host and an IP telephone to the same access port.

Trunk ports

Trunk ports are ports that connect a switch to another switch. By default, switch ports are not configured as trunk ports. You need to configure trunk ports either manually, using the `switchport mode` Cisco IOS command, or automatically, using *Dynamic Trunking Protocol (DTP)*.

Before you configure trunk ports you need to ensure the following:

✦ You have Fast Ethernet (100-Mbps) or Gigabit Ethernet (1-Gbps) ports on your switch. Trunk ports cannot be configured on normal Ethernet ports (10-Mbps) because they are not fast enough to carry the additional traffic load generated by several VLANs.

✦ You interconnect your switches using crossover cables. Switches are always interconnected using crossover cables, not straight-through cables. Newer Cisco switches have a feature called SmartPort. SmartPort adapts connection parameters according to the type of cable that is plugged in to the port and according to the device at the other end of the cable. Hence, using the Cisco SmartPort feature, you could theoretically use any cable. However, for the CCNA test purposes, switches are always connected using crossover cables.

To configure trunk ports, you can do either of the following:

✦ Use the `switchport mode` Cisco IOS command.

✦ Use the Dynamic Trunking Protocol (DTP). DTP sets a switch port to be a trunk port if the port connects to another switch. DTP sets the port to be an access port if the port connects to an end device, such as a computer host or an IP telephone.

Trunk ports are members of all VLANs, and they carry traffic for all VLANs. Trunk ports carry traffic in Ethernet frames that are tagged with VLAN ID information. When you create a trunk port, you need to choose one of the frame-tagging methods discussed earlier: the Cisco ISL proprietary tagging method or the IEEE 802.1q tagging standard. You can use the `switchport trunk encapsulation` Cisco IOS command to choose a frame-tagging method.

Switches look at the source field of an Ethernet frame when the frame comes in on a trunk port, and they process the frame. The switch extracts the VLAN ID from the Cisco ISL tag or from the IEEE 802.1q tag:

✦ If the frame destination is an end device on the switch, the switch rebuilds the Ethernet frame without the VLAN ID tag and forwards the frame out on the access port connecting to the end device.

✦ If the frame destination is an end device on another switch, the switch forwards the tagged Ethernet frame on an outgoing trunk port that reaches that destination switch.

Managing VLAN trunk ports

Read the following sections to find out more about DTP and to see a complete example of how to configure a few physical ports in an EtherChannel port trunk. The example then shows how to configure a VLAN port trunk over the EtherChannel port trunk.

Dynamic Trunking Protocol (DTP)

The Dynamic Trunking Protocol (DTP) is used to configure VLAN port trunks automatically. DTP sets a switch port to be a trunk port if the port connects to another switch. It sets the port to be an access port if the port connects to an end device, such as a computer host or an IP telephone.

DTP can also set the VLAN ID tag encapsulation method. Two VLAN ID tag encapsulation methods are available on Cisco switches:

✦ The Cisco ISL proprietary VLAN ID tag encapsulation method

✦ The IEEE 802.1q VLAN ID tagging standard, also known as the *dot1q* encapsulation method

DTP helps two switches negotiate the choice of one of these VLAN ID tagging methods.

Whenever DTP determines that a switch port connects to another switch, it communicates with DTP on the remote switch to set up a VLAN port trunk according to the mode of the ports on each switch.

Configuring switch port DTP operation mode

Switch ports are either ready to set up a trunk with another switch port or not ready to set up a trunk with another switch port. Five operation modes determine whether a switch port becomes a trunk port. You can configure these five modes on each physical port on a switch.

Switch ports can be operating in any of the following five modes.

Access

A port in access mode is a port that is not available to set up a VLAN port trunk, even if DTP on the neighbor switch port tries to set up a VLAN port trunk. You set a port in access operating mode if it connects to end devices, such as computer hosts. A port in access operating mode is a member of a single VLAN, and it carries data only for that VLAN. Access ports do not send or receive any DTP frames: DTP is disabled on these ports.

You can use the `switchport mode access` Cisco IOS command to set up a port in access operating mode.

Trunk

A port in trunk mode is a port that is available to set up a VLAN port trunk, even if DTP on the neighbor switch port does not try to set up a VLAN port trunk. In other words, no matter what the neighbor switch is doing, this port, in trunk operating mode, will try to set up a port trunk. It will succeed if the port on the remote switch is in any operating mode other than access.

You can use the `switchport mode trunk` Cisco IOS command to set up a port in trunk operating mode.

Nonegotiate

A port in nonegotiate mode is a port that does not send or receive any DTP frames: DTP is disabled on these ports. You can set a trunk port or an access port in nonegotiate operating mode. Anytime you set a port in nonegotiate mode, you are expected to set the operating mode of the port manually, instead of relying on DTP to do that.

You can use the `switchport nonegotiate` Cisco IOS command to set up a port in nonegotiate operating mode.

Dynamic desirable

A port in dynamic desirable mode is actively ready to become a trunk port. It sends and receives DTP frames. It actively seeks to set up a trunk with its neighbor port. It sets up a trunk port with its neighbor if the port at the other end of the link is a trunk port, a dynamic desirable port, or a dynamic auto port.

You can use the `switchport mode dynamic desirable` Cisco IOS command to set up a port in dynamic desirable operating mode.

Dynamic auto

A port in dynamic auto mode is passively ready to become a trunk port. It receives DTP frames but does not send any. It sets up a trunk port with its neighbor port if the port at the other end of the link is either a trunk port or a dynamic desirable port. Cisco switch ports operate by default in dynamic auto mode.

You can use the `switchport mode dynamic auto` Cisco IOS command to set up a port in dynamic auto operating mode.

Enabling EtherChannel and port trunking

In the previous chapter, you discovered how to set up an EtherChannel. Here you review how to set up an EtherChannel and you see how to create a VLAN port trunk over that EtherChannel.

Creating port channel (EtherChannel) 1

To use link aggregation on a redundant link between two switches, you need to enable EtherChannel on both switches. You can enable EtherChannel using the `interface port-channel` Cisco IOS command.

To configure EtherChannel on switch SW2 and on switch SW5 and to assign interfaces fa0/3 to fa0/4 to the EtherChannel, run the following commands on SW2 and SW5:

```
SW2>en
SW2#configure terminal (or config t)
SW2(config)#interface port-channel 1 (or int port-channel 1)
SW2(config)#exit
SW2(config)#interface range fastethernet 0/3 - 4
SW2(config-if-range)#channel-group 1 mode on
SW2(config-if-range)#exit
SW2(config)#
```

Here are the details of the preceding commands:

✦ The `interface port-channel 1` command creates the port channel no. 1, also known as EtherChannel 1.

✦ The `interface range fastethernet 0/3 - 4` command selects a range of physical interfaces to work with.

✦ The `channel-group 1 mode on` command assigns the selected interface, or the selected interface range, to port channel group (EtherChannel) 1.

✦ The `channel-group mode` command has a few options that control which port aggregation protocol is used to aggregate the physical ports in the EtherChannel you create. You can choose between two-port (or link) aggregation protocols:

  • Cisco's proprietary Port Aggregation Protocol (PAgP)

  • IEEE's 802.3ad Link Aggregation Control Protocol (LACP) standard

Table 5-1 summarizes the options available with the `channel-group mode` Cisco IOS command.

Table 5-1	Choosing a Port (Link) Aggregation Protocol	
Channel-group command	*Protocol*	*Behavior*
`channel-group <channel #> mode on`	LACP	Sends LACP frames to the neighbor switch
`channel-group <channel #> mode off`	None	Port (link) aggregation is off
`channel-group <channel #> mode auto`	PAgP passive	Waits for the neighbor switch to send PAgP frames
`channel-group <channel #> mode passive`	LACP passive	Waits for the neighbor switch to send LACP frames
`channel-group <channel #> mode desirable`	PAgP active	Sends PAgP frames to the neighbor switch
`channel-group <channel #> mode active`	LACP active	Sends LACP frames to the neighbor switch

Configuring a VLAN port trunk over port channel (EtherChannel) 1

To manually configure port trunking over EtherChannel 1, run the following commands on SW2 and SW5:

```
SW2>en
SW2#configure terminal (or config t)
SW2(config)#interface port-channel 1 (or int port-channel 1)
SW2(config-if)#switchport trunk encap dot1q
```

```
SW2(config-if)#switchport mode trunk
SW2(config-if)#switchport nonegotiate
SW2(config-if)#exit
SW2(config)#
```

Here are the details of the preceding commands:

✦ The `switchport trunk encap dot1q` command sets the IEEE 802.1q VLAN ID tagging standard on the VLAN port trunk.

✦ The `switchport mode trunk` command enables port trunking over the selected port channel group.

✦ The `switchport nonegotiate` command disables automatic port negotiation on the trunk port that you just created over the port channel group (EtherChannel) 1.

You did everything manually here:

✦ You used the `switchport nonegotiate` command to disable DTP negotiation.

✦ You set the operating mode of the EtherChannel port manually, using the `switchport mode trunk` command.

Alternately, you can use DTP to automatically create the VLAN port trunk over the EtherChannel and to automatically negotiate the VLAN ID tagging method used by SW2 and SW5. To do this, you would need to

✦ Set at least one of the EtherChannel ports to dynamic desirable

✦ Set the other port to either dynamic auto or dynamic desirable

To let DTP automatically configure port trunking over EtherChannel 1, run the following commands:

```
SW2>en
SW2#configure terminal (or config t)
SW2(config)#interface port-channel 1 (or int port-channel 1)
SW2(config-if)#switchport mode dynamic desirable
SW2(config-if)#exit
SW2(config)#
```

You need to run the previous commands on SW5 as well. However, you can leave the SW5 port in dynamic auto operating mode because the SW2 port is dynamic desirable: SW2 initiates the DTP negotiation (dynamic desirable) while SW5 can just wait (dynamic auto).

VLAN Trunking Protocol (VTP)

You previously discovered how to create VLANs manually, using the `vlan` Cisco IOS command. Read the following sections to see how you can use the VLAN Trunking Protocol (VTP) to create and manage VLANs automatically.

VTP creates and manages VLANs

VTP is a data-link (Layer 2) protocol that facilitates the management of VLANs across several switches in a network. Using VTP, you do not need to log in to each switch to create and name each VLAN manually. Managing VLANs manually on each switch in your network works well for a few switches. VTP is a better solution in large enterprise networks.

VTP does not manage VLAN port membership

You still need to assign ports to each VLAN either manually or automatically:

+ **Manually:** You can assign ports to each VLAN on each switch, using the `switchport access vlan <vlan #>` Cisco IOS command.

+ **Automatically:** You can let VMPS (VLAN Membership Policy Server) assign ports to each VLAN across your network according to the MAC address of each device connecting to the LAN.

VTP benefits

Here are the advantages of using VTP to manage VLANs in your network:

+ **Simplified VLAN management:** Managing VLANs manually on each switch in a large network can become a management nightmare. VTP solves this problem by centralizing VLAN management on a single switch, or a few switches, and keeping all other switches in sync, automatically.

+ **Flexible VLAN management:** VTP keeps track of any VLAN change. Whenever a VLAN is created or removed, VTP notifies all switches in the network about the change with no intervention of the network administrator.

VTP domain

VTP works with VTP domains: group of switches that have the same VTP domain name. VTP domains allow a network administrator to have different VLAN management policies for different parts of the network. VTP manages switches within each VTP domain. So, you can set certain management rules for one VTP domain that includes switches at the head office, for example. You can set different management rules for VTP domains that include switches at branch offices. A switch can only be in one VTP domain at a time.

VTP server

VTP manages VLANs using a switch that acts as the VLAN manager in the VTP domain. This switch is called the *VTP server* or *VTP domain controller.*

VTP switch operating mode

A switch can operate in three modes in VTP: server, client, and transparent.

Server mode

A switch in server mode is the VLAN manager in the domain, the VTP domain controller. The VTP server can create, change, and delete VLANs in the VTP domain and propagate VLAN changes to the other switches in the VTP domain.

You can use the `vtp mode server` Cisco IOS command to configure a switch to be a VTP server.

VLAN configurations are saved in NVRAM. This is the default mode for all Cisco switches.

Client mode

A switch in client mode gets VLAN configuration information from the VTP server and sends and receives updates to/from other switches. A VTP client cannot create, change, or delete VLANs.

You can use the `vtp mode client` Cisco IOS command to configure a switch to be a VTP server.

VLAN configuration is *not* saved in NVRAM.

Transparent mode

A switch in transparent mode does not take into account VLAN configuration information pushed by the VTP server. It maintains its own isolated list of VLANs. A VTP transparent switch sends updates to other switches about its own VLANs. However, it does not accept VLANs pushed by the VTP server. A VTP transparent switch can create, change, or delete its own local VLANs.

You can use the `vtp mode transparent` Cisco IOS command to configure a switch to be a VTP server.

VLAN configuration is saved in NVRAM.

Best practice for VTP switch operating mode

It is best practice to configure a core switch as a VTP server and configure all other switches as VTP clients. Core switches are faster, more resilient, and more easily accessed by all switches in the network. Always configure the VTP server on a core switch or on the fastest switch in your network.

Cisco switches are by default configured to be a VTP server. Anytime a new switch is added to the network, configure it as a VTP client before connecting it to the network. This is to avoid the new switch pushing out its empty VLAN configuration before it gets the current VLAN configuration from the VTP server in the network. If the new switch pushes out its empty VLAN configuration before it gets the current VLAN configuration from the VTP server, it can erase all VLAN information in the network.

VTP updates

The VTP server distributes information about new VLANs defined in the VTP domain using a VTP notification. VTP notifications are sent to all switches in the domain. VTP client switches forward the VTP notification on their downstream trunk ports. Each VTP client switch updates its VLAN database when it receives a VTP update notification.

Each VTP notification frame has a *VTP revision number.* Every time the VTP server sends new information, it increases the VTP revision number. VTP client switches keep track of the VTP revision number to make sure that they update their VLAN information with each VTP revision.

VTP pruning

VTP pruning saves some bandwidth on trunk ports and on switches by limiting the number of VTP-update transmissions. When the VTP pruning option is enabled in a VTP domain, VTP client switches only receive VTP-update frames for VLANs that are enabled on each switch.

In other words, if a VTP client switch has ports in the Sales VLAN and in the Marketing VLAN, but has no ports in the Engineering VLAN, that switch will only receive VTP updates for the Sales and Marketing VLANs.

The VTP pruning option is disabled by default, but it's a very useful option, so it is best practice to enable it.

VLAN ID range

Two ranges of VLAN IDs are available:

✦ The normal VLAN range is comprised of VLANs with IDs of 1 to 1005.

✦ The extended VLAN range is comprised of VLANs with IDs of 1006 to 4094.

VTP only manages VLANs in the normal range, with VLAN ID 1–1005. Because VLAN 1 is reserved for administrative purposes, you can only use VLANs 2–1005 with VTP. If you configure a switch in transparent VTP operating mode, you can use the additional VLAN IDs 1006–4094 locally on that switch.

VTP requirements

Before you set up VTP in your network, your switches need to satisfy a few requirements:

✦ **Have a few switches in your network:** This is not really a requirement, but rather a recommendation. VTP works best when you have at least two or three switches in your network. Actually, with two switches, you could probably get away without VTP, but if you plan to scale up your network, you might as well configure VTP from the start. It doesn't make sense to configure VTP when you have just one switch in your network.

✦ **Interconnect switches with crossover cables:** You always connect switches using crossover cables.

 The Cisco SmartPort feature in newer switches enables interswitch connectivity even if you don't use crossover cables. However, the CCNA test expects you to know that switches are always interconnected using crossover cables.

✦ **Interconnect switches with VLAN trunk and EtherChannel** over redundant links.

✦ **Configure one VTP server per VTP domain:** Configure your fastest switch as the VTP server, and configure all other switches in your network as VTP clients. You may also configure VTP transparent switches if you need to have a specific isolated list of VLANs, such as in a branch office, for example.

✦ **Ensure that the VTP domain name is identical:** Configure the same VTP domain name on the VTP server and on all VTP client/transparent switches if you want them to have a uniform VLAN database.

✦ **Ensure that the VTP password is identical:** You can optionally configure a password for VTP communication in the VTP domain. All switches in the VTP domain must have the same password to be able to send and receive VTP updates.

Enabling VTP

After you have verified that VTP requirements are satisfied, you can enable VTP by running the following Cisco IOS commands on switches in your network.

**Book III
Chapter 5**

**Virtual Local Area
Networks (VLANs)**

VTP server switch

```
SW1>en
SW1#configure terminal (or config t)
SW1(config)#vtp mode server
SW1(config)#vtp domain my_vtp_domain
SW1(config)#vtp password my_password
```

VTP client switches

```
SW1>en
SW1#configure terminal (or config t)
SW1(config)#vtp mode client
SW1(config)#vtp domain my_vtp_domain
SW1(config)#vtp password my_password
```

Monitoring and troubleshooting VTP

To monitor your VTP configuration, you can use the `show vtp` Cisco IOS commands on switches in your network. Here is an example:

```
SW1#show vtp status
```

The most common source of problems with VTP is having different VTP domain names or different VTP passwords on your switches. Make sure that the `show vtp status` command reports the same VTP domain name and the same VTP password on all switches in your network.

Another source of problems with VTP is having mismatches between the VTP switch operating modes. Make sure that only one of your switches is set to operate in VTP server mode. Set the other switches to operate in VTP client mode or in VTP transparent mode. Remember that Cisco switches are set to operate in VTP server mode by default, so you need to keep your fastest switch in the default VTP server operating mode and set the other switches to operate in VTP client mode or in VTP transparent mode.

Routing Traffic from One VLAN to Another

At the beginning of this chapter, you read that data-link frames do not cross over from one VLAN to another, by default. VLANs break up broadcast domains at the data-link layer (Layer 2).

You need to specifically configure routing between VLANs to allow data-link frames to travel from one VLAN to another.

This section describes how to configure inter-VLAN routing and discusses the various options available to implement inter-VLAN routing using routers, network (Layer 3) switches, or both.

Each VLAN represents it own isolated LAN (virtual LAN). Imagine that you have 15 computers in three different business departments, five computers in each department. You create three networks of five computers. The five computers are interconnected with each other in each network. But, the three networks are not connected. To interconnect the networks, you need a router or a network (Layer 3) switch.

It's the same with VLANs: You have three virtual LANs, isolated logically. They are interconnected physically, but the network is logically divided along three departments just like in the previous example. As in this example, each five computer sets can communicate within their department VLAN, but they cannot communicate with a computer in another department VLAN. To enable inter-VLAN communication, you need to interconnect the VLANs with a router or a network (Layer 3) switch.

One router per VLAN

This method requires one router for each VLAN. You interconnect the routers. You can choose inexpensive routers because you only need one port to connect to the VLAN and one port to connect to another router. However, routers, especially inexpensive ones, are typically slower than switches. So, this solution does not offer the best performance.

✦ Advantages: Easy to set up and can use inexpensive routers.

✦ Disadvantages:

- *Cost:* Even if you use inexpensive routers, the cost still adds up pretty quickly.

- *Speed:* Routers are slower than switches. It is best to do as much as possible with switches.

- *Latency:* Routers have much higher latency than switches. Also, interconnecting several routers, each handling just one VLAN, is a waste of routing capability.

One large router with one port per VLAN

This method requires one large router that has enough ports to connect to each VLAN. Router prices tend to increase proportionately with the number of ports. So, although this solution may be fairly easy to set up and administer, it is more expensive.

✦ Advantages: Easy to set up, easy to maintain, and good performance.

✦ Disadvantages:

- *Cost:* More router ports means higher cost.
- *Speed:* Although performance is good, routers are slower than switches. You may find that you can get a network (Layer 3) switch for less money than a large router and have the same or better performance.

One subinterface per VLAN (router-on-a-stick)

This method has a funny name, but it is an interesting inter-VLAN routing option. *Router-on-a-stick* leverages the capability to configure trunk ports on a router. It requires at minimum one router with one Fast Ethernet physical interface that can be trunked. You configure subinterfaces on one physical router interface and have each subinterface connect to each VLAN. You use the router to route between subinterfaces.

This method provides better performance, and it's cheaper than having one router per VLAN. It's also cheaper than having one large router with enough ports to connect to each VLAN.

✦ Advantages:

- *Cost:* Cheaper than one router per VLAN or one large router.
- *Good performance:* Much better latency than one router per VLAN.

✦ Disadvantages:

- Need to configure subinterfaces on the router.
- Physical interface is a single point of failure.

Network (Layer 3) switch

This method is similar to router-on-a-stick, except that the virtual interfaces connecting to each VLAN are created internally on a network (Layer 3) switch, not on an external router. This provides better performance than router-on-a-stick. The network (Layer 3) switch must also support routing traffic between the virtual interfaces. Some Cisco switches do not support this feature. For example, Cisco Catalyst 2960 series do not support routing traffic between the virtual interfaces. However, Cisco Catalyst 3550 and 3560 series do. It is best practice to use a core switch such as Cisco Catalyst 6500 series to handle inter-VLAN routing.

This method provides the best performance, and it may be cheaper than using routers for inter-VLAN data frame routing. The choice depends on the number of VLANs in the network, the budget available, and performance expectations

In most combinations of these criteria, network (Layer 3) switches are the best choice. The advantages and disadvantages of using a network switch are as follows:

✦ Advantages:

- *Cost:* Cheaper than routing inter-VLAN data frames with routers.

- *Best performance:* Switches are faster than routers.

✦ Disadvantages:

- Not supported on all Cisco switches.

- Need to configure virtual interfaces and routing between virtual interfaces.

Prep Test

1 **Virtual local-area networks (VLANs) allow you to do which of the following?**

A ○ Subdivide a LAN into several logical LANs
B ○ Subdivide a MAC address into several logical MAC addresses
C ○ Subdivide an IP address into several logical IP addresses
D ○ All of the above

2 **Virtual local-area networks (VLANs) limit the _____ domain.**

A ○ collision
B ○ search
C ○ broadcast
D ○ All of the above

3 **What is a benefit of using VLANs?**

A ○ Keeps things well organized by logically grouping your network based on MAC addresses
B ○ Keeps things well organized by logically grouping your network based on business departments and functions
C ○ Keeps things well organized by logically grouping your network based on Web sites names
D ○ All of the above

4 **You create a VLAN using the _____ IOS command.**

A ○ `virtual lan create`
B ○ `vlan create`
C ○ `vlan`
D ○ `virtual lan enable`

5 **Static VLAN membership involves which of the following?**

A ○ Manually assigning a specific port to a specific VLAN
B ○ Automatically assigning a specific port to a specific VLAN using VMPS
C ○ Manually enabling a specific port with the `virtual lan` command
D ○ Automatically enabling a specific port with the `virtual lan` command

6 **How is data-link traffic identified to belong to a specific VLAN?**

A ○ By tagging each data-link frame with the LAN ID

B ○ By tagging each data-link frame with the IP address

C ○ By tagging each data-link frame with the MAC address

D ○ By tagging each data-link frame with the VLAN ID

7 **What do you need to do to create a VLAN trunk over an EtherChannel logical port?**

A ○ Create the EtherChannel logical port first and set it up as a trunk port

B ○ Create the trunk port first and set it up as an EtherChannel logical port

C ○ Create a VLAN first and set it up as a trunk port

D ○ Create a VLAN first and set it up as an EtherChannel logical port

8 **What is the main purpose of the Dynamic Trunking Protocol (DTP)?**

A ○ To configure EtherChannel logical ports automatically

B ○ To configure EtherChannel logical ports and VLAN port trunks automatically

C ○ To configure VLAN port trunks automatically

D ○ All of the above

9 **VTP updates represent the process by which a VTP server does which of the following?**

A ○ Distributes information about new MAC addresses added to MAC address tables in the VTP domain using a VTP notification

B ○ Distributes information about new EtherChannel logical ports defined in the VTP domain using a VTP notification

C ○ Distributes information about new VLAN trunk ports defined in the VTP domain using a VTP notification

D ○ Distributes information about new VLANs defined in the VTP domain using a VTP notification

10 **VTP pruning represents the process by which a VTP server or client does which of the following?**

A ○ Refuses VTP updates for VLANs that are not active on its ports

B ○ Refuses VTP updates for VLAN trunk ports that are not active on its ports

C ○ Refuses VTP updates for EtherChannel logical ports that are not active on its ports

D ○ Refuses VTP updates for MAC addresses that are not active on its ports

Answers

1 **A.** Virtual local-area networks (VLANs) allow you to subdivide a LAN into several logical (virtual) LANs. Refer to *"Benefits of VLANs."*

2 **C.** Virtual local-area networks (VLANs) limit the broadcast domain. Review *"VLANs subdivide the broadcast domain."*

3 **B.** VLANs keep things well organized by logically grouping your network along business departments and functions. Check out *"VLANs keep things tidy."*

4 **C.** You create a VLAN using the `vlan` IOS command. Check out *"Managing VLANs."*

5 **A.** Static VLAN membership involves manually assigning a specific port to a specific VLAN. See *"Static and dynamic VLAN membership."*

6 **D.** Data-link traffic is identified to belong to a specific VLAN by tagging each data-link frame with the VLAN ID. See *"Identifying VLANs."*

7 **A.** To create a VLAN trunk over an EtherChannel logical port, you need to create the EtherChannel logical port first and set it up as a trunk port. Review *"EtherChannel and VLANs are friends."*

8 **C.** The main purpose of the Dynamic Trunking Protocol (DTP) is to configure VLAN port trunks automatically. Check out *"Dynamic Trunking Protocol (DTP)."*

9 **D.** VTP updates represent the process by which a VTP server distributes information about new VLANs defined in the VTP domain using a VTP notification. Look over *"VTP updates."*

10 **A.** VTP pruning represents the process by which a VTP server or client refuses VTP updates for VLANs that are not active on its ports. Review *"VTP pruning."*

Chapter 6: Voice over IP (VoIP)

Exam Objectives

- ✔ Describing the purpose and implications of VoIP
- ✔ Describing the quality of service (QoS) used with VoIP
- ✔ Differentiating between IP priority at network Layer 3 and class of service (CoS) at data link Layer 2
- ✔ Describing how a Cisco IP phone produces VoIP packets
- ✔ Describing how a Cisco IP phone interacts with a Cisco switch
- ✔ Describing how a Cisco IP phone interacts with a computer host connected to its PC port
- ✔ Describing Cisco Discovery Protocol (CDP)
- ✔ Differentiating between trusting and nontrusting switch access ports
- ✔ Configuring switch access ports for VoIP traffic

*R*ead this chapter to find out about Voice over IP (VoIP). VoIP defines a group of network applications, network protocols, and network devices that carry voice signals over the Internet Protocol (IP). More organizations are choosing to use IP telephony to save costs by concentrating their phone and data traffic over the same IP infrastructure.

Using industry standards, Cisco IP phones, Cisco VoIP gateways, Cisco switches, and Cisco routers can provide IP telephony over the same IP network that is used to provide data connectivity. The Cisco IP telephony solution is now part of the Cisco Unified Communications solution framework that provides a very large array of data, storage, and telephony networking solutions. Cisco IP telephony provides advanced features such as voice mail, contact centers, fax services, advanced call routing and call forwarding, caller ID, and global corporate calling extension numbers.

Cisco IP telephony offers all the communications features one has come to expect from a major telephony solutions provider, yet without the cost of a dedicated corporate phone line network.

Introducing Voice over IP (VoIP)

VoIP protocols and network applications digitize the audio signal received from an IP phone handset microphone. Next, VoIP protocols and network applications cut the digital signal into small pieces and wrap those signal bits in IP packets. The IP packets are sent over the network to an IP telephony gateway that forwards those packets to the destination IP telephone. The destination IP telephone unwraps the IP packets, extracts the digital audio bits, reassembles them in order, converts them to analog sound, and sends the analog sound signal out on the handset speaker.

Several networking products and networking protocols work together to provide the link between two IP phones. However, those networking products, networking standards, and networking protocols are beyond the scope of the CCNA test. You need to know though that an IP phone typically connects to an access port on a Layer 2 switch. That access port needs to be configured for VoIP by enabling the VoIP VLAN and configuring quality of service on the switch and on the access port itself.

VoIP Requires Quality of Service (QoS)

Have you ever noticed sound breaking off at times, or poor sound quality, when using audio instant-messaging programs or IP telephony products and services? This is typically due to VoIP without QoS or VoIP with poor QoS configuration.

Without proper QoS configuration, IP packets carrying sound bits are not sent with high priority. They may get sent behind other packets. This causes the sound to break off or be delayed, or be "scratchy." Voice traffic sent over IP networks requires quality of service (QoS) because sound deteriorates if VoIP packets are not transmitted in an orderly and efficient manner.

Consider the following example. When you send an e-mail, the text is cut into smaller pieces and sent over IP. The receiving e-mail application can simply reorder the text before it displays it, if the text arrives out of order. Also, the receiving e-mail application can request a retransmit and wait to receive the whole text before it displays it, if an IP packet got lost in the transmission. IP phones are more sensitive to IP packet transmission errors and delays. If an IP packet carrying part of a sound gets lost, the IP phone can either render the conversation without that sound, in which case the sound breaks off, or the IP phone can request a retransmit of that packet, in which case you hear a pause in the conversation. In both cases, the sound quality is poor. This is why IP telephony packets are always sent with the highest priority. This is also why you need to configure your switch and your access port to support the VoIP VLAN and to enable QoS on the switch and on the access port.

VoIP uses QoS at two OSI layers:

+ IP priority at the network layer (Layer 3)
+ Class of service (CoS) at the data link layer (Layer 2)

Both values are set by default to 0. VoIP sets them to 5: higher priority.

Class of service (CoS) (IEEE 802.1p)

Data-link (Layer 2) frames can be configured with a certain class of service (CoS). By default, CoS is set to 0. Data-link frames carrying VoIP traffic are usually configured with CoS 5 (higher priority). A switch always processes and sends a VoIP data-link frame with CoS 5 before a regular data-link frame with CoS 0.

The class of service (CoS) data-link (Layer 2) option is defined in the IEEE 802.1p standard. Data-link frames are tagged with the VLAN ID, either by the Cisco ISL VLAN ID tagging method or by the IEEE 802.1q (dot1q) VLAN ID tagging standard to identify the VLAN each data link belongs to. The CoS value is the priority field in the 802.1q (do1q) VLAN tag field. Hence, every data-link frame carries a VLAN ID and a CoS value in the VLAN ID 802.1q tag.

Cisco IP Phone

The Cisco IP phone is an end device that connects to a switch access port configured for VoIP. You see how to configure the switch access port for VoIP later in this chapter. Here you discover a bit about the Cisco IP phone device. Figure 6-1 illustrates a Cisco IP phone.

The Cisco IP phone looks and behaves like a normal phone. It has all the features of a typical business-class phone set, such as a large display, hands-free communication, dual or multiple lines, call waiting, call forwarding, caller ID display, and an illuminated keyboard.

The Cisco IP phone is also a three-port Layer 2 switch. Here are the three ports and their usage:

+ **Uplink (10/100 SW) connection:** This port is reserved to connect upstream to the network switch access port.
+ **PC (10/100 PC) connection:** This port can be used to connect a computer host to the phone.
+ **Internal connection:** The third port is an internal port that connects to the IP phone's central processing unit (CPU).

Figure 6-2 illustrates the ports available on a Cisco IP phone.

Figure 6-1:
Cisco IP
phone.

Figure 6-2:
Cisco IP
phone ports.

You connect the uplink port on the Cisco IP phone to the upstream switch access port. The Cisco IP phone operates in the VoIP VLAN.

You can connect a computer host to the PC port on the Cisco IP phone. The computer host operates in the data VLAN configured on the upstream switch access port.

Now, you realize that the uplink port that connects the Cisco IP phone to the upstream switch access port operates like a VLAN trunk port: It interconnects two switches, the upstream network switch and the Cisco IP phone mini-switch, and carries data for two VLANs — the data VLAN and the VoIP VLAN. In the previous chapter, you read that a Cisco switch access port can carry data for two VLANs: a data VLAN and a VoIP VLAN.

Figure 6-3 illustrates a configuration where you have

✦ A Cisco IP phone connected to an upstream switch access port

✦ A computer host connected to the Cisco IP phone

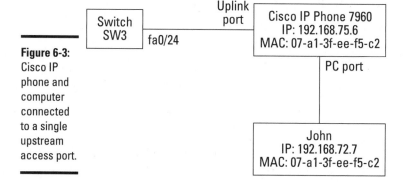

Figure 6-3:
Cisco IP phone and computer connected to a single upstream access port.

The Cisco IP phone builds data-link frames carrying VoIP and sets the CoS at 5 (high priority). It tags the VoIP data-link frames with the VoIP VLAN ID. Next, the Cisco IP phone sends the VoIP frames out on the uplink port to the upstream switch access port.

You would think that the upstream switch processes the VoIP frames with high priority and forwards them to the Cisco VoIP gateway as quickly as possible. Unfortunately, by default, this is not the case. You must specifically configure the upstream switch to trust the IP priority (5) and CoS level (5) set by the Cisco IP phone in the VoIP packets. By default, in untrusted mode, switches override IP priority and CoS values they receive, with the default low priority value (0). You see how to configure the upstream switch in the section "Configuring VoIP on Cisco Switches," later in this chapter.

The Cisco IP phone may receive data frames from the PC port if a computer host is connected. The Cisco IP phone leaves the CoS at 0, the default low-priority value. The Cisco IP phone tags these frames with the data VLAN ID. Next, it sends the data frames on the uplink port to the upstream switch access port. The upstream switch processes the data frames with normal (low) priority and forwards them to the appropriate outgoing switch port.

This is the typical operation flow. You can change the typical operation flow by changing the following:

+ The default configuration of the upstream switch
+ The default configuration of the Cisco IP phone

These configuration options are beyond the scope of the CCNA test, but you do need to know how to configure the upstream switch to trust the IP priority and CoS level set by the Cisco IP phone in the VoIP packets.

Cisco Discovery Protocol (CDP)

Cisco created the Cisco Discovery Protocol (CDP), which allows a Cisco switch to discover the devices connected to its ports. CDP is enabled by default on Cisco switches. CDP is also enabled by default on Cisco IP phones. This protocol is useful in VoIP environments. CDP allows the upstream switch to discover the Cisco IP phone and to negotiate interconnection parameters that are optimum for VoIP.

Negotiating VLAN

The upstream switch communicates with the Cisco IP phone using CDP to set up an interconnection link that allows the Cisco IP phone to send VoIP packets on its uplink port back to the upstream switch, either in the VoIP VLAN or in the data VLAN.

Negotiating CoS

The upstream switch also communicates with the Cisco IP phone using CDP to set up an interconnection link that allows the Cisco IP phone to send VoIP packets on its uplink port back to the upstream switch, either with default CoS level 0 or with high-priority CoS level 5.

Negotiating Cisco IP phone PC port

You can connect a computer host to the PC port on the Cisco IP phone. The computer host operates in the data VLAN configured on the upstream switch access port. By default, the Cisco IP phone leaves the CoS at 0 on data frames received from the PC port. This default option can be changed on the Cisco IP phone. It can also be changed by the upstream switch. The upstream switch can communicate with the Cisco IP phone using CDP to set up the PC port to be trusting or nontrusting:

✦ A *trusting* PC port on the Cisco IP phone trusts the IP priority and CoS level set on incoming IP packets by the computer host connected to the PC port.

   If, for example, the computer host connected in the Cisco IP phone PC port sets the IP priority and the CoS level at 3, and the Cisco IP phone PC port is trusting, it will keep the IP priority and the CoS level at 3.

✦ A *nontrusting* PC port on the Cisco IP phone does not trust the IP priority and CoS level set on incoming IP packets by the computer host connected to the PC port.

   If, for example, the computer host connected in the Cisco IP phone PC port sets the IP priority and the CoS level at 3, and the Cisco IP phone PC port is nontrusting, the Cisco IP phone will reset the IP priority and the CoS level at 0, the default value for IP data packets.

Configuring VoIP on Cisco Switches

Switch access ports can operate in two VLANs: a data VLAN and a VoIP VLAN. This allows you to connect both a computer host and an IP telephone to the same upstream access port. This setup is illustrated in Figure 6-3.

The following sections describe how you configure an access port to support both data and voice VLANs. You also find out how to enable QoS on the switch and on the access port to support high IP priority and high CoS required by VoIP traffic.

Enabling QoS on the upstream switch

To configure VoIP support on the upstream switch, you first need to enable quality of service (QoS) on the switch. To do this, you use the `mls` Cisco IOS command.

For example, to enable QoS on the switch, run the following commands:

```
SW3>en
SW3#configure terminal (or config t)
SW3(config)#mls qos
```

Configuring switch access port to trust CoS

Next, you need to configure the upstream switch access port to trust the IP priority and class of service (CoS) settings of incoming packets from the Cisco IP phone.

For example, to configure the upstream switch access port to trust the CoS level set by the Cisco IP phone on its IP packets, run the following commands:

```
SW3>en
SW3#configure terminal (or config t)
SW3(config)#interface f0/24
SW3(config-if)#mls qos trust cos
SW3(config-if)#switchport priority extend trust
```

Enabling VoIP VLAN on the switch access port

To complete the configuration of VoIP support on the upstream switch, you need to enable the VoIP VLAN on the upstream switch access port. You also configure the VoIP VLAN to use the IEEE 802.1p (CoS) class of service setting to decide the priority of IP packets coming in through the port.

For example, to configure the upstream switch access port to trust the CoS level set by the Cisco IP phone on its IP packets, run the following commands:

```
SW3>en
SW3#configure terminal (or config t)
SW3(config)#interface f0/24
SW3(config-if)#switchport voice vlan dot1p
SW3(config-if)#switchport mode access
SW3(config-if)#switchport access vlan 7
SW3(config-if)#switchport voice vlan 5
```

Here, you configure the upstream switch access port to use CoS to determine the priority of incoming IP packets.

You also set the port to be an access port, and you enable two VLANs on the access port: a VoIP VLAN with VLAN ID 5 and a data VLAN with VLAN ID 7.

Prep Test

Voice over IP (VoIP)

1 What is VoIP?

A ○ A group of network applications and protocols that carries voice over IP networks

B ○ A group of network applications and protocols that allows a Cisco switch port to connect to a Cisco IP phone

C ○ A group of network applications and protocols that allows cell phone service providers to use Cisco IP phones for in-house cell phone network communications

D ○ All of the above

2 Why does VoIP traffic require quality of service (QoS)?

A ○ Because VoIP is unreliable

B ○ Because it is best practice to use QoS, generally, in IP networks

C ○ Because VoIP is not fast enough

D ○ Because sound deteriorates if VoIP packets are not transmitted orderly and efficiently

3 How is VoIP packet priority determined?

A ○ By VLAN ID tagging

B ○ By STP priority and MAC address of the switch

C ○ By IP priority setting on IP packets and CoS setting on data frames

D ○ By IP priority setting on data frames and CoS setting on IP packets

4 The Cisco IP phone sends which of the following?

A ○ VoIP packets with high priority and data packets with default priority

B ○ VoIP packets with high priority and data packets with either default priority or priority set by the computer host connected to the PC port

C ○ VoIP packets with high priority and data packets with priority set by the computer host connected to the PC port

D ○ VoIP packets with default priority and data packets with high priority

5 How is the Cisco Discovery Protocol (CDP) used?

A ○ To help a switch update its MAC address table

B ○ To allow a switch to discover the devices connected to its ports

C ○ To help a switch negotiate connection settings with devices connected to its ports

D ○ All of the above

Answers

1 **A**. VoIP is a group of network applications and protocols that carries voice over IP networks. Refer to *"Introducing Voice over IP (VoIP)."*

2 **D**. VoIP traffic requires quality of service (QoS) to ensure that VoIP packets are transmitted orderly and efficiently to avoid sound deterioration. Review *"VoIP Requires Quality of Service (QoS)."*

3 **C**. The priority of VoIP packets is determined by the combination of IP priority setting on IP packets and CoS setting on data frames. Check out *"VoIP Requires Quality of Service (QoS)."*

4 **B**. The Cisco IP phone sends VoIP packets with high priority and data packets with either default priority or priority set by the computer host connected to the PC port. Read *"Cisco IP Phone."*

5 **D**. All of the above. CDP allows the switch to discover devices connected to its ports. After a device is discovered, CDP helps the switch to get the MAC address of this device and update its MAC address table. The switch also uses CDP to communicate with devices connected to its ports, to negotiate connection parameters and other settings. Look over *"Cisco Discovery Protocol (CDP)."*

Chapter 7: Troubleshooting a Switch Using Cisco IOS

Exam Objectives

- ✔ Describing Cisco hardware and software products and their purposes
- ✔ Gathering troubleshooting information about a Cisco switch
- ✔ Inspecting Cisco switch memory contents
- ✔ Using the show tech-support and the debug commands to inspect a Cisco switch
- ✔ Troubleshooting switch connectivity
- ✔ Gathering troubleshooting information about your network
- ✔ Discovering your network using Cisco Discovery Protocol (CDP)
- ✔ Troubleshooting the startup configuration
- ✔ Troubleshooting the running configuration

*T*roubleshooting a Cisco switch is very similar to troubleshooting a Cisco router. Most IOS troubleshooting commands, such as the debug command, are the same for switches and routers, but the output differs in some cases. Most troubleshooting tools are available for both switches and routers, such as the ping and trace route tools, or the Cisco Network Assistant (CNA). Some troubleshooting tools are only available for routers, such as the Cisco Router and Security Device Manager (SDM) and SDM Express. Other troubleshooting tools are only available for switches, such as the Cisco Device Manager. You learn about switch troubleshooting tools and IOS commands in this chapter.

Troubleshooting Cisco Switches

Read this section to find out how to troubleshoot your Cisco switch using IOS commands and graphical user interface tools, such as the Cisco Device Manager and the Cisco Network Assistant (CNA).

Gathering information about the switch

There are several commands that allow you to gather information about your switch. You review information gathering and troubleshooting commands in this section and find out about some additional commands. You can also use the IOS graphical user interfaces (GUI tools) to gather information about your switch.

Obtaining the IOS version

The first step of the troubleshooting process is finding the particular version of the Cisco IOS that operates your switch. There are several ways to find out the IOS version on your switch:

✦ The boot process output messages display the IOS version.

✦ The IOS image file name contains the IOS version.

✦ The `show version` IOS command displays the IOS version.

✦ GUI tools display the IOS version.

Obtaining IOS version from boot output

The Cisco IOS version and release numbers are displayed during the startup process. Here is an example of the boot loader output displayed on the console of a Cisco Catalyst 2960 switch. The lines in bold font show the version and release numbers of the IOS installed on this switch.

```
Loading "flash:c2960-lanlite-mz.122-37.EY/c2960-lanlite-mz.122-37.EY.bin"...@@@@
   @@@@@@@@@@@@@@@@@@@@@@@@@@@@@@@@@@@@@@@@@@@@@@@@@@@@@@@@@@@@@@@@@@@@@@@@@@@@@@@@@@
   @@@@@@@@@@@@@@@@@@@@@@@@@@@@@@@@@@@@@@@@@@@@@@@@@@@@@@@@@@@@@@@@@@@@@@@@@@@@@@@@@
File "flash:c2960-lanlite-mz.122-37.EY/c2960-lanlite-mz.122-37.EY.bin"
   uncompressed and installed, entry point: 0x3000
executing...

            Restricted Rights Legend
Use, duplication, or disclosure by the Government is
subject to restrictions as set forth in subparagraph
(c) of the Commercial Computer Software - Restricted
Rights clause at FAR sec. 52.227-19 and subparagraph
(c) (1) (ii) of the Rights in Technical Data and Computer
Software clause at DFARS sec. 252.227-7013.

            cisco Systems, Inc.
            170 West Tasman Drive
            San Jose, California 95134-1706

Cisco IOS Software, C2960 Software (C2960-LANLITE-M), Version 12.2(37)EY,
   RELEASE SOFTWARE (fc2)
Copyright (c) 1986-2007 by Cisco Systems, Inc.
Compiled Thu 28-Jun-07 18:07 by antonino
Image text-base: 0x00003000, data-base: 0x00D00000
```

Obtaining IOS version from the IOS image file name

Observe that the Cisco IOS c2960-lanlite-mz.122-37.EY.bin image file is loaded in the preceding example. You can see the Cisco IOS version and release numbers in the filename of the Cisco IOS image file. The image file is named according to the:

✦ Model of the Cisco switch: Catalyst 2960 (c2960)

✦ Edition of the IOS (lanlite)

✦ Version, release of the IOS: Version 12.2 release 37.EY (122-37.EY)

Obtaining IOS version using the Show version command

You can use the show version IOS command to verify the IOS version and release numbers of the IOS running on a Cisco switch. You run the show version IOS command in privileged EXEC mode, as shown in the following example. The lines in bold show:

✦ The version of the Cisco IOS

✦ The version of the Boot loader (bootstrap) program

✦ The Cisco IOS image file that was loaded

```
SW1>en
Password:
SW1#sh version
Cisco IOS Software, C2960 Software (C2960-LANLITE-M), Version 12.2(37)EY, RELEASE
    SOFTWARE (fc2)
Copyright (c) 1986-2007 by Cisco Systems, Inc.
Compiled Thu 28-Jun-07 18:07 by antonino
Image text-base: 0x00003000, data-base: 0x00D00000

ROM: Bootstrap program is C2960 boot loader
BOOTLDR: C2960 Boot Loader (C2960-HBOOT-M) Version 12.2(44r)SE1, RELEASE SOFTWARE
    (fc2)

SW1 uptime is 13 minutes
System returned to ROM by power-on
System image file is "flash:c2960-lanlite-mz.122-37.EY/c2960-lanlite-mz.122-37.
    EY.bin"

cisco WS-C2960-24-S (PowerPC405) processor (revision C0) with 61440K/4088K bytes
    of memory.

[... some output cut ...]

1 Virtual Ethernet interface
24 FastEthernet interfaces
The password-recovery mechanism is enabled.

64K bytes of flash-simulated non-volatile configuration memory.

[... some output cut ...]
```

```
Switch   Ports  Model          SW Version    SW Image
------   -----  -----          ----------    ----------
*   1    24     WS-C2960-24-S  12.2(37)EY    C2960-LANLITE-M

Configuration register is 0xF
```

Obtaining IOS version using the GUI tools

Cisco GUI tools also display the IOS version. The Cisco Device Manager and the Cisco Network Assistant (CNA) show the version of the IOS operating system running on your switch.

Figure 7-1 illustrates the Cisco Device Manager Dashboard screen showing the version of the IOS running on a Cisco Catalyst 2960 switch. The IOS version shows in the *Switch Information* frame.

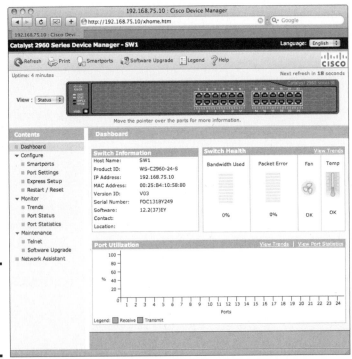

Figure 7-1: Cisco Device Manager Dashboard.

Figure 7-2 illustrates the Cisco Device Manager Software Upgrade screen showing the version of the IOS running on a Cisco Catalyst 2960 switch. The Software Upgrade Web form allows you to upgrade the Cisco Internetworking Operating System (IOS) installed on your switch. Here is the procedure you need to follow to upgrade the IOS on your switch:

✦ Click on the www.cisco.com/public/sw-center/ URL link to access the latest version of the Cisco IOS on Cisco's Web site.

✦ Download the Cisco IOS image (tar file) to your computer hard drive.

✦ Click on *Choose File* and browse to the location where you saved the Cisco IOS image (tar file) on your computer hard drive.

✦ Select the Cisco IOS image (tar file) on your computer hard drive.

✦ Click *Upgrade* to upgrade the Cisco IOS on your switch with the Cisco IOS image file you just downloaded to your computer hard drive.

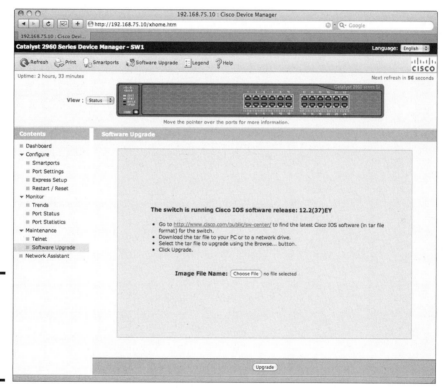

Figure 7-2:
Cisco
Device
Manager
Software
Upgrade.

Book III
Chapter 7

Troubleshooting a
Switch Using
Cisco IOS

Figure 7-3 illustrates a screenshot of the Cisco Network Assistant (CNA) Device Properties showing the version of the IOS running on a Cisco Catalyst 2960 switch. You access the *Device Properties* in CNA by right-clicking the device in the *Topology View* or in *Front Panel View* and selecting the Properties… menu item.

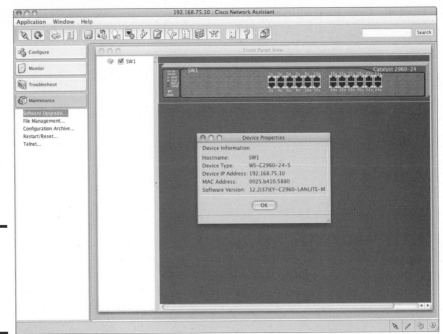

Figure 7-3:
Cisco
Network
Assistant
Device
Properties.

Inspect Cisco switch configuration and memory contents

During the troubleshooting process you need to know the particular configuration of your switch. You also need to know the configuration data stored in the memory of the switch. There are several methods to inspect the configuration of your switch and the data stored in the switch memory:

✦ Use the `show flash` command to inspect flash memory contents.

✦ Use the `show running-config` command to inspect the current running configuration in RAM.

✦ Use the `show startup-config` command to inspect the startup configurations in NVRAM.

✦ Use the `show tech-support` command to inspect all technical parameters on your switch.

✦ Use the Cisco IOS File System (IFS) commands to inspect RAM, NVRAM and flash contents.

Let's review each of these tools.

Inspecting Cisco switch memory contents using the show flash command

You can verify the following technical aspects of your switch using the `show flash` IOS command:

✦ **Presence of a Cisco IOS image file:** You should have at least one Cisco IOS image file in flash memory on your switch.

✦ **Presence of `config.text`:** This is the startup-configuration file. When the switch is started up, the flash memory area that stores `config.text` is mapped as NVRAM and the `config.text` file is mapped as the `nvram:startup-config` file by the Cisco IOS File System (IFS). Hence, if you do not have a `config.text` file in flash memory, the switch does not have a startup configuration: It starts in Setup mode.

✦ **Presence of `private-config.text`:** This file is used to store secured configuration data such as cryptographic encryption keys used for SSH. This file should be there in flash memory when `config.text` is there.

✦ **Presence of `config.text.renamed`:** This file is created whenever you, or the switch IOS, erase the startup configuration file. Recall that you can erase the startup configuration file using the `erase startup-config` IOS command. The switch erases the startup configuration file whenever you reset the switch using the Mode button. In both cases, the startup configuration file is not really removed from flash memory, but rather, renamed to `config.text.renamed`. This ensures that the switch IOS will not find `config.text` when it reboots, but it provides a safety net in case you erase the startup configuration file by mistake.

✦ **Presence of `private-config.text.renamed`:** This file is a hidden version of the `private-config.text` file. The file `private-config.text` is renamed to `private-config.text.renamed` whenever you, or the switch, remove the startup configuration file.

✦ **Presence of `vlan.dat`:** This file stores VLAN data on your switch. The IOS creates some default VLANs that do not require the presence of the `vlan.dat` file. However, if you create additional VLANs, the `vlan.dat` file should be there.

✦ **Free space available in flash memory:** The show flash IOS command displays the free space available in flash memory. It is useful to know how much free space you have in flash memory whenever you want to upload several Cisco IOS image files to the flash memory of your switch. For example, you may want to upload a Cisco IOS image that supports encryption to enable SSH access on your switch. Before you do that, you need to verify that you have enough room in flash memory for both the current Cisco IOS image file and the new one.

You can run the `show flash` IOS command both in user EXEC mode and in privileged EXEC mode. The following example shows the contents in flash memory of a Cisco Catalyst 2960 switch.

```
SW1>show flash
Directory of flash:/
  2 -rwx 1993 Mar 1 1993 00:30:29 +00:00 private-config.text.renamed
  3 -rwx 1398 Mar 1 1993 00:30:29 +00:00 config.text.renamed
  4 -rwx 1398 Mar 1 1993 00:30:29 +00:00 config.text
  5 drwx 512 Mar 1 1993 00:11:25 +00:00 c2960-lanlite-mz.122-37.EY
539 -rwx Mar 1 1993 00:30:29 +00:00 private-config.text

27998208 bytes total (19307520 bytes free)
```

Observe the Cisco IOS image file named `c2960-lanlite-mz.122-37.EY`. This is the IOS image file that is loaded by default when the switch is started up.

Note that you have both a `config.text` file and a `config.text.private.renamed` file in flash memory on this switch. This shows that the switch was reset at some point: This is when the `.renamed` files where created. At that point there was no `config.text` file and no `private-config.text` file in flash memory, just the `.renamed` files. Then, a new startup configuration was created. At that point the `config.text` and the `private-config.text` files were created. However, the `.renamed` files were not removed. This is why you see both the `config.text`, `private-config.text` files and the corresponding `.renamed` files in flash memory.

Inspecting Cisco switch current configuration using show running-config

You can use the `show running-config` IOS command to verify the current running configuration on your switch. You run the `show running-config` command in privileged EXEC mode. The example shows the running configuration of a Cisco Catalyst 2960 switch.

```
SW1>enable
Password:
SW1#show running-config
Building configuration...

Current configuration : 1398 bytes
!
version 12.2
no service pad
service timestamps debug uptime
service timestamps log datetime
no service password-encryption
service sequence-numbers
!
hostname SW1
!
enable secret 5 $1$/nQO$AJ.w7nP4fVgH44NU4gzkZ1
enable password my_priv_password
!
no aaa new-model
system mtu routing 1500
ip subnet-zero
!
!
!
```

```
no file verify auto
spanning-tree mode pvst
spanning-tree extend system-id
!
vlan internal allocation policy ascending
!
interface FastEthernet0/1
!
 [... some output cut ...]

interface FastEthernet0/24
!
interface Vlan1
 ip address 192.168.75.10 255.255.255.0
 no ip route-cache
!
ip default-gateway 192.168.75.1
ip http server
!
control-plane
!
!
line con 0
 exec-timeout 0 0
line vty 0 4
 password my_telnet_password
 login
line vty 5 15
 password my_telnet_password
 login
!
end
SW1#disable
SW1>
```

Inspecting Cisco switch startup configuration using show startup-config

You can use the `show startup-config` IOS command to verify the startup configuration on your switch. You run the `show startup-config` command in privileged EXEC mode. The following example shows the startup configuration of a Cisco Catalyst 2960 switch.

```
SW1>enable
Password:
SW1#show startup-config
Using 1398 out of 65536 bytes
!
version 12.2
no service pad
service timestamps debug uptime
service timestamps log datetime
no service password-encryption
service sequence-numbers
!
hostname SW1
!
enable secret 5 $1$/nQO$AJ.w7nP4fVgH44NU4gzkZ1
enable password my_priv_password
!
no aaa new-model
```

```
system mtu routing 1500
ip subnet-zero
!
!
!
no file verify auto
spanning-tree mode pvst
spanning-tree extend system-id
!
vlan internal allocation policy ascending
!
interface FastEthernet0/1
!
 [... some output cut ...]

interface FastEthernet0/24

 !
interface Vlan1
 ip address 192.168.75.10 255.255.255.0
 no ip route-cache
!
ip default-gateway 192.168.75.1
ip http server
!
control-plane
!
!
line con 0
 exec-timeout 0 0
line vty 0 4
 password my_telnet_password
 login
line vty 5 15
 password my_telnet_password
 login
!
end
SW1#disable
SW1>
```

Inspecting RAM, NVRAM and flash memory contents using the Cisco IFS

You can use Cisco IOS File System (IFS) commands to verify the contents of the RAM, NVRAM, and flash memory areas on your switch. You run Cisco IFS command in privileged EXEC mode.

To see the Cisco IFS directories available on your switch, execute the dir all file-systems Cisco IFS command, as shown in the following example:

```
SW1>enable
Password:
SW1# dir all-filesystems
Directory of nvram:/

    27  -rw-    0   <no date>  startup-config
    28  ----    0   <no date>  private-config

29688 bytes total (29636 bytes free)
Directory of system:/
```

```
    10  drwx   0              <no date>  its
     2  dr-x   0              <no date>  memory
     1  -rw-   582            <no date>  running-config
     9  dr-x   0              <no date>  vfiles

No space information available
Directory of flash:/

     1  -rw-  15572992   <no date>  c2600-ik9o3s3-mz.123-1a.bin

16777216 bytes total (1204160 bytes free)
SW1#disable
SW1>
```

Observe the three main directories on your Cisco switch:

✦ `nvram`: This is the Non-Volatile Random Access Memory (NVRAM), storing the startup-config file, and the private-config file.

✦ `system`: This is the Random Access Memory (RAM), containing the running-config file.

✦ `flash`: This is the flash memory containing the Cisco IOS operating system image. This is the Cisco IOS image that the bootstrap program loads in RAM when the switch boots up.

Observe how the Cisco IFS maps a portion of flash memory as NVRAM during the switch boot process. When you run the `show flash` command, you see the `config.text` and the `private-config.text` files in the listing. These files correspond to the `nvram:startup-config` file and to the `nvram:private-config`, respectively. The `dir all-filesystems` IFS command only lists the Cisco IOS image file in flash, because the other files stored in flash memory are mapped to the `nvram:` directory.

You can list the contents of any of these main directories (file systems) individually using the `dir` Cisco IFS command. You can change your current working directory to any of the main directories using the `cd` Cisco IFS command.

For example, to list the contents of NVRAM specifically, execute the following command:

```
SW1# dir nvram:
Directory of nvram:/
    27  -rw-   0              <no date>  startup-config
    28  ----   0              <no date>  private-config
29688 bytes total (29636 bytes free)
```

Now, change directory to the RAM directory (`system`) and look at the files and directories available there:

```
SW1# cd system:
SW1# dir
Directory of system:/
    10  drwx   0  <no date>   its
     2  dr-x   0  <no date>   memory
     1  -rw-  582  <no date>    running-config
     9  dr-x 0       <no date>         vfiles
```

Finally, to list the contents of flash memory, as seen by IFS, execute the following command:

```
SW1# dir flash:
Directory of flash:/
1  -rw-  15572992  <no date>  c2600-ik9o3s3-mz.123-1a.bin
16777216 bytes total (1204160 bytes free)
```

Inspecting all technical parameters on your switch using show tech-support

The show tech-support IOS command collects and displays information about all technical parameters on a switch. You run the show tech-support command in privileged EXEC mode.

The show tech-support command executes IOS commands to collect and display as much troubleshooting data as possible on your switch, such as these:

+ show clock: Displays the switch system date and time.

+ show version: Displays the version of the IOS operating on the switch. Also shows the version of the bootstrap program, the CPU model, the switch onboard memory and various data about the motherboard.

+ show running-config: Displays the current running configuration on the switch.

+ show stacks: Displays the size and free space on processor and interrupt stacks. This would be the first place to look if you ever get a stack overflow error message. You should always have some free space on all processor and interrupt stacks. Troubleshooting of processor and interrupt stacks is beyond the scope of CCNA.

+ show interfaces: Displays configuration data about interfaces on your switch. This command displays IP configuration data, duplex mode, speed, media type, queue configuration and input and output rates. This data is different from the data returned by the next command (show controllers). Here is the difference: The show interfaces command shows configuration data, whereas the show controllers command shows real time operating statistics collected and summarized by the IOS. Also, note that show interfaces shows configuration data about both the VLAN (port trunk) logical interfaces and the underlying physical interfaces (ports on the switch). The show controllers command only shows statistics about physical interfaces (ports on the switch).

✦ `show controllers`: Displays statistics about interfaces on the switch. These statistics are useful to troubleshoot various network problems. For example, high values in the collision frames and excessive collisions stats indicate poor network segmentation: Verify and minimize the use of hubs in the network. Similarly, an excessive number of Multicast and Broadcast frames indicate potential broadcast storms: Verify the configuration of STP (Spanning Tree Protocol), EtherChannels and VLANs on your switches.

✦ `show user`: displays the users you created on your switch. There are no users by default. You can login to your switch using the various access lines and corresponding passwords if you defined any. However, you can create users on your switch if you have, for example, several network administrators. This is common in large environments.

✦ `show file systems`: displays statistics about the IFS file systems. Note that, unlike the `dir all-filesystems` command that displays the contents of each file system (directory), the `show file systems` command only displays stats about each file system (directory) such as, size, free space, type, and whether you can write to that file system (directory). The output of this command is useful to verify whether you have free space in you file systems. You should have some free space in the `flash:` and `nvram:` file systems. You can also verify whether you can write to each file system: You should see `rw` (read/write) access to the `flash:`, `system:`, `tmpsys:`, `nvram:`, `tftp:`, `rcp:`, `http:`, `ftp:`, and `null:` file systems.

✦ `show flash`: Displays the contents of flash memory on your switch. You learned how to interpret `show flash` command output earlier in this *Troubleshooting* section.

✦ `dir nvram`: Displays the contents of NVRAM file system (directory) on your switch.

✦ `show data-corruption`: Displays whether the switch logged any data corruption. If data corruption was logged this command displays details about the event. This command is beyond the scope of CCNA.

✦ `show memory statistics`: Displays statistics about the memory on your switch. This command is beyond the scope of CCNA.

✦ `show process memory`: Displays statistics about the memory used by each process on your switch. These statistics are useful to troubleshoot some switch performance issues. For example, if your switch underperforms and you notice that one or some processes are using excessive memory (Holding statistic), it is an indication that the process may be leaking memory. This command is beyond the scope of CCNA.

✦ `show process cpu`: Displays statistics about the CPU resources used by each process on your switch. This command is beyond the scope of CCNA.

✦ `show process cpu history`: Displays statistics about the CPU resources used in the last 60 seconds, in the last 60 minutes and in the last 72 hours. The data is displayed in ASCII graphics for each time range. This command is beyond the scope of CCNA.

✦ `show logging`: Displays messages logged in the switch system log file. This command is very useful, because it shows what happened since the switch powered up.

✦ `show env all`: Displays environment data about your switch, such as temperature, fan status, and power supply status.

✦ `show interfaces status`: Displays the state of interfaces on your switch.

✦ `show interfaces status err-disabled`: Displays the state of interfaces that transitioned to `err-disabled` state. An interface transitions to `err-disabled` state if it was configured to be up and `connected`, but something prevented it from transitioning to the "up" state.

✦ `show interfaces switchport`: Displays VLAN and port trunk data about the interfaces on your switch.

✦ `show interfaces trunk`: Displays data about port trunks on your switch, if you created any.

✦ `show vlan`: Displays data about VLANs on your switch.

✦ `show mac-address-table`: Displays data about the MAC address table on your switch. This is a good place to look if you see an excessive number of Multicast and Broadcast frames reported by the `show controllers` command. The MAC address table should contain the MAC addresses of all computer hosts in your LAN. If it doesn't, then, nodes that need to send frames to computers that are not known by your switch, need to send multicast or broadcast frames in the network to find the MAC address of the target. You can ping target hosts from the switch to manually help the switch complete its MAC address table. This would cause the switch to register in its MAC address table the MAC address of the hosts you ping.

✦ `show spanning-tree`: Displays data about STP (Spanning Tree Protocol) on your switch.

✦ `show etherchannel summary`: Displays data about EtherChannels on your switch.

✦ `show ipc nodes`: Displays data about IPC nodes on your switch. IPC nodes are beyond the scope of CCNA.

✦ `show ipc ports`: Displays data about IPC ports on your switch. IPC ports are beyond the scope of CCNA.

✦ `show ipc status`: Displays data about IPC status on your switch. IPC status is beyond the scope of CCNA.

✦ `show cef linecard`: Displays data about Cisco Express Forwarding card status on your switch. CEF line cards are beyond the scope of CCNA.

✦ `show ip mds stats linecard`: Displays data about line cards on MDS (Multicast Distributed Switches) switch. MDS line cards status is beyond the scope of CCNA.

✦ `show sdm prefer`: Displays data about SDM (Switch Database Management) templates on your switch. SDM templates are beyond the scope of CCNA.

✦ `show buffers`: Displays statistics about memory buffers on your switch. Memory buffers are beyond the scope of CCNA.

✦ `show inventory`: Displays the standard UDI (Unique Device Identifier) elements on your switch: PID (product ID), VID (vendor ID), and SN (serial number). UDIs uniquely identify networking devices in a network. UDIs are beyond the scope of CCNA.

✦ `show region`: Displays statistics about memory areas on your switch. This command is beyond the scope of CCNA.

Some commands do not return any output, because the technical aspect they would normally show does not apply to the switch being inspected.

Inspect Cisco switch logs and system messages

System messages and log files are the most useful troubleshooting tools. Cisco switches register events and errors in the system log files as they happen. Each event or error message is logged with a timestamp. Hence, you can look at the log files to know what happened since the switch started. Cisco provides several methods to inspect system event messages and alerts in log files:

✦ Using the `show logging` IOS command

✦ Using the Cisco Network Assistant (CNA)

Let's review each of these tools.

Inspecting the switch logs and system messages with show logging

You can run the `show logging` IOS command both in user EXEC mode and in privileged EXEC mode. The following example shows the results returned by `show logging` on a Cisco Catalyst 2960 switch.

```
SW1>show logging
 Syslog logging: enabled (0 messages dropped, 0 messages rate-limited, 0 flushes,
     0 overruns, xml disabled, filtering disabled)
 Console logging: level debugging, 7 messages logged, xml disabled, filtering
     disabled
 Monitor logging: level debugging, 0 messages logged, xml disabled, filtering
     disabled
 Buffer logging: level debugging, 7 messages logged, xml disabled, filtering
     disabled
 Exception Logging: size (4096 bytes)
 Count and timestamp logging messages: disabled
 File logging: disabled
 Trap logging: level informational, 10 message lines logged

Log Buffer (4096 bytes):

00:00:29: %LINEPROTO-5-UPDOWN: Line protocol on Interface Vlan1, changed state to
     down
00:00:29: %SPANTREE-5-EXTENDED_SYSID: Extended SysId enabled for type vlan
000003: *Mar  1 00:00:31: %SYS-5-CONFIG_I: Configured from memory by console
000004: *Mar  1 00:00:31: %SYS-5-RESTART: System restarted --
Cisco IOS Software, C2960 Software (C2960-LANLITE-M), Version 12.2(37)EY, RELEASE
     SOFTWARE (fc2)
Copyright (c) 1986-2007 by Cisco Systems, Inc.
Compiled Thu 28-Jun-07 18:07 by antonino
000005: *Mar  1 00:00:33: %LINK-3-UPDOWN: Interface FastEthernet0/1, changed
     state to up
000006: *Mar  1 00:00:34: %LINEPROTO-5-UPDOWN: Line protocol on Interface
     FastEthernet0/1, changed state to up
000007: *Mar  1 00:01:04: %LINEPROTO-5-UPDOWN: Line protocol on Interface Vlan1,
     changed state to up
```

Observe log messages 5 and 6 in bold font type. These messages show that the first physical interface (FastEthernet0/1) was started up (connected). Message 7 shows that the VLAN1 logical interface also started up.

Managing the logging system

Cisco switches enable logging by default. All log messages are sent to the console and to the internal log buffer by default. You can use the `logging` IOS command in privileged EXEC configuration mode to control logging settings on a Cisco switch. For example:

- ✦ `logging on`: Enables logging

- ✦ `no logging on`: Disables logging

The `logging` command also allows you to control where system event messages and alerts are logged. Log messages can be sent to the:

✦ **Console:** All system event messages and alerts are displayed on the switch console by default. The `logging console [<level>]` command enables logging to the console and sets the logging `level`. The *logging level* defines which messages are logged. Logging levels are explained further in this section. The `no logging console` command disables logging to the console.

✦ **Internal log buffer:** All system event messages and alerts are written to the internal log buffer by default. The `logging buffered [<level>]` command enables logging to the internal log buffer. The `no logging buffered` command disables logging to the internal log buffer.

✦ **VTY session (Telnet/SSH):** System event messages and alerts are not displayed in virtual terminal (VTY) sessions by default. The `logging monitor [<level>]` command enables logging to Telnet/SSH sessions. The `no logging monitor` command disables logging to Telnet/SSH sessions.

✦ **File in flash memory:** As mentioned earlier, system event messages and alerts are written to the internal log buffer by default. You can configure the logging system to write system event messages and alerts to a specific file in flash memory using the `logging file [flash:<filename>]` command. The `no logging file` command disables logging to a specific file in flash memory.

✦ **Syslog server:** You can configure the SYSLOG protocol on Cisco switches to log system events and alerts to an external computer system. As mentioned earlier, system event messages and alerts are written to the internal log buffer by default. However, this buffer can contain only a limited number of messages, due to the limited amount of memory on a Cisco switch. Configuring a Syslog server allows you to leverage larger hard drive storage available on a management computer system and to centralize system events and alerts logging from several switches onto that single computer host. The `logging trap [<level>]` command enables logging to a Syslog server. The `no logging trap` command disables logging to a Syslog server. The `logging [<IP address>]` command identifies the IP address of the destination Syslog server where system events and alerts are logged. You also need to configure the SYSLOG protocol on the Syslog server computer. You can log system events and alerts to more than one Syslog server by executing the `logging [<IP address>]` command with the IP address of each destination Syslog server. To remove a Syslog server from the logging destination list, execute `no logging [<IP address>]` with the IP address of the Syslog server to be removed from the list.

Cisco logging levels are designed to control the verbosity of the logs. Table 2-4 illustrates the seven log levels.

Table 7-1		Logging Levels	
Level	*Severity*	*Description*	*Syslog Type*
Emergencies	0	Switch is unusable	LOG_EMERG
Alerts	1	Switch requires immediate attention	LOG_ALERT
Critical	2	Switch experienced critical condition	LOG_CRITICAL
Errors	3	Switch experienced error condition	LOG_ERROR
Warnings	4	Switch experienced warning condition	LOG_WARNING
Notifications	5	Switch experienced normal significant condition	LOG_NOTICE
Informational	6	Information message	LOG_INFO
Debugging	7	Debugging message	LOG_DEBUG

Lower severity number means higher severity. This is a bit confusing. Think of it this way:

✦ Severity 0: You have 0 functionality: Switch is unusable due to fatal condition.

✦ Severity 7: You have maximum functionality and log verbosity.

So, for example, if you set logging level 3 (Errors) on the virtual terminal lines (Telnet/SSH sessions) using the command, `logging monitor 3` or `logging monitor errors` the switch only logs messages with severity 3, 2, 1 or 0 out on the virtual terminal lines (Telnet/SSH sessions). It only logs errors, critical events, alerts, and emergency events.

Understanding the output of the show logging command

Observe the first lines of output of the `show logging` command:

```
SW1>show logging
 Syslog logging: enabled (0 messages dropped, 0 messages rate-limited, 0 flushes,
    0 overruns, xml disabled, filtering disabled)
 Console logging: level debugging, 7 messages logged, xml disabled, filtering
    disabled
 Monitor logging: level debugging, 0 messages logged, xml disabled, filtering
    disabled
 Buffer logging: level debugging, 7 messages logged, xml disabled, filtering
    disabled
 Exception Logging: size (4096 bytes)
 Count and timestamp logging messages: disabled
 File logging: disabled
```

```
Trap logging: level informational, 10 message lines logged

Log Buffer (4096 bytes):
[… some output cut …]
```

These lines provide important information about the configuration of the logging system on your switch.

✦ `Syslog logging`: Shows the configuration of the Cisco *system logging process*. This refers to the logging system as a whole on a Cisco switch, not to the SYSLOG protocol and destination Syslog servers. The `Trap logging` field in the `show logging` output refers to the SYSLOG protocol and Syslog server configuration.

✦ `Console logging`: Shows configuration of logging to console.

✦ `Monitor logging`: Shows configuration of logging to virtual terminal lines (Telnet/SSH session).

✦ `Buffer logging`: Shows the configuration of logging to internal log buffer.

✦ `Exception logging`: Shows size of exception logging buffer. This is the size of the internal log buffer.

✦ `Count and timestamp logging`: When enabled this option counts every log message and timestamps last occurrence of each message. This option is disabled by default: Messages are not counted, they are logged and time stamped as events occur. If an event occurs more than once, you see one message logged for each occurrence of the event.

✦ `File logging`: Shows configuration of logging to specific file in flash memory.

✦ `Trap logging`: Shows configuration of logging to Syslog server(s).

✦ `Log buffer`: Shows size of internal log buffer.

Book III
Chapter 7

Troubleshooting a
Switch Using
Cisco IOS

The term *syslog* refers to two different concepts on Cisco switches:

✦ The Cisco *System Logging Process* is the process that manages logging on Cisco switches. Cisco sometimes abbreviates *System Logging Process* to *syslog*. You may also see the term SEMs (system error messages). The term SEMs refers to system error messages generated by the Cisco *System Logging Process*. The `Syslog logging` field in the output of `show logging` refers to the Cisco *System Logging Process*.

✦ SYSLOG is a protocol that allows computer systems to exchange log messages. Cisco supports the SYSLOG protocol to send log messages to a Syslog server to leverage larger hard drive storage available on a management computer system and to centralize system events and alerts from several switches onto that single computer host. The `Trap logging` field in the output of `show logging` refers to the SYSLOG protocol configuration on the Cisco switch.

You can distinguish between the two meanings of *syslog* based on the context of the discussion.

Inspecting the switch logs and system messages with CNA

You learned so far how to inspect system messages in log files using the show logging Cisco IOS command. Read this section to find out how to inspect system messages in log files using the Cisco Network Assistant (CNA).

Figure 7-4 illustrates the System Messages Monitoring tool in the Cisco Network Assistant (CNA) GUI.

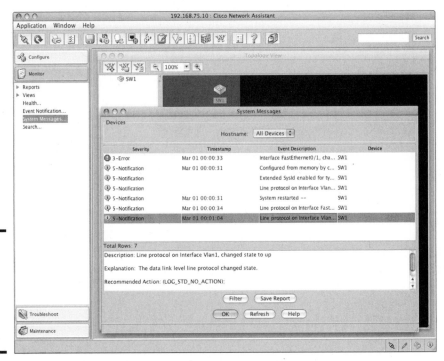

Figure 7-4: Cisco Network Assistant (CNA) – System Messages.

To access the System Messages of a particular switch you need to:

✦ Select the switch you want to inspect in *Topology* or *Front Panel* view.

✦ Select the *Monitoring* tab in the menu.

✦ Click *System Messages…*

Observe that each message line displays:

+ **Severity of the message:** One of the 7 severity levels indicating whether this is warning, an error, a critical condition, or just and informational message, or a debugging message.

+ **Timestamp of the event:** Data and time when event occurred.

+ **Event description:** Short description of what happened.

+ **Device:** Host name of device where the event occurred.

If you click any message line, CNA displays event details in the message details text box, under the message list:

+ **Description:** This is the event description displayed on each message line.

+ **Explanation:** This explains the event providing more details about what happened.

+ **Recommended Action:** This displays a recommended action for events that require the network administrator to remediate a situation that caused the event. Note that in Figure 7-4, the recommended action for the selected message line is LOG_STD_NO_ACTION. This is normal, because the message selected is simply a notification.

Troubleshooting switch connectivity

To troubleshoot connectivity problems on a Cisco switch you need to:

+ Verify cables and patch panels involved in the link.

+ Verify the status of ports on your switch.

+ Test connectivity using `ping` and `traceroute` tools.

Verify cables and patch panels

To verify connectivity between your switch and another device in the network, you first need to verify that you have a valid physical connection between the switch and that device. You need to:

+ Ensure cable connectors are not physically damaged. Pay close attention to the clip securing the connector in the switch port. Look also at the contact lids of the connector to ensure they are not physically damaged and to ensure that they are clean.

+ Ensure the contact lids of the switch port are not physically damaged and that they are clean.

✦ Ensure cable connectors are properly inserted in the switch port and in the device at the other end of the cable.

✦ Ensure cables are not physically damaged. Pay close attention to the cable section exiting the connector; make sure the cable sleeve is not damaged in any way at the junction point in the connector.

✦ Use valid Ethernet cabling: Recall that Ethernet comes in several versions. Each version recommends a specific Unshielded Twisted Pair (UTP) cable. Most network installations today use at least UTP Category 5e (shortly known as Cat5e) cabling. Cat5e cables are well suited for most Ethernet standards. There are several tools that allow you to verify connectivity from one end of the cable to the other. Those tools are beyond CCNA.

When you suspect a broken cable segment (that is, there's no connectivity within that segment), you can replace the broken cable with a cable you know is healthy. This helps you eliminate a potential connectivity trouble. If the switch still experiences connectivity problems, you need to continue the troubleshooting process.

✦ Ensure the link does not extend beyond the distance supported by the Ethernet standard and type of cabling used to connect your switch.

✦ Ensure patch panels are operating within specification.

✦ Ensure distance added by the patch panels does not extend the link beyond the distance supported by the Ethernet standard and type of cabling used to connect your switch.

Verify the ports status on your switch

Once you eliminated cabling from the list of culprits, you verify the status of the ports on your switch. You can either use IOS commands or use Cisco GUI tools to verify port status on your switch.

Verify the ports status on your switch with IOS commands

You can use the following IOS commands to verify port status on your switch:

✦ `show interfaces status`: Displays the state of interfaces on your switch.

✦ `show interfaces status err-disabled`: Displays the state of interfaces that transitioned to `err-disabled` state. An interface transitions to `err-disabled` state if it was configured to be `up` and connected, but something prevented it from transitioning to the "up" state.

✦ `show interfaces switchport`: Displays VLAN and port trunk data about the interfaces on your switch.

✦ `show interfaces trunk`: Displays data about port trunks on your switch, if you created any.

✦ `show vlan`: Displays data about VLANs on your switch.

✦ `show ip interface`: Displays IP information about interfaces on your switch.

✦ `show logging`: Displays system messages logged in the system log since the switch started up. These system messages include port transitions from `down` state to `up` state and vice versa. In some cases, you can also see a port transition to `err-disabled` state if there were any errors preventing the port to open `up`.

Here is an example of `show logging` command:

```
SW1>enable
Password:
SW1#show logging
Syslog logging: enabled (0 messages dropped, 0 messages rate-limited, 0 flushes,
    0 overruns, xml disabled, filtering disabled)
 Console logging: level debugging, 7 messages logged, xml disabled, filtering
    disabled
 Monitor logging: level debugging, 0 messages logged, xml disabled, filtering
    disabled
 Buffer logging: level debugging, 7 messages logged, xml disabled, filtering
    disabled
 Exception Logging: size (4096 bytes)
 Count and timestamp logging messages: disabled
 File logging: disabled
 Trap logging: level informational, 10 message lines logged

Log Buffer (4096 bytes):

00:00:29: %LINEPROTO-5-UPDOWN: Line protocol on Interface Vlan1, changed state to
    down
00:00:29: %SPANTREE-5-EXTENDED_SYSID: Extended SysId enabled for type vlan
000003: *Mar  1 00:00:31: %SYS-5-CONFIG_I: Configured from memory by console
000004: *Mar  1 00:00:31: %SYS-5-RESTART: System restarted --
Cisco IOS Software, C2960 Software (C2960-LANLITE-M), Version 12.2(37)EY, RELEASE
    SOFTWARE (fc2)
Copyright (c) 1986-2007 by Cisco Systems, Inc.
Compiled Thu 28-Jun-07 18:07 by antonino
000005: *Mar  1 00:00:33: %LINK-3-UPDOWN: Interface FastEthernet0/1, changed
    state to up
000006: *Mar  1 00:00:34: %LINEPROTO-5-UPDOWN: Line protocol on Interface
    FastEthernet0/1, changed state to up
000007: *Mar  1 00:01:04: %LINEPROTO-5-UPDOWN: Line protocol on Interface Vlan1,
    changed state to up
SW1#disable
SW1>
```

Observe log messages 5 and 6 in bold font type. These messages show that the first physical interface (FastEthernet0/1) was started up (connected). Message 7 shows that the VLAN1 logical interface also started up.

Book III
Chapter 7

Troubleshooting a
Switch Using
Cisco IOS

Since physical interface FastEthernet0/1 (fa0/1) is "powering" logical interface VLAN 1, as soon as physical interface fa0/1 starts up, logical interface VLAN 1 also automatically starts. If physical interface fa0/1 was shut down, logical interface VLAN 1 also would shut down, unless there are other physical interfaces "powering" it up.

Here is an example of the `show interface status` command:

```
SW1>enable
Password:
SW1#show interfaces status
Port Name  Status      Vlan      Duplex Speed Type
Fa0/1      connected   1         a-full a-100 10/100BaseTX
Fa0/2      notconnect  1         auto   auto  10/100BaseTX
Fa0/3      notconnect  1         auto   auto  10/100BaseTX

[... some output cut ...]

Fa0/24     notconnect  1         auto   auto  10/100BaseTX
SW1#disable
SW1>
```

Observe physical interface (port) FastEthernet0/1 (fa0/1) is:

+ Connected

+ Member of VLAN 1

+ Running in Full Duplex Mode

+ Running at 100Mbps (maximum bandwidth for FastEthernet)

+ Type: 10/100BaseTx (compliant to FastEthernet standard)

All other ports are currently in `notconnect` state: Ports 2 to 24 are not connected right now.

Here is an example of the `show interface switchport` command:

```
SW1>enable
Password:
SW1#show interfaces switchport
Name: Fa0/1
Switchport: Enabled
Administrative Mode: dynamic auto
Operational Mode: static access
Administrative Trunking Encapsulation: dot1q
Operational Trunking Encapsulation: native
Negotiation of Trunking: On
Access Mode VLAN: 1 (default)
Trunking Native Mode VLAN: 1 (default)
Administrative Native VLAN tagging: enabled
Voice VLAN: none
Administrative private-vlan host-association: none
```

```
Administrative private-vlan mapping: none
Administrative private-vlan trunk native VLAN: none

[... some output cut ...]

Name: Fa0/24
Switchport: Enabled
Administrative Mode: dynamic auto
Operational Mode: down
Administrative Trunking Encapsulation: dot1q
Negotiation of Trunking: On
Access Mode VLAN: 1 (default)
Trunking Native Mode VLAN: 1 (default)
Administrative Native VLAN tagging: enabled
Voice VLAN: none
Administrative private-vlan host-association: none
Administrative private-vlan mapping: none
Administrative private-vlan trunk native VLAN: none
[... some output cut ...]

SW1#disable
SW1>
```

Compare the text in bold font type between physical interface FastEthernet0/1 (fa0/1) and physical interface FastEthernet0/24 (fa0/24):

Both physical interfaces are `enabled`: If you plug a network cable in the corresponding fa0/1 or fa0/24 port, you get connectivity through that interface.

Both physical interfaces are member of VLAN 1 (`Access Mode VLAN`). Out of factory, all Cisco switches have a few VLANs pre-created. VLAN 1 is one of them. These pre-created VLANs are reserved for special purposes. VLAN 1 contains all switch ports by default.

The `Operational mode` of physical interface fa0/1 is `static access`. This means that the physical interface (port) fa0/1 is currently connected with a network cable to another device. You see static (or dynamic) access operational mode, as soon as you connect a cable into a physical interface (port) that is enabled and member of a VLAN that is configured for IP networks.

The `Operational mode` of physical interface fa0/24 is `down`. This means that the physical interface (port) fa0/24 is currently not connected with a network cable to another device.

When troubleshooting connectivity, the interface (port) should show up as fa0/1, not as fa0/24. If the operational mode is down, as with fa0/24, either there is no cable connected, or there is a connectivity problem with the cable or patch panels. If you know for sure that a cable is connected in the fa0/24 port and that there are no connectivity problems within the cable or the patch panels, you need to verify the IP configuration of the VLAN where physical interface (port) fa0/24 is assigned. In this case, fa0/24 is assigned to

VLAN 1. Note that, in this case, you know for sure that VLAN 1 is configured properly for IP, because physical interface (port) fa01/1 is also assigned to VLAN 1: If there was a problem with VLAN 1, the operational state of fa0/1 would also be down, and you wouldn't have any connectivity over fa0/1, either. This tells you for sure that fa0/24 is down, because there is no cable connected into that port.

Here is an example of the `show vlan` command:

```
SW1>enable
Password:
SW1#show vlan
VLAN Name                     Status   Ports
---- ------------            -------  --------------------------
1    default                  active Fa0/1, Fa0/2, Fa0/3, Fa0/4
                                     Fa0/5, Fa0/6, Fa0/7, Fa0/8
                                     Fa0/9, Fa0/10, Fa0/11, Fa0/12
                                     Fa0/13, Fa0/14, Fa0/15, Fa0/16
                                     Fa0/17, Fa0/18, Fa0/19, Fa0/20
                                     Fa0/21, Fa0/22, Fa0/23, Fa0/24
1002 fddi-default            act/unsup
1003 token-ring-default      act/unsup
1004 fddinet-default         act/unsup
1005 trnet-default           act/unsup
[... some output cut ...]

SW1#disable
SW1>
```

This switch has 24 ports, all members of VLAN 1, the default VLAN on Cisco switches. Observe that VLAN 1 status is `active`. This command helps you verify that:

✦ The physical interface (Fa0/1) was assigned to a VLAN on the switch.

✦ The VLAN status is active for the VLAN powered by the interface.

If you created additional VLANs, they would appear in this list.

Now, you need to verify that the VLAN powered by this interface has a valid IP address. You can do this by using the `show ip interface` IOS command:

```
SW1>show ip interface
Vlan1 is up, line protocol is up
  Internet address is 192.168.75.10/24
  Broadcast address is 255.255.255.255
  Address determined by non-volatile memory
  MTU is 1500 bytes
[... some output cut ...]
FastEthernet0/1 is up, line protocol is up
  Inbound  access list is not set
FastEthernet0/2 is down, line protocol is down
```

```
     Inbound   access list is not set
[... some output cut ...]
FastEthernet0/24 is down, line protocol is down
   Inbound   access list is not set
```

The lines in bold font type show that VLAN 1 is assigned a valid IP address (192.168.75.10) and that the underlying physical interface (port Fa0/1) is up.

Verify the ports status on your switch with Cisco Device Manager

You can use the Cisco Device Manager Graphical User Interface to verify port status on your switch. You need to:

✦ Browse to the IP address of the switch.

✦ Expand the *Monitor* tab in the *Contents* section.

✦ Select *Port Status* in the *Monitor* tab.

Figure 7-5 illustrates the *Port Status* screen in the Cisco Device Manager.

**Book III
Chapter 7**

**Troubleshooting a
Switch Using
Cisco IOS**

Figure 7-5:
Cisco
Device
Manager –
Port Status.

Verify the ports status on your switch with Cisco Network Assistant (CNA)

You can use the Cisco Network Assistant (CNA) Graphical User Interface to verify port status on your switch.

First, you can verify the port is enabled and that its speed and media type are set to auto-negotiate:

✦ Start CNA and Logon to the switch using `level_15_access` (privileged EXEC mode).

✦ Select the *Configure* tab.

✦ Expand the *Ports* tab.

✦ Select *Port Settings...*

Figure 7-6 illustrates the *Port Settings* screen in CNA.

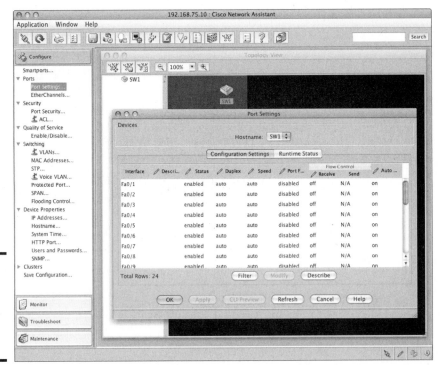

Figure 7-6:
Cisco
Network
Assistant –
Port
Settings.

Next, you verify that the physical interface was assigned to a VLAN on the switch and that the status of that VLAN is active.

✦ Start CNA and Logon to the switch using `level_15_access` (privileged EXEC mode).

✦ Select the *Configure* tab.

✦ Expand the *Switching* tab.

✦ Select *VLANs…*

Figure 7-7 illustrates the *VLANs* screen in CNA.

Book III
Chapter 7

Troubleshooting a
Switch Using
Cisco IOS

Figure 7-7:
Cisco
Network
Assistant –
VLANs.

Now, you verify that the VLAN powered by the physical interface has a valid IP address.

✦ Start CNA and Logon to the switch using `level_15_access` (privileged EXEC mode)

✦ Select the *Configure* tab.

✦ Expand the *Device Properties* tab.

✦ Select *IP Addresses…*

Figure 7-8 illustrates the *IP Addresses* screen in CNA.

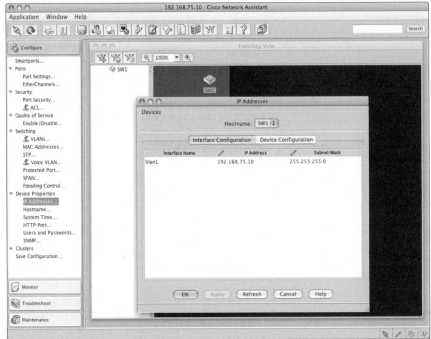

Figure 7-8:
Cisco
Network
Assistant – IP
Addresses.

You can look at Port Statistics to get some performance data about your physical interface. Note that this not only tells you whether you have connectivity over a particular physical interface, it also tells you how fast that interface is.

✦ Start CNA and Logon to the switch using `level_15_access` (privileged EXEC mode).

✦ Select the *Monitor* tab.

✦ Expand the *Reports* tab.

✦ Select *Port Statistics...*

Figure 7-9 illustrates the *Port Statistics* screen in CNA.

Testing connectivity with ping and trace route tools

Finally, you verify that the switch can reach a particular device over the TCP/IP network using the `ping` and `traceroute` IOS commands.

Let's look at each of these tools.

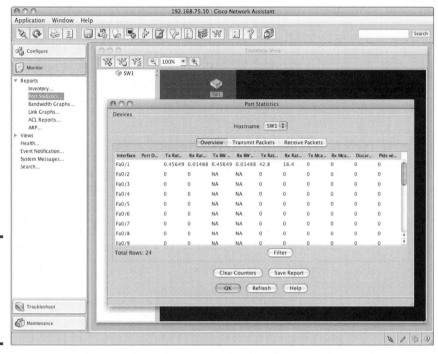

Figure 7-9:
Cisco
Network
Assistant –
Port
Statistics.

Ping tool

The *Ping* tool is an IOS command and CNA tool allowing you to send IP packets to an IP address to test end-to-end connectivity. This is very often the first command that you use to test connectivity between two nodes on a network when you suspect connectivity problems. The nodes can be network devices (switches, routers), computer hosts, IP phones, or any other device that supports TCP/IP network connectivity. Note that the target device must have a valid IP address to use the ping tool. You use the ping in two situations:

✦ Before the troubleshooting process to confirm that there is a connectivity problem. If the ping tool reports failure to send and receive IP packets, you need to troubleshoot connectivity as explained in the *Troubleshooting Switch Connectivity* section.

✦ After the troubleshooting process to confirm that connectivity has been restored and that you can send and receive IP packets between your switch and the remote node. If the ping tool successfully sends and receives IP packets between your switch and the remote node, you successfully restored connectivity.

Here is an example of the `ping` IOS command:

```
SW1>ping 192.168.75.100
Type escape sequence to abort.
Sending 5, 100-byte ICMP Echos to 192.168.75.100, timeout is 2 seconds:
!!!!!
Success rate is 100 percent (5/5), round-trip min/avg/max = 1/2/8 ms
```

To use the `ping` tool in CNA:

✦ Start CNA and Logon to the switch using `level_15_access` (privileged EXEC mode).

✦ Select the *Troubleshooting* tab.

✦ Select *Ping and Trace*...

✦ Select *Ping* tool in the *Ping and Trace* screen.

✦ Enter the *Destination (IP Address/Hostname)*.

✦ Click *Start*.

Figure 7-10 illustrates the *Ping* screen in CNA.

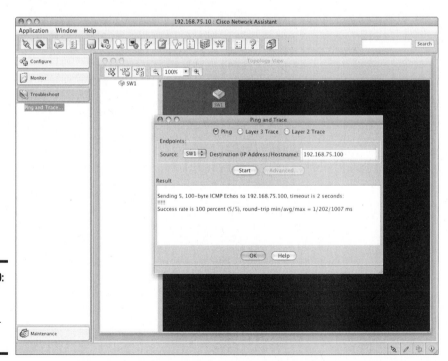

Figure 7-10:
Cisco
Network
Assistant –
Ping.

Trace route tool

The *Trace Route* tool is an IOS command (`traceroute`) allowing you to trace the IP route between two nodes on a TCP/IP network. The nodes can be network devices (switches, routers), computer hosts, IP phones, or any other device that supports TCP/IP network connectivity. Note that the target device must have a valid IP address to use the Layer 3 (Network) `traceroute` tool.

You can also use the Layer 2 (data link) `traceroute mac` tool to trace the Layer 2 (data link) route between two nodes on an Ethernet network. The Layer 2 (data link) `traceroute mac` tool requires that:

✦ Both nodes have valid MAC addresses.

✦ CDP is configured properly and running on your switch.

✦ You execute the `traceroute mac` IOS command in privileged EXEC mode.

The *Trace Route* tool is exposed in the CNA Graphical User Interface (GUI). To use the Layer 3 (network) `traceroute` tool in CNA:

✦ Start CNA and Logon to the switch using `level_15_access` (privileged EXEC mode).

✦ Select the *Troubleshooting* tab.

✦ Select *Ping and Trace...*

✦ Select *Layer 3 Trace* tool in the *Ping and Trace* screen.

✦ Enter the *Destination (IP Address/Hostname)*

✦ Click *Start*.

Figure 7-11 illustrates the *Layer 3 Trace Route* screen in CNA.

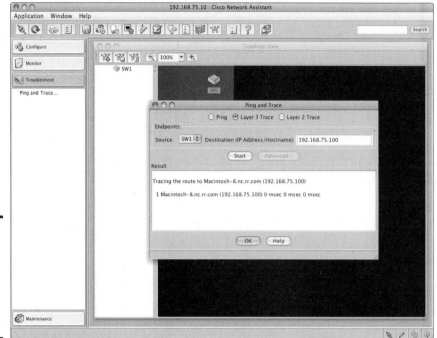

Figure 7-11:
Cisco
Network
Assistant –
Layer 3
Trace
Route.

Gather information about your network

So far, you learned how to gather information about your switch and how to troubleshoot connectivity on a Cisco switch. In this section, you find out how to gather information about the network where your switch connects.

There are several methods allowing you to gather information about your network. You have already seen some of them in previous sections in this chapter. You review information gathering and troubleshooting commands in this section and find out about some additional commands. You can use both IOS commands and graphical user interfaces (GUI tools) to gather information about your network.

Using ICMP

The Internet Control Message Protocol (ICMP) is designed to send control and test IP packets on IP networks. ICMP is a Layer 3 (Network) TCP/IP protocol. Think of an ICMP packet as a specialized IP packet used to discover and control IP network services. Any device that supports IP connectivity also supports ICMP. However, ICMP, or parts of ICMP, can be disabled on a network for security reasons.

Both the *Ping* tool and the *Trace Route* tool are using the Internet Control Message Protocol (ICMP). If ICMP is disabled, the *Ping* tool and the *Trace Route* tool fail. This doesn't mean that there is no connectivity. It is just not possible to verify connectivity using `ping` and `traceroute` on a network where ICMP is disabled.

Typically, ICMP is:

✦ Enabled inside the firewall, within the internal network: ICMP is useful to troubleshoot IP connectivity and performance problems using the *Ping* and *Trace Route* tools. So, it makes sense to enable these tools within a local, firewall-protected network.

✦ Disabled for incoming requests through the firewall: The *Ping* and *Trace Route* tools can be used to find out about the nodes and configuration of a network. Hence, hackers can use these tools to build a "map" of your network. If the firewall allows outside `ping` and `traceroute` requests to flow into your network and if the firewall allows `ping` and `traceroute` results to be returned out of your network, hackers can use the *Ping* and *Trace Route* tools to discover your network.

The *Ping* and *Trace Route* tools can be used on most devices that support TCP/IP connectivity. All UNIX, Linux, Mac OS X, and Windows-based computers provide the *Ping* and *Trace Route* tools. Hence, you can test connectivity and discover your network using these tools both ways between a Cisco switch and a computer host.

Book III
Chapter 7

Troubleshooting a
Switch Using
Cisco IOS

Here is an example of the `ping` command executed on a Mac OS X computer host to test connectivity to the SW1 (`192.168.75.10`) switch.

```
Macintosh-8:~ silange$ ping 192.168.75.10
PING 192.168.75.10 (192.168.75.10): 56 data bytes
64 bytes from 192.168.75.10: icmp_seq=0 ttl=255 time=0.546 ms
64 bytes from 192.168.75.10: icmp_seq=1 ttl=255 time=0.532 ms
[... some output cut ...]
```

The `ping` output shows computer host Macintosh-8 can reach switch SW1 within approximately 0.5 milliseconds (`time=0.546 ms`, `time=0.532 ms`). Observe that `ping` sends each ICMP packet from the Macintosh-8 computer host to the SW1 switch with a sequence number (`icmp_seq=0`, `icmp_seq=1`, ...)

Here is another example of the `ping` command this time executed on a Cisco switch to test connectivity to the Dummies Web site (www.dummies.com):

```
SW1>ping www.dummies.com
Translating "www.dummies.com"...domain server (255.255.255.255) [OK]

Type escape sequence to abort.
Sending 5, 100-byte ICMP Echos to 208.215.179.139, timeout is 2 seconds:
.....
Success rate is 0 percent (0/5)
```

The `ping` output shows that switch SW1 cannot reach the Dummies Web site (`Success rate is 0 percent (0/5)`). This is bizarre, because I can browse to www.dummies.com from SW1's network. Any ideas why `ping` reports no connectivity? If you answer because incoming `ping` (`ICMP` echo) requests are disabled through the firewall of the www.dummies.com network, you are right.

Here is an example of the `traceroute` command executed on a Cisco switch to trace the IP route to the *Dummies* Web site (www.dummies.com):

```
SW1>traceroute www.dummies.com
Translating "www.dummies.com"...domain server (255.255.255.255) [OK]

Type escape sequence to abort.
Tracing the route to dummies.com (208.215.179.139)

  1 192.168.75.1 1007 msec 0 msec 0 msec
  2 cpe-174-099-120-001.nc.res.rr.com (174.99.120.1) 9 msec 8 msec 8 msec
  3 ten13-0-0-202.rlghnca-rtr1.nc.rr.com (66.26.32.65) 17 msec 8 msec 17 msec

[... some output cut ...]

  9 ae-2-79.edge1.Washington3.Level3.net (4.68.17.75) 25 msec
    ae-4-99.edge1.Washington3.Level3.net (4.68.17.203) 25 msec
    ae-1-69.edge1.Washington3.Level3.net (4.68.17.11) 42 msec

[... some output cut ...]

 13 gar3.nw2nj.ip.att.net (12.122.130.109) 25 msec 34 msec 50 msec
 14 12.88.61.178 34 msec 34 msec 33 msec
 15  *   *   *
```

The results returned by the *Trace Tool* show that the SW1 switch reached the www.dummies.com site server through several network routers through the `rr.com`, `Level3.net`, and `att.net` networks. This helps you define where your network sits within the larger global networks. You can see that:

- ✦ Switch SW1 connects into Local Area Network (LAN) 192.168.75.0.

- ✦ The LAN 192.168.75.0 connects to the `rr.com` network through gateway (router) 192.168.75.1.

- ✦ The `rr.com` network connects to the `Level3.net` global network.

- ✦ The `Level3.net` global network is interconnected with the `att.net` global network.

- ✦ The www.dummies.com site server connects into the `att.net` global network.

Here is an example of the `traceroute` command executed on a Mac OS X computer host to trace the IP route from computer host `Macintosh-8` to router RT1 (`192.168.75.40`):

```
Macintosh-8:~ silange$ traceroute 192.168.75.40
traceroute to 192.168.75.40 (192.168.75.40), 64 hops max, 40 byte packets
 1  192.168.75.40 (192.168.75.40)  1.661 ms * 1.227 ms
```

Here is an example of the `traceroute` command executed on a Mac OS X computer host to trace the IP route from computer host `Macintosh-8` to switch `SW1`:

```
Macintosh-8:~ silange$ traceroute 192.168.75.10
traceroute to 192.168.75.10 (192.168.75.10), 64 hops max, 40 byte packets
 1  192.168.75.10 (192.168.75.10)  0.990 ms * 0.826 ms
```

Observe the preceding performance figures in bold font type. Why are switch `SW1` times faster than router `RT1` times? If you answer, because a switch is typically faster than a router, because it doesn't need to process IP packets, just data-link frames, you are right.

Here is an example of the `traceroute` command executed on a Mac OS X computer host to trace the IP route to the Dummies Web site (www. dummies.com):

```
Macintosh-8:~ silange$ traceroute dummies.com
traceroute to dummies.com (208.215.179.139), 64 hops max, 40 byte packets
 1  192.168.75.1 (192.168.75.1)  2.454 ms  1.891 ms  1.686 ms
 2  cpe-174-099-120-001.nc.res.rr.com (174.99.120.1)  9.994 ms  11.131 ms  10.260
    ms
 3  ten13-0-0-202.rlghnca-rtr1.nc.rr.com (66.26.32.65)  26.870 ms  13.329 ms
    13.247 ms

[... some output cut ...]

 9  ae-2-79.edge1.Washington3.Level3.net (4.68.17.75)  25.284 ms ae-4-99.edge1.
    Washington3.Level3.net (4.68.17.203)  26.751 ms ae-3-89.edge1.Washington3.
    Level3.net (4.68.17.139)  37.998 ms

[... some output cut ...]

13  gar3.nw2nj.ip.att.net (12.122.130.109)  32.668 ms  31.946 ms  31.588 ms
14  12.88.61.178 (12.88.61.178)  34.915 ms  32.394 ms  31.880 ms
15  * * *
```

The output of `traceroute dummies.com` on the Mac OS X computer host is very similar to the output of `traceroute dummies.com` on the SW1 switch.

The `traceroute` command on Windows is actually named `tracert`. So, you execute `tracert` instead of `traceroute` on Windows-based computer hosts.

Here is an example of the `tracert` command executed on a Windows computer host to trace the IP route to the *eTips Dummies* Web site (etips. dummies.com):

```
C:\> tracert etips.dummies.com

Tracing route to etips.dummies.com [12.165.240.180] over a maximum of 30 hops:

 1   2.200 ms   1.649 ms   1.726 ms 192.168.75.1 [192.168.75.1]
 2   9.315 ms   8.800 ms   9.282 ms cpe-174-099-120-001.nc.res.rr.com [174.99.120.1]
 3  13.422 ms  15.031 ms  13.974 ms ten13-0-0-202.rlghnca-rtr1.nc.rr.com
     [66.26.32.65]

 [... some output cut ...]

 9  32.835 ms  31.070 ms  36.398 ms ae-61-61.ebr1.Washington1.Level3.net
     (4.69.134.129)

 [... some output cut ...]

16  72.789 ms  59.959 ms  60.742 ms gar1.ipsin.ip.att.net [12.122.133.109]
17  62.420 ms  59.553 ms  61.310 ms 12.86.112.170 [12.86.112.170]
18   *  *  *
```

Observe that Windows writes the performance statistics before the hop
host name and IP address. Note also that Windows writes the IP addresses
between square brackets instead of curved brackets. Otherwise, the *Trace
Route* tool results are similar on all platforms.

Using CNA

You can use the Cisco Network Assistant to discover the network surrounding your switch. CNA provides a Graphical User Interface (GUI) allowing the
network administrator to have both a global and detailed views of the Cisco
networking environment.

Although CNA monitors and manages both Cisco switches and Cisco routers, it is intended more for switches than for routers. Routers are typically
monitored and managed using either the Cisco SDM (Security and Device
Manager) tool, or the Cisco SDM Express tool.

You download the CNA software package from Cisco Web site (cisco.com).
CNA is provided for free by Cisco.

Here are the features of CNA that allow you to discover the network surrounding your switch:

✦ **Topology View:** The topology view provides a global view of your Cisco
   network. You see both the switch you connect to and network devices
   that are connected to the switch. Figure 7-12 shows the SW1 switch and
   its neighbor router RT1. Observe that router RT1 is not supported by
   CNA. RT1 is an older Cisco 2621 series router that is unsupported by
   CNA version 2.5.

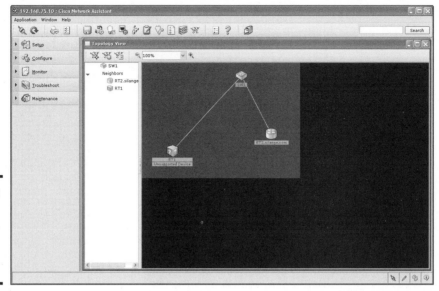

Figure 7-12:
Cisco
Network
Assistant –
Topology
View.

✦ ***Ping and Trace* tools:** The *Ping and Trace* tools are used to verify connectivity to neighboring devices from your switch. The topology view provides you a quick overview of your network. The ping and trace route tools allow you to verify connectivity to those devices. You learned previously how to use the Ping and Trace tools in the section "Using ICMP to Discover Network," and in the section "Testing connectivity using `ping` and `traceroute` tools."

Using CDP

The *Cisco Discovery Protocol (CDP)* is a proprietary Cisco Layer 2 (data link) protocol. CDP is enabled by default on most Cisco switches and routers.

CDP is designed to enable Cisco networking devices to discover each other. The CDP protocol is used, for example, to build the topology view in CNA. Recall that the CNA topology view shows the neighbors of a Cisco switch or router.

CDP is very useful to discover the landscape of your network. Assume that you know the IP address of only one switch or only one router in your network. To discover other devices in your network, you can:

✦ Connect to the IP address of the switch or router you know.

✦ Use CDP IOS commands to discover:

   • CDP configuration

   • Devices in the network

**Book III
Chapter 7**

**Troubleshooting a
Switch Using
Cisco IOS**

Configure CDP

For example, to view the CDP configuration on your switch, execute the `show cdp` IOS command:

```
SW1>show cdp
Global CDP information:
    Sending CDP packets every 60 seconds
    Sending a holdtime value of 180 seconds
    Sending CDPv2 advertisements is  enabled
```

If the CDP protocol is not enabled on your switch or router, the `show cdp` command reports "`% CDP is not enabled`". You can enable CDP using the `cdp run` IOS command like this:

```
SW1> enable         (or en)
Password: my_priv_encrypt_password
SW1# configure terminal      (or config t, or conf t)
SW1(config)# cdp run
SW1(config)# exit
SW1# copy running-configuration startup-configuration
Destination filename [startup-config]?  <press Enter>
Building configuration...
[OK]
SW1# disable
SW1>
```

To see available CDP IOS commands, use the contextual help system:

```
SW1> enable         (or en)
Password: my_priv_encrypt_password
SW1# configure terminal      (or config t, or conf t)
SW1(config)# cdp ?
  advertise-v2 CDP sends version-2 advertisements
  holdtime     Specify the holdtime to be sent in packets
  run          Enable CDP
  timer        Specify the rate at which CDP packets are sent
```

Observe that you need to be in privileged EXEC global configuration mode to execute CDP configuration commands.

There are two CDP parameters that you can control with the `cdp` command:

✦ `holdtime`: CDP packets have a hold time value (in seconds) that determines how long the receiver keeps packets. This helps receivers that keep CDP information about their neighbors, even if CDP momentarily stops sending updates.

✦ `timer`: CDP packets are constantly exchanged between CDP-enabled switches and routers to keep track of changes in the network. The *timer* parameter determines the frequency (in seconds) at which these packets are sent.

You can enable or disable CDP individually on each interface. To do so, you:

✦ Select the interface on which you want to enable or disable CDP.

✦ Execute `cdp enable` to enable CDP on that interface.

✦ Execute `no cdp enable` to disable CDP on that interface.

By default, CDP is enabled globally on Cisco devices: CDP is enabled on all interfaces on Cisco devices. CDP consumes some bandwidth sending packets about networking devices in the LAN. You may choose to disable CDP on certain interfaces if, for example, you need those interfaces to perform at top speed.

Discover your network using CDP

When CDP is enabled and configured, you can use it to discover the landscape of your network. There are several discovery options for the `show cdp` command. Read on to find out about each of these CDP network discovery commands.

Discover neighbor devices

To discover the neighbors of switch SW1, use the `show cdp neighbors` IOS command:

```
SW1>sh cdp neighbors
Capability Codes:
R-Router, T-Trans Bridge, B-Source Route Bridge
S-Switch, H-Host, I-IGMP, r - Repeater, P - Phone

Device ID  Local Intrfce  Holdtme  Capability  Platform  Port ID
RT2.silange.com  Fas 0/7  175  R S I  1801  Fas 7
RT2.silange.com  Fas 0/5  175  R S I  1801  Fas 1
RT1  Fas 0/1  146  R I  2621  Fas 0/0
```

The output shows that switch SW1 is connected to:

✦ Router RT2 using two interfaces:

  • SW1 interface 7 (Fas 0/7) connects to RT2 interface 7 (Fas7)

  • SW1 interface 5 (Fas 0/5) connects to RT2 interface 1 (Fas1)

✦ Router RT1 using one interface:

  • SW1 interface 1 (Fas 0/1) connects to RT2 interface 0 (Fas 0/0)

Observe that you see both the local interface on SW1 (`Local Intrfce`) and the remote interface on RT2 (`Port ID`) in the output of `show cdp neighbors`.

The show cdp neighbors IOS command reports the platform and capabilities of each remote device:

✦ RT2 is reported to be an 1801 series router with router (R), switch (S) and ICMP (I) capabilities.

✦ RT1 is reported to be a 2621 series router with router (R) and ICMP (I) capabilities.

To get more details about the remote RT2 router, use the detail argument with the show cdp neighbors command.

You can also execute the show cdp entry * command on SW1 to view details about devices in the vicinity of switch SW1. The show cdp entry * command and the show cdp neighbors detail command display the same output.

Here are the items that are reported by the show cdp neighbors detail command, in addition to the summary command:

✦ IP address of remote device

✦ Cisco IOS software version of remote device

✦ CDP advertisement version

✦ VTP (VLAN Trunk Protocol) Management Domain of remote device

✦ Native VLAN of remote device

✦ Duplex mode of the link to the remote device

You can use either the show cdp neighbors detail command or the the show cdp entry * command to view details about devices in the vicinity of the switchswtich or router where you run the show cdp command.

The show cdp entry * command can filter the output if you use one of the following arguments:

✦ protocol: Shows only the IP address of each remote node.

✦ version: Shows only the Cisco IOS software version of each remote node.

Viewing interface status and configuration

To discover the status and configuration of interfaces on switch SW1, use the show cdp interface IOS command.

Troubleshooting the startup configuration

If your switch has trouble starting up, there may be problems with the startup configuration. To verify whether the startup configuration is causing problems during startup, you can:

✦ Boot the switch loading a known good startup configuration file, if you have one. You should have one if you followed the best practice to backup your startup configuration file to a backup computer host. If the switch starts up fine when you load the known good startup configuration file, you can simply replace the faulty startup configuration file with the known good one.

✦ Boot the switch without loading the startup configuration file. If the switch starts up fine when you do not load the startup configuration, chances are there is something wrong in the startup configuration, or the startup configuration file is corrupted.

To boot the switch without loading the startup configuration file, you need to interrupt the automatic boot process using one of these methods:

✦ Use the `boot` command to enable manual booting.

✦ Press the Mode button during the boot process.

✦ Press Ctrl-Break during the boot process.

Either of these methods brings you at the `switch:` manual boot prompt. The manual boot prompt allows you to control the boot process of the switch. Here are the steps to boot up the switch manually, without loading the startup configuration file from NVRAM:

✦ Manually initialize the flash file system:

```
switch: flash_init

Initializing Flash...
mifs[2]: 0 files, 1 directories
mifs[2]: Total bytes     :    3870720
mifs[2]: Bytes used      :       1024
mifs[2]: Bytes available :    3869696
mifs[2]: mifs fsck took 0 seconds.
mifs[3]: 518 files, 19 directories
mifs[3]: Total bytes     :   27998208
mifs[3]: Bytes used      :    8687616
mifs[3]: Bytes available :   19310592
mifs[3]: mifs fsck took 5 seconds.
...done Initializing Flash.
```

✦ Hide the startup configuration file to prevent the IOS from loading it.

```
switch: rename flash:config.text flash:config.text.old
```

✦ Boot the switch manually and wait for IOS to finish loading in RAM.

```
switch: boot
```

If the switch starts up fine, you need to rebuild a new, valid startup configuration file, using the setup utility:

✦ Execute the setup utility to setup your switch.

```
SW1>enable              (or en)
SW1# setup
--- System Configuration Dialog ---
Continue with configuration dialog? [yes/no]: yes

[… some output cut …]
```

✦ Save the current running-configuration over the startup configuration file in NVRAM.

```
SW1#copy running-config startup-config
Destination filename [startup-config]?
Building configuration...
[OK]
```

✦ Reboot your switch.

```
SW1# reload
```

Troubleshooting the running configuration

If your switch reports errors, alerts, or warnings during normal operation, there may be something wrong with the running configuration. To verify whether the running configuration is causing problems, you can:

✦ Boot the switch loading a known good startup configuration file, if you have one. You should have one if you followed the best practice to backup your startup configuration file to a backup computer host.

  • If the switch operates fine when you load the known good startup configuration file, you can simply replace the faulty startup configuration file with the known good one.

  • If the switch still reports errors, alerts, or warnings when you load the known good startup configuration file, the problem may not be related to the running configuration. Read on.

✦ If problems persist even after you start the switch with a known good startup configuration, boot the switch without loading a startup configuration at all.

- If the switch starts up and operates fine without a startup configuration, chances are there is something wrong in the startup configuration, or the startup configuration file is corrupted. You need to fix the startup configuration. Refer to the section "Troubleshooting the startup configuration" to see how to fix the startup configuration.

- If the switch still reports errors, alerts, or warnings, even without a startup configuration, the problem may not be related to the startup configuration. Read on.

If problems persist when you start the switch without a startup configuration, the startup and the running configurations are not the cause of the problems. You need to use other troubleshooting tools to find out the culprit:

✦ **Inspect the logs and system messages:** First, look at the logs and system messages, searching for any error messages, fatal exceptions, alerts, and warnings. Refer to the section "Inspect Cisco switch logs and system messages" earlier in this chapter to see how to manage and inspect the logs and system messages.

- If you notice any error message, fatal exception, alert, or warning in the logs or in the system messages, you need to correct that issue.

- If you do not notice error messages, fatal exceptions, alerts, and warnings in the logs or in the system messages, read on.

✦ **Use the** `show tech-support` **command:** You can use this command to inspect many technical aspects on your switch. Look out for any error messages, fatal exceptions, alerts, or warnings in the output of the `show tech-support` command. Refer to the section "Inspect Cisco Switch Configuration and Memory Contents" earlier in this chapter to see how to use the `show tech-support` command and how to interpret its output.

✦ **Use the** `debug` **command:** This command provides a wealth of technical information about the operation of your switch.

Using the Debug command

The `debug` command is a very useful troubleshooting tool. This command enables *debug mode* on the switch. In debug mode, the switch displays and logs detailed information about ongoing operations, including any error messages, fatal exceptions, alerts, and warnings.

Best practice

You can enable debug mode using the `debug` command on specific components and protocols. It is best practice to enable debug mode selectively on certain components or protocols that you suspect are troublesome. It is not recommended to enable debug mode on all components, features and protocols, because the debug process has priority over all other processes on your switch. This may severely impact the performance of your switch, to the point of rendering it unusable.

You execute the `debug` command in privileged EXEC mode.

To enable debug mode on a specific component, feature, or protocol, execute the `debug` command suffixed by the component, feature, or protocol name. Many components, features and protocols have various items that can be monitored in debug mode. For example, there are several aspects of STP (Spanning Tree Protocol) that you can debug:

```
SW1#debug spanning-tree ?
  all              All Spanning Tree debugging messages
  backbonefast     BackboneFast events
  bpdu             Spanning tree BPDU
  bpdu-opt         Optimized BPDU handling
  config           Spanning tree config changes
  csuf/csrt        STP CSUF/CSRT
  etherchannel     EtherChannel support
  events           Spanning tree topology events
  exceptions       Spanning tree exceptions
  general          Spanning tree general
  mstp             MSTP debug commands
  pvst+            PVST+ events
  root             Spanning tree root events
  snmp             Spanning Tree SNMP handling
  switch           Switch Shim debug commands
  synchronization  STP state sync events
  uplinkfast       UplinkFast events
SW1#
SW1# debug spanning-tree general
Spanning Tree general debugging is on
SW1#
```

You just enabled general debugging for STP. Now, you will see the following messages displayed on the switch console and logged in the system logs whenever connected switch ports return STP statistics:

```
SW1#
000012: 00:18:35: Returning spanning tree port stats: FastEthernet0/1 (1A32264)
000013: 00:18:35: Returning spanning tree port stats: FastEthernet0/5 (1A2E790)
000014: 00:18:35: Returning spanning tree port stats: FastEthernet0/7 (1A330B0)
000015: 00:19:35: Returning spanning tree port stats: FastEthernet0/1 (1A32264)
000016: 00:19:35: Returning spanning tree port stats: FastEthernet0/5 (1A2E790)
000017: 00:19:35: Returning spanning tree port stats: FastEthernet0/7 (1A330B0)
```

To disable debugging of a specific component, feature, or protocol, execute the `no debug` command followed by the component, feature, or protocol. For example, to disable general STP debugging, execute:

```
SW1# no debug spanning-tree general
Spanning Tree general debugging is off
SW1#
```

To disable all debugging, execute:

```
SW1# no debug all
All possible debugging has been turned off
SW1#
```

Prep Test

1 **You can obtain the version of the IOS on your switch by looking at**

- **A** ○ The output messages displayed during the boot process
- **B** ○ The IOS image file name
- **C** ○ The show version command output
- **D** ○ All of the above

2 **You can inspect the contents stored in the flash memory of a Cisco switch by using**

- **A** ○ The show flash and show tech-support IOS commands
- **B** ○ Cisco IFS (IOS file System) commands
- **C** ○ Cisco Network Assistant (CNA)
- **D** ○ All of the above

3 **You can inspect the inspect the configuration of a Cisco switch by using**

- **A** ○ The show flash IOS command
- **B** ○ The show startup-config command and the show running-config command
- **C** ○ The Cisco Router and Security Device Manager (SDM)
- **D** ○ All of the above

4 **You can inspect the log files and system messages on a Cisco switch by using**

- **A** ○ The show logging IOS command
- **B** ○ The show log-config IOS command
- **C** ○ The Cisco Router and Security Device Manager (SDM)
- **D** ○ All of the above

5 **You can configure the logging system on a Cisco switch by using**

- **A** ○ The log-config IOS command
- **B** ○ The logging IOS command
- **C** ○ The Cisco Router and Security Device Manager (SDM)
- **D** ○ All of the above

6 **To troubleshoot connectivity on a Cisco switch, you need to verify**

- **A** ○ Continuity of signal through cables and patch panels involved in the link
- **B** ○ Connectors involved in the link are properly making contact
- **C** ○ Switch ports involved in the link are up, and properly configured
- **D** ○ All of the above

7 **The ICMP (Internet Control Message Protocol) is designed to send**

A ○ HTTP text over IP networks

B ○ E-mail messages over IP networks

C ○ Control and test IP packets over IP networks

D ○ All of the above

8 **The ping and trace route tools use**

A ○ The ICMP protocol

B ○ The DHCP protocol

C ○ CHAP authentication

D ○ All of the above

9 **The ping tool allows you to**

A ○ Discover the network hops in a WAN

B ○ Send IP packets to an IP address to test end-to-end connectivity

C ○ Trace the IP route between two nodes on a TCP/IP network

D ○ All of the above

10 **The trace route tool allows you to**

A ○ Discover the network hops in a WAN

B ○ Send IP packets to an IP address to test end-to-end connectivity

C ○ Trace the IP route between two nodes on a TCP/IP network

D ○ All of the above

Answers

1 **D.** All of the above

2 **D.** All of the above

3 **B.** Using show startup-config command and the show running-config command

4 **A.** The show logging IOS command

5 **B.** The logging IOS command

6 **D.** All of the above

7 **C.** Send control and test IP packets over IP networks

8 **A.** Use the ICMP protocol

9 **B.** An IOS command and CNA tool allowing you to send IP packets to an IP address to test end-to-end connectivity

10 **C.** An IOS command and CNA tool allowing you to trace the IP route between two nodes on a TCP/IP network

Book IV

Routing with Cisco Routers

"I didn't know they made skins for mainframes."

Contents at a Glance

Chapter 1: Introducing Layer 3 Routers

Exam Objectives

✔ Describing network OSI Layer 3 and how it relates to Layer 3 routers

✔ Describing the purpose of a Layer 3 router

✔ Differentiating a Layer 3 router from a Layer 2 switch

✔ Describing basic Layer 3 router functions

*R*ecall that Layer 3 in the Open Systems Interconnection (OSI) model is the network layer. The main function of network layer devices and protocols is to *route data packets* between hosts. Routing means choosing the best route to send packets between two hosts. The hosts can be next to each other or across the globe. Whereas the data link layer (Layer 2) routes data frames locally between two devices in the same LAN, the network layer (Layer 3) routes data packets between two devices in separate LANs. In other words, the data link layer sends data *within* the same LAN, whereas the network layer routes data *between* LANs.

Layer 3 — Network Layer Review

The network layer assigns logical addresses (IP addresses) to all devices in the network to be able to identify each source host, each destination host, as well as each network through which packets need to be routed. Logical addresses are assigned at the network protocol level as opposed to physical addresses, which are assigned on a physical device, such as a network card.

The network layer does the following:

✦ Receives each data segment from the transport layer on the sending host

✦ Wraps up the segment in a *data packet* along with global routing data (source and destination logical IP addresses)

✦ Sends the data packet down to the data link layer to prepare it to be sent over the LAN connection

The data link layer does the following:

+ Receives each packet from the network layer on the sending host
+ Wraps up the packet in a *data frame* along with local routing data (source and destination physical MAC addresses)
+ Sends the data frame down to the physical layer to code an electrical or optical signal

The physical layer transmits the data frame over a wire or over the air in wireless networks.

On the receiving host, the data link layer does the following:

+ Unwraps the data frame received
+ Extracts the packet out of the data frame
+ Sends the packet up to the network layer

On the receiving host, the network layer does the following:

+ Unwraps the data packet received
+ Extracts the data segment from the data packet
+ Sends the data segment up to the transport layer

The Internet Protocol (IP) is the TCP/IP protocol that operates at Layer 3 to handle network functions. Hence, whenever you consider Layer 3 in TCP/IP, you need to think about IP and logical IP addresses. Also, keep in mind that Layer 3, the network layer, is concerned with routing data between LANs interconnected in global networks. The mission of the network layer is to handle the routing of data packets between two devices connected in different local-area networks (LANs) that are interconnected by global wide-area networks (WANs). The network layer does the following:

+ Routes data packets between LANs
+ Uses the Internet Protocol (IP)
+ Identifies hosts using logical IP addresses

Logical addressing at the network layer is *hierarchical:*

+ A limited range of IP addresses identifies a few global networks.
+ Global networks interconnect large- and medium-size networks that use another specific range of IP addresses.
+ Large- and medium-size networks interconnect smaller networks that use yet another specific range of IP addresses.

Hierarchical logical addressing involves assigning a network layer address to each network, network device, and host device.

The hierarchical IP addressing scheme facilitates routing. This is very similar to the hierarchy of real street addresses, which are composed of information such as street number, street name, neighborhood name (for larger cities), city name, state name, and country name.

The advantage of using hierarchical street addresses is that you do not need to know exactly where your destination is. All you need to know is the location of the nearest mailbox. The post office routes your package to the destination from there. Suppose you are in Australia and you need to send something to Japan. The Australian post office employees don't need to know where the destination city and street are located *within* Japan. All they need to know is that they must send your package to Japan. The Japanese post office will route your packet to the Japanese destination when the packet reaches Japan. This is the power of hierarchical addressing: Anyone can send anywhere without knowing exactly where the destination is.

Routing at the network layer in computer networks works similarly to courier services:

✦ A few extremely large global networks (think countries) interconnect other large networks.

✦ Large-sized networks (think states or provinces) interconnect medium-sized networks (think cities).

✦ Medium-sized networks interconnect smaller networks (think neighborhoods).

✦ Small-size networks interconnect mini-networks (think streets).

✦ Finally, there are computer hosts within each of the mini-networks (think street numbers).

Computer hosts embed the sender and receiver IP address in each data packet they send to another computer:

✦ If the receiving computer host is in the same network as the sender (living on the same street), the packet is simply routed locally at the data link layer using the physical address (the MAC address).

✦ If the receiving computer host is not in the same network as the sender, the packet is handed off to a *gateway* to be routed outside the network.

A gateway is a *router* that links a network to another network.

✦ The gateway looks at the logical address (IP address) of the receiving computer host and determines in which network it is located (on which street):

• If the gateway knows about the network of the receiving computer host (it knows the street; it's in the same city), it sends the data packet to that network.

• If the gateway does not know the destination network, it hands the packet to the higher-up gateway.

Layer 3 routers relate to networks like courier services routing and distribution centers. Layer 3 routers inspect the destination IP address of each data packet they receive to determine where to send that packet:

✦ If they know the destination network, they send the packet on a port that links to the destination network.

✦ Otherwise, they hand off the packet to the next higher-up router.

Routers remember the networks they are connected to. This helps them route data packets to the ports that reach those networks. Whenever a router receives a packet bound for a network it has never "heard about," the router sends the packet to its own gateway, the outbound router that reaches out to other unknown networks.

Purpose of a Layer 3 Router

A Layer 2 switch is a network device that creates one collision domain per port and forwards data frames only on the outbound port that reaches the destination of the frame.

 Considering the post office analogy, a Layer 2 switch is like a postman that delivers the package on a given street or in a given neighborhood. Routers are like the postal routing and distribution centers that group (route) the packets by neighborhood and street and hand the packets off to the postman (the Layer 2 switch) to deliver them to their local destinations.

Layer 2 switches are typically faster than routers because they do not need to look at the network layer (Layer 3) IP packet header. They only inspect the data-link (Layer 2) frame to look at the source and destination MAC address of the frame. This is why they are called Layer 2 switches: They only operate on the data-link (Layer 2) frame.

Figure 1-1 illustrates how data packets are processed by an intermediary node (a router) on their journey between two hosts in different LANs. The router needs to inspect the packet that it extracts from the data-link frame.

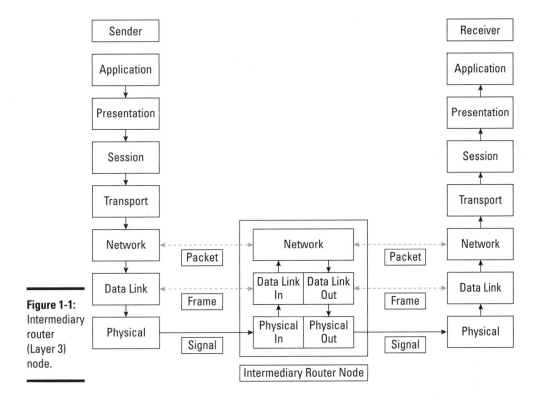

Figure 1-1:
Intermediary router (Layer 3) node.

By contrast, a switch only needs to look at the data frame, as shown in Figure 1-2. Switches do not analyze the IP packet that is encapsulated in the Layer 2 data frame.

The purpose of a router is to route data packets between networks:

✦ The router inspects the IP header of each data packet that passes through it.

✦ The router extracts the destination IP address and inspects the address to determine the destination network of the data packet.

✦ If the router knows the destination network, it sends the data packet to that destination network.

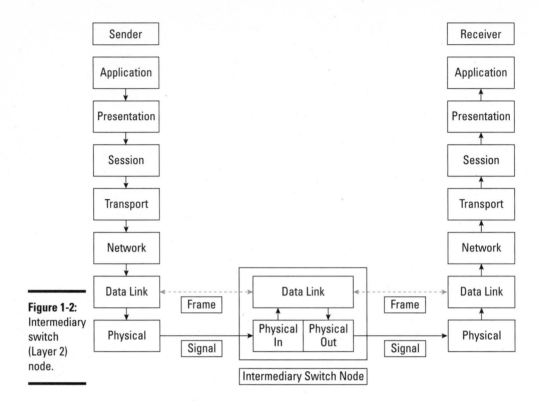

Figure 1-2:
Intermediary
switch
(Layer 2)
node.

+ If the router does not know the destination network, it sends the packet to the outbound gateway of the router:

  • The outbound gateway is also a router. Hence, when the outbound gateway receives the data packet, it goes through the same process to determine where to send the packet.

  • The outbound gateway extracts the destination IP address and inspects the address to determine the destination network of the data packet.

  • If the outbound gateway knows the destination network, it sends the data packet to that destination network.

  • If the outbound gateway does not know the destination network, it sends the packet to the higher-up outbound gateway.

Eventually, an outbound gateway that is high enough in the network hierarchy knows the destination network.

So, how does a router know about a network? By keeping *routing tables* in memory.

Routing tables keep track of the following:

✦ Each network known

✦ Router interface through which each network can be reached

✦ Metrics associated with each route

Routers keep one routing table for each protocol, because each protocol has its own addressing scheme and metrics.

Routers use routing tables to keep information about the networks they know. Routers build their routing tables by exchanging information about the networks they know about. Over time, as each router finds out about new networks, and new routes to those networks, the collective information about networks and routes gets more accurate.

Two types of protocols operate at the network layer: routed protocols and routing protocols:

✦ *Routed protocols* are used to route *data packets.* Routed protocols also identify nodes (hosts) in global networks by assigning a unique logical network address to each node in the network.

For example, IP (IPv4) is a routed protocol that uses IP addresses to identify each node in the global IP network. IPv6, AppleTalk, IPX, and SNA are other routed protocols that operate at the network layer.

✦ *Routing protocols* are used to send and receive *route update packets.* Route update packets carry information about new networks and new routes. Routers send each other route update packets whenever a new network is created or a new route is enabled. Some of the most common routing protocols are Routing Information Protocol (RIP), RIPv2, Enhanced Interior Gateway Routing Protocol (EIGRP), and Open Shortest Path First (OSPF). Different routing protocols use different metrics to decide which routes are better than others.

Basic Router Functions

A Layer 3 router must accomplish four basic functions:

✦ Manage routing protocols

✦ Build routing tables using routing protocols

✦ Route packets using routed protocols and routing tables

✦ Maintain routing tables

Book IV
Chapter 1

Introducing Layer 3
Routers

IP addresses are hierarchical. They have

✦ A part that identifies the network

✦ A part that identifies the host device

For example, a network may be identified by network IP address 192.168.25.0 (subnet mask 255.255.255.0). All hosts in this network have an IP address that starts with 192.168.25.

Another network may be identified by network IP address 192.168.67.0 (subnet mask 255.255.255.0). All hosts in this network have an IP address that starts with 192.168.67.

In these two small networks, the first three numbers (192.168.25 and 192.168.67) identify the network. The last number identifies each host within its network.

Layer 2 switches interconnect hosts locally in networks 192.168.25.0 and 192.168.67.0.

Managing routing protocols

How can hosts on different networks send a data packet to each other? The routers for the two networks need to learn about each other's network. But even before that happens, they need to set up their routing protocols. Think of it in human communication terms: Before you can speak with someone in a foreign language, you need to "set up your language": learn the foreign language.

Setting up a routing protocol on a router typically involves the following:

✦ Starting up the routing protocol on each router

✦ Enabling the routing protocol on interfaces on each router

✦ Configuring routing protocol options

You need to execute these setup steps manually on each router. Some routing protocols can automatically negotiate certain configuration options. You read about some of these options later in this book.

Building routing tables

Routing tables keep track of networks, paths to networks, and *metrics* for each path.

Routing protocols exchange information about the networks in the immediate vicinity of each router, after the protocols are activated on each router.

The following information is exchanged:

✦ Each network known by each router

✦ The router interface through which each network can be reached

✦ Metrics associated with each route

Routing packets

Eventually, each router knows about its own networks (that is, networks in its immediate vicinity) and about networks in the immediate vicinity of its partner router. After routing update packets have been exchanged between routers, the routing tables contain information about the following:

✦ All networks known by each router

✦ Routes to those networks

✦ Metrics for each route

Prep Test

1 **Which of the following describes the network layer?**

A ○ Routes data frames between devices in the same local-area network (LAN)

B ○ Routes data packets between devices in separate local-area networks (LANs)

C ○ Routes data segments between MAC addresses on the same device

D ○ All of the above

2 **How does the network layer identify devices?**

A ○ By assigning a physical address, also known as a MAC address, to each device in the LAN

B ○ By assigning a world-wide port name (WWPN) to each node in the LAN

C ○ By assigning a logical address, also known as an IP address, to each device in the network

D ○ All of the above

3 **IP addresses are organized hierarchically to facilitate which of the following?**

A ○ Video streaming

B ○ Audio streaming

C ○ Routing

D ○ Switching

4 **What is the purpose of a router?**

A ○ To route data packets between networks

B ○ To switch data frames between nodes in a specific local network

C ○ To segment data into small chunks to facilitate routing

D ○ All of the above

5 **How does a router know the destination of each data packet?**

A ○ It inspects the data-link frame header of each data packet and extracts the destination MAC address from the header.

B ○ It inspects the IP header of each data packet and extracts the destination IP address from the header.

C ○ It inspects the TCP header of each data packet and extracts the destination TCP port from the header.

D ○ All of the above.

6 **Which of the following occurs whenever a router does not know the destination network of a data packet?**

   A ○ It sends the data packet to the default outbound gateway.

   B ○ It sends the data packet to the nearest Layer 2 switch.

   C ○ It discards the data packet.

   D ○ All of the above.

7 **How do routers keep track of networks?**

   A ○ By saving the TCP port of each network in the TCP port routing table

   B ○ By saving the MAC address of each network in the MAC address routing table

   C ○ By saving data about each network in routing tables

   D ○ All of the above

8 **Name one of the basic functions of a router.**

   A ○ Maintains TCP port tables

   B ○ Maintains routing tables

   C ○ Maintains MAC address tables

   D ○ Manages the STP protocol operation

9 **How does a router determine the quality of each network route to reach a certain destination?**

   A ○ By calculating metrics (costs) associated with each route

   B ○ By sending the first data packet on all routes at the same time and picking the quickest route to send all the following packets

   C ○ By inspecting the IP address of the destination network

   D ○ All of the above

10 **How are routing protocols used?**

   A ○ To send and receive MAC address updates between routers

   B ○ To send and receive data frames between routers

   C ○ To send and receive data packets between routers

   D ○ To send and receive route update packets between routers

Answers

1 **B.** The network layer routes data packets between devices in separate local-area networks (LANs). See *"Layer 3 — Network Layer Review."*

2 **C.** The network layer identifies devices by assigning a logical address, also known as an IP address, to each device in the network. Refer to *"Layer 3 — Network Layer Review."*

3 **C.** IP addresses are organized hierarchically to facilitate the routing of data packets through networks. Read *"Layer 3 — Network Layer Review."*

4 **A.** The purpose of a router is to route data packets between networks. Look over *"Purpose of a Layer 3 Router."*

5 **B.** A router knows the destination of each data packet by extracting the destination IP address from the IP header of each data packet. Review *"Basic Router Functions."*

6 **A.** A router sends a data packet to the default outbound gateway if the router does not know the destination network of a data packet. Check out *"Basic Router Functions."*

7 **C.** Routers keep track of networks by saving data about each network in routing tables. Refer to *"Basic Router Functions."*

8 **B.** One of the basic functions of a router is to maintain routing tables. Read *"Basic Router Functions."*

9 **A.** A router determines the quality of each network route by calculating the metrics (costs) associated with each route. Look over *"Basic Router Functions."*

10 **D.** Routing protocols send and receive route update packets between routers to help routers keep track of their neighbors and of routes available. Review *"Basic Router Functions."*

Chapter 2: Managing a Router Using Cisco IOS

Exam Objectives

✔ **Connecting to a Cisco router**

✔ **Understanding the startup process of a Cisco router**

✔ **Configuring a Cisco router**

✔ **Managing Cisco router configurations**

✔ **Managing Cisco router authentication**

*R*ead this chapter to find out how to use the Cisco Internetwork Operating System (IOS) to manage Cisco routers. The following topics are covered:

✦ Local and remote router connectivity options

✦ How to use the IOS command-line interface (CLI) as well as the graphical user interface (GUI) to manage Cisco routers

✦ How to secure access to Cisco routers using passwords

✦ How to manage configurations on Cisco routers

Managing a Cisco router is very similar to managing a Cisco switch. Most IOS commands are the same for switches and routers, but the output differs in some cases. Most IOS commands and GUI tools are available for both switches and routers. Some GUI tools are only available for routers, such as the Cisco Router and Security Device Manager (SDM) and SDM Express. Other GUI tools are only available for switches, such as the Cisco Device Manager. You find out about router management IOS commands and GUI tools in this chapter. You can skip over or skim through sections covering tools that you already read about in Book III, Chapter 2.

Best Practices for Using Cisco Routers

You need to understand best practices for using entry-level and top-of-the-line products. For example, top-of-the-line routers are best suited for the *core layer* or for the *distribution layer* of the network. Entry-level and mid-range routers are best suited for the *access layer* or for the *distribution layer*. Cisco defines three layers in a network: core layer, distribution layer, and access layer.

Top-of-the-line routers manage the following specialized services in a network:

✦ Open Shortest Path First (OSPF) designated router (DR)

✦ OSPF backup designated router (BDR)

✦ Inter-VLAN routing

✦ WAN gateway connectivity

These services are used throughout the network. Hence, they need to run on a highly efficient and highly available router. You find out about these services in this book.

Figures 2-1 and 2-2 show the front and rear panels, respectively, of a Cisco 2621 entry-level router.

Figure 2-1:
Cisco 2621
router and
accessory
items —
Front panel.

Figure 2-2:
Cisco 2621
router and
accessory
items —
Rear panel.

Connecting to a Cisco Router

Unlike a computer host, Cisco routers do not have a keyboard, a monitor, or a mouse device to allow direct user interaction. Cisco routers can be managed by connecting either locally or remotely to the router from a computer host. You basically leverage the computer host user interface to interact with the Cisco router.

Connecting locally

Cisco routers have several ports. Think of router ports as plugs where you either connect computer hosts or other network devices.

Some router ports are reserved for other purposes than network connectivity. These are the *console* port and the *auxiliary* port on a Cisco router.

Console port

The *console port* is used to connect a management computer host to the router using a rollover cable. You use this port whenever you want to connect locally to the console of your router. The console is the default monitoring and configuration input and output facility of the router. All Cisco devices have a *console facility,* where the Cisco operating system (IOS) displays status messages, error messages, diagnostic messages, and user prompts.

Think of the console facility as a virtual computer monitor and keyboard:

+ Router output messages are going to the virtual computer monitor.

+ Router user input is gathered using the virtual keyboard.

To access the console facility, you need to connect to the console port on your router. You use a rollover cable connected at one end to the console port of your router and connected at the other end to the management computer host.

Figure 2-3 illustrates a Cisco 2621 router with a management computer host connected to the router console port using a rollover cable. This figure illustrates the rear panel of the router.

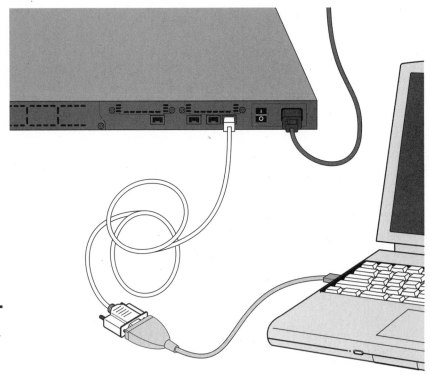

Figure 2-3:
Cisco router
console
connection.

After you physically connect the router to your computer using a rollover cable, you need to use a terminal emulation application on your management computer to open a serial terminal connection to your router. The following applications support terminal emulation:

+ HyperTerminal

+ TeraTerm

+ SecureCRT

You need to configure a connection profile for your Cisco router using specific RS232 serial communication parameters:

+ Baud rate: 9600

+ Data bits: 8

+ Parity: none

+ Stop bits: 1

+ Flow control: none

Serial communications (RS232) are governed by these parameters. Older computer hosts used to have serial communications ports (RS232) named COM1, COM2, COM3, and so on. Since the invention of USB, serial ports are being phased out. Your laptop probably boasts several USB ports but no serial port. If you do not have a serial port on your computer, you need a RS232 serial/USB port adapter.

Figure 2-4 illustrates a DB9 serial-to-USB converter (on the right in the picture). The router rollover cable (on the left in the picture) plugs in to the converter. The converter plugs in to one of the USB ports on the laptop.

Figure 2-4:
Serial-to-
USB port
adapter.

Book IV
Chapter 2

Managing a Router
Using Cisco IOS

Auxiliary port

The *auxiliary* port is used to connect a management computer host to the router using a rollover cable, similarly to the *console* port. However, you use this port whenever you want to connect a modem locally to the auxiliary port. Next, you configure the modem to receive calls from a management computer host over a telephone line. After the management computer host establishes a modem connection to the router, you are connected to the *console facility* of the router. This port is really used for remote connections to your router, but you still need to connect an answering modem locally in the auxiliary port of the router.

It is important to configure passwords to challenge console port and auxiliary port connections.

Figure 2-5 illustrates a Cisco router with a management computer host connected to the router auxiliary port using two modems.

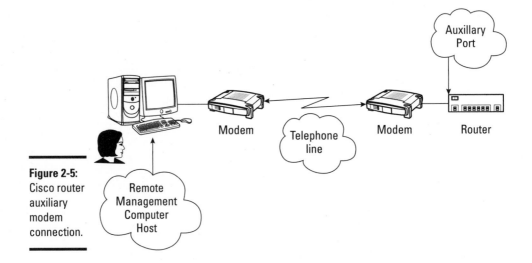

Figure 2-5:
Cisco router
auxiliary
modem
connection.

Connecting remotely

You can connect remotely to a Cisco router. You can connect both to the router console and to its terminal window from a remote management computer host.

You can connect remotely to Cisco routers in several ways:

+ Connect to the auxiliary port of the router using a modem connection. This connects you to the console of the router from a remote location.

✦ Connect to the network IP address of the router using a Telnet or secure Telnet application. Each router has a network IP address that identifies the router as an IP node in the network. You can connect to this IP address using any Telnet or secure Telnet application, just as you connect to a computer host using Telnet or secure Telnet.

✦ Connect to the console IP address of the router using a Console Terminal Server. You can configure a Console Terminal Server that makes the router console facility available at a specific IP address and at a specific TCP/IP port number in the network. You can connect to this `IP:port` address using any Telnet application.

It is important to configure passwords to challenge console port, auxiliary port, and Telnet connections. You see how to configure console, auxiliary, and VTY (virtual terminal) passwords in the "Configuring a Cisco Router" and the "Managing Cisco Router Authentication" sections, later in this chapter.

Figure 2-6 illustrates a Cisco router with a management computer host connected to the router IP address using Telnet.

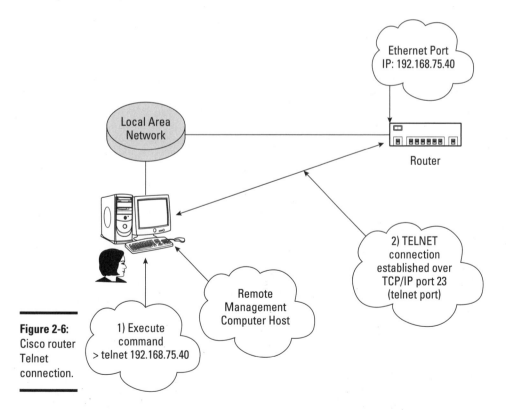

Figure 2-6: Cisco router Telnet connection.

Figure 2-7 illustrates a Cisco router with a management computer host connected to the router console via a Terminal Server.

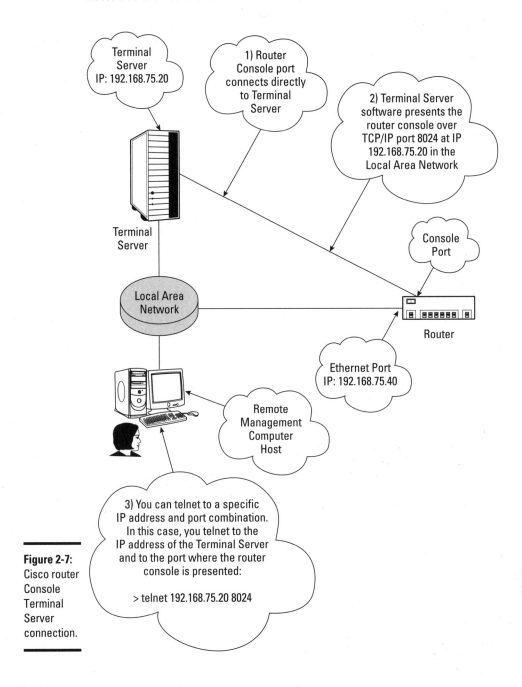

Figure 2-7:
Cisco router
Console
Terminal
Server
connection.

Cisco Router Startup Process

A Cisco router always follows the same process when it is powered up. The steps of this process are:

1. **Run the POST: The Cisco router runs the power-on self test.**

The POST is a microprogram, stored in ROM, that is used to verify basic functionality of the Cisco router hardware.

2. **Boot up: The Cisco router runs the *bootstrap program,* also known as the *boot loader software.***

The boot loader is a microprogram, stored in ROM, that is used to bring up the router and transition it to normal operation mode by loading the Cisco IOS from flash memory. If the boot loader does not find a valid Cisco IOS in flash memory, it tries to load the IOS from a TFTP server or from ROM.

3. **Load the IOS: The Cisco IOS loads into RAM.**

By default, the Cisco IOS is loaded from flash memory. However, as mentioned earlier, if the bootstrap program does not find a valid IOS in flash memory, it tries to load from a TFTP server, if one is configured. If no TFTP server is configured, or if no valid IOS is on the TFTP server, the bootstrap program loads the Rx-boot image from ROM. Recall that the Rx-boot image is a subset of the Cisco IOS operating system. The Rx-boot image is used to manage the boot process. The Rx-boot image comes up with the (boot)> prompt, where you can run various commands to manage the boot process. For instance, you can manually specify a location from which to load the IOS image.

4. **Load the startup configuration: After the Cisco router loads the IOS in RAM, the IOS loads the device** startup-configuration **file from NVRAM.**

The *startup configuration* is loaded into RAM and becomes the *running configuration,* the configuration that changes dynamically while the Cisco device is running.

At this point, the Cisco device is in normal operation mode, ready for business.

The following IOS CLI segment shows a Cisco 2621 router starting up for the first time.

```
System Bootstrap, Version 11.3(2)XA4, RELEASE SOFTWARE (fc1)
Copyright (c) 1999 by Cisco Systems, Inc.
TAC:Home:SW:IOS:Specials for info
C2600 platform with 65536 Kbytes of main memory

program load complete, entry point: 0x80008000, size: 0xed9ee4

Self decompressing the image : ##############################################
   [OK]
```

**Book IV
Chapter 2**

Managing a Router
Using Cisco IOS

The first part of the preceding example shows the following output from the bootstrap program:

+ The version of the bootstrap program: 11.3(2)XA4

+ The router platform: C2600 platform with 65K of system memory

+ The IOS image size: 0xed9ee4

+ The IOS image loading: Self decompressing the image : ####### ...

The output you see in the preceding example starts at the second step in the process (bootup). You do not see the output from the first step of the process (POST) here. The first part of the POST only displays messages upon test failures.

```
Cisco Internetwork Operating System Software
IOS (tm) C2600 Software (C2600-IK9O3S3-M), Version 12.3(1a), RELEASE SOFTWARE
    (fc1)
Copyright (c) 1986-2003 by Cisco Systems, Inc.
Compiled Fri 06-Jun-03 22:08 by dchih
Image text-base: 0x80008098, data-base: 0x819BD990
```

This part loads the Cisco IOS from flash memory and executes it in RAM. The bootstrap program loads the C2600-IK9O3S3-M Cisco IOS image.

```
cisco 2621 (MPC860) processor (revision 0x102) with 60416K/5120K bytes of memory.

Processor board ID JAD04410AGK (901795976)
M860 processor: part number 0, mask 49
Bridging software
X.25 software, Version 3.0.0.
2 FastEthernet/IEEE 802.3 interface(s)
32K bytes of non-volatile configuration memory.
16384K bytes of processor board System flash (Read/Write)
```

This part shows some information about the router hardware and software installed:

+ This is a Cisco 2621 router with an MPC860 CPU.

+ It has 65K of system memory.

+ It has bridging software installed.

+ It supports the X.25 WAN protocol.

+ It has two Fast Ethernet interfaces.

+ It has 32K of system memory configured as NVRAM.

+ It has 16K of system memory configured as flash memory.

Next, the IOS prompts you to start the initial configuration dialog:

```
--- System Configuration Dialog ---

Would you like to enter the initial configuration dialog? [yes/no]: no

Press RETURN to get started!

Cisco Internetwork Operating System Software
IOS (tm) C2600 Software (C2600-IK9O3S3-M), Version 12.3(1a), RELEASE SOFTWARE
    (fc1)
Copyright (c) 1986-2003 by Cisco Systems, Inc.
Compiled Fri 06-Jun-03 22:08 by dchih

Router>
```

This part shows the final stage of the boot process (load startup configuration). Because this is a new router, no startup configuration exists.

The IOS asks whether you would like to enter the initial configuration dialog. This dialog allows you to quickly configure the router:

+ IP address
+ Default gateway (router)
+ Subnet mask
+ Console password
+ Host name
+ Telnet password

If you choose not to run the initial configuration dialog at this time, you can press Enter to access the `Router>` prompt. When you're at the `Router>` prompt, you can run IOS commands to monitor and manage the router.

Routers that have Cisco SDM (Router and Security Device Manager) preinstalled, such as the 1800 series, require that you create an administrator user before you are allowed to run the initial configuration dialog. These routers provide a default administrator user named "cisco," identified by password "cisco," that can only be used one time to create your personalized administrator user. Here is the last part of the boot process on a Cisco 1801 router that has SDM preinstalled:

```
------------------------------------------------------------
Cisco Router and Security Device Manager (SDM) is installed on this device. This
    feature requires the one-time use of the username "cisco" with the password
    "cisco". The default username and password have a privilege level of 15.
    Please change these publicly known initial credentials using SDM or the IOS
    CLI.
```

```
Here are the Cisco IOS commands.

username <myuser>  privilege 15 secret 0 <mypassword>

no username cisco

Replace <myuser> and <mypassword> with the username and password you want to use.

For more information about SDM please follow the instructions in the QUICK START
    GUIDE for your router or go to http://www.cisco.com/go/sdm
------------------------------------------------------------

User Access Verification

Username: cisco
Password: cisco
```

The router informs you about the "cisco" default temporary administrator user and prompts you to create a new personalized administrator user. To create the new personalized administrator user, use the `username` command:

```
Router> configure terminal
Router(config)# username Admin007 privilege 15 secret 0 Admin007Password
```

This command creates a new user named Admin007, identified by password Admin007Pasword, with level_15_privilege access permission. From now on, you can log in to your router using this new administrator user. You are ready to set up your router at this point.

The next section describes how to configure a Cisco router.

Configuring a Cisco Router

Read this section to find out how to initially set up a Cisco router. You also see how to manage startup and running configurations.

Cisco routers ship with several items, as shown in Figure 2-8:

✦ Console rollover cable: This is the cable you need to connect to the console port on the router.

✦ AC power cord.

✦ 19-inch rack mounting brackets.

✦ Getting Started documentation CD.

✦ Router and Security Device Manager (SDM) CD.

Figure 2-8:
Cisco 2621
router and
accessory
items.

These items are needed to initially power up and configure the router. First, use the mounting brackets to mount the router into a standard EIA-310-D data center rack. Next, connect the power cord to the power feed of the EIA-310-D data center rack.

Initial router configuration

Cisco routers are not configured when they are new, out of the box. They do not have a startup configuration, so you need to create one.

Cisco routers revert to setup mode anytime that no startup configuration is saved in NVRAM. This happens in two situations:

✦ The device is new: No startup configuration exists on new devices.

✦ The startup configuration has been deleted: You can delete the startup configuration using IOS commands.

You can create a startup configuration using one of the following methods:

✦ Using the initial configuration dialog

✦ Using the Cisco IOS setup mode commands

**Book IV
Chapter 2**

Managing a Router
Using Cisco IOS

Initializing the router using the initial configuration dialog

The first time you power on a Cisco router, it has no startup configuration in NVRAM. You can connect to the console of the router to get access to the IOS prompt. The router will be in *setup mode* because no startup configuration exists. In setup mode, the IOS asks you to configure the following:

+ IP address

+ Default gateway (router)

+ Subnet mask

+ Enable and enable secret password

+ Host name

+ Telnet password

If choose not to configure the router and use it without a startup configuration, you can avoid or abort setup mode using one the following methods:

+ Exit setup mode by pressing Ctrl+C

+ Answer no when setup mode asks whether you want to configure the router

+ Answer no when setup mode asks whether you want to save the configuration at the end of the series of setup questions

Although you can use a router without creating a startup configuration, it is best practice to verify the router and to create a startup configuration before you start using the router. Using the router without a startup configuration allows you to initially test the basic functionality of the router. However, you should always have a startup configuration and, specifically, console, auxiliary, and privileged mode passwords configured before you start using the router in a production environment.

Here is an example of the initial setup mode dialog on a Cisco 2621 router:

```
System Bootstrap, Version 11.3(2)XA4, RELEASE SOFTWARE (fc1)
Copyright (c) 1999 by Cisco Systems, Inc.
TAC:Home:SW:IOS:Specials for info
C2600 platform with 65536 Kbytes of main memory

program load complete, entry point: 0x80008000, size: 0xed9ee4

Self decompressing the image : ################################################
    [OK]

[ ... some boot messages cut ... ]
```

The first part of the output shown in the preceding example displays various boot messages. The router is now up and running.

Because no startup configuration exists in NVRAM, the IOS asks whether you want to run the initial configuration dialog. You type **yes** as follows to run the initial configuration dialog:

```
        --- System Configuration Dialog ---

Would you like to enter the initial configuration dialog? [yes/no]: yes

At any point you may enter a question mark '?' for help.
Use ctrl-c to abort configuration dialog at any prompt.
Default settings are in square brackets '[]'.

Basic management setup configures only enough connectivity
for management of the system, extended setup will ask you
to configure each interface on the system

Would you like to enter basic management setup? [yes/no]: yes
Configuring global parameters:

  Enter host name [Router]: RT1

  The enable secret is a password used to protect access to
  privileged EXEC and configuration modes. This password, after entered, becomes
    encrypted in the configuration.
  Enter enable secret: my_priv_encrypt_password

  The enable password is used when you do not specify an
  enable secret password, with some older software versions, and some boot
    images.
  Enter enable password: my_priv_password

  The virtual terminal password is used to protect
  access to the router over a network interface.
  Enter virtual terminal password: my_telnet_password
  Configure SNMP Network Management? [no]:
```

The second part of the output shown in the preceding example prompts you to set a host name and passwords on your router. In this example

Book IV
Chapter 2

Managing a Router
Using Cisco IOS

✦ You name the router RT1.

✦ You set the encrypted privileged mode password to my_priv_ encrypt_password.

✦ You set the unencrypted privileged mode password to my_priv_ password.

✦ You set the VTY access lines password to my_telnet_password.

The next section of the initial configuration dialog, shown in the following example, displays a summary of the Ethernet interfaces (ports) available on the router:

```
Current interface summary

Any interface listed with OK? value "NO" does not have a valid configuration

Interface       IP-Address  OK? Method Status   Protocol
FastEthernet0/0 unassigned  YES unset  down     down
FastEthernet0/1 unassigned  YES unset  down     down

Enter interface name used to connect to the
management network from the above interface summary: fastethernet0/0

Configuring interface Fastethernet0/0:
Use the 100 Base-TX (RJ-45) connector? [yes]:
  Operate in full-duplex mode? [no]: yes
  Configure IP on this interface? [yes]:
    IP address for this interface: 192.168.75.40
    Subnet mask for this interface [255.255.255.0] :
    Class C network is 192.168.75.0, 24 subnet bits; mask is /24
```

The third part of the output shown in the preceding example prompts you to set up a management interface for the router. You choose the first Fast Ethernet interface: Fast Ethernet 0/0. You set an IP address and subnet mask on the management interface.

The next section of the initial configuration dialog, shown in the following example, displays a summary of the configuration that will be created on the router.

Only the secret password is encrypted by default: the encrypted privileged mode password.

You can also encrypt the other passwords for increased security.

```
The following configuration command script was created:

hostname RT1
enable secret 5 $1$3GJW$pVC5U4qVd1bzy5x8kDkwa.
enable password my_priv_password
line vty 0 4
password my_telnet_password
no snmp-server
!
no ip routing
!
interface FastEthernet0/0
no shutdown
media-type 100BaseTX
full-duplex
ip address 192.168.75.40 255.255.255.0
!
```

```
interface FastEthernet0/1
shutdown
no ip address
!
end
```

The last section of the initial configuration dialog, shown in the following example, prompts you to do one of the following:

+ Save the configuration you just created to NVRAM.

+ Return to the setup without saving the configuration you just created.

+ Go straight to the IOS prompt without saving the configuration you just created.

Choose "2" in the following example to save the configuration you just created to NVRAM. This configuration becomes the startup configuration.

```
[0] Go to the IOS command prompt without saving this config.
[1] Return back to the setup without saving this config.
[2] Save this configuration to nvram and exit.

Enter your selection [2]:

Building configuration...
[OK]
Use the enabled mode 'configure' command to modify this configuration.

RT1>
```

Initializing the router using Cisco IOS setup mode commands

You can also configure router settings manually using Cisco IOS setup mode commands at any time.

The following sections show you a few basic Cisco IOS configuration commands that you can use at any time to configure your Cisco device.

Naming the router

Book IV
Chapter 2

You can name your router using the `hostname` Cisco IOS command. You should name all your routers using meaningful names to ease identification and management of each router.

This is particularly important in large networks.

To configure the host name of the router, run the following commands:

```
Router>enable (or en)
Router#configure terminal (or config t)
Router(config)#hostname SW1
```

Managing a Router
Using Cisco IOS

```
RT1(config)#exit
RT1#disable
RT1>
```

Configuring the management IP address for the router

You can configure an IP address and an IP gateway for your router using the `ip address` and `ip default-gateway` Cisco IOS commands. This allows you to connect to the router from remote locations using either Telnet or HTTP.

To configure the management IP address and default gateway on your router, run the following commands:

```
RT1>enable (or en)
RT1#configure terminal (or config t)
RT1(config)#interface fastethernet0/0 (or int fe0/0)
RT1(config-if)#ip address 192.168.75.40 255.255.255.0
RT1(config-if)#no shutdown
RT1(config-if)#exit
RT1(config)#ip default-gateway 192.168.75.1
RT1(config)#exit
RT1#disable
RT1>
```

The first two commands (`enable` and `configure terminal`) set the IOS in privileged global configuration mode. You can now run commands that configure global router settings, that is, settings that apply to the whole router.

The `interface fastethernet0/0` command selects an interface to work with. In this example, you select the first Ethernet interface of the router (Fast Ethernet 0/0).

The `ip address 192.168.75.40 255.255.255.0` command sets the IP address and the subnet mask on the interface that you selected previously. Observe that the IOS prompt now shows `RT1(config-if)#`. Config-if means that you are configuring an interface (`if`) now.

The `no shutdown` command starts up the Fast Ethernet 0/0 interface. Recall that you enable components and services on a Cisco router using the component or service name. You disable components and services on a Cisco router using the component or service name prefixed with the no keyword. Here, shutdown is actually a state, not a component or service. An interface is either shut down or not shut down (started up). To summarize:

✦ To shut down an interface, select it and execute `shutdown`.

✦ To start up an interface, select it and execute `no shutdown`.

The ip default-gateway 192.168.75.1 command sets the default gateway for the router. Observe that you first exit from interface configuration mode (RT1(config-if)#exit) because the default gateway applies to the whole router, not just to an interface. Now, you are back in global configuration mode (RT1(config)#).

The Cisco IOS prompt is designed to show you the configuration mode you're in:

✦ (config): You are in global configuration mode.

In this mode, you can execute commands that configure global router settings, that is, settings that apply to the whole router.

✦ (config-if): You are in interface configuration mode.

In this mode, you can execute commands that configure router interface settings, that is, settings that apply to just one interface of the router. You select the interface to work with using the interface command.

✦ (config-if-range): You are in interface range configuration mode.

In this mode, you can execute commands that configure a range of router interfaces, that is, settings that apply to a range of interfaces on the router. You select the range of interfaces to work with using the interface range command.

Configuring passwords

You can configure authentication passwords for your router using the password and login Cisco IOS commands. By default, new Cisco devices do not have a password configured.

You can configure several passwords for different types of access:

✦ **Console password:** Used for console access through the console port or through a Console Terminal Server.

✦ **Auxiliary password:** Used for console access through the auxiliary port using a modem.

✦ **VTY lines password:** Virtual type terminal (VTY) lines are used for Telnet and Secure Shell (SSH) access. They are called virtual type terminal lines because no physical terminal is connected to the router. Rather, you connect a computer host to the network and access the router remotely using the router management IP address. A terminal emulation program on the computer host emulates a physical terminal (TTY).

✦ **Privileged password:** Used for privileged mode access. Privileged mode is an "expert" management operation mode used to run some Cisco IOS commands.

The console port and the auxiliary port are enabled by default, even if no password is specified for them. This is a security risk. It is best practice to specify at least a console password on new Cisco devices.

The VTY lines (Telnet and Secure Shell) are disabled by default. You need to specify a password for the VTY lines to enable them.

To configure passwords, you need to instruct the Cisco device to prompt for authentication. You use the login Cisco IOS command to do this.

Best practice

You should at least set passwords for console and VTY access to secure access through the console port and to enable and secure remote access through Telnet or SSH.

The following sections describe how to configure passwords for console and VTY access using Cisco IOS commands.

Console password

To configure the console password, run the following commands:

```
RT1>enable (or en)
RT1#configure terminal (or config t)
RT1(config)#line console 0 (or line con 0)
RT1(config-line)#password my_password
RT1(config-line)#login
RT1(config-line)#exit
RT1(config)#exit
RT1#disable
RT1>
```

The first two commands (enable and configure terminal) set the IOS in privileged global configuration mode. You can now run commands that configure global router settings, that is, settings that apply to the whole router.

The line console 0 command selects the console line. Cisco devices have only one console line: console 0.

The password my_password command sets the my_password password on the console access line.

Finally, instruct the Cisco device to prompt for authentication by entering the login Cisco IOS command. From now on, anytime you connect to the console line you will be prompted to provide a password. The password you provide must be my_password. To disable the authentication prompt, issue line console 0 again and enter the no login command.

You use the exit commands to exit the config-line mode and to exit the config global configuration mode.

Telnet password

To configure a password for the VTY lines, run the following commands:

```
RT1>enable (or en)
RT1#configure terminal (or config t)
RT1(config)#line vty 0 ?
    <0-4> last line number
RT1(config-line)#line vty 0-4
RT1(config-line)#password my__telnet_password
RT1(config-line)#login
RT1(config-line)#exit
RT1(config)#exit
RT1#disable
RT1>
```

The first two commands (enable and configure terminal) set the IOS in privileged global configuration mode. You can now run commands that configure global router settings, that is, settings that apply to the whole router.

The line vty 0 ? command asks the Cisco IOS how many VTY lines are available. The response (<0-4> last line number) shows that five VTY lines exist on this particular router (you can have five simultaneous Telnet sessions opened to this router). Now, you can configure a password either on one of the VTY lines, by selecting that particular line, or on all VTY lines, by selecting the whole 0–4 line range.

The line vty 0-4 command selects the whole 0–4 VTY line range. Cisco devices have several VTY *access lines.* Older routers have only five VTY lines. Newer routers have as many as 1,180 VTY lines. It is best practice to query the Cisco IOS about how many VTY lines are available.

Two main reasons exist to have several VTY access lines on a Cisco device:

✦ **Allowing you to connect to the router and connect to another device from the router:** Two VTY lines are needed in this case: one to connect into the router and another one to connect out of the router to another device.

✦ **Allowing several administrators to work on the router:** In large networks, more than one administrator may manage the network. More than one administrator may need to connect from a remote location to the same router using Telnet or SSH. This is typical with large core routers.

The password my_telnet_password command sets the my_telnet_ password password on the VTY access lines. You can set a different password on each line. However, this is not recommended, because you don't know which VTY line you on are when you log in, so you wouldn't know which password to enter. Best practice is to select the whole range of VTY lines and to set the same password on all of them.

Finally, instruct the Cisco router to prompt for authentication by entering the `login` Cisco IOS command. From now on, anytime you connect to any of the VTY lines, you will be prompted to provide a password. The password you provide must be `my_telnet_password`. To disable the authentication prompt, issue `line vty 0-4` again and enter the `no login` command.

After you run the initial setup IOS commands, the router has a startup configuration saved in NVRAM. The router is reachable on the IP network. You can now connect to the router either locally to its console or auxiliary port, or remotely to its IP address, as explained previously in the section "Connecting to a Cisco Router."

Configuring banners

You can optionally configure a banner for your router using the `banner` Cisco IOS command. The purpose of a banner is to display a brief message about the router when you log in. This is useful when you have many routers spread out across multiple sites. It helps identify the router you log in to and see its configuration and usage guidelines. Banners are also useful for legal reasons: You can add a security warning in the banner message to warn users against unauthorized logins to the router. Although this does not prevent the user from logging in to the router, it does provide ground for legal action in the case of unauthorized logins. Always use passwords to secure your routers.

Four types of banners are available:

+ **Message of the day (MOTD) banner:** This is the first banner to display when a user connects to a router, regardless of the type of connection. This banner is used to display a message for all users that connect to the router, before they log in. This is typically used for an unauthorized access warning.

+ **Login banner:** This banner is displayed on TTY or VTY terminals after the MOTD banner. This banner is typically used to display information about the router and to provide guidelines on how to log in and use the router.

+ **Incoming terminal connection banner:** This banner is displayed on reverse TTY or VTY terminals after the MOTD banner. This banner is used for the same reasons as the login banner. The only difference is the type of terminal connection: You can specify additional information in this banner for users that connect with reverse TTY or VTY terminals.

✦ **EXEC process creation banner:** This banner is displayed whenever an EXEC process is created, after the user is logged in. An EXEC process is created for each user EXEC prompt. User EXEC prompts are established for each user connected to the router, after the user logs in successfully. Hence, the EXEC process creation banner is displayed after the login/incoming banners and after the MOTD banner.

To configure an MOTD banner on your router, run the following commands:

```
RT1>enable (or en)
RT1#configure terminal (config t)
RT1(config)#banner motd -
Enter TEXT message. End with character '-'.
$This router is property of silange.com networks. Unauthorized access is
    prohibited. Please disconnect if you are not a silange.com employee,
    customer, or business partner.
-
RT1(config)#
```

The `banner motd -` command starts the banner text editor using `'-'` as the delimiting character. The delimiting character is used by the IOS to determine when you are done typing the banner text. You enter the banner text of your choice and finish by typing the delimiting character (`'-'` in this case) and pressing Enter. The delimiting character can be any character, but you cannot use that character within the text of the banner. Cisco IOS would interpret that as the end of the banner text.

Resetting a Cisco router

Cisco routers revert to setup mode anytime no startup configuration exists in NVRAM. Normally, this only happens when the router is new and not yet configured.

However, you may want to clear the current configuration in NVRAM and start a new configuration from scratch. This is typically a last-resort trouble-shooting method: When problems affect the router and no troubleshooting method fixes the problems, your last resort is to reset the router and recon-figure it.

Resetting the router clears the configuration of the router.

After it is reset, the router is in the state it was when you purchased it:

✦ No IP address

✦ No host name

✦ No default gateway (router)

+ No subnet mask

+ No console password

+ No Telnet password

+ No startup configuration

It is best practice to back up the startup configuration of a router to a backup computer host before resetting the router.

To reset a router, you need to clear its startup configuration from NVRAM:

```
RT1>enable (or en)
RT1#erase startup-config
Erasing the nvram filesystem removes all configuration files!
Continue? [confirm] <press Enter to confirm>
[OK]
Erase of nvram: complete
RT1#
```

Observe that the erase command warns you that the NVRAM contents will be reinitialized and prompts you to confirm. The default answer is confirm. To confirm, just press Enter.

Managing Cisco router configuration

Ongoing, you can manage your router using the following:

+ Cisco IOS commands

+ The Cisco Network Assistant (CNA) GUI tool

+ The Cisco Router and Security Device Manager (SDM) GUI tool

+ The Cisco Router and Security Device Manager (SDM) Express Web tool

The Cisco Network Assistant (CNA) tool, the Cisco Router and Security Device Manager (SDM) tool, and the Cisco Router and Security Device Manager (SDM) Express tool are graphical user interface (GUI)–based tools that allow you to manage your router and its startup and running configurations from a remote location using a computer host. Their GUI interfaces are much easier to use and more intuitive than Cisco IOS commands.

Recall that although the Cisco Network Assistant (CNA) tool can monitor and manage both switches and routers, it is typically used with Cisco switches, rather than with Cisco routers. The Cisco Router and Security Device Manager (SDM) and the Cisco Router and Security Device Manager (SDM) Express are the preferred router monitoring and management tools.

You read about the Cisco Network Assistant (CNA) tool, the Cisco Router and Security Device Manager (SDM) tool, and the Cisco Router and Security Device Manager (SDM) Express in Book I, Chapter 10. You find out about Cisco IOS router configuration management commands in the following sections.

Managing the router boot process

Cisco routers always follow the same boot process when they are powered up. This process contains four stages:

1. **Run the POST:** The Cisco router runs the power-on self test to verify basic functionality of the Cisco router hardware.

2. **Boot up:** The Cisco router runs the *bootstrap program* to bring up the router and transition it to normal operation mode by loading the first Cisco IOS image from flash memory.

3. **Load the IOS:** The Cisco IOS loads into RAM from flash memory.

4. **Load the startup configuration:** After the Cisco router loads the IOS in RAM, the IOS loads the device *startup configuration* from NVRAM. The startup configuration is loaded into RAM and becomes the *running configuration,* the configuration that changes dynamically while the Cisco router is running. At this point, the Cisco router is in normal operation mode, ready for business.

This process is also called the *automatic boot process:* The router automatically boots up with current options and loads the startup configuration.

Boot command

Recall that the Cisco bootstrap program loads the first Cisco IOS image file from flash memory, by default, when the router is powered up. In some cases, you may need to boot a specific IOS image file from flash memory. For example, suppose that you download a new Cisco IOS image file that contains additional features, but you would like to test it on your router before you remove the original IOS image file. You can configure the router to boot with the new IOS image file using the boot command.

The boot command allows you to configure the boot process of a Cisco router. You can control the following:

✦ Which Cisco IOS image file is loaded

✦ Which startup configuration file is loaded

You can use the Cisco IOS contextual help to see the options available with the `boot` command:

```
RT1>enable (or en)
Password: my_priv_encrypt_password
RT1#configure terminal (or config t, or conf t)
RT1(config)#
RT1(config)#boot ?
  bootstrap  Bootstrap image file
  host       Router-specific config file
  network    Network-wide config file
  system     System image file
RT1(config)#exit
RT1#disable
RT1>
```

Observe that you need to be in privileged global configuration mode to execute the `boot` command.

The `bootstrap`, `host`, and `network` options are beyond the scope of the CCNA test.

The `service-config` command enables loading of router startup configuration files from remote servers. If loading of configuration files from remote servers is not enabled with the `service-config` command, the router ignores the `boot host` and `boot network` options and looks for a startup configuration file in its NVRAM instead.

Loading startup configuration files from remote servers is done in two phases:

1. **The IOS loads the** `network` **configuration file.** The `network` configuration file contains configuration settings that apply to all routers in your network that are loading their startup configuration from a network configuration server. You would typically have only one `network` configuration file for all your routers. The `network` configuration file name is `network-config` by default.

2. **The IOS loads the** `host` **configuration file.** The `host` configuration file contains configuration settings that apply to a specific router. You may have as many `host` configuration files as you have routers in your network, if each router needs specific settings. The `host` configuration file name is `<router_hostname>-config` by default. It is comprised of the router host name (in lowercase characters) and the `-config` suffix.

The `boot host` option sets the location of the `host` configuration file of the router.

The `boot network` option sets the location of the `network` configuration file of the router.

Using the `host` and `network` boot options in conjunction with the `service-config` command is useful in large environments where you have a lot of routers to manage. It's more efficient to manage the routers' network and host startup configuration files on a central management computer than to keep track of the files on each router. It is best practice to back up the configuration server host to avoid losing the configuration files.

The `system` option allows you to boot a specific Cisco IOS image file. This is useful in cases when, for example, you download a new Cisco IOS image file, containing additional features, and you would like to test it on your router.

The `system` option allows you to boot a specific Cisco IOS image file either from local flash memory on the router or from a remote server.

Here is an example in which you set the router to boot with a specific Cisco IOS image file stored in flash memory:

```
RT1>enable (or en)
Password: my_priv_encrypt_password
RT1#configure terminal (or config t, or conf t)
RT1(config)#
RT1(config)#boot system flash:/c2600-ik9o3s3-mz.123-1a.bin
RT1(config)#exit
RT1#disable
RT1>
```

Observe that you need to be in privileged global configuration mode to execute the `boot` command.

You can use the `show running-configuration` command to verify the current boot options on a router:

```
RT1>enable (or en)
Password:my_priv_encrypt_password
RT1#show running-configuration | include boot
boot-start-marker
boot system flash c2600-ik9o3s3-mz.123-1a.bin
boot-end-marker
RT1#disable
RT1>
```

Observe that you need to be in privileged EXEC mode to execute the `show running-configuration` command.

Note also that you filter the output to display only lines that contain the word *boot* using the `| include boot` suffix.

**Book IV
Chapter 2**

**Managing a Router
Using Cisco IOS**

This command shows the current boot options. All options can be changed with the corresponding `boot` command, as explained earlier. After you change a boot option, you need to reboot your router using the `reload` command in privileged EXEC mode.

Managing the router boot process with the configuration register

In Book I, Chapter 10, you read that the configuration register is a 2-byte (16-bit) area of NVRAM that holds a numeric value defining how the Cisco router starts up.

By default, the value stored in the configuration register instructs the bootstrap program to load the Cisco IOS from flash memory and to load the startup configuration from NVRAM.

You can change the value of the configuration register from the ROMMON prompt. To get to the `rommon >` prompt, you need to break out of the bootstrap process by pressing Ctrl+Break from a console connection while the Cisco router is booting up.

The configuration register can be set to various values, but the following three values are important to remember:

✦ **0x2100:** This value instructs the bootstrap program to boot to the ROMMON prompt. This is equivalent to pressing Ctrl+Break from a console connection while the Cisco router is booting up to break out of the bootstrap process and exit to the `rommon>` prompt.

✦ **0x2101:** This value instructs the bootstrap program to boot to the `(boot)>` Rx-boot prompt.

✦ **0x2102 to 0x210F:** These values instruct the bootstrap program to boot the Cisco IOS from flash memory. Observe that there are 14 possible values (2 to F). The value that you specify determines which copy of the IOS is loaded. You can have up to 14 different copies (versions) of the Cisco IOS in flash memory. The value that you set in the configuration register determines which copy is loaded. *The configuration register is set to 0x2102 by default.* The bootstrap program loads the first copy of the Cisco IOS from flash memory.

So, what are the other configuration register values that you can set? The configuration register is comprised of 2 bytes or 16 bits, which means 2^{16} (65,536) possible values. This is a lot of possible configuration variations, but in reality, only a small number of these values are used.

Table 2-1 illustrates the default value of the configuration register (0x2102) in binary and hexadecimal values.

Table 2-1				Configuration Register											
	Nibble 1				*Nibble 2*				*Nibble 3*				*Nibble 4*		
Bit	15	14	13	12	11	10	9	8	7	6	5	4	3	2	1	0
Bin	0	0	1	0	0	0	0	1	0	0	0	0	0	0	1	0
Hex			2				1				0				2

Each binary nibble (each group of 4 bits) is a digit in hexadecimal. You read this table by nibble:

+ The value of nibble 1 is 0010_2, which is 2_{16}.
+ The value of nibble 2 is 0001_2, which is 1_{16}.
+ The value of nibble 3 is 0000_2, which is 0_{16}.
+ The value of nibble 4 is 0010_2, which is 2_{16}.

Next, you put the value of each nibble side by side to obtain the hexadecimal number: 0x2102.

Now, how would you express 0x2102 in binary? Each digit is a nibble in binary:

+ The value of nibble 1 is 2_{16}, which is 0010_2.
+ The value of nibble 2 is 1_{16}, which is 0001_2.
+ The value of nibble 3 is 0_{16}, which is 0_2.
+ The value of nibble 4 is 2_{16}, which is 0010_2.

Next, you put the value of each nibble side by side to obtain the binary number: $0010\ 0001\ 0000\ 0010_2$.

By turning bits on and off in the configuration register, you configure the behavior of the bootstrap program. Each bit-set combination corresponds to a number in hexadecimal. You set the configuration register to that bit set by initializing the configuration register with the corresponding hexadecimal number.

Table 2-2 lists the purpose of some of the bits of the configuration register.

**Book IV
Chapter 2**

**Managing a Router
Using Cisco IOS**

Table 2-2		Configuration Register Bit Purpose
Bit	*Hexadecimal Value*	*Purpose*
0–3	0x0000–0x000F	Boot option
6	0x0040	Do not load startup configuration from NVRAM
8	0x0100	Disable break
11,12	0x0800, 0x1000	Set console line speed
13	0x2000	Boot from ROM if TFTP boot fails
15	0x8000	Enable diagnostic messages

Bit 0 instructs the bootstrap program to load a specific operating system. The default value of bit 0 (0x0002) instructs the bootstrap program to load the first copy (version) of the Cisco IOS from flash memory. Recall that you can have 14 different copies (versions) of the Cisco IOS in flash memory. Table 2-3 summarizes the values of bit 0 and their purpose.

Table 2-3		Configuration Register: Bit 0 — Boot Option
Bit 0 Value	*Hex*	*Purpose*
0	0x0000	Boot to `rommon>` prompt
1	0x0001	Boot to `(boot)>` prompt
2	0x0002	Boot first copy of Cisco IOS from flash memory
3	0x0003	Boot second copy of Cisco IOS from flash memory
4	0x0004	Boot third copy of Cisco IOS from flash memory
F	0x000F	Boot 14th copy of Cisco IOS from flash memory

Bit 6 is important for recovering lost passwords. Bit 6 instructs the bootstrap program to avoid reading the startup configuration from NVRAM. This allows you to recover lost or forgotten passwords. You find out how to do this in the section "Recovering router passwords," later in this chapter.

Bit 8 instructs the bootstrap program to disable the break key (Ctrl+Break) during normal operation. Note that you can always break out of the boot process to the `rommon>` prompt if you press Ctrl+Break from a console connection during the first 60 seconds while the router boots up, regardless of this setting. Setting bit 8 to 1 really means that Ctrl+Break is disabled during normal operation. Bit 8 is set by default.

Bits 11 and 12 instruct the bootstrap program to use a certain speed for the console line. By default, these two bits are not set: Bit 11 is 0 and bit 12 is also 0. Here are the values and meanings for bits 11 and 12:

+ **00:** Speed is 9600 baud

+ **01:** Speed is 4800 baud

+ **10:** Speed is 1200 baud

+ **11:** Speed is 2400 baud

The console line speed is 9600 baud by default; both bits are 0 by default. There is no reason to change the speed unless you use a computer host that cannot connect at 9600 baud to the console line. You can set a lower speed in that case.

Bit 13 instructs the bootstrap program to boot the default Cisco IOS from ROM if booting from flash memory fails and if booting from a TFTP network boot server also fails.

Bit 15 instructs the bootstrap program to enable diagnostic messages and to ignore the contents of NVRAM. This option is useful for troubleshooting the router.

These values can be combined. For example, the configuration register is set by default to 0x2102. Referring to Table 2-2, bits 13 and 8 are set to 1. Referring to Table 2-3, bit 0 is set to 2. This means the following:

+ **Bit 13:** 0x2000 instructs the bootstrap program to boot the default Cisco IOS from ROM if booting from flash memory fails and if booting from a TFTP network boot server also fails.

+ **Bit 8:** 0x0100 instructs the bootstrap program to disable the break key (Ctrl+Break) during normal operation. Note that you can always break out of the boot process to the rommon> prompt if you press Ctrl+Break from a console connection during the first 60 seconds while the router boots up, regardless of this setting. Setting bit 8 to 1 means that Ctrl+Break is disabled during normal operation.

+ **Bit 0:** 0x0002 instructs the bootstrap program to load the first copy (version) of the Cisco IOS from flash memory. Recall that you can have 14 different copies (versions) of the Cisco IOS in flash memory. The value you set in bit 0 in the configuration register determines which copy is loaded. Table 2-3 summarizes the values of bit 0 and their meaning.

You can change the value of the configuration register using the `config-register` Cisco IOS command. You need to reboot the router for the change to take effect.

Here is an example:

```
RT1>enable (or en)
RT1#configure terminal (or config t)
RT1(config)#config-register 0x2100
RT1(config)#exit
RT1#show version (or sh ver)
…
Configuration register is 0x2102 (will be 0x2100 at next reload)
```

Here you set the configuration register to 0x2100 to boot to the ROM Monitor `rommon>` prompt at next reboot. Observe that the `show version` Cisco IOS command shows you the current value of the configuration register and the future value at next reboot, if you change it.

Managing configurations

Two configurations exist on any Cisco router: the startup configuration and the running configuration. The following sections review the characteristics of startup and running configurations and describe how to manage them on a Cisco router.

Startup configuration

The startup configuration is the configuration that the Cisco IOS loads when it boots up. The startup configuration is stored in NVRAM, which keeps its contents even when the Cisco device is powered down.

Recall that whenever no startup configuration exists in NVRAM, the router starts in setup mode to allow you to create a startup configuration. After you complete the setup mode, you are prompted to save the configuration to NVRAM. If you answer yes, the configuration you created is saved to NVRAM; it becomes the startup configuration. You can also manually save the current configuration to NVRAM by using the `copy running-config startup-config` Cisco IOS command.

Cisco devices use the startup configuration data to configure the device before normal operation starts. The Cisco IOS loads the startup configuration from NVRAM into RAM. At that point, the startup configuration becomes the running configuration. The router is up and ready in normal operation mode.

Running configuration

The running configuration is the dynamic data that changes while the Cisco device is in normal operation mode. This includes the following:

+ Routing tables
+ VLAN data
+ Routing protocol configuration data
+ Temporary buffers

The Cisco IOS loads the startup configuration from NVRAM into RAM during the boot process. After it is in RAM, the startup configuration becomes the running configuration and can change dynamically.

You can save the running configuration into NVRAM to replace the startup configuration with updated data. To do this, use the `copy running-config startup-config` Cisco IOS command. You can also save the running configuration to a file on a computer host.

Saving the running configuration to NVRAM

To save the running configuration to NVRAM, run the following command:

```
RT1>enable (or en)
RT1#copy running-config startup-config (or copy run start)
Destination filename [startup-config]? <press Enter>
Building configuration . . .
[OK]
RT1#
```

The second line shows the `copy` command. You can also use the short form of this command (`copy run start`).

The third line asks where you want to copy the running configuration to. You have several possible destinations:

+ `startup-config`: Use this keyword to copy the current running configuration over the startup configuration in NVRAM.

+ `flash`: Use this keyword to copy the current running configuration to a file in flash memory, alongside the Cisco IOS.

+ `ftp`: Use this keyword to copy the current running configuration to an FTP server. This option is useful to back up the router configuration to a remote computer host.

+ `archive`: This is similar to the ftp option, except that you archive to a tape- or disk-based backup system directly, instead of passing through a computer host.

The default destination is the `startup-config` file in NVRAM. To keep the default answer, just press Enter. Sometimes, the Cisco IOS prompts you to enter a value, and it shows the default answer in between brackets [ ]. To keep the default answer, just press Enter.

Monitoring the running configuration

To monitor the running configuration, run the following command:

```
RT1#show running-config (or sh run)
```

Monitoring the startup configuration

To monitor the startup configuration, run the following command:

```
RT1#show startup-config (or sh start)
```

Deleting the startup configuration

Upon reboot, a router starts in setup mode if no startup configuration exists in NVRAM. You can manually delete the startup configuration from NVRAM. This allows you to start a new configuration from scratch. This is typically a last-resort troubleshooting method: When problems affect the router and no troubleshooting method fixes the problems, your last resort is to reset the router and reconfigure it.

It is best practice to back up the startup configuration to a backup computer host before deleting it. You find out how to back up the configuration to a backup computer host in the section "Back up the router running configuration to a computer host," later in this chapter.

To delete the startup configuration, run the following command:

```
RT1>enable (or en)
RT1#erase startup-config
Erasing the nvram filesystem removes all configuration files!
Continue? [confirm] <press Enter to confirm>
[OK]
Erase of nvram: complete
RT1#
```

Observe that the `erase` command warns you that the NVRAM contents will be reinitialized and prompts you to confirm. The default answer is `confirm`. To confirm, simply press Enter.

Router configuration backup and recovery best practice

It is best practice to save the running configuration to both

+ The startup configuration file in NVRAM on the router itself

+ To a computer host

This protects you against a total failure of the router. If the router fails and you need to replace it with a new one, you don't want to have to re-create the startup configuration from scratch. If you have that configuration saved on a computer host, you can load the startup configuration from the computer host and onto the new router, and you're ready to go in production with the new router.

Back up the router running configuration to a computer host

To back up the running configuration to a computer host, run the following command:

```
RT1>enable (or en)
RT1#copy running-config tftp (or copy run tftp)
Address or name of remote host []? 192.168.75.5
Destination filename [RT1-config]? <press Enter>
812 bytes copied in 0.910 secs (892 bytes/sec)
RT1#
```

The `copy running-config tftp` Cisco IOS command on the second line initiates the copy process of the router running configuration to a TFTP server.

The third line prompts you for the IP address or host name of the remote host destination. Observe that the IOS does offer a suggested IP address or host name. You can configure a default TFTP server. The IP address or host name of that default TFTP server then shows up as a suggestion in line 3.

The fourth line prompts you for the filename you want to give to the configuration file saved on the remote host. The router name, followed by the suffix `-config`, is suggested by default. You simply press Enter to accept the suggested filename.

Now your running configuration is saved in a file named `RT1-config` on the remote computer host with IP address 192.168.75.5.

Recover a router configuration from a computer host

Suppose that you need to load a configuration from a remote host to your router. The same `copy` Cisco IOS command allows you to recover a configuration from a remote host:

```
RT1>enable (or en)
RT1#copy tftp running-config (or copy tftp run)
Address or name of remote host []? 192.168.75.5
Source filename []? RT1-config
Destination filename [running-config]? <press Enter>
Accessing tftp://192.168.75.5/RT1-config...
Loading RT1-config from 192.168.75.5
[OK - 812 bytes]
812 bytes copied in 10.120 secs (80 bytes/sec)
RT1#
```

The `copy tftp running-config` Cisco IOS command on the second line initiates the copy process of the router running configuration from a TFTP server.

The third line prompts you for the IP address or host name of the remote host destination. Observe that, in this example, the IOS does not suggest any source IP address or hostname "[]". You can configure a default TFTP server on your router. The IP address or hostname of that default TFTP server will then show up suggested between the square brackets.

The fourth line prompts you for the source filename of the configuration file that you want to load from the remote host. Enter the name of a configuration file that you saved previously on the TFTP server. In this example, you enter the name of the configuration you just copied to the TFTP server in the previous example ("RT1-config").

The fifth line prompts you for the destination filename. The `running-config` filename is suggested. This means that the configuration you load from the TFTP server will replace the current running configuration. Press Enter to accept the suggested choice.

Next, the `copy` command displays a few status messages.

At this point, your running configuration has been loaded from a file named `RT1-config` from a remote TFTP server host with IP address 192.168.75.5.

Managing router configurations using the Cisco IOS File System (IFS)

This section shows how to manage the memory of a Cisco router using Cisco IOS File System (IFS) commands.

Know that you can manage the memory of a Cisco router like a file system on a computer host. The Cisco IFS presents the memory of a Cisco router as directories (or folders) and files within those directories, just like Microsoft Windows, Apple Mac OS X, Linux, or any other computer operating system presents the hard drive of a computer host as directories (or folders) and files.

The Cisco IFS commands are only available in privileged mode. So, you need to run the `enable` command first (or en in its short form).

First, verify the current directory:

```
RT1>enable (or en)
RT1#pwd
flash:
```

You are currently in the flash main memory directory, as shown by the pwd command. Next, run the `dir` Cisco IFS command to see the contents of flash memory on your router:

```
RT1#dir
Directory of flash:/
   1  -rw-  15572992  <no date>  c2600-ik9o3s3-mz.123-1a.bin
16777216 bytes total (1204160 bytes free)
```

This shows that the flash memory on your router contains a single Cisco IOS image named `c2600-ik9o3s3-mz.123-1a.bin`.

You can easily find other directories and files by using the `dir all-filesystems` Cisco IFS command:

```
RT1#dir all-filesystems
Directory of nvram:/
27  -rw-  0          <no date>  startup-config
28  ----  0          <no date>  private-config

29688 bytes total (29636 bytes free)

Directory of system:/
10  drwx  0          <no date>  its
 2  dr-x  0          <no date>  memory
 1  -rw-  582        <no date>  running-config
 9  dr-x  0          <no date>  vfiles

No space information available
Directory of flash:/
1  -rw-  15572992    <no date>  c2600-ik9o3s3-mz.123-1a.bin

16777216 bytes total (1204160 bytes free)
```

Observe that you have three main directories (file systems) on your Cisco router:

✦ `nvram`: Stores the `startup-config` and the `private-config` files.

✦ `system`: This is the RAM, which contains the `running-config` file.

✦ `flash`: This is the flash memory, which contains the Cisco IOS operating system image. This is the Cisco IOS image that the bootstrap program loads in RAM when the router boots up.

You can list the contents of any of these main directories (file systems) individually using the `dir` and `cd` Cisco IFS commands. You can change your working directory from `flash:` to any of the main directories using the `cd` Cisco IFS command.

For example, list the contents of NVRAM:

```
RT1#dir nvram:
Directory of nvram:/
  27  -rw-  0    <no date>  startup-config
  28  ----  0    <no date>  private-config
29688 bytes total (29636 bytes free)
```

**Book IV
Chapter 2**

**Managing a Router
Using Cisco IOS**

Now, change to the RAM directory (system) and look at the files and directories available there:

```
RT1#cd system:
RT1#dir
Directory of system:/
   10  drwx   0    <no date>   its
    2  dr-x   0    <no date>   memory
    1  -rw-   582  <no date>   running-config
    9  dr-x   0    <no date>   vfiles
```

Observe the running-config file. This is the current running configuration. You can copy a configuration file from a computer host to system:/running-config to load a configuration on the router from a configuration backup file on a computer host.

To load a configuration on the router from a configuration backup file on a computer host, run the following Cisco IFS commands:

```
RT1#copy tftp://192.168.75.5/RT1-confg system:/running-config
Destination filename [running-config]? <press Enter>
Accessing tftp://192.168.75.5/RT1-confg...
Loading RT1-confg from 192.168.75.5
[OK - 812 bytes]
812 bytes copied in 10.120 secs (80 bytes/sec)
RT1#
```

The copy tftp://192.168.75.5/RT1-confg system:/running-config command you use here is very similar to the copy tftp running-config command that you used in the previous section. The only difference is that you specify the path to the source and the path to the destination when you use the Cisco IFS version of the copy command.

You can also use this command to copy a configuration from a configuration backup file on a computer host to the startup-config file in NVRAM. Here is an example:

```
RT1#copy tftp://192.168.75.5/RT1-confg nvram:/startup-config
Destination filename [startup-config]? <press Enter>
Accessing tftp://192.168.75.5/RT1-confg...
Loading RT1-confg from 192.168.75.5
[OK - 812 bytes]
812 bytes copied in 10.120 secs (80 bytes/sec)
```

Managing Cisco Router Authentication

You can configure several passwords for different types of access to your router:

✦ **Console password:** Used for console access through the console port or through a Console Terminal Server.

✦ **Auxiliary password:** Used for console access through the auxiliary port using a modem.

✦ **VTY lines password:** Virtual type terminal (VTY) lines are used for Telnet and Secure Shell (SSH) access. They are called virtual type terminal lines because no physical terminal is connected to the router. Instead, you connect a computer host to the network and access the router remotely using the router management IP address. A terminal emulation program on the computer host emulates a physical terminal (TTY).

✦ **Privileged password:** Used for privileged mode access. Privileged mode is an "expert" management operation mode used to run some Cisco IOS commands.

The console port and the auxiliary port are enabled by default, even if no password is specified for them. This is a security risk. It is best practice to specify at least a console password on new Cisco devices.

Privileged EXEC mode is *not* secured with a password by default on Cisco routers. By default, you can access privileged mode by executing the enable IOS command at the user EXEC prompt. It is best practice to configure a privileged mode password to secure access to advanced IOS commands that can adversely affect the functionality of the router, if misused.

The VTY lines (Telnet and Secure Shell) are disabled by default. You need to specify a password for the VTY lines to enable them.

To configure passwords, you need to instruct the Cisco device to prompt for authentication. You use the login Cisco IOS command to do this.

Console password

This section reviews how to configure a console password. To configure the console password, run the following commands:

```
RT1>enable (or en)
RT1#configure terminal (or config t)
RT1(config)#line console 0 (or line con 0)
RT1(config-line)#password my_password
RT1(config-line)#login
RT1(config-line)#exit
RT1(config)#exit
RT1#disable
RT1>
```

The first two commands (`enable` and `configure terminal`) set the IOS in privileged global configuration mode. You can now run commands that configure global router settings, that is, settings that apply to the whole router.

The `line console 0` command selects the console line. Cisco devices have only one console line: console 0.

The `password my_password` command sets the `my_password` password on the console access line.

Finally, you instruct the Cisco router to prompt for authentication by entering the `login` Cisco IOS command. From now on, anytime you connect to the console line, you will be prompted to provide a password. The password you provide must be `my_password`. To disable the authentication prompt, issue `line console 0` again and enter the `no login` command.

You use the `exit` commands to exit the `config-line` mode and to exit the `config` global configuration mode.

Telnet password

This section reviews how to configure a password for the VTY access lines. To configure a password for the VTY lines, run the following commands:

```
RT1>enable (or en)
RT1#configure terminal (or config t)
RT1(config)# line vty 0 ?
   <0-4> last line number
RT1(config-line)#line vty 0-4
RT1(config-line)#password my_telnet_password
RT1(config-line)#login
RT1(config-line)#exit
RT1(config)#exit
RT1#disable
RT1>
```

The first two commands (`enable` and `configure terminal`) set the IOS in privileged global configuration mode. You can now run commands that configure global router settings, that is, settings that apply to the whole router.

The `line vty 0 ?` command asks the Cisco IOS how many VTY lines are available. The response (`<0-4> last line number`) shows that five VTY lines are available on this particular router. Now you can configure a password on any one of the VTY lines (by selecting that particular line) or on all VTY lines (by selecting the whole 0–15 line range).

The `line vty 0-4` command selects the whole 0–4 VTY line range. Cisco routers have several VTY *access lines*. Older routers have only five VTY lines. Newer routers have as many as 1,180 VTY lines. It is best practice to query the Cisco IOS about how many VTY lines are available.

Two main reasons exist to have several VTY access lines on a Cisco router:

✦ **Allowing you to connect to the router and connect to another device from the router.** Two VTY lines are needed in this case: one to connect into the router and another one to connect out of the router to another device.

✦ **Allowing several administrators to work on the router.** In large networks, more than one administrator may manage the network. More than one administrator may need to connect from a remote location to the same router using Telnet or SSH. This is typical with large core routers.

The `password my_telnet_password` command sets `my_telnet_ password` password on the VTY access lines. You can set a different password on each line. However, this is not recommended. You don't know which VTY line you are on when you log in, so you wouldn't know which password to enter. Best practice is to select the whole range of VTY lines and to set the same password on all of them.

Finally, instruct the Cisco router to prompt for authentication by entering the `login` Cisco IOS command. From now on, anytime you connect to any of the VTY lines, you will be prompted to provide a password. The password you provide must be `my_telnet_password`. To disable the authentication prompt, issue `line vty 0-15` again and enter the `no login` command.

Auxiliary password

If your router has an auxiliary port, it is best practice to secure access to the auxiliary port using a password. To configure the auxiliary password, run the following commands:

```
RT1>enable (or en)
RT1#configure terminal (or config t)
RT1(config)#line auxiliary 0 (or line aux 0)
RT1(config-line)#password my_aux_password
RT1(config-line)#login
RT1(config-line)#exit
RT1(config)#exit
RT1#disable
RT1>
```

**Book IV
Chapter 2**

**Managing a Router
Using Cisco IOS**

The first two commands (`enable` and `configure terminal`) set the IOS in privileged global configuration mode. You can now run commands that configure global router settings, that is, settings that apply to the whole router.

The `line auxilary 0` command selects the auxilary line. Cisco routers have only one auxilary line: auxilary 0.

The `password my_password` command sets the `my_password` password on the auxilary access line.

Finally, instruct the Cisco router to prompt for authentication by entering the `login` Cisco IOS command. From now on, anytime you connect to the auxilary line, you will be prompted to provide a password. The password you provide must be `my_password`. To disable the authentication prompt, issue `line auxilary 0` again and enter the `no login` command.

You use the `exit` commands to exit the `config-line` mode and to exit the `config` global configuration mode.

Privileged password

It is best practice to set up a privileged password to secure access to advanced IOS commands that can adversely affect the functionality of the router if misused. You can use two different commands to configure a privileged password:

+ `enable password my_priv_password`: This command sets `my_priv_password` as the privileged password. This password is not encrypted by default. This command is supported in all IOS versions.

+ `enable secret my_priv_encrypt_password`: This command sets `my_priv_ encrypt_password` as the privileged password. This password is encrypted. This command is supported in newer IOS versions.

Using the `enable secret` or the `enable password` commands, you configure a privileged password that is stored locally on your router. The only difference between the two commands is that `enable secret` stores the password on the router in encrypted form, which is more secure than `enable password`, which stores the password on the router in unencrypted form.

Always use the Cisco IOS help to determine whether the `enable secret` command is available. If it is, use it to set the privileged password. It is best practice to encrypt the privileged password using the `enable secret` command whenever this command is available.

You can also configure your privileged password to be stored on a *Terminal Access Controller Access Control System (TACACS)* server. This is a good option in larger networks with many routers when it is better to configure the privileged password once, centrally, on a TACACS server, instead of configuring passwords on each of your routers.

To configure an encrypted privileged mode password, run the following commands:

```
RT1>enable (or en)
RT1#configure terminal (or config t)
RT1(config)#enable secret my_priv_encrypt_password
RT1(config)#exit
RT1#disable
RT1>
```

Encrypting passwords

By default, passwords are stored in plain text in the running configuration in RAM and in the startup configuration file in NVRAM. You can view the passwords on your router in plain text, using either the show running-config command or the show startup-config command. This is a security risk. It is best practice to encrypt all passwords on your router.

The privileged password is encrypted if you use the enable secret command. It is best practice to set a privileged password using the enable secret command to make sure that it is encrypted. So, if you use enable secret instead of enable password to set a privileged password, your privileged password is encrypted.

How about other passwords? Console, auxiliary, and virtual terminal (VTY) passwords are *not* encrypted, even if you use the enable secret command for the privileged password. You need to encrypt them using the service password-encryption command.

To encrypt passwords on your router, run the following commands:

```
RT1>enable (or en)
RT1#configure terminal (or config t)
RT1(config)#service password-encryption
RT1(config)#exit
RT1#disable
RT1>
```

The first two commands (enable and configure terminal) set the IOS in privileged global configuration mode. You can now run commands that configure global router settings, that is, settings that apply to the whole router.

The service password-encryption command asks the Cisco IOS to encrypt all passwords except the privileged password that is already encrypted if the enable secret command was used.

**Book IV
Chapter 2**

**Managing a Router
Using Cisco IOS**

Enabling Secure Shell (SSH)

Secure Shell (SSH) is similar to Telnet: It allows remote users to connect to the router by using the router IP address. SSH is more secure than Telnet, because it encrypts data exchanged between the remote management computer and the router.

It is best practice to encrypt data exchanged between the remote management computer and the router.

Consider this example: You need to change the passwords on a router located in a remote data center. The data center is too far to walk to, so you need to connect to the router remotely from your computer. While changing the passwords, you enter the passwords on the keyboard of your computer. If you are connected to the router using Telnet, the data exchanged between your computer and the router is in clear text. That data includes the new passwords that you type at your computer keyboard. Hence, passwords are sent over the Internet in clear text. This is a security risk. SSH avoids this security risk by encrypting data exchanged between your computer and the router.

SSH uses encryption keys to encrypt the data exchanged in an SSH session. Cisco supports both SSH version 1.0 (also known as SSH v1 or SSH.1) and SSH version 2.0 (also known as SSH v2 or SSH.2). Cisco started to support SSH v2 with IOS Release 12.1(19)E on some router models.

If you get a `%Invalid input` error when you execute the `crypto key generate rsa` command, the Cisco IOS version on your router does not support SSH. You may need to download the cryptographic software image from Cisco. To download the cryptographic IOS software image for your router, log in to `www.cisco.com/public/sw-center/index.shtml`. Note that you need to register at Cisco.com before downloading. Some software export limitations may apply.

Figure 2-9 shows the Cisco 2621 series router software download section at Cisco.com.

Observe that various packages are available for each release. Each package enables certain features for typical usages of the router. You choose the IOS image that corresponds to your needs. For example:

+ **IP/IPX/APPLETALK:** You choose this Cisco IOS image if you use your 2621 router to route data for IP, IPX, or AppleTalk network protocols. If you do not have any computer hosts using the NetWare IPX protocol and if you do not have any hosts using the AppleTalk protocol, it wouldn't make sense to use this image, because enabling support for more protocols than necessary slows your router.

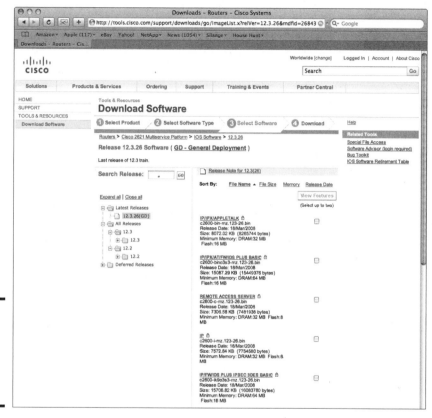

Figure 2-9:
Down-
loading
Cisco 2621
router IOS
images.

✦ **IP:** You choose this Cisco IOS image if all computer hosts in your network are using the Internet Protocol. Contrary to the previous IOS
image, which enabled support for IP, IPX, and AppleTalk, this image only
enables IP. If all your hosts are using IP, this is the image you want.

Scrolling down the list, you find images that enable encryption. You need to
download and install one of those encryption-enabled IOS images.

To enable SSH, you need to

✦ Ensure that the Cisco IOS image on your router supports SSH.

✦ Ensure that you assigned a host name to your router: SSH needs the
host name to generate the encryption keys.

✦ Ensure that you assigned an IP domain name to you router: SSH needs
the IP domain name to generate the encryption keys.

✦ Create a local or TACACS administrator user and assign it a password:
SSH cannot use the Telnet password that you assigned to the VTY

access lines. You need to create a specific user that will be used to authenticate SSH sessions.

✦ Create the encryption keys.

✦ Configure SSH options such as session timeout and number of login retries.

✦ Enable SSH on the VTY lines of your router.

Let's look at an example:

```
RT1> enable                      (or en)
RT1# configure terminal          (or config t)
```

The first two commands (`enable` and `configure terminal`) set the IOS in privileged global configuration mode. You can now run commands that configure global router settings: settings that apply to the whole router.

```
RT1(config)# ip domain-name silange.com
```

The command `ip domain-name silange.com` sets the IP domain-name for this router. SSH needs the hostname and the IP domain name to generate the encryption keys. Observe that you did not use the `hostname RT1` command here, since the router already has a hostname that is different from the default Cisco "Router " hostname. If your router was still named "Router " and you try to run the crypto command, the IOS would prompt you to assign a hostname to your router.

```
RT1(config)# username Admin007 password Admin007Passwrd
RT1(config)# line vty 0 4
RT1(config-line)# login local
RT1(config-line)# exit
```

The commands `line vty 0 4` and `login local` enable local authentication on VTY lines 0 to 4.

You could also use *Terminal Access Controller Access-Control System* (TACACS) authentication by executing `login tacacs` instead of `login local`. However, you would need to configure a TACACS server, which is beyond the scope of CCNA.

Next, you exit the line configuration mode by executing `exit` at the `(config-line)` prompt.

Now, it's time to create the SSH encryption keys for your router. You execute the `crypto key generate rsa` command. This command generates public and private encryption keys based on the RSA encryption algorithm. It uses the hostname.domain-name combination of the router to generate the keys. The crypto command also uses a modulus number to generate the keys. You can choose the number of bits used for the modulus number: between 360 and 2048. The higher the number of bits in the modulus number, the harder it is for a hacker to break the keys. So, it is better to have more bits in the modulus number. However, the more bits in the modulus number, the longer it takes to generate it. Modulo 1024 is used in this example: good compromise between security and performance.

```
RT1(config)# crypto key generate rsa
The name for the keys will be: RT1.silange.com
Choose the size of the key modulus in the range of 360 to 2048 for your General
    Purpose Keys. Choosing a key modulus greater than 512 may take a few minutes.

How many bits in the modulus [512]: 1024
% Generating 1024 bit RSA keys ...[OK]
*Mar  1 00:14:40.071: %SSH-5-ENABLED: SSH 1.5 has been enabled
```

Next, you look at the current SSH configuration on the router using the `show ip ssh` command. Observe that you prefix this command with the `do` keyword since you cannot run `show ip ssh` in configuration mode. The `do` prefix allows you to run a Privileged EXEC command from the Privileged EXEC configuration prompt.

```
RT1(config)# do show ip ssh
SSH Enabled - version 2.0
Authentication timeout: 120 secs; Authentication retries: 3

RT1(config)# ip ssh time-out 60
RT1(config)# ip ssh authentication-retries 2
```

The commands `ip ssh time-out 60` and `ip ssh authentication-retries 2` configure a 60 seconds SSH session timeout and configures SSH to allow 2 login retries. Observe that default timeout is 120 seconds and default number of retries is 2 as shown by the `show ip ssh` command in the previous step.

Finally, you need to enable SSH as an input transport protocol on the VTY access lines as shown in the example below. The commands `line vty 0 4` and `transport input ssh telnet` accomplish this.

Note that you enabled both SSH and Telnet as input transport protocols on the VTY access lines. If you removed the `telnet` keyword from the `transport input` command below, only SSH would be enabled.

```
RT1(config)# line vty 0 4
RT1(config-line)# transport input ssh telnet
RT1(config-line)# exit
```

The next two commands show the current SSH configuration on the router (`show ip ssh`) and the status of current SSH connections if any (`show ssh`).

```
RT1(config)# do show ip ssh
SSH Enabled - version 2.0
Authentication timeout: 60 secs; Authentication retries: 2
RT1(config)# do show ssh
```

Book IV
Chapter 2

Managing a Router
Using Cisco IOS

```
%No SSH server connections running.
RT1(config)# exit
RT1# disable
RT1>
```

Recovering router passwords

The Cisco IOS provides a mechanism to recover passwords, in case you lost them or you do not remember them.

You need to have physical access to the router to connect to its console port. This is a good thing, because you don't want anyone else connecting from a remote location through Telnet to be able to reset the passwords on your routers.

The key point of the password recovery process is to boot up the Cisco router ignoring its current startup configuration, which contains the current passwords. To boot up the Cisco router ignoring its current startup configuration you need to change the value in the configuration register. You can set bit 6 in the configuration register to instruct the bootstrap program to avoid reading the startup configuration from NVRAM. By doing this, you boot up the router as if it had no startup configuration — as if the router were new, coming out of the box.

Password recovery process

Follow these steps to recover passwords on a Cisco router:

1. **Change the configuration register to 0x2142.**

2. **Reboot the router.**

3. **Upon reboot, exit from setup mode.**

The router ignores the startup configuration in NVRAM, so it automatically starts in setup mode. You need to exit setup mode because your router is already set up. You just want to reset the passwords in the current startup configuration, not to reset the whole configuration.

4. **Enable privileged EXEC mode.**

5. **Load the startup configuration manually from NVRAM to RAM.**

6. **Enable global configuration mode.**

7. **Change the passwords.**

8. **Save the running configuration over the startup configuration in NVRAM.**

9. **Change the configuration register back to the default value of 0x2102.**

10. **Reboot the router.**

Here is an example:

```
RT1> enable                          (or en)
RT1# configure terminal              (or config t)
```

The first two commands (`enable` and `configure terminal`) set the IOS in privileged global configuration mode. You can now run commands that configure global router settings: settings that apply to the whole router.

```
RT1(config)# config-register 0x2142
RT1(config)# do show version         (or sh ver)
...
Configuration register is 0x2102 (will be 0x2142 at next reload)
```

Next, you change the configuration register to 0x2142 to set bit 6 on to avoid loading up the startup configuration during the next reboot. Observe that you use the `config-register` command here at the global (`config`) privileged mode prompt to do this. You could also exit out to the `rommon>` prompt and use the `confreg` ROM monitor command to change the value of the configuration register. The advantage of using `config-register` at the global (`config`) privileged mode prompt instead of using `confreg` at the `rommon>` prompt is that you avoid a reboot cycle: to load the ROM monitor, you must reboot the router and break out of the bootstrap program. You avoid this initial boot cycle, just to get to the `rommon>` prompt, by changing the configuration register value using `config-register` at the global (`config`) privileged mode prompt.

```
RT1(config)# exit
RT1# reload
```

Once you changed the configuration register value, you need to reboot your router using the `reload` command. The next few lines show the reload command and the "Reload requested by console" message. Now, you see your router reboot. Boot messages were cut from the output.

```
System configuration has been modified. Save? [yes/no]: yes
Proceed with reload? [confirm] <press Enter>
*Mar  1 00:09:58.659: %SYS-5-RELOAD: Reload requested by console.

[... boot messages output cut ...]

RT1> enable
RT1# copy startup-config running-config
    Destination filename [running-config]?  <press Enter>
    582 bytes copied in 0.984 secs (591 bytes/sec)
```

When the router comes up to the User EXEC prompt, you enable Privileged EXEC Mode and load the startup configuration manually into RAM. As mentioned earlier, you want to keep the startup configuration as it is. You just need to reset the password. Loading the startup-config manually allows you to re-save it to NVRAM, later, with the new password.

```
RT1# configure terminal             (or config t)
RT1(config)# enable secret my_secret_password
```

Next, you change the console password using the enable secret command.

```
RT1(config)# exit
RT1# copy running-config startup-config
   Destination filename [startup-config]?  <press Enter>
   Building configuration...
   [OK]
```

Once the new password is configured in the running configuration in RAM, you save the running-config to NVRAM, overwriting the startup-config already there. You use the copy running-config startup-config command to do this. The current running-config is almost the same as the startup-config you're overwriting. The only difference is the new password.

```
RT1# configure terminal             (or config t)
RT1(config)# config-register 0x2102
RT1(config)# exit
RT1# show version                   (or sh ver)
…
Configuration register is 0x2142 (will be 0x2102 at next reload)
RT1# reload
System configuration has been modified. Save? [yes/no]: yes
Proceed with reload? [confirm] <press Enter>
*Mar  1 00:09:58.659: %SYS-5-RELOAD: Reload requested by console.

[… boot messages output cut …]
```

Finally, you set the configuration register back to its default value of 0x2102 and reboot the router.

Prep Test

1 What is the Cisco IOS (Internetwork Operating System)?

A ○ Cisco's proprietary router graphical user interface

B ○ Cisco's proprietary router operating system

C ○ Cisco's proprietary router console facility

D ○ All of the above

2 Name some of the graphical user interface(s) that you can use to manage a Cisco router.

A ○ Cisco Network Assistant (CNA)

B ○ Cisco Router and Security Device Manager (SDM)

C ○ Cisco Router and Security Device Manager (SDM) Express

D ○ All of the above

3 What is the main purpose of the ROM Monitor microprogram, also known as ROMMON?

A ○ To maintain, test, and troubleshoot the power consumption of a Cisco device

B ○ To maintain, test, and troubleshoot the console port of a Cisco device

C ○ To maintain, test, and troubleshoot the configuration stored in ROM and in the flash memory of a Cisco device

D ○ To maintain, test, and troubleshoot the ROM port of a Cisco device

4 When does the power-on self test (POST) run?

A ○ Immediately after the Cisco IOS loads on a router

B ○ Immediately after the startup configuration loads on a router

C ○ Immediately after the startup configuration loads on a router

D ○ Immediately after a Cisco router is powered up

5 What is the main purpose of the bootstrap program, also known as the boot loader?

A ○ To bring up a Cisco router by loading the startup configuration from flash memory to RAM

B ○ To bring up a Cisco router by loading the Cisco IOS from flash memory to RAM

C ○ To bring up a Cisco router by loading the running configuration from flash memory to RAM

D ○ To bring up a Cisco router by loading the Cisco Device Manager from flash memory to RAM

6 It is best practice to use entry-level routers, such as the Cisco 2600 series or the Cisco 2800 series, at what layer(s)?

A ○ Access and distribution layer

B ○ Distribution and core layer

C ○ Core layer

D ○ Access and core layer

7 What does the flash memory on a Cisco router store?

A ○ The startup configuration of a Cisco router

B ○ The image file of the Cisco IOS operating system

C ○ The Cisco Device Manager software application

D ○ All of the above

8 On Cisco routers, where is the running configuration loaded from?

A ○ The running configuration file during startup

B ○ Cisco's Web site during startup

C ○ The startup configuration file during startup

D ○ All of the above

9 The Cisco IOS command-line interface operates in setup mode to do which of the following?

A ○ Initially configure the ROM Monitor (ROMMON) microprogram

B ○ Initially configure the Device Manager software application

C ○ Initially configure the IOS

D ○ Initially configure the router

10 The Cisco IOS command-line interface operates in privileged configuration mode to do which of the following?

A ○ Configure the ROM Monitor (ROMMON) microprogram

B ○ Configure the Device Manager software application

C ○ Configure the IOS

D ○ Configure the router

11 You can connect locally to your router to manage it using the _____ port.

A ○ Fast Ethernet 24 (fa0/24)

B ○ console

C ○ auxiliary

D ○ Fast Ethernet 0 (fa0/0)

Answers

1 **B.** Cisco's proprietary router operating system. The Cisco IOS (Internetworking Operating System) is Cisco's proprietary switch and router operating system. Review the chapter introduction.

2 **D.** All of the above. Some of the Graphical User Interfaces that you can use to manage a Cisco router are the Cisco Network Assistant (CNA), the Cisco Router and Security Device Manager (SDM), and the Cisco Router and Security Device Manager (SDM) Express edition. Review the chapter introduction.

3 **C.** Maintain, test, and troubleshoot the configuration stored in ROM and in the flash memory of a Cisco device. The ROM monitor micro-program, also known as ROMMON, is used to maintain, test and troubleshoot the configuration stored in ROM and in the Flash memory of a Cisco device. Check *"Cisco router startup process"* and *"Managing Cisco Router Configuration."*

4 **D.** Immediately after a Cisco router is powered up. The Power-On-Self-Test runs immediately after a Cisco router is powered up. Review *"Cisco router startup process."*

5 **B.** Bring up a Cisco router by loading the Cisco IOS from flash memory to RAM. The main purpose of the bootstrap program, also known as the boot loader, is to bring up a Cisco router by loading the Cisco IOS from Flash memory to RAM. See *"Cisco router startup process."*

6 **A.** Access and distribution layer. It is best practice to use entry-level routers, such as the Cisco 2600 series or the Cisco 2800 series at the access and distribution layers. Review *"Best Practice For Using Cisco Routers."*

7 **D.** All of the above. The flash memory on a Cisco router stores the startup configuration of the router, the image file of the Cisco IOS operating system, and the Cisco Device Manager software application program. See *"Cisco router startup process."*

8 **C.** Is loaded from the startup configuration file during startup. The running configuration of a Cisco router is loaded from the startup configuration file during startup. Review *"Cisco router startup process."*

9 **D.** Initially configure the router. The Cisco IOS command line interface operates in setup mode to initially configure the router. Review *"Initial router configuration."*

10 **D.** Configure the router. The Cisco IOS command line interface operates in privileged configuration mode to configure the router. Review *"Managing Cisco Router Authentication."*

11 **B.** Console. You can connect locally to your router to manage it using the console port. Check *"Connecting to a Cisco Router."*

Chapter 3: Network Routing

Exam Objectives

✓ Describing the types of network routes and knowing when to use them

✓ Describing routing and routed protocols, their characteristics, and purpose

✓ Describing routing decision criteria

✓ Distinguishing distance vector routing from link-state routing

✓ Describing route updates and convergence

✓ Describing routing administrative distance

✓ Describing common routing protocol metrics

✓ Describing the general process to enable and configure a routing protocol

*R*ead this chapter to find out about Layer 3 routing. Routers route data packets between networks. Routers do the following:

✦ Manage routing protocols

✦ Build routing tables using routing protocols

✦ Route packets using routed protocols and routing tables

✦ Maintain routing tables

Introducing Network Routes

A *network route* is a data transmission path through one or more networks between two end nodes. The end nodes can be any computer device that supports IP connectivity, such as computer hosts, IP phones, digital video consoles, and smartphones.

More than one route can exist between two end nodes. The main purpose of a router is to find the best route to reach a destination node. The best route is calculated according to *route metrics:* the cost in time and resources to send a data packet over that route.

More than one router can exist in the data transmission path between the sending and the receiving nodes. For example, when you connect to an Internet Web site from your home computer, your computer sends data packets to your home router. Your home router routes those packets to the default outbound gateway of your Internet service provider. The default outbound gateway of your Internet service provider, also a router, sends your data packets to the network of the Internet Web site. In this example, at least three routers are involved:

✦ Your home router

✦ Your Internet service provider's router

✦ The inbound router of the Internet Web site

You find three types of network routes:

✦ Static routes

✦ Default routes

✦ Dynamic routes

Static routes

You define static routes manually on a router. Static routes are best suited for small networks, such as LANs, where routes rarely change. If routes change, you need to update your routes to reflect the new data transmission paths.

Advantages

Some of the advantages of using static routes are as follows:

✦ **Routing efficiency:** By defining static routes, you can leave the routing protocols disabled on your router. This saves some bandwidth. Dynamic routing requires routing protocols to be enabled. Routing protocols consume some bandwidth because they constantly send route update packets between routers.

✦ **Security:** In some cases, you may want to define static routes to control the data transmission paths used by your data. This may be useful in highly secure environments. Keep the following in mind though:

  • You can filter routing data using firewalls at the network perimeter.

  • You can use Virtual Private Networking (VPN) to secure your data transmissions, no matter which data path they travel on.

Hence, you can mitigate security risks involving dynamic routes using either firewalls or VPNs or both. You read about firewalls and VPN in Book VI.

Disadvantages

Some of the disadvantages of using static routes are as follows:

✦ **Maintenance:** If routes change, you need to update your routes to reflect the new data transmission paths. This adds some management overhead.

✦ **Accuracy:** If your network changes and you do not update the static routes, your router does not have an accurate knowledge of your network. This can result in lost or delayed data transmissions.

✦ **Scalability:** Large networks have hundreds, even thousands, of alternate routes to reach other networks. It is practically impossible to define all these routes statically. Even if you define all alternate routes statically, as soon as a change occurs in the overall network topology, you would need to update the static routes. This is a maintenance nightmare. Hence, static routes are best suited for small networks.

Configuring static routes

You can configure static routes using the `ip route` Cisco IOS command in global configuration mode. The syntax of this command is as follows:

```
ip route dest-ip subnet {next-hop-ip | interface}
```

✦ `dest_ip`: This is the IP address of the destination network. You are registering a static route to the destination network.

✦ `subnet`: This is the IP subnet mask of the destination network that defines which part of the IP address identifies the network and which part identifies the hosts in that network.

✦ `{next-hop | interface}`: This is the IP gateway (router) through which you reach out to the destination network. You have to specify either the IP address of the next hop on the route to the destination network, or the outbound interface on your router through which the router can reach the destination network.

The {} notation means that you must specify something. The | (pipe) sign means that you need to choose either one of those options. Think of the | (pipe) sign as an "or." Think of the {} notation as a "must."

To remove a static route, you can use the usual no prefix with the `ip route` command: `no ip route dest-ip [subnet] {next-hop-ip | interface}`

Here is an example:

```
RT6751>enable (or en)
RT6751#configure terminal (or config t)
RT6751 (config)#ip route 192.168.25.0 255.255.255.0 serial 0/1
```

**Book IV
Chapter 3**

Network Routing

```
RT6751 (config)#exit
RT6751#disable
RT6751>
```

In this example, you define a static route on router RT6751 to network 192.168.25.0 through serial interface 0/1.

Default routes

Default routes are static routes that you define for packets bound to a destination network that is not found in any of the routing tables on the router. Whenever the router receives packets bound to a network the router doesn't know, it sends the packet out on the default route.

It is best practice to define a default route to ensure that data packets bound for networks unknown to your router are forwarded to a default gateway.

Default routes are related to default gateways: A default route is a data transmission path to the default outbound gateway in a network. For example, in a LAN with network IP address 192.168.25.0, the default gateway is typically 192.168.25.1. The default route is the data transmission path that reaches 192.168.25.1, the default gateway.

Configuring default routes

You configure default routes using the same `ip route` Cisco IOS command in global configuration mode. However, the IP address and the subnet mask of the destination network are 0.0.0.0. Here is an example:

```
RT6751>enable (or en)
RT6751#configure terminal (or config t)
RT6751 (config)#ip route 0.0.0.0 0.0.0.0 serial 0/0
RT6751 (config)#exit
RT6751#disable
RT6751>
```

In this example, you define a default route on router RT6751 to outbound serial interface 0/0. Router RT6751 now sends data packets bound for unknown networks out on serial interface 0/0.

You can also use the IP address of the default gateway to configure a default route, as shown here:

```
RT6751>enable (or en)
RT6751#configure terminal (or config t)
RT6751 (config)#ip route 0.0.0.0 0.0.0.0 192.168.67.1
RT6751 (config)#exit
RT6751#disable
RT6751>
```

In this example, you define a default route on router RT6751 to outbound IP address 192.168.67.1. Router RT6751 now sends data packets bound for unknown networks out to the default gateway of network 192.168.67.0.

Dynamic routes

Dynamic routes are routes that change over time. Routing protocols define and maintain dynamic routes. Routes change due to the following:

+ Network topology updates

+ Network traffic updates

+ Available bandwidth

+ Link state

Some of the advantages of using dynamic routes are as follows:

+ **Low maintenance:** You do not need to update your routes whenever data transmission paths change when using dynamic routing. Routes are automatically updated by routing protocols that exchange route update packets. All you need to do is to configure routing protocols on your router.

+ **Accuracy:** Routing protocols keep track of network changes. This improves routing accuracy because routers send packets over the best routes available at any time.

+ **Scalability:** Large networks have hundreds, even thousands, of alternate routes to reach other networks. It is practically impossible to define all these routes statically. Even if you define all alternate routes statically, as soon as a change occurs in the overall network topology, you would need to update the static routes. This is a maintenance nightmare. Dynamic routing avoids this problem by using routing protocols to allow routers to communicate about routes they know, new routes they discover, and routes that became unavailable or overloaded. Thus, networks using dynamic routing can scale out much better than networks that solely use static routes.

Disadvantages

Overhead is a disadvantage of using dynamic routes. Dynamic routing protocols consume some bandwidth because they regularly send route update packets between routers.

Configuring dynamic routes

You configure dynamic routes using routing protocols.

Book IV
Chapter 3

Network Routing

Routing Protocols

Routing protocols exchange network, routes, and metric information between routers to help find optimal routes as fast as possible. Routers use the information provided by routing protocols to build their *routing tables* for each *routed protocol* to keep track of networks, paths to networks, and *metrics* associated with each route.

Several routing protocols exist. Most routers support more than one routing protocol. Several routing protocols can be simultaneously enabled on a router. Routing protocols do not interfere and do not communicate with each other.

The most widely used routing protocols, and the ones you need to know for the test, are as follows:

✦ Routing Information Protocol (RIP); see Chapter 4

✦ Enhanced Interior Gateway Routing Protocol (EIGRP); see Chapter 5

✦ Open Shortest Path First (OSPF); see Chapter 6

Routed Protocols

Routed protocols tag each data packet with source and destination hierarchical addresses to allow the routing of data packets through networks as needed. Routed protocols also assign a unique logical address to each node in the network to identify each source and each destination in the network.

Here are some routed protocols that you may encounter in the field:

✦ Internet Protocol version 4 (IPv4, commonly referred to as just IP)

✦ Internet Protocol version 6 (IPv6)

✦ AppleTalk

✦ Novell Netware Internetwork Packet Exchange (IPX)

Routing Decision Criteria

Routers may pick different network routes to a destination for a given packet depending on various decision criteria. Some routes may be deemed faster than others by different routing protocols. Routers keep separate routing tables for each protocol. A route that is best now may not be best in a few minutes, depending on various criteria such as traffic, available bandwidth, and link state. Routers adapt to changes in traffic, available bandwidth, and link state by constantly monitoring the state of each route they know.

Routing tables keep track of networks, paths to networks, and metrics associated with each route.

Routers consider two aspects when deciding which network routes are best at a given moment:

✦ **Administrative distance:** How reliable is the information source that provided the data about the network route?

✦ **Routing protocol metrics:** What are the costs associated with each network route?

Administrative distance

The administrative distance determines the reliability of the information source that provided the data about the network route. Routers learn about network routes using various methods:

✦ **Router connects directly to a network.** The router learns about the network firsthand, because it connects to it.

✦ **Router does not connect to the network, but a static route exists to that network.** The router does not "see" the network, but it's been informed about its existence by a fairly reliable source (the static route).

✦ **Router is connected indirectly, through other router(s), to a network.** The router does not "see" the network, but it "heard" about it from another router.

Routers trust routes according to how reliable the source of information is. A router always prefers routes learned from reliable information sources. Cisco defined the concept of administrative distance to measure this trust. Various sources get different administrative distance values, as shown in Table 3-1.

Table 3-1	Administrative Distances
Routing Information Source	*Administrative Distance*
Directly connected	0
Static route	1
EIGRP (internal)	90
OSPF	110
RIP (v1 and v2)	120
EIGRP (external)	170

Routers prefer sources with lower administrative distances. In other words, a router trusts a static route more than a route learned from OSPF. On the other hand, a router trusts a route learned from OSPF more than it trusts a route learned from RIP.

If the same routing protocol finds two different routes to the same destination, the administrative distance is the same. In this case, other *metrics* are considered to decide on which route to use.

Routing protocol metrics

You read that routers may pick different network routes to a destination for a given packet depending on various decision criteria, such as traffic, available bandwidth, and link state.

Each routing protocol calculates the efficiency (the cost) of a route differently. Hence, decision differences may exist. For example, considering two different routes to the same destination, route A and route B, OSPF may find that route A is better than route B. However, RIP may find that route B is better than route A. So which route does the router choose? Route A or route B? If you answered route A, you are right: Whenever routing protocols contradict each other, the one with the lowest administrative distance is preferred. However, what if the same routing protocol finds two (or more) routes to the same destination? How would the routing protocol choose one of the routes? By using specific decision criteria to evaluate the quality of each route.

Routing decision criteria are quantified by measurements, or metrics. Each routing protocol uses some metrics to determine the quality, or efficiency, or cost of a certain network route.

I now look at the various metrics that routing protocols consider when calculating the cost of a given route.

Hop count

The hop count is the number of routers that need to be traversed to get to the destination network. Routing protocols prefer routes with fewer hops because a certain delay is always involved at every hop to route the packet between network segments.

Think of flying: For the same cost, most people prefer flights with fewer stops, because time is wasted at every stop.

RIP uses the hop-count metric to choose network routes. RIP prefers routes with fewer hops.

Bandwidth

Bandwidth is the throughput of the network route to the destination. Bandwidth is typically measured in bits per second (bps). Routing protocols prefer routes with larger bandwidth because it is very likely that packets reach the destination faster. This is not a guarantee though. For example, if a large-bandwidth route suddenly becomes congested, routers start sending on alternate routes.

Think of driving: For a comparable distance, most people prefer driving on a freeway because it has more lanes and higher speed limits than a normal road, and no street crossings. However, freeways are not always faster — just ask anyone stuck in rush-hour traffic.

EIGRP uses the bandwidth metric to pick network routes. EIGRP prefers routes with larger bandwidth.

Delay

Delay is the time it takes a data packet to reach the destination. Total delay is calculated based on the following:

+ **Processing delay:** The time routers need to inspect the destination of the data packet

+ **Queuing delay:** The time a packet sits in the inbound or outbound queue of the router before being processed or before being sent to the next hop

+ **Transmission delay:** The time it takes to send the packet onto the link to the next hop

+ **Propagation delay:** The time the signal takes to propagate through the transmission media

EIGRP uses the delay metric to pick network routes. EIGRP prefers routes with shorter delay.

Reliability

Reliability is the percentage of time the route is available.

EIGRP considers the reliability metric to pick network routes. EIGRP prefers routes with higher reliability.

Load

Load measures the bandwidth consumed by current traffic on a given route. Load is the difference between the total bandwidth and the available bandwidth of the route.

Book IV Chapter 3

Network Routing

EIGRP considers the load metric to pick network routes. EIGRP prefers routes with lower load.

Maximum transmission unit (MTU)

MTU is the size, in bytes, of each data packet. Each network route has a certain MTU value. The higher the MTU, the more data can be transferred at once.

EIGRP considers the MTU metric to pick network routes. EIGRP prefers routes with higher MTU.

Cost

Cost is calculated based on the bandwidth of a network route. Cost is 10^8/bandwidth.

The OSPF protocol considers the cost metric to pick network routes. OSPF prefers routes with lower cost.

Routing Methods

Routing protocols exchange network, route, and metric information between routers to help routers build their routing tables. Earlier you saw that routing protocols use different metrics to evaluate the quality of a route. Routing protocols also use different methods to exchange information about network routes.

Distance vector routing

Some routing protocols use the distance to a network to evaluate the quality of a network route. Shorter routes (routes with fewer hops) are considered better than longer routes.

Routers using these protocols build their routing tables based on route distance, and they exchange and combine their routing table with their neighbors. Neighbor routers trust each other's route information, and they relay the combined information farther. These protocols are using *distance vector routing*.

Distance vector routing is also known as *rumor routing,* because routers "hear" about routes from their neighbors and they relay this information to other neighbor routers. Routing tables are combined and relayed to all routers in the network.

Convergence

The initial routing information exchange between routers is called *convergence*. When routers finish exchanging data about networks and routes they know, the routers have *converged*. Because distance vector routing protocols combine the routing tables of all routers and propagate them to all neighbors, the convergence process can be fairly long in larger networks. That is one reason why it is not best practice to enable distance vector routing protocols on core layer routers. Distance vector routing is best suited for access or distribution layer routers.

Route updates

After they have converged, routers continue to update each other about network routes they know. These route updates keep track of route changes. Distance vector routing protocols send updates that contain the whole routing table.

Because this is the combined routing table of all routers in the network, the same combined routing table ends up being sent to all routers at predefined time intervals. This consumes more resources on routers and more bandwidth than link-state routing protocols, which do not send the whole routing table to neighbor routers at predefined time intervals.

Although each router sends a route update at predefined time intervals, you must understand that routers do not necessarily send their route updates at the same time. Hence, variations may exist in the knowledge about routes among the routers in the network.

Distance vector routing protocols

The following protocols use distance vector routing:

✦ Routing Information Protocol (RIP)

✦ Interior Gateway Routing Protocol (IGRP)

   IGRP is no longer supported by Cisco. It has been replaced by EIGRP (Enhanced IGRP). EIGRP is considered a hybrid protocol: It has both distance vector and link-state characteristics.

Routing loops

Distance vector routing can cause routing loops. Routing loops route data packets, in a loop, continuously, between neighbor routers. This occurs when routers do not all have the same knowledge of the network.

Route updates send the combined routing table to all routers at predefined intervals. However, routers do not send their route updates at the same time. Hence, variations may exist in the knowledge about routes among the routers in the network.

For example, if a network route becomes unreachable, the router that links to that route knows about it. However, a router that is farther from the failed route still thinks that the route is up. It takes some time before all routers in the network know about the failed route.

Figure 3-1 illustrates an example of a routing loop.

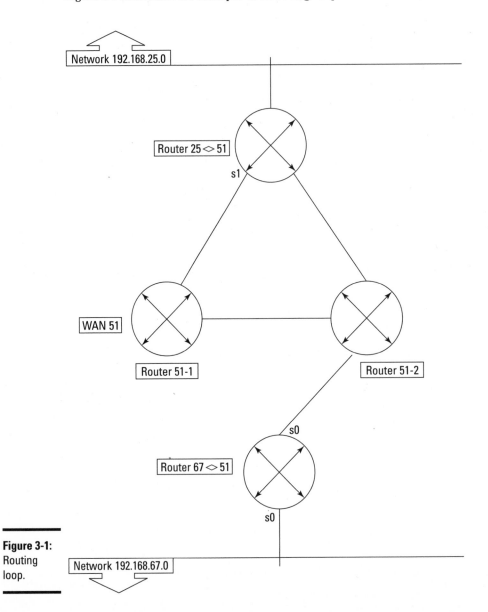

Figure 3-1:
Routing
loop.

Here is what is shown in this figure:

✦ Two networks, 192.168.25.0 (network 25) and 192.168.67.0 (network 67).

✦ Net 25 and net 67 are interconnected through WAN 51.

✦ Router 25<>51 routes data packets in and out of net 25 and WAN 51.

✦ Router 67<>51 routes data packets in and out of net 67 and WAN 51.

✦ WAN 51 provides two routes between net 25 and net 67:

  • One route through router 51-1

  • One route through router 51-2

All routers know about net 25 and net 67, after they all converged their routing tables. Router 25<>51 can get to net 67 through two alternate routes: through router 51-1 and through router 51-2. Now suppose that net 67 becomes unreachable:

✦ Router 67<>51 sends a packet to router 51-1 to inform it that net 67 is unavailable: It sends the routing table without a route to net 67.

✦ Router 51-2 stops sending packets to router 67<>51.

✦ Routers 25<>51 and 51-2 do not know yet that net 67 is unavailable.

✦ Router 51-1 sends a route update to router 51-1 to inform it that net 67 is unavailable.

✦ Assume that router 25<>51 still doesn't know that net 67 is unavailable: It sends an update to routers 51-1 and 51-2 that includes a route to net 67 through 25<>51.

✦ At this point, router 51-1 received the following:

  • A route update "Net 67 down" from Router 51-2.

  • Followed by a route update "Net 67 up" from Router 25<>51.

  • Router 51-1 thinks that net 67 is reachable through router 25<>51.

✦ At this point, router 51-2 received the following:

  • A route update "Net 67 down" from router 67<>51.

  • Followed by a route update "Net 67 up" from router 25<>51.

  • Router 51-2 also thinks that net 67 is reachable through router 25<>51.

  • Router 51-2 did not have the chance to send a route update to router 25<>51 to let it know that net 67 is down.

**Book IV
Chapter 3**

Network Routing

Now, assume that a data packet is sent to net 67 from net 25:

✦ Router 25<>51 still thinks that net 67 is reachable through either 51-1 or 51-2: It sends the packet to either one of them (perhaps 51-1).

✦ Router 51-1 still thinks that net 67 is reachable through router 25<>51: It sends the packet to 25<>51.

✦ And so on. The three routers send this packet in an infinite loop.

This is a problem because sending this packet continuously in an infinite loop between the routers wastes bandwidth and resources on the routers. Luckily, distance vector routing protocols use some tricks to avoid these routing loops:

✦ Maximum hop count

✦ Split horizon

✦ Route poisoning

✦ Poison reverse

✦ Hold-down timer

✦ Triggered update

Maximum hop count

The *maximum hop count* feature ensures that a data packet never takes a route that counts more than a predefined maximum number of hops.

In the example shown previously, the packet will loop indefinitely, which means that it will traverse an infinite number of hops. The maximum number of hops feature attempts to stop this infinite loop. Each protocol has a pre-defined maximum number of hops. Routers consider a destination network to be unreachable if the number of hops associated with the route to that network exceeds the maximum number of hops allowed by the routing pro-tocol. Table 3-2 lists the predefined maximum hop count for each routing protocol.

Table 3-2	Maximum Hop Count
Routing Protocol	*Maximum Number of Hops*
RIP	15
EIGRP	255 (can be configured between 1 and 255; default is 100)
OSPF	Unlimited, because this is a link-state protocol

Split horizon

The *split horizon* feature prevents a route from being advertised back to its advertiser. Here is how this works: Consider two routers, 67<>51 and 51-2. Router 67<>51 advertises the existence of network 67 to router 51-2. Next, router 51-2 advertises network 67 to other routers: router 51-1 and router 25<>51. Without the split horizon feature, router 51-2 would also advertise network 67 back to router 67<>51. This would confuse router 67<>51 because it would think that there is an alternate route back to network 67 through router 51-2. If you assume that the split horizon feature does not exist, this can cause a routing loop:

✦ This would cause router 67<>51 to think that an alternate route exists back to network 67 through router 51-2.

✦ Router 51-2 knows about network 67 from router 67<>51.

✦ Assume that router 67<>51 lost its connection to network 67.

✦ Router 67<>51 thinks that an alternate route exists back to network 67 through router 51-2, because router 51-2 advertised network 67 back to router 67<>51 (no split horizon feature).

✦ Now, router 67<>51 sends packets bound for network 67 to the alternate route to network 67 through router 51-2.

✦ Router 51-2 knows about network 67 from router 67<>51, so it sends packets bound for network 67 back to router 67<>51.

✦ And so on. The data packets bound for network 67 bounce infinitely between routers 67<>51 and 51-2.

You see now how the split horizon feature allows routers to avoid this situation by preventing router 51-2 from advertising "network 67 reachable through router 51-2" back to router 67<>51.

Route poisoning

The *route poisoning* feature changes the hop count associated with a route that becomes unreachable: It sets the hop count to the maximum hop count plus 1. This effectively tells all routers in the network that the route is unreachable because the hop count exceeds the maximum hop count

Book IV
Chapter 3

Network Routing

allowed by the routing protocol. It is a method of disabling an unavailable route in the routing tables as quickly as possible.

In the preceding example, when network 67 becomes unreachable, router 67<>51 sends a packet to router 51-2 advertising network 67 with a hop count of MaxHopCount+1. Right away, router 51-2 considers network 67 unreachable. This prevents router 51-2 from getting confused by router 25<>51 when it advertises "network 67 up" right after router 67<>51 advertises "network 67 down": Even if router 51-2 thinks that network 67 is up and reachable through router 25<>51 now, the hop count is larger than the maximum hop count allowed by the routing protocol, so 51-2 would never send to network 67.

Poison reverse

The *poison reverse* feature is similar to router poisoning but in the reverse direction. In the preceding example, when router 67<>51 sends a packet to router 51-2 advertising network 67 with a hop count of MaxHopCount+1, router 51-2 sends back a packet to router 67<>51 advertising network 67 with a hop count of MaxHopCount+1. This basically breaks the split horizon rule, but that's okay, because the whole purpose of all of these rules is to prevent routing loops from happening. By using poison reverse, the routers ensure that all neighbors know as quickly as possible that network 67 is down.

Hold-down timer

The *hold-down timer* prevents a router from accepting updates about a route for a certain time if that route was advertised as unavailable. This prevents routing loops by ensuring that when a route has been advertised as being unreachable, it is not readvertised as being back up by a router that did not receive the "route down" message yet.

For example, router 51-2 is confused by router 25<>51 when 25<>51 advertises "network 67 up" right after router 67<>51 advertises "network 67 down." The hold-down timer feature avoids this confusion by preventing router 51-2 from accepting the "network 67 up" update sent by router 25<>51, right after router 67<>51 sent a "network 67 down" update.

Triggered update

The *triggered update* feature allows routers to update each other as soon as a change occurs in the network, as opposed to waiting until the scheduled route updates to be exchanged.

By default, distance vector routing protocols combine and exchange the routing tables of all routers at predefined time intervals. If a network fails right after the router sent its scheduled route update, the other routers won't know about the failed network until the next route update sent by the router that connects to the failed network. This opens a large window of time when routers in the network think that a route is up when in fact it is down. Triggered updates fix this by causing the router to send its update to neighbors as soon as it detects that the route is down.

Link-state routing

Link-state routing protocols build their routing tables independently based on route updates they receive from their neighbors. Link-state protocols do not merge the routing tables of neighbor routers. Rather, they enable routers to have a clear image of their neighbors, network topology, and routes to their neighbors and beyond.

Here are the main characteristics of link-state protocols:

✦ Route updates are only sent when routes change, as opposed to distance vector protocols, which send route updates periodically.

✦ Route updates contain information about the route that changed only, as opposed to distance vector protocols, which send route updates that contain the whole combined routing table.

✦ Routers first exchange "Hello" messages to get acquainted with their neighbors, as opposed to distance vector protocols, which exchange and combine their routing tables from the get-go.

✦ Routers maintain neighbor and topology tables in addition to routing tables to help routers keep track not only of routes but also of the topology of the network and of their neighbor routers.

Convergence

Routers execute an initial exchange of routing information when they power up and join the network. This initial exchange is called the *convergence* process. When routers finish exchanging data about networks and routes they know, the routers have *converged*.

Because link-state routing protocols only exchange "Hello" messages initially and because link-state protocols do not merge their routing tables, they converge faster than distance vector protocols.

It is best practice to use link-state routing protocols or hybrid protocols on core layer routers. Distance vector routing is best suited for access or distribution layer routers.

Route updates

Similar to distance vector protocols, link-state routing protocols continue to update routers about available routes after they have converged. These route updates keep track of route changes. Contrary to distance vector routing protocols, link-state protocols do not send regular updates that contain the whole routing table. Link-state routing protocols send route updates that contain only information about the route that changed.

Because link-state route updates are relatively infrequent and contain only a small advertisement about the route that changed, they consume fewer resources on routers and less bandwidth than distance vector routing protocols, which send the whole routing table to neighbor routers regularly, at predefined time intervals.

Link-state routing protocols

The Open Shortest Path First (OSPF) protocol uses link state routing.

Hybrid routing

Hybrid protocols have both distance vector and link-state characteristics:

✦ Like distance vector protocols, hybrid protocols use distance to evaluate the quality of routes.

✦ Like link-state protocols, hybrid protocols use other metrics in addition to distance to evaluate the quality of routes, such as available bandwidth, delay, reliability, load, and MTU.

Convergence

Similar to link-state routing protocols, hybrid protocols only exchange "Hello" messages initially. Hence, they converge faster than distance vector protocols.

Hybrid protocols are well suited for core layer, distribution layer, and even access layer routers.

Route updates

Similar to distance vector protocols, hybrid routing protocols send route updates that contain the whole routing table. However, unlike distance vector protocols, hybrid protocols do not send route updates regularly at predefined time intervals. They only send updates when routes change, like link-state protocols.

Hybrid routing protocols

Enhanced IGRP (EIGRP) is considered a hybrid routing protocol.

Configuring Routing Protocols

The procedure to configure routing protocols on Cisco routers is the same for all protocols. Follow these steps to enable any given routing protocol on a Cisco router:

1. Start up the routing protocol on each router.

2. Enable the routing protocol on interfaces on each router.

3. Configure routing protocol options.

You need to execute these setup steps manually on each router. Some routing protocols can automatically negotiate certain configuration options.

Prep Test

1 **Describe a network route.**

   A ○ A set of metrics that routers use to evaluate distance to a network

   B ○ A data transmission path through one or more networks between two end nodes

   C ○ A Layer 3 protocol

   D ○ All of the above

2 **Describe a static route.**

   A ○ It is predefined on your router.

   B ○ You create it manually on your switch.

   C ○ You create manually on your router.

   D ○ All of the above.

3 **What is the main advantage of static routes?**

   A ○ Routing efficiency: fewer resources consumed on your router and less bandwidth spent for routing

   B ○ Maintenance: easier to maintain than dynamic routes

   C ○ Scalability: static routes scale out very well, even in large networks

   D ○ All of the above

4 **Describe a dynamic route.**

   A ○ It is predefined on your router.

   B ○ Routes are dynamically created and maintained on your router.

   C ○ It is manually created on your router.

   D ○ All of the above.

5 **Dynamic routes are necessary for network environments that need which of the following?**

   A ○ Adaptive routing accuracy: routes are updated as they change by routing protocols

   B ○ Low maintenance: easier to maintain than static routes

   C ○ High scalability: dynamic routes scale out very well, even in large networks

   D ○ All of the above

6 **Define a default route.**

A ○ It is a predefined route on your router.

B ○ Routing protocols are created and maintained on your router.

C ○ It is a static route that defines the destination of any packets whose destination network is unknown

D ○ All of the above

7 **Routing protocols have which of the following features?**

A ○ Exchange network, routes, and metric information between routers

B ○ Help routers build their routing tables

C ○ Do not route data packets

D ○ All of the above

8 **Describe routed protocols.**

A ○ They tag each data packet with the source and destination hierarchical addresses.

B ○ They assign a unique logical address to each node in the network.

C ○ They route data packets.

D ○ All of the above.

9 **The administrative distance defines which of the following?**

A ○ How reliable is the information source that provided the data about the network route

B ○ How far is the next router on a given route

C ○ How far is the next administration service point on a given route

D ○ All of the above

10 **When the administrative distance of two routes to the same network is the same, routing protocols use _____ to evaluate the quality of each route**

A ○ Helper agents

B ○ Metrics

C ○ Switch modules

D ○ All of the above

11 **Describe the hop-count metric.**

A ○ It is the number of routers and networks that need to be traversed to get to the destination network.

B ○ It is the number of ports on a router.

C ○ It is the number of links between two networks.

D ○ All of the above.

Answers

1 **B.** A network route is a data transmission path through one or more networks between two end nodes. Read *"Introducing Network Routes."*

2 **C.** You create manually on your router. A static route is a route that you manually create on your router. See the *"Introducing Network Routes"* section.

3 **A.** Routing efficiency: fewer resources consumed on your router and less bandwidth spent for routing. The main advantage of static routes is their efficiency. Static routes consume very few resources on the router since you don't need to run routing protocols to maintain static routes the way you do for dynamic routes. See the *"Introducing Network Routes"* section.

4 **B.** Routing protocols create and maintain on your router. A dynamic route is a route that routing protocols create and maintain on your router. See the *"Introducing Network Routes"* section.

5 **D.** All of the above. Dynamic routes are well suited for network environments that need adaptive routing accuracy, low maintenance, and high scalability. See the *"Introducing Network Routes"* section.

6 **C.** Is a static route that defines the destination of any packets whose destination network is unknown. A default route is a static route that defines where packets are sent when the router cannot find any route for them. See the *"Introducing Network Routes"* section.

7 **D.** All of the above. Routing protocols exchange network, routes and metric information between routers to help routers build their routing tables. Routing protocols do not route packets. Routed protocols route packets. Review the *"Routing Protocols"* section.

8 **D.** All of the above. Routed protocols tag each data packet with the source and destination hierarchical addresses. They assign a unique logical address to each node in the network and they route data packets. Review the *"Routing Protocols"* section.

9 **A.** How reliable is the information source that provided the data about the network route. The administrative distance defines how reliable is the information source that provided the data about the network route. Review the *"Routing Decision Criteria"* section.

10 **B.** Metrics. When the administrative distance of two routes to the same network is the same, routing protocols use metrics to evaluate the quality of each route. Review the *"Routing protocol metrics"* section.

11 **A.** The number of routers and networks that need to be traversed to get to the destination network. The hop count metric measures the number of routers and networks that need to be traversed to get to the destination network. Review the *"Routing protocol metrics"* section.

Chapter 4: Routing Information Protocol (RIP)

Exam Objectives

✓ Defining distance vector and interior gateway protocols

✓ Examining routing updates and convergence

✓ Understanding hop-count metrics, routing loops, and split horizon

✓ Comparing RIPv1 and RIPv2

✓ Detailing RIP packet structures

✓ Defining autonomous systems

✓ Configuring RIP

✓ Verifying RIP installations

The Routing Information Protocol, or RIP for short, is a dynamic local- and wide-area network distance vector, interior gateway protocol. The distance vector routing algorithm on which RIP is based has been in use since the mid-1950s. Known originally as the Bellman-Ford algorithm, it was first used for the ARPANET computer networks in 1968. This distance vector algorithm is used in packet-switched networks to calculate paths and distances to target networks by mathematically comparing multiple routes to the same destination. RIP uses these calculations to determine the best path to the target network.

Distance vector protocols such as RIP are required to periodically announce any known network topology changes to other neighboring routing devices. Because distance vector protocols do not have knowledge of the entire network topology, these updates are repeated at regular intervals on User Datagram Protocol (UDP) port 520. Also, during network topology configuration changes, these updates are recorded in the routing table of each connected network router. Routing updates continue between network routers with the goal of having all routing tables in complete agreement with one another, or matching. This is known as *convergence*. Without convergence, it is impossible for distance vector protocols to function properly.

Introducing Routing Information Protocol (RIP)

Because routers initially have only information pertaining to directly attached interfaces, neighboring routes must be discovered. Routers use distance vector algorithms (such as RIP) and routing tables to discover, analyze, and record distances between possible destinations.

Each router periodically sends a list of all known routes and announces these routes to all other neighboring routers (on directly attached segments). Distance vector protocols do not maintain a map of the entire network, just neighboring next-hop addresses. This differs from link-state protocols, which contain the entire network map and include updates to remote router segments. So, a general overview of RIP may be consolidated as follows:

✦ Each router on an internetwork has an individual identity and advertises directly attached links using a zero metric.

✦ During the router bootup process, the complete routing table is forwarded to all neighboring routers.

✦ Routing updates are propagated (sent to other neighboring routers) every 30 seconds, or they may be forwarded automatically when topology changes are detected.

✦ Each router calculates which neighbor may be used to reach a destination network using the shortest available path.

Due to protocol limitations, RIP is known to have slow convergence times and is considered a poor choice for large-scale WANs. RIP is best suited for smaller-scale deployments isolated within a single autonomous system (AS).

An interior gateway protocol

RIP is also defined as an interior gateway protocol and was originally designed for smaller networks, with similar network topology and specifications. This means that the routing protocol is contained within the same routing domain, or autonomous system. Autonomous systems are considered to be a single network or multiple groups of networks under the control of the same administrative structure. For example, the IT department of a single university tasked with the administration of multiple campus networks is considered a single autonomous system. The routers inside these interior networks use interior gateway protocols such as RIP to communicate and share routing information between subnets.

Communication outside or between autonomous systems is handled by a Border Gateway Protocol (BGP), formerly known as an Exterior Gateway Protocol. To separately distinguish and uniquely identify each AS on the

Internet, autonomous systems are assigned an Autonomous System Number (ASN) by the Internet Assigned Numbers Authority (IANA) or individual Regional Internet Registries (RIRs).

Cisco routers use a number of different protocols to transfer data. Multiple protocols may be activated simultaneously and run independently of one another. To decide which methods of communications to use, protocols are weighted by administrative distance (AD). The higher the AD value, the less likely that the protocol will be chosen by the IOS. For example, RIP carries an AD value of 120, with Open Shortest Path First (OSPF) assigned a value of 110. If two routes exist on a router (using RIP and OSPF in this example) to a particular destination network, the lowest AD, OSPF, is selected. The default assigned vales for administrative distance are listed in Figure 4-1. The `distance` command may be used to change these default values.

Administrative Distance	Routing Method
0	Direct Connection
1	Static Route
5	Enhanced IGRP Summary Route
20	External BGP
90	Internal Enhanced IGRP
100	IGRP
110	OSPF
115	IS-IS
120	RIP
140	EGP
160	On Demand Routing
170	External Enhanced IGRP
200	Internal BGP
255	Unknown

Figure 4-1: Cisco default administrative distances.

Book IV
Chapter 4

Routing Information
Protocol (RIP)

Routing tables, updates, and hop count

RIP relies heavily on a metric hop count to determine the path and distance to the destination network. The optimal route to a destination is decided by RIP's calculated number of hops it must make to deliver data to the target network. To RIP, less hops means less stops and shorter distances to the destination. The lowest metric value is considered by RIP to be the best route available. For example, a route with five hops to a target network will be preferred over a different six-hop route leading to the same destination.

This method of route determination by RIP may also prove dramatically inefficient. For example, the speed of both links has not been taken into consideration. RIP considers the five-hop route closer in distance than the six-hop route and chooses the shortest metric for delivery. This would prove to be a poor choice if the six-hop route were established over high-speed connections while the five-hop route used much slower WAN links.

RIP limits the hop count to eliminate the condition known as "counting to infinity." By assigning each IP packet a starting default Time-To-Live (TTL) value of 15, a packet "life span" is established. Every packet must reach its final destination in 15 hops or less. As a packet progresses through a gateway, a hop is recorded, and the TTL value is reduced by 1. Each router along the path to the destination is considered a hop and decreases the TTL value inside the IP packet by 1. If the packet's TTL value equals 0 and still has not reached its final destination, it is discarded. This eliminates routing loops and prevents undeliverable packets from remaining on the internetwork indefinitely.

When a routing table update is received, the router checks for changes by comparing the update to the currently existing routing table. If a new route is announced in an update, it is added to the existing routing table. This increases the metric value by a factor of 1, and the sender's IP address is assigned as the next-hop address. To ensure proper convergence, the router then sends this new update to all neighboring routers right away and separately from any other regularly scheduled routing updates. If an identical route exists in both the update and current routing table (but includes a lower metric for the route), the lower metric is used by replacing the existing routing table entry with the updated route (smaller metric value).

Routing error mitigation methods

RIP depends on neighboring routing devices and gateways to announce routing table updates (every 30 seconds) and uses the best route to a destination. Problems arise when a gateway or router along the destination path fails. In such cases, these newly unreachable gateways are unable to announce their "downed" status:

✦ If communication to a router is not made after 90 seconds, the route is considered invalid.

✦ After 180 seconds, the hold-down timer is reached, and RIP determines that the route is no longer available.

Neighboring gateways are contacted with an update regarding the unavailable route.

✦ After 270 seconds, if no other information is received regarding the failed route, the flush timer removes the route from the routing table.

RIP also prevents the possibility of routing loops by limiting the hop count value to 15. A routing loop is an error occurring in the routing algorithm, causing an endless, infinite loop that designates a remote destination network as unreachable. To examine the RIP routing table update process and looping problem, refer to Figure 4-2. Three subnets are connected using two routers. The routing table on the Alpha router contains information on how to reach the accounting and IT department, while the Bravo router knows routes for the IT department as well as the human resources subnet. After routing table updates are exchanged between routers, each router will have a defined map to reach all three subnets.

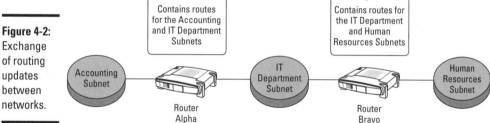

Figure 4-2:
Exchange
of routing
updates
between
networks.

Routing Table A
Contains routes
for the Accounting
and IT Department
Subnets

Routing Table B
Contains routes for
the IT Department
and Human
Resources Subnets

Accounting
Subnet

Router
Alpha

IT
Department
Subnet

Router
Bravo

Human
Resources
Subnet

Now, a user on the accounting subnet wants to communicate with a user on the human resources subnet. Complications begin in this scenario when an interface on a router fails. The user's packet reaches the Bravo router, but the Bravo router's interface to the human resources subnet goes down and has no possibility of delivering the packet. If the Alpha router is advertising an alternate route to the human resources department, the Bravo router will forward the packet back to the Alpha router, figuring that the packet will be deliverable through the Alpha route. The Alpha router will then do a routing table lookup and determine that the next-hop path to the human resources department is through router Bravo. As shown in Figure 4-3, without the hop-count limitation, this loop would continue to infinity.

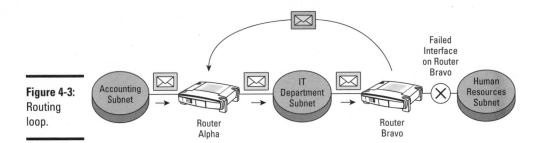

Figure 4-3:
Routing
loop.

Split horizon

RIP provides other preventive measures to eliminate routing loops. Split horizon is a method that prevents a router from advertising a route back out of the same interface on which the route was received, or learned on.

This would eliminate the problem from the previous example. Router Alpha knows the path to the human resources department only because of router Bravo's routing table announcements, and therefore does not send routing information to router Bravo regarding the human resources network. Likewise, Router Bravo has discovered the accounting subnet only because of the broadcasted announcements of router Alpha and — using the split horizon rules of communication — does not send its routing table information regarding the accounting department to router Alpha. Split horizon is thus enabled by default on interfaces running RIP, Interior Gateway Routing Protocol (IGRP) and Enhanced IGRP (EIGRP).

Split horizon with poison reverse is a slightly modified version of the split horizon loop-mitigation method previously mentioned. In standard split horizon, router Alpha's path to the human resources subnet is not advertised to router Bravo. Likewise, router Bravo's known route to the accounting subnet is not advertised to router Alpha. Instead of not advertising the path to prevent the loop as with standard split horizon, poison reverse inexplicably denies the path. This is done by assigning the route with a TTL metric of 16. When the router reads this in its routing table, the route is ignored.

Convergence and timers

RIP relies on convergence and timers to keep routing tables between interconnected routing devices on a WAN current and accurate.

Convergence allows all routing devices to be in complete synchronization with one another. Convergence may prove to be more difficult to achieve in larger-scale network deployments. As an internetwork grows, more routing tables must be updated and kept in agreement with all other gateways. When a change inside the internetwork topology is detected, a new routing table update is triggered. This "triggered update" occurs independently from the repetitive, regularly scheduled 30-second automatic routing table updates and improves convergence times. For example, when a router detects a link failure to a neighboring router of a gateway, a routing update is triggered, notifying all other neighboring routing devices of the failed link. Each contacted router then informs its own neighbors regarding the link failure until all devices converge (are in agreement).

Problems may arise if all routers do not converge in a timely fashion. If a neighboring router has not yet been informed and is unaware of the link failure, and its own (outdated) routing table update is sent to a router that has already been notified of the link failure, a reactivation of the failed link by means of an unwanted routing table update (reinserting the route to the bad link) could happen. Timers, such as the hold-down timer, are used in preventing the reactivation of failed links. Hold-down timers deny propagation of dead routes via updates for specific periods of time, allowing proper network convergence to occur.

Keep the following points in mind regarding the Routing Information Protocol:

✦ Hop count limit of 15.

✦ RIP broadcasts routing updates every 30 seconds.

✦ Sends routing table updates on UDP port 520.

✦ Inefficient routing decisions. Best path determined by smaller metric.

✦ Slow convergence in large-scale networks.

✦ Uses minimal CPU and memory resources.

✦ Efficient in single autonomous systems or small-scale networks.

✦ Universal interoperability protocol support between hardware manufacturers and software developers allows interconnecting legacy and newer hardware.

RIPv1

The original RIP specification, created by Xerox Corporation, is known as RIP version 1.

The major difference between RIPv1 and RIPv2 is that routing updates in RIP version 1 cannot contain subnet information.

As shown in Figure 4-4, RIPv1 is known as a classful routing protocol. You cannot use RIPv1 in a classless routing environment. Because all subnets must be of the same size, creating unequal-sized subnets with variable-length subnet masking (VLSM) is not possible using RIPv1. RIPv1 also supports no method to authenticate router updates, which leaves the network vulnerable to malicious attacks.

Figure 4-4:
RIPv1
classful
internetwork.

204.218.209.0/24   204.218.210.0/24   204.218.211.0/24   204.218.212.0/24

Router   Router   Router
Alpha   Bravo   Charlie

RIPv1 transports routing table updates in IP packets reaching 512K in size. The structure of these individual packets is shown in Figure 4-5. Following are the descriptions of the various fields that comprise a RIPv1 packet:

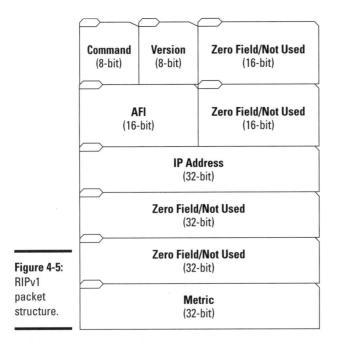

Figure 4-5:
RIPv1
packet
structure.

✦ **Command:** Field distinguishing the type of packet being transmitted. Request packets are used to poll other routers for routing table updates. Response packets are either generated due to a request packet or as a normally scheduled routing table update.

✦ **Version Number:** Field displaying the RIP version number currently in use. For RIPv1, this value is set to 1. A value of 2 indicates RIPv2.

The version number field may be used in troubleshooting scenarios, allowing administrators to pinpoint potential incompatibility problems between RIP versions.

✦ **Zero/Unused:** Unused field holding a default value of 0.

✦ **Address-Family Identifier (AFI):** Because RIP is able to transport routing information for multiple protocols, this field is used to designate the address family, or advertised protocol, used by RIP.

Each AFI number identifies the address being used by its value, with 2 representing IP addressing.

✦ **Address:** Field holding the IP address.

✦ **Metric:** The number of hops encountered along the way to a particular destination. A reachable route always uses a metric of 15 hops or less. Any destination requiring more than 15 hops is considered unreachable.

RIPv2

RIPv2 builds on the existing structure of RIPv1 by adding the following features:

✦ **Enhanced security measures:** Provides support for message digest algorithm 5 (MD5) and plain-text password authentication.

✦ **Support for classless addressing schemes:** Classless interdomain routing (CIDR) and VLSM are supported by adding a subnet mask field to the RIPv2 packet structure.

✦ **Route Tag field:** Separator for internal and external RIP routes.

✦ **Next Hop field:** Allows packet forwarding to the immediate next-hop address.

✦ **Multicasting:** RIPv2 supports multitasking using IP address 224.0.0.9.

The RIPv2 packet structure is similar in size to the RIPv1 packet but replaces the zero fields with router tag, subnet mask, and next-hop addressing information.

The changes to the packet structure allow RIPv2 to provide authentication security and VLSM/CIDR support, which are not available in RIPv1. The RIPv2 packet structure is shown in Figure 4-6, and the following descriptions explain the various fields that comprise a RIPv2 packet:

**Book IV
Chapter 4**

**Routing Information
Protocol (RIP)**

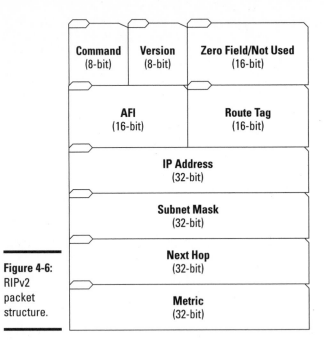

Figure 4-6:
RIPv2
packet
structure.

+ **Command:** As with RIPv1, this field is used to distinguish the type of packet being transmitted. Request packets are used to poll other routers for routing table updates. Response packets are either generated due to a request packet or as a normally scheduled routing table update.

+ **Version:** Denotes the RIP version used. For RIPv2, this value is set to 2.

+ **Zero/Unused:** Unused field holding a default value of 0 and implemented only for backward compatibility with nonstandard (outdated) RIP versions.

+ **Address-Family Identifier (AFI):** Shows the address family used by RIP. The AFI field of RIPv2 functions similarly to RIPv1.

   One difference between RIPv1 and RIPv2 is the use of authentication. If the AFI hex message entry in the first message equals 0xFFFF, the remaining entries will contain authentication information consisting of a simple password.

+ **Route Tag:** Field used to show whether the route is an internal or external route. Internal routes are discovered by RIP alone, whereas external routes are discovered via non-RIP protocols.

+ **IP Address:** Field used for IP address information.

+ **Subnet Mask:** Field used for subnet mask information.

A subnet mask field value of 0 means that no subnet mask addressing information has been given. This field is not available in RIPv1.

✦ **Next Hop:** IP address of the next-hop address.

✦ **Metric:** The number of hops encountered along the way to a particular destination. A reachable route always uses a metric of 15 hops or less. Any destination requiring more than 15 hops is considered unreachable.

The maximum number of router table entries in a RIPv1 or RIPv2 packet is 25. Using RIPng (see the next section), there is no longer a limit for routing table entries and is only limited by the maximum transmission unit (MTU).

RIPng

Routing Information Protocol Next Generation, or RIPng, is intended for IPv6 networks. Based on the RIP IPv4 algorithm, RIPng is designed for medium-sized autonomous systems using interior gateway protocols.

The following are key differences in implementation between IPv4 and IPv6:

✦ RIPng does not need to implement authentication on packets.

If authentication is required, it is performed by IP Security (IPsec), increasing efficiency.

✦ Packets use the Prefix Length field instead of a subnet mask.

✦ Next-hop addresses are contained in a separate routing entry to conserve space.

✦ Uses multicasts for transmissions using FF02::9.

✦ Uses UDP port 521 instead of 520.

The packet structure of IPv6 compared to IPv4 is shown in Figure 4-7. An explanation of the RIPng packet fields follows:

✦ **Command:** Distinguishes between request and response messages. Request messages seek information for the router's routing table and contain the value of 1. A value of 2 indicates response messages, sent periodically or when a request message is received.

✦ **Version Number:** Specifies the version of RIPng that the originating router is running. This will be set to 1 because this is the first version of the RIPng protocol.

✦ **Zero/Unused:** An unused, reserved field set with a default value of 0.

Book IV
Chapter 4

Routing Information
Protocol (RIP)

RIP IPv4 Packet Header

RIPng IPv6 Packet Header

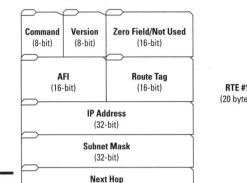
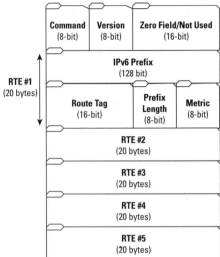

Figure 4-7:
RIP IPv4
versus IPv6
packet
structure.

✦ **Route Table Entries:** A 20-byte routing table entry field containing information regarding reachable routes. Each RIPng packet contains a variable amount of routing table entries (RTEs). RTE subfields include the following:

- *IPv6 prefix:* The 128-bit network address.

- *Route Tag:* Distinguishes between internal and external routes.

- *Prefix Length:* An 8-bit prefix length field analogous to an IPv4 subnet mask. The prefix length is used to separate the network and host portion of the address.

- *Metric:* A value of 15 or less, designating a valid route. Invalid routes are marked with an unreachable value of 16, or infinity.

Configuring RIP

Matching the simplistic characteristics of the protocol, RIP configuration is also simple and easy to implement. There are two main requirements when configuring RIP on a Cisco router:

✦ The `router rip` command is used to enable RIP on the router.

✦ The `network` command is issued to designate the networks that allow RIP traffic.

Execute the following IOS commands to enable RIP on a Cisco router:

1. **In global configuration mode, assign IP addresses to the router interfaces (if not already configured):**

```
Router>enable
Router#config t
Router(config)#interface ethernet 0
Router(config-if)#ip address 192.168.10.1
Router(config-if)#no Shutdown
Router(config-if)#interface ethernet 1
Router(config-if)#ip address 192.168.11.1
Router(config-if)#no shutdown
Router(config-if)#exit
```

2. **Enable RIP:**

```
Router(config)#router rip
```

3. **Specify a network to associate with RIP routing (from Step 1):**

```
Router(config-router)#network 192.168.10.0
Router(config-router)#network 192.168.11.0
Router(config-router)#exit
```

Although not mandatory, quite a few additional configuration options are available for RIP.

The following options may be used after RIP has been enabled on the Cisco router:

✦ **Permit unicast updates:** RIP is considered a broadcast protocol. To allow the exchange of routing updates between broadcast and nonbroadcast networks, issue the following command in router configuration mode:

```
Router(config-router)#neighbor ip-address
```

RIP router table updates will now be sent to the nonbroadcast neighboring router.

✦ **Prevent updates on a specified interface:** In certain cases, limiting router updates from reaching certain interfaces may be warranted. For example, preventing the advertisement of local routes from Ethernet (LAN) interfaces to be sent to serial (WAN) interfaces may be required, thus regulating advertised routes. To disable RIP updates to a specified interface, use the following command in router configuration mode:

```
Router(config-router)#passive interface type number
```

✦ **Routing metric offsets:** Allows increasing incoming and outgoing metric values learned by RIP. In the following example, an incoming offset of 10 is established to any routes learned from the Ethernet 0 interface (using access-list number 50):

```
Router(config-router)#offset-list 50 in 10 ethernet 0
```

✦ **Timer adjustments:** Interval settings may be adjusted for the frequency of outgoing routing updates, specified time period until a route becomes invalid, and the elapsed time until a dead route is removed from the routing table. To adjust timers, use the `timers basic` command in router configuration mode:

```
Router(config-router)#timers basic 30 90 180 270 0
```

Listed here are the default timer interval settings:

- *Update (30 seconds):* Time interval between routing table updates

- *Invalid (90 seconds):* Time interval during which a route is considered invalid

- *Holddown (180 seconds):* Time interval during which routing information regarding better paths is ignored, or suppressed

- *Flush (270 seconds):* Amount of time elapsed before a route is removed from the routing table

- *Sleeptime (0 milliseconds):* Amount of time in which routing updates will be postponed

✦ **RIP version:** Specifies the sending and receiving of RIPv1 or RIPv2 updates. By default, Cisco routers receive incoming RIPv1 and RIPv2 router table updates, but send outgoing RIPv1 updates only.

To specify the required RIP version, use the `ip rip send version` and `ip rip receive version` IOS commands in interface configuration mode:

- To send and receive RIPv1 packets only:

```
Router(config-if)#ip rip send version 1
Router(config-if)#ip rip receive version 1
```

- To send and receive RIPv2 packets only:

```
Router(config-if)#ip rip send version 2
Router(config-if)#ip rip receive version 2
```

- To send and receive both RIPv1 and RIPv2 packets:

```
Router(config-if)#ip rip send version 1 2
Router(config-if)#ip rip receive version 1 2
```

✦ **Enable RIP authentication:** Because RIP authentication is not possible in version 1, sending and receiving of RIPv2 packets must be enabled to use this option. RIP authentication only applies to RIPv2. Plain text (used by default and is a security risk) and message digest algorithm 5 (MD5) are the two types of authentication methods.

MD5 authentication is enabled in interface configuration mode as follows:

```
Router(config-if)#ip rip authentication mode md5
    keychain NAMEOFCHAIN
```

✦ **Disable route summarization:** When disabled, subnet and host routing information is transmitted across classful network boundaries. RIPv2 supports route summarization by default.

To disable this feature, use the `no auto-summary` command in router configuration mode:

```
Router(config-router)#version 2
Router(config-router)#no auto-summary
```

✦ **Disable source IP address validation:** By default on Cisco routers, incoming RIP routing updates are validated by source IP address. This allows verification of the sender's address. If the IP address is determined to be from an unauthorized source (mismatching IP), the update is discarded.

To disable this feature (not recommended), enter the following in router configuration mode:

```
Router(config-router)#no validate-update-source
```

✦ **Split horizon:** Used to prevent routing loops. The rule of split horizon specifies that no received inbound routing updates may be sent back outbound on the same interface. This feature improves network communications and is enabled by default for all encapsulation types other than nonbroadcast networks such as Frame Relay.

In the case of nonbroadcast network types, it may be advantageous to disable split horizon in interface configuration mode as follows:

```
Router(config-router)#no ip split horizon
```

To enable split horizon, enter the following:

```
Router(config-router)#ip split horizon
```

Verifying RIP

A few methods exist to verify the functionality of RIP on Cisco devices. Basic IOS commands such as `ping` and `traceroute` are invaluable troubleshooting aids regarding connectivity issues and the routes packets take to reach a destination. Many additional and helpful clues may be learned from various `show` and `debug` commands. Listed here are the most helpful IOS commands when troubleshooting RIP:

✦ `show ip protocols`: Used in EXEC mode to display the state and parameters of the active routing protocols.

This allows a network administrator to verify that RIP (or other IP protocols) is actively running on a router and to view the configured timers and networks, as shown here:

```
Router#show ip protocols
Routing Protocol is "rip"
  Sending updates every 30 seconds, next due in 5 seconds
  Invalid after 180 seconds, hold down 180, flushed after 240
  Outgoing update filter list for all interfaces is not set
  Incoming update filter list for all interfaces is not set
  Redistributing: rip
  Default version control: send version 2, receive version 2
    Interface         Send  Recv  Key-chain
    Ethernet0         2     2     trees
    Fddi0             2     2
  Routing for Networks:
    10.0.0.0
  Routing Information Sources:
    Gateway     Distance      Last Update
    10.1.2.1    120           00:00:13
    10.1.5.2    120           00:00:07
  Distance: (default is 120)
```

Quite a bit of information is given from the sample output shown here regarding RIP (because RIP is the only configured protocol in the example). The first line states that the routing protocol is RIP. Routing updates are being sent every 30 seconds (default), with the next update arriving in 5 seconds. The intervals for invalid, hold-down, and flush timers are 180, 180, and 240 (nondefault), respectively. Incoming and outgoing filter lists specify whether filters have been set, and the default version control displays that sending and receiving of RIPv2 packets are active. Routing for networks displays the IP addresses of networks into which the routing process is currently injecting routes. Routing information sources shows any address, distance, and last update of routing sources used in compiling the routing table.

✦ `show ip route`: Displays the routing table. A sample output is shown here:

```
Router#show ip route
Codes: C - connected, S - static, I - IGRP, R - RIP, M - mobile, B - BGP
       D - EIGRP, EX - EIGRP external, O - OSPF, IA - OSPF inter area
       N1 - OSPF NSSA external type 1, N2 - OSPF NSSA external type 2
       E1 - OSPF external type 1, E2 - OSPF external type 2, E - EGP
       i - IS-IS, L1 - IS-IS level-1, L2 - IS-IS level-2, * - candidate
default
       U - per-user static route, o - ODR

Gateway of last resort is not set

     172.16.0.0/24 is subnetted, 2 subnets
C       172.16.1.0 is directly connected, Ethernet0
C       172.16.2.0 is directly connected, Ethernet1
```

As shown in this code, both Ethernet networks are directly attached to the router

✦ `show ip rip database`: Displays summary address entries in the RIP routing database, as shown here:

```
Router#show ip rip database
172.18.0.0/16     auto-summary
172.18.0.0/16
    [1] via 172.16.1.2, 00:02:44 (permanent), Serial1/0
    * Triggered Routes:
    - [1] via 172.16.1.2, Serial1/0
172.19.0.0/16     auto-summary
172.19.0.0/16
    [1] via 172.16.1.2, 00:02:45 (permanent),Serial1/0
    * Triggered Routes:
    - [1] via 172.16.1.2, Serial1/0
```

✦ `debug ip rip`: Used to display information on RIP events and issues a log message for each RIP update:

```
R1#debug ip rip
RIP protocol debugging is on

RIP: received v1 update from 192.168.1.2 on Ethernet0
    192.168.2.0 in 1 hops
    192.169.2.0 in 1 hops

RIP: sending v1 update to 255.255.255.255 via Ethernet0 (192.168.1.1)
    network 192.169.1.0, metric 1

RIP: sending v1 update to 255.255.255.255 via Loopback0 (192.169.1.1)
    network 192.168.1.0, metric 1
    network 192.168.2.0, metric 2
    network 192.169.2.0, metric 2
```

The first section displays routing updates received from the source network, and the next two RIP updates are sent to destination addresses.

To disable debugging, enter the following:

```
Router#undebug all
All possible debugging has been turned off
```

Additionally, the `debug ip rip` command contains many keywords to specify certain criteria. A few of these are listed here:

- `debug ip rip events`: Displays information regarding RIP routing transactions

- `debug ip rip trigger`: Provides information on RIP triggered packet events

- `debug ip rip database`: Displays information regarding RIP database events

Disable debugging output with the `undebug all`, `no debug all`, and `no debug ip rip` commands.

Prep Test

1 **Which types of protocol is RIP? (Choose two.)**

A ○ Interior gateway protocol
B ○ External gateway protocol
C ○ Distance vector protocol
D ○ Link-state protocol

2 **Which statement is true regarding RIPv1?**

A ○ RIP does not use subnet masks.
B ○ All subnets must use the same subnet mask.
C ○ Subnets may use variable subnet masks.
D ○ VLSM support is built into all versions of RIP.

3 **Which features allow RIP to prevent routing loops? (Choose two.)**

A ○ VLSM
B ○ Authentication
C ○ Split horizon
D ○ CIDR
E ○ Hold-down timers

4 **Which method best describes RIP's best-path route determination?**

A ○ Fastest link
B ○ Administrative distance (AD)
C ○ Bandwidth allocation
D ○ Hop count

5 **Which of the following are disadvantages of RIPv1? (Choose three.)**

A ○ Slow convergence
B ○ Classless routing
C ○ Poor performance in large-scale networks
D ○ No security features

6 **Which commands are used to configure RIP? (Choose two.)**

A ○ `configure rip`
B ○ `network`
C ○ `rip enable`
D ○ `route rip`
E ○ `router rip`

7 **What is the administrative distance for RIP?**

A ○ 110
B ○ 120
C ○ 140
D ○ 130

8 **By default, at what intervals are RIP routing updates broadcast?**

A ○ Every 30 seconds
B ○ Every 45 seconds
C ○ Every 60 seconds
D ○ Every 90 seconds
E ○ Every 180 seconds

9 **What is the difference between split horizon and split horizon with poison reverse?**

A ○ Poison reverse ignores routes learned from the destination router.
B ○ Poison reverse inexplicably denies the path using a 16 metric.
C ○ Poison reverse allows advertisements back out the same interface it was learned on.
D ○ Poison reverse inexplicably denies the path using a 1 metric.

10 **Which command is best used to display whether RIP is running on the router?**

A ○ `show ip route`
B ○ `debug ip rip`
C ○ `show ip running config`
D ○ `show ip protocols`

11 **Which command is used to prevent updates on certain interfaces?**

A ○ `passive interface`
B ○ `no auto-summary`
C ○ `rip authentication`
D ○ `router rip no update`

Answers

1 **A, C.** Distance vector and interior gateway protocol. RIP is designed for containment within an autonomous system and is used in packet-switched networks to calculate paths and distances to target networks. Review *"Introducing Routing Information Protocol (RIP)."*

2 **B.** RIPv1 is a classful routing protocol, and all subnets using RIPv1 must be configured with identical subnet masks. See *"RIPv1"* and *"RIPv2."*

3 **C, E.** Split horizon and hold-down timers are used to prevent routing loops. Split horizon prevents advertisements back out the same interface in which the route was originally learned on. Hold-down timers prevent the reactivation of a dead link. Refer to *"Split horizon"* and *"Convergence and timers."*

4 **D.** RIP uses a hop-count metric to determine the shortest path to the destination. Read *"Routing tables, updates, and hop count."*

5 **A, C, D.** Slow convergence and poor performance in large-scale networks, along with lack of authentication methods, are all disadvantages of RIPv1. RIP was designed for deployment in small-scale, single autonomous systems. See *"Convergence and timers"* and *"RIPv1."*

6 **B, E.** `router rip` and `network` are the IOS commands used to enable RIP. Examine *"Configuring RIP."*

7 **B.** 120 is the administrative distance for RIP. Review *"An interior gateway protocol."*

8 **A.** RIP routing table updates are sent every 30 seconds. Read *"Routing error mitigation methods."*

9 **B.** Instead of not advertising the path to prevent the loop as with standard split horizon, poison reverse inexplicably denies the path. Review *"Split horizon."*

10 **D.** The `show ip protocols` command is used to determine whether RIP is enabled and running on a Cisco Interface. Read *"Verifying RIP."*

11 **A.** To disable RIP updates to a specified interface, use the `passive interface` command. Check out *"Configuring RIP."*

Chapter 5: Enhanced Interior Gateway Routing Protocol (EIGRP)

Exam Objectives

✔ Describing the features and characteristics of EIGRP

✔ Distinguishing EIGRP from IGRP

✔ Describing EIGRP routing decision criteria

✔ Describing EIGRP route updates and convergence

✔ Describing EIGRP routing tables and operation

✔ Understanding the Diffusing Update Algorithm (DUAL)

✔ Deploying EIGRP

✔ Verifying and troubleshooting EIGRP on a Cisco router

As the name implies, the Cisco-proprietary Enhanced Interior Gateway Routing Protocol (EIGRP) is an interior gateway protocol that contains many advantages over Routing Information Protocol (RIP) and its superseded predecessor, the Interior Gateway Routing Protocol (IGRP). EIGRP is the enhanced version of IGRP. Like RIP, IGRP is known as a distance vector protocol, but it uses a dramatically improved distance vector algorithm to determine the best path to a particular destination. IGRP relies more heavily on the bandwidth and delay metrics of a route as opposed to RIP, which relies on the distance of a route.

EIGRP includes features commonly found in more advanced link-state protocols. EIGRP also uses a more advanced method of loop mitigation than both RIP and IGRP, providing a 100-percent loop-free environment.

Other benefits of EIGRP include high scalability with minimal network overhead and very fast convergence speeds. To fully understand the capabilities of EIGRP, it is beneficial to first take a look at the protocol on which it is based, namely IGRP.

IGRP — The Foundation of EIGRP

The Interior Gateway Routing Protocol was originally developed in the mid-1980s by Cisco Systems to exchange routing information between IP-based networks. A major reason for the development of IGRP was to overcome the limitations of RIP. A protocol was needed that would support larger-scale networks not limited by the 15-hop-count metric of RIP. By introducing a complex formula for route calculations, IGRP replaced the single routing metric employed by RIP, and combined multiple metrics (such as bandwidth, delay, load, MTU, and reliability) into a single unit.

IGRP uses the following metrics:

✦ **Default metrics:** Bandwidth, delay

✦ **Optional metrics:** Load, reliability, MTU

IGRP still imposed limitations on network topologies by limiting routing to classful networks. Because IGRP did not contain a field for the subnet mask inside the packet, support for variable-length subnet masks (VLSMs) and classless networking was not available. These classful protocols, such as IGRP and RIP, assume that all networks are using the same subnet mask. This imposes a huge waste of IP addresses and proves highly inefficient, considering the constant depletion of IPv4 address space.

Enhanced IGRP replaced IGRP. IGRP is no longer supported by Cisco Systems. RIP also has many disadvantages compared to the more powerful EIGRP. Here are some of the limitations of both RIP and IGRP:

✦ Slow convergence

✦ No CIDR/VLSM support

✦ Hop-count limitation of 15 (RIP)

✦ Not 100-percent loop-free

✦ Broadcasts complete routing table during updates

EIGRP Benefits

Cisco developed EIGRP to overcome IGRP limitations, so EIGRP:

✦ Converges quickly

✦ Supports CIDR and VLSM

✦ Hop count can be configured between 1 and 255, with a default of 100

✦ Uses the more advanced DUAL (Diffusing Update Algorithm) to evaluate the quality of each route

✦ Can leverage routes maintained by other routing protocols

✦ Is compatible with existing IGRP and can route Internet Protocol (IP), Novell Netware Internetwork Packet Exchange (IPX), and Apple AppleTalk routed protocols

Characteristics of EIGRP

Although EIGRP evolved out of IGRP, which is a *distance vector protocol,* EIGRP is considered to be a *hybrid routing protocol* because it provides many advanced features that are typically found in *link-state protocols.*

Whenever you are asked about EIGRP on the CCNA test, always think of it as a *hybrid routing protocol.* In fact, EIGRP performs as well, and sometimes better than, Open Shortest Path First (OSPF), which is a link-state protocol. So, EIGRP is in the OSPF and other link-state protocols' league, not in the distance vector protocols' league.

Here are the main characteristics of EIGRP:

✦ EIGRP uses many metrics to evaluate the quality of a route, in addition to the distance of the route:

- Bandwidth and delay (these are EIGRP default metrics)

- Reliability, load, MTU (these are EIGRP optional metrics)

- Evaluates quality of routes using DUAL (Diffusing Update Algorithm)

✦ EIGRP, like OSPF and other link-state routing protocols, sends route updates only when changes occur in the network.

RIP and IGRP broadcast the routing table periodically to all routers in the network.

✦ EIGRP, like OSPF and other link-state routing protocols, exchanges only "Hello" messages and routing updates, rather than the entire routing table, between routers during the convergence process.

✦ EIGRP is not supported on non-Cisco routers, because it is a Cisco-proprietary routing protocol.

✦ EIGRP uses two administrative distance values:

- 90 for routes learned with EIGRP

- 170 for routes learned from other routing protocols

EIGRP Operation

To understand EIGRP operation, you need to understand its components.

Basic components

EIGRP consists of four basic components:

✦ **Neighbor discovery/recovery:** Technology used by Cisco routers to discover the presence of neighboring routers on direct-attached networks. The discovery process allows Cisco routers to use small-sized, low-overhead hello packets to contact other routers. The sending and receiving of these efficient hello packets determine whether a neighbor is functioning properly or whether a routing device has become unreachable. Routers acknowledge their presence to other networks with these packets, and after they are exchanged, communications may begin. If no hello packet is received from a neighboring router, it is considered unreachable.

✦ **Reliable Transport Protocol (RTP):** Provides reliable and guaranteed delivery of EIGRP multicast or unicast packets to all neighboring routers. To maintain protocol efficiency, RTP only transmits packets reliably when required. Certain multicast-capable networks such as Ethernet do not require guaranteed delivery or acknowledgment of hello packets to and from neighbors, and is indicated as such inside the packet header. Packets that contain routing table updates do require acknowledgment.

✦ **DUAL finite-state machine:** Routing algorithm used by EIGRP to compute, select, and track loop-free routes. DUAL uses a metric to determine least-cost routes based on feasible successors. Feasible successors are considered guaranteed, loop-free routing neighbors that will be used to forward packets reliably to the end destination.

✦ **Protocol-dependent modules:** Independent modules used by a particular protocol at the OSI network layer for sending and receiving packets.

The IP protocol-dependent module for EIGRP is called IP-EIGRP and is tasked with delivering and receiving EIGRP packets encapsulated using IP. IP-EIGRP communicates with DUAL to compute routes that are then stored in the routing table.

Routing tables

Information regarding neighboring routers and the topology of the network is collected by EIGRP and is stored in a series of tables. Three main types of tables are used by EIGRP:

✦ **Neighbor table:** Contains information regarding neighboring routers that are accessible through directly connected interfaces. All collected information is added to the neighbor table, to include interface and addressing values. Each router running EIGRP maintains its own neighbor table. Thus:

- Each router has a clear picture of its peer routers.

- Each router has a clear picture of the network topology in its immediate vicinity.

✦ **Topology table:** A collection of EIGRP routing tables received from routing neighbors. The topology table lists EIGRP-routable destination networks and their metric calculations. If available, a successor and feasible successor are also listed for each destination in the topology table. Each destination is marked either in an active or passive state. A passive state means that the router knows the route to the destination, while an active state denotes a topology change in which the router is currently updating its routing information for a particular route. Each router running EIGRP maintains its own link-state table. Thus:

- Each router has a clear picture of the topology in the immediate vicinity of its neighbors.

- Using the neighbor table and the link state, each router has a two-level knowledge of the network topology: the topology in its immediate vicinity and the topology in the vicinity of its neighbors.

For each destination network, the topology table keeps track of the following:

- *The successor route:* This is the best route to the destination as evaluated by DUAL.

- *The feasible successor route:* This is the next best route to the destination as evaluated by DUAL.

✦ **Routing table:** A map of all known destination routes. The routing table is built using information collected from the topology table. Whereas the neighbor and link-state tables are used to quantify routes, the routing table is used to qualify each route:

- Only the *successor route* is copied from the topology table to the routing table, and this route is used as long as it's available.

- Whenever the *successor route* is down, the *feasible successor route* is copied from the topology table to the routing table and is used as the alternate route.

**Book IV
Chapter 5**

**Enhanced Interior
Gateway Routing
Protocol (EIGRP)**

Neighboring successors

Two main types of neighboring devices (next-hop routers) are used in EIGRP-based networks. Both types guarantee that they will not be part of a routing loop:

+ **Successor:** A next-hop router that provides the shortest distance to a destination network. In other words, this neighbor provides the best route to the destination network.

+ **Feasible successor:** A next-hop router that provides the next shortest distance to a destination network. In other words, this neighbor provides the next best route to the destination network.

ElGRP packet types

EIGRP uses five types of packets:

+ **Hello/ACKs:** Unacknowledged, multicast hello packets used in the process of neighbor discovery and recovery. Any hello packet empty of data is considered an acknowledgment, or ACK. ACKs are unicast addressed packets specified by a nonzero acknowledgment number.

+ **Updates:** Reliable unicast packets that contain routing advertisements that are received by neighboring devices to build and maintain a map (routing table) of the network topology. If an update contains a cost change for a particular link, the update will be included in a multicast packet.

+ **Queries:** Multicast packet queries transmitted when the destination node enters an active state. If the query is sent in response to a received query, it is formatted as a unicast packet.

+ **Replies:** Reliable unicast packets transmitted in response to queries. Replies indicate to the originator that feasible successors are available and it should not enter an active state.

+ **Requests:** Unreliable multicast or unicast packets used to gather information from neighboring devices.

Convergence

EIGRP converges much faster than RIP and IGRP because neighbor routers only exchange "Hello" messages initially as opposed to typical distance vector routing protocols, which need to merge and distribute their routing tables among them during the convergence process.

Using EIGRP, the routers get to know each other during the convergence process, exchanging communication parameters and setting up their *neighbor table.* This is similar to OSPF and other link-state routing protocols' convergence process.

Two routers can only become neighbors if the following things occur:

✦ They successfully exchanged "Hello" messages.

✦ They have interfaces in the same routing domain (that is, in the same autonomous system).

✦ They use the same metrics: EIGRP uses bandwidth and delay metrics by default. If you decide to also use the optional metrics, such as load, reliability, and MTU, you need to do this on both routers.

✦ They have their hello timers set to same values for

  • The frequency at which routers send "Hello" messages to each other.

  • How long neighbors wait before they consider a router out of network.

Hello messages are not only sent during the convergence process but also afterward to keep track of which routers are still there in the network. If a router becomes unavailable and stops sending "Hello" messages, one of the hello timers defines how long neighbor routers wait for a "Hello" message before they consider the unavailable router out of the network.

Route updates

EIGRP continues to update routers about available routes after they have converged. This allows routers to maintain their *link-state tables.*

After they have built their neighbor and link-state tables, routers know their neighbors, the network topology in their immediate vicinity, and the network topology in the vicinity of their neighbors.

Next, each router evaluates the quality of each route registered in the link-state table. EIGRP uses DUAL (Diffusing Update Algorithm) to evaluate the quality of each route in the link-state table.

DUAL — Diffusing Update Algorithm

Cisco leverages the *Diffusing Update Algorithm,* shortly known as *DUAL,* to evaluate the quality of network routes maintained by EIGRP.

DUAL improves the efficiency of EIGRP over IGRP, most notably avoiding routing loops altogether. Here are some of the characteristics of DUAL:

✦ For each destination network, it calculates a *successor route* (the best route to the destination s evaluated by DUAL) and a *feasible successor route* (the next best route to the destination as evaluated by DUAL).

✦ DUAL supports variable-length subnet masking (VLSM), allowing EIGRP to route across networks with different subnets.

✦ DUAL provides alternate routes very quickly in case the best route to a destination is down. DUAL provides two features that enable a very quick alternate route calculation:

  • The successor and feasible successor routes: For each route, an alternate route is already available and ready to kick in.

  • If both the successor and the feasible successor routes are down, DUAL enables routers to communicate with their neighbors to find an alternate route.

  Because neighbors also have a successor and a feasible successor route to each destination, an alternate route borrowed from a neighbor can be readily used to reach the destination network.

Classful and classless routing

EIGRP supports both classful and classless routing. By default, like RIPv1 and IGRP, EIGRP is a *classful routing protocol:*

✦ It does not send subnet information in the route updates.

✦ It automatically summarizes routes on boundary routers based on the IP address class that each network belongs to. For example, if a router sends an update for network 172.16.50.0, EIGRP summarizes this route to 172.16.0.0. This works if the router that receives the update is also in the 172.16.0.0 IP address class. Intermediary routers also need to be in the same IP address class.

EIGRP can be configured to run in classless mode by executing the no auto-summary Cisco IOS command in router configuration mode. *Classless routing protocols* have the following features:

✦ Send subnet information in the route updates.

✦ Do not automatically summarize routes on boundary routers based on the IP address class each network belongs to. For example, if a router sends an update for network 172.16.50.0, EIGRP does not summarize the route in classless mode; it really sends 172.16.50.0. This works even if the router that receives the update, or the intermediary routers, are not in the 172.16.0.0 IP address class.

Networks that contain multiple subnets in different IP address classes are called *discontiguous networks*. Discontiguous networks require classless routing (that is, with RIPv2 and with EIGRP, you need to execute the `no auto-summary` command). You can still summarize routes manually.

You find out about manual route summarization in Book IV, Chapter 6. The OSPF protocol does not automatically summarize routes: OSPF is a classless routing protocol.

Configuring EIGRP

You configure EIGRP on a Cisco router similarly to RIP:

+ Start up EIGRP on each router
+ Enable EIGRP on interfaces on each router
+ Configure EIGRP options

Figure 5-1 shows an example of a network that you will configure with EIGRP. This network spans three subnets:

+ 192.168.25.0/24
+ 192.168.67.0/24
+ 51.10.1.0/24

Observe that these networks are in different IP address classes. Hence, this is a *discontiguous network*. You need to disable autosummarization of routes in this setup to set EIGRP in classless routing mode.

Start up EIGRP

To start EIGRP, you run the `router eigrp as_id` Cisco IOS command in global configuration mode.

The `as_id` is the autonomous system (AS) number, also known as the routing domain ID. You need to set a common autonomous system number on all routers that will exchange EIGRP routing data. EIGRP routing data can only be exchanged between routers with the same autonomous system number. The EIGRP AS is a number between 1 and 65535.

Book IV
Chapter 5

Enhanced Interior Gateway Routing Protocol (EIGRP)

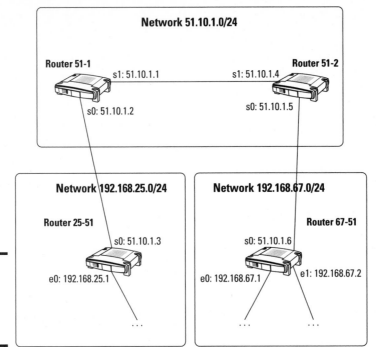

Figure 5-1:
EIGRP
routing
configura-
tion.

Enable EIGRP on router interfaces

To enable EIGRP on interfaces on your router, you run the `network int_IP` Cisco IOS command in global configuration mode.

The `int_IP` is the IP address that identifies the interface on which you enable OSPF.

Configuring EIGRP on Router 2551

```
R251>enable (or en)
R2551#configure terminal (or config t)
R2551(config)#router eigrp 1
R2551(config-router)#network 192.168.25.0
R2551(config-router)#network 51.0.0.0
R2551(config-router)#no auto-summary
R2551(config-router)#exit
R2551(config)#exit
R2551#disable
R2551>
```

Configuring EIGRP on Router 6751

```
R6751>enable (or en)
R6751#configure terminal (or config t)
R6751(config)#router eigrp 1
R6751(config-router)#network 192.168.67.0
R6751(config-router)#network 51.0.0.0
R6751(config-router)#no auto-summary
R6751(config-router)#exit
R6751(config)#exit
R6751#disable
R6751>
```

Configuring EIGRP on Router 51-1

```
R51-1>enable (or en)
R51-1#configure terminal (or config t)
R51-1(config)#router eigrp 1
R51-1(config-router)#network 51.0.0.0
R51-1(config-router)#no auto-summary
R51-1(config-router)#exit
R51-1(config)#exit
R51-1#disable
R51-1>
```

Configuring EIGRP on Router 51-2

```
R51-2>enable (or en)
R51-2#configure terminal (or config t)
R51-2(config)#router eigrp 1
R51-2(config-router)#network 51.0.0.0
R51-2(config-router)#no auto-summary
R51-2(config-router)#exit
R51-2(config)#exit
R51-2#disable
R51-2>
```

Verifying and Monitoring EIGRP Operation

You can verify a few elements to monitor EIGRP operation and ensure optimum routing.

Inspect the routing table

You look at the routing tables on a Cisco router using the `show ip route` Cisco IOS command in privileged EXEC mode. The output includes the following:

✦ Network IP information

✦ Available subnets

**Book IV
Chapter 5**

**Enhanced Interior
Gateway Routing
Protocol (EIGRP)**

✦ Routes currently stored in the routing table. For each route, the command displays the following:

- The IP address of the destination network reached by that route

- The word *connected,* if the router you run the command on is directly connected to the destination network of that route

- The IP address of the gateway (router) to the destination network of that route if the router you run the command on is not directly connected to the destination network of that route

- The router interface that connects either to the destination network or to the gateway that reaches the destination network

Inspect EIGRP protocol configuration

You use the `show ip protocols` Cisco IOS command in privileged EXEC mode to look at the IP routing protocol configuration on a Cisco router.

The output displays one section for each IP routing protocol enabled on your router. For EIGRP, it shows the following:

✦ EIGRP process ID

✦ Whether an outgoing update filter is set

✦ Whether an incoming update filter is set

✦ Whether automatic network summarization is active

✦ Destination networks

✦ Information sources about destination networks

✦ Current administrative distances: internal and external

Inspect EIGRP topology table configuration

You use the `show ip eigrp topology` Cisco IOS command in privileged EXEC mode to look at the EIGRP topology table. The command displays the following:

✦ Destination networks and for each destination network:

- *The successor route:* Shows the interface name and its IP address to reach that route

- *The feasible successor route:* Shows the interface name and its IP address to reach that route

✦ Whether the destination network is A (active) or P (passive)

Passive destination networks are networks that converged. In other words, the successor and the feasible successor routes to that network have converged. All routers know those routes; they are not exchanging route updates about them. After the routers have converged, destination networks show up as passive.

Active destination networks are networks that have not converged yet (the successor and the feasible successor routes to that network have not converged). Routers are still exchanging route updates about them. A destination network would show up as active, after routers have converged, if either the successor or the feasible successor route becomes unavailable and the router needs to exchange data with its neighbors about alternate routes to the destination network.

Inspect EIGRP neighbor information

You use the `show ip eigrp neighbors` Cisco IOS command in privileged EXEC mode to look at information about the EIGRP neighbors of your router. The command shows the following information:

+ EIGRP process ID.

+ Order of discovery of each neighbor.

+ IP address of each neighbor.

+ Interface reaching each neighbor.

+ Hold time, also known as the Hello timer: This determines how long the router waits for a Hello message from its neighbor.

+ SRTT — Smooth Round-Trip Timer: This is the time it takes for a packet to make a round trip from the router to the neighbor and back to the router.

   This used to determine how long the router should wait for replies from its neighbor: It should wait at least as long as it takes a packet to do a round trip.

+ RTO — Retransmission Timeout: This timeout value determines how long the router waits before retransmitting a packet for which it received no acknowledgment from its neighbor.

+ Q Cnt — Queue Count: This shows how many packets are waiting to be sent in the router's queue.

   If the queue count is consistently high, it shows that some communication problems exist between the router and its neighbor. One of the following is occurring:

   • The router is sending too much to its neighbor.

   • Its neighbor is not fast enough.

   • Something is wrong with the link between the router and its neighbor.

Troubleshooting EIGRP

Whenever you notice EIGRP routing malfunctions, you use the `debug eigrp` Cisco IOS command in privileged EXEC mode to look at information about EIGRP operation on your router.

The `debug` command enables *debug mode* on specific components and protocols. In this case, you enable debug mode on EIGRP to capture detailed troubleshooting data about EIGRP. You execute the `debug eigrp` command in privileged EXEC mode.

To disable debugging, execute the `no debug eigrp` command in privileged EXEC mode.

Prep Test

1 **EIGRP is which of the following?**

- **A** ○ A hybrid protocol
- **B** ○ A proprietary protocol that was developed by Cisco
- **C** ○ An interior gateway protocol (IGP)
- **D** ○ All of the above

2 **What does the EIGRP neighbor table keep track of?**

- **A** ○ Routers in the vicinity of a router
- **B** ○ Neighboring cables in an unshielded twisted-pair (UTP)
- **C** ○ Patch panels in the vicinity of a router
- **D** ○ All of the above

3 **What does the EIGRP topology table keep track of?**

- **A** ○ The routes on neighbor patch panels
- **B** ○ Destination networks and best and next-best routes to them
- **C** ○ The cable links to the default gateway
- **D** ○ All of the above

4 **How does EIGRP converge?**

- **A** ○ Slowly, because it needs to merge routing tables from all routers and exchange them between all routers
- **B** ○ Quickly, because it only exchanges hello packets to allow routers to build their neighbor tables
- **C** ○ Never, because routers running EIGRP do not need to exchange information about their routes
- **D** ○ All of the above

5 **To evaluate the quality of each route in the topology and routing tables, EIGRP uses which of the following?**

- **A** ○ The Diffusing Update Algorithm (DUAL)
- **B** ○ The distance of the route
- **C** ○ Both the bandwidth and the distance of a route
- **D** ○ All of the above

6 **EIGRP uses the _____ and the _____ metrics by default to calculate the quality of each route.**

   A ○ load, MTU

   B ○ reliability, load

   C ○ bandwidth, delay

   D ○ All of the above

7 **Which of the following is an EIGRP feature?**

   A ○ Does not support route summarization

   B ○ Automatically summarizes routes by default, but can be configured for manual summarization as well

   C ○ Only summarizes feasible successor routes

   D ○ All of the above

8 **EIGRP does which of the following?**

   A ○ Can leverage routes found by other routing protocols

   B ○ Communicates with RIP and IGRP on neighbor routers

   C ○ Shares its routing tables with RIP and IGRP

   D ○ All of the above

9 **EIGRP can route packets for which of the following protocols?**

   A ○ IP (Internet Protocol)

   B ○ IPX (Novell Netware Internetwork Packet Exchange) protocol

   C ○ AppleTalk protocol

   D ○ All of the above

10 **You need to do which of the following to configure EIGRP in your network?**

   A ○ Start up EIGRP on each router in your network

   B ○ Enable EIGRP on interfaces on each router in your network

   C ○ Configure optional routing protocol parameters

   D ○ All of the above

Answers

1 **D.** EIGRP is a proprietary protocol that was developed by Cisco. Check out *"Characteristics of EIGRP."*

2 **A.** The EIGRP neighbor table keeps track of the routers in the vicinity of the router that owns the EIGRP neighbor table. Review *"Routing tables."*

3 **B.** The EIGRP topology table keeps track of the destination networks and best and next-best routes to them from the router that owns the EIGRP topology table. Look over *"Routing tables."*

4 **B.** EIGRP converges quickly because it only exchanges hello packets to allow routers to build their neighbor tables. See *"Convergence."*

5 **A.** EIGRP uses the Diffusing Update Algorithm (DUAL) to evaluate the quality of each route in the topology and routing tables. Check out *"DUAL — Diffusing Update Algorithm."*

6 **C.** EIGRP uses the bandwidth and the delay metrics by default to calculate the quality of each route. Read *"Characteristics of EIGRP."*

7 **B.** EIGRP automatically summarizes routes by default, but can be configured for manual summarization as well. Review *"Classful and classless routing."*

8 **A.** EIGRP can leverage routes found by other routing protocols. Refer to *"EIGRP Benefits."*

9 **D.** All of the above. EIGRP can route packets for IP, IPX, and AppleTalk. Check out *"EIGRP Benefits."*

10 **D.** All of the above. To configure EIGRP in your network, you need to start up EIGRP on each router in your network, enable EIGRP on interfaces on each router in your network, and configure optional routing protocol parameters. Look over *"Configuring EIGRP."*

Chapter 6: Open Shortest Path First (OSPF) Protocol

Exam Objectives

✔ Describing the features and characteristics of OSPF

✔ Describing OSPF routing decision criteria

✔ Describing OSPF route updates and convergence

✔ Distinguishing OSPF designated and backup designated routers

✔ Understanding the Dijkstra shortest path first (SPF) routing algorithm

✔ Describing OSPF route summarization

✔ Configuring OSPF on a Cisco router

✔ Verifying and troubleshooting OSPF on a Cisco router

*O*SPF is a link-state routing protocol. OSPF was developed based on an open standard and is supported by several router manufacturers. OSPF is widely used as an *interior gateway protocol (IGP),* especially in large network environments. Interior gateway protocols, including OSPF, route within a single routing domain. A *single routing domain,* also known as an *autonomous system (AS),* is a group of routers and network addresses that use a common routing system. For example, a network that uses OSPF on all routers is an autonomous system. This network can be connected to a large service provider network that is using another routing protocol such as *IS-IS (Intermediate System–to–Intermediate System).* The service provider's IS-IS network is another autonomous system. The protocol used to route between autonomous systems and between large Internet service providers is called *Border Gateway Protocol (BGP).* It is not necessary to know all the details about IGPs and BGPs, but it is important to know that OSPF is classified as an interior gateway protocol.

Introducing Open Shortest Path First (OSPF)

Link-state routing protocols build their routing tables independently based on route updates they receive from their neighbors. Link-state protocols do not merge the routing tables of neighbor routers. Link-state protocols enable routers to have a clear image of neighbors, network topology, and routes to their neighbors and beyond by maintaining not just routing tables but also topology and neighbor tables. OSPF complies with all these link-state routing protocol characteristics.

Routing tables

OSPF maintains these routing tables:

+ **Neighbor table:** This table keeps track of the neighbors of a router. Each router running OSPF maintains its own neighbor table. Thus, each router has a clear picture of its peer routers, and each router has a clear picture of the network topology in its immediate vicinity.

+ **Link-state table:** This table keeps track of the state of the links on neighbor routers. In other words, this table keeps track of the state of the routes on neighbor routers. Each router running OSPF maintains its own link-state table. Thus:

  • Each router has a clear picture of the topology in the immediate vicinity of its neighbors.

  • Using the neighbor table and the link state, each router has a two-level knowledge of the network topology: the topology in its immediate vicinity and the topology in the vicinity of its neighbors.

+ **Routing table:** This table keeps track of the metrics of each link tracked by the link-state table. Hence, whereas the neighbor and link-state tables are used to quantify routes, the routing table is used to qualify each route.

Characteristics of OSPF

Here are the main characteristics of the OPSF protocol:

+ Route updates are only sent when routes change. Each router sends a *link-state advertisement (LSA)* whenever a change occurs in one of the routes known to the router.

+ LSAs contain information about the route that changed only.

+ Routers exchange "Hello" messages during the convergence process to build their neighbor tables.

+ OSPF, like RIP, is supported on non-Cisco routers.

+ OSPF supports variable-length subnet masking (VLSM).

+ OSPF supports an unlimited number of network hops.

+ OSPF scales out very well because

  • It divides the routing domain (autonomous system) into areas.

  • It classifies routers hierarchically.

- It converges very quickly.

- It sends routes updates (LSAs) only when routes change, minimizing route change traffic.

- LSA packets have a small footprint.

- LSA traffic is consolidated to the designated router.

- LSA traffic is minimized when routes are summarized.

Convergence

The OSPF routing protocol converges within seconds because neighbor routers only exchange "Hello" messages initially. During the convergence process, routers get to know each other, exchanging communication parameters and setting up their *neighbor table*.

Routers can only become neighbors if the following things occur:

✦ They have successfully exchanged "Hello" messages

✦ They have interfaces in the same routing domain (that is, in the same autonomous system)

✦ They have their hello timers set to the same values. Hello timers define the following:

- The frequency at which routers send each "Hello" message to each other

- How long neighbors wait before they consider a router out of network

Hello messages are not only sent during the convergence process but also afterward to keep track of which routers are still in the network. If a router becomes unavailable and stops sending Hello messages, one of the hello timers defines how long neighbor routers wait for a Hello message before they consider the unavailable router out of the network.

Route updates

OSPF continues to update routers about available routes after they have converged. These route updates are sent in the form of link-state advertisement (LSA) packets. Routers exchange LSA packets to maintain their *link-state tables*. After they have built their neighbor and link-state tables, routers know the following:

✦ Their neighbors

✦ The network topology in their immediate vicinity

✦ The network topology in the vicinity of their neighbors

Next, each router evaluates the quality of each route registered in the link-state table.

Cost metric

OSPF uses the *cost* metric to evaluate the quality of each link.

Route cost is a metric calculated based on the bandwidth of each link. Cisco routers calculate the cost by dividing a default bandwidth of 100 Mbps (100 million bits per second) by the actual bandwidth of the link.

For example, the following list illustrates the default OSPF cost calculated by Cisco routers for various bandwidths:

+ 64-Kbps (64,536-bits-per-second) link: 100,000,000 / 64,536 = 1,562

+ 1.544-Mbps (T1) link: 100,000,000 / 1,544,000 = 64

+ 10-Mbps link: 100,000,000 / 10,000,000 = 10

+ 100-Mbps link: 100,000,000 / 100,000,000 = 1

+ 1-Gbps link: 100,000,000 / 1,000,000,000 = 0.1

+ 10-Gbps link: 100,000,000 / 10,000,000,000 = 0.01

OSPF chooses the route with the lowest cost. You can modify the default reference bandwidth used to calculate the OSPF cost using the `auto-cost reference-bandwidth` Cisco IOS command in global configuration mode. It is very important to set the same reference bandwidth on all routers in your network.

For example, if most links in your network are 1 Gbps, you set the reference bandwidth to 1 Gbps instead of 100 Mbps using the following commands:

```
RT6751>enable (or en)
RT6751#configure terminal (or config t)
RT6751(config)#auto-cost reference-bandwidth 1000000000
RT6751(config)#exit
RT6751#disable
RT6751>
```

OSPF Routing Hierarchy

OSPF uses the *Dijkstra shortest path first (SPF)* routing algorithm to calculate the shortest path from a router to each destination network.

The Dijkstra SPF routing algorithm does the following:

✦ Considers the router to be the root of a tree

✦ Considers each destination network (router) to be a branch or a leaf in that tree

✦ Calculates the shortest route from the root of the tree (the router) to each branch and to each leaf (to each destination network)

Effectively, the Dijkstra SPF algorithm calculates the shortest route from each router to each network in the OSPF routing domain (or autonomous system), because each router is the root of its own tree. This creates a shortest-path tree for each router.

However, OSPF does not need to calculate the shortest path from each router to each destination if the network is designed in a hierarchical fashion.

Router trees overlap in a hierarchical design. This improves the efficiency of OSPF because after the Dijkstra SPF algorithm calculates the shortest routes for a branch of the tree, it doesn't need to recalculate those routes as you move up the tree to the root router.

Figure 6-1 shows the recommended network topology for OSPF.

Observe the following:

✦ One router is the root of the OSPF tree (although you can configure more than one root router).

✦ The OSPF routing domain (or autonomous system) is divided into areas with at least one *designated router (DR)* in each area. It is best practice to have a *backup designated router (BDR)* in each area as well.

In this example, the tree that starts at router 10-1, going down, is

✦ Part of the DR-10 router tree in area 10

✦ Part of the BDR-10 router tree in area 10

✦ Part of the root tree in the area 0

This is good, because after OSPF (the Dijkstra SPF algorithm) calculates the shortest route from router 10-1 to each destination underneath, the DR-10 router, the BDR-10 router, and the root router can readily use those shortest routes to destinations under the 10-1 router.

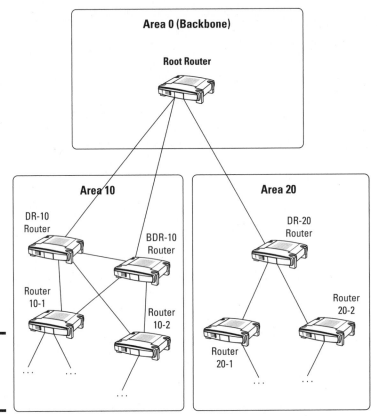

Figure 6-1:
OSPF
routing
hierarchy.

OSPF route summarization

The reuse of previously calculated shortest routes is leveraged by *route summarization*. Route summarization allows routers to identify common network IP address spaces and create a summarized route for the IP address space as opposed to creating a route for each IP address individually. This improves network throughput because routers sharing a summarized route send LSA packets upstream only when the summarized route changes, as opposed to sending LSA packets upstream for each of their (internal, or downstream) routes. For example, in Figure 6-1:

✦ The tree underneath router DR-10 is one IP address space (subnet).

✦ The tree underneath router BDR-10 is another IP address space (subnet).

✦ The tree underneath router 10-1 is one IP address space (subnet).

✦ The tree underneath router 10-2 is another IP address space (subnet).

However, the DR-10 tree includes the 10-1 and the 10-2 trees. Similarly, the BDR-10 tree includes the 10-1 and the 10-2 trees.

Suppose that networks in area 10 have the following IP addresses:

+ Router DR-10: 172.10.75.0

+ Router BDR-10: 172.10.76.0

+ Router 10-1: 172.10.77.0

+ Router 10-2: 172.10.78.0

The first 2 bytes are the same for all subnets in area 10: 172.10. The third byte is different. Table 6-1 examines these IP addresses in binary.

Table 6-1	**Route Summarization**			
IP Address	*Byte 1 (172)*	*Byte 2 (10)*	*Byte 3 (75, 76, 77, 78)*	*Byte 4 (0)*
172.10.75.0	1100 0000	0000 1010	0100 1011	0000 0000
172.10.76.0	1100 0000	0000 1010	0100 1100	0000 0000
172.10.77.0	1100 0000	0000 1010	0100 1101	0000 0000
172.10.78.0	1100 0000	0000 1010	0100 1110	0000 0000

Observe that the IP address of these networks is almost the same except for byte 3. Now from the perspective of the root router in area 0, this difference is irrelevant because the DR-10 and BDR-10 trees both include the 10-1 and the 10-2 trees. Hence, if the root router in area 0 knows how to get to DR-10 and to BDR-10, it knows how to get to everyone underneath. So, it makes sense to expose only one route up to the root router instead of exposing all four. That is exactly what route summarization accomplishes.

So how do you summarize these routes? Table 6-1 shows that only byte 3 varies. Specifically, only the second nibble in byte 3 varies. Assume that nibble 2 in byte 3 would be the same for all routers (for example, 0100 1011, which is 75). You would have IP address 172.10.75.0 for all networks. However, you can only do this if you modify the subnet mask.

The subnet mask changes from 255.255.255.0 (/24) to 255.255.240.0 (/20), because the variable part of the IP address now includes 4 more bits in byte 3. Table 6-2 details the following:

✦ The original subnet mask, where bytes 1 and 2 represent the network IP address and bytes 3 and 4 are used for variable intranetwork addresses.

✦ The new subnet mask for the summarized route, where byte 1 and the first nibble in byte 2 represent the network IP address. The second nibble of byte 2 and bytes 3 and 4 represent the variable intranetwork IP addresses.

Table 6-2	Subnet Mask for Summarized Route			
Mask	Byte 1	Byte 2	Byte 3	Byte 4
255.255.255.0	1111 1111	1111 1111	1111 1111	0000 0000
255.255.240.0	1111 1111	1111 1111	1111 0000	0000 0000

Now you can expose route 172.10.75.0/20 up to the root router in area 0. You are telling the root router in area 0 to keep track of route 172.10.75.0/20 to get to any of the networks in area 10.

In fact, you can have two summarized routes in this example, because both DR-10 and BDR-10 connect to the root router in area 0:

✦ One route to reach the tree under router DR-10: 172.10.75.0/20

✦ One route to reach the tree under router BDR-10: 172.10.76.0/20

Now instead of exposing four routes up to the root router in area 0, you only expose one (or two) summarized routes. This improves the efficiency of the root router because it needs to maintain only one (or two) route(s) for area 10 instead of maintaining four routes.

OSPF designated router (DR)

The OSPF protocol elects a *designated router* that is responsible for keeping all routers updated on shortest routes. Instead of exchanging route information with ever other router in the network, routers only communicate their routes to the designated router. The designated router then updates everyone on the routes available. Consolidating the exchange of information about routes to the designated router improves the efficiency of the network because less bandwidth is consumed by having each router communicate its routes only to the designated router, instead of communicating with every other router in their area.

Routers send their LSA packets to a multicast address (224.0.0.6). The DR listens to this multicast IP address. The DR relays routing information back to the routers by sending route updates to the multicast address 224.0.0.5. All routers running OSPF are listening to the 224.0.0.5 multicast IP address.

Selecting a designated router

The designated router is elected based on the *OSPF priority*. The OSPF priority is a value between 0 and 255 assigned to a router interface using the `ip ospf priority value` Cisco IOS command. The default OPSF priority is set to 1.

The router with the highest OPSF priority becomes the designated router. If two routers have the same OPSF priority, the *router ID (RID)* is used to decide which one becomes the DR.

It is best practice to configure a core router — or the largest, most highly available, and most powerful router — in your network to be the designated router. You can control which router is elected DR using either of the following:

✦ **Loopback interfaces:** Create loopback interfaces on each router in your network, and set the highest IP address on the one you want to become the DR.

✦ **OSPF priority:** Set the highest OPSF priority on the router and interface you want to become the DR.

Router ID (RID)

The router ID is one of the IP addresses of the router that has been chosen to identify the router. The IP address can be set by one of the following methods:

✦ Manually, using the `router-id` Cisco IOS command

✦ Automatically, using either

- The highest IP address assigned to a loopback interface on your router

- The highest IP address of an active interface on your router

Keep in mind that if a loopback interface is defined, its IP address is used as the router ID, even if it is not the highest IP address defined on the router.

Creating loopback interfaces

Loopback interfaces are software-based logical interfaces that point back to the router where they are created. These interfaces are used as interface support for certain features, including the OSPF DR/BDR election process.

Book IV
Chapter 6

Open Shortest
Path First (OSPF)
Protocol

To create a loopback interface on your router, use the `int loopback` Cisco IOS command in global configuration mode. You need to assign an IP address to your loopback interface. However, the IP address you assign is not really important:

✦ The loopback interface is local to your router: The IP interface is not visible to other routers, switches, or hosts on the network as a normal physical interface is.

✦ Even if the IP address is lower than another IP address on your router, the router always uses a loopback interface, if available, to set its RID before the IP addresses of any physical interface are compared.

OSPF backup designated router (BDR)

The backup designated router becomes the designated router in case the designated router is down. The BDR receives the route updates (LSA packets) that routers send to the DR. In fact, routers send their LSA packets to a multicast address (224.0.0.6). Both the DR and the BDR listen to the multicast address 224.0.0.6. Hence, both the DR and the BDR receive the LSA packets. The routing information is in sync on the DR and on the BDR.

The router with the second-highest OSPF priority becomes the backup designated router.

Configuring OSPF

You configure OSPF on a Cisco router similarly to RIP and EIGRP. Follow these steps:

1. Start up OSPF on each router.

2. Enable OSPF on interfaces on each router.

3. Configure OSPF options.

The following sections outline the details of these steps.

Start up OSPF

To start OSPF, run the `router ospf process_id` Cisco IOS command in global configuration mode.

The `process_id` is a number between 1 and 65536 that identifies the OSPF routing process on the router. The OSPF process ID can be a different number on routers that communicate using OSPF.

Enable OSPF on router interfaces

To enable OSPF on the interfaces of your router, run the `network int_IP wildcard_mask area area_id` Cisco IOS command in global configuration mode:

+ The `int_IP` portion is the IP address that identifies the interface on which you enable OSPF.

+ The `wildcard_mask` portion identifies which IP addresses are part of this network. In other words, OSPF exposes to a certain network area all interfaces identified by the IP addresses represented by the wildcard mask. For example, the 172.10.75.0 0.0.0.255 `int_IP wildcard_mask` combination configures the router to expose all addresses in the space 172.10.75: any router interface in the 172.10.75 network.

+ The `area area_id` portion is the OSPF operation area. Recall that OSPF divides the routing domain (or autonomous system) into areas.

Understanding wildcards

The 172.10.75.0 0.0.0.255 int_IP/wildcard_mask combination configures the router to expose all addresses in the space 172.10.75: any router interface in the 172.10.75 network. Read on to find out more about wildcards.

Wildcards are essentially bit masks. A *bit mask* is a set of bits that are either 0 or 1. In this case, OSPF wildcard bits have the following meaning:

+ Number 0 means to match exactly the corresponding bit in the IP address.

+ Number 1 means that the corresponding bit in the IP address can be any number.

If you look at the IP address as a whole, divided into 4 bytes (8 bits each), you can specify wildcards between 0.0.0.0 and 255.255.255.255 with the `network` command:

+ Number 0 means to match exactly the corresponding byte in the IP address. Here, a 0 in decimal represents eight 0s in binary.

+ Number 255 means that the corresponding byte in the IP address can be any number. Here, 255 in decimal represents eight 1s in binary.

For example, wildcard 0.0.0.0 matches exactly the IP address specified in the `network` command. In other words, if you use 172.10.75.0 0.0.0.0, only address 172.10.75.0 is exposed as a route. This may be what you want in some cases. However, usually you want to match a range of addresses as opposed to a specific address when using the `network` command. In other words, you tell OSPF to expose all router interfaces that match the wildcard.

Referring to Figure 6-1, recall the IP addresses of each router:

+ Router DR-10: 172.10.75.0

+ Router BDR-10: 172.10.76.0

+ Router 10-1: 172.10.77.0

+ Router 10-2: 172.10.78.0

The following sections describe configuring OSPF on router interfaces in area 10.

Enable and configure OSPF on router DR-10

```
DR-10>enable (or en)
DR-10#configure terminal (or config t)
DR-10(config)#router ospf 1
DR-10(config-router)#network 172.10.75.0 0.0.0.255 area 10
DR-10(config-router)#network 172.10.75.0 0.0.15.255 area 0
DR-10(config-router)#exit
DR-10(config)#exit
DR-10#disable
DR-10>
```

You configure the DR-10 router to expose interfaces to area 10 and to area 0:

+ **Area 10:** DR-10 exposes to area 10 any address in the IP space 172.10.75: any router interface in the 172.10.75 network using the 172.10.75.0 0.0.0.255 IP/wildcard_mask combination.

+ **Area 0:** DR-10 exposes to area 0 any address in the IP space 172.10.7_: any IP address that starts with 172.10.7. In other words, you expose to area 0 a summary route that reaches area 10. You use the 172.10.75.0 0.0.15.255 IP/wildcard_mask combination.

So, why did you use a 0.0.15.255 wildcard here? Consider the subnet mask of the summary route that you determined earlier (255.255.240.0), which is shown in binary in Table 6-3.

Table 6-3	Subnet Mask for Summarized Route			
Subnet Mask	**Byte 1**	**Byte 2**	**Byte 3**	**Byte 4**
255.255.240.0	1111 1111	1111 1111	1111 0000	0000 0000

This subnet mask tells the router that this summarized route represents an IP address space with

+ Byte 1 constant: 172

+ Byte 2 constant: 10

+ Byte 3, nibble 1 constant: 7

+ Byte 3, nibble 2 variable: 5 to 8

+ Byte 4 variable: any number (0 to 254)

To represent the same filter with a wildcard mask, you need to replace all 0s with 1s and all 1s with 0s, because in a wildcard, 0 means "match exactly" and 1 means "could be anything." The wildcard value is shown in Table 6-4.

Table 6-4	Wildcard Mask for Summarized Route			
Wildcard Mask	*Byte 1*	*Byte 2*	*Byte 3*	*Byte 4*
0.0.15.255	0000 0000	0000 0000	0000 1111	1111 1111

Next, you need to run similar configuration commands on routers BDR-10, 10-1, and 10-2.

Enable and configure OSPF on router BDR-10

```
BDR-10>enable (or en)
BDR-10#configure terminal (or config t)
BDR-10(config)#router ospf 1
BDR-10(config-router)#network 172.10.76.0 0.0.0.255 area 10
BDR-10(config-router)#network 172.10.75.0 0.0.15.255 area 0
BDR-10(config-router)#network 172.10.75.0 0.0.0.255 area 10
BDR-10(config-router)#exit
BDR-10(config)#exit
BDR-10#disable
BDR-10>
```

Router BDR-10, like router DR-10, exposes interfaces to area 10 and to area 0, because it connects both to area 10 and to area 0. Router BDR-10 also defines a route to router DR-10 (172.10.75.0) by registering a route with the 172.10.75.0 0.0.0.255 IP/wildcard_mask combination.

Enable and configure OSPF on router 10-1

```
10-1>enable (or en)
10-1#configure terminal (or config t)
10-1(config)#router ospf 1
10-1(config-router)#network 172.10.77.0 0.0.0.255 area 10
```

**Book IV
Chapter 6**

**Open Shortest
Path First (OSPF)
Protocol**

```
10-1(config-router)#network 172.10.75.0 0.0.0.255 area 10
10-1(config-router)#network 172.10.76.0 0.0.0.255 area 10
10-1(config-router)#exit
10-1(config)#exit
10-1#disable
10-1>
```

Router 10-1 exposes interfaces to area 10 only because it doesn't connect to area 0. Router 10-1 also defines routes to router DR-10 (172.10.75.0) and to router BDR-10 (172.10.76.0) using the 172.10.75.0 0.0.0.255 and the 172.10.76.0 0.0.0.255 IP/wildcard_mask combinations, respectively.

Enable and configure OSPF on router 10-2

```
10-2>enable (or en)
10-2#configure terminal (or config t)
10-2(config)#router ospf 1
10-2(config-router)#network 172.10.78.0 0.0.0.255 area 10
10-2(config-router)#network 172.10.75.0 0.0.0.255 area 10
10-2(config-router)#network 172.10.76.0 0.0.0.255 area 10
10-2(config-router)#exit
10-2(config)#exit
10-2#disable
10-2>
```

In this configuration, router 10-2, like router 10-1, does the following:

+ Exposes interfaces to area 10 only, because it doesn't connect to area 0.

+ Defines a route to router DR-10 (172.10.75.0) using the 172.10.75.0 0.0.0.255 IP/wildcard_mask combination

+ Defines a route to router BDR-10 (172.10.76.0) using the 172.10.76.0 0.0.0.255 IP/wildcard_mask combination

Configure OSPF options

Now you can configure optional parameters to customize the operation of OSPF on your routers.

OSPF priority

You can manually set the *OSPF priority* of a router interface using the `ip ospf priority value` Cisco IOS command in global configuration mode.

Changing the OSPF priority allows you to control the OSPF DR (designated router) and BDR (backup designated router) election process. OSPF elects the DR and the BDR based on the OSPF priority of the router interface.

OSPF cost

You can manually set the *OSPF cost* of an interface on your router using the `ip ospf cost value` Cisco IOS command in global configuration mode.

Verifying and Monitoring OSPF Operation

You can verify the following elements to monitor OSPF operation and ensure optimum routing:

+ Inspect the routing table

+ Inspect the OSPF protocol configuration

+ Inspect the OSPF interface configuration

+ Inspect the OSPF neighbor information

+ Inspect the OSPF routing database

Inspect the routing table

This is not an OSPF-specific technique: Inspecting the routing table shows you all IP routing protocols enabled on your router and the state of their routing tables. You look at the routing tables on a Cisco router using the `show ip route` Cisco IOS command in privileged EXEC mode. The output includes the following:

+ Network IP information

+ Available subnets

+ Routes currently stored in the routing table

  For each route, the command displays these items:

  • The IP address of the destination network reached by that route

  • The word *connected,* if the router you run the command on is directly connected to the destination network of that route

  • The IP address of the gateway (router) to the destination network of that route if the router you run the command on is not directly connected to the destination network of that route

  • The router interface that connects either to the destination network or to the gateway that reaches the destination network

Inspect the OSPF protocol configuration

This is not an OSPF-specific technique: Inspecting the IP routing protocols shows you all IP routing protocols enabled on your router and their configuration. You use the `show ip protocols` Cisco IOS command in privileged EXEC mode to look at the IP routing protocol configuration on a Cisco router. The output displays one section for each IP routing protocol enabled on your router. For OSPF, it shows these items:

✦ OSPF process ID

✦ Whether an outgoing update filter is set

✦ Whether an incoming update filter is set

✦ RID (router ID)

✦ Number of OSPF areas active on the router where you run the command

✦ IP and OSPF area of networks registered for OSPF routing

✦ Reference bandwidth used to calculate the cost of each route

✦ Routing information sources: neighbor routers that exchange OSPF LSA packets with the router where you run the command

✦ Current administrative distance

Inspect the OSPF interface configuration

You use the `show ip ospf interface` Cisco IOS command in privileged EXEC mode to look at interface-specific OSPF configuration:

✦ If you run the command specifying a particular interface, it shows data only about that interface.

✦ Otherwise, the command displays one section for each interface enabled for OSPF on your router.

Inspect the OSPF neighbor information

You use the `show ip ospf neighbor` Cisco IOS command in privileged EXEC mode to look at information about the OSPF neighbors of your router.

Inspect the OSPF routing database

You use the `show ip ospf database` Cisco IOS command in privileged EXEC mode to inspect data stored in the OSPF routing database. The command displays information about neighboring routers and the state of the links to them.

Troubleshooting OSPF

Whenever you notice routing malfunctions that are related to OSPF, you use the `debug ip ospf` Cisco IOS command in privileged EXEC mode to look at information about the OSPF operation on your router.

The `debug` command enables *debug mode* on specific components and protocols. In this case, you enable debug mode on the OSPF protocol to capture detailed troubleshooting data about OSPF. You execute the `debug ip ospf` command in privileged EXEC mode.

To disable debugging, execute the `no debug ip ospf` command in privileged EXEC mode.

**Book IV
Chapter 6**

**Open Shortest
Path First (OSPF)
Protocol**

Prep Test

1 **The OSPF protocol is which of the following?**

   A ○ A link-state protocol

   B ○ A protocol that was developed based on open standards

   C ○ An interior gateway protocol (IGP)

   D ○ All of the above

2 **What does the OSPF neighbor table keep track of?**

   A ○ Routers in the vicinity of a router

   B ○ Neighboring cables in an unshielded twisted-pair (UTP)

   C ○ Patch panels in the vicinity of a router

   D ○ All of the above

3 **What does the OSPF link-state table keep track of?**

   A ○ The state of the links on neighbor patch panels

   B ○ The state of the routes on neighbor routers

   C ○ The state of the cable links to the default gateway

   D ○ All of the above

4 **What does the OSPF routing table keep track of?**

   A ○ Metrics for each link on neighbor patch panels

   B ○ Metrics for each cable link to the default gateway

   C ○ Metrics for each route on neighbor routers

   D ○ All of the above

5 **Describe OSPF link-state advertisement (LSA) packets.**

   A ○ They are sent whenever a route changes.

   B ○ They contain information about the route that changed only.

   C ○ They are sent by the route that detected a change in the state of one of its directly connected routes.

   D ○ All of the above.

6 **How does OSPF converge?**

A ○ Slowly, because it needs to merge routing tables from all routers and exchange them between all routers

B ○ Quickly, because it only exchanges hello packets to allow routers to build their neighbor tables

C ○ Never, because routers running OSPF do not need to exchange information about their routes

D ○ All of the above

7 **Using OSPF, routers have knowledge about which of the following?**

A ○ The network topology in their immediate vicinity

B ○ Their neighbors

C ○ The network topology in the vicinity of their neighbors

D ○ All of the above

8 **How is the OSPF cost metric calculated?**

A ○ Based on the bandwidth of the route

B ○ Based on the distance of the route

C ○ Based on both the bandwidth and the distance of a route

D ○ All of the above

9 **OSPF uses the *Dijkstra shortest path first (SPF)* routing algorithm to calculate the shortest path from a router to each destination network. The Dijkstra SPF algorithm does which of the following?**

A ○ Considers each router to be the root of a tree

B ○ Considers each destination network (router) to be a branch or a leaf in that tree

C ○ Calculates the shortest route from the root of the tree (the router) to each branch and to each leaf (to each destination network)

D ○ All of the above

10 **You need to do which of the following to configure OSPF in your network?**

A ○ Start up OSPF on each router in your network

B ○ Enable OSPF on interfaces on each router in your network

C ○ Configure optional routing protocol parameters

D ○ All of the above

Answers

1 **D.** All of the above. The OSPF protocol is a link-state protocol, a protocol that was developed based on open standards, and an interior gateway protocol (IGP). Refer to *"Introducing Open Shortest Path First (OSPF)."*

2 **A.** The OSPF neighbor table keeps track of routers in the vicinity of the router that owns the neighbor table. Review *"Routing tables."*

3 **B.** The OSPF link-state table keeps track of the state of the routes on neighbor routers. Check out *"Routing tables."*

4 **C.** The OSPF routing table keeps track of the metrics for each route on neighbor routers. Read *"Routing tables."*

5 **D.** All of the above. OSPF link-state advertisement (LSA) packets are sent whenever a route changes. They contain information about the route that changed only, and they are sent by the route that detected a change in the state of one of its directly connected routes. Refer to *"Route updates."*

6 **B.** OSPF converges quickly because it only exchanges hello packets to allow routers to build their neighbor tables. Look over *"Convergence."*

7 **D.** All of the above. Using OSPF, routers have knowledge about their neighbors, the network topology in their immediate vicinity, and the network topology in the vicinity of their neighbors. Review *"Route updates."*

8 **A.** The OSPF cost metric is based on the bandwidth of the route. See *"Cost metric."*

9 **D.** All of the above. The Dijkstra SPF algorithm considers each router to be the root of a tree and considers each destination network (router) to be a branch or a leaf in that tree. It then calculates the shortest route from the root of the tree (the router) to each branch and to each leaf (each destination network). Look over *"OSPF Routing Hierarchy."*

10 **D.** All of the above. To configure OSPF in your network, you need to start up OSPF on each router, enable OSPF on interfaces on each router, and configure optional routing protocol parameters. Refer to *"Configuring OSPF."*

Book V

Wireless Networks

NETWORK ADMIN

"We found where the security breach in the WLAN was originating. It was coming in through another rogue robot-vac. This is the third one this month. Must have gotten away from its owner, like all the rest."

Contents at a Glance

Chapter 1: Introducing Wireless Networks

Exam Objectives

↳ Describing standards associated with wireless media

↳ Identifying some of the governing bodies that are involved with WLANs, such as the IEEE Wi-Fi Alliance and the ITU/FCC

*I*t would be rare for a networking specialist in the current networking environment to not have to work with wireless devices or wireless networking. This mobile technology has gone way beyond the brick-like phones of the 1980s and has invaded all aspects of our society. This chapter reviews where this technology stands today and where it has come from.

Wireless technologies have been around for more than a hundred years, with the beginnings of commercial wireless technologies starting with Nikola Tesla and Guglielmo Marconi around the beginning of the 20th century. With each major increase in technology through the 20th century, many of these technologies were used to improve wireless communications. Just as early wireless was used to transmit traditional telegraph signals wirelessly, current wireless is used to transmit traditional networking signals wirelessly.

Purpose of Wireless Networks

The main goal of wireless networking is to provide mobility to network users, regardless of where their network access devices may be. Within an office, this may mean that moving users from one office to another becomes easier, or when planning to move into new offices, you can avoid the costly and manual job of running cables through the ceilings and walls. Outside your office, wireless networks give you access to the Internet or even to corporate resources on an as-needed, where-needed basis.

With the wide variety of networking devices that are in use in the world today, from smart phones to netbooks to media players, as well as people's reliance on getting data directly from the Internet using high-speed connections, we have become a world of users who do not download and store information, but rather grab it from where it is and use it where we are. As a result of this, an ever-increasing desire exists to be able to access this information in more and more locations, wherever we may be.

Going over the Air, Locally or Globally

When wireless networks first emerged onto the market, the technologies were only good for limited distances. As the technologies have improved, so has the range where they can be used. Four main classes of wireless networks exist based on range and geographical areas:

✦ Wireless personal-area network (WPAN)

✦ Wireless local-area network (WLAN)

✦ Wireless metropolitan-area network (WMAN)

✦ Wireless wide-area network (WWAN)

Wireless personal-area network (WPAN)

The WPAN makes use of short-range wireless technologies, usually less than 10 meters, or 11 yards. These technologies include IrDA, Bluetooth, and ZigBee. Bluetooth has replaced IrDA as the main WPAN technology in use today, while ZigBee is an up-and-comer in that arena. Personal-area networks join devices such as cell phones to computers to sync data and wireless earpieces to phones.

Wireless local-area network (WLAN)

WLANs make use of LAN technologies and cover a larger area than that of the WPAN. A WLAN typically provides network connectivity throughout an office, building, or several buildings within a small geographical area, with all the networking components connected with LAN technologies. The technology used for a WLAN is short range and typically includes, but is not limited to, 802.11 networking components.

Wireless metropolitan-area network (WMAN)

With another increase in the geographical area, you deal with the WMAN. The technologies used in a WMAN allow wireless connections over longer ranges than the WLAN, which are limited to several hundred meters or yards. The WMAN uses technologies such as WiMAX, which can cover several kilometers or miles. The distinction between the WLAN and WMAN is made primarily by the types of technology used.

Wireless wide-area network (WWAN)

The largest area covered is the WWAN, which uses public carriers rather than private equipment. They may make use of WiMAX but most often make use of other cellular network technologies such as GPRS, HSDPA, and 3G to communicate. When using a device on a WWAN, the user can connect to his office network via a secured connection or connect two offices within the area of the cellular network provider.

Sharing the Airwaves

When you move into a new neighborhood, sometimes you have good neighbors who respect your property boundaries, while other times, your neighbors encroach on your property and are a general nuisance; the same is true when your property is your wireless network. When working with wireless networks, your neighbors may interfere with your network by generating traffic on the same frequencies as you are, or by using devices that encroach on the frequencies that you are using. This is especially true when using unlicensed radio bands, but it is easier to deal with when using the limited licensed radio bands.

Using unlicensed radio bands

When hearing a term like *unlicensed,* you may think there are no laws or that it is like the "wild west" and people can do as they like; but that is not completely the case, as you must follow several regulations that cover the use the unlicensed radio bands. The big difference between licensed and unlicensed bands is that the licensed bands are only allowed to be used by the company that licensed them, while the unlicensed bands are used by anyone who wants to use them. Wireless phone companies, such as Sprint or Rogers, have specific frequencies that only they are allowed to use by leasing them from the government; IEEE 802.11 networks have several choices of wireless bands that are available to them to use, without the requirement to lease the frequencies from the government. The downside of the unlicensed frequencies or bands is that anyone else can use the same frequency ranges; which can cause interference for the signals you are trying to transmit. Users of both licensed and unlicensed bands are required to follow a series of government regulations, but the unlicensed bands may be used by anyone who follows the guidelines and regulations. These guidelines cover issues like encroaching on neighboring frequencies and causing interference; so if everyone follows these rules they will all be good neighbors, which is not always the case.

Some groups have helped to develop standards so that all users can be good neighbors with others that use those radio bands. These groups and standards bodies include the following:

✦ **FCC (Federal Communications Commission):** Manages and sets standards with regard to the spectrum use

✦ **IEEE (Institute of Electrical and Electronics Engineers):** A leading standards organization which publishes standards that are adopted across industries

✦ **Wi-Fi Alliance:** An organization that attempts to create a single standard for WLANs, thereby ensuring interoperability

✦ **ETSI (European Telecommunications Standards Institute):** Another standards organization that has contributed many worldwide standards

✦ **ITU-R (International Telecommunication Union, Radiocommunication Sector):** With the FCC, defines how WLANs should operate from a regulatory perspective, such as operating frequencies, antenna gain, and transmission power

✦ **WLANA (WLAN Association):** Provides information resources related to WLANs with regard to industry trends and usage

Licensed radio bands

To use licensed radio bands, a license must be obtained from a government agency. This is true of all users of these radio spectrums. A few of the uses of licensed radio bands are as follows:

✦ AM broadcast

✦ FM broadcast

✦ Cellular phones (840 MHz)

In the larger electromagnetic spectrum, which includes the radio spectrum, the licensing of infrared and X-ray spectrums also exists.

Unlicensed radio bands

Unlicensed radio bands have been allocated to certain users by the government, but to be able to use and broadcast on these bands, you do not need to have a license; you only need to create compliant devices that are to be used. Regulations exist around these bands, so it is not a free-for-all. In the United States, the FCC regulates all the electromagnetic spectrum, but it has set aside several ranges for public use.

Some of the types of unlicensed radio bands are as follows:

✦ **Industrial, Scientific, Medical (ISM):** This includes several medical monitors and other devices that operate in the 900-MHZ, 2.4-GHz, and 5-GHz bands.

✦ **Unlicensed National Information Infrastructure (U-NII):** This defines the specifications for the use of wireless devices such as WLAN access points and routers in the 5-GHz band.

✦ **Unlicensed Personal Communications Services (UPCS):** This defines the specifications for devices operating in the 1.9-GHz band, where DECT6 cordless phones operate.

Modulating the Airwaves

When sending data over radio frequencies (RF), there are several things to remember:

✦ A lot of other traffic is out there, as well as natural phenomena that can cause interference with these signals, either by sending data on the same frequencies or by blocking the signals.

✦ You need to modify a standard signal to transmit data. There are many standard methods to perform this task.

✦ RF bands are only so wide, and therefore can only handle so many discrete sessions or channels at a time.

It is not necessary to understand all the details of signal processing for the CCNA certification test, but you need to know a few things about signals and their characteristics.

Introducing signals

When referring to a *signal* when discussing wireless communications, I am talking about an electromagnetic field with specific characteristics. If I were working with a different medium, the signal could be comprised of light (an optical signal), sound (an airwave signal), or electricity (an electrical signal). When working with computer data, copper wires are used to send electrical signals; fiber-optic cables can send optical signals. If you want to send wireless signals, you use light for line-of-sight technologies such as IrDA or RF for non-line-of-sight technologies.

You surely have listened to a radio station in your local area. This radio station broadcasts its content over a radio-wave signal that operates at a base waveform. This wave can be modified through one of the modulation techniques to change its form, and thereby transmit information. The two modulation techniques that you have heard the most about are likely amplitude modulation (AM) and frequency modulation (FM). The base waveform to which data will be added is referred to as the *carrier signal*. In the case of broadcasting a radio show, the added information is voices or music, while in the case of computer data, it is a series of 1s and 0s that represent binary data.

All signal waves have the same common characteristics, as shown in Figure 1-1. These are as follows:

✦ Amplitude, or height of the wave

✦ Period, or length of the wave to repeat one cycle

✦ Phase, or the offset of the wave from zero, or how far a wave is through its cycle

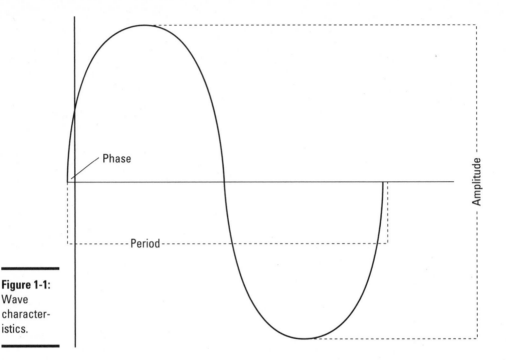

Figure 1-1:
Wave character-
istics.

Many ways exist to measure the amplitude of the wave. Some people measure from either peak (which is peak-to-peak), while others measure from
the center of the wave to the peak (which is peak or semiamplitude). The
frequency of the wave is the number of times it repeats over a given time
frame.

Modulating signals

Because you can now identify a waveform at a frequency, modulation allows
you to add data to that waveform by changing its basic form. The changes
that you can make include the amplitude, the frequency, and the phase. In
all cases, what you do to the wave prior to transmitting it (modulating) can
then be undone by the receiver (demodulating), assuming that it knows
what type of modification you are performing. When dealing with computers, which are composed of circuits that are either open or closed, you only
deal with two states, so as long as you can create two distinct states in the
waveform, you can identify them as open or closed, on or off, or 0 or 1. This
then allows you to transmit binary data over RF. Figure 1-2 shows two basic
types of modification of the initial carrier wave, which could be used to
show binary number patterns.

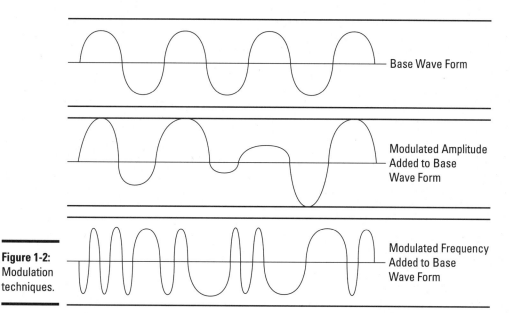

Base Wave Form

Modulated Amplitude
Added to Base
Wave Form

Modulated Frequency
Added to Base
Wave Form

Figure 1-2:
Modulation
techniques.

Using RF channels

When a national regulatory body (such as the FCC in the United States) allocates a frequency range to be used for a function, it can also specify how it is used or shared. So, in the case of the 5-GHz range that is used by cordless phones and 802.11a wireless devices, the frequency band is defined as 5.170 GHz–5.835 GHz, but is then divided into 24 channels, each 20 MHz wide. This allows 24 unique conversations or communications to take place in that frequency range in the same physical area. If you are using 802.11a wireless networking, in a single room, you can operate 24 access points without interference between devices (not that you would likely want to do that).

Transmission channels in the 2.4-GHz radio frequency range

When working with the 2.4-GHz portion of the RF spectrum, the actual range that you are working with is 2.4000–2.4835 GHz. This range is broken up into 14 unique channels, with each one 22 MHz wide, but the center of each of these channels is only 5 MHz apart. This means that an overlap exists between consecutive channels, which would result in interference and prevent proper communication. In the United States, the FCC has only allowed 11 of these channels to be used.

Due to the overlapping of channels, if you are using multiple devices in a small geographical area where the devices' RF may come in contact with each other, there is a maximum of three nonoverlapping channels that you can choose from — 1, 6, and 11. This is illustrated in Figure 1-3, which shows each of the 14 channels defined in the range, while only channels 1–11 are used in the United States.

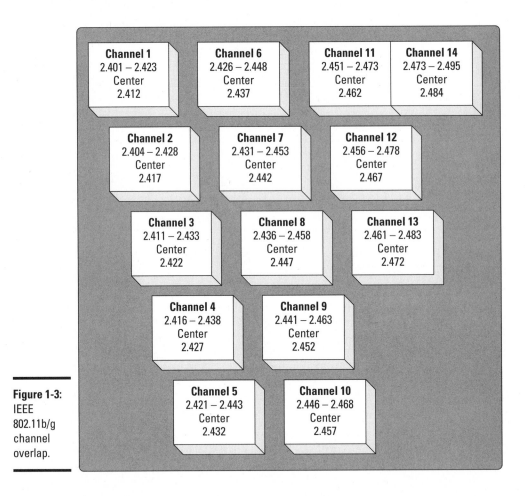

The 2.4-GHz RF band is used by IEEE 802.11 b/g/n networking, as well as Bluetooth and many cordless phones. This has caused issue, because in any given area, you can expect something to generate signal traffic in that frequency range, and poorly designed devices can bleed beyond their specified RF ranges and create additional interference for other devices. The 2.4-GHZ RF band is heavily congested.

Transmission channels in 5-GHz radio frequency

When working with the 5-GHz portion of the RF spectrum, you are primarily working with the range of 5.170–5.835 GHz. This range is broken up into 24 unique channels, with each one being 20 MHz wide and the center of each channel is at least 20 MHz apart. Most countries use 20-MHz wide channels but often authorize different frequencies to be used for the channels that can go as low as 4.905 GHz. For simplicity, I limit my discussion to the authorized channels in the United States.

For an IEEE 802.11a wireless network, the list of available channels includes 36, 40, 44, 48, 52, 56, 60, 64, 149, 153, 157, 161, and 165. Now this gets more confusing when dealing with IEEE 802.11n, because the specifications for the standard allow the use of either 20-MHz channels or 40-MHz channels; this increases the amount of data that can sent over the channel.

The biggest benefits of the 5-GHz portion of the spectrum are the nonoverlapping channels and the lack of competition for channel space. As in addition to IEEE 802.11a/n networking, this RF band is primarily only used by cordless phones.

Introducing RF modulation techniques

In preparation for your CCNA exam, you should know something about the different RF modulation techniques that are implemented in IEEE 802.11 networking. Do not worry about knowing everything about them; just be familiar with the terminology that is used in the following sections.

Frequency-hopping spread spectrum (FHSS)

This modulation technique uses the available channels to transmit and receive data, but rather than staying on any one channel, it rapidly switches between channels using a pseudorandom pattern that is based on an initial key; this key is shared between the participants of the communication session. If interference affects only a few of the channels, this interference is minimized because each channel is only used briefly. If the interference is broad, it can still affect all the channels that are in use. This modulation technique requires that the initial seed or key be shared, but after that has happened, it is very difficult to eavesdrop on.

IEEE 802.11 wireless networks use this technique for modulation, while Bluetooth uses an adaptive version of this technique that stops using channels where interference or weak signals exist.

Direct-sequence spread spectrum (DSSS)

Rather than rapidly swapping between several channels, DSSS spreads the carrier signal across the entire 22-MHz frequency range of its channel. For example, a device sending over channel 1 would spread the carrier signal across the 2.401- to 2.423-GHz frequencies (the full 22-MHz range of channel 1). At the same time it is transmitting the data over this channel, it also, at a faster rate, generates a noise signal in a pseudorandom pattern. This noise signal is known to the receiver, which can reverse or subtract this signal from the data signal. This process allows the carrier signal to be spread over the entire spectrum. With the entire spectrum being used, the effect of narrow-spectrum interference is reduced. Also, if the channel is being used by other devices, the effect of their signal is reduced because they will not be using the same pseudorandom noise pattern.

DSSS has an advantage over FHSS in that it has better resistance to interference. It is used primarily by IEEE 802.11b networks and cordless phones operating in the 900-MHz, 2.4-GHz, and 5-GHz spectrums. It is also sometimes used by IEEE 802.11g/n networks, but these newer networks tend to prefer OFDM.

Orthogonal Frequency Division Multiplexing (OFDM)

The slower that data is transmitted, the less likely that interference or line noise will cause a problem with the transmission. Multiplexing allows you to take several pieces of data and combine them into a single unit that can then be sent over the communication channel. In this case, OFDM takes the data that needs to be transmitted and breaks it into a large number of subcarrier streams (up to 52 subcarriers) that can then all be multiplexed into a single data stream. Because 52 subcarriers exist, the final data stream can be sent at a slower rate, while still delivering more data than other methods in the same time period.

This multiplexing process gives OFDM an advantage over DSSS because it allows higher throughput (54 Mbps instead of 11 Mbps) and it can be used both in the 2.4-GHz frequency range and in the 5-GHz frequency range. Multiplexing has many uses, and OFDM is used in any technology that needs to send large amounts of data over slower transmission lines or standards. You will find that OFDM is used with IEEE 802.11g/a/n networking as well as with ASDL and digital radio.

Multiple-in, multiple-out (MIMO)

MIMO allows multiple antennas to be used when sending and receiving data. The concept of spatial multiplexing allows these multiple signals to be multiplexed or aggregated, thereby increasing the throughput of data. To improve the reliability of the data stream, MIMO is usually combined with OFDM.

When using multiple antennas, you can achieve higher transmission speeds —
more than 100 Mbps.

MIMO is used in both WiMAX and IEEE 802.11n networks, allowing these networks to achieve their high speeds.

Introducing Wireless Local Area Network (WLAN) Standards (IEEE 802.11)

Early in WLAN development, many people were trying different technologies
to achieve the goal of wireless LAN communication. As some clear winners
started to emerge, a need existed for interoperation among these technologies. This desire for interoperation led to the development of standards
around WLAN communications. As with all other standards in communications, standards allow all companies involved to build equipment to a level
that allows their equipment to be used with equipment made by other vendors. This was not necessarily true in the beginning, but by the time IEEE
802.11a and IEEE 802.11b emerged, the standards were set, and all hardware
vendors were able to build to a level that allowed interoperability.

2.4-GHz band

Many of the wireless standards that emerged were designed to operate in
the already crowded 2.4-GHz band. Whether this was a good idea does not
matter; it is what happened. The following sections take a closer look at the
standards in this category.

IEEE 802.11

As with the early days of any technologies, a number of players in the industry were looking at different methods of transferring LAN data without wires.
As things moved along, a few groups emerged at the top of the pile. These
groups used technologies that were not compatible with each other, and the
most popular of these was collectively called 802.11-1997 or 802.11 Legacy.
It is odd that these were referred to as collective, because they were not
compatible with each other. The common factors of this standard were the
communication rates and base technology components that are common to
all IEEE 802.11 networks.

Terminology that arose from this specification applies to all IEEE 802.11 networks. This includes the following:

✦ Access point (AP)
✦ Basic Service Set (BSS)

+ Distribution System (DS)

+ Extended Service Set (ESS)

+ Service set identifier (SSID)

+ Frame structure (defining MAC and physical layers)

+ Distributed Coordination Function, which is carrier sense multiple access collision avoidance (CSMA/CA)

+ Dynamic rate shifting (DRS)

+ Beacon frames

+ Wired Equivalent Privacy (WEP)

+ Ad hoc networking

+ Infrastructure networking

These terms are fully described in the later chapters of this book, but you should be aware that they date back to the first IEEE 802.11 wireless networks.

The specifications for IEEE 802.11 define three possible physical layer systems that can be used:

+ Frequency-hopping spread spectrum (FHSS) in the 2.4-GHz band

+ Direct sequence spread spectrum (DSSS) in the 2.4-GHz band

+ InfraRed (which is in the specification but was not adopted by the industry)

In addition to defining the physical layer protocols, the specification defines the communication speed as 1or 2 Mbps.

The main benefit of IEEE 802.11 was that it offered RF wireless networks with greater range and throughput than other wireless technologies at the time, which were primarily infrared-based and thereby line-of-sight. Because this networking was based in the crowded 2.4-GHz spectrum, a great deal of interference existed, which was only partly minimized by FHSS and DSSS.

All the IEEE 802.11 networking standards use carrier sense multiple access collision avoidance (CSMA/CA). This is different from the Ethernet LAN standard, which uses carrier sense multiple access collision detect (CSMA/CD). In both cases, *carrier sense* means that all devices can sense or see other traffic that is transmitting, and *multiple access* means that multiple (or all) devices can access the media at the same time, but only one computer is allowed to send data at a time.

The difference starts there. With LAN technologies, when a computer wants to send a frame on the network, it uses its carrier sense to see whether anyone is using the network. If not, it then sends a network frame onto the wire, and the signal goes to the end of the wire, where it bounces and returns to the sending computer. The maximum length of an Ethernet cable is set to require the bounce signal to return within a specified time limit. When the computer sees what it sent, it knows that it was sent without a collision. But if what it sees is garbled, it knows that a collision occurred, and it then waits a random period of time and repeats the process. This system of collision detection works because the physical media allows the sending computer to verify that its data was correctly sent on the media.

When working with WLAN technologies, the frame is sent on the network, which has no mechanism to allow a signal to bounce, and as such, it relies on collision avoidance. The method of sending data still starts with listening to the network to see whether anyone is using the media, and if no frames are detected for a specified period of time (known as the *distributed inter-frame space [DIFS]*), it is allowed to send its frame. The receiving station performs the CRC (cyclic redundancy check) of the received packet and sends back an ACK (acknowledgment) frame when the media is free. After the sending station receives its ACK frame, it knows that the data was sent correctly.

This collision-avoidance process generates more network frames to send data, but it follows a more orderly process than collision detection. When the network is under high utilization, the collision-detection process tends to move more data than collision avoidance; this is likely due to mandatory wait states that occur by devices honoring the DIFS.

Dynamic rate shifting (DRS) allows an AP to rate-shift to a lower bandwidth when the signal weakens. The signal becomes weaker proportionally to the distance between the AP and the target wireless device. In other words, the farther you go from the AP, the weaker the wireless signal becomes and the lower the transmission speed becomes because DRS automatically rate-shifts to a lower speed when the signal weakens.

IEEE 802.11b

In the 2.4-GHz spectrum, the first major upgrade to the WLAN specification is IEEE 802.11b, which raised the maximum bandwidth to 11 Mbps. This standard also relied primarily on Complementary Code Keying (CCK) as its modulation technique, which was a modified form of DSSS, while it would use DSSS when using slower connection speeds via DRS. The typical range for IEEE 802.11b is about 100 feet (30 meters) when operating at 11 Mbps.

Expect the exam to refer to the modulation used for IEEE 802.11b as DSSS rather than the modified subtype of CCK.

The benefit of this standard over its predecessor is primarily in the maximum network speed, while it still suffered from interference on a crowded RF spectrum. The other drawback that this standard suffered from was a slower transmission speed than the other standard at the time (IEEE 802.11a, which had a rated bandwidth of 54 Mbps). Even though IEEE 802.11a had higher throughput, IEEE 802.11b emerged as the dominant standard.

IEEE 802.11g

The next major improvement in WLAN networking in the 2.4-GHz band is IEEE 802.11g, which increases the maximum bandwidth to 54 Mbps and primarily makes use of the RF modulation technique of Orthogonal Frequency Division Multiplexing (OFDM) in addition to CCK and DSSS when speeds are reduced.

IEEE 802.11g offered an easy upgrade path for users of IEEE 802.11b as older devices were able to connect to newer radios, although this caused the radio to automatically fall back to the slower technology for all users. This issue was mitigated by many hardware vendors by including multiple radios in their APs, allowing one to be set to IEEE 802.11g only and one to be set to IEEE 802.11b. When using IEEE 802.11g transmission standards, a modified collision avoidance system is used, thereby reducing the delays and the wait states required for transmission.

5-GHz band

At the same time that IEEE 802.11b was being implemented in the 2.4-GHz RF band, IEEE 802.11a was being implemented in the 5-GHz band.

IEEE 802.11a

IEEE 802.11a offered several advantages over IEEE 802.11b. It had a maximum transmission rate of 54 Mbps and operated in the less cluttered 5-GHz RF band. It uses OFDM as its RF modulation technique.

The biggest drawback is that IEEE 802.11a is not compatible with devices that run in the 2.4-GHz spectrum, primarily IEEE 802.11b/g devices.

2.4-GHz and 5-GHz bands

The latest technologies for WLAN allow you to operate in both of the major RF frequencies. This provides you the best of both worlds and will likely be the trend moving forward.

IEEE 802.11n

In early versions of the draft specifications, this standard was only to use the 2.4-GHz RF spectrum. However, the final specification was ratified in September 2009 and allowed operating in the 5-GHz RF spectrum as well. By allowing both of the previous RF spectrums to be used, it allows IEEE 802.11n devices to be backward compatible with both IEEE 802.11b/g and IEEE 802.11a devices and maximizes its possible acceptance.

IEEE 802.11n uses both OFDM and multiple-in, multiple-out (MIMO) RF modulation techniques. While ranges are comparable with the IEEE 802.11 network specifications, it allows a maximum throughput of 600 Mbps when using four MIMO streams, or 150 Mbps for a single stream.

IEEE 802.11n offers nothing but advantages over the previous IEEE 802.11 network specifications because it operates in both major RF bands, is backward compatible with other standards, and operates at higher data speeds. Because it has only recently been ratified, many of the existing devices on the market conform to draft specifications, but you can expect that these will be upgraded through 2010.

If you are using a device that supports IEEE 802.11n that you purchased before September 2009 when the standard was ratified, make sure to update the device firmware to bring it up to the final IEEE 802.11n specification.

Prep Test

1 **What is the greatest benefit for wireless implementations?**

A ○ Increased security

B ○ Reduced cost

C ○ Increased mobility

D ○ Business continuity

2 **What technology does IEEE 802.11 networking use to control data on the network?**

A ○ CSMA/CW (carrier sense multiple access collision warning)

B ○ CSMA/CA (carrier sense multiple access collision avoidance)

C ○ CSMA/CD (carrier sense multiple access collision detect)

D ○ CSMA/CP (carrier sense multiple access collision prevention)

3 **What is the name of the organization that defines 802.11 networking standards?**

A ○ WiMAX

B ○ FCC

C ○ Wi-Fi Alliance

D ○ IEEE

4 **What wireless networking standard operates in both the 2.4-GHz and 5-GHz RF ranges?**

A ○ 802.11a

B ○ 802.11b

C ○ 802.11n

D ○ 802.11i

5 **What wireless networking technologies offer the highest networking through-put? (Choose two.)**

A ○ 802.11a

B ○ 802.11b

C ○ 802.11g

D ○ 802.11i

Answers

1 **C.** Increased mobility is the largest benefit to wireless networking. Peek at *"Purpose of Wireless Networks."*

2 **B.** CSMA/CA (Carrier Sense Multiple Access with Collision Avoidance) is the data control technology on IEEE 802.11 networks. Review *"IEEE 802.11."*

3 **D.** IEEE is the body that defines the standard of the 802.11 networking components. Peruse *"Using unlicensed radio bands."*

4 **C.** The only technology that works in both 2.4 GHz and 5 GHz RF ranges is IEEE 802.11n. Look at *"2.4-GHz and 5-GHz bands."*

5 **A, C.** Both IEEE 802.11a and 802.11g both operate at a rated 54 Mbps. Take a look at *"802.11a" and "802.11g".*

Chapter 2: Wireless Local Area Network (WLAN) Security

Exam Objective

✔ **Comparing and contrasting wireless security features and capabilities of WPA security (including open, WEP, WPA, and WPA2)**

*N*ow that you are interested in working with wireless networking, you need to know how to secure the wireless network that you are working with. Many options are available to you to secure various aspects of your wireless network. This chapter examines some of the main methods and options that are available to you when securing wireless networks.

Securing a wireless network, like any network, would be done to ensure that your data and private information remain private. The difference is that with wireless networks, you can never be sure where the users may be. I review some of the risks that you have to deal with as well as discuss the steps that you can take to reduce your risks.

Recognizing Security Risks

As with any wired network, any number of attacks can be perpetrated on you if an unauthorized computer is allowed to connect to your network. This is why on secure networks, all unauthorized ports of network switches are disabled or disconnected. However, this is not possible when dealing with wireless networks, where the access point (AP) radio is either on or off.

When a computer is on your network, it is capable of sniffing packets, perpetrating man-in-middle attacks, spoofing valid network packets, capturing passwords and other sensitive information, and causing a denial of service. If you are able to control which computers are allowed to connect to your network, you can reduce your exposure to these security issues. Most networks have removed all their network hubs and replaced them with switches, which are more secure.

A switch treats each network switch port as a separate collision domain (in the carrier sense multiple access collision detect [CSMA/CD] sense), which means that when a device on port 1 sends frames to a device on port 2, and both MAC addresses are known to the switch, those frames only travel along the cables connected to port 1 and port 2. However, when a hub is used, the frame travels to every device connected to every port on the hub. When dealing with wireless networks, an AP operates in the same manner as a hub, so all devices that are connected wirelessly to a single AP radio can see all traffic that is sent on that radio. If a device is allowed to join a wireless network, it can perpetrate any number of attacks on the devices connected to the same AP, as well as other attacks that only require it to be on the same network segment.

Introducing Security Risk Mitigation Methods

Although there are inherent security risks with everything that we do in life, steps can be taken to reduce the risks. If you are going for a walk in a strange town, you may stay on well-lit roads, carry only a limited amount of cash and credit cards, walk with other people, and stay aware of your surroundings. All these things may limit what might happen to you on your walk, while not going at all is also an option.

In the computer world, if you don't network your computers, you reduce or all but eliminate the risk of what can happen to your computer by undesirable elements, but you also reduce its functionality. So to increase its functionality, you add a modem or a network card and attach your computer to other computers to share data and perform remote operations. You then mitigate the risk of having these computers connected to each other, and possibly the Internet, by using antivirus software, software and hardware firewalls, intrusion detection hardware and software firewalls and hardware, and other security and monitoring devices. When you decide to add a wireless network to this mix, you have many of the same issues, but these are now compounded because people can have local access to the network without actually being in your building or offices. This added functionality of mobility needs to be weighed against the added risks of remote users exploiting security holes and getting to your private data.

When working with most wireless networking equipment, you have the following ways to protect your network data:

+ Authentication and data encryption
+ MAC address filtering
+ Intrusion detection and intrusion prevention
+ Hiding the service set identifier (SSID)

The following sections examine each of these in detail.

Authentication and data encryption

Authentication and data encryption comprise a large topic. I start by taking a look at the most common techniques and then move on to other techniques that are equally good, but used less frequently.

WEP, WPA, and WPA2

One of the first major complaints that arose from wireless networking was from the security community. Quite rightly, the complaint was that with RF signals being broadcast over the air, nothing can stop someone from reaching out and grabbing them. At least with wired networking, a person had to physically be connected to the same hubs or switches to be able to eavesdrop on a network conversation.

To deal with this issue, Wired Equivalent Privacy (WEP) was introduced. The goal of WEP is to provide the same level of privacy that you would have if you were still connected to a wired network. The goal was good, but as with a better-built mousetrap, you end up with smarter mice.

The basis of WEP involved two sets of mechanisms:

✦ **Authentication:** You need to prove your identity before participating in the network.

✦ **Encryption:** You want everything you send over the airwaves to be encrypted.

The basis of WEP encryption is tied to an encryption key; today you typically see either 64-bit WEP or 128-bit WEP encryption keys. With 64-bit WEP, you use a 40-bit key that is joined with a 24-bit initialization vector (IV) to generate an RC4 (Rivest Cipher 4) stream cipher. A 128-bit WEP uses a 104-bit encryption key, which is then joined with the 24-bit IV to create the RC4 cipher.

While this gives you a quick and efficient way to encrypt and decrypt traffic at high speed, it has some serious flaws. Even if you cannot read the data, you can still capture data packets off a wireless network, because they are just traveling over the air. One of the issues is that the IV must be unique for every packet that is sent over a time period, and because it is only 24 bits long, it can start repeating in as little as 5,000 packets, making it not as random or secure as it can be. WEP has consistently been proven to be broken in as little as 1 minute and can be broken with readily available software. Given this, it is not considered to be reliably secure for networks. Payment Card Industry (PCI), which sets standards for credit and debit card transactions, prohibits the use of WEP in any part of a credit card transaction.

The authentication part of WEP can be a configured as an open system, which does not require authentication but rather starts a conversation with any device. That device still would be required to know the WEP key if encryption is enabled.

If shared key authentication is being used, all devices start their communication with the AP with a four-way handshake process that starts with the client sending an authentication request. The AP would send a challenge (a random piece of data) that the client then encrypts by using the WEP key and returns to the AP. The AP decrypts the data it receives and does a comparison with the data it sent in the initial challenge. If the data matches, the device is sent an acknowledgment; if it does not match, it is sent a refusal. If the client is authenticated, it can start sending data to the AP, likely encrypting it using its WEP key.

Due to the limitations of WEP, Wi-Fi Protected Access (WPA) was developed. WPA makes use of most of the recommendations that are included in the IEEE 802.11i specification, which lays out security standards for wireless networks. WPA2 followed later, implementing all the IEEE 802.11i mandatory elements. Rather than using a static encryption key, as is used with WEP, WPA makes use of Temporal Key Integrity Protocol (TKIP), which can easily be implemented because it is a minor but effective upgrade to WEP. Rather than using a plain text IV, it combines the IV with a secret root key. It also implements a sequence counter, so all packets must arrive at the AP in the correct order, or they are rejected. Finally, it provides a method of rekeying or updating the encryption key, neutralizing people trying to break the key.

There are still many documented attacks that can be successfully carried out on a WPA network using TKIP, and as such, it required additional updating. The implementation of AES (Advanced Encryption Standard) increased the level of encryption to a level that is still considered to be the safest on the market, while the initial key was set with either certificate-based authentication or a shared secret. When security is initialized with a shared secret, entrance to the secured network provides a breach point, while certificate-based authentication provides a less vulnerable option. Certificate-based authentication is available when using enterprise-mode authentication, while shared secret or Pre-Shared Key (PSK) is used for personal-mode authentication.

Virtual Private Network (VPN)

Many companies or organizations operate a VPN to allow their users to securely gain access to network resources when operating their mobile computers on a remote and unsecured network. This allows them to isolate their computers from the local network that they are on and connect them to their corporate network. Using this same mentality, they can operate their wireless network is a less secure manner, but separate from their main corporate network. When their users are on this network, they can then use their VPN solution to make a connection back to their corporate network in a secured manner, as shown in Figure 2-1.

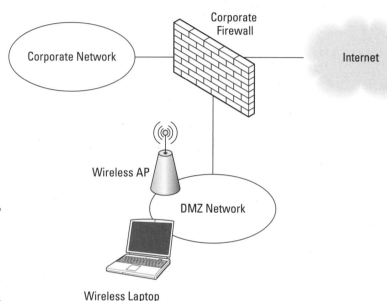

Figure 2-1:
Corporate
wireless
access over
a VPN.

This solution allows a secure connection to their corporate resources without worrying about the absolute security of their wireless network because any secure data will be communicated through the VPN connection.

SSH, SSL, TLS, HTTPS

Secure Shell (SSH), Secure Socket Layer (SSL), TLS (Transport Layer Security), and HTTPS all represent technologies that can be used to secure communication between a client and a server. Each has proven itself as a method of securing data and keeping it safe, whether that data is wireless or wired. So when using wireless networking, these technologies should be always be used.

Secure Shell is the secure replacement for Telnet. Unlike Telnet, which transmits its data in clear text over the network, SSH encrypts all data that it sends between clients and servers. It also allows you to authenticate with either a username and password or by using certificate-based authentication. This has become the de facto standard when communicating with UNIX/Linux servers and network devices such as routers and switches.

TLS is the replacement for SSL and is the standard method of encrypting client/server data that starts with a key exchange, authentication, and the implementation of standard ciphers. Many IP-based protocols support the use of TLS to encrypt data, such as HTTP (HTTPS), SMTP, POP3, FTP, and NNTP. Because most major protocols support this method of encryption, when using these protocols over wireless, TLS should be used if the server supports it.

MAC address filtering

When attempting to secure a wireless network, in addition to encryption and authentication of WEP and WPA, you can also filter users from connecting to your WLAN if they do not have a registered or authorized MAC address associated with their network card. In addition to adding a list of authorized MAC addresses to the individual APs that make up your wireless network, you can centrally maintain a list of authorized MAC addresses via a Remote Authentication Dial-In User Service (RADIUS) or authentication, authorization, and accounting (AAA) server on your network.

Because many operating systems allow you to locally set your MAC address on your network card, this security should only be considered as light security, like WEP. If an intruder knows a valid MAC address on your network, either by social engineering or by capturing wireless network frames, he can use that to gain access to your network by manipulating his own MAC address.

Hiding the service set identifier (SSID)

Each WLAN AP sends out regular broadcasts that include the name of the network, or SSID. Knowing the SSID of a network allows you to connect to the network. Most APs allow you to disable the broadcasting of the SSID, which prevents people from knowing your network name and makes it difficult for them to connect to your network. Tools like Network Stumbler are designed to monitor RF WLAN signals and can easily identify whether WLAN networks exist in your area; this is shown in Figure 2-2. Other tools, such as AirCrack, can help you identify the SSID.

As with MAC address filtering, disabling the broadcasting of the SSID does not provide you with strong security; it only keeps the casual passerby from connecting to your WLAN.

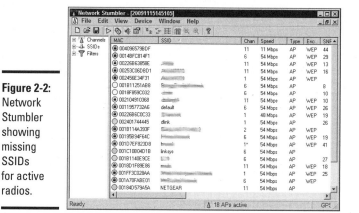

Figure 2-2:
Network
Stumbler
showing
missing
SSIDs
for active
radios.

Intrusion detection and intrusion prevention

Intrusion detection systems (IDSs) and intrusion prevention systems (IPSs)
monitor network traffic and traffic to these systems to locate devices on
your network that may be attempting infiltrate your network. When people
are attempting to gather information about your network, they will run tools
that leave a signature on your network or will send specific types of traffic to
devices on the network. Having devices for intrusion detection allows them
to see who is scanning, which allows you to locate them and block them.
When the intrusion detection system reacts to the intrusion and attempts to
block the attempt automatically, the system is usually referred to as an IPS.

Most network providers like Cisco have a full range of IDSs and IPSs that run
either on a network gateway or inside the network. These systems range in
price based on the features they offer and how they integrate into the network.

Changing default passwords

All network devices — be they switches, routers, wireless LAN controllers,
or access points — all ship with a default system configuration that includes
IP address configuration, SSID, users, and administration password. Because
this information is documented in the devices owner's manual and on the
manufacturer's Web site, you should change these items prior to deploying
these devices on your network; otherwise, unknown people will be able to
change your device configurations.

Years ago, this was not identified as a major concern. It caused many APs to
be deployed with default SSIDs, allowing the manufacturer of that AP to be
identified and the default username and password to then be known. This

would then lead to security breaches for those networks. Most manufacturers now promote the fact that security is important and, in some cases, require all configuration to be manually set up before the AP or network devices can be used.

Management access

When dealing with a residential-grade AP, you usually only have one networking interface that is used for both data access as well as for management. When dealing with commercial- or enterprise-grade access points, you usually have the option of supporting virtual local-area networks (VLANs) right at the AP. This allows you to support multiple SSIDs over a single radio, which are then assigned to separate VLANs to isolate the traffic for each SSID. With VLAN support comes the ability to assign the management network interface to a separate VLAN. If the management interface is on a separate VLAN, security can be assigned at routers or firewalls to restrict which network devices can connect to the management interface. Some wireless devices also allow you to prevent management access through their own radios so that a user on the wireless network cannot manage that AP.

Prep Test

1 **Which of the following is true when comparing WPA and WPA2?**

   A ○ WPA uses 802.1x for authentication while WPA2 uses AES.

   B ○ WPA uses personal mode while WPA2 uses enterprise mode.

   C ○ WPA offers higher security options than WPA2.

   D ○ WPA2 uses AES for encryption while WPA uses TKIP for encryption.

2 **In what situation should WEP be used as a security method for a network?**

   A ○ WEP should be used anytime there is a need for high security on a wireless network.

   B ○ WEP should only be used when existing hardware offers it as the most secure option available.

   C ○ WEP should be used when AES encryption is required.

   D ○ WEP should always be used.

3 **What methods should be used to secure an access point? (Choose all that apply.)**

   A ○ Isolate the management interface on a private VLAN

   B ○ Enable SSID broadcasting

   C ○ Change the default administrative password

   D ○ Enable WEP or WPA encryption on the management interface

4 **What is the purpose of an IDS implementation?**

   A ○ An IDS offers an upgrade to CSMA/CA LAN technologies.

   B ○ An IDS identifies attackers and takes steps to disable their access to your network.

   C ○ An IDS allows you to integrate biometrics into your network security.

   D ○ An IDS detects when a network attack or penetration is happening on your network.

5 **MAC address filtering can be used to do which of the following?**

   A ○ Prevent your SSID from being detected by unauthorized devices

   B ○ Can be used to detect attacks or infiltration on your network

   C ○ Restrict access to your network to only specific wireless network cards

   D ○ Offer the most secure cipher available, because it is keyed with the MAC address of your network card

Answers

1 **D.** WPA2 can make use of the more secure AES encryption, while WPA only offers TKIP for encryption. Peek at *"WEP, WPA, and WPA2."*

2 **B.** WEP should only be used when wireless clients that are required on your network offer it as the highest encryption available; otherwise, WPA or WPA2 should be used. Study *"WEP, WPA, and WPA2."*

3 **A, C.** Protecting the management interface of the AP and changing the default administrative password can help to secure the AP from unauthorized changes. Refer to *"Management access."*

4 **D.** An IDS is an intrusion detection system. It is like an alarm system for network attacks or penetration. Take a look at *"Intrusion detection and intrusion prevention."*

5 **C.** MAC address filtering restricts access to a WLAN to a specific list of MAC addresses. Examine *"MAC address filtering."*

Chapter 3: Wireless Local Area Network (WLAN) Operation Modes

Exam Objectives

✔ Identifying the basic parameters to configure on a wireless network

✔ Identifying and describing the purpose of the components in a small wireless network — including SSID, BSS, ESS

✔ Identifying common issues with implementing wireless networks

*W*hen working with wireless LANs, you need to know their operating modes as well as how to lay out access points (APs) to allow maximum coverage while reducing internal conflicts. This chapter examines the basic options for WLAN operation and describes how to lay out a basic wireless network. If you focus on these key facts, you should breeze through the related questions on the exam.

When you are working with a traditional wired network, you connect your computer to a network switch to interconnect all devices on your network. Or, you use crossover network cables to directly connect two computers. In the case of wireless networking, you still have two choices: You can connect two devices directly or you can connect your devices using a central device, mainly an access point. These two methods are referred to as *ad hoc mode* when the devices are directly connected or *infrastructure mode* when using an AP. This chapter takes a look at both of these options.

Ad Hoc Mode

When working with networking in ad hoc mode, you are connecting to another device that has the same wireless settings as the settings on your own device. The benefit of this networking is that you do not need to pre-configure your network infrastructure to support a temporary group of users, while these users (or rather their devices) are able to share information among themselves. A sample ad hoc wireless network is shown in Figure 3-1. This networking required very little configuration to get it started.

Figure 3-1:
A sample
wireless
ad hoc
network.

In addition to device-to-device connections, you will find that this type of networking is also used in wireless mesh devices, in which all devices connect to the mesh (that being a few devices that are located near each other), and data will pass from device to device through the mesh, until it reaches its final destination. The advantage of using this type of technology is that all nodes can be provided with rudimentary routing information that allows the device to handle not only routing changes as needed but also to determine the best way to pass packets, or to be able to pass packets due to a hardware failure in one of the devices. After the hardware failure, all other wireless devices determine or update their paths for data.

When dealing with ad hoc mode WLAN technology, focus on device-to-device connections, because the wireless mesh overlays the ad hoc networking with additional software to support the mesh.

In most cases, when discussing ad hoc mode wireless networking, you will be dealing with device-to-device connections. These are easy enough to set up with the following process. In Windows XP, follow these steps:

1. **Choose Start⇨Control Panel.**

2. **Select Network and Internet Connections.**

3. **Choose Network Connections.**

4. **In the Wireless Network Connection Properties dialog box, locate your wireless network card in the list; then select it and click the Properties button. The Wireless Network Connection Properties dialog box opens, as shown in Figure 3-2.**

5. **In the Wireless Network Connection Properties dialog box, click the Wireless Networks tab.**

6. **Click the Add button.**

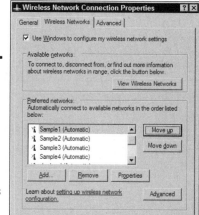

Figure 3-2:
Wireless
settings
for each
network
connection
are found in
the network
connection's
Properties
dialog box.

7. **In the Wireless Network Properties dialog box, provide a name for your new ad hoc network or type the name of an existing network.**

8. **At the bottom of the dialog box, select the This Is a Computer-to-Computer (Ad Hoc) Network check box.**

9. **Choose the Network Authentication and Data Encryption settings that you would like to use.**

   If the WEP key is not provided for you automatically, deselect the The Key Is Provided for Me Automatically check box and type the WEP key into the Network Key and Confirm Network Key fields.

   A completed dialog box with these settings is shown in Figure 3-3.

10. **Click the OK button to save your changes and close the Wireless Network Properties dialog box.**

11. **If this is the first device that you have set up for this network, repeat the steps for your second device.**

    The second computer will see the network show up in its list of available wireless networks.

By default, the TCP/IP settings for each network card will be set to use Automatic Private IP Addressing (APIPA), so since there will not be a DHCP server on your ad hoc network, both of your devices will choose a random address in the 169.254.0.0/16 network. This should be fine, as you will be able to then connect to the devices by either their computer name or IP address.

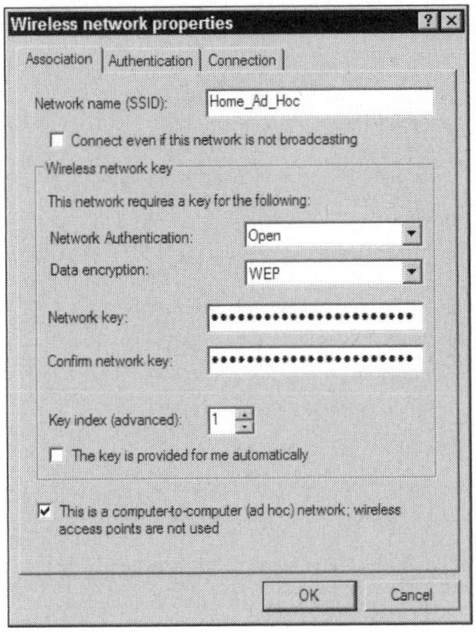

Figure 3-3:
Only a few
pieces of
information
are required
to set up
an ad hoc
network.

To activate your new ad hoc network, you need to let Windows know that you want to use it now. It is set up as an on-demand wireless connection. To do this, follow these steps:

1. **Choose Start⇨Control Panel.**

2. **Select Network and Internet Connections.**

3. **Choose Network Connections.**

4. **In the Wireless Network Connection Properties dialog box, click the View Wireless Networks button.**

   The Choose a Wireless Network dialog box appears, as shown in Figure 3-4.

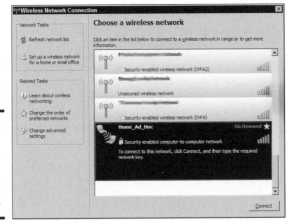

Figure 3-4:
Connecting
to an
on-demand
wireless
connection.

5. **Select your new ad hoc network connection and click the Connect button.**

    This changes this connection to Automatic so that it can then automatically connect when within range.

Rather than creating an on-demand connection, when you were creating the initial ad hoc connection, you can choose "Connect when this network is in range" on the Connection tab (refer to Figure 3-3).

These ad hoc networks are good to use when you are in a location where you have no infrastructure to which you can connect. This is sometimes the case in boardrooms or meeting spaces that have not been set up to support computers (either wired or wireless), or any other place where you need to connect a few computers. If someone has a small switch and cables with him, you can use those to set up a small temporary network. Otherwise, wireless ad hoc is the next best thing.

If you are using Windows to set up your ad hoc networking and you have a computer with a second network card that has an Internet connection, you can use Internet Connection Sharing to allow all the other computers on the ad hoc network to use your Internet connection.

Beware of ad hoc networks that you do not know the source of. I have often gone to public locations, such as airports and coffee houses, and checked for public wireless access. This is common in these locations. You should check these broadcasted networks prior to connecting to them. Any connection that is ad hoc, shown in Figure 3-4 as two computers rather than the wireless antenna, is likely not legitimate, and a person can attempt to gather information from your computer or from sites you are connecting to.

If you connect to a wireless network in ad hoc mode that also allows you to connect to the Internet, or any unknown network, you could be subject to a man-in-the-middle attack using network-auditing software such as Cain and Able from Oxid.it. All your passwords can be exposed, including those for secured HTTPS Web sites.

Infrastructure Mode

As opposed to ad hoc mode networks, infrastructure mode wireless networks use networking infrastructure. In this case, *infrastructure* refers to switches, routers, firewalls, and access points (APs).

At a minimum, the only network infrastructure component that is required for infrastructure mode is an access point, but if an AP is all you have, you have no more than you would have had when using ad hoc mode. However, most implementations include other components from your traditional network infrastructure, as shown in Figure 3-5.

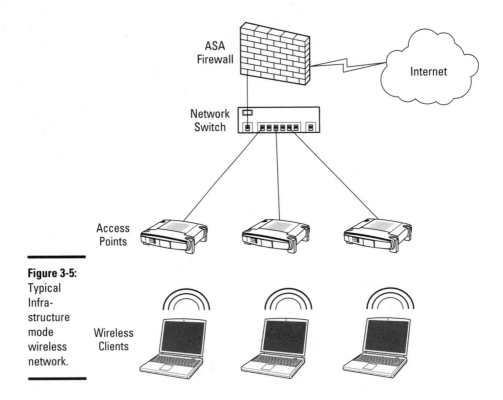

ASA Firewall

Internet

Network Switch

Access Points

Figure 3-5: Typical Infra-structure mode wireless network.

Wireless Clients

To connect to a wireless network that is broadcasting its SSID using Windows XP, follow these steps:

1. **Choose Start➪Control Panel.**

2. **Select Network and Internet Connections.**

3. **Choose Network Connections.**

4. **In the Network Connection window, locate your wireless network card and right-click➪View Wireless Networks.**

The Choose a Wireless Network dialog box appears, as shown in Figure 3-6.

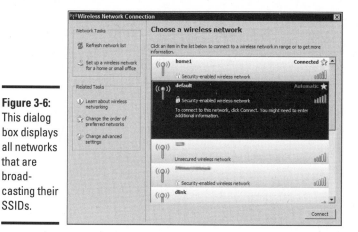

Figure 3-6:
This dialog box displays all networks that are broadcasting their SSIDs.

5. **Select a wireless network from the list and click the Connect button.**

If the network uses WEP or WPA, you will be prompted to enter the network key; then click the OK button.

Infrastructure mode wireless networking is the mode that you most often encounter in your work as a CCNA supporting networks for clients or in a corporate environment.

Autonomous mode

When 802.11 networking began, all APs were autonomous mode, which means that each AP worked as a stand-alone unit, with no knowledge of or interaction among other APs. This was fine in the beginning when wireless networking was often limited to providing network access in common areas or boardrooms, and continuous roaming was not a requirement. This meant that a typical network might deploy from one to ten access points across the network environment, and an environment of that size is still easily managed. Figure 3-5 showed an example of an autonomous mode wireless network.

Lightweight mode

Rather than using autonomous mode APs, you can also use lightweight mode APs if you have a network component that offers wireless LAN controller services. Cisco offers the lightweight mode option on most of its APs, so they can be purchased with either a controller-based software image (using Lightweight Access Point Protocol [LWAPP]) or a stand-alone software image (Cisco IOS software image). A sample of how this fits together in your network is shown in Figure 3-7. Some wireless LAN controllers have Power over Ethernet (PoE) ports that allow you to connect APs to; you can also connect the AP to any other PoE switch on your network.

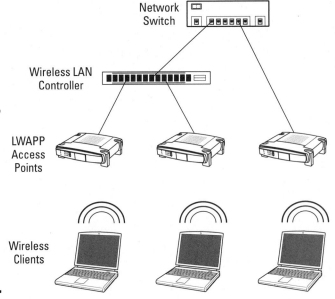

Figure 3-7: Lightweight APs require a wireless LAN controller to be available on the network in order to function.

To have wireless LAN controller (WLC) services on your network, you can use any of the following:

✦ Cisco 2100 series controller

✦ Cisco 4400 series controller

✦ Catalyst 6500 series Wireless Services Module (WiSM)

✦ Cisco 7600 series Router Wireless Services Module (WiSM)

✦ Cisco 28/37/38xx series Integrated Services Router with Controller Network Module

✦ Catalyst 3750G Integrated Wireless LAN Controller Switch

In this scenario, the access points all have their configuration managed by the WLC. A single policy can be set on that WLC, and that configuration setting can be deployed to all managed access points, reducing the workload of managing hundreds of lightweight access points (when using the Cisco 7600 series Router Wireless Services Module). Also, in this configuration, some of the processing work that would normally be done at the AP can be offloaded to the WLC, leaving more CPU cycles available on the AP.

Service set

Service set refers to all the wireless devices that participate in a specific wireless LAN. This wireless LAN may be a local WLAN or an enterprise WLAN, spanning several buildings or areas. Each service set is identified by a service set identifier, or SSID. The SSID should directly relate to the network that the WLAN or AP will connect the wireless device to:

♦ If you have multiple networks within an enterprise environment, multiple SSIDs can exist.

♦ If you only have one network, you should only have one SSID.

Figure 3-8 shows multiple access points hosting connections to multiple networks. This means that in a single area, you will likely have multiple APs using the same SSID.

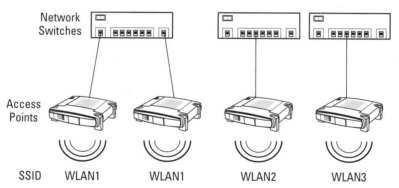

Figure 3-8:
Each SSID
should
identify a
different
or unique
physical
network that
is allowing
connections.

While the SSID can be up to 32 characters long, it is usually made up of human-readable ASCII characters, but it could contain any of the possible 256 values in those 32 digits. When users connect to the WLAN identified by the SSID, they can make the connection automatically or manually.

In addition to multiple access points broadcasting or using the same SSID, an option also exists for a single access point to use multiple SSIDs. This only makes sense if the AP allows you to map each of these SSIDs to a different network connection. This would typically be accomplished through the use of VLAN tagging, as shown in Figure 3-9. If the user associates with a particular SSID, this traffic is then passed to the network switch destined for a specific VLAN. This allows each network to have a different set of security standards surrounding it. You may have a wireless network, CorpSSID, which uses certificate-based authentication via WPA2 and AES encryption; while using the same APs to provide a second wireless network, GuestSSID, which uses only WEP. Even though you are providing two wireless networks, you are able to isolate guest traffic from the rest of corporate network and only allow them to use some services.

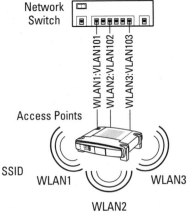

Figure 3-9: A single AP can supply access for multiple SSIDs.

Basic service set (BSS)

In simple terms, the BSS is one AP and its collection of clients. The AP is identified by a basic service set identifier (BSSID), which is a unique identifier for an AP and is usually a 48-bit MAC address of the AP. This allows each AP to be uniquely identified, even though they all may be providing service for the same SSID. The BSSID is only used on beacon frame as a means of identifying each AP.

Extended service set (ESS)

Extended service set extends the BSS to more than one AP that shares the same logical link control layer. So effectively, if these APs share the same physical connection to the network or exist on the same physical segment, they can act as one unit with multiple radios, thereby increasing the possible throughput available on that AP. All of the BSS units that make up the ESS would share the same SSID and can work on the same or different channels.

The benefit of the ESS is that it allows client roaming without reconfiguration of the client.

Network planning and layout

You have many factors to consider when planning a wireless network, from external sources of broad-spectrum interference to the characteristics of building materials that are in use to channel selection and range.

RF signal factors

Many things influence RF signals. You may get signal loss from building materials that usually comes from three main sources that are based on the types of materials used. These three sources are as follows:

✦ **Absorption:** Absorption occurs when RF waves are absorbed by the materials that they are attempting to pass through. Absorption typically occurs when the waves pass through walls or dense materials. Water and concrete have high RF absorption properties.

✦ **Reflection:** Reflection occurs when RF waves cannot penetrate a surface and are returned or bounced off the surface. This is common with metal and glass surfaces.

✦ **Scattering:** Scattering occurs when the reflective surface is uneven, which causes many random bounces. A reflective signal may still have enough of its original properties to be used, but a scattered signal will not.

The more issues you have with your signal between the client and the AP, the higher the noise level of the signal. Other sources of noise include other devices that operate in the same wireless band as your AP and devices that may cause broad-spectrum interference. Some level of noise always exists, but if the level is too high, the signal-to-noise ratio will be too low to sustain a proper connection.

Due to unexpected signal loss, a site survey is standard practice prior to deploying access points. A site survey allows you to

✦ Identify other wireless networks in the area that may conflict with your network

✦ Place a temporary AP and measure the signal strength from different areas

This predeployment step can answer many of the unknowns and allow you to have a successful deployment.

AP layout

The simplest wireless network would contain only one AP. The issues that you need to deal with for one AP are generally placement and signal loss. Figure 3-10 shows a centrally located AP in an office with a few obstructions that may cause signal loss in the areas specified.

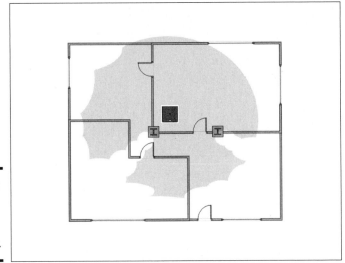

Figure 3-10:
Signal loss
in a single
AP WLAN
deployment.

Ignoring signal loss from building materials, if you have three APs in your layout and no outside interference, you should use all three of the non-overlapping channels (1, 6, and 11). The only exception to this would be if you had a more linear layout, where the APs at either end of the line were isolated by the middle AP. A typical pattern may give you a layout that resembles what is shown in Figure 3-11. Cisco recommends a 10–15 percent overlap between APs to allow complete coverage in the interim area.

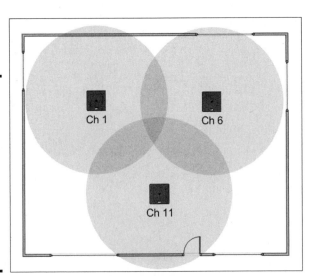

Figure 3-11:
Three APs
on your
wireless
network
usually
require that
all three
nonover-
lapping
channels be
used.

This deployment would be more complex if you had to provide coverage using four APs. In that case, you would have to reuse at least one of the nonoverlapping channels to complete the deployment. You can do this by isolating the reused channel from the other AP on that channel by stronger signals from the intermediary APs. Staggering these AP channels allows you to provide coverage on all your network APs. An example of this is shown in Figure 3-12.

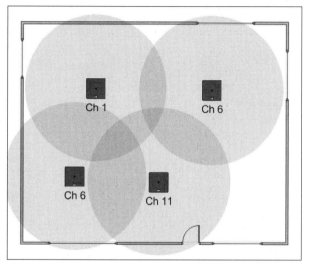

Figure 3-12: Isolating reused channels by using stronger AP signals in between.

Now if the area gets even more crowded, in an attempt to provide better coverage or to support higher client density, you may need to take additional steps. In Figure 3-13, notice that an AP on channel 6 separates the two channel 1 APs, allowing that channel to be reused, while all three channel 6 APs are primarily separated by the channel 11 AP. In addition to the physical placement, the power levels on the channel 6 APs have been reduced to provide a lower radius of coverage, thus preventing these APs from touching each other.

Having been involved in some large wireless rollouts, I can tell you that this gets even more complicated when you have to do this type of RF management across a three-story building. In that case, you not only have to keep your channels separated per floor but also between floors.

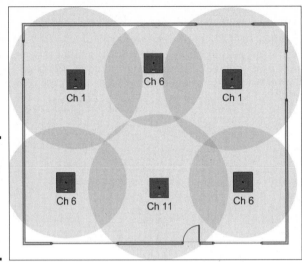

Figure 3-13:
Tuning radio
strength or
power can
also isolate
duplicate
channels.

Automatic tuning

Some APs on the market support automatic tuning, but in challenging environments, you may need to actively manage them. Systems like Cisco's Wireless LAN Controller, which knows about all internal network APs and can detect external APs, give you a good option for automatic tuning of channels and signal strength. Each AP goes off-channel for a short period of time to allow it to scan all channels to look for interference. Because the Wireless LAN Controller also knows about all other APs that exist on the network, it can determine the strength and visibility of the surrounding APs. This allows it to recalculate the channel selection and radio strength of all APs on the network, thereby optimizing coverage over the whole network.

Prep Test

1 What of the following items is never used in an ad hoc wireless network?

A ○ WEP

B ○ Wireless client

C ○ Access point

D ○ SSID

2 When a DHCP server is unavailable, Automatic Private IP Addressing will choose an address from which network block?

A ○ 169.254.0.0/16

B ○ 172.16.0.0/16

C ○ 192.168.254.0/24

D ○ 169.254.0.0/24

3 What factor does not influence wireless signals?

A ○ Scattering

B ○ Absorption

C ○ Displacement

D ○ Reflection

4 Why would you choose to use an ad hoc mode network over an infrastructure mode network?

A ○ Better security

B ○ Requirement for static IP addressing

C ○ Invalid SSID names

D ○ Lack of an available AP

5 What is a drawback of using autonomous mode APs?

A ○ Lack of roaming

B ○ Support for multiple radios

C ○ Lack of backward compatibility

D ○ Managing of multiple devices

Answers

1 **C.** An access point is not used in ad hoc mode wireless networking. See *"Ad Hoc Mode."*

2 **A.** 169.254.0.0/16 is the network range that addresses are chosen from when using APIPA. Review *"Ad Hoc Mode."*

3 **C.** Displacement is not one of the factors that affects RF signals. Peek at *"RF signal factors."*

4 **D.** Ad hoc mode networking would be used if no APs are available to support your wireless networking requirements. Reread *"Infrastructure Mode."*

5 **D.** One of the drawbacks of autonomous mode APs is management overhead when you have a large number of APs. Peruse *"Autonomous mode."*

Chapter 4: Managing Cisco Wireless Local Area Networks

Exam Objective

✔ **Understanding the infrastructure of a Cisco Wireless Local Area Network**

So as a CCNA, you will need to understand which components make up a standard Cisco wireless network. This chapter will prepare you for the exam by providing you an overview of the components and let you know how they work together. With this information you should be able to meet the challenges of the exam.

This chapter will review all of the components that make up a standard Cisco wireless network and provide you with necessary information you will need in order to know how all of these components function in order to provide wireless network services to your entire network.

Introducing the Cisco Unified Wireless Network Architecture (CUWN)

In today's market, the driving force behind mobile computing is actually mobile computer users. These users have been finding it more and more convenient to be able to use their computing devices wherever they need to. The more places that they are able to use them, the more places they want to be able to use them. This gives corporate IT staff a challenge in that they are typically concerned with the integrity, safety, and security of corporate data; allowing users in an ever widening geographical area to have access to this data goes against the goals of corporate IT staff. To alleviate some of this concern, Cisco released information on the Cisco Unified Wireless Network. The unified part of this solution is that it incorporates a standard management methodology and goal across all the products that Cisco provides for both wired and wireless data communication, with data security in the front of all development thoughts.

So the Cisco Unified Wireless Network takes data from a client, through wireless access points, through the wired infrastructure, to the servers or devices that will ultimately hold the data. As such, this makes use of networking devices at all levels of the process, and Cisco has released tools to allow for central management of all of these devices through a series of management tools.

The Cisco Unified Wireless Network uses some or all of the following components:

✦ Cisco Wireless Control System (WCS)

✦ Cisco WCS Navigator

✦ Cisco Wireless LAN Controller

✦ Cisco Wireless LAN Controller Module (WLCM)

✦ Cisco Wireless Service Module (WiSM)

✦ Cisco Catalyst 2750G Integrated Wireless LAN Controller

✦ Cisco Lightweight Access Points

✦ Cisco Aironet Wireless Bridge

✦ Cisco Aironet 1500 Series Lightweight Outdoor Mesh Access Points

✦ Cisco Client Devices

So now we can take a look at some of these components in more detail.

Cisco Wireless LAN Controller

Management of wireless LAN can be challenging today with the widespread deployment of access points (AP). In networks where there is currently no wireless, there is pressure to deploy a wireless solution; in established networks, the pressure is usually to increase coverage in the current solution.

To have Wireless LAN Controller (WLC) services on your network, you can use any of the following:

✦ Cisco 2100 series controller

✦ Cisco 4400 series controller

✦ Catalyst 6500 Series Wireless Services Module (WiSM)

✦ Cisco 7600 Series Router Wireless Services Module (WiSM)

✦ Cisco 28/37/38xx Series Integrated Services Router with Controller Network Module

✦ Catalyst 3750G Integrated Wireless LAN Controller Switch

The Cisco Wireless LAN Controller is used to manage all aspects of multiple APs and can also take care of all your Radio Resource Management.

The two WLC devices that you will likely encounter most often are the Cisco 2100 series controller or the Cisco 4400 series controller.

The Cisco 2100 series controller has eight network ports on it; two ports support POE (Power-Over-Ethernet) to power APs, while the other ports can be assigned as management interfaces, or assigned to support various VLAN and network connections that you may be using to isolate traffic for your SSIDs. This WLC can manage up to six APs.

Depending on the model of the Cisco 4400 series controller you look at, you can manage up to 100 APs through up to four network ports, which are used as distribution system ports. This series of controller is typically connected to a network switch, which would provide network services for your APs.

Most of these WLC support the following features:

✦ Distribution System Ports used to connect the WLC to a network switch and act as a path for data.

✦ Service Port used as a management or console port. This port is active during the boot mode of the WLC.

✦ Management Interface, which is used for in-band management and provides connectivity to network devices (such as DHCP servers or Radius servers). If you want to connect to the controller's web management interface, it would be through this interface. The management interface is assigned an IP address and is the initial point of contact for LWAPP communication and registration.

✦ AP-Manager Interface is used to control and manage all Layer 3 communications between the WLC and lightweight APs. For the best AP association results, it is recommended that the AP-Manager Interface be assigned to the same IP subnet as the Management Interface.

✦ Virtual Interface is used to support mobility management features, such as DHCP relay and Guest Web Authentication.

✦ Service-Port Interface is used to communicate to the Service Port and must have an IP Address that belongs to a different IP Subnet than that of the AP-Manager Interface and any other dynamic interface.

✦ Dynamic Interfaces are VLAN interfaces created by you to allow for communication to various VLANs.

Some features that are available to you when working with the WLC and LWAP include:

+ Controller port mirroring allows you to copy data on one port of your controller to another port for diagnostics.

+ Controller link aggregation (LAG) allows you to bond multiple ports together on your controller to allow multiple physical ports to be treated as a single logical port. With LAG enabled, you can support 100 APs on a single 4404 WLC, which still follows the recommendation of 48 APs per port.

+ DHPC Proxy allows you to forward DHCP requests to the normal DHCP servers existing on your network.

+ Aggressive load balancing distributes wireless clients between APs, rather than waiting for clients to naturally migrate between APs. This provides better performance on the overall WLAN.

+ Client roaming support between AP on the same ESS, and also between controllers and subnets, as well as Voice-over-IP Telephone Roaming.

+ Integrated security solutions built around 802.1x and AAA or Radius servers.

+ Rogue device management.

+ Cisco IDS and IPS support.

+ Internal DHCP server support, as well as requiring all clients on the network to have DHCP assigned IP addresses for additional security.

+ MAC filtering for WLAN access, which can be managed through AAA servers.

+ Dynamic transmit power control allows the radio strength to be tuned to allow for maximum coverage with minimal interference between APs.

+ Dynamic channel assignment allows for regular checks of RF channels in use in the area, and assigning channels that provide the least amount of interference or noise.

+ Coverage hole detection and correction allows for clients that detected to be getting weak coverage to trigger a process that will re-evaluate the overall channel and signal strength on the network to correct the holes.

+ Rogue AP detection allows you to identify non-managed APs in your area, and determine whether they are actually on your local network. If they are found to be on your local network, then remedial action may be taken.

Cisco WLAN Access Point (AP) Devices

Cisco Aironet Access Points are designed to support a variety of environments from indoor to outdoor. The lightweight access points allow users to make use of all mobility features of Cisco's Unified Wireless Network and support all of the standards of 802.11a/b/g/n. These devices offer reliable and secure communications using either single or double radios, while the greatest advantage is with "zero-touch" configuration, allowing you to deploy APs right out of the box, with no initial prep work.

Cisco's product line of APs includes:

✦ Cisco Aironet 1130AG Series, which is designed for indoor office environments and includes integrated antennas.

✦ Cisco Aironet 1230AG and 1240AG Series are for factories and warehouses. They offer rugged metal cases with external antennas.

✦ Cisco Aironet 1250 Series APs are based on the IEEE 802.11n specifications and provide reliable coverage for all standards based on 802.11 a/b/g/n. This support allows for the use of high bandwidth applications, such as voice.

✦ Cisco Aironet 1500 Series lightweight outdoor mesh access points are the ideal solution for outdoor areas.

Cisco Wireless Control System (WCS)

The Cisco Wireless Control System (WCS) is a control system for a wireless network. It is designed to help you design, plan, control, and troubleshoot a multi-controller wireless environment.

Think of WCS as a controller for the WLC.

Unlike the other products listed previously in this chapter, WCS is primarily a software solution that runs on a server.

Lightweight Access Point Protocol (LWAPP)

The LWAPP runs on WLAN controller and on APs to route packets in and out of the WLAN on optimal routes. In other words, the WLAN controller is the gateway of the WLAN to the LAN. The key fact here is that if you do not have a functioning WLC running on your network, then none of your lightweight APs will be able to function. So once your wireless network hits a level that it is considered to be mission critical, then it is imperative that you have more than one WLC to which your APs can connect to. When you configure your

APs on your network, you can assign primary, secondary, and tertiary controllers for your network. If the primary controller is unavailable, the backup controller will be used until the primary becomes available on the network again.

The controller and APs run protocols that route packets in and out of the WLAN and LAN, using optimum path through the wireless mesh network and through the wired network linking the WLAN controller to other WLAN controllers, or to Layer 2 switches or Layer 3 routers.

When working with the WLC and APs, a function called Split MAC is used to determine which functions are performed by the AP and which functions are performed by the WLC.

The WLC usually performs these functions:

+ 802.11 authentication
+ 802.11 association
+ 802.11 frame translation and bridging
+ 802.1x/EAP/RADIUS processing
+ Termination of 802.11 traffic on a wired interface

The AP usually performs time sensitive operations, such as:

+ Frame exchange handshake between a client and AP
+ Transmission of beacon frames
+ Buffering and transmission of frames for clients in power save mode
+ Response to probe request frames from clients
+ Provision of real-time signal quality information to the switch with every received frame
+ Monitoring each of the radio channels for noise, interference, and other WLANs
+ Monitoring for the presence of other APs
+ Encryption and decryption of 802.11 frames

If you have already purchased all of your access points and they are autonomous, but you now wish to roll out a WLC, then you are able to convert your APs to lightweight mode by running a Cisco-supplied upgrade tool on your compatible Cisco AP. This process can be reversed by reapplying the latest Cisco ISO for that Cisco AP.

Adaptive Wireless Path Protocol (AWPP)

When dealing with Cisco Wireless Mesh APs, you require a method to allow you to pass data through the mesh. In the case of Cisco, the method that is used is AWPP, which runs on Mesh Access Points (MAP) and Rooftop Mesh Access Points (RAP). AWPP routes data packets through the wireless mesh between MAPs, RAPs, and the wired data network.

Prep Test

1 The Cisco Wireless LAN Controller is not found in which of the following products?

A ○ Cisco 4404 Wireless LAN Controller

B ○ Cisco 7600 Series Router Wireless Services Module

C ○ Cisco 18xx Series Integrated Services Router

D ○ Catalyst 3750G Integrated Wireless LAN Controller Switch

2 How many ports on the Cisco 2100 series WLC support POE?

A ○ 2

B ○ 4

C ○ 6

D ○ None

3 The Cisco 4404 WLC is capable of managing how may lightweight APs?

A ○ 6

B ○ 25

C ○ 50

D ○ 100

4 Which interface is used for Guest Web Authentication?

A ○ Management Interface

B ○ AP-Manager Interface

C ○ Virtual Interface

D ○ Service-Port Interface

5 What configuration option in the Cisco 4400 Series WLC allows for combining multiple network ports?

A ○ Controller port mirroring

B ○ Controller link aggregation

C ○ Aggressive load balancing

D ○ Dynamic transmit power control

Answers

1 **C.** The Cisco 18xx Series Integrated Services Router does not contain a Cisco Wireless LAN Controller. Review *"Introducing the Cisco Unified Wireless Networks Architecture (CUWN)."*

2 **A.** The Cisco 2100 series WLC has 2 POE ports. See *"Cisco Wireless LAN Controller."*

3 **D.** The Cisco 4404 WLC is capable of managing 100 lightweight APs. Scan *"Cisco Wireless LAN Controller."*

4 **C.** The Virtual Interface is used for Guest Web Authentication. Peek at *"Cisco Wireless LAN Controller."*

5 **B.** Multiple network ports on the Cisco 4400 Series WLC are combined using controller link aggregration. Study *"Cisco Wireless LAN Controller."*

Chapter 5: Configuring Cisco Wireless Local Area Networks

Exam Objective

✔ **Performing a basic configuration of a Cisco wireless network**

In preparation for your CCNA exam, you should know how to do some of the basic configurations for a wireless network. This chapter focuses on the management and configuration of a wireless network based on the Cisco Wireless LAN Controller. If you review the information found in this chapter, you shouldn't have issues with these topics on the exam.

Configuration Flow

The following sections give you an overview of the basic process for setting up your wireless LAN. In this case, I focus on a WLAN that will be functioning with a Cisco Wireless LAN Controller (WLC).

Set up and verify the wired LAN to which the WLAN will connect

This process assumes the following:

✦ You have already planned the number and type of service set identifiers (SSIDs) that you will be supporting.

✦ You have the VLANs that are required to support them.

✦ You have security parameters around the VLANs.

✦ You have conducted a site survey so that you know where each AP will be mounted.

Knowing all of these items ahead of time can ease and speed the deployment of your wireless infrastructure.

Set up the Cisco Wireless LAN Controller (s)

After unpacking your WLC, connect the console cable to the service port and set your computer's terminal settings to the following:

+ 9600 baud
+ 8 data bits
+ 1 stop bit
+ No parity
+ No hardware flow control

When powering up your WLC, you need to perform some configuration. You are presented with the Startup Wizard, which prompts you for the following information and verifies its accuracy:

+ Ensures that the controller has a system name, up to 32 characters.
+ Adds an administrative username and password, each up to 24 characters.
+ Ensures that the controller can communicate with the GUI, CLI, or Cisco WCS through the service port by accepting a valid Dynamic Host Configuration Protocol (DHCP) configuration or manual IP address and netmask. Entering **0.0.0.0** for the IP address and netmask disables the service port.
+ Ensures that the controller can communicate with the network (802.11 distribution system) through the management interface, having you assign a static IP address, netmask, default router IP address, VLAN identifier, and physical port assignment.
+ Prompts for the IP address of the DHCP server used to supply IP addresses to clients and the controller management interface.
+ Asks for the Lightweight Access Point Protocol (LWAPP) transport mode.
+ Collects the virtual gateway IP address — any fictitious, unassigned IP address (such as 1.1.1.1) to be used by Layer 3 security and mobility managers.
+ Allows you to enter the mobility group (RF group) name.
+ Collects the wireless LAN 802.11 SSID, or network name.
+ Asks you to indicate whether clients can use static IP addresses. Allowing this is more convenient for some users but offers less security. Disallowing this requires that all devices get their IP configuration from a DHCP server.

✦ Asks whether you want to configure a Remote Authentication Dial-In User Service (RADIUS) server from the Startup Wizard, the RADIUS server IP address, communication port, and secret.

✦ Collects the country code to ensure that it configures the radios for the local region.

✦ Enables or disables the 802.11a/n and 802.11b/g/n lightweight access point networks.

✦ Enables or disables Radio Resource Management (RRM).

Verify connectivity to the wired LAN

At this point, you should have the WLC configured and supporting at least one SSID that will be valid for your network. If you choose to, you would be able to perform configuration changes from a remote terminal or via the Web-based GUI. The following sections allow you to configure additional SSIDs.

Enable the 802.11 bands

Using the command-line interface (CLI), you can enable or disable the supported radios with the following commands:

```
config 802.11a disable network
config 802.11b disable network
config 802.11a enable network
config 802.11b enable network
config {802.11a | 802.11b} 11nsupport {enable | disable}
```

To save and view your configuration changes, use the following commands:

```
save config
show {802.11a | 802.11b}
```

You then see output that looks something like this:

```
802.11a Network.............................. Enabled
11nSupport................................... Enabled
802.11a Low Band............................. Enabled
802.11a Mid Band............................. Enabled
802.11a High Band............................ Enabled
802.11a Operational Rates
802.11a 6M Rate.............................. Mandatory
802.11a 9M Rate.............................. Supported
802.11a 12M Rate............................. Mandatory
802.11a 18M Rate............................. Supported
802.11a 24M Rate............................. Mandatory
802.11a 36M Rate............................. Supported
802.11a 48M Rate............................. Supported
802.11a 54M Rate............................. Supported
...
```

Configure the SSID

In the case of Cisco Wireless LAN Controllers, an SSID is configured as part of a WLAN, so each WLAN maps to an SSID. Within the WLAN settings, you can configure security, quality of service (QoS), radio policies, and other wireless network settings. Each controller supports up to 16 WLANs.

The following commands allow you to configure an additional SSID:

```
show wlan summary
config wlan create wlan_id profile_name ssid
```

When the WLAN is created, it is automatically disabled for security. After you have completed all your security settings, you can enable the WLAN with the following commands:

```
config wlan enable wlan_id
save config
```

Configure WLAN security

Configuring security settings on WLAN sets is for all your associated access points. You can configure either static WEP or WPA for wireless security.

To configure static WEP keys, follow these steps based on a specific WLAN ID:

1. **Disable 802.1x encryption:**

   ```
   config wlan security 802.1X disable wlan_id
   ```

2. **Configure the WEP key as 40/64-, 104/128-, or 128/152-bit:**

   ```
   config wlan security static-wep-key encryption wlan_id
       {40 | 104 | 128} {hex | ascii} key key_index
   ```

   The default key level is 104, which requires you to enter 26 hexadecimal or 13 ASCII characters for the key.

3. **To configure WPA1 or WPA2, use the following commands:**

   ```
   config wlan disable wlan_id
   config wlan security wpa {enable | disable} wlan_id
   config wlan security wpa wpa1 {enable | disable} wlan_
       id
   ```

4. **To enable WPA2, use the following command:**

   ```
   config wlan security wpa wpa2 {enable | disable} wlan_
       id
   ```

5. **Choose Advanced Encryption Standard (AES) or Temporal Key Integrity Protocol (TKIP) for data encryption:**

```
config wlan security wpa wpa1 ciphers {aes | tkip}
    {enable | disable} wlan_id
config wlan security wpa wpa2 ciphers {aes | tkip}
    {enable | disable} wlan_id
```

The default values are TKIP for WPA1 and AES for WPA2.

6. **Choose a system for authenticated key management, which would be 802.1X, Pre-Shared Key (PSK), or Cisco Centralized Key Management (CCKM):**

```
config wlan security wpa akm {802.1X | psk | cckm}
    {enable | disable} wlan_id
```

The default value is 802.1X.

7. **When using PSK, set a preshared key:**

```
config wlan security wpa akm psk set-key {ascii | hex}
    psk-key wlan_id
```

WPA preshared keys must be 8 to 63 ASCII text characters or 64 hexadecimal characters long.

8. **Enable the WLAN:**

```
config wlan enable wlan_id
```

9. **Save your settings:**

```
save config
```

Set up Cisco access point (s)

If you are using a Cisco lightweight AP, this process takes you through the setup of the WLC to accept registration of APs. This is all part of the controller discovery process.

As previously mentioned, Cisco's lightweight access points (LWAPs) use the Lightweight Access Point Protocol (LWAPP) to communicate between the components of the wireless network infrastructure. In this environment, your access point needs to be associated or linked with a controller to properly function. The discovery process allows this association to occur. After an access point is associated with a WLC, its full potential can be reached. This process starts with the lightweight access point sending a join request to the controller. The controller acknowledges this request by sending a join response to the lightweight access point, which then gives the lightweight access point permission to become associated with the controller. After this process is complete, the controller can manage all aspects of the lightweight access point, such as its configuration, firmware, control transactions, and data transactions.

A lightweight access point can be discovered in the following ways:

✦ **Layer 3 LWAPP discovery:** This occurs when the LWAP is on a different subnet from the WLC and the AP uses the IP address rather than the Layer 2 MAC address.

✦ **Layer 2 LWAPP discovery:** This occurs when the LWAP and WLC are on the same subnet and the discovery data is placed in Ethernet frames that contain the MAC addresses of the two devices. Layer 2 LWAPP discovery cannot be used in Layer 3 environments.

✦ **Over-the-air provisioning (OTAP):** This option is only supported by Cisco 4400 and Cisco 2100 series WLCs. If the option is enabled, all associated access points send neighbor messages. This then allows new LWAP devices to receive the WLC's IP address, where they can conduct the rest of the discovery process. After this process has been completed, the option on the controller should be disabled.

✦ **Locally stored controller IP address discovery:** After a discovery has been completed, the AP stores the addresses for its controllers in non-volatile memory so that for later deployment, it has all the necessary controller information. This process is called *priming the access point.*

✦ **DHCP server discovery:** This option allows the DHCP option 43 to provide controller IP addresses to the access points.

✦ **DNS discovery:** Domain Name System (DNS) information for the controller can be stored in your DNS zone. The record should be called `CISCO-LWAPP-CONTROLLER.`*`localdomain`*`,` where *`localdomain`* is the access point domain name. After the AP knows the IP address of the controller, it can connect to the controller to complete the registration process.

From time to time, you may need to locate a specific lightweight access point on your network. The easiest way to do this is to configure the access point to flash its LEDs. This feature is supported on any controller software Release 4.0 or later and all lightweight access points. To flash an access point's LEDs, issue the following command:

```
debug ap enable Cisco_AP
```

To cause a specific access point to flash its LEDs for a specified number of seconds, issue this command:

```
debug ap command "led flash seconds" Cisco_AP
```

You can enter a value between 1 and 3600 for the *seconds* parameter. To disable LED flashing for a specific access point, use the following command:

```
debug ap command "led flash disable" Cisco_AP
```

Configuring backup controllers

Due the importance of having an active controller on your network to support your wireless network, you should not rely on only having a single controller on your network. Controllers may be distributed between a central site and regional sites and still manage all APs anywhere on the network. Controllers at the central site and regional sites do not need to be in the same mobility group, and using the CLI on the controller, you can specify a primary, secondary, and tertiary controller for your lightweight access points.

Starting with controller software Release 5.0, you can configure timers for the primary and secondary backup controllers so that the time taken to discover a failed primary controller is reduced. If, during that timed interval, a controller has not received any data packets from the other controller, it then sends an echo request to the controller. If there are no results from the echo, the controller considers the other controller to be failed. From the lightweight access point's perspective, if a controller fails two consecutive discovery requests, it is considered to be failed.

In all failure cases, the secondary and then the tertiary controllers are attempted to be contacted. When the primary controller comes back on line, the access points automatically fail back over to the primary controller. To configure backup controllers, follow these steps:

1. **Configure a primary controller for a specific access point:**

```
config ap primary-base controller_name Cisco_AP
    [controller_ip_address]
```

2. **Configure a secondary controller for a specific access point:**

```
config ap secondary-base controller_name Cisco_AP
    [controller_ip_address]
```

3. **Configure a tertiary controller for a specific access point:**

```
config ap tertiary-base controller_name Cisco_AP
    [controller_ip_address]
```

4. **Configure a primary backup controller for a specific controller:**

```
config advanced backup-controller primary backup_
    controller_name backup_controller_ip_address
```

5. **Configure a secondary backup controller for a specific controller:**

```
config advanced backup-controller secondary backup_
    controller_name
backup_controller_ip_address
```

6. **Configure the fast heartbeat timer for local, hybrid-REAP, or all access points:**

```
config advanced timers ap-fast-heartbeat {local | hreap
    | all} {enable | disable} interval
```

7. **Configure the access point primary discovery request timer:**

```
config advanced timers ap-primary-discovery-timeout
    interval
```

8. **Save your changes:**

```
save config
```

9. **Verify the configuration changes that you made by using these commands:**

```
show ap config general Cisco_AP
show advanced backup-controller
show advanced timers
```

Web authentication process

The Web authentication process is a Layer 3 security function that allows the controller to block all client IP traffic with the exception of DHCP traffic. After the client has obtained an IP address, the only action that is open to the user is to attempt to connect to a Web site. Any HTTP-related traffic is then captured. The user's Web browser session is redirected to a default or custom login page, where the user is prompted for authentication information in the form of a username and password.

Because this system includes a self-signed certification, the first time that this process takes place, the user is prompted with a security alert, which should be accepted.

You have a few options for the login page: The basic controller administration page allows some simple modification of the page text and the presentation of the Cisco logo. The following options are available as login pages:

✦ The default login page

✦ A modified version of the default login page (as shown in Figure 5-1)

✦ A customized login page that you configure on an external Web server

✦ A customized login page that you download to the controller

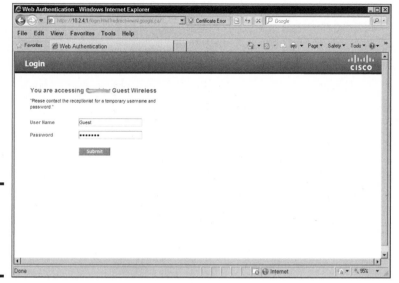

Figure 5-1:
The default
Web
authentica-
tion page.

After the user successfully logs in, he is presented with a successful login
page and then automatically redirected to the originally requested URL.

Example using the Cisco graphical user interface (GUI)

For both the wireless LAN controller and autonomous APs, you also have
an option of using the GUI to perform your configuration. This GUI is Web
based and can be configured to operate over HTTP or HTTPS. In some cases,
some devices also support the use of Cisco's Security Device Manager (SDM)
or Adaptive Security Device Manager (ASDM). The SDM can be launched
from the Web management interface of Cisco's Integrated Services Router
(ISR), while the ASDM is the main management interface for Cisco's Adaptive
Security Appliance (ASA) firewalls and is also launched through the Web
management interface.

Figure 5-2 shows a sample of the Web interface used for managing the Cisco
2106 WLC; the interface for the 4400 series WLC would be similar.

Figure 5-3 shows the management interface for the autonomous mode Cisco
1250 Series Access Point. Note that its interface appears quite different from
that of the WLC, which can be seen from the list of menu items. In this case,
the SSID management is found in the SSID Manager on the Security menu
(located in the left hand menu), while the WLC has SSID settings on the
WLAN menu.

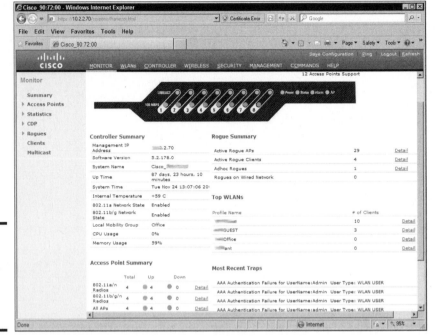

Figure 5-2:
The administration GUI on the Cisco 2106 WLC.

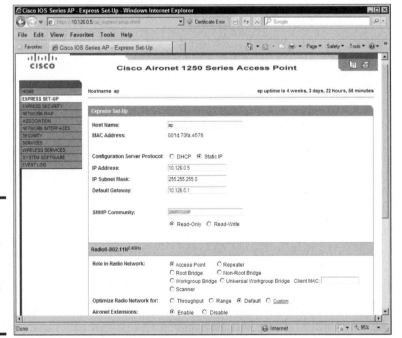

Figure 5-3:
The administration GUI on the Cisco 1250 Series Access Point.

The other interface that is quite different is that of the Cisco ASA firewalls using the ASDM, which is shown in Figure 5-4. This is shown only to illustrate the differences in Cisco's management tools, because the company has a wide set of tools for its appliances.

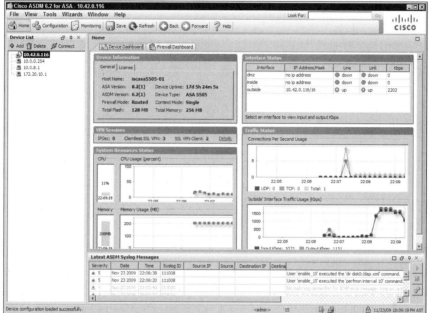

Figure 5-4: The administration GUI on the Cisco ASA 5505 firewall.

Prep Test

1 What is not a possible security option for authentication and encryption?

A ○ 802.1X

B ○ WEP

C ○ CCKM

D ○ WPA2

2 How many characters long is a WPA PSK?

A ○ 3

B ○ 6

C ○ 63

D ○ 127

3 What is not an LWAPP discovery method?

A ○ LWAPP sequential discovery

B ○ Layer 3 LWAPP discovery

C ○ Layer 2 LWAPP discovery

D ○ Over-the-air provisioning (OTAP)

4 When using Web authentication, what is not a valid option for a login page?

A ○ A customized login page that you configure on an external Web server

B ○ A customized login page that you download to the controller

C ○ The default login page

D ○ A customized login page that you download to a Cisco AAA server

5 The WLC has a GUI management tool that is accessed in what manner?

A ○ ASDM

B ○ SDM

C ○ Telnet or SSH

D ○ HTTP or HTTPS

Answers

1 **C.** CCKM is an RF modulation technique and not a WLAN security option. See *"Configure WLAN security."*

2 **C.** The WPA PSK length is between 8 and 63 ASCII characters or 64 hexadecimal characters. Review *"Configure WLAN security."*

3 **A.** LWAPP sequential discovery is not one of the LWAPP discovery methods. Peruse *"Set up Cisco access point(s)."*

4 **D.** A Cisco AAA server cannot be used to house a Web authentication login page. Peek at *"Web authentication process."*

5 **D.** The GUI management interface for a WLC is accessed via HTTP or HTTPS. Study *"Example using the Cisco graphical user interface (GUI)."*

Book VI

Network Security

Contents at a Glance

Chapter 1: Network Security Basics

Exam Objectives

- ✔ Identifying security threats
- ✔ Recognizing the need to implement comprehensive security policies
- ✔ Understanding network zones
- ✔ Describing common security appliances and applications
- ✔ Differentiating between internal and external networks
- ✔ Understanding firewalls, access control lists (ACLs), Network Address Translation (NAT), and Virtual Private Networks (VPNs)
- ✔ Mitigating security threats
- ✔ Taking steps to secure network devices

A structured threat targeting a vulnerable organization's computer network is likely taking place as you read this. Due to the rapid growth of the Internet, many forms of security threats have emerged. Viruses, Trojan horse attacks, malicious hackers, and even an organization's own employees are potential security hazards to corporate networks. These threats have the potential to steal and destroy sensitive corporate data, tie up valuable resources, and inflict major damage due to network downtime. This may lead to a cost crisis and cripple the company financially. Security breaches are also encountered more frequently in home or private networks these days. We all have a reason to be concerned.

A crucial component of protecting internetworks is identifying and understanding the need to implement strong security measures. By preventing security breaches generating from outside users and mitigating unauthorized access to the physical networking equipment — and the digital data it transmits — from inside users, steps are taken to ensure the safety of electronic information. Network security is a culmination of many different preventive measures all working together to protect valuable data from intruders. I examine these steps and their implementation methods in this chapter.

Network Zoning

A *network zone* is a collection of resources that share the same security risk and exist together in the same subnetwork, or *security zone.* Each zone may be logically and physically segmented from the rest of the network infrastructure, specifying its own security policy and sharing the identical exposure to risk. This segregation allows a security breach to occur in one zone while having no effect on the security of the other zones, as shown in Figure 1-1. All members of the same zone are usually considered of equal value, or peer members. This means that high-risk candidates such as Web, e-mail, and FTP servers are not included in zones with common LAN clients. Hosts that communicate with the Internet are likely placed in different zones than non-Internet-connected hosts. By separating these various devices based on function, networks can be better planned and implemented. This leads to a more secure, stable, and highly scalable infrastructure.

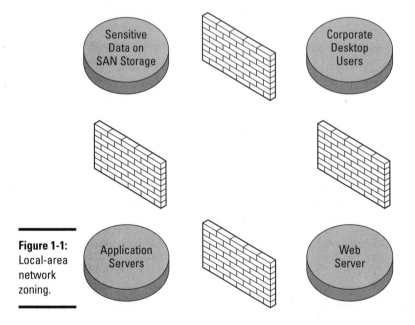

Figure 1-1: Local-area network zoning.

The core internal network must maintain the highest level of security and typically does not want or allow external public access. LAN clients reside on the internal or private side of the network and have some of the greatest security requirements. For maximum protection, highly sensitive resources that provide only internal services should be zoned separately. Other highly visible servers that offer services to the outside world carry an even higher risk of attack, and therefore are also placed in separate zones. Access can be controlled to these zones using authentication methods and defined rules implemented on firewalls, routers, or other security appliances such as the following:

✦ **Perimeter routers:** The first line of defense against external attacks and reside closest to untrusted networks. Any traffic denied at the perimeter router never arrives inside the organization's private network. This is accomplished by screening and controlling the flow of incoming traffic based on information contained inside each packet and then comparing each packet to a specified set of rules. These rules define who is allowed or denied access into the router's interface. Or course, you may want or need certain kinds of public access into your network. Maybe access to the corporate Web or e-mail server is needed. Beware that any traffic that passes through the perimeter router is a potential security hazard. Strategically placed internal routers and firewalls, along with additional hardened security appliances, can provide added protection from traffic allowed inside the perimeter.

✦ **Internal routers:** Interconnect segments of the private network and filter traffic between locally segregated subnets. Internal routers are always placed behind perimeter routers in an organization's network topology and can further define access permissions. Internal routers may be set up to perform the functionality of a firewall device.

✦ **Firewall routers:** Provide a secure boundary that filters network traffic between untrusted and trusted networks. Firewall routers are zone separators and are usually placed behind perimeter routers. Firewall routers are used for filtering traffic based on access policies between subnets. These policies may state who is allowed or denied access to the demilitarized zone (DMZ), locally protected file servers, or other LAN resources. Firewall routers not only protect access from public networks into the private network, but they also can be used to deny unauthorized internal corporate access.

✦ **Demilitarized zone (DMZ):** Resides between the internal and external network and offers external services for outside access through one or more firewalls. The DMZ is less secure than the internal network but more secure than the external network. Higher-risk nodes such as HTTP Web servers and FTP servers are placed in the DMZ. For additional protection, each server can be placed in its own zone based on functionality. If one server is compromised, the security breach will not impact the other zoned servers. All connectivity allowed to the DMZ ends at the DMZ also.

You have the following approaches to setting up a DMZ:

• **Single firewall, or three-legged firewall:** One router serving as a single firewall, using three firewall-configured interfaces. Each interface segments traffic into a particular zone. This approach allows each zone to have its own specified security on the same router. A major downside is the single point of failure from one device.

Also, this device has the additional burden of managing all traffic through these interfaces. You can see an example of the three-legged approach in Figure 1-2.

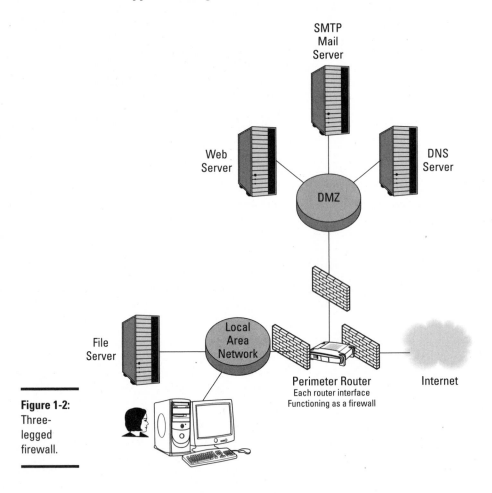

Figure 1-2:
Three-legged firewall.

- **Dual firewall:** A much stronger and more robust security implementation method. The dual-firewall approach consists of two firewall devices called a *front-end firewall* and a *back-end firewall* used in creating the DMZ. The front-end firewall is the first line of defense and allows network traffic destined for both the DMZ and local network. The back-end firewall allows permitted traffic to the internal private network only. A dual-firewall setup is shown in Figure 1-3.

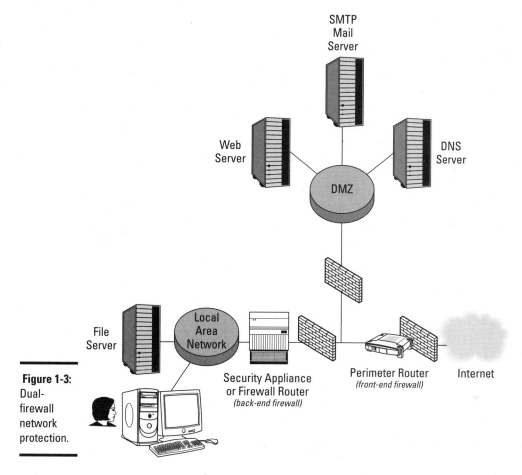

SMTP
Mail
Server

Web
Server

DNS
Server

DMZ

File
Server

Local
Area
Network

Perimeter Router
(front-end firewall)

Internet

Figure 1-3:
Dual-
firewall
network
protection.

Security Appliance
or Firewall Router
(back-end firewall)

Using a firewall or Secure Shell (SSH)–encrypted authentication method
allows a LAN administrator to protect network configuration files from outside public security threats.

Recognizing Security Risks

Threats to network security come in many forms. It is vital that you understand and recognize the type of attack used and its origin. Both *structured*
and *unstructured* attacks originate from *internal* and *external* sources:

✦ External structured attacks are implemented by knowledgeable hackers who are proficient and highly skilled; they desire the "keys to your organization's castle."

✦ Compared to unstructured attacks, structured attacks are more difficult to recognize and prevent. Unstructured attacks are usually poorly planned by amateur "wanna-be" hackers using hacking tools that are easily downloadable by anyone with Internet access. These attacks are usually motivated by the thrill of hacking, a quest for knowledge, or just outright malicious intent.

External attacks originate outside of the private network structure. Internal attacks are usually conceived by employees or individuals who have physical proximity to the servers, storage, and resources in the network. They may have digital access to network files, passwords, and highly sensitive information — maybe even domain administrative privileges. Internal attacks are implemented by using knowledge and information gained over a period of time.

Information collectors

Gathering reconnaissance information is usually the first step in a planned attack on an organization's network. Pieces are individually collected until the complete "network puzzle" can be fitted together. After the preliminary survey is assembled, a structured attack follows in a variety of forms.

Reconnaissance attacks

Reconnaissance attacks are attempts to collect information about a target network topology and its hardware. This indirect attack is often used just for intelligence gathering, which can help the intruder in future attacks. Reconnaissance attacks may go undetected for long periods of time. Due to the nature of the attack, some traces of hacker activity may be left behind in system log files.

A typical reconnaissance attack is known as a *ping sweep* and attempts to contact each node on the network, creating a detailed map of every live system (responding to the ping request). This map lists each network host and all available services, ports, operating systems, and applications currently running. *Port scans* are performed to identify all running programs on each host. *Domain Name System (DNS) lookup queries* may also be done to discover the domain owner and assigned IP addresses. This gives the attacker a detailed blueprint on how to proceed with the attack.

Access attacks

An *access attack* is any attempt to gain information from the organization's network by unauthorized personnel. These attacks exploit vulnerabilities in services and applications that rely on authentication methods for network security. Access attacks may also include authorized personnel inside the organization attempting to increase their network privileges for higher-level access to unauthorized data. Some methods of access attacks are as follows:

+ **Password attacks:** Attempts to crack the users' passwords to gain access to network resources:

  • The most common type of password attack is *password guessing,* which attempts to manually or automatically find at least one weak password in a network.

  • Hardware- and software-based utilities called *keyloggers* attempt to intercept typed passwords input by the user (from the keyboard) and return them to the malicious attacker.

  The user is unaware of the logging activity unless *antispyware* or other keylogging-detection methods are used.

+ **Brute-force attacks:** A trial-and-error method of decoding passwords and encryption keys that will always succeed, given enough time. A brute-force utility or cracking application uses a sequential order to try every possible combination of characters until all possible key combinations are exhausted.

  A *dictionary attack* is a common form of these types of attacks and relies on the weakness of users' passwords for success by trying every known word in the dictionary.

+ **Trojan horse attacks:** Malicious code disguised as a dormant or inactive program. A digital Trojan horse is often disguised by a fake identity and resembles a harmless program. After it is executed, the malicious intent may go undetected and unknown for a long time. Preventing Trojan horse attacks is as simple as not executing or running programs from untrusted or unknown origins.

+ **Trust exploitation attacks:** Uses trust relationships established between two computer systems or trusting networks to implement an attack. Because communication between hosts in a network topology depends on trust, an attacker will attempt to appear to other hosts as a trusted member of the network.

  For example, if an unauthorized user gains access to a trusted machine, he may forge his identity and appear just as the trusted machine does on the network. All traffic originating from the attacker will seem to come from the trusted host.

Denial of service (DoS) attacks

A *DoS attack* attempts to crash or render a system, service, network resource, or the entire network infrastructure unstable by systematically and repeatedly attacking the target with large volumes of traffic. This form of attack is designed to be highly devastating and grind the system to a halt, denying services to its users.

DoS attacks use a simple form of establishing the maximum amount of available connections with a Web or network server. By stealing all open connections, no connections are made available for legitimate hosts.

Denial of service attacks are usually performed by running an automated script or program that pings the target host until its resources are rendered unavailable. This is widely known as *The Ping of Death.* Internet Control Message Protocol (ICMP) packets overrun and flood the target while the target machine attempts to respond to these requests.

IP header manipulation is another form of DoS attack that deceives the target machine into believing that packets are much larger than they really are. This causes system instability and eventually results in a system crash.

Another attack method that is even more severe than a DoS attack is known as a *distributed denial of service (DDoS)* attack. DDoS recruits compromised systems to conduct a synchronized attack on the target node. These breached machines generate the traffic used to attack the target and are described as *handlers* and *agents.* The attacking client node infiltrates the master or handler machines and executes a program that controls additional recruited slave machines. These agents, or *zombies,* are then used as the malicious foot soldiers and march into battle.

IP spoofing

IP spoofing is a tactic employed by a malicious user that tricks the target host into believing it is actually a trusted host on the network, thereby gaining unauthorized access. For this type of attack to be successful, the attacker must have collected prior reconnaissance information such as the trusted host's IP address. The hacker then modifies the IP header information so that packets sent from the malicious user appear to be originating from the trusted host. The underlying attack method is the established trust relationship exploitation between network hosts.

The steps in IP spoofing are quite simple:

1. A target host is chosen, and a trust pattern is identified.

2. The trusted host is then disabled with a *SYN flood.*

   These synchronization packets flood the trusted host and render it temporarily inoperable while it waits for an acknowledgment (ACK). These ACKs never get delivered, causing connections to remain open.

3. *TCP sequence numbers* from individual packet headers are examined.

4. The malicious user node impersonates the trusted node and contacts a target service using the trusted IP address, predicting the next sequence numbers.

SYN packets are sent when a client wants to establish a TCP connection. The target host then returns a SYN/ACK with a special identification number called the Initial Sequence Number (ISN). Both the client machine and the host machine exchange sequence numbers (SQNs) for error-checking and reporting purposes.

Man-in-the-middle attacks (IP packet sniffing)

The terms *IP packet sniffing* and *man-in-the-middle attacks* are used to describe an unauthorized user who intercepts and places false data into the communications stream between two nodes. Also known as *TCP session hijacking,* the attacker establishes a connection and sniffs out messages on the network between two systems. Next, these messages are modified in some way and returned to the network. The network nodes trust that these messages are originating from one another, not from the unknown attacker.

This type of attack targets TCP applications such as Telnet, FTP, and HTTP Web browsers.

Introducing Security Risk Mitigation Methods

When discussing the subject of security risk mitigation, the desired result always involves reducing the impact and severity of a malicious attack. No network is guaranteed 100-percent foolproof. Proactive steps must be taken to secure the network as much as possible and minimize damage when an organization does become compromised. It's not a matter of whether your organization will be attacked, but when. By having a sound security structure in place and isolating high-risk areas through zoning, organizations can save many hours in downtime and financial costs.

IP access control lists (ACLs)

ACLs are one of the most important and highly used features in the Cisco IOS. The main purpose of IP access control lists is to allow or deny network traffic by packet or protocol type. ACLs function in Layers 2, 3, and 4 of the OSI reference model and perform similarly to a network firewall. ACLs are used as a packet-filtering firewall when applied to a router's interface. ACLs perform this traffic filtering based on a defined set of rules specified by the network administrator.

You find many different types of ACLs, but for now, I briefly focus on IP's two major types, *standard* and *extended* access control lists:

✦ **Standard ACL:** Permits or denies incoming packets that match the specifically stated *source IP addresses only.* Each newly defined standard IP ACL is given a number for system identification, ranging from 1 to 99 and 1300 to 1999. Routers process access control lists starting at the top of the list and working downward.

Implement a standard ACL using the following code:

```
Router(config)#access-list 1 permit 192.168.1.0
    0.0.0.255
```

In this example, a standard access list is created (defined by the number 1), allowing all traffic from the 192.168.1.0 network. The value 0.0.0.255 is called an *inverse subnet mask,* or *wildcard mask,* and determines the IP traffic allowed or denied, based on which bits of the IP address are read and which bits are ignored.

The 0 bits in the inverse subnet mask specify that the bit will be read. A value of 1 in the wildcard mask is ignored and skipped. Matching the binary IP address and the inverse mask, you can determine the traffic rules. This means that any wildcard mask value of 0 tells the ACL to consider and process this portion of the address. ACLs do not care about the 1 bits, and they are not filtered.

New entries to ACLs are always added to the end of the list. Another important issue to remember is that ACLs always end with an *implicit deny* statement. The IOS inserts this statement by default. You can see how this works by viewing the previously created access list:

```
Router#show access-list 1
Standard IP access list 1
1 permit 192.168.1.0
1 deny any
```

The first `permit` statement allows all traffic from the 192.168.1.0 network. The second line denies, or blocks, all other traffic.

You must have at least one `permit` statement per ACL; otherwise, all traffic is implicitly denied!

✦ **Extended ACL:** Provides greater flexibility than standard ACLs by filtering traffic based on *source IP address, destination IP address, source port,* or *destination port.* This gives you a much more specific way to protect your network. Extended ACLs are considered packet-filtering firewalls, using numbers 100–199 and 2000–2699 as their identification range. Extended access control lists are processed just like standard ACLs, from top to bottom. A sample extended ACL looks like this:

```
Router(config)#access-list 101 permit 192.168.1.0
    0.0.0.255 any eq 80
```

In this example, access list 101 specifies that traffic on the 192.168.1.0 network will allow access to port 80 (HTTP) only. Remember that an unseen implicit deny statement exists at the end of every access list. In Book VI, Chapter 2, I examine ACLs in greater detail and describe how ACLs are applied to inbound and outbound traffic.

If a network administrator wants to prevent pings into the corporate network, ICMP may be blocked using ACLs.

Keep the "three *ps*" in mind when designing ACLs. One ACL may be created *per protocol, per interface,* and *per direction.* You cannot combine multiple router interfaces, multiple protocols (IP and IPX), and directions (inbound and outbound) in the same ACL!

NAT — The great masquerader

Network Address Translation (NAT) is generally used as an *IP masquerading* technique to hide private network IP address space. NAT rewrites the header information from IP packets while they are in transit, essentially hiding the source IP address and issuing a single public address in its place. NAT is typically found in private LANs, where many hosts need Internet connectivity but very few routable IPs are available. All internal private traffic using NAT appears (to public networks) to be coming from a single source, usually the IP address of the perimeter router.

A typical home user with four computers may only be issued one IP address from his or her ISP. NAT allows each device to use a private IP address on the local network. When the private IP address wants to connect with the outside world, NAT intercepts the outbound packet. NAT then modifies the IP header information and replaces the private IP address with the router's public address. These four private nodes all appear as a single global (routable) IP address.

To receive packets into the private network, this process is reversed. Using a stateful translation table, NAT can keep track of which traffic is originating from and destined to which private address. You find out more about Network Address Translation in Book VI, Chapter 3.

Virtual Private Networks (VPNs)

Virtual Private Networks are wide-area networks constructed by connecting private networks and/or remote users using a public network, such as the Internet. Cost savings gives VPN technology a huge advantage over expensive long-distance leased circuits. Instead of using a permanently established circuit, such as a dedicated point-to-point leased line, a virtual connection is established over an existing public infrastructure. This flexibility is called *tunneling,* and it allows private network connectivity to exist over huge distances, which would be otherwise impossible. VPNs provide major scalability at minor costs to an organization.

Security is a major concern using this type of technology. VPN security measures such as *content encryption* and *authentication* are used to protect data and ensure privacy. Content encryption takes standard, readable data and renders the information unreadable to unauthorized users. The most popular authentication methods used with VPNs are typically user password authentication and biometric input.

In Book VI, Chapter 4, I examine VPNs in greater detail.

Cisco IOS Firewall

The Cisco IOS Firewall is an extra feature set available and built in to many Cisco routers today. When enabled, this IOS option incorporates a fully functional, connection-aware firewall operating at the upper OSI layers. Standard ACLs provide a good measure of security and operate at the lower OSI layers. The Cisco IOS Firewall adds extra security features at the application layer by using stateful inspection techniques to track TCP and UDP connections.

Unlike *stateless* packet inspection, which operates at the network layer (and only looks at the IP packet header), the stateful functionality of the Cisco IOS allows TCP connections to remain open and tracked. The IOS monitors outgoing traffic and opens inbound ports for the return traffic automatically. This is a major difference from stateless or *static* packet filtering, which provides less security than stateful inspection.

Stateless IP filtering allows direct external host–to–internal host connections, and is vulnerable to IP spoofing attacks. Static filtering can also be more difficult to maintain and offers no method of authentication. As you have seen with ACLs, a static map is created and specifies which traffic is allowed or denied. With ACLs and the Cisco IOS Firewall feature set, network security is increased further.

For example, a network user establishes an FTP data session using port 20. The Cisco IOS Firewall tracks and records the client's information (IP address, port number, and so on) using the state routing table, and dynamically opens and monitors a connection for returning traffic. Return traffic must match the state information stored in the router to be allowed back into the network. After a connection is terminated, ports are closed by the IOS. This is also known as Context-Based Access Control (CBAC).

The Cisco IOS Firewall does not protect against threats coming from inside the organization. Only traffic passing through the router's IOS firewall interface can be mitigated!

Packet filtering and inspection can be done on incoming and/or outgoing packets, depending on the interface and direction applied.

A few Cisco IOS Firewall highlights are as follows:

✦ **Application-level traffic filtering and inspection:** Allows TCP and UDP incoming packets to be permitted access (dynamically) into the network *if* the connection/traffic originated from inside the same network. This is done by inspecting the state of the application layer protocol session information. By implementing stateful packet inspection, detection and blocking of SYN flooding and denial of service attacks can be achieved. Also, TCP sequence numbers can be monitored to ensure that all packets are within expected ranges. Alerts and audits can be set up to warn system administrators regarding suspicious activity.

✦ **Built-in intrusion detection system (IDS) using common attack signatures:** Limited feature set for detecting various TCP/IP, VDP, FTP, RCP, SMTP, and other attacks. The IDS contains 59 of the most common attack signatures and drops any threatening connections that are detected.

✦ **Protects network resources using existing routing hardware:** The Cisco IOS Firewall is an extra feature set add-on for the Cisco IOS. Although the IOS Firewall uses additional memory and CPU resources, no additional hardware is required. This is cheaper than purchasing dedicated firewall appliances, providing cost savings to an organization. However, for increased security mitigation benefits, organizations may still want to invest in additional, dedicated security appliances.

Book VI
Chapter 1

Network Security Basics

Intrusion detection systems (IDSs) and *intrusion prevention systems (IPSs)* are two key types of network security. Intrusion detection systems are passive and monitor packets of data traversing the network. Using an IDS, traffic is compared to configured rules and sets off alarms if suspicious activity is detected. Intrusion prevention systems are active devices that intercept incoming traffic and shut down any real-time detected threats.

Cisco IOS Firewall — A sample configuration

Before the Cisco IOS Firewall can be configured to protect the internal network from external threats, verification must be done to ensure that it is a part of the current IOS feature set. To do this, enter the following command in global configuration mode:

```
Router(config)#ip inspect ?
```

If a list of IP inspection options appears, the feature set is enabled, and you may proceed. If an Unrecognized command error is received, the feature set is not enabled in the IOS, and no configuration is possible.

After the IOS Firewall is enabled, you can prepare to block all inbound traffic on an external router interface using an extended ACL. This will still allow CBAC return traffic originating from inside the network. Follow these basic steps:

1. Block all TCP and UDP traffic:

```
Router(config)#access-list 100 deny tcp any any
Router(config)#access-list 100 deny udp any any
```

2. Specify the interface to be configured:

```
Router(config)#interface serial0
```

3. Specify the access group number and the direction of the ACL (inbound):

```
Router(config-if)#ip access-group 100 in
```

The above configuration instructs the IOS Firewall to inspect all forms of TCP and UDP traffic when it reaches the router. If the router determines that traffic originated from the internal private network, the return traffic is allowed to pass through. All other traffic is blocked.

The Cisco IOS Firewall consumes more CPU and memory resources than standard ACLs! Be sure that your router is adequately equipped to handle the extra duties!

Physically securing networking equipment and restricting access from unauthorized users are key components to a comprehensive security plan.

Security checklist

✔ Plan and implement a complete network security solution.

✔ Continuously assess this plan to improve security and to discover weaknesses.

✔ Disable unneeded network services that can be exploited by an attacker.

✔ Require users to create and use strong alphanumeric passwords consisting of at least eight characters.

✔ Require mandatory password changes every 90 days.

✔ Install antivirus and antispam software on all network nodes.

✔ Keep antivirus and antispam updated with the latest updates and versions.

✔ Educate employees regarding security issues. Warn users about opening e-mail attachments.

✔ Regularly update Web server software.

✔ Use firewalls.

✔ Back up data regularly.

✔ Keep remote traffic separated from general network traffic.

✔ Disable and/or delete any user accounts not in use or no longer needed.

Prep Test

1 Which security mitigation method provides stateful packet inspection at the application layer?

A ○ NAT

B ○ VPN

C ○ Cisco IOS Firewall

D ○ Access control lists

2 Which of the following is an example of a brute-force attack?

A ○ Dictionary attack

B ○ Information gathering

C ○ Exploiting trusts

D ○ Ping sweep

3 What are important reasons for zoning a network? (Choose three.)

A ○ Ease of management

B ○ Mitigating security risks

C ○ Hackproofing the network

D ○ Separating high-risk hosts from low-risk hosts

E ○ Specifying trusted hosts

4 What are the purposes of a port scan? (Choose two.)

A ○ Retrieve IP address

B ○ Establish connection with host

C ○ Network discovery

D ○ Reveal running programs

5 Which is always the last item executed in an access list?

A ○ Extended list

B ○ Last statement specified by the administrator

C ○ Sequence number

D ○ Implicit deny statement

6 What are methods of a denial of service attack? (Choose two.)

A ○ Reconnaissance and information gathering

B ○ Overwhelming target with data traffic

C ○ Hacking users' passwords and data

D ○ Occupying all open connections

7 **An access control list numbered 100 falls into which category?**

A ○ Extended

B ○ Named

C ○ Standard

D ○ Enhanced

8 **What are examples of VPN security? (Choose two.)**

A ○ Encryption

B ○ Handshaking

C ○ Sequencing

D ○ Authentication

9 **Which technology uses tunneling to ensure data security?**

A ○ Cisco IOS Firewall

B ○ VPN

C ○ ACL

D ○ NAT

10 **Which answer best describes a three-legged firewall?**

A ○ Three perimeter routers with back-end firewall routers

B ○ Three firewall appliances

C ○ One router using three firewall-configured interfaces

D ○ One router using three security appliances

11 **Which technology allows private traffic to appear as if it originates from a public source?**

A ○ NAT

B ○ VPN

C ○ Firewall

D ○ ACLs

Answers

1 **C.** Cisco IOS Firewall. The Cisco IOS Firewall operates at the network, transport, and application layers and provides stateful packet inspection at Layer 7. Review *"Cisco IOS Firewall."*

2 **A.** Dictionary attack. An attacker systematically uses every known word in the dictionary to crack a user password over an extended duration of time. See *"Access attacks."*

3 **A, B, D.** Ease of management, mitigating security risks, and separating high-risk nodes from low-risk nodes are all good reasons to establish zoning. Refer to *"Network Zoning."*

4 **C, D.** Network discovery and revealing running applications are the reasons an attacker port scans a network. Take a look at *"Information collectors."*

5 **D.** Implicit deny statement. The last item processed in an ACL is always the implicit deny statement. See *"IP access control lists (ACLs)."*

6 **B, D.** By overwhelming the target with data traffic and stealing all available connections, an attacker may render a target system inoperable. Look over *"Denial of service (DoS) attacks."*

7 **A.** Extended. Extended ACLs range from 100 to 199 and 2000 to 2699, with standard ACLs ranging from 1 to 99 and 1300 to 1999. Check out *"IP access control lists (ACLs)."*

8 **A, D.** Encryption and authentication are two methods used to provide VPN security mitigation. See *"Virtual Private Networks (VPNs)."*

9 **B.** VPN. Virtual Private Networks rely on tunneling to transmit data safely over public networks. Read *"Virtual Private Networks (VPNs)."*

10 **C.** One router using three firewall-configured interfaces is know as a three-legged firewall. Refer to *"Internal and external network access."*

11 **A.** NAT. Network Address Translation allows multiple private IP addresses to use a single public IP address. Read *"NAT — The great masquerader."*

Chapter 2: Introducing IP Access Lists (IP ACLs)

Exam Objectives

✔ Describing the purpose and different types of access lists

✔ Understanding traffic filtering using security appliances

✔ Investigating the Cisco SDM

✔ ACL inbound and outbound configurations

✔ Managing ACLs

✔ Monitoring and verifying ACLs in a network environment

✔ Troubleshooting ACL issues

*M*anaging and troubleshooting enterprise networks can be a real challenge. Besides delivering data, a router is one tool that can provide additional benefits to network administrators, such as isolating broadcast messages and subnet traffic. You can break a single organization's network into logical segments, which helps in isolating problems and confining misbehaving hosts. Integration of security mitigation methods into this topology planning and design should be a major concern for every organization.

Routers should not only transfer and segment data traffic but also provide some reliable measure of protection against all forms of attack. The router is the first line of defense against network intruders, and properly configured, it can provide a strong method of security mitigation. A router needs a way to identify traffic that is wanted — or allowed to pass through the router's interface — and which data is undesirable, or rejected by the router. Network administrators can achieve basic traffic management control and high network availability by defining a list of networks that are allowed or denied access to the organization's private network.

Characteristics of Access Lists

Access control lists (ACLs), also called access lists, take data management a step further by filtering inbound and/or outbound packets based on a specified set of rules put in place by the network administrator. Although not as sophisticated as a dedicated security appliance, ACLs provide powerful protection when properly configured and applied to a router's interface. ACLs can prevent traffic from entering and leaving the networks, limit the amount of traffic on the network, and prevent IP spoofing or denial of service (DoS) attacks.

ACL location

It is important to determine the best interface and router for ACL placement. The location of the ACL is a crucial factor that decides the eventual success or failure of the ACL. The direction, either inbound or outbound, is another crucial factor to consider when configuring ACLs. Keep the following rules in mind when determining ACL placement:

✦ ACLs should always be implemented on border (perimeter) routers to provide a minimum measure of firewall protection from outside threat. These ACLs filter traffic between the internal and external network. Every enabled protocol on each interface of the router should have its own inbound and outbound access list.

✦ Another good location for ACLs is on routers specifically tasked with segmenting internal network traffic. Dividing a private network into certain groups allows an administrator more control over the network environment. This funnels control of data traffic even further and provides an additional layer of security inside the network.

ACL purpose and benefits

The major ACL duties and benefits are as follows:

✦ **Filtering IP packets:** Blocking or allowing network traffic with inbound or outbound destinations is possible by filtering methods based on source IP address, destination IP address, type of traffic, protocol, or interface used.

For security reasons, an administrator may wish to permit only one specified remote terminal access to an inbound *VTY* session (Telnet) and disallow all other Telnet traffic entering or leaving the network.

✦ **Reducing routing table updates:** Routers send and receive periodic routing table updates. This can saturate and cause performance issues if allowed to enter into your private networks. You can specify how to limit or deny these updates from propagating uncontrollably.

ACLs can be used to control which networks are to be advertised by dynamic routing protocols. The ACL is applied to a protocol instead of an interface and is called a *distribute list*. A distribute list is then applied to a routing protocol to control the content of the traffic.

✦ **Prioritizing traffic:** ACLs are a series of IF/THEN statements evaluated sequentially:

- Routing traffic can be prioritized, allowing certain types of specified data to be processed by the router before other traffic is analyzed. This is called *priority queuing* and ensures that high-priority packets are given attention first.

- A network administrator may also want to prioritize traffic based on the type, protocol, or purpose of the data. *Custom queuing* allows balancing of traffic in this way.

✦ **Controlling traffic:** Applying an ACL on a slow link allows a network administrator more control over traffic on that link. This improves performance and decreases excess traffic. An ACL may also specify which addresses are serviced by *Network Address Translation (NAT)* or which type of data triggers a *Dial –on-Demand Routing (DDR)* session to a remote network. This ensures that only certain types of traffic initiate a WAN link connection. In this way, ACLs are used to identify interesting traffic for DDR sessions.

✦ **Mitigating security risks:** It is possible and desired to block denial of service and IP spoofing attacks before theyhave a chance to attack your network. ACLs can be used to prevent connection flooding by controlling the *Transmission Control Protocol (TCP) Intercept* feature. When enabled, TCP Intercept analyzes SYN packets between two host interfaces, determined by an extended ACL. The software then establishes a transparent connection between client and server machine, and it forwards packets between the two until the connection ends, removing the possibility of establishing unauthorized connections.

✦ **Authentication:** Incoming *remote shell (RSH)* and *remote copy (RCP)* protocols may be allowed into the router using a configured database for authentication. This database is set up by the network administrator and is used by ACLs to control router access.

How is an ACL processed?

Each ACL is defined by a name or number, and is processed in an orderly, top-down, first-come, first-served fashion. For ACL processing to occur, each ACL must be applied to either an inbound or outbound interface. After it is applied, an ACL is processed in the following way:

1. Packet header information is read on any packet received (inbound) or delivered (outbound) through a configured interface on the router.

2. The packet is then compared to each statement in the ACL. The ACL statement matching process starts at the top of the ACL. The ACL statement on top of the list is analyzed first. If a packet does not match the current ACL statement in the list, the current statement is skipped and the packet is checked against the next ACL statement underneath. This process continues until either a match is found or the bottom of the ACL is reached.

3. If the packet header matches an ACL statement, the packet is either allowed or blocked to flow through the interface where the ACL was created, based on the matching ACL statement. Once the packet matched an ACL statement, the ACL matching process terminates, even if there are more matches for this packet, further down in the ACL. The ACL matching process stops as soon as it finds an ACL statement that matches the packet being analyzed.

It is important to understand that if an ACL statement matches the packet before the list ends, the packet is either allowed or blocked to flow through the interface where the ACL was created, based on the matching ACL statement, no matter the ACL statements that follow underneath.

4. If the IOS blocks a packet from flowing through an interface, based on a matching ACL statement, the IOS issues an Internet Control Message Protocol (ICMP) *"Host Unreachable"* message. If the IOS does not find a matching ACL for the packet analyzed, the implicit deny statement always rejects the packet. The IOS automatically creates an implicit *deny all* entry at the bottom of each ACL.

If you do not have at least one *permit* ACL statement in your ACL, the default *deny all* entry at the bottom of the ACL blocks all packets from flowing through the interface.

Using ACLs, you can allow or deny packets from different hosts or networks. Incoming traffic is compared to ACL entries based on the order of the entries' occurrence in the router. This order is important. New statements get added to the end of the list, and the router continues to process the ACL until it finds a match. If the router reaches the end of the ACL with no match found, the traffic is denied. For this reason, place all frequent entries near the top of the ACL.

Types of ACLs

The two main categories of access control lists are *standard* and *extended.* Each standard or extended ACL must be identified using either a name or number. *Named* access lists support additional features not found in *numbered* ACLs. To provide packet-filtering capabilities, the ACL must be applied to either an *inbound* or *outbound* interface. Each category of ACL is described as follows:

✦ **Standard ACLs:** These access lists are the easiest to configure. Standard ACLs are used to filter packets on *source IP address only* and are applied on interfaces near the destination. Standard numbered ACLs range from 1 to 99 and 1300 to 1999 in the expanded range. A standard ACL using the extended range functions identically to ACLs numbered in the 1–99 range.

Two exceptions can allow standard ACLs to filter by a value other than source IP address:

- For VTY purposes, the *destination address* is used (instead of the source IP address) when applying an ACL to an outbound interface.

- Filtering route advertisements is done using the *network address* instead of the source IP address.

✦ **Extended ACLs:** These access lists provide additional flexibility and features that are not included with standard ACLs. Extended ACLs may be either named or numbered. Extended numbered ACLs range from 100 to 199 or 2000 to 2699 and are used for detailed filtering based on source IP address, destination IP address, type of protocol used, port number, hop count (TTL), and other options, as follows:

- *Source address:* Filters traffic by packet source address.

- *Destination address:* Filters packets by destination address.

- *Protocol:* Filters traffic by protocol type. Extended ACLs add features not available with standard ACLs which allow filtering of TCP/IP family protocols such as TCP, UDP, ICMP, IGMP, EIGRP, and OSPF.

- *Port:* Filters traffic by TCP or UDP port address. This simple type of filtering is useful when a network administrator would like to block HTTP, FTP, or TELNET access.

- *TTL:* Filters traffic based on the hop count, or Time to live of the packet.

✦ **Named ACLs:** These access lists are functionally similar to extended ACLs but are identified by a name rather than a number. Named ACLs are supported in Cisco IOS version 11.2 or later and use slightly different command syntax than numbered access lists. Using a specified, practical name assigned by the network administrator, named ACLs become easier to remember and identify.

Some benefits of named ACLs over numbered ACLs are as follows:

- *TCP flags:* Read and filter traffic based on flags set in TCP header information. TCP flags may be used to eliminate *false synchronization* packets from entering the configured interface. TCP flags are used in named ACLs.

- *IP options:* Filter data based on specific IP options, which may help prevent bogus packets from flooding the network.

- *Reflexive access lists:* Dynamically created ACL entries that are temporarily stored in extended ACLs. These work similarly to the *established* ACL operator, which allows packets back into the network from already-established connections. The established command does not work with applications that change the source port dynamically or with UDP/ICMP traffic. Reflexive ACLs support both ICMP and UDP packets, and work with programs that automatically change ports.

**Book VI
Chapter 2**

Introducing IP
Access Lists (IP
ACLs)

- *Noncontiguous ports:* Allow support for noncontiguous port assignment using one *access control entry (ACE).* This reduces the size of the ACL and eliminates the need for multiple entries of the same source, destination, or protocol.

- *Delete ACL entries:* With named ACLs, specific entries may be removed using the *no permit* or *no deny* commands without having to delete and re-create the entire ACL. This is not possible with numbered ACLs using older IOS versions. Cisco IOS versions 12.2(14) S and later allow addition, deletion, and modification of individual statements in named or numbered ACLs using sequence numbers. For the exam, remember that individual ACE entries may be manipulated on named lists but not on numbered lists.

✦ **Inbound ACLs:** Apply to data traffic entering a router's interface. An inbound ACL is implemented to allow or deny external (public) network traffic into the private (internal) network.

✦ **Outbound ACLs:** Apply to data traffic exiting a router's interface. An outbound ACL is used to allow or restrict hosts on the internal (private) network from reaching external (public) networks or hosts.

Managing ACLs — Best Practices

There are many helpful tips to keep in mind when creating and managing access lists. Implementing the following best practices can provide a solid foundation for understanding and designing access lists, and provide the core knowledge needed to ace the ACL portion of the CCNA exam:

✦ **Order ACLs by placing specific, *most restrictive* access list entries before more general or *less restrictive* entries.** Also, place frequently used entries ahead of less frequent entries. For instance, ACL entries that will likely have a match sooner than others should be placed higher in the ACL. This saves router resources because ACL processing is halted when the first matching entry is found.

New ACL entries are always placed at the end of the access list.

✦ **Place standard ACLs as close as possible to the destination.** Standard ACLs filter traffic based on source IP address — not destination address — and should be placed near the destination. This prevents unnecessary routing table lookups (and additional router resource usage) by filtering traffic *before* the routing decision is made.

Network administrators can only apply ACLs to router interfaces in their control.

✦ **Place extended ACLs as close as possible to the source.** ACLs must be placed where they have the greatest impact and have the most efficiency. Proper placement of the ACL is crucial in saving router resources and routing the packet unnecessarily. There is no need to allow traffic to be routed through the network, just to have it denied by an ACL right before it reaches the destination.

Extended ACLs should be assigned to the interface closest to the source, which prevents unwanted traffic from traversing the network. Extended ACLs may filter traffic on source or destination addresses, port, protocol, or other factors.

✦ **Use at least one permit statement.** An ACL without at least one permit statement denies all traffic. Because there is an implicit deny rule at the end of an ACL list, if a packet is not processed by any of the ACL rules, it will be discarded.

**Book VI
Chapter 2**

✦ **Never make the first ACL entry a** *permit any any* **statement.** This allows all traffic to pass through the router's interface. No other entries can be processed after the permit any any statement.

Be careful where this command is placed in the ACL. The permit any any statement allows all traffic to pass through that was not already specifically denied in a previous access list entry. Placing this rule as the last line in an ACL negates the implicit deny statement.

✦ **Use an explicit deny statement.** Placing the `deny ip any any` command at the end of an ACL has more benefit than relying on the implicit deny statement. Using an explicit deny statement and the `show access-list` command, you can view the count of rejected packets by the router. This assists with troubleshooting issues and network monitoring. Denied packets from the implicit deny statement are not shown by the `show access-list` IOS command.

✦ **Create the ACL first, and then apply it to an interface.** You can apply a nonexistent (or empty) ACL to an interface.

Don't do it! An empty ACL permits all traffic! Naturally, this can be very dangerous. During the creation process, if the empty ACL is already applied to the interface, the IOS will start filtering traffic only after the first statement is specified. Then, the unwritten implicit deny statement will be executed. This can cause serious network access issues for the duration of the ACL creation process.

✦ **Use only one inbound ACL per interface.** Multiple inbound ACLs cannot be assigned to the same interface and in the same direction. Only one inbound and one outbound ACL are allowed per interface.

To save router resources, an inbound ACL is executed *before* the routing table lookups.

✦ **Use only one outbound ACL per interface.** Multiple outbound ACLs cannot be assigned to the same interface. You can combine one inbound and one outbound ACL per interface. The filtering process on outbound traffic is done *after* the routing table lookup is performed.

✦ **Use a text editor to edit and order the ACLs.** Notepad (Windows), vi (UNIX), or any standard text editor may be used to add, delete, or modify an access list entry. Follow these steps:

1. Execute the `show running-config` command.

2. Copy the ACL entries and paste them into a text editor.

3. After the required changes are made to the ACL in the text editor, remove the applied ACL from the interface using the `no ip access-group` *access-list-name/number in/out* command.

4. Delete the access list using the `no access-list` *access-list-name/number* command.

5. Paste the newly edited ACL back into the router's global configuration mode, which verifies each statement individually and warns if any errors are encountered.

6. Reapply the ACL to the interface by using the `ip access-group` command in interface configuration mode.

✦ **Delete ACL entries.** Entries belonging to numbered access lists cannot be individually deleted in IOS versions prior to 12.2(14)S. The entire numbered access list must be deleted and re-created from scratch. Deleting single entries on named ACLs is possible using the `no permit` and `no deny` commands. In IOS versions supporting ACL sequence numbers, all types of access lists may be edited.

✦ **Use the** `remark` **command.** Using this command, nonexecuted remarks can be added before or after any command in an ACL.

✦ **Deny all inbound IP packets from the Internet that contain reserved private IP addresses.** Private IP addresses are not routable and should not be allowed as inbound network traffic. Some examples of IPs that should be blocked using ACLs are 0.0.0.0/8, 10.0.0.0/8, 169.254.0.0/16, 172.16.0.0/20, and 192.168.0.0/16. Packets attempting to enter the network using 127.0.0.0/8 (loopback) should also be denied access.

✦ **Deny all inbound IP packets from the Internet that contain IP multicast addresses.** Block unnecessary multicast traffic from entering and possibly flooding the network. Also block unwanted broadcast traffic from crossing perimeter border routers.

✦ **Deny all inbound IP packets from the Internet that contain source addresses of internal networks or hosts.** An intruder may initiate an IP spoofing or TCP sequence number guessing attack using the same private IP addresses (in packet headers) that are in use on the trusted private network. This protection should be applied to interfaces facing untrusted networks.

Creating ACLs

Creating ACLs is not difficult if you understand the many ACL rules and know how to apply them. When creating access lists, be sure to keep in mind the tips from the previous section. The other important concept to understand is that of *inverse subnet masks,* or *wildcard IP masks.*

Wildcard IP masks

The ACL filtering process relies on wildcard IP masks to identify which IP address bits of the filtered packet should be read or ignored by the IOS. This process compares the address bits of the filtered packet to the address bits specified in the ACL. Wildcard masks use *0* and *1* bits to determine which bits of the IP address are to be processed or ignored, as follows:

Book VI
Chapter 2

Introducing IP
Access Lists (IP
ACLs)

✦ 0 bits are read and specify to the IOS that the corresponding IP address bits must match. The filtering process is activated for 0 bits.

✦ 1 bits tell the router to ignore the corresponding IP address bit value. These 1 bits are "I don't care" bits — they are ignored by the IOS and not filtered.

Wildcard IP masks are exactly the opposite of subnet masks, hence the name *inverted subnet mask.* In standard subnetting, the mask is read from left to right. The 1 bits are read as network bits, and the 0 bits are ignored. With wildcard masks, you start reading from the right and move left. There is another important difference between subnet masks and wildcard masks. With subnet masks, network and subnet bits are always contiguous. Inverted masks may contain bits that are *not* right next to each other (noncontiguous). Figure 2-1 shows an example of typical wildcard match results.

The wildcard IP mask rules to follow are

✦ **0 bit:** Match

✦ **1 bit:** Ignore

The wildcard mask targets the following addresses:

✦ **A single host or IP address:** Specifies that all bits in the host IP must match and all are checked. Wildcard masks for single host matches are designated as *0.0.0.0* in dotted-decimal notation.

✦ **A subnet or an entire network:** Every subnet or network portion of the IP address must match.

IP Address	Wildcard Mask	Description
0.0.0.0	255.255.255.255	All IP addresses ignored. Same as permit any any.
128.10.0.0/16	0.0.255.255	Network 128.10.0.0 will be processed. Third and fourth octets are ignored.
200.100.1.15/24	0.0.0.255	Network 200.100.1.0 will be processed. Fourth IP octet is ignored.
200.100.1.15/24	0.0.0.0	ACL processing is done on the single host only! IP 200.100.1.15
204.1.1.16/28	0.0.0.15	Only subnet 204.1.1.16 (204.1.1.17 to 204.1.1.30) will be processed.

Figure 2-1: Wildcard match examples.

For standard Class A networks, the wildcard mask value of *0.255.255.255* is inverse to the standard subnet mask of 255.0.0.0. *0.0.255.255* is the wildcard mask for Class B networks, and *0.0.0.255* is used for Class C networks.

A slightly different approach is needed to reveal the inverse mask for subnetted networks. First, write the classless interdomain routing (CIDR) notation in decimal format. For example, to figure out the wildcard mask for subnet 204.1.1.16/28, take the subnet mask value of 255.255.255.240 and subtract it from 255.255.255.255. This provides the inverse mask value of 0.0.0.15. You can see a binary example of the inverted subnet mask in Figure 2-2.

Figure 2-2: Wildcard mask in binary.

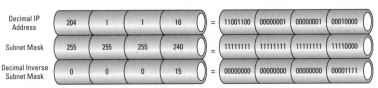

+ **A specific range of IP addresses:** Targets only a specified range of IP addresses. This allows targeting of particular subnets. For example, you might like to filter all nodes included on the 204.1.1.0 and 204.1.1.16 subnets. To target these two networks only, first view these subnets in binary, as shown in Figure 2-3. You want to match on each of the first three octets, but you must go a little farther, to the 27th bit location. This specifies networks 204.1.1.0 and 204.1.1.16, excluding 204.1.1.32. You then convert /27 into decimal and invert to get the wildcard mask of 0.0.0.31.

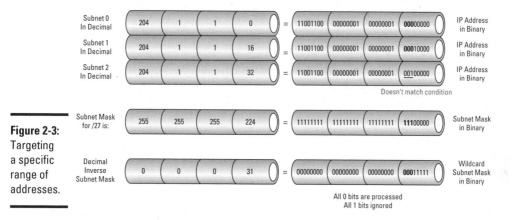

Figure 2-3:
Targeting a specific range of addresses.

Using another example, you can target networks 192.168.1.0 and 192.168.2.0 by matching on all bit locations up to the 23rd bit position. A /23 prefix length is equal to 255.255.254.0 in decimal. The decimal subnet mask is then inverted to 0.0.1.255. This can be achieved by subtracting 255.255.254.0 from 255.255.255.255.

You do not have to assign a wildcard mask to a specific source or destination *host* address in an ACL. The IOS automatically assigns an implicit wildcard mask of 0.0.0.0, which requires all bit values in the IP address to match.

Creating and applying the ACL

When creating an access list, it is important to remember two basic steps:

1. Create the ACL.

2. Apply it to an interface.

To prevent access problems, always create the ACL before applying it to the interface. Another major concern is where to apply the ACL, either to inbound or outbound traffic. Each ACL contains a listing of logical access control entries that are implemented on either incoming or outgoing data. Each ACE in the ACL defines whether the packet is allowed access or denied entry, and the ACL stops processing on the first ACE match.

Filtered packets are always processed by the inbound access list prior to being routed. Packet filtering is checked against a specific access list only once.

Packets traversing through a router may be checked multiple times using *different* access lists, depending on the interface and direction chosen.

Creating standard ACLs

Standard ACLs filter packets using the source IP address and are applied to interfaces nearest the destination. Standard numbered ACLs range from 1 to 99 and 1300 to 1999. A sample standard (numbered) ACL is listed here:

1. **Enter privileged EXEC/global configuration mode and permit access to user *Dummy* with the IP address of 172.210.1.5:**

   ```
   Router>enable
   Router#configure terminal
   Router(config)#access-list 1 remark Permit access to
       Dummy
   Router(config)#access-list 1 permit 172.210.1.5
   ```

2. **Deny access to user *Smarty* and log any access attempts:**

   ```
   Router(config)#access-list 1 remark Deny access to
       Smarty and log any access attempts by Smarty
   Router(config)#access-list 1 deny 194.168.10.3 0.0.0.0
       log
   ```

3. **Permit access to the remaining network users:**

   ```
   Router(config)#access-list 1 remark Permit access to
       rest of network
   Router(config)#access-list 1 permit 194.168.10.0
       0.0.0.255
   ```

4. **Apply and activate the inbound ACL to interface serial 0:**

   ```
   Router(config)#interface serial 0
   Router(config-if)#ip access-group 1 in
   ```

In this example, I entered global configuration mode and added a REM statement (a nonprocessed note supported by named and numbered access lists) to remind you that user Dummy is allowed access inside the network. So far, only this specific IP address is permitted traffic into your private network. Next, another REM statement provides a reminder that you are blocking user Smarty from having access into the network, and have decided to log any of his unsuccessful attempts to gain network access. The next permit statement allows access to all other hosts from the 194.168.10.0 network. The exception is user Smarty.

Keep in mind that when a match is found in an ACL, processing is halted. Looking at this standard ACL, you can see how important the order of entries in the ACL is. For instance, if the network permit statement for 192.168.10.0 was placed before the deny statement for the single user Smarty, all traffic coming from the 192.168.10.0 network, including Smarty, would be allowed network entry. This is because all ACL processing is done from the top down, and halted when a match is found. The last two statements in the example apply and activate the inbound ACL to interface serial 0. The `ip access-group` command takes all the ACEs with the same list number and groups them together, applies them in the order they were issued to the IOS, and activates them on interface serial 0. Finally, any packets not specified on an ACE are implicitly denied.

The 0.0.0.0 wildcard mask after the user's IP address specifies that all bits of the address should be processed. Because you are filtering on a host IP alone, the 0.0.0.0 wildcard mask is not mandatory. The IOS inputs this value automatically. Another method is to use the *host* keyword, which precedes the IP address.

To view the newly created access list, execute the following command:

```
Router#show ip access-list 1
Standard IP access list 1
    permit 172.210.1.5
    deny 194.168.10.3
    permit 194.168.10.0, wildcard bits 0.0.0.255
```

Creating extended ACLs

To properly configure extended ACLs, you must first understand the terminology used. Refer to the sidebar "Extended ACL command syntax" box for clarification of the parameters used in the next example. Following is a sample of how an extended ACL may be designed to protect and block certain kinds of traffic on a perimeter, or border, router. The following is an example for blocking some reserved and private IP addresses:

1. **Enter privileged EXEC/global configuration mode and block private and special-use IPs:**

   ```
   Router>en
   Router#conf t
   Router(config)#access-list 100 remark Block special use
       and private addresses
   Router(config)#access-list 100 deny ip 127.0.0.0
       0.255.255.255 any log
   Router(config)#access-list 100 deny ip 255.0.0.0
       0.255.255.255 any log
   ```

```
Router(config)#access-list 100 deny ip 224.0.0.0
   7.255.255.255 any log
Router(config)#access-list 100 deny ip host 0.0.0.0 any
   log
Router(config)#access-list 100 deny ip 10.0.0.0
   0.255.255.255 any
Router(config)#access-list 100 deny ip 172.16.0.0
   0.15.255.255 any
Router(config)#access-list 100 deny ip 192.168.0.0
   0.0.255.255 any
Router(config)#access-list 100 deny ip [your network IP
   address] any
```

2. Permit established traffic:

```
Router(config)#access-list 100 remark Permit
   established traffic
Router(config)#access-list 100 permit ip any [your
   network IP address][your network mask] est
Router(config)#access-list 100 remark Permit FTP data
   connection
Router(config)#access-list 100 permit tcp any eq 20
   host [host IP address] gt 1023
```

3. Group and apply the ACL to an interface:

```
Router(config)#interface serial 2/0
Router(config-if)#ip access-group 100 in
```

The first access list command contains a note that all specified special and private addresses are to be blocked. The next eight deny statements block these reserved addresses to any internal destination. IP addresses such as loopback, broadcasts, reserved multicasts, and private Class A, B, and C network addresses are blocked. Also, an organization's own private internal addresses should be blocked on the inbound ACL. Incoming network traffic should not be using your private IP addresses as the source IP address. This helps prevent IP spoofing or other attacks on the network. Any attempt by these addresses to enter your network will be logged.

The next remark and permit statements allow already-established connections (originating from the private network) back inside the internal network. This ensures that the firewall does not block expected return traffic from an already-allowed, established connection. The following two remark and permit statements are used for FTP. A specific node on the private network may receive incoming FTP data transmitted on port 20 from any data source, using any TCP port greater than 1023. Finally, the ACL is grouped and applied to a serial interface. The show ip access-list command can then be given to display the contents of the ACL.

ACL commands

`show access-lists`: Allows an administrator to view all currently configured access lists on the router. The `show access-lists` command does not specify which interface the ACL is assigned to.

`show access-list` *[list #]*: Provides details for a specific access list by using the ACL number.

`show ip access-list`: By not including the name or number of a specific access list, the `show ip access-list` command lists all IP access lists configured on the router.

`show ip interface`: Shows all interfaces that have been configured with an IP access list.

`show running-config`: Displays the access lists currently configured on the router and indicates which interfaces are assigned ACLs.

`clear access-list counter` *[list#]*: Clears the counters used in extended access lists. These counters indicate the number of matches identified per line in an ACL.

`ip access-group`: Applies an IP ACL to an interface.

A standard access list should be located nearest to the destination. Implement extended access lists as near to the source of the traffic as possible. Standard access lists match against the source IP address, while extended access lists are used to deny or permit certain traffic to certain hosts or networks.

A standard access list and an extended access list cannot have the same name. Access lists specified by name are not compatible with Cisco IOS releases prior to 11.2.

Creating Telnet/SSH ACLs

This type of ACL blocks access and enforces security on the router itself. Telnet and Secure Shell (SSH) access lists are used to specify who is allowed to establish these types of connections and from where.

In this case, a standard ACL is created and applied to the virtual type terminal (VTY) lines:

1. **Enter privileged EXEC/global configuration mode and specify the IP address to permit for Telnet and SSH access:**

```
Router>en
Router#conf t
Router(config)#access-list 5 remark Permit Telnet/SSH
    session for hosts 192.168.10.100, 192.168.10.101,
    and 192.168.10.102
Router(config)#access-list 5 permit 192.168.10.100
```

```
Router(config)#access-list 5 permit 192.168.10.101
    0.0.0.0
Router(config)#access-list 5 permit host 192.168.10.102
```

2. Deny all other access and log any access attempts:

```
Router(config)#deny any log
```

3. Specify the line and access class:

```
Router(config)#line vty 0 4
Router(config-line)#access-class 5 in
```

This ACL allows only hosts 192.168.10.100, 192.168.10.101, and 192.168.10.102 VTY access to the router, and denies all other requests. Notice there are three different (legal) ways to specify a host IP address. After the three nodes are permitted access, the *deny any* statement bans all other access and logs any attempts to establish connection to the console. The access-class command is used to restrict incoming and outgoing connections between a virtual type terminal (VTY) and the addresses in an ACL. There is also a major difference between the previous two standard and extended ACL examples and this one. The first two ACLs were applied to a router interface. This Telnet/SSH ACL is applied to the inbound VTY terminal lines on the router, which affects traffic destined to the router, not traffic flowing through the router attempting to reach the internal network.

Placing an outbound ACL on the router restricting Telnet/SSH connectivity would prevent virtual terminal sessions from originating at the router. For example, hosts 192.168.10.100, 101, and 102 have been allowed Telnet access into the router but would be prevented from establishing a Telnet session from the same router to other hosts.

Creating named ACLs

Named ACLs are functionally identical to standard and extended access lists, but use a descriptive name instead of a number to identify the ACL. You can add, remove, and edit line-item entries in a named ACL without having to re-create the entire access list. Creating named ACLs is also slightly different than creating numbered ACLs. I create both standard and extended named ACLs. First, a standard named access list is as follows:

ACL keywords

any: Keyword specifying all hosts or networks. Used as a shortcut replacement for 0.0.0.0 255.255.255.255 in an access control list.

host: Keyword specifying a single host. Uses wildcard mask of 0.0.0.0, which designates one host only.

ACL command syntax

ACL number: A number extended between 100 and 199 or 2000 and 2699 for the extended range that denotes the "name" of the access list.

Permit/deny statement: Specifies whether to permit or deny a packet based on matched conditions, or rules, in an ACL.

Protocol: Specifies the type of protocol filtered (that is, IP, ICMP, UDP, TCP, and so on).

Source IP address: Network or host IP address that the packet originates from. The keyword *any* may be used as an abbreviation for the 0.0.0.0/255.255.255.255 "all networks" address. The any keyword represents all networks. The *host* keyword may also be used with a dotted-decimal address to denote a host address. This means matching will be done on one specific host only.

Source mask: A wildcard mask (also known as an inverse mask) used to determine which bits of source address are read and which bits are skipped. 0 bits are "significant" bits and 1 bits are ignored.

Destination address: The IP address of the destination network. The keyword any may also be used to denote all networks.

Destination mask: The destination network mask. An optional destination address may be used with the mask.

Operator (optional): Applies only to TCP or UDP ports:

- ✔ eq = equal

- ✔ lt = less than

- ✔ gt = greater than

- ✔ neq = not equal to

- ✔ range = a range of port numbers using a beginning and ending port number

- ✔ est = established connections

Port (optional): Assigns the destination port number or service (TCP/UDP traffic).

Log: Used to record access list activity when the logging feature is enabled on the router.

**Book VI
Chapter 2**

Introducing IP Access Lists (IP ACLs)

1. **Enter privileged EXEC/global configuration mode and specify the network addresses to permit access:**

```
Router>en
Router#conf t
Router(config)#ip access-list standard Permit_4_Subnets
Router(config-std-nacl)#permit 192.168.10.0 0.0.0.255
Router(config-std-nacl)#permit 192.168.21.0 0.0.0.255
Router(config-std-nacl)#permit 192.168.34.0 0.0.0.255
Router(config-std-nacl)#permit 192.168.68.0 0.0.0.255
```

2. **Specify the interface and apply the ACL (inbound):**

```
Router(config-std-nacl)#int s0
Router(config-if)#ip access-group Permit_4_Subnets in
```

The first `ip access-list` command creates a standard ACL called *Permit_4_Subnets* and puts the IOS in *named access control list (NACL)* mode. The next four ACEs specify the source IP addresses of the allowed networks. The unwritten implicit deny statement then blocks all other traffic. I then apply the NACL to the inbound serial interface.

With named access lists, the name identifier is an alphanumeric string and is used instead of a number. Named access lists allow you to configure more IP access lists in a router than numbered access lists. If you identify your access list with a name rather than a number, the mode and command syntax are slightly different.

In the next example, I want to prevent the user *Dummy* (192.168.10.15) from accessing the Web server (192.168.11.5) via port 80:

1. **Enter privileged EXEC/global configuration mode and create an extended ACL:**

```
Router>en
Router#conf t
Router(config)#ip access-list extended Block_Dummy
```

2. **Block user from accessing the Web server on port 80 and allow all other traffic:**

```
Router(config-ext-nacl)#deny tcp host 192.168.10.15
    host 192.168.11.5 eq 80
Router(config-ext-nacl)#permit ip any any
```

3. **Apply the inbound NACL to the interface:**

```
Router(config-ext-nacl)#int e0
Router(config-if)#ip access-group Block_Dummy in
```

The first `ip access-list` command creates an extended ACL called *Block_Dummy* and puts the IOS in named access control list mode. Next, specify that host Dummy is denied access to the Web server via port 80. Any other types of traffic from Dummy to the Web server (not equal to port 80) will be allowed. The next ACE permits all other IP traffic. The NACL is then applied and enabled on the inbound Ethernet interface. Don't forget that the implicit deny blocks everything else.

The `ip access-group` command is used to enable an ACL on an interface and define which direction the ACL is applied, either inbound or outbound. Inbound traffic is packets arriving at the router interface and has not yet been processed by the router. Outbound traffic is packets that the router has already processed and is leaving the router interface.

To view the newly created named access list, execute the following command:

```
Router#show ip access-list Block_Dummy
Extended IP access list Block_Dummy
   10 deny tcp host 192.168.10.15 host 192.168.11.5 eq 80
   20 permit ip any any
```

You have just created a named ACL but would like to add an additional access control entry to your ACL, which would block all Telnet traffic from any source or destination. Here's how:

```
Router(config)#ip access-list extended Block_Dummy
Router(config-ext-nacl)#5 deny tcp any any eq telnet
Router(config-ext-nacl)#exit
Router(config)#exit
```

Now take another look at the ACL using the `show access-list` command:

```
Router#show access-list Block_Dummy
Extended IP access list Block_Dummy
5 deny tcp any any eq telnet
10 deny tcp host 192.168.10.15 host 192.168.11.5 eq 80
20 permit ip any any
```

In the `show access-list` command output, the sequence number *5* is added as the first entry in the extended access list called *Block_Dummy*.

You may or may not recognize the line numbering in the above `show` output. If the IOS version running on the router supports line sequence numbering, the IOS automatically adds ACE line numbers to each entry. This is done in increments of ten or can be specified by the administrator. Using newer revisions of the 12.2 and XE IOS software, administrators can add, remove, and reorder sequence numbers manually from named access lists. This prevents having to delete and re-create the entire ACL from scratch when changes to the ACL are necessary.

There is also a method for editing numbered access lists, which recognizes a numbered ACL as if it were a named ACL. This is done by editing the numbered ACL in NACL subconfiguration mode. For the exam, the standard answer is that numbered access lists *cannot* be edited without erasing all data and starting over. Named access lists *can* be edited per access entry.

Creating time-oriented ACLs

Access control lists that filters traffic based on specific times of the day or week are called *time-oriented ACLs.*

With time-oriented ACLs, the *time range* defines when the permit or deny statements in the ACL are activated. Calculations to determine the time are made by the router's internal clock, but really should be left to Network Time Protocol (NTP) synchronization. In the previous examples, all access control entries are in effect after the ACL is applied to an interface.

Here is an example of a time-oriented ACL:

1. Define the time range:

```
Router(config)#time-range BLOCK_HTTP
Router(config-time-range)#periodic weekdays 8:00 to
    17:00
Router(config-time-range)#exit
```

2. Create the ACL and deny hosts using the specified time range:

```
Router(config)#ip access-list extended DENY_WEB
Router(config-ext-nacl)#deny tcp any host
    192.168.10.200
0.0.0.255 eq www time-range BLOCK_HTTP
```

3. Permit all other traffic and apply to the interface (inbound):

```
Router(config-ext-nacl)#permit ip any any
Router(config-ext-nacl)#exit
Router(config)#int s0
Router(config-if)#ip access-group DENY_WEB in
```

This example shows how you can limit access to certain resources during specific times and days of the week. I have defined a time-oriented ACL that denies access to the specified HTTP Web server during company business hours. The first step in creating a time-oriented ACL is specifying a time range. The `time-range` command defines a named time range. Then, the periodic days and times are selected by the administrator. After this is done, an extended named (or numbered) ACL is created. All Web traffic destined to 192.168.10.200 is denied during duty hours by specifying the *BLOCK_HTTP* parameter. I then specify that all other IP traffic is allowed to pass through the ACL filter, and assign the ACL to the inbound serial interface. To view the details of the time range in the IOS, run the `show time-range` command.

Creating switch port ACLs

Port ACLs are configured on Layer 2 switches and only support inbound traffic filtering. Port ACLs (PACLs) may be configured as standard, extended, or MAC-extended access lists.

The major benefit of port ACLs over router ACLs is that IP traffic using IP access lists and non-IP traffic using MAC access lists may be filtered. This allows a physical Layer 2 interface to have both an IP and a MAC ACL applied to it simultaneously.

PACLs use the following modes:

✦ **Prefer port mode:** This mode overwrites all other Cisco IOS ACLs or VLAN ACLs (VACLs) using PACL on Layer 2 devices. In instances where PACL is not setup on the interface, other features are merged and applied on the interface.

✦ **Merge mode:** This default mode combines PACL, VACL, and Cisco IOS ACLs and merges them in the ingress direction.

Keep the following guidelines in mind when configuring PACLs:

✦ A maximum of one IP access list and one MAC access list may be applied to the same Layer 2 interface.

✦ Only named MAC access lists are allowed. A MAC access list is not applied to IP, IPv6, MPLS, or ARP messages.

✦ The hardware resources on the switch determine the number of ACLs and ACEs that can be configured. If there are insufficient hardware resources to program a PACL in hardware, the PACL is not applied.

✦ The access group mode may alter the way PACLs interact with other ACLs. For consistent results across different Cisco platforms, use the default merge mode.

The following example configures an extended named IP ACL called *permit-tcp-acl,* which permits all TCP traffic and implicitly denies all other IP traffic:

```
Switch(config)#ip access-list extended permit-tcp-acl
Switch(config-ext-nacl)#permit tcp any any
Switch(config-ext-nacl)#end
```

The following is an example of how to configure an extended named MAC ACL called *permit-host-acl* to permit source host 000.000.011 to any destination host:

```
Switch(config)#mac access-list extended permit-host-acl
Switch(config-ext-macl)#permit host 000.000.011 any
Switch(config-ext-macl)#end
```

The following example shows how to configure an interface to use prefer port mode:

```
Switch#configure terminal
Switch(config)#interface gigabitEthernet 6/1
Switch(config-if)#access-group mode prefer port
```

The following example shows how to configure an interface to use merge mode:

```
Switch#configure terminal
Switch(config)#interface gigabitEthernet 6/1
Switch(config-if)#access-group mode merge
```

If a switch port ACL is applied to a trunk port, the ACL filters traffic on every VLAN contained in that trunk port. If a switch port ACL is applied to a VLAN with voice capability, the ACL filters both voice and data.

Managing, Verifying, and Troubleshooting ACLs

To mitigate security problems, the network administrator should have a firm understanding of ACL management and troubleshooting techniques. ACLs always reveal the configuration problem by what traffic is allowed or denied. You just need the eye and the tools to spot the problem. For example, when ACL configuration errors deny authorized user access to trusted resources, there are some weapons an administrator may use to manage, test, verify, and troubleshoot the misconfigured ACL.

The basic commands to be aware of are as follows:

✦ `show access-list`: Displays which ACLs are currently configured on the router.

✦ `show ip access-list`: Displays IP ACLs only.

✦ `show running-config access-list`: Displays the running configuration access list. This is beneficial for verifying and changing ACLs *before* saving them to the startup config file using the `copy running-config startup-config` command.

✦ `show access-list ACL_name detail`: Shows detailed information of an ACL specified by name. The command will list ACE entries, hit count, and MD5 hashes, which help with troubleshooting issues.

✦ `show ip interface`: Displays the ACL direction (either inbound or outbound) and interface assignment.

✦ `show resource usage`: Allows an administrator to verify that sufficient resources are available for the configured ACLs on the router.

Logging ACL IP matches

The *log* keyword after a permit or deny statement provides message-logging capability and informs the administrator about packets that match the access list rules. This causes an informational logging message about the packet to be sent to the console. The number of messages logged to the console is specified by the `logging console` global configuration command. The first packet triggers an instantaneous logging message. Each additional logging message is gathered in a *logging buffer* over a 5-minute interval and then displayed collectively to the console. Each logging message includes the ACL number, source IP address, whether the packet was allowed or denied, and the total number of packets received in the 5-minute interval.

Access control lists — Rules to guide you!

✔ Keep in mind that you can have only one ACL "per direction, per protocol, per interface".

✔ There is one unwritten command at the bottom of every ACL called the "implicit deny statement". This command denies traffic.

✔ Each ACL must contain a minimum of one permit statement; otherwise, the implicit deny blocks all traffic.

✔ The main purpose of ACLs is to filter incoming and outgoing traffic on intermediary and destination routers. ACLs do not filter traffic on the entry point router.

✔ Standard ACLs and Extended ACLs must have unique names.

✔ Be wary of empty ACLs! An empty ACL will allow all traffic traveling through the interface where the ACL is created. Referring to an un-existing ACL by name allows all traffic.

✔ Proper ACL ordering is critical for reliable filtering. ACLs stop processing an IP packet as soon as a match is found. The process of allowing or denying a packet is based on the first conditional match.

✔ Inbound ACLs are designed to filter packets arriving on an inbound interface before allowing packets to traverse the router. If the ACL allows a packet, the router forwards it to an outbound interface. Because packet forwarding between inbound and outbound interfaces only happens if the packet is allowed by the ACL, ineligible packets are dropped before router resources are consumed. This process saves CPU cycles and memory allocation on the router, by only forwarding permitted traffic to the outbound interface.

✔ Outbound ACLs filter packets just before sending them out of a routers interface. This means that incoming packets destined for outside networks traverse the router from an inbound interface to the outbound interface before the ACL is verified. Router resources are used even if the packet is eventually filtered and dropped by the outbound ACL.

✔ ACLs are just one method to mitigate network security threats. You should also deploy anti-virus protection, and design and implement backup and disaster recovery policies to protect against data loss and data center disasters.

The `show logging` EXEC command displays statistics and the *level* of logging configured. Specifying a certain level allows messages at that level and all lower levels to be sent to the console. Each level is listed here from most significant to least significant:

✦ **Level 0:** Emergencies: System unusable

✦ **Level 1:** Alerts: Immediate action needed

✦ **Level 2:** Critical: Critical conditions

✦ **Level 3:** Errors: Error conditions

✦ **Level 4:** Warnings: Warning conditions

✦ **Level 5:** Notifications: Normal but significant conditions

✦ **Level 6:** Informational: Informational messages only

✦ **Level 7:** Debugging: Debugging messages

The results of the *log* keyword with an extended IP access list depend on the setting of the logging console command. The log keyword only takes effect if the logging console level is set to 6 or 7. If a level is specified lower than 6 using the log keyword with the extended IP access list command, no information will be logged and sent to the console.

Configuring firewalls and ACLs with Cisco SDM GUI

The Cisco Security Device Manager (SDM) is a Java-based Web application used to ease the configuration methods of Cisco devices. It provides administrators with an easy-to-use graphical user interface that is less intimidating than the IOS command-line interface. The *Cisco SDM Firewall Wizard* walks you through several graphical user interface (GUI) dialogs to easily step through the process of configuring your firewalls and ACLs.

Prep Test

1 **Which type of access list can filter only by source IP address?**

- **A** ○ Extended ACL
- **B** ○ Standard ACL
- **C** ○ Time-oriented ACL
- **D** ○ Named ACL

2 **What functions are provided by the** `ip access-group` **command? (Choose two.)**

- **A** ○ Enables the ACL on an interface
- **B** ○ Enables the ACL for VTY filtering
- **C** ○ Defines ACL direction
- **D** ○ Displays content of ACL

3 **Which statement is always the last ACL statement?**

- **A** ○ Deny any any
- **B** ○ Visible implicit deny statement
- **C** ○ Permit any any statement
- **D** ○ Unwritten implicit deny statement

4 **Which function will the *deny tcp any any eq telnet* access list entry provide?**

- **A** ○ Deny all TCP traffic
- **B** ○ Deny all protocols other than Telnet
- **C** ○ Deny source and destination addresses from passing Telnet traffic
- **D** ○ Deny source addresses from Telnet access

5 **Which statements regarding time-oriented ACLs are true? (Choose three.)**

- **A** ○ Filter traffic based on specific times of the day or week
- **B** ○ Filter traffic based on actual time in packet header
- **C** ○ Use NTP to keep time
- **D** ○ Use router internal clock
- **E** ○ Set time using the `show time-range` command

6 **Which type of ACL is used to protect the router itself?**

- **A** ○ Time-oriented ACL
- **B** ○ Telnet/SSH ACL
- **C** ○ Inbound ACL
- **D** ○ PACL

7 **Which keyword is used to generate informative messages displayed to the console?**

A ○ log

B ○ est

C ○ alert

D ○ warn

8 **When are packets processed in an inbound ACL?**

A ○ Multiple times until packets reach the destination

B ○ Depends on the interface configuration

C ○ After they are routed to an interface

D ○ Before packets are routed to an outbound interface

9 **What are rules for proper ACL placement? (Choose two.)**

A ○ Place standard ACLs closest to the source.

B ○ Place standard ACLs closest to the destination.

C ○ Place extended ACLs closest to the source.

D ○ Place extended ACLs closest to the destination.

10 **Which bits are read and ignored in the wildcard mask? (Choose two.)**

A ○ 0 bits are read.

B ○ 0 bits are ignored.

C ○ 1 bits are read.

D ○ 1 bits are ignored.

11 **What functions are not provided by ACLs? (Choose two.)**

A ○ Comprehensive virus protection

B ○ IPS

C ○ Filter unwanted traffic

D ○ Triggering DDR calls

Answers

1 **B.** Standard ACL. Standard ACLs filter by source IP address. Extended ACLs are more flexible and filter on a variety of factors such as source and destination IP address, port, protocol, or hop count. Review *"Types of ACLs."*

2 **A, C.** Enables the ACL on an interface and defines whether the ACL is applied to the inbound or outbound direction. Take a look at *"Creating ACLs."*

3 **D.** Unwritten implicit deny statement. The implicit deny is always the last statement in an ACL and is included automatically by the IOS. Examine *"How an ACL is processed."*

4 **C.** Deny source and destination addresses from passing Telnet traffic. This ACL statement specifies that all TCP traffic consisting of the Telnet protocol should be denied, by either source or destination IP address. See *"Creating named ACLs."*

5 **A, C, D.** Time-oriented ACLs filter traffic based on specific times of the day or week and use the router's internal clock or another NTP time source to set the time. Examine *"Creating time-oriented ACLs."*

6 **B.** Telnet/SSH ACL. The Telnet/SSH ACL is used to filter traffic destined to create a session with the router itself, not at traffic attempting to flow through the router. Check out *"Creating Telnet/SSH ACLs."*

7 **A.** log. The log keyword in an ACL provides message-logging capability and informs the administrator about packets that match the access list rules. This causes an informational logging message to be sent to the console in 5-minute intervals. Review *"Logging ACL IP matches."*

8 **D.** Packets are inspected before they are routed to an outbound interface. Read *"Creating and applying the ACL."*

9 **B, C.** Place standard ACLs closest to the destination and extended ACLs closest to the source. This prevents needless routing lookups and saves router resources. Also, standard ACLs filter on source address only, and extended ACLs filter on either source and/or destination address. Check out *"Managing ACLs — Best Practices."*

10 **A, D.** The 0 bits are read by the IOS, and the 1 bits are ignored. Filtering is only done on inverse mask 0 bits. Review *"Wildcard IP masks."*

11 **A, B.** Comprehensive virus protection and intrusion prevention system functionality are not part of ACL features. ACLs allow some specific types of threats to be filtered. Read the sidebar *"Access control lists — Rules to guide you!"*

Chapter 3: Introducing Network Address Translation (NAT)

Exam Objectives

✔ Identifying the purpose of Network Address Translation

✔ Describing the different types of NAT

✔ Explaining the basic operation of NAT

✔ Configuring NAT

✔ Describing NAT management

✔ Troubleshooting NAT issues

The short supply and high demand of IPv4 address space have led to the development of IPv6, which now provides more address space than we will ever need. Implementing IPv6 is not without hurdles of its own. Migrating to IPv6 has proven to be a slow, time-consuming process. It can take years to finally realize a new Internet infrastructure based solely on IPv6. Until then, certain tools can minimize the limitations brought on by the IPv4 address space. One of these tools, developed by Cisco, is *Network Address Translation (NAT),* sometimes referred to as the Network Address Translator. Think of NAT as a "middleman" that resides on a device (typically a router, firewall, or computer) between internal and external internetworks, translating private, nonroutable IP addresses into publicly registered IP addresses allocated by the IANA. This creates a binding between a public and private IP address. Only one routable IP address is required to provide an entire NAT-enabled network with access to publicly held resources.

Purpose of NAT

There is more to Network Address Translation than just the benefits of saving IPv4 address space. Security and administration features are also benefits of NAT. The three main purposes of NAT are as follows:

✦ **Minimize IPv4 address shortage:** Network address translation is implemented on a private network when a network administrator does not have enough publicly registered IP addresses available for each host on the internal network. This shortage of publicly registered IP addresses could prevent some hosts from accessing outside resources such as the Internet. Dynamic NAT and port address translation allow all configured private hosts access to public resources with minimal use of publicly registered IP addresses. It is possible to use one routable IP address to represent an entire private network. Setting up a network in this way allows an administrator to preserve and prevent the exhaustion of available IP addresses.

✦ **Add security:** Provides a firewall type of protection against network attack, which helps mitigate security breaches. NAT improves network security by hiding private source IP addresses from public view and can replace or mask internal IP addresses with publicly registered IP address. This is accomplished by replacing the private source IP address in the data packet with a publicly registered, routable IP address. Outside public networks view this traffic as originating from the router itself and not from the private hosts on the internal network.

Permitted traffic is generated from the inside private network, not from the outside, and is considered *trusted* traffic. This trusted traffic is allowed to return inside the internal network, while all other traffic that originates from outside sources remains blocked. This means that only traffic initiated from the inside network is permitted entry into the private network. NAT also provides filtering, which may be set up to specifically allow users to access certain types of data content, or to prevent or restrict access to harmful or unwanted traffic.

✦ **Provide administration:** NAT eases administration duties by providing network organization features. Because one IP address may represent an entire network or subnet, hosts may be added or removed from the private network without impacting the configuration of connected external networks. Using *inbound mapping,* Web services may be relocated to another server without requiring reconfiguration of external hosts. Inbound mapping allows external clients to gain access to private network resources. Additionally, some NAT gateways contain *Dynamic Host Configuration Protocol (DHCP) servers,* providing automatic IP configuration to client machines. NAT may also be used to separate different portions of the private network into zones based on security requirements. *Traffic logging* may be implemented to record all packets going into or out of the NAT gateway.

NAT protects an organization's private addressing scheme from public view. To do this, NAT should be configured on the border router or firewall that resides between the private network and the Internet.

The internal network is known as the *stub domain.* A stub domain is a private LAN that uses nonroutable, internal IP addresses. The majority of traffic on the stub domain stays local and does not traverse the router.

Types of Network Address Translation

Different methods are available to set up NAT bindings between internal and external networks. The three major types of NAT are as follows:

✦ **Static NAT:** Maps a private IP address to a public IP address on a fixed, one-to-one basis. Static NAT is generally used when private hosts on the internal network need permanently established connections to external networks. As shown in Figure 3-1, static NAT allows the mapping of the public and private IP address to remain constant. Private hosts using static NAT retain the same publicly registered IP address for all internetwork communication.

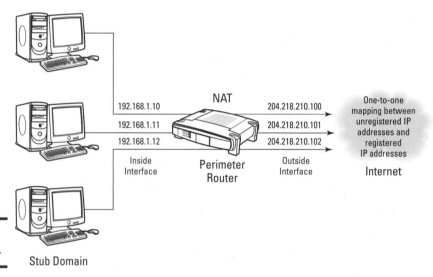

Figure 3-1:
Static NAT.

✦ **Dynamic NAT:** Binds an unregistered IP address to a registered IP address, allocated from a specific range of registered addresses. Dynamic NAT NAT is designed to share a pool of public IP addresses with the local subnet of private IP hosts. Publicly registered IP addresses are issued to requesting hosts from the configured range pool. The issuing of IP addresses to private hosts is dependant on availability at the time of request and issued on a first-come, first-served basis. As shown in Figure 3-2, these private-to-public bindings are recorded in a NAT lookup table. As long as the connection is maintained, the bindings are kept and remain valid. After the connection is dropped, the public address is released from use and returned to the pool of available IP addresses. The IP address is no longer assigned to a specific host and may be reissued to the next requesting host. If a permanent mapping between public and private IP addresses is needed, static NAT should be used instead of dynamic NAT.

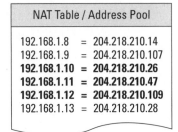

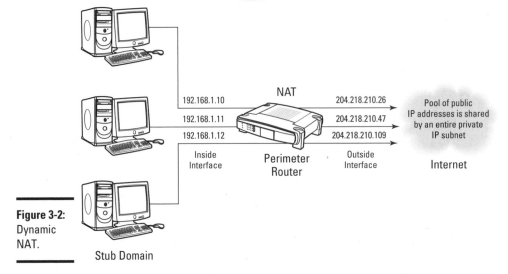

Figure 3-2:
Dynamic
NAT.

✦ **Port Address Translation (PAT):** Maps multiple private IP addresses to one publicly registered IP address using multiple ports. PAT uses port information collected from the transport layer to dynamically create NAT entries which is known as *port multiplexing.* PAT implements port multiplexing by allowing concurrent streams of UDP and TCP data to share one publicly registered IP address. This method of network address translation is known as *overloading.* PAT is often used by organizations or home users with more hosts on a private network than their public IP addresses can accommodate. Figure 3-3 shows an example of port address translation.

Port Address Translation uses port information from the transport layer to dynamically create NAT entries. PAT, also known as one-to-many Network Address Translation, allows many private network hosts to share a single IP address for public Internet access.

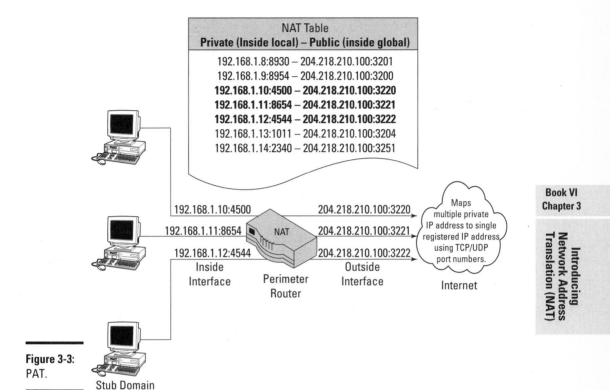

Figure 3-3:
PAT.

Local and global addresses

Cisco defines four different types of NAT addresses:

+ **Inside local address:** Internal (private) address used by a computer or host located on a private network. These addresses are issued internally. They are not assigned by an outside agency.

+ **Inside global address:** This is a globally routable external (public) IP address that is used to represent one or more internal (private) local IP addresses to external public networks. An Internet service provider (ISP) issues and registers these addresses with a local Internet registry (LIR).

+ **Outside local address:** This is the IP address of an external host mapped to an IP address on the internal network. The Outside local address must be routable on the internal network, but does not have to be a public IP address registered with an LIR.

+ **Outside global address:** This is the IP address of an external host that is routable globally. An Internet service provider (ISP) issues and registers these addresses with a local Internet registry (LIR).

A *local address* consists of any IP addresses that reside on the inside (internal or private) network. A *global address* is always located on the outside (external or public) of the network.

Operational Flow of NAT

NAT uses *local* and *global* addresses during packet delivery. Packets that originate from the inside private network use an *inside local* address as the source address. The packet also contains an *outside local* address which represents the destination address. During the delivery process, the packet reaches the outside network and a change occurs in regards to the IP source and destination addresses. The source IP address of the packet changes from the inside local to the *inside global* address, while the destination IP address morphs from the outside local to the *outside global* address.

Reversing this process, a packet originating from the outside network has an outside global source address and an inside global destination address. When this packet enters the inside network, the source address becomes the outside local address. The destination address becomes the inside global address.

Figure 3-4 shows a slightly modified example of this process. In this case, both the inside and outside networks are using a NAT-enabled router for translation services.

Static NAT

The easiest Network Address Translation method to understand is static NAT. Static NAT is almost completely transparent to outside networks and uses a manual method of mapping IP addresses on a one-to-one basis. To provide Internet access to all stub hosts, equal amounts of public IP (inside global) addresses are required. Each stub host must be statically assigned one public IP address. After a NAT rule is configured by the administrator, static NAT maintains a permanent connection between an inside local IP address and an inside global IP address. NAT provides this connectivity to local network (nonroutable) hosts by maintaining a static map of nonroutable-to-registered IP addresses. Communications can be initiated from either the inside or outside network. Here's how basic Network Address Translation works:

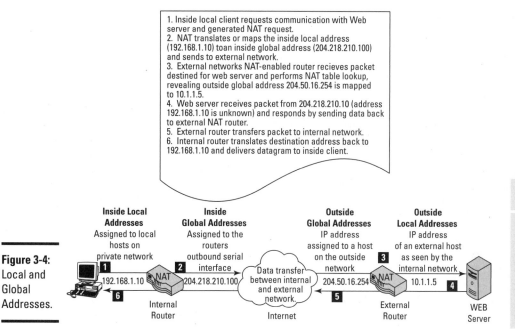

1. Inside local client requests communication with Web server and generated NAT request.
2. NAT translates or maps the inside local address (192.168.1.10) toan inside global address (204.218.210.100) and sends to external network.
3. External networks NAT-enabled router recieves packet destined for web server and performs NAT table lookup, revealing outside global address 204.50.16.254 is mapped to 10.1.1.5.
4. Web server receives packet from 204.218.210.10 (address 192.168.1.10 is unknown) and responds by sending data back to external NAT router.
5. External router transfers packet to internal network.
6. Internal router translates destination address back to 192.168.1.10 and delivers datagram to inside client.

Book VI Chapter 3

Introducing Network Address Translation (NAT)

Figure 3-4: Local and Global Addresses.

Inside Local Addresses Assigned to local hosts on private network

192.168.1.10

1

NAT

Internal Router

Inside Global Addresses Assigned to the routers outbound serial interface

2

204.218.210.100

6

Data transfer between internal and external network.

Internet

Outside Global Addresses IP address assigned to a host on the outside network

204.50.16.254

5

External Router

Outside Local Addresses IP address of an external host as seen by the internal network

3

NAT

10.1.1.5

4

WEB Server

1. The internal private network, also known as the *stub domain*, consists of a series of computer hosts using either non-routable private IP addresses (inside local addresses) or globally routable IP addresses (inside global addresses). Only hosts with non-routable private IP addresses (inside local addresses) need to have their IP address translated if they need to communicate outside the stub domain. Hosts with inside global addresses do not require NAT when they need to communicate outside the stub domain because their IP address is globally routable.

2. Packets from inside interfaces on the stub domain destined for outside public hosts are delivered to the default gateway.

3. The NAT router maintains a translation table that keeps track of each inside local address and their corresponding inside global address. When the NAT router receives an outbound packet from the stub domain, it tries to match its destination address to a destination in its routing table. If a match is not found the packet is dropped. If a match is found, NAT examines the address translation table looking to match the inside local address to its corresponding inside global address.

4. Inside local to inside global address translation occurs. The packet is forwarded to the destination network using an inside global source address. Any packets not having an address translation entry are forwarded along without any translation services being rendered.

5. The packet is received by the NAT-enabled gateway on the outside net-work and is checked against the routing and address translation tables to find the destination address.

6. The destination computer receives the data and returns a packet for the originating stub host. The source address of the packet is an outside global address with a destination address of the inside global address.

7. The router using NAT services on the inside network receives the packet and consults the address translation table for a match on the inside global address. The inside global address is matched to the stub computer's inside local address, and the packet is delivered. The rout-ing table is checked before it sends it to the destination computer. If an entry is not found in the address translation table, no translation is pro-cessed. The routing table is then checked for the destination address. If no route is found in the routing table for the destination address, the packet is discarded.

Dynamic NAT operation

Here is how dynamic NAT operates in a stub domain using inside local addresses connected to a NAT-enabled router:

1. The local router is configured with a pool of publicly registered IP addresses provided by the IANA or other issuing authority.

2. A stub domain computer requests contact with an outside host.

3. The local router receives a packet from the stub domain host.

4. The local router consults its routing table and verifies that the host is allowed access to translation services. The inside local IP address is saved to the address translation table and then replaced (in the packet header) with the first available publicly registered IP address (from the address pool). This routable IP address (inside global address) is then mapped to the nonroutable IP address of the host in the NAT translation table.

5. The packet is forwarded to the destination network using an inside global source address.

6. The packet is then sent to the external network using the publicly regis-tered IP address as the source address. The destination host is not aware of the inside local address or port that sent the packet. Only the newly NAT router issued IP address and port are known to the destination.

7. The destination host transmits a reply packet to the router on the source network. The packet is inspected, and the destination IP address is read. The address translation table is consulted to find the previously saved inside local address of the originating stub domain host. If no match is found in the lookup table, the packet is discarded. If the lookup results in a match, the destination address is then changed from the inside global address back to the inside local address and the packet is delivered.

8. This process continues until communications between the two systems terminate. After communication is finalized, the inside global address is returned to the IP address pool for reissue.

How overloading (PAT) operates

PAT implements two important changes not found with dynamic NAT:

✦ The address pool allocation employed with dynamic NAT is not used. Instead, the pool of IP addresses is replaced with a single routable IP address. All inside local addresses share one inside global address for external data communications.

✦ Multiplexing is implemented to allow each local host separate communications using a unique TCP or UDP port address.

This process works as follows:

1. The local router is configured with a single publicly registered IP address known as the inside global address.

2. A stub domain computer requests contact with an outside host.

3. The local router receives a packet from the stub domain host.

4. After routing and verifying the packet for translation, the inside local address and port number (of the stub domain host) are recorded in the address translation table. The inside local address is then replaced with the router's external IP address, and the original source port is swapped for a port in the router's reserved port range. This range is exclusively used for NAT masquerading. The new IP address and port are recorded and mapped to the original address and port in the address translation table.

5. The packet is then sent to the external network using the router's newly issued IP address and port number. The destination host is not aware of the mapped IP address and port information for packet delivery.

6. The destination host transmits a reply packet to the router on the source network. The router inspects the inbound packet's port address and consults the address translation table to determine the mapped IP address and port information for packet delivery. If no match is found, the packet is discarded. If a match is found, the destination address and port are stripped out of the packet header and replaced with the mapped address found in the NAT lookup table. The packet is then forwarded to the assigned host.

7. This process continues until communications between the two systems terminate. Communications may be interrupted due to a certain time period of inactivity between the two hosts. A timer is used and is reset after each address translation lookup, and the timeout countdown begins. If an entry is not consulted in the specified amount of elapsed time, the entry is removed from the lookup table.

**Book VI
Chapter 3**

Introducing
Network Address
Translation (NAT)

Configuring NAT

As with all network security mitigation methods, proper planning is necessary when implementing NAT.

Keep these key concepts in mind when deploying NAT:

✦ **Define inside and outside interfaces:** Decide which interfaces need to be configured for NAT. Find out on which interfaces the stub hosts are located, and whether multiple interfaces require configuration. Generally, inside interfaces are considered internal networks, and outside interfaces are thought of as external networks. NAT uses the `ip nat inside` and the `ip nat outside` commands to configure the router's interfaces.

✦ **Define the purpose:** Figure out which stub hosts require access to which external resources. Decide which traffic will be allowed access to which resources back inside the private network. Maybe TCP traffic redirection to an alternate port or IP address is required. For example, a Web server may have been reconfigured with a new IP address. NAT can be deployed to allow nonupdated clients continued access using the old IP address until they are reconfigured by the system administrator. This can allow uninterrupted network services to continue during network redesign phases.

✦ **Choose the method:** Review the purpose of NAT deployment. Select one address translation method, or a combination approach of static, dynamic, and/or NAT overloading.

✦ **Implement NAT:** Proper configuration and verification procedures must be followed to ensure correct operation of NAT. The procedures to implement and manage NAT are discussed in the following sections.

Configuring static NAT

Determining inside and outside interfaces is the most important part of any NAT deployment. The configuration differs depending on the type of deployment selected. For static NAT, entries are created manually by the administrator in the address translation table.

Here is an example of adding static NAT entries in the IOS:

1. **Configure the inside interface:**

```
Router(config)#int fastethernet0/0
Router(config-if)#ip address 192.168.1.1 255.255.255.0
Router(config-if)#ip nat inside
```

Assign an internal private IP address to an interface, and designate it as the NAT inside interface. This interface will be used by hosts on the stub domain to access external resources made possible by the outside interface.

2. **Configure the outside interface:**

```
Router(config)#int serial0/0
Router(config-if)#ip address 204.218.10.1 255.255.255.0
Router(config-if)#ip nat outside
```

I have assigned a publicly registered IP address to the serial interface, and designated the interface as the NAT outside interface.

3. **Specify IP addresses to static NAT:**

```
Router(config)#ip nat inside source static 192.168.10.10 204.218.10.10
Router(config)#ip nat inside source static 192.168.10.11 204.218.10.11
Router(config)#ip nat inside source static 192.168.10.12 204.218.10.12
Router(config)#ip nat inside source static 192.168.10.13 204.218.10.13
```

The `ip nat inside source static` and `ip nat outside source static` commands enable NAT on the inside or outside interface. Four inside local stub domain hosts (192.168.10.10–192.168.10.13) now have individual static NAT mappings to corresponding inside global addresses (204.218.10.10–204.218.10.13). These IP addresses are added to the NAT address translation table statically by executing the four previous commands. The four internal hosts now have access to external resources (Internet) and are also permanently reachable from public networks. The four hosts remain reachable until these commands are removed from the router's IOS using the `no ip nat inside source static` command shown here:

```
Router(config)#no ip nat inside source static 192.168.10.10 204.218.10.10
Router(config)#no ip nat inside source static 192.168.10.11 204.218.10.11
Router(config)#no ip nat inside source static 192.168.10.12 204.218.10.12
Router(config)#no ip nat inside source static 192.168.10.13 204.218.10.13
```

Static configurations may coexist with other types of NAT configurations simultaneously, such as dynamic NAT or Port Address Translation.

Using another example, perhaps an organization has configured the company Web server to listen to internal traffic on TCP port 8080. The administrator would like to make the Web server accessible to public users on standard port 80. The administrator creates a static NAT entry for the Web server (200.100.100.3):

1. **Configure the inside interface:**

```
Router(config)#int fastethernet0/0
Router(config-if)#ip address 200.100.100.1 255.255.255.0
Router(config-if)#ip nat inside
```

Assign the private IP address to an interface. The `ip nat inside` command denotes the NAT inside interface. This interface will be used by hosts on the stub domain to access external resources made possible by the outside interface.

2. **Configure the outside interface:**

```
Router(config)#int serial0/0
Router(config-if)#ip address 204.218.10.1 255.255.255.0
Router(config-if)#ip nat outside
```

I will now assign a publicly registered IP address to the serial interface, and designate it as the NAT outside interface.

3. **Specify the IP addresses and TCP ports of the Web server:**

```
Router(config)#ip nat inside source static tcp 200.100.100.3 8080
    200.100.100.3 80 extendable
```

This command configures a static NAT mapping for the Web server IP address 200.100.100.3.

This example shows the Web server IP address as both the internal address and the public address. All traffic that uses the TCP source port number 8080 from the inside network is translated to port 80 for outgoing traffic (to the outside network). Likewise, port 80 traffic going from the outside to the inside network is translated to the destination port number of 8080. The extendable keyword specifies that port forwarding is required and extends the translation to another port.

Configuring dynamic NAT

Configuring dynamic NAT differs from static NAT in two ways:

✦ No static IP assignments are given by the administrator. All inside global addresses are issued dynamically from a pool of addresses using the `ip nat pool` command.

✦ The static NAT address translation table fills as each entry is input by the administrator. With dynamic NAT, this table remains empty until traffic starts passing through the interface. As traffic is processed, entries to the NAT table are recorded. These entries stay in the NAT table until a specified *timeout value* is reached, either 24 hours for TCP or 5 minutes for UDP. During this timeout value, the translated (inside global) address is not available for any other host and remains assigned until the timeout value expires. Remember that static table entries remain in effect indefinitely until they are manually removed by the administrator.

The timeout value can be set in the IOS by using the `ip nat translation timeout` *timeout value*, `ip nat translation tcp-timeout` *timeout value*, or `ip nat translation udp-timeout` *timeout value* command.

Here's how to configure dynamic Network Address Translation on a Cisco router for two stub domains that require Internet access:

1. **Configure the inside interfaces:**

```
Router(config)#int fastethernet0/0
Router(config-if)#ip address 192.168.1.1 255.255.255.0
Router(config-if)#ip nat inside
Router(config)#int fastethernet1/0
Router(config-if)#ip address 192.168.2.1 255.255.255.0
Router(config-if)#ip nat inside
```

Assign an internal private IP address to each Ethernet interface, and designate both as NAT inside interfaces. This allows stub domain hosts on both interfaces to access external resources made possible by the outside interface.

2. **Configure the outside interface:**

```
Router(config)#int serial0/0
Router(config-if)#ip address 204.218.9.1 255.255.255.0
Router(config-if)#ip nat outside
```

I have assigned a publicly registered IP address to the serial interface, and designated the interface as the NAT outside interface.

3. **Configure the NAT address pool:**

```
Router(config)#ip nat pool DYN_POOL 204.218.10.1 204.218.11.254 netmask
    255.255.254.0
```

The `ip nat pool` command defines the pool name (DYN_POOL) and IP address pool range (204.218.10.1–204.218.11.254). The pool range must contain one or more IP publicly registered and routable IP addresses. The `netmask` parameter specifies the valid subnet mask for the IP address. The `prefix-length /13` syntax may also be used in its place.

The `ip nat inside` and `ip nat outside` commands are issued in interface configuration mode and specify which interface is performing which role in address translation. The `ip nat pool` command is used in global configuration mode to define a pool of IP addresses for NAT.

4. **Create the ACL:**

```
Router(config)#ip access-list 1 permit 192.168.1.0 0.0.0.255
Router(config)#ip access-list 1 permit 192.168.2.0 0.0.0.255
```

This standard ACL permits NAT services to all hosts on the private 192.168.1.0 and 192.168.2.0 networks.

5. **Assign the ACL to the NAT address pool:**

```
Router(config)#ip nat inside source list 1 pool DYN_POOL
```

Executing this command, all hosts specified in ACL 1 now have access to the publicly registered pool of IP addresses and are enabled for address translation services.

Using another example, I now want to limit the number of hosts allowed access to the Internet. I have chosen to allow a limited number of hosts from each stub domain access to the dynamic address pool. Here's how I configure this access:

1. **Configure the inside and outside interfaces:**

```
Router(config)#int fastethernet0/0
Router(config-if)#ip address 192.168.1.1 255.255.255.0
Router(config-if)#ip nat inside

Router(config)#int fastethernet1/0

Router(config-if)#ip address 192.168.2.1 255.255.255.0
Router(config-if)#ip nat inside

Router(config)#int serial0/0
Router(config-if)#ip address 204.218.10.1 255.255.255.0
Router(config-if)#ip nat outside
```

2. **Configure the NAT address pool for a specified range:**

```
Router(config)#ip nat pool DYN_POOL 204.218.10.101 204.218.10.130 prefix-
    length /24
```

Again, the `ip nat pool` command defines the pool name (DYN_POOL), but in this example, the IP address pool range (204.218.10.101–204.218.10.130) has been reduced. I only have 30 available IP addresses to issue to requesting hosts. I can now choose which hosts to grant NAT services to by configuring the ACL.

3. **Create the ACL:**

```
Router(config)#ip access-list 1 permit 192.168.1.0 0.0.0.15
Router(config)#ip access-list 1 permit 192.168.2.0 0.0.0.15
```

This standard ACL permits NAT services to the first 15 hosts on each of the private 192.168.1.0 and 192.168.2.0 networks. All other hosts on the two private networks are denied NAT services.

4. **Assign the ACL to the NAT address pool and add the static route:**

```
Router(config)#ip nat inside source list 1 pool DYN_POOL
```

Configuring Port Address Translation (PAT)

Another popular method of NAT configuration is Port Address Translation. This method is usually implemented when only one routable IP address is available for use. PAT allows all inside local hosts to use one inside global address and separate ports. With *overloading,* each address can theoretically support up to 65,536 ports. Here's how to configure NAT overloading on a Cisco router:

1. **Configure the inside interface:**

```
Router(config)#int fastethernet0/0
Router(config-if)#ip address 192.168.1.1 255.255.255.0
Router(config-if)#ip nat inside
```

**Book VI
Chapter 3**

An internal private IP address is assigned to the Fast Ethernet interface and designated as the NAT inside interface.

2. **Configure the outside interface:**

```
Router(config)#int serial0/0
Router(config-if)#ip address 204.218.10.1 255.255.255.0
Router(config-if)#ip nat outside
```

Introducing
Network Address
Translation (NAT)

The inside global IP address is assigned to the serial interface and designated as the NAT outside interface.

3. **Configure the NAT address pool:**

```
Router(config)#ip nat pool PATOVLD 204.218.10.254 204.218.10.254 netmask
   255.255.255.0
```

The pool name (PATOVLD) and single IP address pool range (204.218.10.254) is specified. This means that all private network hosts will use the same IP address to communicate with any external networks.

Each host is provided multiplexing capabilities and uses different ports to separate network traffic. This is achieved by appending different port numbers to the end of the IP address, creating a unique connection.

4. **Create the ACL:**

```
Router(config)#ip access-list 1 permit 192.168.1.0 0.0.0.255
```

This standard ACL permits NAT services to all hosts on the private 192.168.1.0 network.

5. **Assign the ACL to the NAT address pool:**

```
Router(config)#ip nat inside source list 1 pool PATOVLD overload
```

All hosts on the 192.168.1.0 network now have access to the single routable IP address specified in the pool name PATOVLD and are enabled for address translation services. The overload syntax simply states that NAT translations will be overloaded. This allows multiple inside local addresses to be translated using one shared inside global address.

Be wary of any questions that involve the NAT pool and network hosts that are not able to access the Internet. If the overload keyword is not specified, always verify that enough IP addresses are available in the NAT pool to accommodate all hosts!

Managing NAT

As with access control lists, Network Address Translation may be managed from either the command-line interface (CLI) or the Security Device Manager (SDM). The SDM provides an easy-to-use graphical user interface that may be preferred by some administrators, compared to the standard CLI. Keep in mind that all SDM configuration parameters are sent to the IOS as a series of CLI commands and function identically. Now I examine a few ways to monitor and troubleshoot NAT.

Monitoring and troubleshooting NAT

One of the biggest obstacles a network administrator faces when connectivity issues arise is determining the source of network translation problems. When communication failure occurs in a NAT-enabled environment, address translation services are often the first area inspected for faults. The Cisco IOS provides tools that an administrator can use to narrow the suspected culprits and rule out any NAT-induced problems. How do administrators rule out NAT? These steps can help:

1. **Review the configuration.** For what purpose is NAT implemented, and what is it supposed to accomplish?

2. **Review the translation table.** Make sure address translation is working by consulting the NAT address translation table for translation entries. This verification process of actual table entries tells the administrator that translation is occurring.

3. **Use CLI commands.** Use the `show` and `debug` commands to verify that NAT is executing translations. Some of these popular commands are:

   - `debug ip nat`: Used to troubleshoot NAT and to verify NAT is operating correctly. The display output of this command contains IP packet translation information.

- `show ip nat statistics`: Displays statistics and a general overview associated with NAT translation. Information provided by the `show ip nat statistics` command includes ACL packet matches, ACL packet mismatches, and inside and outside interface information.

- `show ip nat translations`: Allows the administrator to view the contents of the address translation table. The type of protocol in use, along with inside local, inside global, outside local, and outside global addresses are given for all active NAT translations.

- `show ip route`: Gives a listing of the IP routing table.

- `clear ip nat translation`: Erases dynamic NAT translations from the translation table. Keep in mind that static entries must be removed manually.

4. **Follow the packet.** Analyze the path that the packet takes and verify the functionality of established routes to ensure proper traffic flow.

Book VI
Chapter 3

Introducing
Network Address
Translation (NAT)

Using the CLI commands

Earlier in the chapter, you configured static NAT, dynamic NAT, and Port Address Translation. Now I take a look at the commands used to verify and troubleshoot the NAT implementation. First, use the `show ip nat translations` command to verify whether NAT is functioning properly:

```
Router#show ip nat translations
Pro  Inside global     Inside local   Outside local   Outside global
---   204.218.10.1      192.168.1.1    ---             ---
```

The results of the `show` command indicate that a one-to-one mapping exists. Now you see how this same command displays the results for Port Address Translation (PAT):

```
Router#show ip nat translations
Pro   Inside global      Inside local       Outside local       Outside global
tcp   204.218.10.1:5000  192.168.1.14:5000  200.200.200.5:25    200.200.200.5:25
tcp   204.218.10.1:2320  192.168.1.15:2320  200.200.200.5:25    200.200.200.5:25
```

Notice that the inside local address is unique but the inside global address remains the same and is shared by all hosts. Only the TCP port number changes to facilitate individual multiplexed communications.

If the `show ip nat translations` command results display a blank table, the interfaces are not properly configured for NAT.

The next step is to verify that translation is actually taking place. To verify translation, use the `show ip nat statistics` command. Another troubleshooting aid, the `clear ip nat statistics` command, may be used to reset all NAT statistics. These two commands provide a helpful method of troubleshooting NAT problems. The following code shows how this works:

```
Router#show ip nat statistics
 Total active translations: 1 (1 static, 0 dynamic; 0 extended)
 Outside interfaces:
 Serial0
 Inside interfaces:
 Ethernet 0 Ethernet1
 Hits: 15  Misses: 0
 Expired translations: 0
 Dynamic mappings:
 -- Inside Source
 access-list 1 pool dyn_pool refcount 0
 pool test: netmask 255.255.255.0
 start 204.218.10.101 end 204.218.10.135
 type generic, total addresses 35, allocated 0 (0%), misses 0
```

Now clear all NAT statistics by running the `clear ip nat statistics` command. Notice that the hit counter resets to 0:

```
Router#clear ip nat statistics
Router#show ip nat statistics
 Total active translations: 1 (1 static, 0 dynamic; 0 extended)
 Outside interfaces:
 Serial0
 Inside interfaces:
 Ethernet 0 Ethernet1
 Hits: 0  Misses: 0
 Expired translations: 0
 Dynamic mappings:
 -- Inside Source
 access-list 1 pool dyn_pool refcount 0
 pool test: netmask 255.255.255.0
 start 204.218.210.101 end 204.218.210.135
 type generic, total addresses 35, allocated 0 (0%), misses 0
```

The general idea is to clear all NAT statistics and then generate traffic through the translated interfaces. Using a ping or other traffic-generation method, this can advance the hit counter and shows that traffic is being translated by executing the `show ip nat statistics` command again.

Next, verify that the router has the properly assigned routes to reach all outside interfaces:

```
Router#show ip route
Codes: C - connected, S - static, I - IGRP, R - RIP, M - mobile, B - BGP
       D - EIGRP, EX - EIGRP external, O - OSPF, IA - OSPF inter area
       N1 - OSPF NSSA external type 1, N2 - OSPF NSSA external type 2
       E1 - OSPF external type 1, E2 - OSPF external type 2, E - EGP
       i - IS-IS, L1 - IS-IS level-1, L2 - IS-IS level-2, ia - IS-IS inter area
       * - candidate default, U - per-user static route, o - ODR
       P - periodic downloaded static route

Gateway of last resort is not set
```

```
       204.218.10.0/24 is subnetted, 4 subnets
C         204.218.11.0 is directly connected, Serial0.4
C         204.218.9.0 is directly connected, Serial0.5
C         204.218.10.0is directly connected, Serial0.6
C         204.218.17.0 is directly connected, Ethernet0
```

Another useful command is the `debug ip nat` or `debug ip nat detailed` option. The `debug` command should be run as a last resort and uses a large amount of router resources. This can prove disastrous to network performance in a production environment, so use it only when absolutely necessary.

Configuring NAT with the Cisco SDM GUI

The Cisco Router and Security Device Manager (SDM) GUI provides an easy-to-use method of configuring various key router components such as Network Address Translation. Using the SDM *NAT Configuration Wizard,* you can:

✦ View and manage NAT rules and address pools

✦ Designate interfaces as inside or outside

✦ Set translation timeouts

Prep Test

1 **On which type of router should NAT always be implemented?**

- **A** ○ Departmental router
- **B** ○ Perimeter or border router
- **C** ○ Internal router
- **D** ○ External router

2 **NAT overload allows what important feature?**

- **A** ○ Many-to-many static address translation
- **B** ○ One-to-one Port Address Translation
- **C** ○ One-to-many dynamic Port Address Translation
- **D** ○ Static Port Address Translation

3 **What is the function of the** `ip nat pool quizme 192.168.10.100 192.168.10.200 netmask 255.255.255.0` **command?**

- **A** ○ Defines static NAT range
- **B** ○ Defines dynamic inside local and inside global addresses
- **C** ○ Defines PAT port pool ranges
- **D** ○ Defines a pool of IP addresses for dynamic NAT

4 **Which type of NAT is used when permanent entries are needed?**

- **A** ○ Overloading
- **B** ○ PAT
- **C** ○ Static NAT
- **D** ○ Dynamic NAT

5 **What is the inside global address?**

- **A** ○ A host IP address
- **B** ○ A unique IP address located on an internal network
- **C** ○ A nonroutable private IP address
- **D** ○ A publicly registered address representing an inside host to external networks

6 **What is the purpose of the overload keyword?**

- **A** ○ To share one public IP address with many private hosts
- **B** ○ To configure dynamic port addresses
- **C** ○ To enable static, dynamic, and PAT interoperability
- **D** ○ To share many IP addresses in a pool range

7 The `show ip nat translations` **command would be useful in revealing which type of NAT problem?**

A ○ Unconfigured interfaces
B ○ No route to destination
C ○ Not enough IP addresses
D ○ Invalid pool range

8 **Which types of Network Address Translation require ACLs? (Choose all that apply.)**

A ○ Static NAT
B ○ Dynamic NAT
C ○ PAT
D ○ Overloading

9 **What is the source address of a packet originating from an external network?**

A ○ Inside global
B ○ Outside global
C ○ Inside local
D ○ Outside local

10 **Which method does PAT use to update the address translation table?**

A ○ Manually.
B ○ Dynamically.
C ○ Statically.
D ○ PAT does not update the NAT table.

11 **What is the standard timeout value for a dynamic TCP entry in the address translation table?**

A ○ 24 hours
B ○ 5 minutes
C ○ 5 hours
D ○ 2 minutes

Answers

1 **B.** Perimeter or border router. NAT should always be implemented on the router that resides between the Internet and the internal private network. Review *"Purpose of NAT."*

2 **C.** One-to-many dynamic Port Address Translation. PAT, or dynamic NAT over-loading, allows many hosts using private IP addresses to share one publicly registered IP address. See *"Types of Network Address Translation."*

3 **D.** The `ip nat pool` command defines a pool of IP addresses for Dynamic NAT. Refer to *"Configuring dynamic NAT."*

4 **C.** Static NAT. Static NAT allows the administrator to specify manual NAT entries and input them directly in the IOS. These static commands remain in effect until they are removed using the `no ip nat inside source static` or `no ip nat outside source static` command. Read *"Configuring static NAT."*

5 **D.** An inside global address is a publicly registered address that represents an inside host to external networks. See *"Local and global addresses."*

6 **A.** Overloading allows many private hosts to share a single IP address. Communication is performed individually by TCP port multiplexing. Take a look at *"Configuring Port Address Translation (PAT)."*

7 **A.** Unconfigured interfaces. If the `show ip nat translations` command output displays a blank table, the interfaces are not properly configured for NAT. Look over *"Managing NAT."*

8 **B, C, D.** Dynamic NAT, PAT, also known as NAT overloading use access lists to define networks and hosts for translation. Static NAT is input manually by the system administrator and does not require an ACL. Check out *"Configuring NAT."*

9 **B.** Outside global address. A packet originating from the outside network has a source address of the outside global address. Read *"Operational Flow of NAT."*

10 **B.** Dynamically. The inside local address and port number are recorded in the address translation table, which is then replaced with the router's external IP address. The original source port is swapped for a port in the router's reserved port range. The new IP address and port are mapped to the original address and port in the address translation table. Review *"How overloading (PAT) operates."*

11 **A.** A standard TCP entry is held in the NAT table 24 hours. UDP entries are held for 5 minutes. Read *"Configuring dynamic NAT."*

Chapter 4: Introducing Virtual Private Networks (VPNs)

Exam Objectives

- ✓ Understanding Virtual Private Networks
- ✓ Identifying VPN types
- ✓ Understanding VPN implementation methods
- ✓ Creating Virtual Private Networks using Cisco SDM
- ✓ Examining SDM quality of service features
- ✓ Reviewing VPN Management

Mobile users and telecommuters today make up an increasingly larger part of the corporate workforce. To provide corporate intranet resources to mobile employees, organizations are requiring more flexible, elaborate, and wider connectivity options. At the same time, companies attempt to remain cost conscious, eliminating any unnecessary and wasteful forms of communications. This balancing act between flexibility and cost has turned corporate attention away from expensive leased lines and Frame Relay circuits to more cost-effective and dynamic alternatives.

Rather than implementing dedicated lines that prove to be a huge financial burden, Virtual Private Networks (VPNs) provide companies with a secure connectivity solution between corporate sites. A VPN is a private network established using a public network infrastructure, such as the Internet. Remote users may access corporate LAN resources by connecting directly to local ISPs, thereby reducing long-distance telephone charges. By dismissing cost-intensive and highly inflexible communications methods for cheaper, more robust, and manageable solutions, the need for VPNs soon becomes very clear.

Purpose of VPNs

The main purpose of Virtual Private Networks is to provide a cost-effective, secure, and highly scalable means of connecting remote sites, while maintaining an acceptable level of performance. VPNs use the existing Internet infrastructure to establish links between corporate sites, placing the burden of data delivery on local and remote ISPs. Because the Internet is an open, public resource, sensitive corporate data must be protected. VPNs provide methods to ensure that data is protected from eavesdropping, manipulation, and outright theft.

VPNs prove to be more dynamic and flexible than dedicated leased lines by not requiring permanent links between corporate network endpoints. Establishing this virtual connection between two endpoints is known as *tunneling.* This dynamic, or virtual, tunneling method allows VPN connections to be established as they are needed, and then terminated after data transmission is complete, thus saving corporate bandwidth.

While implementing VPN security does provide valuable safeguards against attack, it does not necessarily mitigate all network risks. The effectiveness of the security relies on the strength of the implementation. By attacking a misconfigured VPN gateway or flaws in encryption algorithms and software, malicious users may intercept and decode encrypted keys or data traffic, or forge the identity of a legitimate user. VPNs offer a wide variety of configuration options and must be designed and implemented with a meticulous eye for security.

The most critical requirement when implementing corporate site-to-site connectivity using public infrastructures is security mitigation. Methods must be enforced to derail malicious users from accessing confidential data. To be effective, VPNs must provide secure lines of communications by implementing the following security measures:

✦ **Access control:** Denying unauthorized user access to the corporate network. Connections may be controlled and verified by maintaining a user accounts database on a VPN server. This method is susceptible to keylogging, password cracking, and other attacks and should not be relied on as a sole source of security.

✦ **Data origin authentication:** Method of verifying sender identity to prevent spoofing or other attacks. Data origin authentication uses IP Security (IPsec), certificates, or the exchange of pre-shared keys.

✦ **Data confidentiality:** Because VPNs transfer private data over public networks, enforcing data encryption and encapsulation techniques is essential for data confidentiality. Encryption allows encoding and decoding of data transmissions by the sending and receiving machines only, which ensures that sensitive corporate data is not copied or read by unauthorized users. Data tunneling may be used to hide the originator of the source packet. Popular encryption protocols include IPsec, PPTP, and L2TP.

✦ **Data integrity:** Ensuring that source data reaches the proper destination unaltered while in transit over public infrastructures. IPsec provides security mechanisms to ensure that data packets are not tampered with or changed. If any changes to the data or packet are detected, the packet is discarded.

The encryption algorithm and encapsulation protocol are two vital components that must be addressed when planning a VPN.

Type of VPNs

Three primary models of VPN architecture are known as remote-access, site-to-site, and business partner VPNs. Each type should be deployed based on the role the VPN will play in the organization:

Book VI
Chapter 4

Introducing Virtual
Private Networks
(VPNs)

✦ **Remote-access VPNs:** Also known as a user-to-LAN or host-to gateway VPN. Remote-access VPNs provide company resources (by virtually extending an organization's work environment) to mobile users who connect from remote locations. Remote-access VPNs are client-initiated, secure connections that enable data transfer between a third-party service provider and the corporate network. Remote-access VPNs function by installing special software on the client computer, allowing an encrypted, authenticated session to the remote LAN's VPN gateway.

✦ **Site-to-site VPNs:** Connect fixed sites using existing public networks as the main connectivity backbone. Site-to-site VPNs are also known as gateway-to-gateway VPNs or intranets. Links are established between fixed sites (such as branch offices) that belong to the same company, but in geographically different locations. Each site may use separate and different Internet connections to establish a seamless virtual connection between routers. Site-to-site VPNs use IPsec methods and provide an alternative to dedicated leased lines and Frame Relay circuits. To establish connectivity, a typical site-to-site deployment involves setting up a VPN gateway on each network. These two VPN gateways negotiate an IPsec connection and allow the passing of secure information between each other. This intranet connectivity is seamless to users and does not require installation of VPN client software.

✦ **Business partner VPNs:** Another type of secure site-to-site network known as an extranet VPN, which is used to connect corporate partner sites to their business partners or customers. IPsec-based security is ideal for extranet connectivity, due to the inexpensive and quick deployment possibilities of IPsec-based devices.

Choosing a VPN Implementation Method

IT managers typically have two choices to consider when deciding on a VPN implementation method, namely, *IPsec* and *Secure Socket Layer (SSL)*. IPsec-based VPNs enable encryption on any application by installing separate client software on every remote device requiring VPN access. SSL VPNs do not require client software and work using any standard HTTP Web browser. IPsec is used more for site-to-site VPNs, while SSL is better suited for remote client access VPNs.

VPNs feature *symmetric* and *asymmetric* cryptography. Symmetric cryptography uses the same key to encrypt and decrypt data. Also known as public/private key cryptography, asymmetric cryptography uses separate keys for encryption and decryption, or to digitally sign or verify a signature. Symmetric cryptography is generally used for encrypting the majority of VPN traffic. Some popular algorithms used in implementing symmetric cryptography are Digital Encryption Standard (DES), Triple DES (3DES), Advanced Encryption Standard (AES), Hash Message Authentication Code (HMAC), message digest algorithm 5 (MD5), and Secure Hash Algorithm (SHA-1). Asymmetric cryptography uses two separate keys to encrypt and decrypt data. One key is used to encrypt or digitally sign the data. The second key is used to decrypt the data or verify a digital signature. Only a matching private key from the same user is able to decode the public key encryption. IPsec employs both symmetric and asymmetric cryptography. Identity authentication is performed by asymmetric cryptography, and symmetric cryptography is used for protecting the actual data.

Using IPsec

Internet Protocol Security (IPsec) is a suite of protocols that provides security mitigation features at the Internet layer of the TCP/IP model (the OSI model's network layer). IPsec enforces data confidentiality, integrity, encryption, and authentication features between communication endpoints across IP-based networks.

IPsec enables organizations to establish secure VPN links with remote branch offices and mobile users, saving the costs of expensive ATM or Frame Relay WAN links.

The main goal of IPsec is to provide communications protection. To use IP security, devices must be deemed IPsec compliant. These IPsec-compliant devices implement security measures by sharing *certificates* or *keys* using either 56-bit (single DES) or 168-bit (triple DES) encryption. Advanced Encryption Standard (AES) is another algorithm used by IPsec to encrypt user data.

IPsec provides security for IP packets only!

IPsec is based on the following cryptographic technologies:

✦ **Diffie-Hellman key exchange:** Method of digital encryption used between source and destination peer computers to share a private (secret) key over a public (insecure) network. This key is then used to decode further communications between hosts.

✦ **Public key cryptography:** Digitally signing Diffie-Hellman key exchanges to verify the identity of communications partners, which helps prevent man-in-the-middle attacks.

✦ **Data Encryption Standard (DES):** A secret encryption algorithm shared between hosts using a 56-bit cipher key.

✦ **Keyed hash algorithms:** Use Hash Message Authentication Code (HMAC), MD5, and SHA-1 algorithms to verify authenticity and integrity of data packets. Keyed hash algorithms combine cryptographic hash functions with a secret key for making calculations.

✦ **Digital certificates:** Validate the identity of a sending host and enable the receiver to encode and send a reply. Digital certificates contain identification information contained in a public key, which is obtained from an issuing certificate authority (CA).

Three algorithms used to encrypt user data in an IPsec VPN framework are DES, AES, and 3DES.

IPsec advantages are as follows:

✦ **Performance:** Only IP packets traversing public (insecure) networks are encrypted. This provides high performance by only encrypting necessary data between insecure networks.

✦ **Network layer security:** IPsec operates at the network layer and does not require modification of TCP/IP applications to secure them.

✦ **Scalability:** IPsec VPNs may be implemented over any IP-capable network backbone such as the Internet. Simple deployment also provides organizations with operational cost reduction benefits.

✦ **Versatile:** Implements various security mechanisms such as data authentication, encryption, digital integrity checking, and replay protection, which prevents duplication of old transactions and mitigates denial of service attacks.

✦ **Universal acceptance:** IPsec is an industry-recognized IETF standard and is supported by most operating systems.

✦ **Application independence:** IPsec is transparent to applications (and upper OSI layers) and is not assigned to any one specific application.

IPsec disadvantages are as follows:

✦ **Performance:** IPsec may require large amounts of processing power on VPN endpoints (gateways) to encrypt, decrypt, and authenticate traffic.

✦ **Security:** Because IPsec relies on public keys, security mitigation depends on secure key management. Compromised security keys eliminate the security integrity and benefits of IPsec. Also, vulnerabilities existing at the IP layer of the remote network can be inherited by the corporate network through the IPsec tunnel.

IPsec VPN best practices

✔ Establish an IPsec deployment plan. Create and test each policy thoroughly before deploying in a production environment.

✔ Encryption must be enabled to provide confidentiality protection for traffic traversing VPNs.

✔ For stronger authentication, use certificates instead of pre-shared keys.

✔ VPNs should always provide data integrity protection by implementing a data integrity algorithm such as HMAC-SHA-1 or HMAC-MD5.

✔ A VPN must use an encryption algorithm such as 128-bit AES or 168-bit 3DES to provide VPN security mitigation. 56-bit standard DES is vulnerable to attack and is generally not recommended.

✔ Do not allow unsecured communications from public, remote-site VPNs. Make sure that security policies are tightened as much as possible.

✔ A VPN should feature replay protection, which allows each transaction (or packet) to be processed only once, regardless of the number of times it is received.

✔ The maximum value for IKE lifetime security associations (SAs) settings should be 24 hours. Maximum IPsec SA values should be 8 hours.

✦ **Complexity:** The vast configuration options of IPsec make it very flexible, but also overly complex. Configuration errors can expose the corporate network to unnecessary security risks and introduce weaknesses in the VPN.

✦ **Firewall restrictions:** Connecting to an organization's own network from an off-site location may not be possible due to corporate firewall restrictions (blocking IPsec-specific UDP ports).

✦ **Management:** IPsec employs digital signature authentication, which relies on a public key infrastructure (PKI). PKI requires considerable implementation planning and administrative management. The majority of IPsec VPN solutions have third-party hardware and software installation requirements. IPsec client software is required on each computer that needs access to an IPsec-enabled VPN. This is both an advantage (increased security) and a disadvantage (financial cost and extra VPN management).

Using Secure Socket Layer (SSL)

SSL operates at Layer 4 (transport) of the OSI model to authenticate and encrypt Hypertext Transfer Protocol (HTTP) traffic. By allowing secure VPN communications from any Web-based browser between the internal corporate network and the remote user, SSL eliminates the IPsec installation requirement of third-party VPN client software. Some advantages and disadvantages compared to IPsec are listed here.

SSL advantages are as follows:

✦ **Interoperability:** Part of TCP/IP de facto standard. SSL is supported by a variety of device and software manufacturers and allows operability between different vendors and applications.

✦ **Management:** SSL makes deployment, management, and administration tasks extremely simple and effective. No additional client software installation is required, which saves corporate dollars. Certificate management may also be reduced by installing certificates only on required servers.

✦ **Cost:** The clientless architecture of SSL allows a cheaper deployment alternative than IPsec-based VPNs. No special client software licenses or other expensive hardware is needed.

✦ **Granular structure:** Provides finely detailed client access policies based on user identity and profile. This allows an administrator to be very specific when defining the corporate VPN. SSL allows narrowing down authenticated user access to specific data, applications, and servers.

✦ **Firewall and NAT operation:** SSL uses TCP port 443 (HTTPS), which is open on most networks, allowing SSL VPNs to operate without extra administrative overhead.

✦ **Security:** By only allowing access to certain applications, security mitigation is increased, and the threat of attack is minimized.

✦ **Application layer functionality:** Unlike IPsec, which operates at the OSI network layer, SSL eliminates IP-based address management problems by operating at the transport layer and provides services to the upper layers.

SSL disadvantages are as follows:

✦ **Web-based:** Works best with HTTP, although in theory, SSL can support any application layer protocol because SSL operates at the transport layer below.

✦ **Security:** SSL user authentication is optional, which can introduce major network security breaches. Also, standard SSL encryption is 56-bit DES. IPsec uses DES, 3DES, or AES encryption. SSL provides access to the VPN gateway from any Web-enabled host, which introduces additional intruder vulnerabilities.

✦ **Performance:** Under extremely high loads, SSL VPNs may overtax the corporate VPN gateway. High CPU overhead may result from public key operations.

✦ **Additional software downloads:** Access to non-Web-enabled applications may require Java and Active X software downloads to function properly. This can cause a problem if a firewall is set to block access to these types of applications.

Using tunneling

Tunneling protocols provide secure paths between insecure networks and are used to transport multiple, dissimilar network protocols using the same transport mechanism. Tunneling enables VPN endpoints to transmit encrypted traffic between one another by encapsulating packets at peer layers or below. Tunneling is based on three primary components:

✦ The *passenger* protocol is the protocol being encapsulated, such as IP or IPX.

✦ The *transport* protocol is used to encapsulate the passenger protocol.

✦ The *carrier* protocol is the means of transporting both protocols.

Two popular types of point-to-point tunneling (carrier) protocols are *L2TP* and *GRE:*

✦ **Layer 2 Tunneling Protocol (L2TP):** Tunneling protocol created by Cisco and Microsoft that is derived from two older proprietary tunneling protocols, namely, Microsoft's Point-to-Point Tunneling Protocol (PPTP) and Cisco's Layer 2 Forwarding (L2F) technology. L2TP is a mechanism to tunnel Point-to-Point Protocol (PPP) traffic over non-PPP-enabled links using UDP port 1701. PPP is used for POTS and ISDN remote dialup access. Primarily used for remote-access VPNs, L2TP allows an L2TP-enabled client remote access into the corporate network. L2TP does not provide its own method of encryption and may rely on IPsec for security. Commonly called L2TP over IPsec, IPsec security is provided over the tunneling functionality of L2TP.

✦ **Generic routing encapsulation (GRE):** Tunneling protocol developed by Cisco that is used to transport data packets from one network through another network. This transport is accomplished by allowing other protocols to be encapsulated in IP tunnels. GRE is used with IPsec to transmit routing protocol data between gateways that IPsec does not natively support. For example, GRE encapsulates a clear text packet. Then IPsec encrypts the packet using either transport or tunnel mode. IPsec over GRE allows routing updates, which are generally multicast, to be passed over an encrypted link. IPsec cannot provide this functionality alone because it does not support multicast. Valid uses of GRE include transporting multiprotocol and IP multicast traffic between two sites that have only IP unicast connectivity. Because IPsec encryption only works on IP unicast frames, tunneling is a crucial VPN element. Tunneling allows the encryption and transportation of multiprotocol traffic across the VPN. Packets traversing between tunnel endpoints appear to the IP network as an IP unicast frame.

- *Pros:* Tunneling works with any type of network. Non-IP-based networks can be secured using tunneling.

- *Cons:* Not as ubiquitous as IPsec. Some devices and software may not work optimally with tunneling.

When establishing a VPN tunnel through public networks, data protection is extremely important to prevent unauthorized data interception. VPN clients and gateways must establish authentication for the channel to be deemed secure. Next, a secret key must be shared between communications partners and an encryption algorithm agreed upon.

Split tunneling

Another tunneling method, called *split tunneling,* allows traffic destined to the corporate network to be encrypted while other public traffic destined for the Internet remains unencrypted. Both the public and private tunnels are implemented through the VPN client on the same physical network connection. This reduces bandwidth usage by not routing public Internet traffic through the VPN server. The disadvantage is that the threat for a security breach is increased because the VPN is accessible through the public network.

Creating and Managing IPsec VPNs

Designing an IPsec-based VPN implementation plan is much like designing any other network deployment. Administrators must have a well-thought-out, step-by-step approach to integrating new technology into existing corporate architectures. This deployment is best realized in phases:

✦ **Identification:** Decide where and how security mitigation methods should be implemented. Identify which data, computer systems, and networks require protection.

✦ **Design:** Plan the architectural requirements, authentication methods, packet filtering, and cryptographic policies needed to deploy IPsec VPNs in the current infrastructure.

✦ **Testing:** Implement and verify design functionality in a test environment before actual corporate deployment.

✦ **Deployment:** After the design is verified, gradually deploy the IPsec-based VPN in stages throughout the enterprise.

✦ **Management:** IPsec provides a vast assortment of configuration options that must be carefully managed to reduce security vulnerabilities. Network inbound and outbound access points, along with all IPsec endpoints, must be carefully controlled.

Book VI
Chapter 4

Introducing Virtual
Private Networks
(VPNs)

It is important for network administrators to protect the network from remote users connecting from unsecured locations. The VPN should be configured to ensure that employees only have access to applications and network resources to which they are authorized. The access should be defined by the employees' job functions.

Introducing IPsec protocols

IPsec implementations use a number of different security protocols to provide transmission encryption, integrity, validation, and source authentication of data. These protocols can be divided into two different types: packet protocols and service protocols. The two major packet protocols, called *Encapsulating Security Payload (ESP)* and *Authentication Header (AH),* are used to provide data security. The primary service protocol is called *Internet Key Exchange (IKE).* The ESP and AH protocols may be implemented separately or together, using either transport or tunnel modes. IPsec is inserted below the IP layer, between the TCP/IP kernel and the link modules. IPsec inserts AH and ESP protocol headers on all outgoing traffic requiring security, also parsing and stripping IPsec headers from incoming IP packets.

A more detailed look at these protocols follows:

✦ **Encapsulating Security Payload (ESP):** Provides message content protection and data-tampering mitigation methods, ensuring confidentiality, authentication, and integrity of packets. ESP functions by encapsulating the entire data portion of the IP packet and adding its own header and trailer information. The ESP header contains the security and sequencing information. The contents of the ESP trailer include variable padding and optional authentication data.

✦ **Authentication Header (AH):** Provides data validation, authentication, and integrity services. AH does not support encryption as does ESP (therefore consuming less router resources) but provides greater IP layer security. AH is mainly concerned with the identity of data exchange partners, and generates hash signatures to ensure that no data modification has taken place during transmission.

✦ **Internet Key Exchange (IKE):** Provides key management and security association (SA) management using Diffie-Hellman key exchange. SAs are IPsec values applied to a connection. IKE authenticates sessions between hosts by using a pre-shared, cryptographic key, and is used to help provide IPsec-protected connections. Using IKE, keys may be validated and refreshed between users to ensure that only keyholders may access secured data.

Choosing transport mode versus tunnel mode

Because packet authentication and encryption are split into two separate functions, IPsec uses two different types of modes for packet transmission.

In tunnel mode, encryption and authentication are performed on the entire IP packet, which includes all Layer 3 data and header information. Tunnel mode also provides protection against an attacker analyzing network traffic. An attacker is only able to determine tunnel endpoints, not the source and destination addresses of tunneled packets.

Transport mode provides end-to-end security and lower overhead than tunnel mode. In transport mode, only the transport layer data, or IP payload, is encrypted and authenticated. This makes transport mode slightly faster than tunnel mode because no IP header encryption is performed on the packet. This also reduces the size of the packets. The disadvantage of not encrypting the IP header is that an attacker may be able to perform some traffic analysis. However, the Layer 4 header will be encrypted. Transport mode also allows devices on the public network to see the final source and destination address of the packet.

Figures 4-1 and 4-2 examine IPsec header and trailer information using transport and tunnel modes.

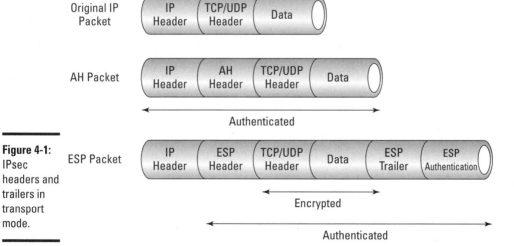

Figure 4-1: IPsec headers and trailers in transport mode.

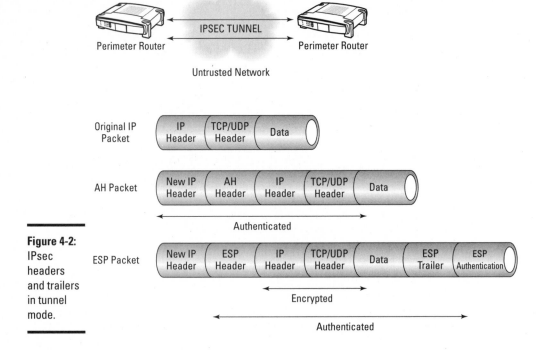

Figure 4-2:
IPsec
headers
and trailers
in tunnel
mode.

Configuring Cisco Virtual Private Networks

The Cisco IOS allows the creation of a remote-access VPN connection. By using the following commands, a secure TCP/IP connection may be established, allowing remote users to gain access to a central site. The basics of VPN configuration are as follows:

1. **Configure two interfaces.** Inside and outside interfaces are configured for VPN access. The inside interface is usually assigned to the private network, and the outside interface faces the public network.

2. **Configure the ISAKMP policy and enable ISAKMP on the outside interface.** The Internet Security Association and Key Management Protocol (ISAKMP), or IKE, is the protocol used to negotiate an IPsec security association between hosts. The negotiation process is split into two phases, Phase 1 and Phase 2:

   - *Phase 1:* Creates a tunnel used in protecting ISAKMP negotiation messages

   - *Phase 2:* Creates a tunnel used in protecting data traveling across the secure connection

3. **Configure the address pool.** Used to assign IP addresses to remote users.

4. **Configure remote users.** Defines the users who are allowed remote access.

5. **Create a transform set.** A combined authentication and encryption method agreed on by peers used to protect data transmission.

6. **Define the tunnel group.** A group of records that define connection policies. Two default tunnel groups exist:

   - *DefaultRAGroup:* The default IPsec remote-access tunnel group

   - *DefaultL2Lgroup:* The default IPsec LAN-to-LAN tunnel group

   These two groups are used during tunnel negotiation to configure default tunnel parameters for remote access and LAN-to-LAN tunnel groups when no specific tunnel group is identified. Three tunnel group attributes are required to establish a remote connection:

   - Set the connection type to IPsec remote access.

   - Configure the address assignment method.

   - Configure an authentication method.

7. **Define the crypto map.** Allows the security appliance to receive connections from peers that have unknown IP addresses, such as remote-access clients. Dynamic crypto map entries identify the connection's transform set. By enabling reverse routing, routing information may be discovered for connected clients and advertised with Routing Information Protocol (RIP) or Open Shortest Path First (OSPF).

8. **Save changes.**

Here is an example of a VPN configuration:

1. **In global configuration mode, configure the inside (private) and outside (public) interfaces:**

   ```
   Router(config)#interface ethernet0
   Router(config-if)#ip address 10.10.4.200 255.255.0.0
   Router(config-if)#nameif outside
   Router(config)#no shutdown
   ```

   First, specify the interface, IP address, and subnet mask. The `nameif` command assigns a name to the interface. The `no shutdown` command enables the interface. Repeat the same process to configure the inside interface.

2. **To verify peer identity, specify the authentication method to use:**

   ```
   Router(config)#isakmp policy 1 authentication pre-share
   ```

   The `isakmp policy` command specifies the terms of IKE negotiation. The priority value is set at 1, and the authentication method will use the pre-shared key.

3. **Specify the encryption type (3DES):**

   ```
   Router(config)#isakmp policy 1 encryption 3des
   ```

4. **Specify the HMAC method (SHA-1):**

   ```
   Router(config)#isakmp policy 1 hash sha
   ```

5. **Specify the Diffie-Hellman group number:**

   ```
   Router(config)#isakmp policy 1 group 2
   ```

6. **Set the encryption key lifetime value in seconds:**

   ```
   Router(config)#isakmp policy 1 lifetime 43200
   ```

7. **Apply ISAKMP to the interface (named "outside"):**

   ```
   Router(config)#isakmp enable outside
   ```

8. **Specify the address pool:**

   ```
   Router(config)#ip local pool dummypool 192.168.1.100-192.168.0.110
   ```

9. **Configure usernames and passwords to identify remote users:**

   ```
   Router(config)#username Dummy password 12345678
   ```

   Repeat this step for each user requiring access.

10. **Specify a transform set to protect data flow, which combines the encryption method and the authentication method:**

    ```
    Router(config)#crypto ipsec transform set DummySet esp-3des esp-md5-hmac
    ```

    The name of the transform set is DummySet. The encryption method is ESP-3DES, and the authentication method is ESP-MD5-HMAC.

11. **Define the tunnel group to establish tunnel connection policies:**

    ```
    Router(config)#tunnel-group dummygroup type ipsec-ra
    Router(config)#tunnel-group dummygroup general-attributes
    Router(config-general)#address-pool dummypool
    Router(config)#tunnel-group dummygroup ipsec-attributes
    Router(config-ipsec)#pre-shared-key 21acbn524896fxxf
    ```

    The first `tunnel-group` command sets the group name to `dummygroup` and the connection type to IPsec remote access. The next command sets the authentication method for the dummygroup and enters general-attributes mode. Next, the address pool is created. The last two statements enter ip-sec attributes mode and define the pre-shared key of 21acbn524896fxxf.

12. **Define the crypto map entries:**

```
Router(config)#crypto dynamic-map dyn1 1 set transform-set DummySet
Router(config)#crypto dynamic-map dyn1 1 set reverse-route
Router(config)#crypto map dummymap 1 ipsec-isakmp dynamic dyn1
Router(config)#crypto map dummymap interface outside
```

The first crypto dynamic map entry is named (dyn1) and identifies the transform set (DummySet). The `dynamic map set reverse-route` command enables reverse route injection (RRI) for the connection. RRI is used to populate the routing table for remote VPN clients. Next, the `crypto map` command is used to create a dynamic crypto map called dummymap, with a sequence number of 1. Finally, the dummymap is applied to the outside interface.

13. **Save changes:**

```
Router(config)#write memory
```

Creating a VPN with the Cisco Security Device Manager (SDM)

The Cisco SDM simplifies router and security configuration by assisting the administrator using several intelligent setup wizards. These wizards allow easy and efficient configuration of key router components such as Virtual Private Networks. Using the SDM Easy VPN Server Wizard, you can:

✦ Choose the router interface to configure as VPN server.

✦ Choose the preferred authentication method.

✦ Select the encryption and authentication algorithms.

✦ Select a method to exchange encryption keys.

✦ Choose the type of data protection in the VPN tunnel.

Enabling quality of service (QoS) in the VPN using Cisco SDM

QoS manages network resources to guarantee high quality data communication. QoS for VPNs examines packet headers and distinguishes the identity of packets before IPsec encryption, allowing more effective packet tunneling. QoS provides the means to prioritize network traffic based on the type of data and set bandwidth allocation limitations. The SDM QoS Wizard provides simple configuration flexibility for implementing QoS policies to prioritize outgoing traffic. Using the SDM QoS Wizard, you can:

✦ Select the outgoing interface on which you wish to apply a QoS policy. Here you want to enable QoS in your VPN: the interface you select is the same interface that you configured for VPN.

✦ Prioritize traffic based on its type.

✦ Set bandwidth allocation limits.

✦ Classify protocols in real time and business critical categories. You may enable more than one protocol on each router interface. This option allows you to prioritize your protocols based on business needs and service level agreements (SLAs).

✦ Enable Network-Based Application Recognition (NBAR) Protocol discovery for the interface.

Prep Test

1 Which key components must be considered when implementing data confidentiality using VPNs? (Choose two.)

A ○ Encryption

B ○ Compression

C ○ Privacy

D ○ Encapsulation

2 Which protocols are used to encapsulate traffic traversing a VPN tunnel? (Choose two.)

A ○ ATM

B ○ IPsec

C ○ PPTP

D ○ TCP

3 Which technology is used to prioritize important traffic?

A ○ IPsec

B ○ TCP

C ○ VPN

D ○ QoS

4 Which statements are true regarding split tunneling? (Choose two.)

A ○ A reduced security risk exists.

B ○ VPN server utilization is increased.

C ○ Traffic to intranet is encrypted.

D ○ Public traffic to the Internet is not encrypted.

5 Which methods allow an administrator to configure a secure VPN for remote home-to-office use? (Choose three.)

A ○ Create remote-access VPN

B ○ Create site-to-site VPN

C ○ Install VPN client on home computer

D ○ Use dedicated T1 leased line

E ○ Implement network management ACL, allowing only home IP address access to management ports on network devices

6 **Which protocols are known as packet protocols and provide data security? (Choose two.)**

A ○ GRE

B ○ L2TP

C ○ AH

D ○ ESP

7 **Which statements are true regarding transport versus tunnel mode? (Choose three.)**

A ○ Transport mode uses higher overhead than tunnel mode.

B ○ Transport mode implements end-to-end security.

C ○ Packet authentication and encryption are split into two separate functions.

D ○ Tunnel mode masks source and destination addresses.

E ○ Tunnel mode does not encrypt or authenticate packets.

8 **Which port does SSL use to establish VPN connectivity?**

A ○ 25

B ○ 443

C ○ 442

D ○ 8080

9 **Single DES and triple DES use which types of encryption?**

A ○ 56-bit (single DES) and 168-bit (triple DES) encryption

B ○ 48-bit (single DES) and 128-bit (triple DES) encryption

C ○ 64-bit (single DES) and 156-bit (triple DES) encryption

D ○ 24-bit (single DES) and 72-bit (triple DES) encryption

Answers

1 **A, D.** Encryption and encapsulation. VPN data confidentiality is provided by encryption and encapsulation methods. Review *"Purpose of VPNs."*

2 **B, C.** IPsec and PPTP. Both IPsec and PPTP are tunneling protocols used to encapsulate VPN traffic. Take a look at *"Using tunneling."*

3 **D.** QoS. Quality of service allows prioritization of traffic based on rules defined by the network administrator. Read *"Enabling quality of service (QoS) in the VPN with the Cisco SDM."*

4 **C, D.** Public Internet traffic is not encrypted, while private intranet traffic is encrypted. The VPN server is taxed less using split tunneling, although security risks are increased. Review *"Split tunneling."*

5 **A, C, E.** Create a remote access VPN, install client VPN software on the home PC, and design an access list that allows only authorized users access to specific ports on networking equipment. Read *"Type of VPNs"* and *"Creating and Managing IPsec VPNs."*

6 **C, D.** AH and ESP. The two major packet protocols, called Encapsulating Security Payload (ESP) and Authentication Header (AH), are used to provide data security. Review *"Introducing IPsec security protocols."*

7 **B, C, D.** Transport mode implements end-to-end security, packet authentication and encryption are split into two separate functions, and tunnel mode hides source and destination addresses. Refer to *"Choosing transport mode versus tunnel mode."*

8 **B.** 443. SSL uses TCP port 443 (HTTPS), which is open on most networks, allowing SSL VPNs to operate without extra administrative overhead. Review *"Using Secure Socket Layer (SSL)."*

9 **A.** 56-bit (single DES) and 168-bit (triple DES) encryption. Read *"Using IPsec."*

Book VII

Wide Area Networks (WAN)

Contents at a Glance

Chapter 1: Wide-Area Networking Basics

Exam Objectives

✔ Defining wide-area networking

✔ Explaining WAN connection types

✔ Describing WAN protocol encapsulation methods

✔ Introducing Cisco router cabling standards

✔ Identifying AUX and COM port connectors

✔ Understanding popular DSL technologies

✔ Recognizing the differences between DCE and DTE devices

Introducing WANs

A wide-area network (WAN) is a connection between two or more local-area networks (LANs) spanning across a large, spread-out geographical area. A single LAN is usually considered to be confined to the same building or office that does not communicate over public transportation methods. A metropolitan-area network (MAN) limits its communications to a specific city function or campus area, while a WAN uses dedicated leased lines from telephone companies to establish links between geographically dispersed LANs and/or MANs. WAN technologies operate at the three lower layers of the OSI model, namely, the network, data link, and physical layers.

The Internet is the best example of a WAN and is the largest public network on the planet. As you can see in Figure 1-1, private WANs are used to establish permanent communications links between company sites and branch offices. Using routers, traffic is managed and sent to the proper destination LAN. The traffic is then transferred to LAN switching devices until the data reaches the intended recipient. Private WANs may use a number of methods to connect to remote sites, such as dedicated telephone lines, ATM, Frame Relay, and satellite links. Private WANs may also use public networks to communicate. Setting up an encrypted VPN over a local ISP's DSL service or dialup connection is another cost-friendly alternative for secure communications.

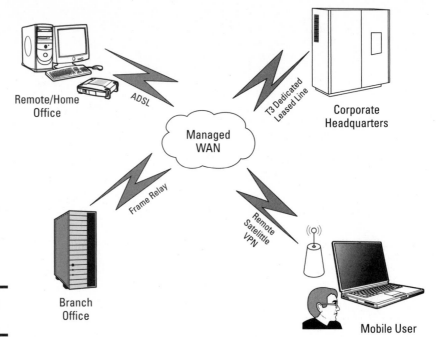

Figure 1-1:
WAN.

Purpose of WANs

A wide variety of options exist to interconnect remote LAN sites. LANs are brought together into WANs for the purpose of sharing network resources between authorized users and devices. Collaborative data and resource sharing between corporate sites and business partners allows WANs to globally interconnect any business.

Data terminal equipment (DTE) and data communications equipment (DCE)

Basic WAN connectivity between the subscriber and provider relies on two types of serial communications devices:

✦ Data terminal equipment (DTE)

✦ Data communications equipment (DCE), also known as data circuit terminating equipment

A DCE device is typically a modem known as either

• Terminal adapter/network termination 1 (TA/NT1)

• Channel service unit/data service unit (CSU/DSU)

These hardware devices are used to establish the WAN communications link and are responsible for translating frames between the local LAN and the ISP or phone company. DCE units are located between the DTE device and the transmission link or circuit, such as a dedicated leased line. The transmission link is the WAN path the data travels to reach other networks.

DCE devices also control the clock rate for DTE devices. DCEs allow the timing for all network devices to remain synchronized by maintaining an accurate bit rate. This ensures that all network data is time synchronized and readable between DCE and DTE devices.

WAN connectivity would not be possible without the services of both DCE and DTE devices. DTEs are known as user-side devices — usually routers or computers — that interconnect packet-switching LANs, converting user data into signals that can be interpreted by DCE devices. Customer devices that connect to the telephone company's (telco's) equipment are known as customer premises equipment (CPE). The site location where the customer equipment (DTE) and telephone equipment (DCE) meet is called the *demarcation point (demarc).* An example of the DCE and DTE arrangement is shown in Figure 1-2.

Figure 1-2:
DTE and DCE devices.

Router (DTE)   Modem (DCE)   Transmission Medium/Telecom Switch   Modem (DCE)   Computer Terminal (DTE)

**Book VII
Chapter 1**

**Wide-Area
Networking Basics**

Cisco serial interfaces

All wide-area networks use serial interfaces as a means of transmission. Serial transmission allows traffic to flow 1 bit at a time over a single channel or link. A few questions must be raised when selecting a serial interface:

+ Will the interface be used by a DTE or a DCE device?

+ Which signaling standard does the serial interface require?

+ What type of connector is required?

    A DTE device typically has a male connector with pins.

    A DCE device typically has a female connector with holes.

The two types of proprietary Cisco WAN connectors are as follows:

+ **Proprietary 60-pin serial connection:** A WAN connection using a 60-pin serial interface developed by Cisco Systems. The opposite end of the

60-pin serial cable may be EIA/TIA-530, EIA/TIA-449, EIA/TIA-232, V.35, or X.21 standard connectors, which I examine in the following section.

✦ **High-Speed Serial Interface (HSSI):** A proprietary *smart-serial* DTE/DCE interface developed by Cisco Systems and T3plus Networking for use in high-speed WAN link communications.

HSSI operates at the physical layer of the OSI model and uses a male, subminiature 50-pin connector with a maximum cable length of 50 feet. HSSI provides data transmission rates approaching 52 Mbps by employing differential emitter-coupled logic (ECL). ECL technology enables low noise and high-speed data communications. HSSI uses a series of four loopback tests and two control signals to validate the communications process. These communication checks provide handshaking, internal self testing, and high reliability features.

DCE serial interfaces

Several types of serial interface standards for WAN communications have been defined by the Electronic Industries Alliance/Telecommunications Industry Association (EIA/TIA). The following connectors may be used to connect to a router's serial port:

✦ **EIA/TIA-530:** The standard for synchronous balanced and unbalanced serial interfaces using inexpensive DB-25 connectors.

EIA/TIA-530 defines a cabling interface standard between a DTE and DCE device. Differential signaling is used to send high-speed data over long cable using a combination of send, receive, clocking, control, and handshaking signals to send high-speed data over long cabling. Even though the EIA/TIA-530 standard reduces the amount of signal pins used from a 37-pin connector to a 25-pin connector, the most critical electrical signals are carried over and maintained on the 25-pin connector.

✦ **EIA/TIA-449:** A synchronous serial interface standard used for data networking communications that uses a smaller and less expensive connector than V.35 types.

EIA/TIA-449 signals may travel greater distances than the EIA/TIA-232 standard and support data transfer rates up to 2Mbit/s. The Cisco CAB-449MT cable uses a male DB-60-pin connector (Cisco end) to a male DB-37-pin connector (network end).

✦ **EIA/TIA-232:** An asynchronous serial interface that uses 9-pin (DB-9) and 25-pin (DB-25) connectors popular on all types of DCE/DTE equipment, personal computers, modems, terminals, and older printers. The EIA/TIA-232 standard is used to transfer binary data between a DCE and DTE device. Generally, computer serial ports use DTE male pins and DCE devices (such as modems and other networking equipment) employ female connectors. Male-to-female and female-to-male gender changers are available. EIA/TIA-232 cable lengths are restricted to 50 feet (15 meters).

✦ **V.35:** The OSI physical layer ITU partially balanced standard that supports high-speed data rates up to 2.048 Mbps (but used mostly for 56kbps and 64kbps communications).

V.35 is a standard for synchronous serial interfaces that has become obsolete in favor of EIA/TIA-449, but it continues to be used and remains popular today. V.35 eliminates line noise by separately twisting the individual wires carrying data and clock information.

Connection Types

Various connection types are available when designing a WAN connection. Each type provides advantages and disadvantages that must be understood prior to implementation. Defining an organization's WAN traffic flow requirements is crucial to the success of the WAN design.

The four common types of WAN connections available are as follows:

✦ **Dedicated leased line connection:** An individual, point-to-point serial connection that uses a permanently established link to provide guaranteed bandwidth between remote networks. These dedicated circuits provide up to 44.736-Mbps speeds over a public carrier's T-1 or T-3 lines.

These types of high-speed connections are "always on" and have the advantage of minimum overhead compared to other connection types. Also, this persistent connection does not require continuous setup and tear down between communication phases. The disadvantage of dedicated leased lines is cost (factored by distance between links and the amount of bandwidth assigned to the single link), because they are more expensive than other connection types.

✦ **Circuit-switched connection:** The most popular type of WAN connection in which a physical circuit is established "as needed" between two endpoints for the duration of the connection. This type of connection requires call setup of the link to occur before any communications may begin. The physical lines remain unavailable for other users until the connection is dropped. The two types of serial circuit-switched connections are

• Asynchronous plain old telephone system (POTS) dialup

• Synchronous Integrated Services Digital Network (ISDN)

✦ **Packet-switched connection:** A point-to-point virtual circuit connection established using a public carrier's network, allowing multiple customers to share carrier resources. The sharing of packet-switched connections between customers remains transparent to the end user. Packet-switched connections provide high bandwidth and reduced cost compared to dedicated leased lines, but are more expensive than ISDN and dialup connections.

Frame Relay and X.25 are known as packet-switched technologies.

**Book VII
Chapter 1**

**Wide-Area
Networking Basics**

✦ **Cell-switched connection:** A type of point-to-point packet-switched connection that uses digital circuits to transmit 53-byte packets called cells.

Asynchronous Transfer Mode (ATM) is an example of a cell-switched WAN.

Encapsulation Types

Encapsulation is the wrapping of data in a particular protocol header to successfully transport the data. Because IP is a network layer protocol, it must be encapsulated when traversing a WAN (data link/physical layer) link. Cisco devices support many WAN encapsulation types. Each encapsulation type must be manually assigned to a router's serial interface, while identically matching the corresponding point-to-point link on the other end of the connection.

The configured encapsulation type must be identical between both endpoints on a single link; otherwise, communications will not be possible.

The following sections describe the most popular encapsulation types used on Cisco devices.

HDLC (High-Level Data Link Control)

Cisco's default encapsulation type for serial interfaces, HDLC is used to encapsulate packets into frames over established, dedicated, point-to-point leased lines. HDLC packets are small and use low overhead, thus making them quite efficient. HDLC also verifies link integrity and communications by implementing keepalives and sequence numbering. A downside of HDLC is that it provides no means for authentication.

The original HDLC specification outlined by the International Organization for Standardization (ISO) did not provide simultaneous support for multiple network layer protocols. Independent vendors took it upon themselves to make improvements to the HDLC protocol, which introduced new functionality and incorporated the use of multiple Layer 3 protocols. Cisco's proprietary version of HDLC (known as cHDLC) is a synchronous, bit-oriented protocol which adds a new frame field in the packet header to allow for multi-protocol support. cHDLC uses a link keepalive method called Serial Line Address resolution Protocol (SLARP) to verify connection availability and integrity.

HDLC encapsulation is the default assignment for serial interfaces. If a non-HDLC encapsulation type is required for link establishment, it must be manually configured by the network administrator on both sides of the link.

PPP (Point-to-Point Protocol)

PPP encapsulates network layer packets and transmits frames over Layer 2 connections used by point-to-point dedicated circuits and asynchronous dialup or ISDN links. PPP features include connection authentication, encryption, and compression.

Two basic PPP sublayers are as follows:

✦ **Network Control Protocol (NCP):** Encapsulates heterogeneous network layer protocols over PPP. This allows multiple, dissimilar protocols to be transmitted by NCP over the PPP link.

✦ **Link Control Protocol (LCP):** Manages initial link setup, handshake negotiations, and ongoing connections during PPP communications. LCP also manages the termination of point-to-point links.

SLIP (Serial Line Internet Protocol)

SLIP is a very simplistic, nonstandard protocol used to frame and transmit IP datagrams over serial connections.

Due to its inflexible design, SLIP does not provide additional features such as encryption, authentication, or error detection and has been widely replaced by PPP.

Frame Relay

Frame Relay is a high-performance packet-switching WAN protocol originally designed for use with ISDN, which has superseded X.25. Frame Relay uses HDLC encapsulation between connected devices at T-1 (1.544-Mbps) and T-3 (45-Mbps) speeds, but is relatively inexpensive compared to ATM or dedicated leased lines.

Frame Relay is an OSI Layer 2 protocol that relies on the upper-layer protocols to handle flow control and error correction responsibilities. Frame Relay uses virtual circuits to multiplex multiple connections over a single transmission link between DTE and DCE devices. Service providers assign connection identifiers to customer DTE devices and map them to outgoing ports.

ATM (Asynchronous Transfer Mode)

ATM is packet-switching digital transmission technology that sends voice, video, and data signals using 53-byte, fixed-length cell relay between end points over a virtual circuit. An ATM cell contains a 5-byte header and a 48-byte payload (user data), which is processed individually (asynchronously). ATM cells are queued before being multiplexed over the connection-oriented transmission path.

Packaging data into smaller fixed-size cell units allows jitter reduction and prevents data-queuing delays known as contention. By preventing contention in applications where timely delivery of data is crucial — such as voice and video applications — jitter is reduced and overall performance is improved.

ATM is a popular Layer 2 WAN protocol that establishes data-link layer communications over physical Layer 1 circuits. The link between endpoints must be established before data transmission may begin. Data bit rates of 155 Mbps over CAT5 cable and 622 Mbps using fiber-optic cable are possible, with ATM network speeds approaching 10 Gbps. ATM is more expensive compared to Frame Relay technology.

An ATM network is comprised of multiple ATM switches interconnected by point-to-point links, which transmits data cells to destination ATM network interface adapters (known as the ATM endpoints). Examples of ATM endpoints include CSUs, routers, switches, computers, and video coder-decoders (codecs). Two types of ATM switch interfaces are known as either UNI or NNI. UNI interfaces interconnect ATM end systems to ATM switches. NNI interfaces connect ATM switches. UNI and NNI interfaces are also classified by the owner of the interface. The telephone company is assigned publicly owned interfaces, with private equipment being assigned to the end user and is known as customer premises equipment (CPE).

The ATM cell headers are defined in either UNI or NNI format, depending on the type of interface used. Some of the ATM cell header fields are as follows:

+ **Generic Flow Control (GFC):** Field used to identify two or more devices on an ATM network that are using the same ATM interface (multiplexing).

+ **Virtual Path Identifier (VPI) and Virtual Channel Identifier (VCI):** Fields used in determining the ATM cell destination while in transit through an ATM switched network. Cells are tagged with VPI and VCI values. A local translation table determines the port address of a particular destination based on the VPI and VCI values.

+ **Payload Type (PT):** Field used to show the type of data carried. Data may be either user data or control data. If the cell is transporting user data, the first bit is always set to 0. The bit value changes to 1 when control data is used. The second bit in the payload type is assigned for congestion. A 0-bit value represents no congestion, and a 1 bit is used to register network congestion. If the third bit is on (a 1 bit), the cell is marked as the last cell in a frame.

+ **Cell Loss Priority (CLP):** Field responsible for management of buffering. If the CLP bit equals 1, the cell will be dropped when congestion on the network is discovered.

+ **Header Error Control (HEC):** Field used in checksum calculations to determine whether problems exist in the header.

Virtual circuit types

WAN circuits are categorized into two kinds of connection types:

+ **Permanent virtual circuits (PVCs):** PVCs establish direct connections between sites and function similarly to a dedicated leased line. The persistent nature of PVC connections allows for a permanent mode of communications where call setup and termination is not required.

A PVC connection guarantees an "always on" communications availability using a manual static setup method.

✦ **Switched virtual circuits (SVCs):** SVCs dynamically generate connections and terminate them after data has been completely transferred, functioning similarly to a telephone call. A signaling protocol is used between the ATM endpoint and the ATM switch to dynamically control the connection.

SVCs provide flexibility and call setup to networking devices, but require additional time and overhead to set up the connection.

Both PPP and ATM WAN encapsulation types support asynchronous communications.

X.25

This is an international WAN protocol family standardized by the ITU's Telecommunication Standardization Sector (ITU-T) that defines how connections are established and maintained between end user devices and networking equipment.

X.25 network devices are categorized into three types:

✦ **Data terminal equipment (DTE):** DTE devices are customer-owned computers, terminals, and routers that communicate across the X.25 network.

✦ **Data circuit-terminating equipment (DCE):** DCE devices are modems and packet switches that reside between DTE devices and PSEs.

✦ **Packet-switching exchange (PSE):** PSEs transfer data between DTE devices over the X.25 network. X.25 was designed before the conception of the OSI layer and has been generally replaced by the more efficient Frame Relay technology, although X.25 is still used in some ISDN scenarios.

Introducing Cable Connections

Cisco routers use either RJ-45 or DB-25 connectors for DCE/DTE console and AUX ports. A terminal DTE device or DCE modem may be connected to these ports using an RJ-45 cable and an RJ-45–to–DB-25 or RJ-45–to–DB-9 connector.

RJ-45 cabling

Twisted-pair cable uses four pairs of eight individual wires twisted together to eliminate electrical interference known as crosstalk. UTP cables feature RJ-45 connectors that contain eight connector pins per connector. RJ-45 cables are categorized into these main types:

✦ **Straight-through:** Standard network cable used to connect source and destination interfaces between hubs and switches. The eight individual wires on both ends of the 8-pin connector are identical. Pins 1 and 2 are used for sending data, and pins 3 and 6 are used for receiving data. Pins 4, 5, 7, and 8 are not used.

✦ **Crossover:** RJ-45 cable used to connect a source and destination interface directly to one another without the need for a hub or switch. The crossover cable cross-connects two pairs of wires, meaning that each end of the cable is wired differently. The white/orange and orange solid set of wires is swapped with the white/green and green solid set of wires on one end of the cable. Pin 1 crosses over to pin 3 and pin 2 crosses to pin 6. This means that one end of the cable is defined as T568A, the other specified as T568B. A crossover cable may be used to connect pairs of computers, hubs, switches, or routers to one another.

✦ **Rollover:** Cisco-proprietary cables used to connect into the console port of a router or a network switch. In an RJ-45 rollover cable, the colored wiring on one end of the cable becomes reversed on the other end. Pin 1 on one end of the cable connects to pin 8 at the other end of the cable. Similarly, pin 2 is wired to pin 7 at the other end, and so on.

Some common uses for twisted-pair cabling in a Cisco wide-area networking environment include the following:

✦ **Serial transmission:** A WAN serial transmission over a single channel consisting of a single 1-bit data transmission. Each bit is transmitted one bit at a time (compared to the multiple 8-bit transmission nature of parallel communications). Even though serial communications may seem to have a disadvantage compared to parallel transmissions, serial communications methods are often faster than parallel communications. Cisco uses a 60-pin serial connector for one end of the serial transmission cable, while the other end of the cable may be EIA/TIA-232, EIA/TIA-449, EIA/TIA-530, V.35, or X.21.

✦ **ISDN connections:** Digital technology that transmits integrated voice and data over a publicly switched network. ISDN was originally designed to provide private customers and small businesses with high-speed Internet access over existing communications infrastructures. ISDN BRI (Basic Rate Interface) is a service that uses two 64-Kbps bearer channels (2B) plus one 16-Kbps data channel (D) used for clocking, and is called "out-of-band" signaling. This basically means that two encapsulation methods are used between the signaling and data channels.

✦ **Console connections:** A DTE terminal session is established and used to deliver commands to the router via a console connection. A rollover cable with an RJ-45 connector is used to connect the PC or terminal to the console port of the Cisco device.

Connecting Cisco routers using a DCE-to-DTE crossover cable

Although Cisco routers are considered DTE devices (Cisco serial interfaces are DTE by default), you can create a simulated lab DCE-to-DTE WAN environment using two Cisco routers and a DCE-to-DTE crossover cable. Because channel service unit/data service unit (CSU/DSU) devices (DCEs) control the timing (clocking) for synchronous serial interfaces, one Cisco router must be configured as a DCE device. Each router's serial interface should be configured depending on which end of the DB-60 cable is plugged in: One interface configured as a DCE and the other end as the DTE device. Make sure that both routers' serial interfaces are configured with the no shutdown command and the proper IP addressing information, and then configure clocking on the DCE device:

```
RouterDCE(config-if)#clock
    rate 64000
```

This command sets the clock rate to 64,000 bits per second. Because no error message was generated by the router, the command executed successfully. What would happen if the same clocking command was mistakenly executed on the DTE device?

```
RouterDTE(config-if)#clock
    rate 64000
%Error: This command applies
    only to DCE interfaces
```

The show controllers command display output allows an administrator to view which interfaces are set up for DCE or DTE operation:

```
RouterDTE#show controllers
    serial 0
HD unit 1, idb = 0x711CD0,
    driver structure at
    0x124140
buffer size 1524 HD unit 1,
    V.35 DTE cable
```

Before connecting a terminal to the console port, configure the terminal to match the router console port settings, typically 9600 baud, 8 data bits, no parity, and either 1 or 2 stop bits (depending on the router model).

DB-25 cabling and adapters

The types of cabling and adapters used for Cisco routers are categorized into these main types:

✦ **RS-232 straight-through cable:** Standard serial cable known as CAB-R23. This Cisco router cable uses a female DB-25 connector on one end and a male DB-25 connector on the other end. Either end may be used by the network or Cisco device, depending on DCE or DTE device designation and assignment. If the Cisco router is designated as a DCE device, the female DB-25 connector is the Cisco end of the cable. If the router is designated as a DTE device, the male DB-25 connector is the Cisco end.

✦ **RJ-45–to–DB-9 adapter:** Connects a router to a PC through a 9-pin COM port.

Book VII
Chapter 1

Wide-Area
Networking Basics

✦ **RJ-45–to–DB-25 adapter:** Connects a router to a PC through a 25-pin serial port.

Introducing Digital Subscriber Line (DSL) Connections

Digital subscriber line (DSL) data transfer is the high-speed transmission of digital data over standard telephone lines. The digital data is transmitted over analog carrier signals using copper wiring. DSL technology enables home and small business customers to use the same phone line for both high-speed Internet access and telephone services. This combination of new DSL technology with older analog signaling (POTS) allows high-speed Internet access without requiring the installation of newer and more expensive communications methods. The most popular types of DSL connections are as follows:

✦ **Asymmetric digital subscriber line (ADSL):** The most common method of DSL communication that transfers both analog and digital information over a pair of copper wires, using either POTS or ISDN signals.

Since a typical home user requires less upstream bandwidth than downstream bandwidth, ADSL allocates the majority of the telephone line frequencies to downstream traffic. This provides a much larger capacity for Internet downloading, while restricting a users' upload bandwidth considerably. This means data downloads to the end user will occur much faster than data being uploaded from the user to the Internet. ADSL line speeds may approach 24 Mbps downstream and 3.5 Mbps upstream, with data transmission rates fluctuating based on the Internet service provider (ISP) and line quality of the link. Distance also plays a factor in data rates. By using a *splitter*, an ADSL subscriber may simultaneously access both the public switched telephone network (PSTN) and the Internet on the same twisted-pair copper cabling. The splitter provides a means to filter between high and low frequencies.

Two DSL modems or ADSL transceiver units (ATUs) are used to establish a link. One unit, located at the service provider's central office, is called the ATU-C; the remote transceiver unit located at the home or business customer is called the ATU-R. The location where the telephone company's copper wires terminate is called the main distribution frame (MDF). The MDF connects incoming public or private lines to the internal telephone company's network inside a wire rack. The digital subscriber line access multiplexer (DSLAM) is connected to the line at the telephone service provider via the MDF, and is used to connect multiple customer DSL connections to the Internet backbone using multiplexing. The DSLAM acts as a Layer 2 switch that collects multiple customer DSL streams and multiplexes the data into a single signal. This multiplexed traffic is then sent over the Internet backbone switch called the Network Service Provider (NSP) at speeds up to 10 Gbps. Figure 1-3 shows an example of a typical ADSL setup.

✦ **PPPoE (Point-to-Point Protocol over Ethernet):** An OSI Layer 2 protocol used to encapsulate PPP frames inside Ethernet frames. PPPoE is typically used by Internet service providers (ISPs) to allow customers to log on to DSL services using broadband modems. Based on the older Point-to-Point Protocol (PPP), ISPs use PPPoE to track an IP address to a specific customer's authenticated username and password. This allows users to establish a virtual point-to-point WAN "dialup" session over Ethernet networks and securely transmit data between endpoints. PPPoE uses tunneling for security purposes and is similar to the Point-to-Point Tunneling Protocol (PPTP) found in virtual private networks. For this reason, PPPoE consumes additional bandwidth and resources.

✦ **Cisco Long Range Ethernet (LRE):** A proprietary broadband Ethernet protocol developed by Cisco Systems that connects LANs or individual computers to LRE-enabled switches over POTS. LRE is based on VDSL technology and supports distances up to 1.5 kilometers over standard phone lines, enabling simultaneous voice, video, and data transfers.

Cisco LRE products are designed to share lines with analog, Integrated Services Digital Network (ISDN), and digital private branch exchange (PBX) switch telephones using the 0- to 700-kHz frequency range, delivering data rates of 5–15 Mbps. This allows Cisco LRE to offer Ethernet-like performance using lower quality and older Category 1/2/3 cabling. LRE is considered a metropolitan-area network protocol and is easy to install and manage. Cisco LRE also provides huge speed advantage over standard Internet dialup connections.

**Book VII
Chapter 1**

**Wide-Area
Networking Basics**

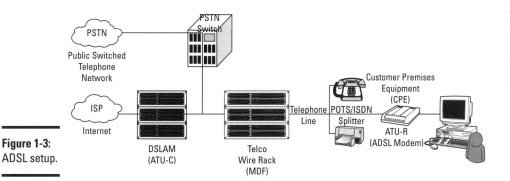

Figure 1-3:
ADSL setup.

Prep Test

1 **Which types of devices control the clock rate and timing synchronization for WAN interfaces? (Choose two.)**

A ○ DTE

B ○ ATM

C ○ MTF

D ○ DCE

E ○ CSU/DSU

2 **Which type of cable is required to configure a simulated WAN environment between two routers?**

A ○ 50-pin HSSI cable

B ○ 60-pin DCE-to-DTE crossover cable

C ○ CAB-449MT cable

D ○ RJ-45 straight-through cable

E ○ RJ-45–to–DB-9 female cable

3 **What is the name for WAN equipment not located at (but connected to) the telephone company?**

A ○ PBX

B ○ Demarc

C ○ Cisco LRE

D ○ Customer premises equipment (CPE)

E ○ MAN

4 **Which protocol would be used by an ISP to establish an authenticated customer dialup session?**

A ○ ATM

B ○ HDLC

C ○ PPPoE

D ○ Frame Relay

E ○ SLIP

5 **Which technology uses separate channels for data and signaling?**

A ○ ISDN

B ○ ADSL

C ○ ATM

D ○ HDLC

6 **Which simplistic, nonstandard protocol is used to frame and transmit IP datagrams over serial connections?**

A ○ ATM

B ○ HDLC

C ○ SLIP

D ○ X.25

7 **Which proprietary interface was developed by Cisco Systems and T3plus Networking for use in high-speed, WAN link communications?**

A ○ HDMI

B ○ HSSI

C ○ 60-pin DCE-to-DTE

D ○ RJ-45–to–DB-9

8 **Which technologies are examples of circuit-switched connections? (Choose two.)**

A ○ Dedicated leased line

B ○ POTS

C ○ Frame Relay

D ○ ATM

E ○ ISDN

9 **Which technologies are examples of packet-switched connections? (Choose two.)**

A ○ ATM

B ○ Frame Relay

C ○ ISDN

D ○ X.25

10 **Which WAN type provides guaranteed bandwidth over an "always on" connection?**

A ○ Packet-switched network connection

B ○ Cell-switched network connection

C ○ Circuit-switched network connection

D ○ Dedicated leased line connection

11 **What is the best example of a cell-switching technology?**

A ○ X.25

B ○ CST

C ○ ATM

D ○ Ethernet

Answers

1 **D, E.** DCE and CSU/DSU. Data communications equipment (DCE), also referred to as a channel service unit/data service unit (CSU/DSU), controls the timing synchronization for WAN devices. Review *"Data terminal equipment (DTE) and data communications equipment (DCE)."*

2 **B.** A 60-pin DCE-to-DTE crossover cable is used to establish a simulated DCE-to-DTE environment using the serial interface between Cisco routers. See *"Cisco serial interfaces"* and *"Introducing Cable Connections."*

3 **D.** Customer premises equipment (CPE) connects to equipment provided by the telephone company at the demarcation point. Refer to *"Data terminal equipment (DTE) and data communications equipment (DCE)."*

4 **C.** PPPoE. Many Internet service providers use PPPoE to authenticate customers using a username and password over dialup connections. Take a look at *"Encapsulation Types."*

5 **A.** ISDN. ISDN BRI (Basic Rate Interface) is a service using two 64-Kbps bearer channels (2B) plus one 16-Kbps data channel (D) used for clocking, and is called "out-of-band" signaling. Read *"Introducing Cable Connections."*

6 **C.** SLIP. Serial Line Internet Protocol is a very simplistic, nonstandard protocol used to frame and transmit IP datagrams over serial connections. See *"Encapsulation Types."*

7 **B.** HSSI. High-Speed Serial Interface (HSSI) is a proprietary smart-serial DTE/DCE interface that uses a male, subminiature 50-pin connector with a maximum cable length of 50 feet. Examine *"Cisco serial interfaces."*

8 **B, E.** POTS and ISDN. The two types of serial circuit-switched connections are asynchronous plain old telephone system (POTS) dialup and synchronous Integrated Services Digital Network (ISDN). Look over *"Connection Types."*

9 **B, D.** Frame Relay and X.25 are known as packet-switched technologies and provide higher bandwidth and cost compared to ISDN and dialup alternatives. Check out *"Connection Types."*

10 **D.** Dedicated leased line. A dedicated leased line establishes a permanent link using a point-to-point serial connection, which provides guaranteed bandwidth to remote networks. Review *"Connection Types."*

11 **C.** ATM. Asynchronous Transfer Mode establishes a point-to-point cell-switched WAN that transmits 53-byte packets called cells. Refer to *"Connection Types."*

Chapter 2: HDLC (High-Level Data Link Control) Protocol

Exam Objectives

✔ Understanding the HDLC Protocol

✔ HDLC framing

✔ Configuring HDLC

✔ Keepalives and SLARP

✔ Monitoring HDLC

Introducing the High-Level DataLink Control Protocol

*H*DLC is a common WAN protocol that operates at the data-link layer and transmits data between network endpoints. HDLC is based on IBM's SDLC protocol and was developed by the International Organization for Standardization (ISO). HDLC data is packed into frames and sent across the network using delivery-verification procedures. HDLC encapsulates data over synchronous point-to-point serial links using framing characters and checksums. These features provide synchronous framing and error detection without windowing or retransmission. HDLC is the default encapsulation type on Cisco router serial interfaces. Cisco HDLC, also known as cHDLC, is a proprietary extension of the HDLC protocol. cHDLC maintains connections by sending a series of keepalive messages between peers. Serial Link Address Resolution Protocol, or SLARP, is another feature used by cHDLC to discover the IP addresses of neighboring routing devices.

HDLC links

HDLC links are set up using two main types of network configurations:

✦ **Point-to-point:** Network setup consisting of two nodes. One node is the controller node, or primary node. The primary node is responsible for setting up and terminating the link, along with link management and control of a peer node, called the secondary node. Secondary nodes must wait for permission from primary nodes before communication is allowed.

✦ **Multipoint:** Instead of a single primary and a single secondary node as in a point-to-point topology, multipoint uses a single primary and multiple secondary nodes.

Data framing

A primary reason for the creation of Cisco's version of HDLC was to address the problem concerning the original HDLC protocol's inability to support multiple protocols. Because cHDLC includes multiprotocol support, the framing structure between the two is slightly different. cHDLC adds a separate field used to identify the encapsulation type employed in the frame. You can see an example of HDLC and cHDLC frames in Figure 2-1.

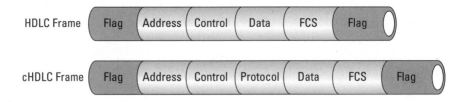

Figure 2-1:
HDLC and
cHDLC
frames.

Opening Flag: 8 bits [01111110], [7E hex]
Address: 8 bits or more
Control: 8 or 16 bits
Data (Payload): Variable, not used in some frames, or padded to fill
Protocol: 16 bits, cHDLC protocol type encapsulated
FCS: Frame Check Sequence - 16 or 32 bits
Closing Flag: 8 bits [01111110], [7E hex]

Header and trailer information is added to data encapsulated by HDLC. HDLC header information includes the HDLC address and HDLC control field. HDLC trailers contain cyclic redundancy check (CRC) information, which discovers any errors during transmission. Individual HDLC frames are separated by HDLC flags used to denote nonframe sequences. A brief description of each field in the HDLC frame is as follows:

✦ **Address field:** Denotes a single, multicast, or broadcast address for a source or destination

✦ **Control field:** Regulates the flow of information being sent using flow control, error checking, and sequence numbering

✦ **Protocol field:** Specifies the encapsulation type used within the cHDLC frame

✦ **Data field:** Contains the user information being transported in the frame

✦ **CRC (cyclic redundancy check) or FCS (frame check sequence) field:** Used to verify that data contained in the frame is error-free

✦ **Flag field:** Marker used to start and stop error checking

The overhead of the HDLC data frame ranges from 7 to 12 bytes, which is quite small and proves to be very efficient.

SLARP

IP address neighbor discovery between routers is made possible by exchanging Serial Link Address Resolution Protocol (SLARP) address request and response messages. HDLC manages serial interface links by sending and receiving these SLARP keepalive messages between peer networking interfaces.

A *keepalive message* is an acknowledgment that an endpoint is still active, thus identifying inactive or failed connections. If a keepalive message is not generated from the router or end point, the connection is considered to be inactive or in a failed state.

A SLARP frame is designated by a specific cHDLC Protocol code field hex value of 0x8035. Three types of SLARP frames are defined as follows:

✦ Address requests (0x00)

✦ Address replies (0x01)

✦ Keepalive frames (0x02)

Keepalive frames operate by passing sequence numbers between the data communications equipment (DCE) side of the link and the data terminal equipment (DTE) side:

✦ If the DCE device receives a sequence number echoed from the DTE side of the link, the link is proven operational.

✦ If the sequence number is not delivered and acknowledged, the router deactivates the link after the third attempt.

HDLC transfer modes

HDLC supports three types of transfer modes:

✦ **Normal response mode (NRM):** Transfer mode that disallows secondary communications with the primary. After the primary authorizes communications, transmission may begin.

✦ **Asynchronous response mode (ARM):** Transfer mode that gives secondaries automatic authorization to primaries. No permission from the primary is required.

✦ **Asynchronous balanced mode (ABM):** Transfer mode that may alter between primary and secondary modes and allows data transmission initiation among all ABM devices.

Configuring HDLC

Because HDLC is the default frame encapsulation type on all Cisco serial interfaces, configuring HDLC is very easy. If HDLC encapsulation configuration is not required, only an IP address needs to be specified on the serial interface. HDLC configuration follows these steps:

1. **Configure HDLC encapsulation:** From the router's interface mode, use the encapsulation hdlc command.

2. **Configure the clock rate:** When setting up a serial link between two routers, the DCE side of the link should be configured to provide the timing between DCE and DTE devices. This is established by using the clock rate command.

Channel service unit/data service unit (CSU/DSU) devices are also DCE devices.

3. **Configure compression (optional):** Enable compression for the serial interfaces on each end of the link by using the compression stac command.

Here is an example of setting up encapsulation on a serial interface:

```
Router(config)#interface s1
Router(config-if)#encapsulation hdlc
Router(config-if)#clock rate 56000
Router(config-if)#ip address 192.168.10.5 255.255.255.0
Router(config-if)#exit
```

The steps listed here explain in further detail the previous serial encapsulation configuration example:

1. **The serial 1 interface is specified, and HDLC encapsulation is enabled on the interface.**

2. **The DCE clock rate is established.**

Do not execute this command for DTE devices. Only DCE devices use this timing mechanism.

3. **The IP address is specified and assigned to the interface.**

Use the no encapsulation hdlc command to disable Cisco HDLC on the interface.

Using HDLC encapsulation provides a fast and efficient means of establishing connections between Cisco routers. This can also be useful when setting up a Cisco lab testing environment using multiple routers to simulate DCE and DTE devices.

Monitoring HDLC

HDLC is a simple protocol that relies on simple commands to monitor functionality.

Verifying that HDLC is enabled and running on a serial interface is quite straightforward using the following show and debug commands:

✦ show interface: Displays the operational status of an interface. The key fields to monitor are the interface line [up | down] and the line protocol [up | down]. An output example of the show interface command is listed here:

```
Router#show interface serial 1
Serial5 is up, line protocol is up
  Hardware is CD2430 in sync mode
  Internet address is 192.168.10.5/24
  MTU 1500 bytes, BW 115 Kbit, DLY 20000 usec, rely 255/255, load 1/255
  Encapsulation HDLC, loopback not set, keepalive set (10 sec)
  Last input 00:00:01, output 00:00:00, output hang never
  Last clearing of "show interface" counters never
  Input queue: 0/75/0 (size/max/drops); Total output drops: 0
  Queuing strategy: weighted fair
Output queue: 0/1000/64/0 (size/max total/threshold/drops)
    Conversations  0/1/256 (active/max active/max total)
    Reserved Conversations 0/0 (allocated/max allocated)
  5 minute input rate 0 bits/sec, 0 packets/sec
  5 minute output rate 0 bits/sec, 0 packets/sec
    4471 packets input, 245871 bytes, 0 no buffer
    Received 2415 broadcasts, 0 runts, 0 giants, 0 throttles
    0 input errors, 0 CRC, 0 frame, 0 overrun, 0 ignored, 0 abort
    2204 packets output, 204505 bytes, 0 underruns
    0 output errors, 0 collisions, 21 interface resets
    0 output buffer failures, 0 output buffers swapped out
    12 carrier transitions
DCD=up  DSR=up  DTR=up  RTS=up  CTS=up
```

✦ show controllers: Displays physical layer information about a serial controller. This information also helps identify the controller's DCE or DTE cable types. A command-line interface (CLI) output example of the show controllers command is listed here:

```
Router#show controllers serial 1
HD unit 1, idb = 0xC6B24, driver structure at 0xCD7B4
buffer size 1524  HD unit 1, V.35 DCE cable, clockrate 56000
cpb = 0x43, eda = 0x2140, cda = 0x2000
RX ring with 16 entries at 0x222000
```

```
00 bd_ptr=0x2000 pak=0x0DF384 ds=0x22C468 status=80 pak_size=0
01 bd_ptr=0x2014 pak=0x0DF1B4 ds=0x22BDB0 status=80 pak_size=0
02 bd_ptr=0x2028 pak=0x0DEFE4 ds=0x22B6F8 status=80 pak_size=0
03 bd_ptr=0x203C pak=0x0DEE14 ds=0x22B040 status=80 pak_size=0
04 bd_ptr=0x2050 pak=0x0DEC44 ds=0x22A988 status=80 pak_size=0
05 bd_ptr=0x2064 pak=0x0DEA74 ds=0x22A2D0 status=80 pak_size=0
06 bd_ptr=0x2078 pak=0x0DE8A4 ds=0x229C18 status=80 pak_size=0
07 bd_ptr=0x208C pak=0x0DE6D4 ds=0x229560 status=80 pak_size=0
08 bd_ptr=0x20A0 pak=0x0DE504 ds=0x228EA8 status=80 pak_size=0
09 bd_ptr=0x20B4 pak=0x0DE334 ds=0x2287F0 status=80 pak_size=0
10 bd_ptr=0x20C8 pak=0x0DE164 ds=0x228138 status=80 pak_size=0
11 bd_ptr=0x20DC pak=0x0DDF94 ds=0x227A80 status=80 pak_size=0
12 bd_ptr=0x20F0 pak=0x0DDDC4 ds=0x2273C8 status=80 pak_size=0
13 bd_ptr=0x2104 pak=0x0DDBF4 ds=0x226D10 status=80 pak_size=0
14 bd_ptr=0x2118 pak=0x0DDA24 ds=0x226658 status=80 pak_size=0
15 bd_ptr=0x212C pak=0x0DD854 ds=0x225FA0 status=80 pak_size=0
16 bd_ptr=0x2140 pak=0x0DD684 ds=0x2258E8 status=80 pak_size=0
cpb = 0x43, eda = 0x2800, cda = 0x2800
TX ring with 2 entries at 0x222800
00 bd_ptr=0x2800 pak=0x000000 ds=0x000000 status=80 pak_size=0
01 bd_ptr=0x2814 pak=0x000000 ds=0x000000 status=80 pak_size=0
02 bd_ptr=0x2828 pak=0x000000 ds=0x000000 status=80 pak_size=0
0 missed datagrams, 0 overruns
0 bad datagram encapsulations, 0 memory errors
0 transmitter underruns
0 residual bit errors
```

✦ debug serial interface: If the show interface command reveals that the line and protocol status are down, the debug serial interface command may be used to isolate timing problems as the cause of a connection failure. If the keepalive values in the myseq, mineseen, and yourseen fields are not incrementing in each subsequent line of output, there is a timing or line problem at one end of the connection.

You can see this problem in the following debug output:

```
Router#debug serial interface
Serial1: HDLC myseq 604562, mineseen 604562, yourseen 259336, line up
Serial1: HDLC myseq 604563, mineseen 604563, yourseen 259337, line up
Serial1: HDLC myseq 604564, mineseen 604564, yourseen 259338, line up
Serial1: HDLC myseq 604565, mineseen 604565, yourseen 259339, line up
Serial1: HDLC myseq 604566, mineseen 604565, yourseen 259340, line up
Serial1: Reset from PC 0x6DEA0
Serial1: HDLC myseq 604567, mineseen 604565, yourseen 259341, line up
Serial1: HDLC myseq 604568, mineseen 604568, yourseen 259342, line up
Serial1: HDLC myseq 604569, mineseen 604569, yourseen 259343, line up
Serial1: HDLC myseq 604570, mineseen 604570, yourseen 259344, line up
Serial1: HDLC myseq 604571, mineseen 604571, yourseen 259345, line up
```

In the above output

✦ Serial1 is the interface used for the connection.

✦ HDLC denotes that the serial connection is HDLC.

- ✦ The myseq counter increases by one every time the router transmits a keepalive packet to the remote router interface.

- ✦ The mineseen value represents the last myseq sequence number the remote router has acknowledged receiving from the router.

  The remote router stores this value in its yourseen counter and transmits that value using a keepalive packet.

  The yourseen counter displays the value of the myseq sequence number it has received in a keepalive packet from the remote router.

- ✦ The line up output shows that the connection between the routers is maintained:

  The value changes to line down if the values of the myseq and myseen fields in a keepalive packet differ by more than three.

  The value changes back to line up when the interface is reset. If the line is in loopback mode, looped is displayed after this field.

Use any debug commands as a last resort, because they can impede router functionality and performance in a production environment.

Prep Test

1 What is the default encapsulation type on Cisco serial interfaces?

A ○ PPP

B ○ SLIP

C ○ ATM

D ○ HDLC

2 Why and how do HDLC frames differ from cHDLC frames? (Choose two.)

A ○ HDLC frames use a protocol field.

B ○ cHDLC frames use a proprietary protocol field.

C ○ To address the cHDLC protocol's lack of multiprotocol support.

D ○ To address the HDLC protocol's lack of multiprotocol support.

3 What does SLARP stand for?

A ○ Serial Line Answering Remote Protocol

B ○ Standard Link Address Redundancy Protocol

C ○ Serial Link Address Resolution Protocol

D ○ Standard Serial-Link Address Removal Protocol

4 What are keepalive messages used for? (Choose two.)

A ○ To debug an interface

B ○ To restrict user access to an interface

C ○ To identify failed interfaces

D ○ To acknowledge that a link is still active

5 A link is deactivated after how many connection attempts?

A ○ Three

B ○ Four

C ○ Six

D ○ Two

6 Which command enables encapsulation on a serial interface?

A ○ `clock rate 56000`

B ○ `interface serial 0`

C ○ `encapsulation hdlc`

D ○ `encapsulation hdlc enable on`

Answers

1 **D.** HDLC. HDLC is enabled as the default encapsulation protocol on serial interfaces. Review *"Introducing High-Level Data Link Control Protocol."*

2 **B, D.** cHDLC frames use a proprietary protocol field, and cHDLC was designed to address the HDLC protocol's lack of multiprotocol support. See *"Data framing."*

3 **C.** SLARP stands for Serial Link Address Resolution Protocol. Refer to *"SLARP."*

4 **C, D.** HDLC manages serial interface links by sending and receiving SLARP keepalive messages between peer networking interfaces. A keepalive message is an acknowledgment that an endpoint is still active, thus identifying inactive or failed connections. Take a look at *"SLARP."*

5 **A.** Three. A link is deactivated after three failed connection attempts. Read *"SLARP."*

6 **C.** The `encapsulation hdlc` command enables HDLC encapsulation on a serial interface. See *"Configuring HDLC."*

Chapter 3: PPP (Point-to-Point Protocol)

Exam Objectives

✓ Understanding PPP

✓ Seeing the operational flow of PPP

✓ Examining the Link Control Protocol and Network Control Protocol

✓ Revealing PAP and CHAP authentication methods

✓ Understanding PPP configuration using the CLI

✓ Examining the Cisco SDM GUI configuration with PPP

✓ Setting up PAP and CHAP authentication

✓ Monitoring and troubleshooting PPP

What Is PPP?

The Point-to-Point Protocol (PPP) is a standard WAN encapsulation method that transports multiprotocol frames between peer connections across full-duplex, bidirectional links. PPP may be used over dedicated serial point-to-point links, Integrated Services Digital Network (ISDN), or asynchronous dialup connections and has superseded the Serial Line Internet Protocol (SLIP) for synchronous and asynchronous communications.

As shown in Figure 3-1, PPP operates at the physical and data link layers of the OSI model to provide data connectivity between endpoints using encapsulation, multiplexing, load balancing, error detection, data compression, and authentication features. Based on the original HDLC specification, PPP adds features such as the Link Control Protocol (LCP) and the Network Control Protocol (NCP). NCP and LCP are key components of PPP and are responsible for proper setup and operation of the Point-to-Point Protocol link between DCE and DTE devices.

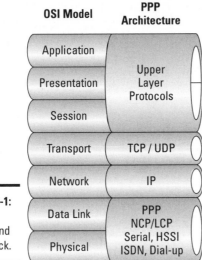

OSI Model **PPP Architecture**

OSI Model	PPP Architecture
Application	Upper Layer Protocols
Presentation	
Session	
Transport	TCP / UDP
Network	IP
Data Link	PPP NCP/LCP
Physical	Serial, HSSI ISDN, Dial-up

Figure 3-1:
The OSI model and PPP stack.

Key features of PPP are as follows:

✦ May be used on all DCE and DTE interfaces.

✦ Supports synchronous and asynchronous communication (ISDN, HSSI, and dialup).

✦ Data load balancing may be enabled across multiple links (link aggregation).

✦ No limits on transmission rates.

✦ Supports clear text PAP and encrypted CHAP authentication.

✦ Offers multiprotocol support.

PPP is divided into three main components:

✦ **Encapsulation:** PPP encapsulates higher-layer multiprotocol datagrams and simultaneously transmits them across either asynchronous or bit-oriented synchronous links. This allows many dissimilar network layer protocols to function independently of one another while still being transported simultaneously over PPP.

As shown in Figure 3-2, PPP uses a frame format for encapsulating data similar to the framing structure used in the HDLC Protocol. The efficient and simple design of the enhanced PPP frame provides a performance boost which maximizes bandwidth speed and data throughput.

The PPP frame fields shown in Figure 3-2 are explained as follows:

- *Flag:* Marks the beginning or ending of a frame using the 8-bit binary value 01111110.

- *Address:* Standard broadcast address using the 8-bit binary value 11111111. PPP uses broadcasting instead of individual node addresses.

- *Control:* Denotes user data in an unsequenced frame represented by the 8-bit binary value 00000011.

- *Protocol:* 16-bit field that identifies the type of protocol data carried by the frame.

- *Data:* Holds up to 1,500 bytes of user data.

- *Frame check sequence (FCS):* 16-bit or 32-bit field used for error detection.

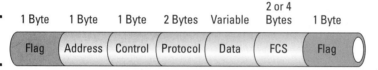

Figure 3-2:
PPP frame.

1 Byte	1 Byte	1 Byte	2 Bytes	Variable	2 or 4 Bytes	1 Byte
Flag	Address	Control	Protocol	Data	FCS	Flag

✦ **Link Control Protocol (LCP):** Allows two endpoints to negotiate data link layer connections. LCP establishes, configures, and verifies the integrity of the data link layer connection by using configuration packets, maintenance packets, and termination packets. These three types of LCP packets allow both ends of a connection to agree upon and use the same set of communication rules regarding the link.

✦ **Network Control Protocol (NCP):** A family of protocols that encapsulates multiple network layer protocols to allow them to communicate over PPP. NCP is known as a data-carrier protocol and is used to configure network layer options between link endpoints. After LCP establishes the rules for link communication between endpoints, control is then passed over to NCP.

PPP is based on the High-Level Data Link Control (HDLC) Protocol but offers several additional features not available with HDLC:

✦ **Authentication:** PPP implements two types of authentication: Password Authentication Protocol (PAP) and Challenge Handshake Authentication Protocol (CHAP). CHAP is encrypted and highly favorable over the less secure, clear text transmission method of PAP authentication.

✦ **Multilink:** Trunking multiple communications channels together to create one logical channel bundle. Multilinking combines allocated bandwidth.

✦ **Compression:** Improves communications efficiency over slow WAN links by enabling Stac or Predictor compression.

✦ **Callback service:** Enhances security by allowing remote PPP callback services. The PPP client first establishes and then terminates a call to the PPP server. After the session has ended, the PPP server reinitializes communications by calling the PPP client back. This provides additional security benefits and reduces telephone billing costs for the PPP client.

✦ **Error detection:** Detects loops and fault conditions within the link to isolate problems and create loop-free environments. Options include a magic number for loop detection and link quality fields.

Operational Flow of PPP

PPP operation consists of several major phases to establish, maintain, and terminate point-to-point links. The operational flow of PPP is shown in Figure 3-3.

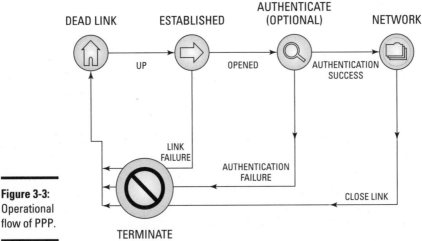

Figure 3-3: Operational flow of PPP.

The main phases of PPP are detailed here:

✦ **Link dead phase:** Each link initially begins with a link-dead state. The link state may proceed to the next phase (established) after signal carriers are detected between peer endpoints. Disconnection of established connections returns the link to the link-dead state.

✦ **Link establishment phase:** After carrier signals are detected between peer endpoints, the Link Control Protocol (LCP) is used to establish the link. By exchanging configuration frames, LCP negotiates link options between peers and sets the rules for communication. This phase is considered to be complete when a configuration-acknowledgment frame has been both sent and received. This phase then initiates the PPP opened state, which allows authentication to occur.

✦ **Link authentication phase (optional):** Authenticates link partners using Password Authentication Protocol (PAP) or Challenge Handshake Authentication Protocol (CHAP) for additional security.

To enter the next phase (network), the authentication process must complete successfully:

- If peer authentication is required, a request is issued and configuration options are negotiated right after the link establishment phase.

- If authentication fails, the link will move to the termination phase.

Only LCP and link quality determinations are read and executed during the authentication phase. All other frames are logged and then dropped.

✦ **Link quality determination phase (optional):** Link quality determination may also occur during the authentication phase and before the network phase. The integrity of the link is checked to decide whether the line quality is reliable enough to support the network layer protocols.

✦ **Link Network Layer Protocol (NLP) phase:** By reaching this phase, the main setup of the link is established and LCP relinquishes control to the network layer protocol. NLP is tasked with network layer session establishment over PPP using Network Control Protocol (NCP) services. NLPs are data-carrying protocols that may use different NCP services depending on the network protocol requiring encapsulation.Available network layer protocols include

- Internet Protocol Control Protocol (IPCP)

- AppleTalk Control Protocol (ATCP)

- Novell IPX Control Protocol (IPXCP)

After LCP has finished the link quality determination test, NCPs take over and network layer protocol configuration negotiation occurs. NCPs may be initiated or terminated at any time. When LCP begins the process of terminating an active link, NCP and the network layer protocols are given ample warning prior to link deactivation.

✦ **Link termination phase:** The Link Control Protocol is responsible for terminating the active link by sending and receiving LCP terminate frames between link end points. These frames may be generated and issued due to a number of different reasons. LCP terminate frames may be triggered because of poor link quality, authentication failure, non-carrier detection, or manual user intervention.

PPP informs upper network layer protocols (NLPs such as IP) regarding the status of link termination. After terminate frames have been exchanged between endpoints, the physical link connection is dropped. Terminate frames consist of Terminate-Requests and Terminate-ACKs, which can be seen in Figure 3-4, along with the entire PPP configuration sequence.

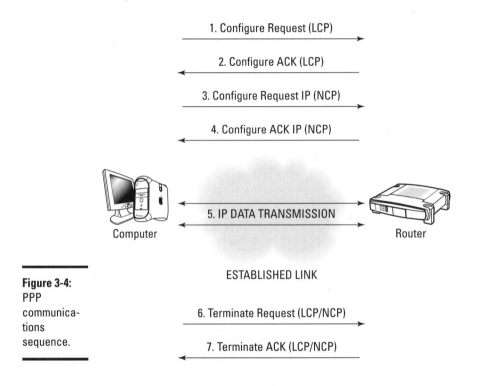

1. Configure Request (LCP)

2. Configure ACK (LCP)

3. Configure Request IP (NCP)

4. Configure ACK IP (NCP)

Computer

5. IP DATA TRANSMISSION

Router

ESTABLISHED LINK

6. Terminate Request (LCP/NCP)

7. Terminate ACK (LCP/NCP)

Figure 3-4:
PPP communications sequence.

PPP links are established by the LCP. NCP links are established within LCP links. Terminating all NCP links does not close the LCP link. The LCP link remains open, although no data will pass through the link until an NCP link is reestablished. PPP links are shut down by terminating the LCP. NCP or LCP packets may be used to deactivate a PPP link.

Link Control Protocol (LCP)

The Link Control Protocol is defined and categorized as having three distinct types of frames. Each LCP frame is responsible for a specific phase in the link communications process. The three categories of LCP frames are:

✦ **Link configuration frames:** These frames provide link establishment and configuration functionality. Frames used for link configuration are Configure-Request, Configure-ACK, Configure-NAK, and Configure-Reject.

✦ **Link maintenance frames:** These frames provide management and link-debugging capabilities. Frames used for link maintenance are Code-Reject, Protocol-Reject, Echo-Request, Echo-Reply, and Discard-Request.

✦ **Link termination frames:** These frames provide link termination services. Frames used for link termination are Terminate-Request and Terminate-ACK.

Purpose of LCP

As seen from the functional types of LCP frames, LCP is responsible for link establishment, configuration and negotiation of optional settings, link management, and link termination. LCP helps routers negotiate and agree upon a specific set of link options. That is why LCP is known as the *link negotiator* because it helps routers negotiate the options of a link. As previously shown in Figure 3-4, LCP link and option negotiation is a series of LCP frames exchanged between PPP peers during data transmission. The LCP negotiation process consists of two separate communications dialogs between PPP peers. To ensure proper communications between endpoints, both peers must agree upon a set of standards which will be used during link establishment, although peers are not required to use the exact same set of LCP options.

Peer A requests, negotiates, and receives confirmation for the set of LCP options to be used for data transmission with peer B. Communication begins with peer A sending a Configure-Request message and ends when peer B sends a Configure-ACK message. Peer B may likewise negotiate the LCP options used for communication with peer A. Peer B initiates communication by sending a Configure-Request message and terminates when peer A sends a Configure-ACK message.

Some common responses to a peer Configure-Request message include the following:

✦ **Configure-ACK:** A positive acknowledgment sent between peers when options received on a link are agreed upon. These values indicate that both parties acknowledge and are in agreement with the configuration options specified. The peer device may transmit data after receiving Configure-ACK acknowledgments.

✦ **Configure-NAK:** Peers send Configure-NAK messages when they do not agree on one or more options. Configure-NAKs trigger peers to resend new Configure-Request messages that offer new link configuration options.

✦ **Configure-Reject:** A rejection acknowledgment. A Configure-Reject is sent when non-negotiable options are received. Options that are unknown to a peer will trigger a new Configure-Request message that contains updated options.

LCP options

An LCP Configure-Request message may contain various options offered by the peer initiator. This allows one peer to let the other peer know what options are requested during link setup. If no value is specified for a particular option, the initiator has no preference on that particular option, and default values are assumed.

LCP negotiable options include the following:

✦ **Compression:** Eliminates redundant data in the protocol field by using compression. This shrinks the 16-bit field inside each PPP frame to 8 bits, saving 1 byte of data in the PPP frame. Compression applied to the address and control fields inside the frame saves additional bandwidth.

✦ **PPP call back:** 8-bit field indicating callback determination.

✦ **Multilink:** Bonding of multiple links using the PPP multilink protocol (MP) creates one virtual link. LCP handles multiple links in a virtual circuit as a single entity. The benefits of bonding include performance improvement and increased bandwidth availability.

✦ **Authentication:** Option used on PPP links for enabling CHAP or PAP authentication.

✦ **Maximum-Receive-Unit (MRU):** Defines the maximum size of a datagram sent over the PPP link. By default, PPP sends datagrams that contain 1500 bytes.

✦ **Quality-Protocol:** Option used for link quality monitoring. This option is disabled by default.

✦ **Magic-Number:** Enables loop and error detection on the link. LCP messages include a magic number that identifies each peer in a PPP link. Whenever a link is in an actively looped state, the node receives an LCP message with its own magic number, instead of receiving a message with the magic number of the peer node. The magic number field allows the sending node to detect the loop and take corrective action.

Network Control Protocol (NCP)

The modular design of PPP allows simultaneous encapsulation and transmission of multiple network layer protocols inside data frames over a WAN link. PPP uses Network Control Protocol (NCP) datagrams to define and configure the network layer protocols to be transferred over the WAN. After the network layer protocols are configured, datagrams are prepared for transmission over the LCP-established link.

NCP is designed as a "packager" that encapsulates multiple network layer protocols and allows simultaneous communications over one active LCP link. LCP does not have to understand nor is concerned with each Layer 3 protocol being transmitted. LCP establishes the link and turns over all network layer encapsulation responsibility to NCP. NCP acts as an interface between the data link layer and the network layer. Although multiple NCPs may be transmitted over a single LCP link, they must be sent during the Network Layer Protocol (NLP) phase of PPP communications.

The Network Control Protocol (NCP) phase is responsible for establishing and configuring network layer protocols such as IP, IPX, and AppleTalk. The Internet Protocol Control Protocol (IPCP) and Internet Protocol Control Protocol version 6 (IPCPv6) are network layer protocols responsible for enabling, configuring, and terminating the Internet Protocol (IP) modules on both ends of the point-to-point link. During the opened state, NCP carries the corresponding network layer protocol packets across the link. During IP encapsulation, normal traffic transfer in the opened state consists of LCP, NCP, and IPCP (or IPCPv6) packets. Network layer protocol packets received when the corresponding NCP is not in the opened state are dropped. The link remains active until LCP or NCP packets specifically terminate the link, or until some other external process shuts down the link.

PAP and CHAP Authentication

To improve security mitigation, the PPP protocol suite was designed to offer the optional feature of user authentication. Devices that initiate a PPP session must pass strict identity verification before link establishment is approved. The link is activated only after the proper credentials have been given and accepted. If PPP authentication fails for any reason, access is denied and the link is promptly terminated. Although proprietary authentication methods may be configured to work with PPP, the two main types of PPP authentication methods are Password Authentication Protocol (PAP) and Challenge Handshake Authentication Protocol (CHAP). CHAP is the preferred authentication method and is considered superior to PAP.

Password Authentication Protocol (PAP)

PAP uses a simple authentication method using Authentication-Request and Authentication-Reply messages to validate the identity of a remote client:

1. The initiator (possibly a remote dialup user) sends an Authentication-Request message consisting of a username and password to a peer device (possibly an ISP).

2. The receiving device validates the username and password, and sends back an Authenticate-ACK approving the connection.

   If the Authentication-Request is disapproved, an Authenticate-NAK message is transmitted back to the source, and link establishment is terminated.

Although the PAP authentication process is simple and efficient, a couple of major security problems exist with PAP:

✦ PAP does not use any type of encryption to send usernames and passwords over the link. All authentication data is sent in clear text over the WAN link, which is a huge security risk.

✦ PAP is extremely vulnerable to various forms of malicious attack, such as password guessing or other brute force attacks.

✦ The PAP remote client controls the amount of authentication attempts to the authentication server. This means an attack could continue indefinitely against a PPP (PAP-enabled) authentication server.

For these reasons, CHAP is often used as a more secure replacement for PAP. Since CHAP has superseded PAP, PAP should only be used in PPP implementations where security is not a concern. An example of a PAP two-way handshake is shown in Figure 3-5.

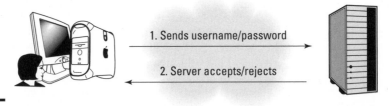

Figure 3-5:
PAP
two-way
handshake.

Remote Host
Sends username/password
as cleartext
Username: PAP
Password: cleartext

ESTABLISHED LINK

Dial-up Server
Authenticates
Username: PAP
Password: cleartext

Challenge Handshake Authentication Protocol (CHAP)

Compared to PAP, CHAP is a more secure method of validating user identities over a PPP link. CHAP provides similar functionality to PAP while increasing security mitigation, and does not send clear text passwords across the WAN link. Instead, CHAP uses a three-way handshake and a shared secret password that is not transmitted over the LCP link.

The three-way handshake process is as follows:

✦ **Challenge:** After the link establishment phase is complete, the authenticating peer generates a *challenge text* message and sends the frame to the peer that initiated the request. These text messages are found on both link peers and consist of identical data.

✦ **Response:** The initiator uses its shared secret password to encrypt the challenge text message received from the authenticating peer and returns the message as an encrypted *response* message. This cryptographic calculation uses a one-way hash function or MD5 checksum hash for encryption. No password is transmitted during the challenge or response stage. Although both link peers know the shared secret information, only the encrypted challenge text message is passed between the link initiator and link authenticator.

✦ **Verification:** The authenticator checks the response message against the known hash value from its own calculations, and a success or failure message is returned to the initiator. If both authentication values match, the same shared secret key is confirmed, and access is granted. If the values do not match, the link is deactivated.

The PPP three-way handshake is done during initial setup of the link. Periodic re-validation may also be performed anytime after the link establishment phase (to provide additional security) by changing the challenge text value. A general CHAP three-way handshake is shown in Figure 3-6.

Book VII Chapter 3

PPP (Point-to-Point Protocol)

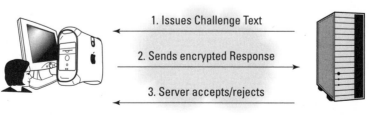

1. Issues Challenge Text

2. Sends encrypted Response

3. Server accepts/rejects

ESTABLISHED LINK

Figure 3-6: CHAP three-way handshake.

Remote Host
Shared secret
(password)
not transmitted
across WAN

Dial-up Server
Shared secret
(password)
not transmitted
across WAN

The secret plain-text values are identical and shared by both peers, but they are never transmitted over the PPP link. Instead, the challenge text message is used to verify that both peers have matching values. Also, remember that the CHAP server (or peer authenticator) controls the authentication process, and differs from the less secure PAP, which provides authentication control to the initiator.

Configuring PPP

HDLC is the default encapsulation protocol on Cisco interfaces but is proprietary to Cisco devices. To establish WAN links using non-Cisco devices, you must enable and configure PPP between peers. PPP links may be established using synchronous, asynchronous, HSSI, and ISDN connections.

The steps to configure PPP using the Cisco command-line interface (CLI) are as follows:

1. **Set up the router host names used for authentication.**
2. **Configure passwords to authenticate between routers.**
3. **Configure PPP encapsulation on router interfaces.**
4. **Configure PAP and CHAP authentication on both routers.**

Set up router host names used for authentication

If the name of the router has not already been set, begin by defining the local router host name and IP address for an interface as follows:

1. **In global configuration mode, specify the host name of the local router:**

```
Router>enable
Router#config term
Router(config)#hostname RT1
```

2. **Specify the interface and IP address:**

```
RT1(config)#interface serial0/0
RT1(config-if)#ip address 10.0.0.1 255.255.255.252
```

3. **Assign the clock rate and issue the** no shutdown **command:**

```
RT1(config-if)#clock rate 64000
RT1(config-if)#no shutdown
RT1(config-if)#exit
```

In this CLI, the host name of the router is specified as RT1, and the serial interface has been assigned an IP address of 10.0.0.1. The same commands may be executed on the remote router, hereby referred to as RT2.

For proper operation, the interfaces that connect the local and remote routers must have identical clock rate settings.

Configure passwords to authenticate between routers

Configure the username and password the remote router will use to authenticate to your local router. Multiple username and password combinations may be created for multiple PPP connections to the same router:

```
RT1(config)#username RT2 password ALLINONE
```

Issue this command for each remote router PPP connection requiring authentication. Also, be sure that the remote router is configured to accept the username and password from the local router:

```
RT2(config)#username RT1 password ALLINONE
```

The `show running-config` command will display the password in clear text, unless the password has been encrypted using the `service password-encryption` command.

Both username and password are case sensitive. Also, the passwords between peer routers must be identical.

Configure PPP encapsulation on the router interface

The default point-to-point protocol enabled on Cisco router interfaces is HDLC (High-Level Data Link Control). HDLC is commonly found on Cisco-proprietary interfaces used for leased lines but does not provide support for authentication.

If authentication is required, PPP is implemented as follows:

1. **In global configuration mode, specify the interface and encapsulation type:**

    ```
    RT1>enable
    RT1#configure terminal
    RT1(config)#interface serial0/0
    RT1(config-if)#encapsulation ppp
    ```

2. **Enable stac or predictor compression:**

    ```
    RT1(config-if)#compress [predictor | stac]
    RT1(config-if)#exit
    ```

**Book VII
Chapter 3**

PPP (Point-to-Point Protocol)

Notice that the optional compression command has been issued. If available bandwidth is minimal, this software compression process removes data redundancy and may improve performance over slow WAN links.

Stacker compression is based on the Lemple Ziv industry-standard algorithm, while the Predictor algorithm is used in older legacy configurations.

Due to increased CPU load, compression may affect overall system performance. Verify CPU load using the `show process cpu` command and disable compression if the CPU load is consistently more than 65 percent.

Both ends of the link must be configured for PPP. If the local router's interface is configured for PPP and the remote router's interface is still set for HDLC, the port status will show that Serial 0 is up but the line protocol is down. This is because the one end of the link is misconfigured and is still set to use HDLC encapsulation.

Configure PAP and CHAP authentication on both routers

By setting up the router host name, IP address, authentication passwords, and encapsulation, PPP is now initialized and enabled on the serial interface. The next step (if required) is to enable the preferred authentication method, either PAP or CHAP. PPP authentication is optional and should only be configured after the circuit is tested and IP connectivity has been established. Delaying the implementation of PPP authentication allows an administrator to verify that PPP is functioning properly before introducing authentication issues, which can complicate troubleshooting of PPP connectivity problems.

You have three options:

✦ Enable PAP at the Cisco CLI:

```
RT1(config)#int s0/0
RT1(config-if)#ppp authentication pap
```

✦ Choose the more secure and recommended CHAP authentication method:

```
RT1(config)#int s0/0
RT1(config-if)#ppp authentication chap
```

✦ Enable both CHAP and PAP authentication:

```
RT1(config-if)#ppp authentication chap pap
```

A remote Cisco router may establish connection to an Internet service provider (ISP) using multiple central routers for authentication purposes.

In certain cases, you must set up additional username authentication that is different from the router's host name. The ISP-assigned username and password may not match the host name of the remote router. Depending on authentication method, the `ppp chap hostname` or `ppp pap sent-username` command is used to specify an alternate username that will be used for authentication.

Using CHAP as an example, multiple remote dialup devices connect to a central site. Each remote device must have its own host name and shared secret password configured and stored on the central router, which provides a management burden for the administrator. By allowing the remote devices to all use usernames other than their host name, only one single user account and password is required, and administrative management is simplified.

The following defines the username and password that the central router will use to authenticate connections with the remote devices:

✦ For PAP authentication, use the following command in interface configuration mode:

```
RT1(config-if)#ppp pap sent-username PAPUSER password PAPPWD
```

✦ For CHAP, issue these commands separately:

```
RT1(config-if)#ppp chap hostname CHAPUSER
RT1(config-if)#ppp chap password CHAPPASS
```

Configuring PPP callback for ISDN Dial on Demand Routing (DDR)

PPP callback allows a router to establish a WAN connection with a peer router and request that a dialup peer router return the call. The callback feature can be used to control access and communications costs between routers. One router must be configured as the PPP callback client issuing requests, while the other router is configured as the PPP callback server, accepting requests and providing the callback functionality. Here is an example of a client and server callback configuration:

1. Specify the interface, IP address, and encapsulation type:

```
RT1(config)#interface bri 0
RT1(config-if)#ip address 10.1.1.10 255.255.255.0
RT1(config-if)#encapsulation ppp
```

2. Enable callback security and the timeout period:

```
RT1(config-if)#dialer callback-secure
RT1(config-if)#dialer enable-timeout 5
```

3. **Specify the dialer map parameters and assign the dialer group:**

```
RT1(config-if)#dialer map ip 10.1.1.11 name NY class DIALGRP 2121234567
RT1(config-if)#dialer-group 1
```

4. **Configure PPP callback:**

```
RT1(config-if)#ppp callback accept
```

5. **Enable CHAP authentication:**

```
RT1(config-if)#ppp authentication chap
```

6. **Specify the dialer class name and callback client name:**

```
RT1(config)#map-class dialer DIALGRP
RT1(config-map-class)#dialer callback-server username
```

First, the encapsulation method and IP address are set up on the callback server's ISDN Basic Rate Interface (BRI). The `dialer callback-secure` command enables optional callback security features forcing authentication. The `dialer enable-timeout` command is also optional and specifies the timeout period in seconds between calls. The `dialer map` command maps the next-hop address to the host name and phone number, referencing the name of the map class (DIALGRP) set for PPP callback. The `dialer group` command assigns the dialer interface to a dialer group. The `ppp callback accept` command allows incoming PPP calls, and PPP authentication is set for CHAP on the interface. The `map-class dialer` command works with the `dialer map` command to specify the dialer class name. The `dialer callback-server` command tells the callback server that the device referenced in the dialer map statement is a callback client.

Here is the configuration on the PPP callback client:

1. **Specify the interface, IP address, and encapsulation type:**

```
RT2(config)#interface bri 0
RT2(config-if)#ip address 10.1.1.11 255.255.255.0
RT2(config-if)#encapsulation ppp
```

2. **Specify the dial map IP, host name, and phone number:**

```
RT2(config-if)#dialer map ip 10.1.1.10 name BOSTON 5551234567
```

3. **Specify the dialer group:**

```
RT2(config-if)#dialer-group 1
```

4. **Select PPP callback and authentication type:**

```
RT2(config-if)#ppp callback request
RT2(config-if)#ppp authentication chap
```

Always execute the `copy running-config startup-config` command to save any configuration changes and make them persistent over router reboots!

Configuring PPP with the Cisco Security Device Manager (SDM)

You can also configure the PPP WAN protocol on your router using the *Cisco SDM WAN Wizard* in the Cisco Router and Security Device Manager (SDM). The Cisco SDM WAN Wizard walks you through several graphical user interface (GUI) dialog boxes to easily step through the process of setting up a PPP, Frame Relay, or HDLC link.

Monitoring and Troubleshooting PPP

The Cisco IOS provides tools to monitor and troubleshoot PPP links. Some of the most useful troubleshooting aids to resolve PPP problems are the `show` and `debug` CLI commands. (See the sidebar "Common PPP troubleshooting and monitoring IOS commands," later in this chapter.) The major difference between `show` and `debug` commands is that `debug` commands operate in real time, while `show` commands do not. After PPP is set up, you should verify PPP link functionality.

Good troubleshooting methods start from the physical layer and work upward through the OSI model:

1. **Verify that all hardware is operating normally.**

2. **Check for configuration errors and use Cisco IOS commands to monitor communications over specific interfaces.**

To verify PPP encapsulation, issue the `show interfaces` command on the configured PPP interface as follows:

```
RT1#show interfaces serial0
Serial0 is up, line protocol is up
  Hardware is HD64570
  Internet address is 192.168.10.5/24
MTU 1500 bytes, BW 64 Kbit, DLY 20000 usec, rely 255/255, load 1/255
Encapsulation PPP, loopback not set, keepalive set (10 sec)
  LCP Open
  Open: IPCP
```

The `show interfaces` command output gives important information regarding the status of PPP:

✦ Both the serial interface and the line protocol must be in the "up" state in order to forward traffic.

If the line is in the "up" state but the protocol is "down," a clocking (keepalive) or framing problem exists. Check that the keepalives, clock rate, and encapsulation types between links match exactly. One end of the link may be set for PPP encapsulation, and the other end may be configured for HDLC.

✦ The configured encapsulation method is set for PPP, and LCP is in an open state. This means that the Layer 2 link establishment phase of LCP is successful.

✦ You can see that NCP Layer 3 IPCP packets are also functioning properly, and in an open state.

Now verify connectivity between link peers (in both directions) using the ping command:

```
RT1#ping 10.10.10.6
Type escape sequence to abort.
Sending 5, 100-byte ICMP Echos to 10.10.10.6, timeout is 5 seconds:
!!!!!
Success rate is 100 percent (5/5), round-trip min/avg/max = 70/70/82 ms
```

PPP link quality monitoring

To monitor the quality of the serial link that is using PPP, enable link quality monitoring (LQM) by issuing the following command on the PPP interface:

```
RT1(config-if)#ppp quality 75
```

Use the no form of this command to disable LQM:

```
RT1(config-if)#no ppp quality
```

The number 75 represents the minimum accepted link quality in both incoming and outgoing directions:

✦ The outgoing quality is calculated by comparing the total number of packets and bytes sent to the total number of packets and bytes received by the destination node.

✦ The incoming quality is calculated by comparing the total number of packets and bytes received to the total number of packets and bytes sent by the destination node.

If the link quality drops below 75 percent, the link is considered unusable and will be shut down. LQM uses a time lag to prevent frame looping so the link does not go up and down continuously.

PPP debug commands

A number of `debug` commands may be used to show the active PPP process on an interface. These commands assist the network administrator with troubleshooting link problems. The most useful PPP `debug` commands are as follows:

✦ `debug ppp authentication`: Outputs CHAP and PAP authentication exchange messages to the console and is used in troubleshooting scenarios to verify that authentication is actually taking place. An example of the `debug ppp authentication` command is as follows and is a subset of the `debug ppp negotiation` command:

```
RT1#debug ppp authentication
Nov 115 08:24:49.237: BR0:1 PPP: Phase is AUTHENTICATING, by both
Nov 115 08:24:49.239: BR0:1 CHAP: O CHALLENGE id 42 len 33 from "RT1"
Nov 115 08:24:49.244: BR0:1 CHAP: I CHALLENGE id 218 len 31 from "RT2"
Nov 115 08:24:49.251: BR0:1 CHAP: O RESPONSE id 218 len 33 from "RT1"
Nov 115 08:24:49.255: BR0:1 CHAP: I SUCCESS id 218 len 4
Nov 115 08:24:49.258: BR0:1 CHAP: I RESPONSE id 42 len 31 from "RT2"
Nov 115 08:24:49.264: BR0:1 CHAP: O SUCCESS id 42 len 4
```

If Configure-NAK messages are received during authentication negotiation, one side of the link is probably configured for PAP, while the other is configured for CHAP password authentication.

✦ `debug ppp chap`: Shows whether CHAP authentication has succeeded or failed. CHAP authentication failures are usually associated with incorrect configurations or configuration mismatches between link peers. Verifying and correcting username and password mismatches normally fix authentication problems.

Here is an example output of a failed CHAP authentication:

```
RT1#debug ppp chap
ppp: received conf.ig for type = 5 (MAGICNUMBER) value = 1E24718 acked
PPP BRI0: B-Channel 1: state = ACKSENT fsm_rconfack(C021): rcvd id E6
ppp: config ACK received, type = 3 (CI_AUTHTYPE), value = C223
ppp: config ACK received, type = 5 (CI_MAGICNUMBER), value = 28CEF76C
BRI0: B-Channel 1: PPP AUTH CHAP input code = 1 id = 83 len = 16
BRI0: B-Channel 1: PPP AUTH CHAP input code = 2 id = 96 len = 28
BRI0: B-Channel 1: PPP AUTH CHAP input code = 4 id = 83 len = 21
BRI0: B-Channel 1: Failed CHAP authentication with remote.
Remote message is: MD compare failed
```

✦ `debug ppp error`: Causes the `debug ppp` command to display protocol errors and error statistics that are relevant to PPP connection negotiation and operation.

The following sample output from the `debug ppp error` command may appear when the Quality Protocol option is enabled on a PPP interface:

```
RT1#debug ppp error
PPP Serial3(i): rlqr receive failure. successes = 12
PPP: myrcvdiffp = 159 peerxmitdiffp = 41091
PPP: myrcvdiffo = 2183 peerxmitdiffo = 1714439
PPP: threshold = 25
PPP Serial4(i): rlqr transmit failure. successes = 12
PPP: myxmitdiffp = 41091 peerrcvdiffp = 159
PPP: myxmitdiffo = 1714439 peerrcvdiffo = 2183
PPP: l->OutLQRs = 1 LastOutLQRs = 1
PPP: threshold = 25
PPP Serial3(i): lqr_protrej() Stop sending LQRs.
PPP Serial3(i): The link appears to be looped back.
```

The rlqr failure message in the second line indicates that the request to negotiate the Link Quality Protocol option is not accepted. The PPP threshold is set at 25, which is the interface's maximum acceptable error percentage. A threshold value of 25 allows the router to maintain a minimum non-error percentage of 75. Anything over the minimum value will render the PPP link to a downed state, and the link will be considered unusable.

✦ `debug ppp negotiation`: Lists PPP negotiation processes between endpoints and allows a network administrator to pinpoint where PPP errors are coming from. The following is an example output of the `debug ppp negotiation` command, with some important areas (which help verify connectivity) highlighted:

```
Router#debug ppp negotiation
08:36:21: %LINK-3-UPDOWN: Interface Serial1/1, changed state to up
08:36:21: Sel1/1 PPP: Treating connection as a dedicated line
08:36:21: Sel1/1 PPP: Phase is ESTABLISHING, Active Open
08:36:21: Sel1/1 LCP: O CONFREQ [Closed] id 5 len 15
08:36:21: Sel1/1 LCP:    AuthProto CHAP (0x0305C22305)
08:36:21: Sel1/1 LCP:    MagicNumber 0x444DB72C (0x0506444DB72C)
08:36:21: Sel1/1 LCP: I CONFREQ [REQsent] id 39 len 15
08:36:21: Sel1/1 LCP:    AuthProto CHAP (0x0305C22305)
08:36:21: Sel1/1 LCP:    MagicNumber 0x5056251B (0x05034145611A)
08:36:21: Sel1/1 LCP: O CONFACK [REQsent] id 39 len 15
08:36:21: Sel1/1 LCP:    AuthProto CHAP (0x0305C22305)
08:36:21: Sel1/1 LCP:    MagicNumber 0x5056251B (0x05034145611A)
08:36:21: Sel1/1 LCP: I CONFACK [ACKsent] id 5 len 15
08:36:21: Sel1/1 LCP:    AuthProto CHAP (0x0305C22305)
08:36:21: Sel1/1 LCP:    MagicNumber 0x444DB72C (0x0506444DB72C)
08:36:21: Sel1/1 LCP: State is Open
08:36:21: Sel1/1 PPP: Phase is AUTHENTICATING, by both
08:36:21: Sel1/1 CHAP: O CHALLENGE id 2 len 25 from "RT1"
08:36:21: Sel1/1 CHAP: I CHALLENGE id 3 len 25 from "RT2"
08:36:21: Sel1/1 CHAP: O RESPONSE id 3 len 25 from "RT1"
08:36:21: Sel1/1 CHAP: I RESPONSE id 2 len 25 from "RT2"
08:36:21: Sel1/1 CHAP: O SUCCESS id 2 len 4
08:36:21: Sel1/1 CHAP: I SUCCESS id 3 len 4
08:36:21: Sel1/1 PPP: Phase is UP
```

```
08:36:21: Se1/1 CDPCP: O CONFREQ [Closed] id 3 len 4
08:36:21: Se1/1 IPCP: I CONFREQ [Not negotiated] id 3 len 10
08:36:21: Se1/1 IPCP:    Address 192.168.10.5 (0x0306C8A84410)
08:36:21: Se1/1 LCP: O PROTREJ [Open] id 6 len 16 protocol IPCP
    (0x80210103000A0306C8A84410)
08:36:21: Se1/1 CDPCP: I CONFREQ [REQsent] id 3 len 4
08:36:21: Se1/1 CDPCP: O CONFACK [REQsent] id 3 len 4
08:36:21: Se1/1 CDPCP: I CONFACK [ACKsent] id 3 len 4
08:36:21: Se1/1 CDPCP: State is Open
08:36:22: %LINEPROTO-5-UPDOWN: Line protocol on Interface Serial1/1,
    changed state to up
```

✦ `debug ppp packet`: Shows the sending and receiving of PPP packets.

The following `debug ppp packet` command output shows incoming and outgoing PPP packet exchanges under normal operation:

```
RT1#debug ppp packet
PPP Serial4(o): lcp_slqr() state = OPEN magic = D21B4, len = 48
PPP Serial4(i): pkt type 0xC025, datagramsize 52
PPP Serial4(i): lcp_rlqr() state = OPEN magic = D3454, len = 48
PPP Serial4(i): pkt type 0xC021, datagramsize 16
PPP Serial4: I LCP ECHOREQ(9) id 3 (C) magic D3454
PPP Serial4: input(C021) state = OPEN code = ECHOREQ(9) id = 3 len = 12
PPP Serial4: O LCP ECHOREP(A) id 3 (C) magic D21B4
PPP Serial4(o): lcp_slqr() state = OPEN magic = D21B4, len = 48
PPP Serial4(i): pkt type 0xC025, datagramsize 52
PPP Serial4(i): lcp_rlqr() state = OPEN magic = D3454, len = 48
PPP Serial4(i): pkt type 0xC021, datagramsize 16
PPP Serial4: I LCP ECHOREQ(9) id 4 (C) magic D3454
PPP Serial4: input(C021) state = OPEN code = ECHOREQ(9) id = 4 len = 12
PPP Serial4: O LCP ECHOREP(A) id 4 (C) magic D21B4
PPP Serial4(o): lcp_slqr() state = OPEN magic = D21B4, len = 48
PPP Serial4(i): pkt type 0xC025, datagramsize 52
PPP Serial4(i): lcp_rlqr() state = OPEN magic = D3454, len = 48
PPP Serial4(i): pkt type 0xC021, datagramsize 16
PPP Serial4: I LCP ECHOREQ(9) id 5 (C) magic D3454
PPP Serial4: input(C021) state = OPEN code = ECHOREQ(9) id = 5 len = 12
PPP Serial4: O LCP ECHOREP(A) id 5 (C) magic D21B4
PPP Serial4(o): lcp_slqr() state = OPEN magic = D21B4, len = 48
PPP Serial4(i): pkt type 0xC025, datagramsize 52
PPP Serial4(i): lcp_rlqr() state = OPEN magic = D3454, len = 48
PPP Serial4(i): pkt type 0xC021, datagramsize 16
PPP Serial4: I LCP ECHOREQ(9) id 6 (C) magic D3454
PPP Serial4: input(C021) state = OPEN code = ECHOREQ(9) id = 6 len = 12
PPP Serial4: O LCP ECHOREP(A) id 6 (C) magic D21B4
PPP Serial4(o): lcp_slqr() state = OPEN magic = D21B4, len = 48
PPP Serial4(i): pkt type 0xC025, datagramsize 52
PPP Serial4(i): lcp_rlqr() state = OPEN magic = D3454, len = 48
PPP Serial4(i): pkt type 0xC021, datagramsize 16
PPP Serial4: I LCP ECHOREQ(9) id 7 (C) magic D3454
PPP Serial4: input(C021) state = OPEN code = ECHOREQ(9) id = 7 len = 12
PPP Serial4: O LCP ECHOREP(A) id 7 (C) magic D21B4
PPP Serial4(o): lcp_slqr() state = OPEN magic = D21B4, len = 48
```

**Book VII
Chapter 3**

**PPP (Point-to-Point
Protocol)**

Common PPP troubleshooting and monitoring IOS commands

`show interfaces`: Provides information regarding configured interfaces. Shows line status, encapsulation type, and the state of LCP and NCP.

`show interfaces serial`: Displays interface configuration for serial interfaces.

`show ip route`: Verifies whether an IP network route exits.

`show controllers`: Shows the interface cable type (DCE or DTE) and clock rate, if available.

`show running-config`: Displays the router's active, running configuration.

`show dialer`: Shows diagnostic information for Dial on Demand Routing (DDR)–configured interfaces.

`show ppp multilink`: Allows an administrator to verify PPP multilink functionality.

`ppp quality`: Denotes the PPP link quality in percentage form. The link is shut down when the line quality drops below the determined acceptable percent value.

`ppp callback accept`: Enables PPP server callback requests from clients. The dialer interface is set up to function as the PPP callback server and accept client requests for callbacks.

`ppp callback request`: Enables PPP clients to request callbacks from servers. The dialer interface is set up to function as the PPP callback client and request PPP callbacks from the server.

`ppp compress`: Enables compression of payload encapsulated in PPP frames.

`ppp multilink`: Enables multilink aggregation into a single virtual circuit on a specific interface used for PPP.

`debug ppp`: Allows an administrator to view and analyze the exchange of PPP frames. Use caution when running `debug` commands in a live production environment. A performance penalty may occur, impacting the router's CPU and memory resources, and can cause slowdowns and other problems on the network.

`debug ppp authentication`: Useful in debugging CHAP and PAP errors by analyzing the packet transfer pertaining to PPP authentication.

`debug ppp chap`: Useful in determining the cause of unsuccessful CHAP authentications.

`debug ppp compression`: Displays useful information regarding PPP packet compression.

`debug dialer`: Shows packet statistics received on a dialer interface.

`debug ppp error`: Displays connection and operational errors on a PPP link.

`debug ppp multilink events`: Shows packet event information regarding a multilink virtual circuit.

`debug ppp negotiation`: Displays packets used during the initial setup and negotiation process of the PPP link.

`debug ppp packet`: Displays incoming and outgoing PPP packets.

`debug ppp pap`: Useful in determining the cause of unsuccessful PAP authentications.

`debug serial interface`: Shows whether a serial interface has failed. Useful for troubleshooting connection and timing issues and knowing whether serial keepalive counters are incrementing.

Prep Test

1 Which features are supported by PPP? (Choose three.)

- **A** ○ Multilink bonding
- **B** ○ Virtual circuits
- **C** ○ Callback
- **D** ○ Authentication security

2 Which PPP subprotocol sets up the PPP link?

- **A** ○ NCP
- **B** ○ IP
- **C** ○ IPCP
- **D** ○ ISDN
- **E** ○ LCP

3 Which PPP subprotocol is responsible for Layer 3 traffic over the PPP link?

- **A** ○ IP
- **B** ○ NCP
- **C** ○ LCP
- **D** ○ ISP
- **E** ○ IPCP

4 Which PPP subprotocol negotiates the options for authentication?

- **A** ○ LCP
- **B** ○ IP
- **C** ○ IPCP
- **D** ○ ISDN
- **E** ○ NCP

5 What is the default encapsulation type on Cisco router interfaces?

- **A** ○ HDLC
- **B** ○ PPP
- **C** ○ ATM
- **D** ○ Frame Relay

6 Which types of commands can assist the administrator in troubleshooting PPP errors? (Choose two.)

A ○ show
B ○ debug
C ○ display
D ○ decode

7 Which are optional phases when establishing a PPP link? (Choose two.)

A ○ Link establishment phase
B ○ Network Link Protocol phase
C ○ Link quality determination phase
D ○ Authentication phase

8 LCP uses which types of frames? (Choose three.)

A ○ Maintenance
B ○ Termination
C ○ Encryption
D ○ Configuration

9 Which authentication method provides poor security measures and sends clear text passwords over the PPP link?

A ○ LCP
B ○ PPP
C ○ CHAP
D ○ NCP
E ○ PAP

10 The CHAP handshake process consists of which of the following steps? (Choose three.)

A ○ Response
B ○ Verification
C ○ Challenge
D ○ Termination

11 Which command is used to display the PPP link establishment process and helps the administrator isolate errors?

A ○ debug ppp negotiation
B ○ debug ppp errors
C ○ debug ppp authentication
D ○ debug ppp packet

Answers

1 **A, C, D.** Multilink bonding, callback, and authentication security are all features of PPP. Review *"What Is PPP?"*

2 **E.** LCP. The Link Control Protocol is responsible for establishing, maintaining, and terminating the PPP link. See *"Purpose of LCP."*

3 **B.** NCP. The Network Control Protocol is responsible for transmitting Layer 3 protocols over the PPP link. Refer to *"Network Control Protocol (NCP)."*

4 **A.** LCP. LCP frames contain configuration options for authentication, compression, multilink, and others. See *"LCP options."*

5 **A.** HDLC. HDLC, not PPP, is the default encapsulation type on Cisco router interfaces. See *"Configuring PPP."*

6 **A, B.** Many show and debug commands provide troubleshooting assistance for the network administrator. Look over *"Monitoring and Troubleshooting PPP."*

7 **C, D.** The link quality determination and authentication are both optional LCP phases. Review *"Operational Flow of PPP."*

8 **A, B, D.** LCP uses maintenance, configuration, and termination frames. Refer to *"Link Control Protocol (LCP)."*

9 **E.** PAP is considered to be an insecure means of authentication and sends passwords across the link in clear text. Read *"PAP and CHAP Authentication."*

10 **A, B, C.** The CHAP three-way handshake consists of a challenge, response, and verification process. See *"Challenge Handshake Authentication Protocol (CHAP)."*

11 **A.** The debug ppp negotiation command displays the PPP negotiation process and allows a network administrator to isolate where the PPP error is occurring. Read *"PPP debug commands."*

Chapter 4: Frame Relay

Exam Objectives

✔ **Understanding Frame Relay WAN connections**

✔ **Examining permanent and switched virtual circuits**

✔ **Defining link status control and LMI**

✔ **Controlling congestion using DE, FECN, and BECN**

✔ **Introducing Frame Relay address resolution using Inverse ARP**

✔ **Managing Frame Relay**

✔ **Configuring Cisco interfaces using Frame Relay**

✔ **Monitoring and troubleshooting Frame Relay**

✔ **Configuring Frame Relay using the Cisco SDM GUI**

Introducing Frame Relay

Frame Relay is an efficient, high-performance, Layer 2 packet-switched WAN technology that shares available bandwidth among users on a packet-switched network medium. Like Point-to-Point Protocol (PPP) and High-Level Data Link Control (HDLC), Frame Relay operates at the physical and data link layers of the OSI model and relies on upper-layer protocols to provide the mechanism for data error correction and flow control. For instance, TCP — not Frame Relay — is responsible for providing the error-checking functionality for IP-based packets. The Frame Relay protocol is also considered to be a replacement for network layer X.25 technology and was originally designed for use with Integrated Services Digital Networks (ISDNs). Today, Frame Relay is a widely popular standard used over a variety of network interfaces and is preferred to X.25 technology. It is a more streamlined, bandwidth-efficient method of connecting local-area networks (LANs) together via wide-area networks (WANs). Frame Relay also provides virtual circuit multiplexing over a single physical link.

Purpose of Frame Relay WAN connections

Frame Relay interconnects several remote sites over a WAN using one or more interfaces from each sites gateway router. Frame Relay devices are categorized as either data terminal equipment (DTE) or data communications equipment (DCE). DTE devices reside at the customer's location where DTE communications originate from. Data terminal equipment consists of computers and data terminals, along with routers, bridges, and other networking devices. Clocking and switching services are provided to data terminal equipment by carrier-owned DCE devices. Data communications equipment is tasked with transmitting the data through the WAN. An example of Frame Relay communications between DCE and DTE devices is shown in Figure 4-1.

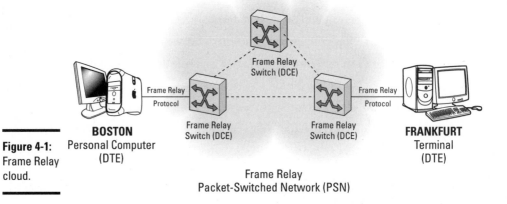

Figure 4-1:
Frame Relay
cloud.

BOSTON
Personal Computer
(DTE)

Frame Relay
Protocol

Frame Relay
Switch (DCE)

Frame Relay
Switch (DCE)

Frame Relay
Switch (DCE)

Frame Relay
Protocol

FRANKFURT
Terminal
(DTE)

Frame Relay
Packet-Switched Network (PSN)

All sites connect to the carrier provider's Frame Relay network infrastructure, or cloud, which is established by interconnecting numerous carrier-owned DCE network devices. The customer has no control over these devices, only their own DTEs. For proper communication to occur between the data terminal equipment located at multiple customer sites, virtual circuits must be established between them.

The clock rate assignment for data transmission is determined by the service provider's DCE device, or channel service unit/data service unit (CSU/DSU). The customer's DTE or customer premises equipment (CPE) has no authority to ignore, dismiss, or invalidate the clock rate specified by the DCE device, and must agree with the chosen settings.

Establishing virtual circuits

Frame Relay connection-oriented communications function by establishing virtual circuits between customer DTEs through the Frame Relay network. To establish communication between DTE endpoints, these virtual or logical connections may traverse numerous intermediate switches, or DCEs, which are transparent to customer's DTEs.

The two main types of virtual circuits are as follows:

✦ **Permanent virtual circuits (PVCs):** PVCs are connections that are maintained on a permanent, always active basis and are never terminated.

PVCs are used to transfer data between DTE devices across the Frame Relay network.

PVCs function in one of two operational states:

- *Data transfer:* Data traffic is flowing between DTE devices using the permanent virtual circuit as the transport mechanism.

- *Idle:* No data transfers are occurring on the active link. However, the connection between DTE devices remains up, ready to transmit data. Although the link is idle, the connection is established, waiting to transfer data. Data may be transmitted at any time without requiring connection reestablishment.

✦ **Switched virtual circuits (SVCs):** SVCs are connections that are maintained on a temporary basis. SVCs are setup to transfer data for a specific time only. Once data is no longer being transmitted over the link, the SVC is closed. After link termination occurs, a new SVC must be re-established to send additional data. SVCs help reduce communications costs to an organization (compared to PVCs) by limiting the lifespan of the link. However, SVCs are not as efficient as PVCs since a connection must be established before data is transmitted.

The four operational phases used to establish and terminate a switched virtual circuit are as follows:

- *Call setup:* During this first phase, a logical circuit is implemented between customer DTE devices.

- *Data transfer:* Once a virtual circuit has been established, data transfer between the DTE devices may begin.

- *Idle:* Idle connection status indicates no data is currently exchanged on the link. With PVCs, DTE devices remain active and are not terminated. SVCs are temporary connections and will be terminated if they remain in an idle state longer than specified.

- *Call termination:* During this final phase, the SVC virtual circuit is shut down. If additional data must be sent between DTE devices after call termination has already taken place, a completely new SVC must be generated. Only then will the additional data be transferred.

Book VII
Chapter 4

Frame Relay

Identifying virtual circuits using data-link connection identifiers (DLCIs)

Frame Relay requires a method to identify single virtual circuits located between customer premises equipment and the service provider's Frame Relay switches. DLCIs are unique numeric values assigned by the service provider to identify individual links. These numbers refer to logical paths through the Frame Relay network, where each segment of the virtual circuit may be assigned different DLCI values for identification and data transmission purposes.

These virtual circuits residing between the local network router (DTE) and the carrier-owned Frame Relay switches (DCE) use DLCI as the main factor for determining data-delivery decisions. The router sending data at one end of a virtual circuit inserts a DLCI number into the Frame Relay frame header, and this DLCI number determines the destination of the frame. Unlike other protocol headers that use a source and destination address, only one DLCI number exists in the Frame Relay frame header. In data transmission and delivery operations, the DLCI number in Frame Relay functions comparably to how Ethernet switches use MAC addresses to deliver data to the proper destination host. DLCI is the Frame Relay equivalent of hardware addresses. Figure 4-2 shows an example of how each end of a Frame Relay virtual circuit uses dissimilar DLCI values to establish connectivity.

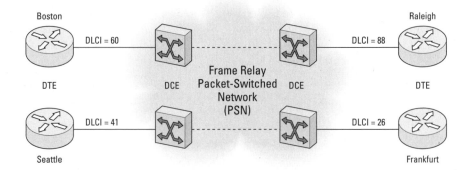

Figure 4-2:
Frame Relay
DLCI.

DLCI Values
0 = Reserved for Call Control Signaling
1 – 15 = Reserved
16 – 1007 = Assignable DLCI Values
1008 – 1022 = Reserved
1023 = Local Management Interface

A DLCI value is bound to the virtual circuit it identifies and to the physical link used by the virtual circuit. Keep in mind that different DTEs assigned to the same virtual circuit can use the same DLCI number. Also, multiple virtual circuits can be active on the same DTE interface by using subinterfaces on the Cisco router.

Reserving bandwidth using access rate and CIR guarantee

Data transmission speeds and bandwidth size allocation are usually negotiated in the WAN planning phase between the customer and service provider prior to implementing Frame Relay. Two important factors that determine data throughput rates are as follows:

✦ **Access rate:** This is the maximum data transfer speed between two DCEs. The access rate is defined on a per port basis on each DCE device. The data transfer speed sets the clock speed of the link between the DCEs and determines how many data frames enter or leave each DCE per second.

✦ **Committed information rate (CIR):** This is the maximum bandwidth size guaranteed by the service provider to the customer for data transmission over the WAN link.

The CIR is in theory "guaranteed," but in reality it is actually a fluctuating value (in bits per second) and cannot be relied upon at 100 percent. The CIR is measured over a period of time. The average measured CIR is called the Committed Rate Measurement Interval (Tc). There may be times when the actual data rate exceeds, or Bursts (Be), over the defined CIR. The Committed Burst (Bc) rate is the maximum number of bits sent during the measured CIR (that is, during the Committed Rate Measurement Interval).

Frame Relay link status control using LMI

Frame Relay uses a signaling control protocol between the customer's DTE device and the provider's DCE device to manage the connection and monitor the device status across the link.

This signaling standard is known as the Local Management Interface (LMI) and was designed by Cisco and a consortium of developers to provide extensions and enhancements to the original Frame Relay protocol. LMI adds the following features:

**Book VII
Chapter 4**

Frame Relay

✦ **Multicasting:** Conserves bandwidth by delivering routing and address resolution updates to specific multicast groups using DLCIs in the 1019–1022 range.

✦ **Global addressing:** Specifies that local DLCIs are uniquely assigned to devices on a global network scale. Each uniquely assigned DLCI represents the DTE address on the Frame Relay network. Global addressing allows one router to be reached by all other remote routers using the same DLCI.

✦ **Virtual circuit status messages:** Provide continuous communication, synchronization, and status monitoring on DLCIs connected from the customer's site's DTE devices to the service provider's DCE devices.

✦ **Keepalive:** A 10-second interval (by default) that determines the time value to wait before declaring the link between the DCE and DTE down or unusable. Data must be received between DTE and DCE devices during this time; otherwise the connection will terminate.

To maintain LMI status message synchronization between the DTE router and the DCE Frame Relay switch, the customer's router keepalive interval value must be equal to or lower than the corresponding keepalive value set on the service provider's switch. If the router's keepalive value is configured with a higher numeric value than the carrier-owned DCE device's keepalive value, sequence number mismatches may occur during the exchange of LMI status messages, interface flapping could result, or the connection might disconnect altogether.

Three types of LMIs exist and are used to listen for specific LMI traffic traveling across reserved DLCIs (0 for ANSI and Q933A; 1023 for Cisco). These LMIs are as follows:

✦ **Cisco:** A Cisco-proprietary LMI type that is set by default on all Cisco routers. It is defined by a consortium of corporations including Cisco, DEC, StrataCom, and Northern Telecom.

✦ **ANSI:** An LMI specification known as Annex D (T1.617) that defines the signaling process without the optional extensions.

✦ **Q933A:** An access signaling specification defined by the International Telecommunications Union (ITU).

Both DTE and DCE devices must use the same type of LMI. Cisco routers allow dynamic detection of the LMI type and are autosensed from the CPE to the provider's DCE Frame Relay switching devices. This autosense feature is activated by default on routers using Cisco IOS Release 11.2 or later. Autosensing will not activate when a manual LMI configuration has been applied to the router.

Frame Relay frame structure

The Frame Relay data frame header is shown in Figure 4-3 and consists of the following fields:

✦ **Flags:** This field is used to mark the start and end points of a frame. This field is always set to the constant binary value 01111110 or 7E in hexadecimal. The DCEs use this field to determine where a Frame Relay frame starts. Keep in mind that there may be electrical noise on a WAN link: some (noise) bits may be received by a DCE at any time. The *Flags* field helps a DCE device determine when an actual Frame Relay frame is being received.

✦ **Address:** A field that contains the following information:

• *DLCI:* A unique 10-bit value identifying a particular virtual circuit. A DLCI value is bound to the virtual circuit it identifies and to the physical link used by the virtual circuit. Both ends of a single virtual circuit may use different DLCI values to establish one link.

- *Command/Response (C/R):* An undefined bit located after the most significant DLCI byte.

- *Extended Address (EA):* Marker used to determine the last addressing field. This bit is usually set to 1. Setting the bit to 1 tags the byte as the last Frame Relay address byte.

- *Congestion Control fields:* These are three 1-bit congestion fields known as FECN, BECN, and DE. Congestion control bits trigger upper layer protocols to mitigate congestion using flow control whenever the WAN link becomes overloaded.

  An explanation of the FECN, BECN, and DE bits is provided in the next section of this chapter.

✦ **Data:** A variable-length field that holds encapsulated user data. The data field is responsible for delivery of upper-layer protocol packet (PDU) through a Frame Relay network.

✦ **Frame check sequence:** This field is used to check the validity of frame. The sending device calculates the initial frame check and stores the calculated value in this field. The destination device verifies the frame by calculating a check sequence based on the frame received and comparing the calculated value with the value stored in this field.

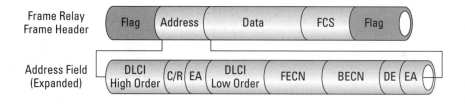

DLCI = Data Link Connection Identifier
C/R = Command / Response Field
EA = Address Extension Field
FECN = Forward Explicit Congestion Notification
BECN = Backward Explicit Congestion Notification
DE = Discard Eligibility

Figure 4-3:
Frame Relay
data frame
header.

Frame Relay flow and congestion control using DE, FECN, and BECN

Frame Relay provides simple and effective mechanisms to combat network congestion, while relying on the upper-layer protocols to handle the responsibility of data flow control. By using basic congestion-notification features instead of assigning specific flow control on every virtual circuit, network overhead is minimized.

Three network congestion-mitigation methods exist for Frame Relay; they are all identified and controlled by a single binary bit located in the address portion of the Frame Relay frame header. The congestion-control methods are as follows:

✦ **Discard eligible (DE):** Any data that exceeds the committed information rate is considered discard eligible (DE) and will be discarded if network congestion occurs. Frames with the DE bit set to 1 (in the address field of the frame header) are given a lower priority than other frames and are the first to be dropped when excessive CIR limits are reached. This helps ensure that less critical frames are dropped first when network congestion occurs.

✦ **Forward explicit congestion notification (FECN):** When network congestion is encountered during communications from source to destination, the Frame Relay switch changes the bit value in the FECN packet header to 1 and forwards the frame on to the destination device. Changing the FECN bit value indicates to the receiving machine that network congestion is occurring starting from the source device or somewhere along the path used to reach the source to destination devices.

✦ **Backward explicit congestion notification (BECN):** When network congestion is detected by a Frame Relay switch, it instructs the DTE device to slow the rate of data transmission by assigning the BECN bit value to 1. This is a warning that the specific path used for data transmission through the network is congested. BECN notifications are issued back to source DTE devices so that DTEs can send out congestion warnings to upper-layer protocols, which will trigger congestion and flow-control remedies.

FECN and BECN frames flow in opposite directions through the Frame Relay network. Frames with the FECN bit set will flow from source to destination, while BECN set bits issue warnings to the source device. An example of FECN and BECN traffic during network congestion is shown in Figure 4-4.

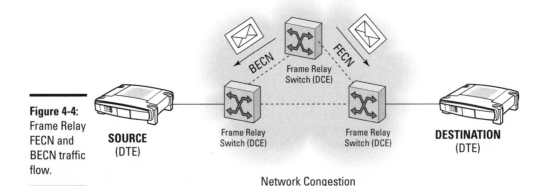

Figure 4-4: Frame Relay FECN and BECN traffic flow.

Frame Relay address resolution using Inverse ARP

There may be instances where a Frame Relay DTE device does not know another remote device's protocol address. Inverse Address Resolution Protocol (Inverse ARP) was developed specifically for Frame Relay networks to reduce traffic congestion during address resolution. In cases where the protocol address is unknown, address resolution is required using Inverse ARP. Inverse ARP is an extension of the existing Address Resolution Protocol, created specifically for Frame Relay networks to discover the protocol (IP, IPX, and so on) address of remote devices.

Inverse ARP dynamically maps protocol addresses (Layer 3) to a DLCI address (Layer 2). After a virtual circuit is established, all routers send an Inverse ARP message identifying itself and its corresponding network layer address. Inverse ARP is enabled by default and Inverse ARP messages are sent between routers every 60 seconds. While Inverse ARP and ARP share the same cache on the router, differences exist between the two. Inverse ARP maps a protocol address to a DLCI address, while standard ARP maps a network layer IP address to a Layer 2 hardware (MAC) address.

Inverse ARP uses dynamic address mapping to request a next-hop protocol address for each active PVC. After a requesting router receives an Inverse ARP response, its DLCI-to-network layer address mapping table is updated. Dynamic address mapping automatically takes place if LMI and Inverse ARP exist on the network. If LMI and Inverse ARP are not supported, a Frame Relay mapping may be statically introduced by the network administrator using the `frame-relay map` command. Once a static mapping is defined, Inverse ARP is automatically disabled for that particular DLCI.

After a router interface is enabled for Frame Relay, Inverse ARP immediately identifies all protocol addresses on startup.

Managing Frame Relay

Minimizing management tasks always begins with a carefully planned network implementation. Proper planning helps mitigate network congestion, bandwidth oversubscription, and additional or unnecessary financial costs to an organization. Knowledge of the protocols, traffic patterns, and network topology before implementation can help construct a successful Frame Relay network.

To manage a Frame Relay network, you must first understand the choice of topologies that can be implemented and the steps involved in the Frame Relay communication process.

Frame Relay topologies

Three main Frame Relay topologies exist for interconnection between remote sites using virtual circuits:

✦ **Star topology:** In this topology, shown in Figure 4-5, Frame Relay endpoints are connected to one central site (switch) using point-to-point links.

The star topology is the most popular Frame Relay method and uses the least amount of PVCs. Also known as the hub-and-spoke topology, the star design simplifies management while reducing operational costs. The hub-and-spoke topology is the most efficient method to connect multiple virtual circuits. One hub device acts as the central communications point, where all other remote routers (known as spoke devices), connect to create a star topology.

Disadvantages to using this approach are

- The central router is a single point of failure on which the entire network depends.

- Data may need to take additional hops to reach a destination.

- Scalability.

- Limited performance.

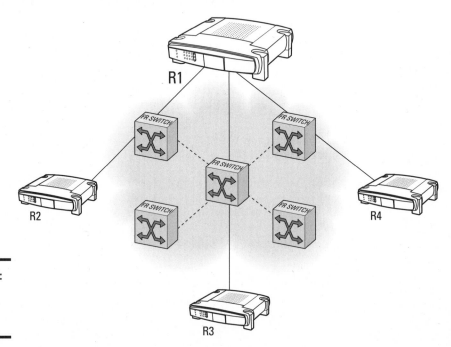

Figure 4-5:
Frame Relay star topology.

✦ **Full mesh topology:** Each DTE device is interconnected to all other routers, providing a direct connection to every known destination. The full mesh topology introduces and allows redundancy that is not available in star topology configurations. If one link in the full mesh network goes down, traffic can be rerouted in another direction to reach its destination.

The drawback is that the full mesh topology is the most costly method. As the number of devices on the network increases, so does the cost, because each device establishes and requires a separate virtual circuit to all other devices on the network. Other disadvantages include

- Complex configuration.

- Larger volumes of traffic and broadcasts.

✦ **Partial mesh topology:** This topology combines Frame Relay devices using the full mesh topology with other devices configured for the star topology. This integration between the full mesh and star topology allows the partial mesh Frame Relay configuration to encompass the optimum balance of performance, cost, scalability, and fault tolerance.

Book VII
Chapter 4

Frame Relay

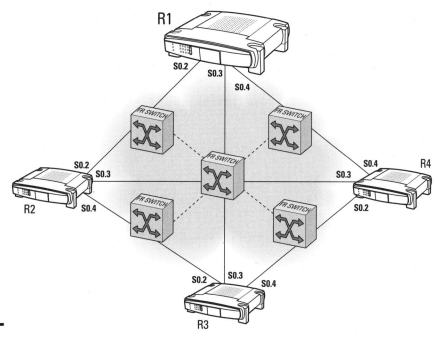

Figure 4-6:
Frame Relay
full mesh
topology.

R = Router (DTE)
FR Switch = Frame Relay Packet-Switched Network (DCE)
SO.x = Subinterface Number

Operational flow of Frame Relay

The overall operation of the Frame Relay Layer 2 protocol is best described in a series of steps as follows:

1. Each customer DTE device (router) connects to a DCE device (Frame Relay switch) and is assigned a DLCI number from the service provider.

2. The DTE device sends a Status Inquiry message containing the status of the router to the DCE device. This message also passes on information about the status of connected routers on the link.

3. The DCE device returns a status message to the requesting DTE device providing DLCI numbers of any connected DTE devices that are available for communication.

4. The requesting DTE device then sends Inverse ARP packets to all remote DTEs announcing itself on the link and requesting each remote router's IP address. Inverse ARP messages are exchanged every 60 seconds between DTE devices on the network.

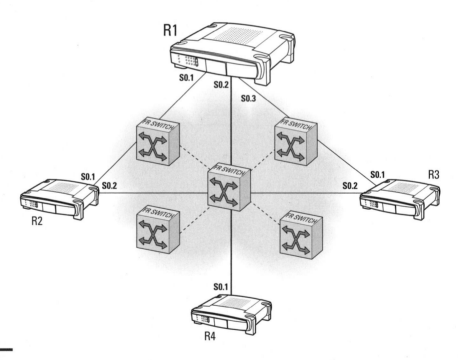

Figure 4-7:
Frame Relay partial mesh topology.

R = Router (DTE)
FR Switch = Frame Relay Packet-Switched Network (DCE)
SO.x = Subinterface Number

5. After the requested IP information is returned to the requesting DTE, Frame Relay map entries are created in the Frame Relay map table. These entries include the DLCI, IP address, and connection status of each DTE.

The three connection states are active, inactive, and deleted. Routers may exchange data in the active state, but not in the inactive or deleted states. If necessary, static routes may be assigned to connect to remote routers. Keepalive messages are used to monitor the state of the connection and are sent every 10 seconds by default.

Split horizon issues in a Frame Relay WAN

Interface configuration is an important issue to remain aware of when designing a Frame Relay network. The amount of broadcast traffic (routing updates), and placement of virtual circuits should be evaluated prior to network implementation to prevent network congestion.

If a single physical router interface is to interconnect multiple sites, consider the following two important factors:

✦ **Split horizon:** Split horizon is used to mitigate routing loops and the counting-to-infinity problem with distance vector routing protocols by limiting routing updates. Split horizon prevents inbound routing updates (or broadcast traffic) received on one interface to be forwarded outbound on the same physical interface:

Book VII
Chapter 4

Frame Relay

- Use the `ip split horizon` command to enable.
- Use the `no ip split horizon` command to disable.

✦ **Nonbroadcast multiple access (NBMA):** Data is transmitted directly from one peer to another over a virtual circuit. NBMA is the opposite of a broadcast network, which means that broadcasted routing updates may not be received by all sites.

By default, Frame Relay uses the NBMA method of communication. Also, with split horizon enabled, routing updates may not be received by all sites located on multiple PVCs. This is not a problem for point-to-point Frame Relay networks using a single virtual circuit, but it does create a problem for delivering broadcast traffic to all locations in a multipoint environment.

Disabling the split horizon feature for IP networks may sound like a good solution, but the problem of routing loops on the network becomes much greater. A better option is to use subinterfaces. Subinterfaces are logically divided, multiple interfaces that reside on a single physical interface.

Keep these two rules in mind when enabling Frame Relay on a physical interface:

✦ **Physical serial interface:** Split horizon is disabled automatically by the router when Frame Relay is configured on an interface. By default, physical serial interfaces are set up for multipoint operation.

✦ **Serial subinterfaces:** Split horizon is enabled by default on subinterfaces.

Using subinterfaces, incoming and outgoing routing updates may be transmitted on the same physical interface, and the split horizon issue is solved. Because split horizon is enabled at the subinterface level, the threat of routing loops occurring is once again minimized.

Subinterfaces may be configured for the following types of Frame Relay connectivity:

✦ **Point-to-point:** A single virtual circuit connection between two end devices that reside on the same subnet. Each configured interface or subinterface contains its own unique DLCI number. Inverse ARP is not needed on point-to-point links.

Point-to-point connections work theoretically like leased lines and establish the link as a complete subnet, eliminating the broadcasting problem. To minimize address space usage, a typical point-to-point connection uses a 30-bit (/30) subnet mask, as shown in Figure 4-8.

When using point-to-point subinterfaces in a Frame Relay network, the subinterfaces will reside in the same IP subnet and have assigned IP addresses. An IP address on the physical interface is not required.

✦ **Multipoint:** Multiple virtual circuits on remote routers that establish connection with a single subinterface on a central router. Each multipoint interface requires a unique DLCI and performs dynamic address mapping using Inverse ARP. Inverse ARP maps the next-hop protocol address to the local DLCI on the router.

Although split horizon is enabled by default on Cisco router interfaces, split horizon is disabled by default on any physical interface configured for Frame Relay. Also, split horizon is enabled by default on Frame Relay subinterfaces.

Configuring single interfaces for Frame Relay over a point-to-point link

The most basic type of Frame Relay network is a point-to-point connection between two end DTE devices.

Referring again to Figure 4-8, you now configure the interfaces on both the Boston and Frankfurt routers for Frame Relay.

Using the Cisco CLI, the configuration is implemented as follows for the Boston router:

1. **In global configuration mode, specify the interface, IP address, subnet mask, encapsulation type, and bandwidth:**

```
Boston#config t
Boston(config)#int s0
Boston(config-if)#ip address 192.168.1.1 255.255.255.252
Boston(config-if)#encapsulation frame-relay
Boston(config-if)#bandwidth 64
```

2. **Specify the LMI type and DLCI number for the interface:**

```
Boston(config-if)#frame-relay lmi-type cisco
Boston(config-if)#frame-relay interface-dlci 100
Boston(config-if)#no shutdown
Boston(config-if)#exit
```

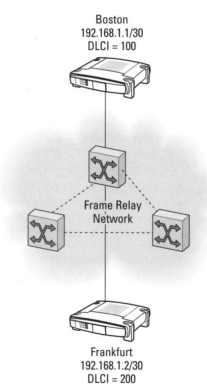

Boston
192.168.1.1/30
DLCI = 100

Frame Relay
Network

Figure 4-8:
Configuring
single
interfaces
over Frame
Relay point-
to-point
connections.

Frankfurt
192.168.1.2/30
DLCI = 200

The configuration is implemented as follows for the Frankfurt router:

1. **In global configuration mode, specify the interface, IP address, subnet mask, encapsulation type, and bandwidth:**

```
Frankfurt#config t
Frankfurt(config)#int s0
```

```
Frankfurt(config-if)#ip address 192.168.1.2 255.255.255.252
Frankfurt(config-if)#encapsulation frame-relay
Frankfurt(config-if)#bandwidth 64
```

2. **Specify the LMI type and DLCI number for the interface:**

```
Frankfurt(config-if)#frame-relay lmi-type cisco
Frankfurt(config-if)#frame-relay interface-dlci 200
Frankfurt(config-if)#no shutdown
Frankfurt(config-if)#exit
```

I examine these steps in greater detail:

1. Both the Boston and Frankfurt routers' serial interfaces are configured with an IP address and subnet mask that belongs to the same subnet.

2. The `encapsulation frame-relay` command is given to denote the use of the Frame Relay encapsulation type, instead of the default HDLC. The `encapsulation frame-relay ietf` command may be used to establish the IETF Frame Relay encapsulation type, allowing connection to non-Cisco DTE devices. Be sure to have matching encapsulation types on both ends of the point-to-point link; otherwise communication failure will occur.

3. The Frame Relay LMI signaling type is specified using the `frame-relay lmi-type cisco` command. LMI is assigned by the Frame Relay service provider and must match on the customer's device. The default LMI type on Cisco DTE routers is always Cisco and is usually autosensed, so it is not always necessary to issue this command.

4. The Frame Relay DLCI numbers are configured on each interface using the `frame-relay interface dlci` command. For both routers to communicate with each other, both ends of the point-to-point link must be configured with unique DLCIs. Each router configuration sets up a one-way virtual circuit to the other.

Because only two communication endpoints exist on a point-to-point Frame Relay virtual circuit, DLCI–to–IP address mappings are not configured, and Inverse ARP is not needed.

Configuring subinterfaces for Frame Relay over multipoint links

Multipoint virtual circuit connections in a full or partial mesh topology are used to connect multiple DTEs over a Frame Relay network, which requires the configuration of subinterfaces. Configuring Frame Relay subinterfaces allows a single physical interface to be treated as multiple virtual interfaces. Incoming data received on one virtual interface may be forwarded through another virtual interface to its destination, even if both virtual interfaces reside on the same physical router interface. This is achieved by assigning each subinterface its own number, which protocols interpret as belonging to individual, separate physical interfaces.

This differs from point-to-point Frame Relay configurations, where subinterfaces do not require unique assigned numbers, and reduces interface management.

Each DTE device shown in Figure 4-9 belongs to the same subnet, excluding the point-to-point link to Frankfurt. Because the devices that belong to the multipoint network are all on the same subnet, DLCIs may be combined onto the same subinterface. Only one subinterface is needed per router to make the multipoint connection. Also, keep in mind that because subinterfaces inherit settings from the parent interface, certain commands already established on the serial interface (such as bandwidth, LMI type, encapsulation type, and the `no shutdown` command) are not required on the subinterface.

To configure subinterfaces in a multipoint (partial mesh) configuration, follow these steps:

1. In global configuration mode, specify the multipoint subinterface, IP address, subnet mask, and DLCIs for the Boston router:

```
Boston#config t
Boston(config)#int s0.3 multipoint
Boston(config-subif)#ip address 10.1.1.1 255.255.255.0
Boston(config-subif)#frame-relay interface-dlci 300
Boston(config-fr-dlci)#exit
Boston(config-subif)#frame-relay interface-dlci 400
Boston(config-fr-dlci)#exit
Boston(config-if)#exit
```

2. In global configuration mode, specify the interface, encapsulation type, bandwidth, and LMI type on the Seattle router:

```
Seattle#config t
Seattle(config)#int s0
Seattle(config-if)#encapsulation frame-relay
Seattle(config-if)#bandwidth 64
Seattle(config-if)#frame-relay lmi-type cisco
Seattle(config-if)#no shutdown
Seattle(config-if)#exit
```

3. Specify the multipoint subinterface, IP address, subnet mask, and DLCIs for the Seattle router:

```
Seattle(config)#int s0.1 multipoint
Seattle(config-subif)#ip address 10.1.1.2 255.255.255.0
Seattle(config-subif)#frame-relay interface-dlci 500
Seattle(config-fr-dlci)#exit
Seattle(config-subif)#frame-relay interface-dlci 600
Seattle(config-fr-dlci)#exit
Seattle(config-if)#exit
```

4. In global configuration mode, specify the interface, encapsulation type, bandwidth, and LMI type on the Raleigh router:

```
Raleigh#config t
Raleigh(config)#int s0
```

Book VII Chapter 4

Frame Relay

```
Raleigh(config-if)#encapsulation frame-relay
Raleigh(config-if)#bandwidth 64
Raleigh(config-if)#frame-relay lmi-type cisco
Raleigh(config-if)#no shutdown
Raleigh(config-if)#exit
```

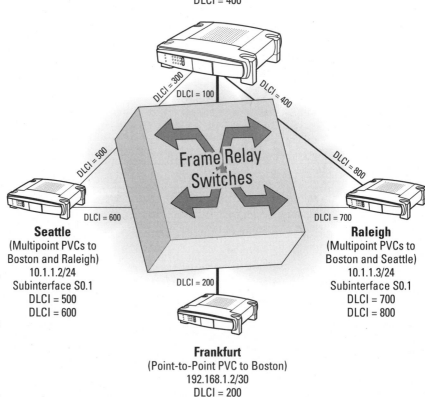

Boston
(Point-to-Point PVC to Frankfurt)
192.168.1.1/30
Subinterface S0.1
DLCI = 100

(Multipoint PVCs to Seattle and Raleigh)
10.1.1.1/24
Subinterface S0.3
DLCI = 300
DLCI = 400

Seattle
(Multipoint PVCs to
Boston and Raleigh)
10.1.1.2/24
Subinterface S0.1
DLCI = 500
DLCI = 600

Raleigh
(Multipoint PVCs to
Boston and Seattle)
10.1.1.3/24
Subinterface S0.1
DLCI = 700
DLCI = 800

Frankfurt
(Point-to-Point PVC to Boston)
192.168.1.2/30
DLCI = 200

Figure 4-9:
Configuring
subinterfaces
over Frame
Relay partial
mesh
topology.

5. **Specify the multipoint subinterface, IP address, subnet mask, and DLCIs for the Raleigh router:**

```
Raleigh(config)#int s0.1 multipoint
Raleigh(config-subif)#ip address 10.1.1.3 255.255.255.0
Raleigh(config-subif)#frame-relay interface-dlci 700
Raleigh(config-fr-dlci)#exit
Raleigh(config-subif)#frame-relay interface-dlci 800
Raleigh(config-fr-dlci)#exit
Raleigh(config-if)#exit
```

In the previous examples, each subinterface is assigned its own IP address. Because IP addresses are not required for Frame Relay links on a physical interface, be sure to remove the IP address on the physical interface prior to configuring subinterfaces. The serial interface from the Boston router in Figure 4-8 is deactivated, and the IP address and DLCI are reconfigured on subinterface s0.1 (as shown in Figure 4-9).

After these configurations have been issued on each router's interface, Inverse ARP is responsible for IP-to-DLCI address resolution across the multipoint network. In certain cases, a network administrator may want to implement static mappings. Creating a static map entry is quite easy and is shown here:

```
Boston(config-subif)#frame-relay map ip 10.1.1.2 500 broadcast
Boston(config-subif)#frame-relay map ip 10.1.1.3 800 broadcast
```

The `frame-relay map` command is used to assign the remote IP address to the local DLCI. The `broadcast` command permits forwarding of routing updates across the NBMA virtual circuit.

Frame Relay is used in mission-critical WAN applications and provides access for multiple locations that connect to a single router port:

✦ Using multiple Frame Relay PVCs, connection to many locations is possible using multiple subinterfaces on one physical interface.

✦ Subinterfaces inherit the settings from the parent interface.

Configuring Frame Relay with the Cisco Router and Security Device Manager (SDM)

You can also configure the Frame Relay WAN protocol on your router using the *Cisco SDM WAN Wizard* in the Cisco Router and Security Device Manager (SDM). The Cisco *SDM WAN Wizard* walks you through several graphical user interface (GUI) dialogs to easily step through the process of setting up a PPP, Frame Relay, or HDLC link.

Monitoring and Troubleshooting Frame Relay

Using `show` and `debug` IOS commands, an administrator may verify and troubleshoot Frame Relay networks. Because `debug` commands heavily tax

**Book VII
Chapter 4**

Frame Relay

the router's hardware resources and may negatively impact network performance, these commands should only be used in troubleshooting instances, not during normal network operation. The show commands may be used whenever needed to display and verify proper Frame Relay operation.

Monitoring and troubleshooting Frame Relay problems may be categorized into four steps:

1. Verify the physical connection between the router and the CSU/DSU.

2. Verify the LMI exchange between the DTE and DCE.

3. Verify that the state of the virtual circuit is set to "active."

4. Verify that encapsulation types are identical between routers.

The following are the most commonly used commands when monitoring and troubleshooting Frame Relay networks:

✦ show interface serial: Lists information on the physical status, line protocol status, and encapsulation type of an interface or subinterface. The show interface serial command allows an administrator to view the type of encapsulation and LMI used, keepalive value, and if the interface is configured as a DCE or DTE device.

The show interface serial command provides functionality verification of the physical connection between the DTE and the CSU/DSU and should be used as the first step when troubleshooting Frame Relay networks. If the serial interface status is down, it could be caused by a faulty cable or interface connector on the router.

The following is sample output from the show interface serial command for the serial1 interface with LMI enabled:

```
Router#show interface serial 1
Serial1 is up, line protocol is down
Hardware is MCI Serial
Internet address is 192.168.200.4, subnet mask is 255.255.255.0
MTU 1500 bytes, BW 1544 Kbit, DLY 20000 usec, rely 246/255, load 1/255
Encapsulation FRAME-RELAY, loopback not set, keepalive set (10 sec)
LMI enq sent  2, LMI stat recvd 0, LMI upd recvd 0, DTE LMI down
LMI enq recvd 266, LMI stat sent  264, LMI upd sent  0
LMI DLCI 200  LMI type is CISCO  frame relay DTE
Last input 0:00:05, output 0:00:03, output hang never
Last clearing of "show interface" counters 0:32:31
Output queue 0/40, 0 drops; input queue 0/75, 0 drops
Five minute input rate 0 bits/sec, 0 packets/sec
Five minute output rate 0 bits/sec, 0 packets/sec
327 packets input, 8648 bytes, 0 no buffer
Received 0 broadcasts, 0 runts, 0 giants
0 input errors, 0 CRC, 0 frame, 0 overrun, 0 ignored, 0 abort
0 input packets with dribble condition detected
282 packets output, 4502 bytes, 0 underruns
0 output errors, 0 collisions, 5 interface resets, 0
     restarts
180 carrier transitions
```

✦ `show frame-relay lmi`: Displays statistics about the Local Management Interface (LMI) for interfaces configured to use LMI. The show frame relay lmi command shows the configured LMI type and the LMI traffic statistics.

The following is sample output from the `show frame-relay lmi` command for a DTE-configured interface:

```
Router#show frame-relay lmi
LMI Statistics for interface Serial1 (Frame Relay DTE) LMI TYPE = ANSI
Invalid Unnumbered info 0      Invalid Prot Disc 0
Invalid dummy Call Ref 0       Invalid Msg Type 0
Invalid Status Message 0       Invalid Lock Shift 0
Invalid Information ID 0        Invalid Report IE Len 0
Invalid Report Request 0       Invalid Keep IE Len 0
Num Status Enq. Sent 4         Num Status msgs Rcvd 0
Num Update Status Rcvd 0       Num Status Timeouts 4
```

✦ `show frame-relay map`: Shows current Frame Relay DLCI map entries and specific configuration information for each entry. The show frame relay map command lists mappings between DLCIs and next-hop addresses. Mappings created by both dynamic Inverse ARP and static assignment (using the `frame-relay map` command) are shown. This command is not available on point-to-point connections.

The following is an example of the `show frame-relay map` command output for a static entry:

```
Router#show frame-relay map
Serial1 (up): IP 192.168.2.2 dlci 200(0x15,0x0444), static CISCO, BW=
    56000, status defined, active
```

Here is an example of a dynamic entry:

```
Router#show frame-relay map
Serial1/2 (up): ip 204.218.210.2 dlci 500(0x182,0x4110), dynamic,
    broadcast,, status defined, active
Serial1/2 (up): ip 204.218.210.3 dlci 700(0x2C4,0x3B42), dynamic,
    broadcast,, status defined, active
```

✦ `show frame-relay pvc`: Displays Frame Relay interface statistics regarding permanent virtual circuits (PVCs) and the state of the connection. The connection may be active, inactive, or deleted. The `show frame-relay pvc` command also shows dropped packets and network congestion from FECN and BECN notifiers.

The following is sample output from the `show frame-relay pvc` command:

```
Router#show frame-relay pvc
  PVC Statistics for interface Serial1 (Frame Relay DCE)
    DLCI = 100, DLCI USAGE = SWITCHED, PVC STATUS = ACTIVE
        input pkts 1210        output pkts 824        in bytes 202402112
        out bytes 18012123     dropped pkts 21        in FECN pkts 120
        in BECN pkts 141       out FECN pkts 214      out BECN pkts 145
        in DE pkts 0           out DE pkts 0
        pvc create time 0:03:03 last time pvc status changed 0:03:03
```

Book VII
Chapter 4

Frame Relay

```
      Num Pkts Switched 0
DLCI = 200, DLCI USAGE = SWITCHED, PVC STATUS = INACTIVE
   input pkts 0           output pkts 0         in bytes 0
   out bytes 0            dropped pkts 0        in FECN pkts 0
   in BECN pkts 0         out FECN pkts 0       out BECN pkts 0
   in DE pkts 0           out DE pkts 0
   pvc create time 0:02:58 last time pvc status changed 0:02:58
   Num Pkts Switched 0
DLCI = 300, DLCI USAGE = SWITCHED, PVC STATUS = DELETED
   input pkts 0           output pkts 0         in bytes 0
   out bytes 0            dropped pkts 0        in FECN pkts 0
   in BECN pkts 0         out FECN pkts 0       out BECN pkts 0
   in DE pkts 0           out DE pkts 0
   pvc create time 0:02:58 last time pvc status changed 0:02:58
   Num Pkts Switched 0
```

The `show frame-relay pvc` command shows each PVC status in an active, inactive, or deleted state. Only PVCs in the active state are functioning normally. The BECN pkts, FECN pkts, and dropped pkts fields are helpful in troubleshooting congestion and dropped packets occurring on the network.

If a Frame Relay DLCI becomes inactive or deleted, there is likely a configuration error on the Frame Relay DTE device (router).

✦ `show frame-relay route`: Shows the status of configured Frame Relay routes.

The sample output from the `show frame-relay route` command follows:

```
Router#show frame-relay route
   Input Intf    Input Dlci    Output Intf    Output Dlci    Status
   Serial1       100           Serial2        200            active
   Serial1       101           Serial2        201            active
   Serial1       102           Serial2        202            active
   Serial1       103           Serial3        203            inactive
   Serial2       200           Serial1        100            active
   Serial2       201           Serial1        101            active
   Serial2       202           Serial1        102            active
   Serial3       203           Serial1        103            inactive
```

✦ `show frame-relay traffic`: Displays the router's global Frame Relay statistics since the last reboot.

The following is sample output from the `show frame-relay traffic` command:

```
Router#show frame-relay traffic
   Frame Relay statistics:
   ARP requests sent 18, ARP replies sent 0
   ARP request recvd 0, ARP replies recvd 11
```

✦ `debug frame-relay events`: Useful for isolating connection-oriented problems between end points during Frame Relay network installation.

The `debug frame-relay events` command shows Inverse ARP traffic generated between the DTE device (router) and the Frame Relay network when dynamic addressing is used.

```
Router#debug frame-relay events
*Mar 12 03:46:39.235: Serial1/2: FR ARP input
*Mar 12 03:46:39.235: datagramstart = 0x7D0DE6E, datagramsize = 34
*Mar 12 03:46:39.235: FR encap = 0x64110300
*Mar 12 03:46:39.235: 80 00 00 03 08 06 00 0F 08 00 02 04 00 08 00 00
*Mar 12 03:46:39.239: AD 10 01 04 18 51 00 00 00 00 01 02 00 00
*Mar 12 03:46:39.239:
*Mar 12 03:46:44.899: Serial1/2: FR ARP input
*Mar 12 03:46:44.899: datagramstart = 0x7D0E0EE, datagramsize = 34
*Mar 12 03:46:44.899: FR encap = 0x30910300
*Mar 12 03:46:44.899: 80 00 00 03 08 06 00 0F 08 00 02 04 00 09 00 00
*Mar 12 03:46:44.899: AD 10 01 02 30 91 AC 10 01 01 01 02 00 00
*Mar 12 03:47:44.911: Serial1/2: FR ARP input
*Mar 12 03:47:44.911: datagramstart = 0x7D0CCEE, datagramsize = 34
*Mar 12 03:47:44.911: FR encap = 0x48D10300
*Mar 12 03:47:44.911: 80 00 00 03 08 06 00 0F 08 00 02 04 00 09 00 00
*Mar 12 03:47:44.911: AD 10 01 02 48 D1 AC 10 01 01 01 02 00 00
```

✦ `debug frame-relay lmi`: Verifies Frame Relay connections and accurate LMI communications processes by examining the exchange of LMI data. Use the `debug frame-relay lmi` command as follows:

```
Router#debug frame-relay lmi
*Mar 14 01:26:16.063: Serial1/2(out): StEnq, myseq 43, yourseen 42, DTE up
*Mar 14 01:26:16.063: datagramstart = 0x7B00E94, datagramsize = 13
*Mar 14 01:26:16.063: FR encap = 0xFCF10309
*Mar 14 01:26:16.063: 00 75 01 01 00 03 02 2B 2A
*Mar 14 01:26:16.063:
*Mar 14 01:26:16.071: Serial1/2(in): Status, myseq 43
*Mar 14 01:26:16.071: RT IE 1, length 1, type 0
*Mar 14 01:26:16.071: KA IE 3, length 2, yourseq 43, myseq 43
*Mar 14 01:26:16.075: PVC IE 0x7 , length 0x6 , dlci 200, status 0x2 , bw 0
*Mar 14 01:26:16.075: PVC IE 0x7 , length 0x6 , dlci 300, status 0x2 , bw 0
*Mar 14 01:26:16.075: PVC IE 0x7 , length 0x6 , dlci 400, status 0x2 , bw 0
*Mar 14 01:26:16.075: PVC IE 0x7 , length 0x6 , dlci 500, status 0x2 , bw 0
```

When issuing the `debug frame-relay lmi` command from a remote Telnet session, use the privileged EXEC `terminal monitor` command to display the output to the VTC. Otherwise, output may not be displayed.

✦ `debug frame-relay packet`: Analyzes each datagram transmitted through a particular Frame Relay interface. The debugging output of this command may grow
rapidly; therefore, it is best to specify a certain interface or DLCI. A shortened `debug frame-relay packet` output is listed here:

```
Router#debug frame-relay packet
*Mar 1 01:37:25.195: Serial1/2(i): dlci 500(0x7C51), pkt type 0x800,
    datagramsize 53
*Mar 1 01:37:28.195: Serial1/2(i): dlci 500(0x7C51), pkt type 0x800,
    datagramsize 53
*Mar 1 01:37:31.203: Serial1/2(i): dlci 500(0x7C51), pkt type 0x800,
    datagramsize 53
*Mar 1 01:37:34.203: Serial1/2(i): dlci 500(0x7C51), pkt type 0x800,
    datagramsize 53
```

Prep Test

1 **What are DLCIs? (Choose two.)**

A ○ Data-link connection identifiers

B ○ Values assigned by the service provider to identify individual links

C ○ Data-link connection interface

D ○ Numeric values assigned by the customer to identify a link

2 **What are the main types of virtual circuits? (Choose two.)**

A ○ DVCs

B ○ PVCs

C ○ BVCs

D ○ LVCs

E ○ SVCs

3 **Frame Relay clocking is determined by which types of devices? (Choose two.)**

A ○ CSU/DSU

B ○ PVC

C ○ DTE

D ○ DCE

4 **Which term describes the maximum bandwidth of data allocated and guaranteed to the customer by the telephone company or service provider?**

A ○ Access rate

B ○ CIR

C ○ Bc

D ○ Tc

5 **LMI is used for which purpose?**

A ○ Manages the connection and monitors the device status on the link

B ○ Debugs and troubleshoots Frame Relay networks

C ○ Defines link segments by a unique numeric value

D ○ Eliminates network congestion

6 Which Frame Replay topology uses a hub-and-spoke system to connect multiple remote links to a central router?

A ○ ATM

B ○ Full mesh

C ○ Partial mesh

D ○ Star topology

7 Subinterfaces may be configured for which types of Frame Relay connectivity? (Choose two.)

A ○ Multipoint

B ○ PVC

C ○ Point-to-point

D ○ SVC

8 What configuration is required on both routers on a point-to-point link before communications may occur?

A ○ Configure DLCI

B ○ Configure IP address

C ○ Inverse ARP request

D ○ Static mapping assignment

9 Which type of commands incur a performance hit on router hardware resources and should be limited in a production environment?

A ○ show commands

B ○ Privileged EXEC commands

C ○ debug commands

D ○ Telnet commands

10 Which command syntax adds a static DLCI-to-protocol map entry?

A ○ frame-relay map ip 192.10.10.1 100 broadcast

B ○ frame-relay pvc ip 192.10.10.1 100 broadcast

C ○ frame-relay static ip 192.10.10.1 100 broadcast

D ○ frame-relay dlci ip 192.10.10.1 100 broadcast

Answers

1 **A, B.** Data-link connection identifiers are unique numeric values assigned by the service provider to identify individual links. Review *"Identifying virtual circuits using data-link connection identifiers (DLCIs)."*

2 **B, E.** Permanent virtual circuits (PVCs) and switched virtual circuits (SVCs) are the two types of Frame Relay circuits. PVCs are always active and do not require constant call establishment and termination. SVCs are temporarily established connections used for data transmission. See *"Establishing virtual circuits."*

3 **A, D.** CSU/DSU, DCE. When connecting a customer's DTE device to a Frame Relay network, the service provider's DCE device (or CSU/DSU) always defines the interface clock rate. Take a look at *"Purpose of Frame Relay WAN connections."*

4 **B.** CIR, or committed information rate, is the maximum bandwidth of data allocated and guaranteed to the customer by the telephone company or service provider. Although the CIR is said to be guaranteed, it is a best-effort value (in bits per second) and is not an absolute guarantee of the provider's bandwidth. See *"Reserving bandwidth using access rate and CIR guarantee."*

5 **A.** LMI, or Local Management Interface, manages the Frame Relay connection and monitors the device status across the link. Examine *"Frame Relay link status control using LMI."*

6 **D.** A star topology, also known as a hub-and-spoke Frame Relay network, is the most efficient method of connecting multiple virtual circuits. One hub device acts as the central communications point and connects the remote routers, or spoke devices. Review *"Frame Relay topologies."*

7 **A, C.** Subinterfaces may be configured for both point-to-point and multipoint connections. Read *"Split horizon issues in a Frame Relay WAN."*

8 **A.** DLCI assignments must be made on both routers before communications may occur. See *"Configuring single interfaces for Frame Relay over a point-to-point link."*

9 **C.** The `debug` commands are used for troubleshooting purposes and increase the burden on router resources. Disable `debug` commands as soon as they are no longer needed. Review *"Monitoring and Troubleshooting Frame Relay."*

10 **A.** The `frame-relay map ip 192.10.10.1 100 broadcast` command creates a static IP (192.10.10.1)–to–DLCI (100) mapping. After a static mapping is enabled for the interface, dynamic Inverse ARP is disabled automatically. Read *"Managing Frame Relay."*

Appendix A: About the CD

On the CD-ROM

✓ **System requirements**

✓ **Using the CD with Windows and Mac**

✓ **Prep Test with hundreds of sample questions to make sure you're ready for the CCNA exam**

✓ **Troubleshooting**

This appendix is designed to give you an overview of the system requirements for your system in order to run the software found on the accompanying CD. I also include a description of what you can find on the CD that will help you prepare for your exam.

System Requirements

Make sure that your computer meets the minimum system requirements shown in the following list. If your computer does not meet most of these requirements, you might have problems using the software and files on the CD. For the latest and greatest information, please refer to the ReadMe file located at the root of the CD-ROM.

◆ A PC running Microsoft Windows 2000 or later

◆ A Macintosh running Apple OS X or later

◆ An Internet connection

◆ A CD-ROM drive

If you need more information on the basics, check out these books published by Wiley: *PCs For Dummies,* 11th Edition, by Dan Gookin; *Macs For Dummies,* 10th Edition, by Edward C. Baig; *Windows XP For Dummies,* 2nd Edition, *Windows 7 For Dummies,* and *Windows Vista For Dummies,* all by Andy Rathbone.

Using the CD

To install the items from the CD to your hard drive, follow these steps.

1. **Insert the CD into your computer's CD-ROM drive to bring up the license agreement.**

   Note to Windows users: The interface won't launch if you have AutoRun disabled. In that case, choose Start⇨Run. In the dialog box that appears, type **D:\start.exe**. Replace D with the proper letter if your CD-ROM drive uses a different letter. If you don't know the letter, see how your CD-ROM drive is listed under My Computer (XP and earlier) or Computer (Vista and 7).

2. **Click OK.**

   Note for Mac Users: The CD icon will appear on your desktop. Just double-click the icon to open the CD and then double-click the Start icon.

3. **Read through the license agreement and then click the Accept button to use the CD.**

   The CD interface appears, from which you can install the programs and run the demos with just a click of a button (or two).

What You Will Find on the CD

The following sections are a summary of the software on the CD-ROM included with this book.

Prep Test

The Prep Test is designed to simulate the actual CCNA test — a question with multiple choice answers. The Prep Test on the CD-ROM is not adaptive, though, and it is not timed, so you might want to time yourself to gauge your speed. After you answer each question, you find out whether you answered the question correctly. And if you answered correctly, you are on your way to A+ success! If you answered incorrectly, you are told the correct answer with a brief explanation of why it is the correct answer.

The Prep Test includes all the Prep Test questions from the end of each chapter in the book as well as hundreds of additional questions. If you perform well on the Prep Test, you're probably ready to tackle the real thing.

Troubleshooting

I tried my best to compile programs that work on most computers with the minimum system requirements. Alas, your computer may differ, and some programs might not work properly for some reason.

The two likeliest problems are that you don't have enough memory (RAM) for the programs you want to use or you have other programs running that are affecting installation or running of a program. If you get an error message such as `Not enough memory` or `Setup cannot continue`, try one or more of the following suggestions and then try using the software again:

✦ **Turn off any antivirus software running on your computer.** Installation programs sometimes mimic virus activity and might make your computer incorrectly believe that it is being infected by a virus.

✦ **Close all running programs.** The more programs you have running, the less memory is available to other programs. Installation programs typically update files and programs; so if you keep other programs running, installation might not work properly.

✦ **Have your local computer store add more RAM to your computer.** This is, admittedly, a drastic and somewhat expensive step. However, adding more memory can really help the speed of your computer and allow more programs to run at the same time.

If you have trouble with the CD-ROM, please call the Wiley Product Technical Support phone number at 1-800-762-2974. Outside the United States, call 1-317-572-3994. You can also contact Wiley Product Technical Support at `http://support.wiley.com`. Wiley Publishing will provide technical support only for installation and other general quality control items. For technical support on the applications themselves, consult the program's vendor or author.

To place additional orders or to request information about other Wiley products, please call 1-877-762-2974.

Appendix B: Cisco CCNA Exam Preparation

Cisco certification is unique in the high tech industry since Cisco networks are at the heart of the Internet and they interconnect a variety of different types of computer systems. Whereas host operating system certifications attest your knowledge about a specific operating system, Cisco certification attests your knowledge about networking concepts and networking devices that interconnect all computer devices, thereby opening many doors for you.

The benefit of the Cisco Certified Network Associate (CCNA) Certification is proof that you know and have validated the ability to install, configure, operate, and troubleshoot medium-size routed and switched networks, including implementation and verification of connections to remote sites in a WAN. The CCNA Certification can be presented to employers and clients alike as proof of competency and skill in this area.

CCNA: Foundation of Cisco Certification Pyramid

Cisco created several certification paths. All start with the CCNA certification. In other words, whether you would like to work on the networks that power the internet, or you would like to work on Voice over IP (VOIP) internet telephony, or you would like to work on storage networks, or on wireless networks, the CCNA certification ensures that you have a common core networking knowledge that can be applied to several networking applications.

CCNA Skills

Once you obtain the CCNA certification, Cisco attests that:

+ At a high level
  • You can install, configure, operate and troubleshoot medium-sized local area networks, wide area networks, as well as wireless networks. This includes switched and routed networks.
  • You can tune parameters on Cisco devices to improve network performance, reliability, and security.

✦ Specifically

- You have a sound knowledge of routed protocols (IP, IPv6) and routing protocols (RIP, RIP v2, EIGRP, OSPF)

- You are comfortable with LAN switching, VLANs, Ethernet, Access Control Lists (ACLs) and network security.

- You can configure Serial Line Interface Protocol, Frame Relay, Cable/DSL, PPP, HLDC

These topics are tested in the CCNA exam. Hence, you need to master these skills before you take the exam. Read this book to acquire these skills. Keep in mind that exam preparation questions at the end of each chapter are extremely important to consolidate your knowledge. Make sure you review all *Prep Test* sections at the end of each chapter in this book.

CCNA Adaptive Testing

You can become CCNA either by taking one composite exam or by taking two exams:

✦ *640-802 CCNA* Composite: This is a single exam that combines testing objectives of the ICND1 and ICND2 exams in a single package. It contains 45 to 55 questions. You have 90 minutes to complete it. Passing mark is 85%. This exam costs $250.

✦ *640-822 ICND1* and *640-816 ICND2*: These are the Interconnecting Cisco Networking Devices Part 1 and Part 2 exams. You get a CCENT certification (Cisco Certified Entry Networking Technician) once you pass ICND1. However, you still need to pass ICND2 to get the CCNA certification. 640-822 ICND1 asks between 50 and 60 questions. You have 90 minutes to complete it. 640-816 ICND2 contains between 45 and 55 questions. You have 75 minutes to complete it. The ICND exams cost $125 each, for a total of $250.

Keep in mind that the duration of the exam and the number of questions vary for each exam. CCNA exams are adaptive computer based tests. The questions asked, and the number of questions asked, depend on how well you are doing on each topic. The answers you give to questions asked early in the exam determine which questions you will be asked next.

The CCNA exams include several types of questions:

✦ Multiple choices with one correct answer

✦ Multiple choices with more than one correct answer

✦ Fill in the blank

✦ Switch and router simulation

✦ Drag and drop

Typical switch and router simulation questions show a switch or a router command-line interface window where you type command(s) to configure a particular feature. Cisco accepts supported command abbreviations. For example, you can type en instead of `enable`, or `config t`, or `conf t` instead `configure terminal`.

CCNA certification lasts for three years. To recertify for CCNA after three years, you can pass any of these exams:

✦ The Interconnecting Cisco Networking Devices Part 2 exam (ICND2)

✦ The current CCNA exam

✦ A CCNA Concentration exam (wireless, security, voice, storage)

✦ The current CCDA exam

✦ Any 642 - XXX professional level or Cisco Specialist exam (excluding Sales Specialist exams)

✦ A current CCIE or CCDE written exam

Using This Book to Prepare for the Exams

Exams are stressful events for most people, but if you are well prepared, your stress level should be much lower. If you read and understand the material in this book, you should have no problem with any of the exams. The review questions and exam test engine on the companion CD are all designed to prepare you for what lies ahead.

Check out the exam objectives and focus your study on those objectives. Cisco's web site lists the CCNA exam objectives. Each chapter in this book starts by listing the exam objectives that are covered in the chapter. Some exam objectives are covered in more than one chapter. Make sure you have a clear understanding of the CCNA exam objectives.

Examine the objectives for each chapter before diving into the content so that you can use them as a guide to which sections you might need to focus on. After thoroughly reading the content of the chapter, attempt the Prep Test section at the end of the chapter. If you do poorly on the Prep Test, go back to the objectives to see where you need more effort. When you re-read the chapter sections, try to examine the content from another viewpoint to help you associate the information with the questions and the objectives. For example, a differing viewpoint might be that of a computer user, a help desk employee, or a desktop support technician. After you can complete the Prep Test in each chapter with an 85% or better score, move on to attempt the exams on the companion CD. If you are unable to achieve a mark of 85% or better, you should continue to review the areas in which you are weak.

Making Arrangements to Take the Exams

The CCNA exam can be scheduled at Pearson VUE testing centers. For more information about scheduling your exam, check

```
http://www.vue.com/cisco/schedule/
```

The cost to take the CCNA exam is $250 (US).

The Day the Earth Stood Still: Exam Day

Knowing what to expect on the day of the exam can take some of the pressure off of you. The following sections look at the testing process.

Before you leave for the test center, make sure you have the necessary credentials and payment:

- ✦ Government-issued ID with your legal name
- ✦ Cisco Certification ID (like CSCO00000001) or Test ID number

  If you have taken a Cisco exam before, using the same Cisco Certification ID avoids duplicate records and delays in receiving proper credit for your exams.
- ✦ Company name
- ✦ Valid email address
- ✦ Method of payment

Arriving at the exam location

Get to the exam location early on the day of the exam. You should arrive at the testing center 15 to 30 minutes before the exam starts. This keeps you from being rushed and gives you some temporal elbow room in case there are any delays. It is also not so long that you will have time to sit and stew about the exam. Get there, get into a relaxed frame of mind, and get into the exam.

When you get to the test site, before you sign in, take a few minutes to get accustomed to the testing center. Get a small drink of water. Use the restroom if you need to. The test will be 90 minutes, so you should be able to last that long before another break. You might want to check the center's policy for bringing a beverage with you; some centers will allow it, and others will not.

Now relax. Getting to the exam site early gives you this privilege. You didn't show up early just to stew and make yourself more nervous.

If you feel prepared and are ready to go, you might want to see whether you can start the test early.

You will not be able to take anything into the testing room. You will not be allowed electronics, paper, and so on. They will provide you with something to write with and to write on, which they will take back at the end of test.

Taking the exam

In the testing room, and depending on the size of the testing center, there will usually be as many as eight computers set up. Each computer represents a testing seat.

Because the exam consists of multiple-choice questions, take it slow — or at least pace yourself. Trying to complete the questions too quickly will no doubt lead you to errors. When you are about to start the exam, you will see onscreen how many questions there will be, and how long you have to complete the exam. Be sure to read the onscreen exam instructions at the start of the exam; they do change from time to time.

Based on the number of questions and your exam time, figure out how long you can spend on each question. On average, you have slightly more than one minute per question. Take your time, but be aware of your time for the exam overall. Think of it this way: When you have completed 25 percent of the exam, you should have used only 25 percent of your allotted time.

Read the entire question and try to decide what the answer should be before looking at the answer choices. In most cases, you will find a few key words that are designed to remove any ambiguity in the question, as well as a few distracters and useless information designed to throw you off. If you do not notice these key words, the question will seem vague. If this is the case, re-read the question and look for the key words. Exam questions are written by many authors, so the style of writing for each question could differ.

Don't overcomplicate the questions by reading too much into them. Besides the key words and the distracters, the question should be straightforward. In some cases, the question might ask for the best choice, and more than one answer might seem correct. Choose the one that is *best* — the quickest, most likely to succeed, least likely to cause other problems, supported by Cisco best practices — whatever the question calls for. The best choice is always the right choice.

After identifying the key words and distracters, follow these additional steps:

1. Eliminate choices that are obviously wrong.

Most questions will ask you to choose one of four answers. Some questions will ask you to choose all that apply and have as many as eight choices. You should be able to immediately eliminate at least one choice — perhaps two. Now the odds of choosing the right answer have gotten substantially better. Re-read the question and the remaining choices carefully, and you should be able to locate the correct answer.

2. If you don't have a clue which of the remaining choices is correct, mark an answer.

On a standard timed exam, you can review your answers. Not answering a question is automatically wrong, so if you at least *have* an answer, it might be right. You might also find information on other questions in the exam that triggers the correct answers for questions you were not sure of.

3. Make your choice and leave it.

Unless you have information that proves your choice is wrong, your first instinct is usually correct.

Your first choice is usually correct — don't second-guess your first choice! Change your answer only if you're absolutely positive it should be changed.

Use supported command abbreviations to increase your speed when answering switch and router simulation questions. Cisco accepts supported command abbreviations as correct answers on the CCNA exams. You can save some time by just typing the abbreviation, instead of typing the full command. Be sure the abbreviation is not ambiguous though. If you are unsure about the abbreviation of a command, use the full command.

At the completion of the exam, you receive a score report along with a score breakout by exam section and the passing score for the given exam.

If you do not pass the exam, you can take the exam again in five days.

You can use this chart to identify which chapters to study in preparation for the Cisco CCNA Certification Exam. If you are planning to take the single CCNA exam (640-802) then you should read the entire contents of this book. If you are planning to take the individual ICND1 (640-822) and ICND2 (640-816) exams, you can use this matrix to determine which chapters you need to read.

After reading the entire volume, you can use this chart as part of your review. If you go through the objectives and find any area you don't think you know, you can immediately turn to the appropriate chapter for in-depth review.

The exams covered in the matrix and their column key identifiers are:

+ **640-802 CCNA Exam (C)**

+ **640-822 ICND1 (1)**

+ **640-816 ICND2 (2)**

2009 Examination Objectives

Domain/Objective/Description	C	1	2	Book-Chapter
Describe how a network works				
Describe the purpose and functions of various network devices	X	X		1-1
Select the components required to meet a network specification	X	X		1-6
Use the OSI and TCP/IP models and their associated protocols to explain how data flows in a network	X	X		1-2, 1-3
Describe common networked applications including web applications	X	X		1-1
Describe the purpose and basic operation of the protocols in the OSI and TCP models	X	X		1-2, 1-3
Describe the impact of applications (Voice Over IP and Video Over IP) on a network	X	X		3-6
Interpret network diagrams	X	X		
Determine the path between two hosts across a network	X	X		1-7
Describe the components required for network and Internet communications	X	X		1-1, 1-3
Identify and correct common network problems at layers 1, 2, 3 and 7 using a layered model approach	X	X		1-2
Differentiate between LAN/WAN operation and features	X	X		1-6, 1-7
Configure, verify and troubleshoot a switch with VLANs and interswitch communications				
Select the appropriate media, cables, ports, and connectors to connect switches to other network devices and hosts	X	X		1-6
Explain the technology and media access control method for Ethernet networks	X	X		1-6

(continued)

Domain/Objective/Description	C	1	2	Book-Chapter
Explain network segmentation and basic traffic management concepts	X	X		1-6
Explain basic switching concepts and the operation of Cisco switches	X	X		3-1
Perform and verify initial switch configuration tasks including remote access management	X	X		3-2
Verify network status and switch operation using basic utilities (including: ping, traceroute, telnet, SSH, arp, ipconfig), SHOW & DEBUG commands	X	X		3-7
Identify, prescribe, and resolve common switched network media issues, configuration issues, auto negotiation, and switch hardware failures	X	X		3-7
Describe enhanced switching technologies (including: VTP, RSTP, VLAN, PVSTP, 802.1q)	X		X	3-5
Describe how VLANs create logically separate networks and the need for routing between them	X		X	3-5
Configure, verify, and troubleshoot VLANs	X		X	3-5
Configure, verify, and troubleshoot trunking on Cisco switches	X		X	3-5
Configure, verify, and troubleshoot interVLAN routing	X		X	3-5
Configure, verify, and troubleshoot VTP	X		X	3-5
Configure, verify, and troubleshoot RSTP operation	X		X	3-4
Interpret the output of various show and debug commands to verify the operational status of a Cisco switched network.	X		X	3-7
Implement and verify basic switch security (including: port security, trunk access, management vlan other than vlan1, port security, deactivate ports, etc.)	X	X	X	3-1, 3-4, 3-5
Implement an IP addressing scheme and IP Services to meet network requirements in a medium-size Enterprise branch office network				
Describe the operation and benefits of using private and public IP addressing	X	X		2-3
Explain the operation and benefits of using DHCP and DNS	X	X		2-2
Configure, verify and troubleshoot DHCP and DNS operation on a router (including: CLI/SDM)	X	X		2-3
Implement static and dynamic addressing services for hosts in a LAN environment	X	X		2-5
Calculate and apply an addressing scheme including VLSM IP addressing design to a network	X	X	X	2-4

Domain/Objective/Description	C	1	2	Book-Chapter
Determine the appropriate classless addressing scheme using VLSM and summarization to satisfy addressing requirements in a LAN/WAN environment	X		X	2-4
Describe the technological requirements for running IPv6 in conjunction with IPv4 (including: protocols, dual stack, tunneling, etc).	X		X	2-5
Describe IPv6 addresses	X		X	2-5
Identify and correct common problems associated with IP addressing and host configurations	X	X	X	2-3
Configure, verify, and troubleshoot basic router operation and routing on Cisco devices				
Describe basic routing concepts (including: packet forwarding, router lookup process)	X	X		4-1
Describe the operation of Cisco routers (including: router bootup process, POST, router components)	X	X		4-2
Select the appropriate media, cables, ports, and connectors to connect routers to other network devices and hosts	X	X		1-6
Configure, verify, and troubleshoot RIPv2	X	X		4-4
Access and utilize the router to set basic parameters.(including: CLI/SDM)	X	X		4-2
Connect, configure, and verify operation status of a device interface	X	X		4-2
Verify device configuration and network connectivity using ping, traceroute, telnet, SSH or other utilities	X	X		3-7
Perform and verify routing configuration tasks for a static or default route given specific routing requirements	X	X		4-3
Manage IOS configuration files. (including: save, edit, upgrade, restore)	X	X		4-2
Manage Cisco IOS	X	X		4-2
Compare and contrast methods of routing and routing protocols	X		X	4-3, 4-4, 4-5, 4-6
Configure, verify, and troubleshoot OSPF	X		X	4-6
Configure, verify, and troubleshoot EIGRP	X		X	4-5
Verify network connectivity (including: using ping, traceroute, and telnet or SSH)	X	X	X	3-7
Troubleshoot routing issues	X		X	4-2, 4-4, 4-5, 4-6

(continued)

Domain/Objective/Description	C	1	2	Book-Chapter
Verify router hardware and software operation using SHOW & DEBUG commands.	X	X	X	4-2, 4-4, 4-5, 4-6
Implement basic router security (including password and physical security)	X	X	X	4-2
Explain and select the appropriate administrative tasks required for a WLAN				
Describe standards associated with wireless media (including: IEEE WI-FI Alliance, ITU/FCC)	X	X		5-1
Identify and describe the purpose of the components in a small wireless network. (Including: SSID, BSS, ESS)	X	X		5-1
Identify the basic parameters to configure on a wireless network to ensure that devices connect to the correct access point	X	X		5-3
Compare and contrast wireless security features and capabilities of WPA security (including: open, WEP, WPA-1/2)	X	X		5-2
Identify common issues with implementing wireless networks. (Including: Interface, misconfiguration)	X	X		5-1, 5-2, 5-3
Identify security threats to a network and describe general methods to mitigate those threats				
Describe today's increasing network security threats and explain the need to implement a comprehensive security policy to mitigate the threats	X	X		6-1
Explain general methods to mitigate common security threats to network devices, hosts, and applications	X	X		6-1
Describe the functions of common security appliances and applications	X	X		6-1
Describe security recommended practices including initial steps to secure network devices	X	X		6-1
Implement, verify, and troubleshoot NAT and ACLs in a medium-size Enterprise branch office network				
Describe the purpose and types of ACLs	X		X	6-2
Configure and apply ACLs based on network filtering requirements.(including: CLI/SDM)	X		X	6-2
Configure and apply an ACLs to limit telnet and SSH access to the router using (including: SDM/CLI)	X		X	4-2, 6-2

Domain/Objective/Description	C	1	2	Book-Chapter
Verify and monitor ACLs in a network environment	X		X	6-2
Troubleshoot ACL issues	X		X	6-2
Explain the basic operation of NAT	X	X	X	6-3
Configure NAT for given network requirements using (including: CLI/SDM)	X	X	X	6-3
Troubleshoot NAT issues	X		X	6-3
Implement and verify WAN links				
Describe different methods for connecting to a WAN	X	X		7-1
Configure and verify a basic WAN serial connection	X	X		7-1
Configure and verify Frame Relay on Cisco routers	X		X	7-4
Troubleshoot WAN implementation issues	X		X	7-2, 7-3, 7-4
Describe VPN technology (including: importance, benefits, role, impact, components)	X		X	6-4
Configure and verify a PPP connection between Cisco routers	X		X	7-3

Index

X

Z

Wiley Publishing, Inc.
End-User License Agreement

READ THIS. You should carefully read these terms and conditions before opening the software packet(s) included with this book "Book". This is a license agreement "Agreement" between you and Wiley Publishing, Inc. "WPI". By opening the accompanying software packet(s), you acknowledge that you have read and accept the following terms and conditions. If you do not agree and do not want to be bound by such terms and conditions, promptly return the Book and the unopened software packet(s) to the place you obtained them for a full refund.

1. **License Grant.** WPI grants to you (either an individual or entity) a nonexclusive license to use one copy of the enclosed software program(s) (collectively, the "Software") solely for your own personal or business purposes on a single computer (whether a standard computer or a workstation component of a multi-user network). The Software is in use on a computer when it is loaded into temporary memory (RAM) or installed into permanent memory (hard disk, CD-ROM, or other storage device). WPI reserves all rights not expressly granted herein.

2. **Ownership.** WPI is the owner of all right, title, and interest, including copyright, in and to the compilation of the Software recorded on the physical packet included with this Book "Software Media". Copyright to the individual programs recorded on the Software Media is owned by the author or other authorized copyright owner of each program. Ownership of the Software and all proprietary rights relating thereto remain with WPI and its licensers.

3. **Restrictions on Use and Transfer.**

   (a) You may only (i) make one copy of the Software for backup or archival purposes, or (ii) transfer the Software to a single hard disk, provided that you keep the original for backup or archival purposes. You may not (i) rent or lease the Software, (ii) copy or reproduce the Software through a LAN or other network system or through any computer subscriber system or bulletin-board system, or (iii) modify, adapt, or create derivative works based on the Software.

   (b) You may not reverse engineer, decompile, or disassemble the Software. You may transfer the Software and user documentation on a permanent basis, provided that the transferee agrees to accept the terms and conditions of this Agreement and you retain no copies. If the Software is an update or has been updated, any transfer must include the most recent update and all prior versions.

4. **Restrictions on Use of Individual Programs.** You must follow the individual requirements and restrictions detailed for each individual program in the "About the CD" appendix of this Book or on the Software Media. These limitations are also contained in the individual license agreements recorded on the Software Media. These limitations may include a requirement that after using the program for a specified period of time, the user must pay a registration fee or discontinue use. By opening the Software packet(s), you agree to abide by the licenses and restrictions for these individual programs that are detailed in the "About the CD" appendix and/or on the Software Media. None of the material on this Software Media or listed in this Book may ever be redistributed, in original or modified form, for commercial purposes.

Business/Accounting & Bookkeeping
Bookkeeping For Dummies
978-0-7645-9848-7

eBay Business
All-in-One For Dummies,
2nd Edition
978-0-470-38536-4

Job Interviews
For Dummies,
3rd Edition
978-0-470-17748-8

Resumes For Dummies,
5th Edition
978-0-470-08037-5

Stock Investing
For Dummies,
3rd Edition
978-0-470-40114-9

Successful Time
Management
For Dummies
978-0-470-29034-7

Computer Hardware
BlackBerry For Dummies,
3rd Edition
978-0-470-45762-7

Computers For Seniors
For Dummies
978-0-470-24055-7

iPhone For Dummies,
2nd Edition
978-0-470-42342-4

Laptops For Dummies,
3rd Edition
978-0-470-27759-1

Macs For Dummies,
10th Edition
978-0-470-27817-8

Cooking & Entertaining
Cooking Basics
For Dummies,
3rd Edition
978-0-7645-7206-7

Wine For Dummies,
4th Edition
978-0-470-04579-4

Diet & Nutrition
Dieting For Dummies,
2nd Edition
978-0-7645-4149-0

Nutrition For Dummies,
4th Edition
978-0-471-79868-2

Weight Training
For Dummies,
3rd Edition
978-0-471-76845-6

Digital Photography
Digital Photography
For Dummies,
6th Edition
978-0-470-25074-7

Photoshop Elements 7
For Dummies
978-0-470-39700-8

Gardening
Gardening Basics
For Dummies
978-0-470-03749-2

Organic Gardening
For Dummies,
2nd Edition
978-0-470-43067-5

Green/Sustainable
Green Building
& Remodeling
For Dummies
978-0-470-17559-0

Green Cleaning
For Dummies
978-0-470-39106-8

Green IT For Dummies
978-0-470-38688-0

Health
Diabetes For Dummies,
3rd Edition
978-0-470-27086-8

Food Allergies
For Dummies
978-0-470-09584-3

Living Gluten-Free
For Dummies
978-0-471-77383-2

Hobbies/General
Chess For Dummies,
2nd Edition
978-0-7645-8404-6

Drawing For Dummies
978-0-7645-5476-6

Knitting For Dummies,
2nd Edition
978-0-470-28747-7

Organizing For Dummies
978-0-7645-5300-4

SuDoku For Dummies
978-0-470-01892-7

Home Improvement
Energy Efficient Homes
For Dummies
978-0-470-37602-7

Home Theater
For Dummies,
3rd Edition
978-0-470-41189-6

Living the Country Lifestyle
All-in-One For Dummies
978-0-470-43061-3

Solar Power Your Home
For Dummies
978-0-470-17569-9

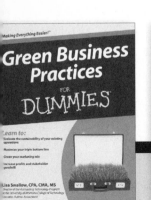

Internet
Blogging For Dummies,
2nd Edition
978-0-470-23017-6

eBay For Dummies,
6th Edition
978-0-470-49741-8

Facebook For Dummies
978-0-470-26273-3

Google Blogger
For Dummies
978-0-470-40742-4

Web Marketing
For Dummies,
2nd Edition
978-0-470-37181-7

WordPress For Dummies,
2nd Edition
978-0-470-40296-2

Language & Foreign Language
French For Dummies
978-0-7645-5193-2

Italian Phrases
For Dummies
978-0-7645-7203-6

Spanish For Dummies
978-0-7645-5194-9

Spanish For Dummies,
Audio Set
978-0-470-09585-0

Macintosh
Mac OS X Snow Leopard
For Dummies
978-0-470-43543-4

Math & Science
Algebra I For Dummies,
2nd Edition
978-0-470-55964-2

Biology For Dummies
978-0-7645-5326-4

Calculus For Dummies
978-0-7645-2498-1

Chemistry For Dummies
978-0-7645-5430-8

Microsoft Office
Excel 2007 For Dummies
978-0-470-03737-9

Office 2007 All-in-One
Desk Reference
For Dummies
978-0-471-78279-7

Music
Guitar For Dummies,
2nd Edition
978-0-7645-9904-0

iPod & iTunes
For Dummies,
6th Edition
978-0-470-39062-7

Piano Exercises
For Dummies
978-0-470-38765-8

Parenting & Education
Parenting For Dummies,
2nd Edition
978-0-7645-5418-6

Type 1 Diabetes
For Dummies
978-0-470-17811-9

Pets
Cats For Dummies,
2nd Edition
978-0-7645-5275-5

Dog Training For Dummies,
2nd Edition
978-0-7645-8418-3

Puppies For Dummies,
2nd Edition
978-0-470-03717-1

Religion & Inspiration
The Bible For Dummies
978-0-7645-5296-0

Catholicism For Dummies
978-0-7645-5391-2

Women in the Bible
For Dummies
978-0-7645-8475-6

Self-Help & Relationship
Anger Management
For Dummies
978-0-470-03715-7

Overcoming Anxiety
For Dummies
978-0-7645-5447-6

Sports
Baseball For Dummies,
3rd Edition
978-0-7645-7537-2

Basketball For Dummies,
2nd Edition
978-0-7645-5248-9

Golf For Dummies,
3rd Edition
978-0-471-76871-5

Web Development
Web Design All-in-One
For Dummies
978-0-470-41796-6

Windows Vista
Windows Vista
For Dummies
978-0-471-75421-3

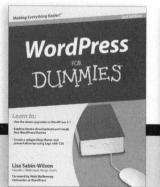